Python®

ALL-IN-ONE

2nd Edition

by John C. Shovic, PhD
Alan Simpson

for
dummies®
A Wiley Brand

Python® All-in-One For Dummies®, 2nd Edition

Published by: **John Wiley & Sons, Inc.**, 111 River Street, Hoboken, NJ 07030-5774, www.wiley.com

Copyright © 2021 by John Wiley & Sons, Inc., Hoboken, New Jersey

Published simultaneously in Canada

For general information on our other products and services, please contact our Customer Care Department within the U.S. at 877-762-2974, outside the U.S. at 317-572-3993, or fax 317-572-4002. For technical support, please visit https://hub.wiley.com/community/support/dummies.

Wiley publishes in a variety of print and electronic formats and by print-on-demand. Some material included with standard print versions of this book may not be included in e-books or in print-on-demand. If this book refers to media such as a CD or DVD that is not included in the version you purchased, you may download this material at http://booksupport.wiley.com. For more information about Wiley products, visit www.wiley.com.

Library of Congress Control Number: 2021932818

ISBN 978-1-119-78760-0 (pbk); ISBN 978-1-119-78761-7 (ebk); ISBN 978-1-119-78762-4 (ebk)

Manufactured in the United States of America

SKY10025752_031921

Contents at a Glance

Table of Contents

Introduction

The power of Python. The Python language is becoming more and more popular, and in 2017 it became the most popular language in the world according to IEEE Spectrum. The power of Python is real.

Python the number-one language because it's easy to learn and use, due partly to its simplified syntax and natural-language flow but also to the amazing user community and the breadth of applications available.

About This Book

This book is a reference manual to guide you through the process of learning Python and how to use it in modern computer applications, such as data science, artificial intelligence, physical computing, and robotics. If you're looking to learn a little about a lot of exciting things, this is the book for you. It gives you an introduction to the topics that you'll need to explore more deeply.

Python All-in-One For Dummies, 2nd Edition guides you through the Python language and then takes you on a tour through some cool libraries and technologies (the Raspberry Pi, robotics, AI, data science, and more) that all revolve around the Python language. When you work on new projects and new technologies, Python is there with a diverse number of libraries just waiting for you to use.

This is a hands-on book, with examples and code throughout. You are expected to enter the code, run it, and then modify it to do what you want. You don't just buy a robot; you build it so you can understand all the pieces and can make sense of the way Python works with the robot to control its motors and sensors. Artificial intelligence is complicated, but Python helps make a significant part of it accessible. Data science is complicated, but Python helps you do data science more easily. Robotics is complicated, but Python gives you the code that controls the robot. And Python even enables you to tie these pieces together and use, say, AI in robotics.

In this book, we take you through the basics of the Python language in small, easy-to-understand steps. After we have introduced you to the language, we step into the world of artificial intelligence, exploring programming in machine learning and neural networks using Python and TensorFlow and working on real problems and real software, not just toy applications.

After that, we're off to the exciting world of big data and data science with Python. We look at big public data sets such as medical and environmental data.

Finally, you get to experience the magic of what we call physical computing. Using the inexpensive, small, and incredibly popular Raspberry Pi computer, we show you how to use Python to control motors and read sensors. This is a lead-up to the final minibook, "Building Robots," where you build a robot and control it with Python and your own programs, even using artificial intelligence. This is not your mother's RC car.

Python data science, robotics, AI, and fun all in the same book.

This book won't make you understand everything about these fields, but it will give you a great introduction to the terminology and the power of Python in all these fields. Enjoy the book and go forth and learn more afterwards.

Foolish Assumptions

We assume that you know how to use a computer in a basic way. If you can turn on the computer and use a mouse, you're ready for this book. We assume that you don't know how to program yet, although you will have some skills in programming by the end of the book. If we're wrong and you already know Python (or some other computer language), jump ahead to minibook 4 and dig right into learning something new. Our intent is to guide you through the language of Python and then through some of the amazing technologies and devices that use Python. We provide complete examples. If you get stuck on something, look it up on the web, read a tutorial, and then come back to it.

What to Buy

To complete the projects in Books 4 through 7, you need a Raspberry Pi 3B+ starter kit at `https://amzn.to/2WzYdoY` or a Raspberry PI 4B Starter Kit at `https://amzn.to/3nIH8W8`. In addition, you need the items listed in this section, organized by minibook.

TIP

If you want to use a Raspberry Pi 4B in the robot in Book 7, it will dramatically reduce the battery life, and with some types of batteries the robot may not be able to boot the Pi 4B.

Book 6

For building the projects in Book 6, you need the following:

» Pi2Grover board at https://shop.switchdoc.com or www.amazon.com. (You can get $5.00 off the board at shop.switchdoc.com by using the discount code PI2DUMMIES at checkout.)

» Grove blue LED module, which includes a Grove cable, at https://shop.switchdoc.com or Amazon.

» A package of Grove male jumper patch cables, specifically the Grove-4-male-pin-to-Grove-conversion cables, at https://shop.switchdoc.com/products/grove-4-pin-male-jumper-to-grove-4-pin-conversion-cable-5-pcs-per-pack and https://amzn.to/3nyGbic.

» A package of female-to-Grove patch cables at https://shop.switchdoc.com/products/grove-4-pin-female-jumper-to-grove-4-pin-conversion-cable-5-pcs-per-pack and https://amzn.to/3jhQmXY.

» Grove HDC1080 I2C temperature and humidity sensor at https://store.switchdoc.com or www.amazon.com. The SwitchDoc Labs HDC1080 sensor comes with a Grove connector. If you buy a non-Grove sensor on Amazon, you'll need a female-to-Grove patch cable, as discussed in Chapter 2 of this minibook. You can get a female-to-Grove patch cable at https://shop.switchdoc.com/products/grove-4-pin-female-jumper-to-grove-4-pin-conversion-cable-5-pcs-per-pack and https://amzn.to/3jhQmXY.

» Grove oxygen sensor at www.seeedstudio.com or www.amazon.com.

» Pi2Grover Raspberry-Pi-to-Grove converter, https://shop.switchdoc.com or www.amazon.com. (You can get $5.00 off the board at shop.switchdoc.com by using the discount code PI2DUMMIES at checkout.)

» Grove four-channel, 16-bit analog-to-digital converter at https://store.switchdoc.com or www.amazon.com.

» Grove I2C motor drive (with a Grove cable) at www.seeedstudio.com or https://amazon.com.

» Two small DC motors at www.adafruit.com/product/711 or https://amazon.com.

» SG90 micro servo motor at www.ebay.com or https://amazon.com. These motors are inexpensive, so you may end up having to buy two or more for under $10.

» 28BYJ-48 ULN2003 5V stepper motor at www.ebay.com or https://amzn.to/2BuNDV1. This type of motor is inexpensive, so you may end up having to buy five for $12. Make sure you get the ones with the driver boards (such as the ones at the Amazon.com link).

Book 7

For the robot in Book 7, purchase the following:

» Adeept Raspberry Pi PiCar-B. Make sure you buy the PiCar-B and *not* the PiCar-A. Look for "Adeept Mars Rover PiCar-B." You can buy the PiCar-B at Amazon.com `https://amzn.to/36dukPU`, `www.ebay.com`, and `www.adeept.com`.

» Two 18650 3.7V LiPo 5000mAh batteries at `https://amazon.com` and many other places.

Icons Used in This Book

What's a *Dummies* book without icons pointing you in the direction of truly helpful information that's sure to speed you along your way? Here we briefly describe each icon we use in this book.

TIP

The Tip icon points out helpful information that's likely to make your job easier.

REMEMBER

This icon marks a generally interesting and useful fact — something you may want to remember for later use.

WARNING

The Warning icon highlights lurking danger. When we use this icon, we're telling you to pay attention and proceed with caution.

TECHNICAL STUFF

When you see this icon, you know that there's techie-type material nearby. If you're not feeling technical-minded, you can skip this information.

Beyond the Book

In addition to the material in the print or e-book you're reading right now, this product also comes with some access-anywhere goodies on the web. To get this material, simply go to `www.dummies.com` and search for "*Python All-in-One For Dummies* cheat sheet" in the Search box. In addition, we provide all the source code for this book at `www.dummies.com/go/pythonaiofd2e`. Click Downloads in the left column, and you'll see the code links organized by minibook.

Where to Go from Here

Python All-in-One For Dummies, 2nd Edition is designed so that you can read a chapter or section out of order, depending on what subjects you're most interested in. Where you go from here is up to you!

Book 1 is a great place to start reading if you've never used Python before. Discovering the basics and common terminology can be helpful when reading later chapters that use the terms and commands regularly!

1

Getting Started

Contents at a Glance

Chapter **1**

Starting with Python

B ecause you're reading this chapter, you probably realize that Python is a great language to know if you're looking for a good job in programming, or if you want to expand your existing programming skills into exciting cutting-edge technologies such as artificial intelligence (AI), machine learning (ML), data science, or robotics, or even if you're just building apps in general. So we're not going to try to sell you on Python. It sells itself.

Our approach leans heavily toward the hands-on. A common failure in many programming tutorials is that they already assume you're a professional programmer in some language, and they skip over things they assume you already know.

This book is different in that we *don't* assume that you're already programming in Python or some other language. We *do* assume that you can use a computer and understand basics such as files and folders.

We also assume you're not up for settling down in an easy chair in front of the fireplace to read page after page of theoretical stuff about Python, like some kind of boring novel. You don't have that much free time to kill. So we're going to get right into it and focus on *doing*, hands-on, because that's the only way most of us learn. We've never seen anyone read a book about Python and then sit at a computer and write Python like a pro. Human brains don't work that way. We learn through practice and repetition, and that requires being hands-on.

Why Python Is Hot

We promised we weren't going to spend a bunch of time trying to sell you on Python, and that's not our intent here. But we would like to talk briefly about *why* it's so hot.

Python is hot primarily because it has all the right stuff for the kind of software development that's driving the software development world these days. Machine learning, robotics, artificial intelligence, and data science are the leading technologies today and for the foreseeable future. Python is popular mainly because it already has lots of capabilities in these areas, while many older languages lag behind in these technologies.

Just as there are different brands of toothpaste, shampoo, cars, and just about every other product you can buy, there are different brands of programming languages with names such as Java, C, C++ (*pronounced C plus plus*), and C# (*pronounced C sharp*). They're all programming languages, just like all brands of toothpaste are toothpaste. The main reasons cited for Python's current popularity are

>> Python is relatively easy to learn.

>> Everything you need to learn (and do) in Python is free.

>> Python offers more ready-made tools for current hot technologies such as data science, machine learning, artificial intelligence, and robotics than most other languages.

HTML, CSS, AND JavaScript

Some of you may have heard of languages such as HTML, CSS, and JavaScript. Those aren't traditional programming languages for developing apps or other generic software. HTML and CSS are specialized for developing web pages. And although JavaScript is a programming language, it is heavily geared to website development and isn't quite in the same category of general programming languages like Python and Java.

If you specifically want to design and create websites, you have to learn HTML, CSS, and JavaScript whether you're already familiar with Python or some other programming language.

Figure 1-1 shows Google search trends over the last five years. As you can see, Python has been gaining in popularity (as indicated by the upward slope of the trend) whereas other languages have stayed about the same or declined. This certainly supports the notion that Python is the language people want to learn right now and for the future. Most people would agree that given trends in modern computing, learning Python gives you the best opportunity for getting a secure, high-paying job in the world of information technology.

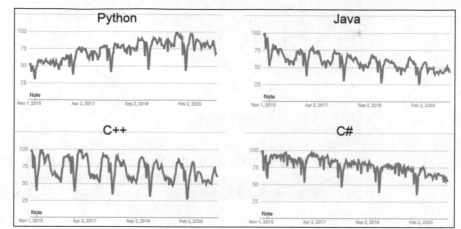

FIGURE 1-1: Google search trends for the last five years or so.

You can do your own Google trend searches at `https://trends.google.com`.

TIP

Choosing the Right Python

There are different *versions* of Python out roaming the world, prompting many a beginner to wonder things such as

» Why are there different versions?

» How are they different?

» Which one should I learn?

All good questions, and we'll start with the first. A version is kind of like a car year. You can go out a buy a 1968 Ford Mustang, a 1990 Ford Mustang, a 2019 Ford Mustang, or a 2020 Ford Mustang. They're all Ford Mustangs. The only difference is that the one with the highest year number is the most current Ford Mustang. That Mustang is different from the older models in that it has some improvements based on experience with earlier models, as well as features current with the times.

Programming languages (and most other software products) work the same way. But as a rule we don't ascribe year numbers to them because they're not released on a yearly basis. They're released whenever they're released. But the principle is the same. The version with the highest number is the newest, most recent model, sporting improvements based on experience with earlier versions, as well as features relevant to the current times.

Just as we use a decimal point with money to separate dollars from cents, we use decimal points with version numbers to indicate how much the software has changed. When there's a significant change, the entire version number is usually changed. More minor changes are expressed as decimal points. You can see how the version number increases along with the year in Table 1-1, which shows the release dates of various Python versions. We've skipped a few releases because there is little reason to know or understand the differences between all the versions. We present the table only so you can see how newer versions have higher version numbers; that's all that matters.

TABLE 1-1 **Examples of Python Versions and Release Dates**

Version	When Released
Python 3.9	October 2020
Python 3.8	October 2019
Python 3.7	June 2018
Python 3.6	December 2016
Python 3.5	September 2015
Python 3.4	March 2014
Python 3.3	September 2012
Python 3.2	February 2011
Python 3.1	June 2009
Python 3.0	December 2008
Python 2.7	July 2010
Python 2.6	October 2008
Python 2.0	October 2000
Python 1.6	September 2000
Python 1.5	February 1997
Python 1.0	January 1994

If you paid close attention, you may have noticed that Version 3.0 starts in December 2008, but Version 2.7 was released in 2010. So if versions are like car years, why the overlap?

The car years analogy just indicates that the larger the number, the more recent the version. But in Python, the year is the most recent within the main Python version. When the first number changes, that's usually a change that's so significant, software written in prior versions may not even work in that version. If you happen to be a software company with a product written in Python 2 on the market, and have millions of dollars invested in that product, you may not be too thrilled to have to start over from scratch to go with the current version. So older versions often continue to be supported and evolve, independent of the most recent version, to support developers and businesses that are already heavily invested in the previous version.

The biggest question on most beginners minds is "what version should I learn?" The answer to that is simple . . . whatever is the most current version. You'll know what that is because when you go to the Python.org website to download Python, it will tell you the most current stable build (version). That's the one they'll recommend, and that's the one you should use.

The only reason to learn something like Version 2 or 2.7 or something else older would be if you've already been hired to work on some project and the company requires you to learn and use a specific version. That sort of situation is rare, because as a beginner you're not likely to already have a full-time job as a programmer. But in the messy real world, some companies are heavily invested in an earlier version of a product, so when hiring, they'll be looking for people with knowledge of that version.

In this book, we focus on versions of Python that are current in late 2020 and early 2021, from Python 3.9 and above. Don't worry about version differences after the first and second digits. Version 3.9.1 is similar enough to version 3.9.0 that it's not important, especially to a beginner. Likewise, Version 3.9 isn't that big a jump from 3.8. So don't worry about these minor version differences when first learning. Most of what's in Python is the same across all recent versions. So you need not worry about investing time in learning a version that is or will soon be obsolete.

Tools for Success

Now we need to start getting your computer set up so you can learn, and do, Python hands-on. For one, you'll need a good Python interpreter and editor. The *editor* lets you type the code, and the *interpreter* lets you run that code. When you run (or execute) code, you're telling the computer to "do whatever my code tells you to do."

TECHNICAL STUFF

The term *code* refers to anything written in a programming language to provide instructions to a computer. The term *coding* is often used to describe the act of writing code. A code editor is an app that lets you type code, in much the same way an app such as Word or Pages helps you type regular plain-English text.

Just as there are many brands of toothpaste, soap, and shampoo in the world, there are many brands of code editors that work well with Python. There isn't a right one or a wrong one, a good one or a bad one, a best one or a worst one. Just a lot of different products that basically do the same thing but vary slightly in their approach and what that editor's creators think is good.

If you've already started learning Python and are happy with whatever you've been using, you're welcome to continue using that and ignore our suggestions. If you're just getting started with this stuff, we suggest you use VS Code, because it's an excellent, free learning environment.

Introducing Anaconda and VS Code

The editor we recommend and will be using in this book is called Visual Studio Code, officially. But most often, it is spoken or written as *VS Code*. The main reasons why it's our favorite follow:

>> It is an excellent editor for learning coding.

>> It is an excellent editor for writing code professionally and is used by millions of professional programmers and developers.

>> It's relatively easy to learn and use.

>> It works pretty much the same on Windows, Mac, and Linux.

>> It's free.

The editor is an important part of learning and writing Python code. But you also need the Python interpreter. Chances are, you're also going to want some Python packages. Packages are simply code written by someone else to do common tasks so that you don't have to start from scratch and reinvent the wheel every time you want to perform one of those tasks.

TIP

Python packages are not a crutch for beginners. They are major components of the entire Python development environment and are used by seasoned professionals as much as by beginners.

Historically, managing Python, the packages, and the editor was a somewhat laborious task involving typing cryptic commands at a command prompt. Although that's not a particularly bad thing, it isn't the most efficient way to do things, especially when you're first getting started. You end up spending most of your time upfront trying to learn and type awkward commands just to get Python to work on your computer, rather than learning Python itself.

An excellent alternative to the old command-line driven ways of doing things is to use a more complete Python development environment with a more intuitive and easily managed graphic user interface, as on a Mac or Windows or any phone or tablet. The one we recommend is Anaconda. It is free and excellent. If you've never heard of it and aren't so sure about downloading something you've never heard of, you can explore what it's all about at the Anaconda website at www. anaconda.com.

Anaconda is often referred to as a data-science platform because many of the packages that come with it are data-science oriented. But don't let that worry you if you're interested in doing other things with Python. Anaconda is excellent for learning and doing all kinds of things with Python. And it also comes with VS Code, our personal favorite coding editor, as well as Jupyter Notebook, which provides another excellent means of coding with Python. And best of all, it's 100 percent free, so it's well worth the effort of downloading and installing it.

We can't take you step-by-step through every part of downloading and installing Anaconda because it's distributed from the website, and people change their websites whenever they feel like it. But we can certainly give you the broad strokes. You should be able to follow along using Mac, Windows, or Linux. Just keep an eye on the screen as you go along, and follow any onscreen instructions as they arise, while following the steps here.

Installing Anaconda and VS Code

To download and install Anaconda, and VS Code, you'll need to connect to the Internet and use a web browser. Any web browser should do, be it Chrome, Firefox, Safari, Edge, Internet Explorer, or whatever. Fire up whatever browser you normally use to browse the web, then follow these steps:

1. **Browse to www.anaconda.com/download to get to their download page.**

   Don't worry about version numbers or dates.

2. **Keep scrolling down or click a Download button, and you should find options that look something like the example shown in Figure 1-2.**

   We can't say exactly what the page will look like the day you visit. We used a Windows computer for that screenshot, but Mac and Linux users will see something similar.

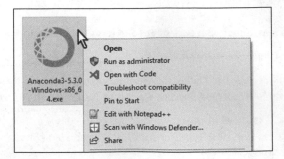

Anaconda Installers

Windows ⊞	MacOS	Linux 🐧
Python 3.8	Python 3.8	Python 3.8
64-Bit Graphical Installer (466 MB)	64-Bit Graphical Installer (462 MB)	64-Bit (x86) Installer (550 MB)
32-Bit Graphical Installer (397 MB)	64-Bit Command Line Installer (454 MB)	64-Bit (Power8 and Power9) Installer (290 MB)

FIGURE 1-2:
Click Download under the largest version number.

3. **Click Download under whichever version number is the highest on your screen.**

   The highest number for us was version 3.8, but a higher-numbered version may be available when you get there. Don't worry about that.

   TIP

   Jot down the Python version number you're downloading for future reference a little later in this chapter. You can also click How to Install ANACONDA (or however the link might be worded when you get there) on the download page if you'd like to see the instructions from the Anaconda team.

4. **Follow any onscreen instructions to download the free version.**

   If you see information about becoming a commercial user (where you have to pay money), follow the onscreen instructions to download the free version. You'll have to set up a user account.

5. **When the download is complete, open your Downloads folder (or wherever you downloaded the file).**

6. **If you're using Mac or Linux, double-click the file you downloaded. If you're using Windows, right-click that file and choose Run as Administrator, as shown in Figure 1-3.**

   TECHNICAL STUFF

   The Run-As-Administrator business in Windows ensures that you can install everything. If that option isn't available to you, double-clicking the file's icon should be sufficient.

FIGURE 1-3:
In Windows, right-click and choose Run As Administrator.

7. **Click Next, Continue, Agree, or I Agree on the first installation pages until you get to one of the pages shown in Figure 1-4.**

Mac is the one on the left, and Windows is on the right.

FIGURE 1-4:
Choose how to install Anaconda.

8. **Choose whichever option makes sense to you.**

If in doubt, Mac users can choose Install on a specific disk and then Macintosh HD. Windows users with Administrator privileges can choose Install for All Users. If the option we suggested isn't available to you, click the one closest to it.

9. **Click Continue or Next and follow the onscreen instructions.**

If you're unsure about what options to choose on any page, don't choose any option. Just accept the default suggestions.

10. **When you come to a page where it asks if you want to install Microsoft VS Code (it may take quite a while), click Install Microsoft VS Code (or whatever option on your screen indicates that you want to install VS Code).**

If VS Code is already installed on your computer, no worries. The Anaconda installer will just tell you that, or perhaps update your version to the more current version.

11. **Continue to follow any onscreen instructions, clicking Continue or Next to proceed through the installation steps, and then click Close or Finish on the last page.**

You may be prompted to sign up with Anaconda Cloud. Doing so is free but not required. Decide for yourself if that's something you want to do.

Opening Anaconda (Mac)

After Anaconda is installed on your Mac, you can open it as you would any other app. Use whichever of the following methods appeals to you:

>> Open Launch Pad and click the Anaconda Navigator icon to open it.

>> Click the Spotlight magnifying glass, start typing **Anaconda**, and then double-click Anaconda Navigator.

>> Open Finder and your Applications folder and double-click the Anaconda Navigator icon.

After Anaconda Navigator opens, right-click its icon in the dock and choose Keep in Dock. That way, its icon will be visible in the dock at all times and easy to find.

Opening Anaconda (Windows)

After Anaconda is installed in Windows, you can start it as you would any other app. Although there are some differences among different versions of Windows, you should be able to use either of these two options:

>> Click the Start button, and then click Anaconda Navigator on the Start menu.

>> Click the Start button, start typing **Anaconda**, and then click Anaconda Navigator on the Start menu when you see it there.

On the Start menu, you can right-click Anaconda Navigator and choose Pin to Start or right-click and choose More⇨Pin to Taskbar to make the icon easy to find in the future.

Using Anaconda Navigator

Anaconda Navigator, as the name implies, is the component of the Anaconda environment that lets you navigate around through different features of the app and choose what you want to run. When you first start Navigator, it opens to the Anaconda Navigator home page, which should look something like Figure 1-5.

If you see a prompt to get an updated version when you open Anaconda, it's okay to install the update. It won't cost anything or affect your ability to follow along in this book.

The left side of the Anaconda Navigator home page has options such as Home, Environments, Learning, and Community. They're not directly related to learning and doing Python, so you're welcome to explore them on your own.

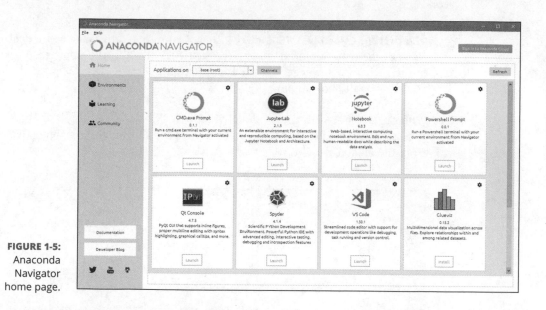

FIGURE 1-5:
Anaconda
Navigator
home page.

Writing Python in VS Code

Most of the Python coding we do here, we'll do in VS Code. Whenever you want to use VS Code to write Python, we suggest that you open VS Code from Anaconda Navigator rather than from the Start menu or Launch Pad. That way, VS Code will already be pointing to the version of Python that comes with Anaconda, which is easier than trying to figure out all that yourself. So the steps are

1. If you haven't already done so, open Anaconda Navigator.

2. Scroll down a little until you see the Launch button under VS Code, if necessary, and then click the Launch button.

ABOUT GIT

Git is a way to store backups of your coding projects and share coding projects with other developers or team members. It's popular with professional programmers, and VS Code has built-in support for it. But Git is optional and not directly related to learning or doing Python coding, so it's perfectly okay to choose Don't Show Again to bypass that offer when it arrives. You can install Git at any time if you later decide to learn about it.

The first time you open VS Code, you may be prompted to make some decisions. None of them are required, so you can just click the X in the upper-right corner of the each one. However, the one that mentions Git will keep popping up unless you click Don't Show Again.

When you're finished, the VS Code window will look something like Figure 1-6. If you don't see quite that many options on your screen, choose Help➪Welcome from the menu bar.

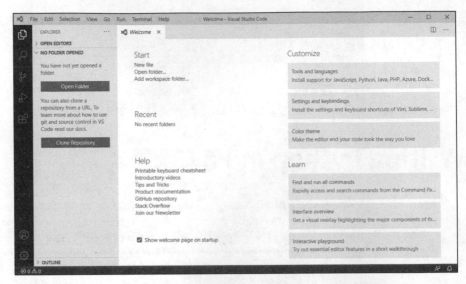

FIGURE 1-6:
The welcome screen of VS Code editor.

Your screen will likely be black with white and colored text. In this book, we show everything as white with black text because it's easier to read on paper that way. You can keep the dark background if you like. If you would rather have a light background, choose Code➪Preferences➪Color Theme (Mac) or File➪Preferences➪Color Theme (Windows). Then choose a lighter color theme; if you choose Light (Visual Studio), your VS Code screens will look more like the ones in this book.

Visual Studio Code is a generic code editor that works with many different languages. To use VS Code with Python and Anaconda, you need some VS Code *extensions*. But you should already have them because they come with your Anaconda download. To verify that, click the Extensions icon in the left pane (it looks like a puzzle piece). You should see at least three extensions listed: Anaconda Extension Pack, Python, and YAML, as shown in Figure 1-7.

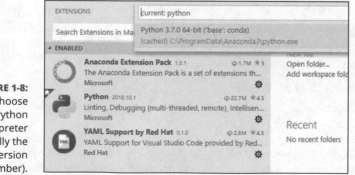

FIGURE 1-7:
VS Code extensions for Python.

Choosing your Python interpreter

Before you start doing any Python coding in VS Code, you want to make sure you're using the correct Python interpreter. To do so, follow these steps:

1. **Choose View ⇨ Command Palette from VS Code's menu.**

2. **Type** python **and then click Python: Select Interpreter.**

Choose the Python version number that matches your download (the one you jotted down while first downloading Anaconda). If you have multiple options with the same version number, choose the one that includes the names *base* and *conda*, as in Figure 1-8.

FIGURE 1-8:
Choose your Python interpreter (usually the highest version number).

Writing some Python code

To ensure that you'll be able to follow along with the examples in this book, let's make sure VS Code is ready for Python coding. Follow these steps:

1. **In VS Code, choose View ⇨ Terminal from the VS Code menu.**

You should see a pane along the bottom-right that looks like one of those shown in Figure 1-9.

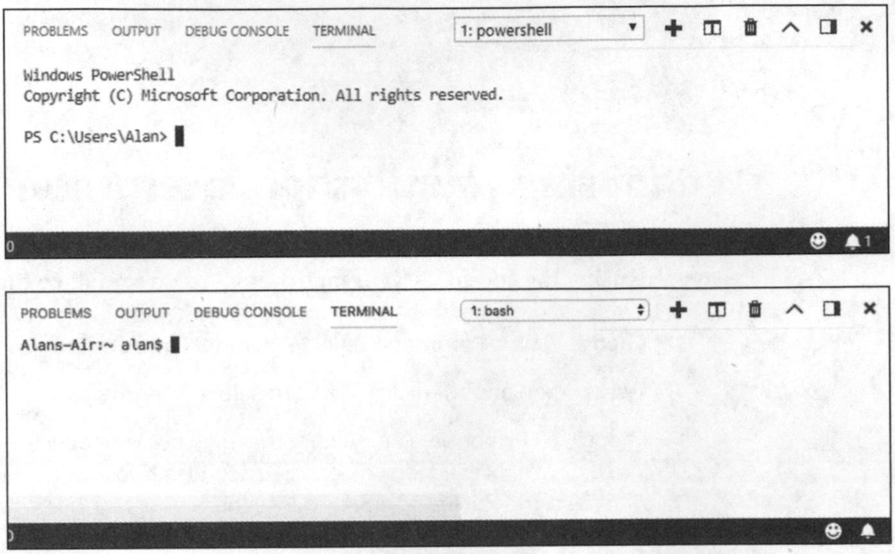

```
PROBLEMS   OUTPUT   DEBUG CONSOLE   TERMINAL        1: powershell       ▼   ✚  ⬚  🗑  ︿  ▢  ✖

Windows PowerShell
Copyright (C) Microsoft Corporation. All rights reserved.

PS C:\Users\Alan> █
```

```
PROBLEMS   OUTPUT   DEBUG CONSOLE   TERMINAL        1: bash             ▼   ✚  ⬚  🗑  ︿  ▢  ✖

Alans-Air:~ alan$ █
```

FIGURE 1-9: Terminal in VS Code (Windows and Mac).

2. **In Terminal, type** python **and press Enter.**

You should see some information about Python followed by a >>> prompt. That >>> prompt is your Python interpreter; if you type Python code there and press Enter, the code will execute.

3. **Type** 1+1 **and press Enter.**

You should now see 2 (the sum of 1 plus 1), followed by another Python prompt, as shown in Figure 1-10.

The 1+1 exercise is about as simple an exercise as you can do. However, all we care about right now is that you saw 2, because that means your Python development environment is all set up and ready to go. You won't have to repeat any of these steps in the future.

```
(base) PS C:\Users\Alan> python
Python 3.8.3 (default, Jul  2 2020, 17:30:36) [MSC v.1916 64 bit (AMD64)] :: Anaconda, Inc. on win32
Type "help", "copyright", "credits" or "license" for more information.
>>> 1+1
2
>>>
```

Now we'll show you how to exit Python and VS Code:

1. **In the VS Code Terminal pane, press CTRL+D or type** exit() **and press Enter.**

   The last prompt at the bottom of the Terminal window should now be whatever it was before you went to the Python prompt, indicating that you're no longer in the Interpreter.

2. **To close VS Code:**

   - *Windows: Click the Close icon (X) in the upper-right corner or choose View ⇨ Exit from the menu.*

   - *Mac: Click the round red dot in the upper-left corner, or choose Code ⇨ Quit Visual Studio Code from the menu.*

3. **Close Anaconda Navigator using a similar technique:**

   - *Window: Click the X in the upper-right corner or choose File ⇨ Quit from the menu bar.*

   - *Mac: Click the red dot or go to Anaconda Navigator in the menu and choose Quit Anaconda Navigator.*

Getting back to VS Code Python

In the future, any time you want to work in Python in VS Code, we suggest you open Anaconda Navigator and then Launch VS Code from there. You'll be ready to roll and do any of the hands-on exercises presented in future chapters.

Using Jupyter Notebook for Coding

Jupyter Notebook is another popular tool for writing Python code. The name *Jupyter* comes from the fact that it supports writing code in three popular languages: **Julia** and **Python** and **R**. Julia and R are popular for data science. Python is a more generic programming language that happens to be popular in data science as well, though Python is good for all kinds of development, not just data science. The *Notebook* part of the name comes from the fact that your code is placed in structures similar to a regular paper notebook.

People often use Jupyter to share code on the Internet. It is free and comes with Anaconda. So if you've installed Anaconda, you already have it and can open it any time by following these simple steps:

1. **Open Anaconda as discussed previously**

2. **Click Launch under Jupyter Notebook, as shown in Figure 1-11.**

   Jupyter notebooks are web-based, meaning that when Jupyter opens, it does so in your default web browser, such as Safari, Chrome, Edge, Firefox, or Internet Explorer. At first, it doesn't look like it has much to do with coding, because it just shows an alphabetized list of folder (directory) names to which it has access, as shown in Figure 1-12. (Of course, the names you see may be different from those in the figure, because those folder names are from our computer, not yours.)

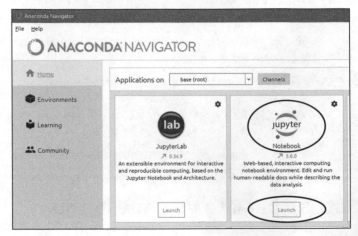

FIGURE 1-11:
Launch Jupyter Notebook from Anaconda's home page.

FIGURE 1-12:
Jupyter Notebook opening page.

3. **Click a folder name of your choosing (the Desktop is fine; we're not making any commitment here).**

4. **Click New, and then choose Python 3 under Notebook, as shown in Figure 1-13.**

   A new, empty notebook named Untitled opens. You should see a rectangle with In [ ]: on the left side. That's called a *cell*, and a cell can contain either code (words written in the Python language) or just regular text and pictures. If you want to write code, make sure the drop-down menu in the toolbar displays Code. Change that menu option to Markdown if you want to write regular text rather than Python code.

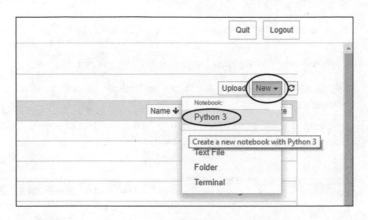

FIGURE 1-13:
Creating a new
Jupyter notebook.

**TECHNICAL
STUFF**

Markdown is a language for writing text that uses fonts, pictures, and such. We'll talk more about that in the next chapter. For now, let's stay focused on Python code, because that's what this book is all about.

A cell is not like the Python interpreter, where your code executes immediately. You have to type some code first (any amount), and then run that code by clicking the Run button in the toolbar. To see for yourself, follow these steps:

1. **Click inside the code cell.**

2. **Type** 1+1.

3. **Press Enter.**

You see 1+1 in the cell, but not the result, 2. To get the result, click Run in the toolbar or put the mouse pointer into the cell and click the Run icon to the left of the cell, as shown in Figure 1-14, or click Run in the toolbar above the cell. You'll see the number 2 to the right of Out[1]. Out indicates that you're seeing the output from executing the code in the cell, which of course is 2 because 1 plus 1 is 2.

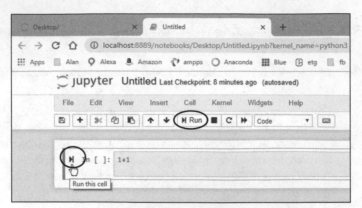

FIGURE 1-14:
Two ways to run code in a Jupyter cell.

To close a notebook, do either of these following:

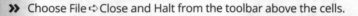

>> Close the tab in the browser that's showing the cell.

>> Choose File ⇨ Close and Halt from the toolbar above the cells.

Figure 1-15 shows an example using Chrome as the browser. Your tabs may look different if you're using a different browser.

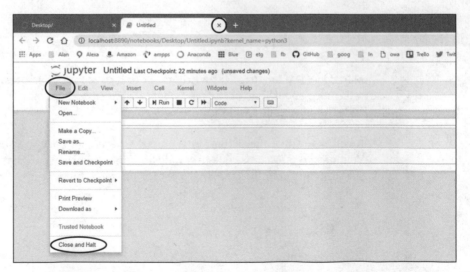

FIGURE 1-15:
Result of running code in a Jupyter Notebook cell.

You may be prompted to save your work. For now, you don't need to save because we're focused on the absolute basics . . . what you'll do every time you run Python code.

Even if you don't specifically save a notebook, you'll see an icon for it in the folder in which you created the notebook. The notebook's name will be Untitled, and if you have filename extensions visible, you'll see the .ipynb filename extension. The *pynb* part is short for Python notebook. The *i* in that extension, in case you're wondering, comes from iPython, which is the name of the app from which Jupyter Notebook was created and is short for interactive.

You can delete a notebook file if you're just practicing and don't want to keep it. Just make sure you close the notebook in the web browser (or just close the browser first) — otherwise, you may get an error message stating that you can't delete the file while it's open.

So now you're ready to go. You have a great set of tools set up for learning Python. The simple skills you've learned in this chapter will serve you well through your learning process, as well as your professional programming after you've mastered the basics. Come on over to Chapter 2 in this minibook now and we'll delve a bit deeper into Python and using the tools you now have available on your computer.

IN THIS CHAPTER

» Using interactive mode

» Creating a development workspace

» Creating a folder for your code

» Typing, editing, and debugging code

» Writing code in a Jupyter

Chapter **2**

Interactive Mode, Getting Help, and Writing Apps

Now that you've installed Anaconda and VS Code, you're ready to start digging deeper into writing Python code. In this chapter, we take you briefly through the interactive, help, and code-editing features of VS Code and Jupyter Notebook to build on what you've learned so far. Most of you are probably anxious to get started on more advanced topics such as data science, artificial intelligence, robotics, or whatever. But learning those topics will be easier if you have a good understanding of the many tools available to you — and the skills to use them.

Using Python's Interactive Mode

Many teachers and authors will suggest that you try things hands-on at the Python prompt, and assume you already know how to get there. We've seen many frustrated beginners complain that trying activities recommended in some tutorial never work for them. The frustration often stems from the fact that they're typing and executing the code in the wrong place. With Anaconda, the Terminal pane in VS Code is a great place to type Python code. So in this chapter that's where you'll start.

Opening Terminal

To use Python interactively with Anaconda, follow these steps:

1. **Open Anaconda Navigator, and then open VS Code by clicking its Launch button on the Anaconda home page.**

2. **If you don't see the Terminal pane at the bottom of the VS Code window, choose View ⇨ Terminal from the VS Code menu bar.**

3. **If the word *Terminal* isn't highlighted at the top of the pane, click Terminal (circled in Figure 2-1).**

```
PROBLEMS   OUTPUT   DEBUG CONSOLE   ( TERMINAL )              1: powershell      ▼   ✚   ⊡

Windows PowerShell
Copyright (C) Microsoft Corporation. All rights reserved.

PS C:\Users\Alan>
```

FIGURE 2-1:
The Terminal pane in VS Code.

The first prompt you see is typically for your computer's operating system, and likely shows the user name of the account you're using. For example, on a Mac, it may look like `Alans-Air:~ alan$` but with the name of your computer in place of `Alans-Air`. In Windows it would likely be `C:\Users\Alan>`, with your user name in place of `Alan`, and possibly a different path than `C:\Users`.

For example, on a Mac, we see this prompt:

```
Alans-Air:~ alan$
```

And in Windows, we see this:

```
C:\Users\Alan>
```

COLORS AND ICONS IN VS CODE

By default, the VS Code Terminal pane displays white text against a black background. We reverse those colors in this book because dark text against a light background is easier to see in a printed book. You can use any color scheme you like. If you want to switch to black on white, as shown in this book, choose File (Windows) or Code (Mac) and then choose Preferences ⇨ Color Theme ⇨ Light (Visual Studio).

If you want your icons in VS Code to match the ones we use, you'll need to download and install the Material Icon theme. You may also want to download the Material Color theme and try it out; we don't use it for the book because it doesn't play well when printed on paper. Follow these steps:

1. **Click the Extensions icon (puzzle piece) in the left pane.**

2. **Type** material, **look for Material Icon Theme, and click its Install option.**

3. **If you see a prompt at the bottom right asking if you want to activate the icons, click Activate.**

4. **Choose File (Windows) or Code (Mac), choose Preferences ⇨ File Icon Theme, and then click Material Icon Theme.**

   If you don't see the Material icon as an option, make sure you've downloaded the extension.

5. **If you'd like to try out the Material color theme, open File (in Windows) or Code (on a Mac), choose Preferences ⇨ Color Theme, and then click Material Icon Theme.**

If at any time you change your mind about the color theme, repeat Step 5 and choose something other than Material Icon Theme.

Depending on your Windows version and current configuration, you might see the following prompt instead, where xxx is your user name:

```
PS C:\Users\xxx>.
```

This just means that you're using PowerShell. You don't need to change anything. The command shown here will work with PowerShell too.

You would see your user name in place of Alan and possibly a different path than C:\Users.

Getting your Python version

At the operating system command prompt, type the following and press Enter to see what version of Python you're using. Note the space before the first hyphen, and no other spaces.

```
python --version
```

You should see something like Python 3.*x.x* (where the *x*'s are numbers representing the version of Python you're using). If instead you see an error message, you're not quite where you need to be. You want to make sure you start VS Code from Anaconda, not just from Launch Pad or your Start menu. Type **python --version** in the VS Code Terminal pane, and press Enter again. If it still doesn't work, choose View ⇨ Command Palette from the VS Code menu bar, type **python**, choose Python: Select Interpreter, and then choose the Python interpreter you downloaded with Anaconda.

Going into the Python Interpreter

When you're able to enter python --version and not get an error, you're ready to work with Python in VS Code. From there you can get into the Python interpreter by entering the command

```
python
```

REMEMBER

When we, or anyone else, says "enter the command," that means you have to type the command and then press Enter. Nothing happens until you press Enter. So if you just type the command and wait for something to happen, you'll be waiting for a long, long time.

A NOTE ABOUT PyLint

PyLint is a feature of Anacaona that helps you find and avoid errors in your code. It's usually turned on by default. The first time you try to use Python, you might see some messages in the lower-right corner of VS Code. If you see a message about *Python Language Server,* click Try It Now and then click Reload. If you see a message that *Linter PyLint Is Not Installed,* click Install.

If you see *Select Python Environment* near the lower-left corner of VS Code's window, click that and choose the Anaconda option from the menu that drops down near the top center. If you see multiple Anaconda options, choose the one with the largest version number.

You should see some information about the Python version you're using and the
>>> prompt, which represents the Python interpreter.

Entering commands

Entering commands in the Python interpreter is the same as typing them anywhere else. You must type the command correctly, and then press Enter. If you
spell something wrong in the command, you will likely see an error message,
which is just the interpreter telling you it doesn't understand what you mean.
But don't worry, you can't break anything. For example, suppose you type the
command

```
howdy
```

After you press Enter, you'll see some techie gibberish that is trying to tell you
that the interpreter doesn't know what "howdy" means, so it can't do that. Nothing has broken. You're just back to another >>> prompt, where you can try again,
as shown in Figure 2-2.

FIGURE 2-2:
Python doesn't
know what *howdy*
means.

Using Python's built-in help

One of the prompts in Figure 2-2 mentions that you can type help as a command
in the Python interpreter. Note that you don't type the quotation marks, just the
word *help* (and then press Enter, as always). This time you see

```
Type help() for interactive help, or help(object) for help about object.
```

Now the interpreter is telling you to type **help** followed by an empty pair of paren-
theses, or help with a specific word in parentheses (*object* is the example given).
Even though you're told to type the command, you should type it and press Enter.
Go ahead and enter the following:

```
help()
```

Note that the line does not have spaces. After you press Enter, the screen provides some information about using Python's interactive help, something like the example shown in Figure 2-3.

PROBLEMS   OUTPUT   DEBUG CONSOLE   TERMINAL   1: python   ∨   +   ⬚   🗑   ∧   ×

```
>>> help()

Welcome to Python 3.8's help utility!

If this is your first time using Python, you should definitely check out
the tutorial on the Internet at https://docs.python.org/3.8/tutorial/.
Enter the name of any module, keyword, or topic to get help on writing
Python programs and using Python modules.  To quit this help utility and
return to the interpreter, just type "quit".

To get a list of available modules, keywords, symbols, or topics, type
"modules", "keywords", "symbols", or "topics".  Each module also comes
with a one-line summary of what it does; to list the modules whose name
or summary contain a given string such as "spam", type "modules spam".

help> █
```

FIGURE 2-3:
Python's interactive help utility.

Seeing help> at the bottom of the window tells you that you're no longer in the operating system shell or the Python interpreter (which always shows >>>) but are now in a new area that provides help. As described on the screen, you can enter the name of any module, keyword, or topic to get help with that term. As a beginner, you might not need help with specifics right at the moment. But it's good to know that the help is there if you need it.

For example, Python uses certain keywords, which have special meaning in the language. To get a list of those, just type the following at the help> prompt:

```
keywords
```

After you press Enter, you'll see a list of keywords, as shown in Figure 2-4.

PROBLEMS   OUTPUT   TERMINAL   ⋯   1: python   ▾   ✚   ⬚   🗑   ∧   ▢   ✖

```
help> keywords

Here is a list of the Python keywords.  Enter any keyword to get more help.

False               class               from                or
None                continue            global              pass
True                def                 if                  raise
and                 del                 import              return
as                  elif                in                  try
assert              else                is                  while
async               except              lambda              with
await               finally             nonlocal            yield
break               for                 not

help> █
```

FIGURE 2-4:
Keyword help.

Above the list of keywords is a message telling you that you can type any keyword at the help> prompt for more information about that keyword. For example, entering the class keyword provides information about Python classes, as shown in Figure 2-5. These are not the kind of classes you attend at school; rather, they're the kind you create in Python (after you've learned the basics and are ready to move onto more advanced topics).

```
PROBLEMS   OUTPUT   TERMINAL   ...        1: python        ▼  ➕ ⬜ 🗑 ∧ ⬜ ✕

Class definitions
*****************

A class definition defines a class object (see section The standard
type hierarchy):

    classdef    ::= [decorators] "class" classname [inheritance] ":" suite
    inheritance ::= "(" [argument_list] ")"
    classname   ::= identifier

A class definition is an executable statement.  The inheritance list
usually gives a list of base classes (see Metaclasses for more
advanced uses), so each item in the list should evaluate to a class
object which allows subclassing.  Classes without an inheritance list
-- More --
```

FIGURE 2-5: Python class help.

All the technical jargon in the help text is going to leave the average beginner flummoxed. But as you learn about new concepts in Python, realize that you can use the interactive help for guidance as needed.

The --More-- at the bottom of the text isn't a prompt where you type commands. Instead, it just lets you know that there is more text, perhaps several pages worth. Press the spacebar or Enter to see it. Every time you see -- More --, you can press the spacebar or Enter to get to the next page. Eventually you'll get back to the help> prompt. If you want to quit rather than keep scrolling, press the letter q.

Exiting interactive help

To get out of interactive help and return to the Python prompt, type the letter **q** (for quit) or press Ctrl+Z. You should be back at the >>> prompt. At the >>> prompt, type exit() or python.

To leave the Python prompt and get back to the operating system, type **exit()** and press Enter. Note that if you make a mistake, such as forgetting the parentheses, you'll get some help on the screen. For example, if you type exit and press Enter, you'll see

```
Use exit() or Ctrl-Z plus Return to exit.
```

You'll know you've exited the Python interpreter when you see the operating system prompt rather than >>> at the end of the Terminal window, as in Figure 2-6.

```
PROBLEMS   OUTPUT   TERMINAL   ...        1: powershell    ▾   ✚ ⊡ 🗑 ⌃ ◻ ✕

See also: **PEP 3115** - Metaclasses in Python 3 **PEP 3129** -
   Class Decorators

Related help topics: CLASSES, SPECIALMETHODS

help> q

You are now leaving help and returning to the Python interpreter.
If you want to ask for help on a particular object directly from the
interpreter, you can type "help(object)".  Executing "help('string')"
has the same effect as typing a particular string at the help> prompt.
>>> exit
Use exit() or Ctrl-Z plus Return to exit
>>> exit()
PS C:\Users\Alan>
```

FIGURE 2-6:
Back to the operating system prompt.

Searching for specific help topics online

Python's built-in help is somewhat archaic because it's text oriented rather than interactive, but it can help you when you need a quick reminder about some Python keyword you've forgotten. But if you're online, you're better off searching the web for help. If you're looking for videos, start at www.youtube.com; if not, https://stackoverflow.com/ is a good place to ask questions and search for help. And of course there's always Google, Bing, and other search engines.

Regardless of what you use to search, remember to start your search with the word *python* or *python 3*. A lot of programming languages share similar concepts and keywords, so if you don't specify the Python language in your search request, there's no telling what kinds of results you may get.

Lots of free cheat sheets

Other good resources for learners are the countless cheat sheets available online for free. Whenever you start to feel overwhelmed by all the possibilities of a language like Python, a cheat sheet summarizing things to a single page or so can help bring information to a more manageable (and less intimidating) size.

Of course, you're not really cheating with a cheat sheet, unless you use it while taking a test that you're supposed to answer from memory. But writing code in real life is much different from answering multiple-choice questions. So what we often call a *cheat sheet* in the tech world is just another tool to help us learn. Many types of cheat sheets are available — what appeals to you depends on your learning style. To see what's available, head to Google or Bing or any search engine you like and search for *free python 3 cheat sheet*. Most are in a format you can download, print, and keep handy as you learn the seemingly infinite possibilities of writing code in Python.

Creating a Python Development Workspace

Although interactive modes and online help are decent support tools, most people want to use Python to create apps. We've found that creating apps is easiest if you set up a VS Code development environment specifically for learning and coding Python. You can set up other development environments for coding in other languages, such as HTML, CSS, and JavaScript for the web, fine-tuning each as you go along to best support whatever language you're working in.

We often switch between Mac and Windows computers, so we have one development environment for each. Alan keeps his in a OneDrive folder so he can get to them from anywhere. Although this is not a requirement, it's handy. If you'll be working strictly from one computer, however, you can put your environment on your computer's hard drive rather than on a cloud drive.

VS Code uses the term *workspace* to define what we call a *development environment.* That environment is the Python interpreter you're using plus any additional extensions you gather along the way.

You can store your workspaces anyplace you like. Do so now, before proceeding with the next set of steps:

1. **If VS Code isn't already open, launch it from Anaconda.**

2. **Choose File ⇨ Save Workspace As, and navigate to the folder where you want to save the workspace settings.**

3. **Type a name for the workspace, and then click Save.**

   In Figure 2-7, Alan is saving his workspace in Windows (top) and then on a Mac (bottom).

4. **Next, do one of the following, depending on whether you're using a Mac or Windows, to adjust some VS Code settings to indicate the location of that saved workspace:**

   - On a Mac, choose Code ⇨ Preferences ⇨ Settings.

   - In Windows, choose File ⇨ Preferences ⇨ Settings.

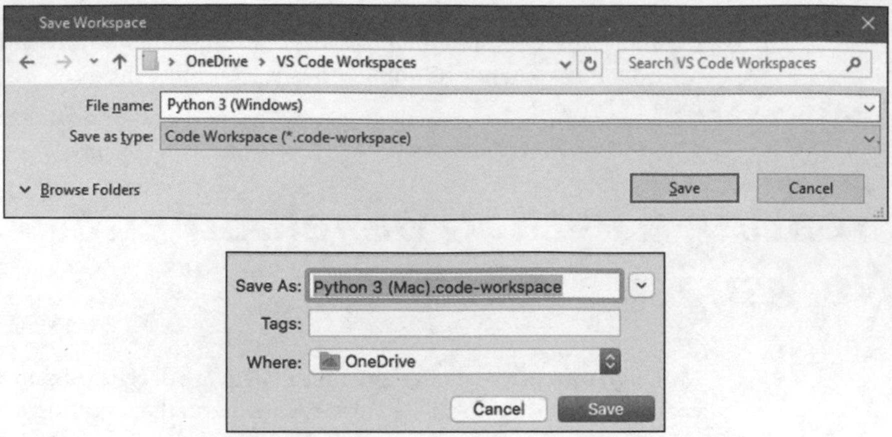

FIGURE 2-7:
Saving
current settings
as workspace
settings.

5. **If you see a page like the one in Figure 2-8, click the Open Settings (JSON) icon near the top-right corner (and circled in the figure).**

   If you don't see that icon, look for one that allows you to open Settings.json.

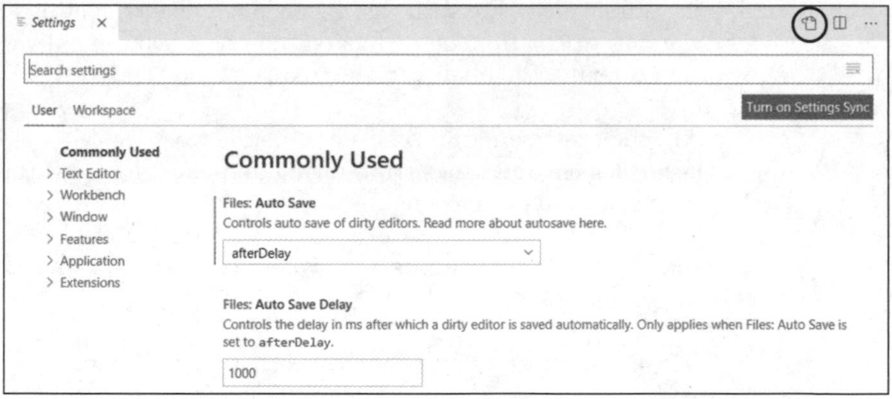

FIGURE 2-8:
VS Code Settings.

6. **In the next window, select the entire line of code that starts with** `python.pythonpath` **(that line tells VS Code where to find the Python interpreter on your computer).**

   You can also select any other command lines that you'd like to make part of the workspace, but don't select the curly braces.

7. **Right-click the selected code and choose Copy to copy it to the clipboard.**

8. **Click the Split Editor Right icon, near the top-right corner.**

   (The icon looks like two side-by-side pages in the version of VS code we're using right now.) Two copies of settings.json appear side-by-side on the screen.

9. **Choose View ⇨ Command Palette. Type** open **and then select Preferences: Open Workspace Settings (JSON).**

10. **Click between the setting's curly braces and paste the lines of code there, as shown in Figure 2-9.**

    All the settings in settings.json (on the top) are copied to the Python 3 settings (on the bottom).

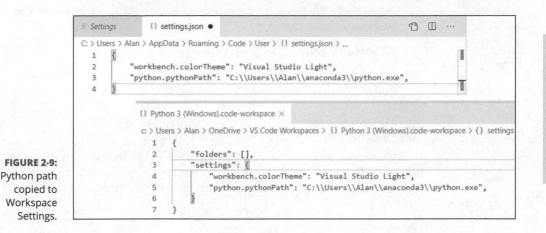

FIGURE 2-9: Python path copied to Workspace Settings.

11. **Choose File ⇨ Save from the VS Code menu.**

12. **Close the Settings and User Settings tabs by clicking the X on the right side of each tab.**

13. **Close VS Code, and then close Anaconda.**

You'll see how to take advantage of the new workspace settings in a moment.

Creating a Folder for Your Python Code

Next, you create a folder to store all the Python code that you write in this book, so it's all together in one place and easy to find when you need it. You can put this folder anywhere you like and name it whatever you like.

In Windows you can navigate to the folder that will contain the new folder (Alan uses OneDrive, but you can use Desktop, Documents, or any other folder). Right-click an empty place in the folder. Then choose New Folder (Mac) or New ⇨ Folder (Windows). Type the folder name and press Enter. To follow along with the examples in this chapter, name your folder *AIO Python*.

Now you should associate this code folder with the VS Code workspace you just created, so that any time you work in the folder you're using the correct Python interpreter and other Python-related settings you choose over time with the files in the code folder. Here's how:

1. **Open Anaconda and launch VS Code from there.**

2. **From the VS Code menu, choose File ➪ Open Workspace.**

3. **Navigate to the folder where you saved your workspace and open the workspace from there.**

4. **Choose File ➪ Add Folder to Workspace.**

5. **Navigate to the folder in which you created the folder for your Python code, click that folder's icon, and choose Add.**

The Explorer bar in VS Code, shown in Figure 2-10, indicates that you've opened both the workspace — Python 3 (Windows) Workspace in the figure — and, under that workspace, the code folder — AIO Python in the figure. If you see something entirely different in the left pane, click the Explorer icon, at the top-left corner of the VS Code window, to make sure you're viewing the Explorer pane.

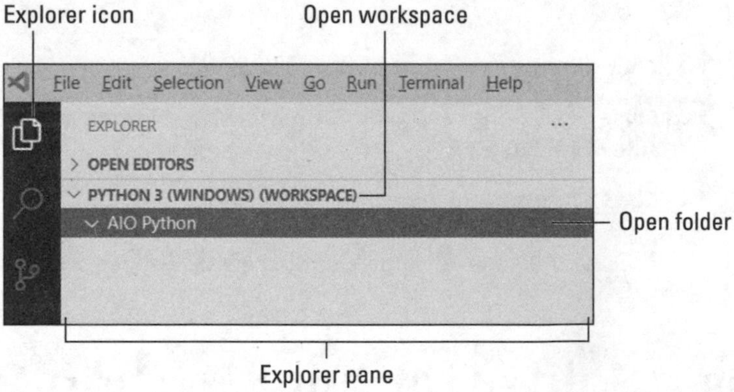

FIGURE 2-10:
Python 3 workspace and AIO Python folder open in VS Code.

When you expand the Open Editors bar, near the top of the Explorer pane, you see files that are currently open in VS Code. Each open file is represented by a tab across the top of the editing area to the right. Right now, in the image, no files were open. But if, say, the VS Code Welcome page is open right now on your own screen, you see Welcome on the right. To close that page, click the X next to its name in the Explorer pane or on the tab. Any time you want to reopen the Welcome page, choose Help ➪ Welcome from the VS Code menu bar.

TIP

If you see a symbol other than a triangle, or no symbol at all, before a folder name, you maybe be using an icon theme that's different from the default. No worries, just click to the left of any folder to expand or collapse it.

You went through quite a few steps to set up your workspace. The benefit, especially if you use VS Code to work in multiple languages, is that any time you want to work with Python in VS Code, all you have to do is follow these steps:

1. **If you've closed VS Code, launch it from Anaconda Navigator.**

2. **Choose File ⇨ Open Workspace from the VS Code menu.**

3. **Open your workspace.**

   The workspace and any folders you've associated with that workspace open, and you're ready to go.

Typing, Editing, and Debugging Python Code

Most likely, you'll write the vast majority of code in an editor. As you probably know, an *editor* enables you to type and edit text. Code is text. The editor in VS Code is set up for typing and editing code, so you may hear it referred to as a *code editor*.

Each Python code file you create will be a plain text file with a .py filename extension. We suggest that you keep any files you create for this book in that AIO Python folder, which you should be able to see anytime VS Code and your Python 3 workspace are open.

To create a .py file at any time, follow these steps:

1. **If you haven't already done so, open VS Code and your Python 3 workspace.**

2. **If the Explorer pane isn't open, click the Explorer icon near the top-left of VS Code.**

3. **To create a file in your AIO Python folder, right-click the folder name and choose New File, as shown in Figure 2-11.**

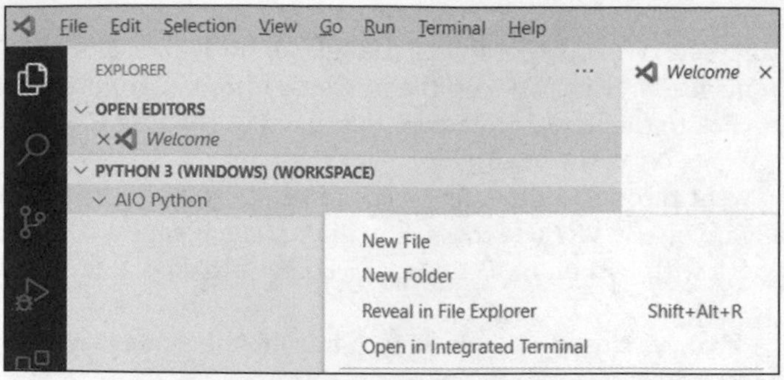

FIGURE 2-11:
Right-click a
folder name and
choose New File.

4. Type the filename with the `.py` **extension (hello.py for this first one) and press Enter.**

The new file opens and you can see its name in the tab on the right, as shown in Figure 2-12. The larger area below the tab is the editor, where you type the Python code. The filename also appears under the AIO Python folder name in the Explorer pane, because that's where it's stored. You can click the Open Editors line to expand and collapse it, which just reveals the names of documents that are currently open for editing.

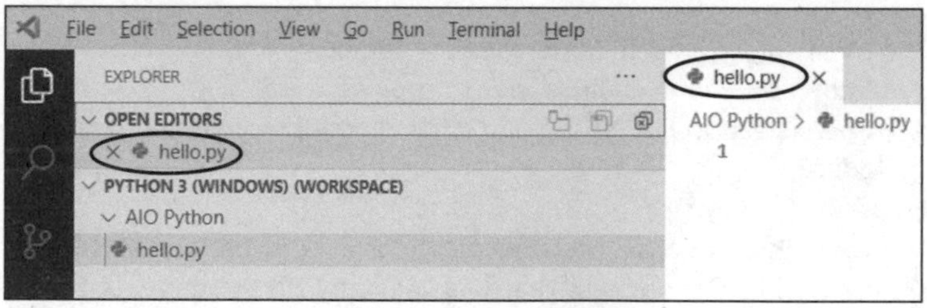

FIGURE 2-12:
New hello.py
file is open for
editing in VS
Code.

Writing Python code

Now that you have a `.py` file open, you can use it to write some Python code. As is typical when learning a new programming language, you'll start by typing a simple Hello World program. Here are the steps:

1. Click just to the right of line 1 in the editing area.

2. Type the following:

```
print("Hello World")
```

As you're typing, you may notice text appearing on the screen. That text is *IntelliSense text,* which detects what you're typing and shows you some information about that keyword. You don't have to do anything with that, though — just keep typing.

3. **Press Enter after you've typed the line.**

The new line of code is displayed on the screen. You may also notice a few other changes, as shown in Figure 2-13:

>> The Explorer icon sports a circled 1, indicating that you currently have one unsaved change.

>> The hello.py name in the tab and the same filename under Open Editors (if that section is expanded) displays a dot, to indicate that the file has unsaved changes.

Unsaved changes indicators

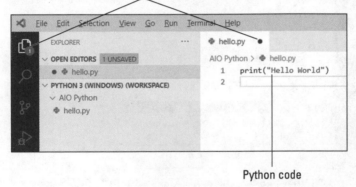

FIGURE 2-13:
The hello.py file contains some Python code and has unsaved changes.

Python code

Saving your code

Code you type in VS Code is not saved automatically. There are two ways to deal with that. One is to try to remember to save any time you make a change that's worth saving. The easiest way to do that is to choose File⇨Save from VS Code's menu bar or press Ctrl+S in Windows or ⌘+S on a Mac.

We prefer the second method, which is to use AutoSave to automatically save changes we make. To enable Auto Save, choose File⇨Auto Save from VS Code's menu bar. The check mark next to Auto Save means that it's turned on. To turn off AutoSave, just choose File⇨Auto Save again. The file is saved automatically as you make changes.

Running Python in VS Code

To test your Python code in VS Code, you need to run it. The easiest way to do that is to right-click the file's name (`hello.py` in this example) and choose Run Python File in Terminal, as shown in Figure 2-14.

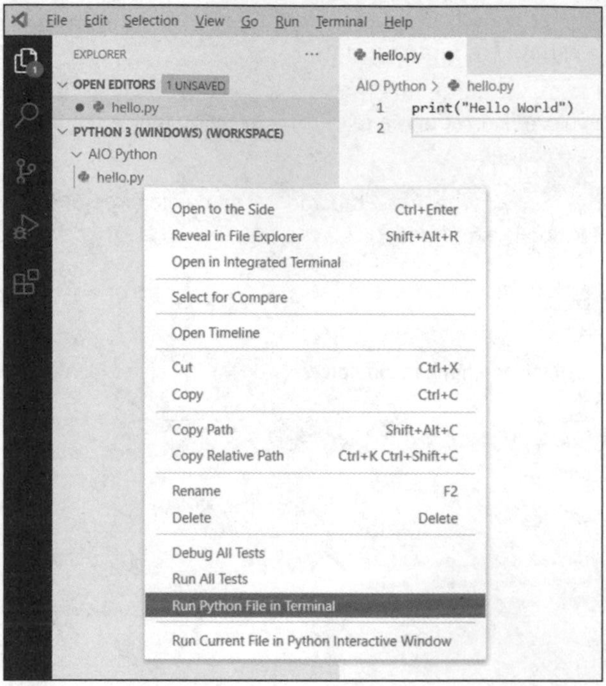

FIGURE 2-14: Run `hello.py`.

The Terminal pane opens along the bottom of the VS Code window. You'll see a command prompt followed by a comment to run the code in the Python interpreter (`python.exe`). And below that, you'll see the output of the program: the words *Hello World*, in this example, and then another prompt, as shown in Figure 2-15. This app is not the most exciting one in the world, but at least now you know how to write, save, and execute a Python program in VS Code, a skill you'll be using often as you continue through this book and through your Python programming career.

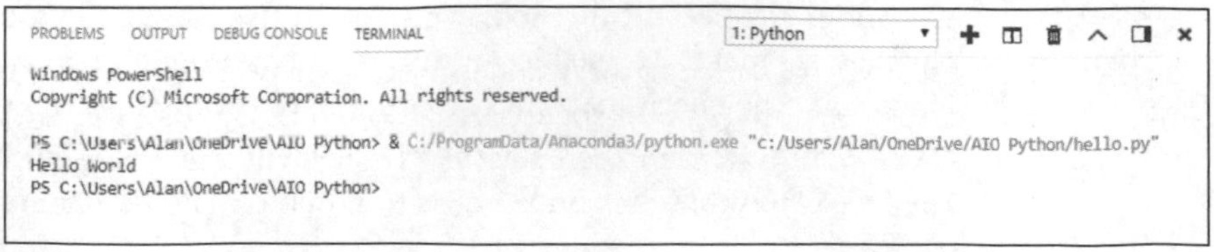

FIGURE 2-15: Output from `hello.py`.

If you're using PowerShell in the Terminal window, you may see a message about switching to the command prompt. Unless you happen to be a PowerShell expert and need it (for whatever reason), you might as well click Use Command Prompt if you see that option so the prompt won't keep pestering you.

Learning simple debugging

When you're first learning to write code, you're bound to make a lot of mistakes. Realize that mistakes are no big deal — you won't break or destroy anything. The code just won't work as expected.

Before you attempt to run some code, you might see several screen indications of an error in your code:

>> The name of the folder and file that contain the error will be red in the Explorer pane.

>> The number of errors in the file will appear in red next to the filename in the Explorer bar.

>> The total number of errors will appear next to the circled X in the bottom left corner of the VS Code window.

>> The bad code will have a wavy red underline.

In Figure 2-16, we typed PRINT in all uppercase, which is not allowed in Python. Python is case-sensitive and the correct command is print. Remember, when we show a command to type in lowercase, you have to type it in lowercase, too.

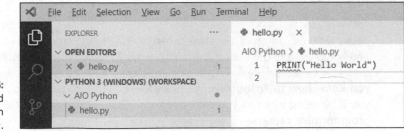

FIGURE 2-16:
PRINT is typed incorrectly in hello.py.

To run the file in Terminal, you must fix the error. Hover the mouse pointer over the word with the red wavy underline to see a brief (and highly technical) description of the problem. In the example shown in Figure 2-16, we would just replace *PRINT* with *print*, and then save the change (unless we've turned on Auto Save). Then we can right-click and choose Run Python File in Terminal to run the corrected code.

Using the VS Code Python debugger

VS Code has a built-in debugger that helps when working with more complex programs and provides a means of testing Python programs in VS Code. You won't be writing anything super complex right now. But there's no harm in getting the debugger set up and ready as part of your Python development workspace. Follow these steps to do so now:

1. **Click the debug icon to the left of the Explorer pane.**

   (The Debug icon is a right-facing triangle with a bug in the corner.) The Debug pane opens.

2. **If you see Create a Launch.json File link, click it.**

3. **Click the drop-down menu at the top of the pane and choose Workspace, and then click Python File Debug the Currently Active Python File, as shown in Figure 2-17.**

4. **Close launch.json by clicking the X on its tab.**

FIGURE 2-17: VS Code Debug pane.

Open Debug pane   Start Debugging

From now on, as an alternative to using the right-click method to run Python code, you can use the Debug pane. The debugger always works with the *current file*, which is whatever file is selected (highlighted) in the Explorer pane. So the usual steps for using the debugger will likely be as follows:

1. **Click the Explorer pane to see a list of all your files.**

2. **Click the icon or file name of the file you want to debug.**

   At the moment you have only one file, `hello.py`. The `hello.py` filename is highlighted in the Explorer pane. The highlight tells you that `hello.py` is the current file that the debugger will run when you tell it to.

3. **Open the Debug pane again by clicking the Debug icon in the left bar of VS Code again.**

4. **Click the Start Debugging icon.**

   The icon is a green triangle next to Python: Current File (workspace).

When you click the Start Debugging icon, the Python code will run as it did when you chose Run Python File in Terminal. If your code has an error, you'll get additional help on the screen describing the error.

If that seems like a lot to remember, for now all you have to remember is that whenever you want to run some Python code in VS Code, you can do either of the following:

» Right-click the .py file's name and choose Run File in Terminal.

» Click the .py file's name in the Explorer bar to select the file, click the Debug icon, and then click the Start Debugging icon, at the top of the Debug pane. Optionally, you can click Run and choose Start Debugging, or press the F5 key.

If you can remember those two options for running Python files, you're well on your way to learning Python.

We're going to look at a different way to write Python code next. So feel free to close any files you have open as well as VS Code.

Writing Code in a Jupyter Notebook

In Chapter 1 of this minibook, you learned that you can write and run Python code in a Jupyter notebook. In this section, we show you how to create, save, and open a Jupyter notebook. For our example, we create a subfolder named *Jupyter Notebooks* inside the AIO Python folder. You can, of course, save your Jupyter notebook wherever you want using any filenames you want.

Creating a folder for Jupyter Notebook

A Jupyter Notebooks folder is no different from any other folder, so you can create it using whatever method you normally use in your operating system. We put ours in the AIO Python folder we created, again just to keep all the files for this book in one place:

1. **Open your AIO Python folder (or whatever folder you created for working with files in this book) in Finder (Mac) or Explorer (Windows).**

2. **Right-click an empty spot in that folder, and choose New ⇨ Folder (Windows) or New Folder (Mac).**

3. **Type** Jupyter Notebooks **as the folder name and press Enter.**

Now that you have a folder in which to save Jupyter notebooks, you can create a notebook, as discussed next.

Creating and saving a Jupyter notebook

To create a Jupyter notebook and save it in a folder, follow these steps:

1. **Open Anaconda (if it isn't already open) and launch Jupyter Notebooks.**

2. **Navigate to the Jupyter Notebooks folder you created in the preceding section.**

   Because the folder is empty, you should see a message stating that the notebook list is empty.

3. **Click New and choose Python 3.**

4. **Near the top of the new notebook that opened, click Untitled, type** 01 Notebook **as the new name, and click Rename.**

   See Figure 2-18. The notebook is created and saved as 01 Notebook.

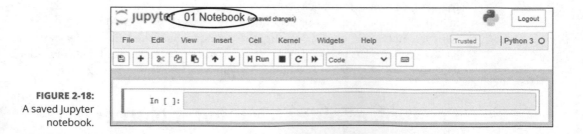

FIGURE 2-18:
A saved Jupyter notebook.

Below the menu bar and toolbar in the notebook you'll see a large rectangular box next to In[]:. That box is a typing area called a *cell*. Next, you'll type some code in that cell.

Typing and running code in a notebook

When your notebook is open, you see at least one cell. When you see Code in the drop-down menu in the toolbar below the menu bar, the active cell is for typing code. To take Jupyter Notebook for a spin, follow these steps:

1. **Click in the Code cell to the right of** In [ ]: **and type the following:**

```
print("Hello World")
```

Don't forget to use lowercase letters for the word *print*.

2. **To run the code, hold down the Alt key (Windows) or Option key (Mac) and press Enter, or click the Run button in the toolbar above the code.**

The output from the code appears below the cell.

Adding Markdown text

As mentioned, you can add text (and pictures and video) to Jupyter notebooks. When typing regular text, you don't need to use any special coding. If you want to format the text or add pictures or videos, however, you'll need to use Markdown tags. *Markdown* is a popular markup language, something similar to a greatly simplified HTML.

We can't go into a lengthy tutorial on Markdown here, and you don't need it to write Python code. And Markdown is easy enough to learn just by searching *Markdown tutorials* in your favorite search engine or on YouTube. But for those who know Markdown already, or are just curious, we'll take you through the steps for creating a cell that contains Markdown text in Jupyter Notebook.

First, make sure you're in your Jupyter Notebook app. If you don't have an empty cell under your Python code, choose Insert ⇨ Insert Cell Below. Then click in that new cell to add content to it. Type your text and Markdown in the cell.

We used the text and Markdown code shown in Figure 2-19.

TIP

If you're interested in learning more about Markdown, check out Alan's free video tutorials in his online school at https://alansimpson.thinkific.com/courses/easy-markdown-with-vs-code.

To run a cell that contains Markdown, click the cell and then click Run in the toolbar. The code is rendered into text and any other content you've put in the cell, as shown in Figure 2-20.

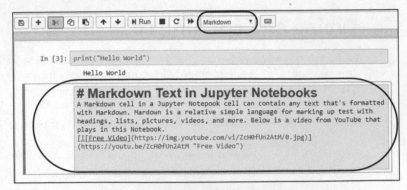

FIGURE 2-19:
A Markdown cell containing some Markdown content.

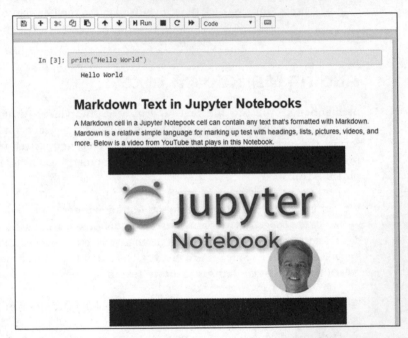

FIGURE 2-20:
A Markdown cell with some Markdown code and text in it.

To change code in a code cell, just click the cell and type your code normally. To change the content of a Markdown cell, first double-click some text or the empty space inside the cell so you can see the code again, and then make your changes.

With either type of cell, click Run again after making your changes. Note that only the cell that contains the cursor will run again. If you want to run all the cells in a notebook, use the double triangle icon in the toolbar. It's just to the left of the icon that lets you choose between a code cell and a Markdown cell.

Saving and opening notebooks

To save a Jupyter notebook, choose File⇨Save and Checkpoint from the menu. Optionally, you can click the little Save and Checkpoint icon (a floppy disk) on the left side of the toolbar.

To close a notebook, choose File⇨Close and Halt from the menu.

Any time that you want to reopen a notebook, open Anaconda and launch Jupyter Notebook. Then navigate to the file you saved and click its filename. The filename will probably have the `.ipynb` filename extension, which is standard for Jupyter notebooks.

It's worth noting that when you open the folder (the one we named AIO Python), you'll see the new Jupyter Notebooks subfolder inside that folder. When you open that subfolder, each notebook will be in there as its own file with the `.ipynb` filename extension.

Okay, so you've dug a little deeper in VS Code and Jupyter Notebook, mostly so you can save and open Python files and Jupyter notebooks. These skills will prove useful when you start getting deeper into writing Python code. See you there!

Chapter **3**

Python Elements and Syntax

Many programming languages focus on things that the computer does and how it does them rather than on the way humans think and work. This one simple fact makes most programming languages difficult for most people to learn. Python, however, is based on the philosophy that a programming language should be geared more toward how humans think, work, and communicate than what happens inside the computer. The Zen of Python is the perfect example of that human orientation, so we start this chapter with that topic.

The Zen of Python

The *Zen of Python*, shown in Figure 3-1, is a list of the guiding principles for the design of the Python language. These principles are hidden in an *Easter egg*, which is a term for something in a programming language or an app that's not easy to find and that's an inside joke to people who have learned enough of the language or app to be able to find the Easter egg. To get to the Easter egg, follow these steps:

1. **Launch VS Code from Anaconda Navigator and open your Python 3 workspace.**

2. **If the Terminal pane isn't open, choose View ➪ Terminal from the VS Code menu bar.**

```
PROBLEMS    OUTPUT    DEBUG CONSOLE    TERMINAL

The Zen of Python, by Tim Peters

Beautiful is better than ugly.
Explicit is better than implicit.
Simple is better than complex.
Complex is better than complicated.
Flat is better than nested.
Sparse is better than dense.
Readability counts.
Special cases aren't special enough to break the rules.
Although practicality beats purity.
Errors should never pass silently.
Unless explicitly silenced.
In the face of ambiguity, refuse the temptation to guess.
There should be one-- and preferably only one --obvious way to do it.
Although that way may not be obvious at first unless you're Dutch.
Now is better than never.
Although never is often better than *right* now.
If the implementation is hard to explain, it's a bad idea.
If the implementation is easy to explain, it may be a good idea.
Namespaces are one honking great idea -- let's do more of those!
>>> █
```

FIGURE 3-1:
The Zen of
Python.

3. **Type** python **and press Enter to get to the Python prompt (>>>).**

If you get an error message after you enter the python command, don't panic. You just need to remind VS Code which Python interpreter you're using. Choose View ⇨ Command Palette from the menu, type **python**, click Python: Select Interpreter, and choose the Python 3 version that came with Anaconda.

4. **Type** import this **and press Enter.**

The list of aphorisms appears. You may have to scroll up and down or make the Terminal pane taller to see them all. The aphorisms are somewhat tongue-and-cheek in their philosophical rhetoric, but the general idea they express is to always try to make the code more human-readable than machine-readable.

The Zen of Python is sometimes referred to as *PEP 20*, where *PEP* is an acronym for *Python enhancement proposals*. The 20 perhaps refers to the 20 Zen of Python principles, only 19 of which have been written down. We all get to wonder about or make up our own final principle.

Many other PEPs exist, and you can find them all on the Python.org website at www.python.org/dev/peps. The one you're likely to hear about the most is PEP 8, which is the *Style Guide for Python Code*. The guiding principle for PEP 8 is "readability counts" — that is, readable by *humans*. Admittedly, when you're first learning Python code, most other peoples' code will seem like some gibberish scribbled down by aliens, and you may not have any idea what it means or does. But as you gain experience with the language, the style consistency will become more apparent, and you'll find it easier and easier to read and understand other peoples' code, which is an excellent way to learn coding yourself.

We'll fill you in on Python coding style throughout the book. Trying to read about it before working on it is sure to bore you to tears. So for now, any time you hear mention of PEP, or especially PEP 8, remember that it's a reference to the Python Coding Style Guidelines from the Python.org website, and you can find it any time you like by doing a web search for *pep 8*. PEP 8 is also referred to as Pycodestyle, especially in VS Code.

This PEP 8 business can be a double-edged sword for learners. On one hand, you don't want to learn a bunch of bad habits only to discover later that you have to unlearn them. On the other hand, the strict formatting demands of PEP 8 can frustrate many learners who are just trying to get their code to work.

To ward off this potential frustration, we follow and explain PEP 8 conventions as we go along. You can take it a step further, if you like, by configuring PyLint to help you. *PyLint* is a tool in Anaconda that makes suggestions about your code as you're typing. (The program adds a little wavy underline near code that may be wrong, and some people think the lines look like lint, hence the name PyLint.)

You can follow these steps to turn on PyLint and PEP 8 now if you'd like to take it for a spin:

1. **Choose File (Windows) or Code (Mac), and then choose Preferences ⇨ Settings.**

2. **Under Search Settings, click Workspace.**

3. **In Search Settings, type** pylint **and select the Python > Linting: Enabled option, as shown in Figure 3-2.**

4. **Type** pycodestyle **in the Search box.**

5. **Scroll down and select the Python > Linting: Pycodestyle Enabled option, as in the bottom half of Figure 3-2.**

6. **Choose File ⇨ Save All or just Save (if Save All isn't available). Then close the Settings page by clicking the X in its tab.**

FIGURE 3-2: Workspace settings with PyLint and Pycodestyle (PEP 8) enabled.

Python › Linting: Enabled
☑ Whether to lint Python files.

Python › Linting: Pycodestyle Enabled *(Also modified in: User)*
☑ Whether to lint Python files using pycodestyle

All the settings you choose in VS Code are stored in a settings.json file. You can make changes to settings also via that file. To get to the file through the Preferences options in VS Code, first choose File (Windows) or Code (Mac) and then choose Preferences⇨Settings. Click the Open Settings (JSON) icon near the top right. The icon looks like a paper document with the top corner folded down, and a rounded arrow near the top.

If the Pycodestyle linting is too demanding, you can change the first line of code to true and the second line to false. (See Figure 3-3.) You can turn off linting altogether by setting the third code line to false as well. There are no right or wrong settings, so try what we have for a while and see how it works for you. If you make any changes to Settings.json, don't forget to save them and close the settings.json tab.

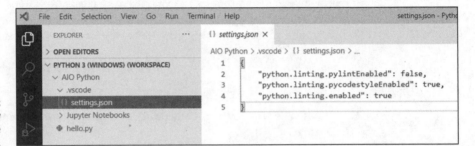

FIGURE 3-3:
A different view
of Workspace
settings.

Introducing Object-Oriented Programming

At the risk of getting too technical or computer science-y, we should mention that there are different approaches to designing languages. Perhaps the most successful and widely used model is *object-oriented programming,* or OOP, which is a design philosophy that tries to mimic the real world in the sense that it consists of objects with properties as well as methods (actions) that those objects perform.

Take a car, for example. Any one car is an object. Not all cars are exactly the same. Different cars have different properties, such as make, model, year, color, and size, which make them different from one another. And yet, they all serve the same basic purpose: to get us from point A to point B without having to walk or use some other mode of transportation.

All cars have certain methods (things they can do) in common. You can drive them, steer them, speed them up, slow them down, control the inside temperature, and more by using controls in the car that you can manipulate with your hands.

An *object* in an object-oriented programming language isn't a physical thing, like a car, because it exists only inside a computer. An object is strictly a software thing. In Python, you can have a *class* (which you can think of as an object creator, such as a car factory) that can produce many different kinds of objects (cars) for varying purposes (sporty, off-road, sedan). All these objects can be manipulated through the controls they all have in common, much as all cars are manipulated by controls such as the steering wheel, brakes, accelerator, and gearshift.

Python is very much an object-oriented language. The core language consists of controls (in the form of words) that allow you to control all different kinds of objects — in your own and other peoples' programs. However, you need to learn the core language first so that when you're ready to start using other peoples' objects, you know how to do so. Similarly, after you know how to drive one car, you pretty much know how to drive them all. You don't have to worry about renting a car only to discover that the accelerator is on the roof, the steering wheel on the floor, and you have to use voice commands rather than a brake to slow it down. The basic skill of driving applies to all cars.

Discovering Why Indentations Count, Big Time

In terms of the basic style of writing code, the one feature that really makes Python different from other languages is that it uses indentations rather than parentheses and curly braces and such to indicate blocks, or chunks, of code. We don't assume that you're familiar with other languages, so don't worry if that statement means nothing to you. But if you are familiar with a language such as JavaScript, you know that you have to do quite a bit of wrangling with parentheses and such to control what's inside of what.

For example, here's some JavaScript code. If you're familiar with the Magic 8 Ball toy, you may have a sense of what this program is doing. But that's not what's important. Just note all those parentheses, curly braces, and semicolons:

```
document.addEventListener("DOMContentLoaded", function () {var question =
    prompt("Ask magic 8 ball a question");var answer = Math.floor(Math.random() *
    8) + 1; if (answer == 1) {alert("It is certain");} else if (answer == 2)
    {alert("Outlook good");} else if (answer == 3) {alert("You may rely on it");}
    else if (answer == 4) {alert("Ask again later");} else if (answer == 5)
    {alert("Concentrate and ask again");} else if (answer == 6) {alert ("Reply
    hazy, try again");} else if (answer == 7) {alert("My reply is no");} else if
    (answer == 8) {alert("My sources say no")} else {alert ("That's not a
    question");}alert("The end");})
```

The code is a mess and not fun to read. We can make reading it a little easier by breaking it into multiple lines and indenting some of those lines. (Note that doing so isn't required in JavaScript.) Following is the reformatted code:

```javascript
document.addEventListener("DOMContentLoaded", function () {
    var question = prompt("Ask magic 8 ball a question");
    var answer = Math.floor(Math.random() * 8) + 1;
    if (answer == 1) {
        alert("It is certain");
    } else if (answer == 2) {
        alert("Outlook good");
    } else if (answer == 3) {
        alert("You may rely on it");
    } else if (answer == 4) {
        alert("Ask again later");
    } else if (answer == 5) {
        alert("Concentrate and ask again");
    } else if (answer == 6) {
        alert("Reply hazy, try again");
    } else if (answer == 7) {
        alert("My reply is no");
    } else if (answer == 8) {
        alert("My sources say no")
    } else {
        alert("That's not a question");}
    alert("The end");
})
```

In JavaScript, the parentheses and curly braces are required because they identify where chunks of code begin and end. The indentations for readability are optional.

The rules are opposite in Python because it doesn't use curly braces or any other special characters to mark the beginning and end of a block of code. The indentations themselves mark those. So those indentations aren't optional — they are required and have a considerable effect on how the code runs. As a result, when you read the code (as a human, not as a computer), it's relatively easy to see what's going on, and you're not distracted by a ton of extra quotation marks. Here is that JavaScript code written in Python:

```python
import random
question = input("Ask magic 8 ball a question")
answer = random.randint(1, 8)
if answer == 1:
    print("It is certain")
elif answer == 2:
    print("Outlook good")
elif answer == 3:
```

```
    print("You may rely on it")
elif answer == 4:
    print("Ask again later")
elif answer == 5:
    print("Concentrate and ask again")
elif answer == 6:
    print("Reply hazy, try again")
elif answer == 7:
    print("My reply is no")
elif answer == 8:
    print("My sources say no")
else:
    print("That's not a question")
print("The end")
```

You may have noticed at the top of the Python code the line that starts with import. Lines that start with import are common in Python, and you'll see why in the next section.

Using Python Modules

One of the secrets to Python's success is that it's comprised of a simple, clean, core language. That's the part you need to learn first. In addition to that core language, many, many modules are available that you can grab for free and access from your own code. These modules are also written in the core language, but you don't need to see that or even know it because you can access all the power of the modules from the basic core language.

Most modules are for some a specific application such as science or artificial intelligence or working with dates and time or . . . whatever. The beauty of using modules is that other people spent a lot of time creating, testing, and fine-tuning that module so you don't have to. You simply import the module into your own Python file, and use the module's capabilities as instructed in the module's documentation.

The preceding sample Magic 8 Ball program starts with this line:

```
import random
```

The core Python language has nothing built into it to generate a random number. Although we could figure out a way to make a random number generator, we don't need to because someone has figured out how to do it and has made the code freely available. Starting your program with import random tells the program that you want to use the capabilities of the random number module to generate a random number. Then, later in the program, you generate a random number between 1 and 8 with this line of code:

```
answer = random.randint(1, 8)
```

Hundreds of free modules for Python are available — you just need to know which ones to import into your program.

Now, you may be wondering where to find all these modules. Well, they're all over the place online. But you'll probably never need to find and download them because you already have the most widely used modules in the world. They were downloaded and installed along with Anaconda. To see for yourself, follow these steps:

1. **Open Anaconda in the usual manner on your computer.**

2. **In the left column, click Environments.**

   On the far right are the Python modules installed on your computer and ready for you to import and use as needed, as shown in Figure 3-4. As you scroll down through the list, you'll see that you already have a ton of them. The rightmost column tells you each module's version.

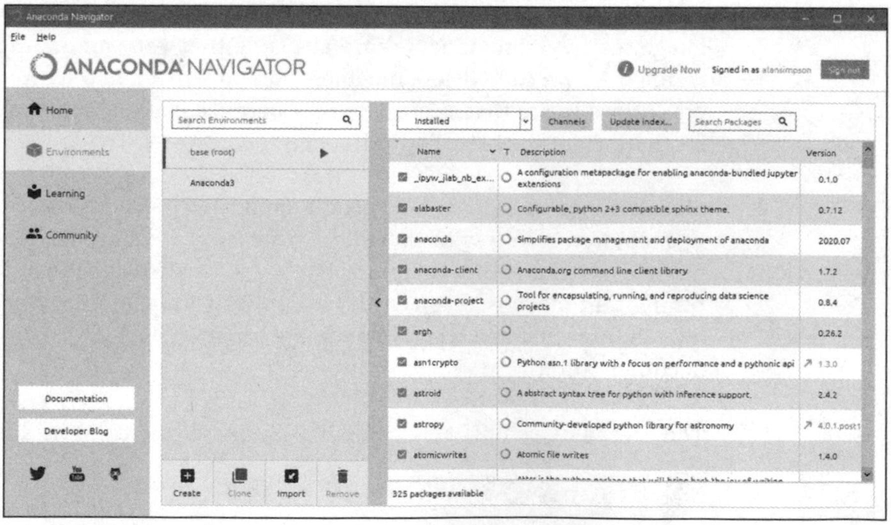

FIGURE 3-4: Installed modules.

You may notice that some version numbers are colored and are preceded with an arrow, which indicates that a more recent version may be available for you to download. As with programming languages, modules evolve over time as their authors improve them and add new capabilities. You're not required to have the latest version, though. If the version you have is working, you might want to stick with it.

One of many nice things about Anaconda is that to get the latest version, you don't have to do any weird `pip` commands, as many older Python tutorials tell you to do. Instead, just click the arrow or version number of the module or modules you want to download, and then click Apply at the bottom-right corner. Anaconda does all the dirty work of finding the current module, determining whether a newer version is available, and then downloading that version, if it is available.

When all the downloads are finished, you see a dialog box like the one shown in Figure 3-5. If no package names are listed, all the selected modules are up-to-date, so click Cancel and then click Home in the left pane to return to Anaconda's home page. If, on the other hand, package names are listed under The Following Packages Will Be Modified, click Apply to install the latest versions.

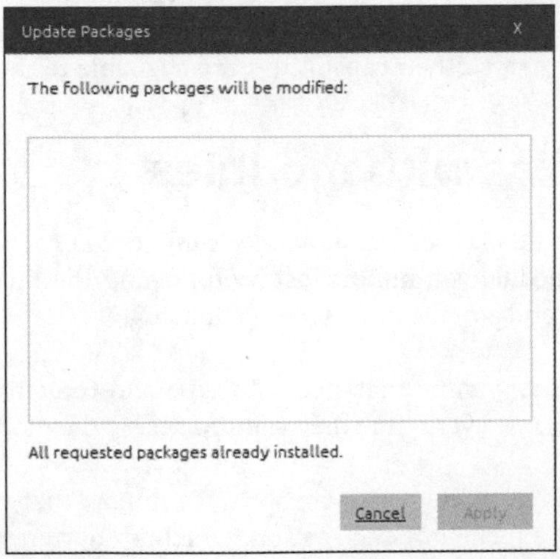

FIGURE 3-5:
All our packages are installed and up-to-date.

Understanding the syntax for importing modules

As mentioned, in your own Python code, you must import a module before you can access its capabilities. The syntax for doing so is

```
import modulename [as alias]
```

Code written in a generic format like that, with some parts in italic, some in square brackets, is sometimes called a *syntax chart* because it's not showing you, literally, what to type. Rather, it's showing the syntax (format) of the code. Here is how information is presented in such a syntax chart:

>> The code is case-sensitive, meaning you must type import and as using all lowercase letters, as shown.

>> Anything in italics is a placeholder for information you should supply in your own code. For example, in your code, you would replace *modulename* with the name of the module you want to import.

>> Anything in square brackets is optional, so you can type the command with or without the part in square brackets.

>> You never type the square brackets in your code because they are not part of the Python language. They are used only to indicate optional parts in the syntax.

You can type the import line any place you type Python code: at the Python command prompt (>>>), in a .py file, or in a Jupyter notebook. In a .py file, always put import statements first, so their capabilities are available to the rest of the code.

Using an alias with modules

As you just saw with the import command's syntax, you can assign an *alias*, or nickname, to any module you import just by following the module name with a space, the word as, and a name of your own choosing.

TIP

Most people use a short name that's easy to type and remember, so they don't have to type a long name every time they want to access the module's capabilities.

For example, instead of typing import random to import that module, you could import it and give it a nickname such as rnd, which is shorter:

```
import random as rnd
```

Then, in subsequent code, you wouldn't use the full name, random, to refer to the module. Instead, you'd use the short name, rnd:

```
answer = rnd.randint(1, 8)
```

Using an alternative short name may not seem like a big deal in this short example. But some modules have lengthy names, and you might have to refer to the modules in many places in your code.

Now that you've learned some background information, it's time to apply it and start getting your hands dirty with some real Python code. See you in the next chapter.

Chapter **4**

Building Your First Python Application

So you want to build an application in Python? Whether you want to code a website, analyze data, or create a script to automate something, this chapter gives you the basics you need to get started on your journey. Most people use programming languages like Python to create *application programs*, which are often referred to as *applications* or *apps* or *programs*. To create apps, you need to know how to write code inside a code editor. You also need to start learning the language in which you'll be creating those apps (Python, in this book).

Like any language, you need to understand the individual words so that you can start building sentences and, finally, the blocks of code that will enable your app to work. First, we walk you through creating an app file in which you will create your code. Then you learn the various data types, operators, and variables, which are the words of the Python language, and then Python syntax. Along the way, you see how to save your app, catch mistakes with linting, and comment your code so that you and others can understand how you built it and why.

Are you ready?

Opening the Python App File

You'll be using the ever-popular Visual Studio Code (VS Code) editor in this book to learn Python and create Python apps. We assume that you've already set up your learning and development environment, as described in previous chapters of this minibook, and know how to open the main tools, Anaconda Navigator and VS Code. To follow along in this chapter, start with these steps:

1. **Open Anaconda Navigator and launch VS Code from there.**

2. **If your Python 3 workspace doesn't open automatically, choose File ➪ Open Workspace from the VS Code menu and open the Python 3 workspace you created in Chapter 2.**

3. **Click the `hello.py` file you created in Chapter 2.**

4. **Select all the text on the first line and delete it, so you can start from scratch.**

At this point, `hello.py` should be open in the editor, as shown in Figure 4-1. If any other tabs are open, close them by clicking the X in each.

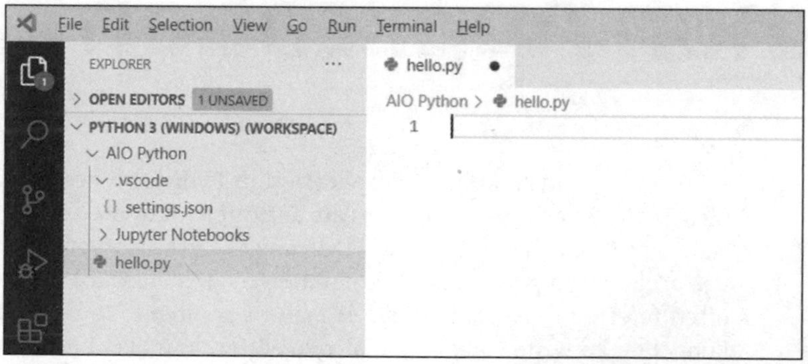

FIGURE 4-1: The `hello.py` file, open for editing in VS Code.

Typing and Using Python Comments

Before you type any code, let's start with a programmer's comment. A *programmer's comment* (usually called a *comment* for short) is text in the program that does nothing. Which brings up the question," If it doesn't *do* anything, why type it in?" As a learner, you can use comments in your code as notes to yourself about what the code is doing. These can help a lot when you're first learning.

However, comments in code aren't strictly for beginners. When working in teams, professionals often use comments to explain to team members what their code is doing. Developers will also put comments in their code as notes to themselves, so that if they review the code in the future, they can refer to their own notes for reminders on why they did something in the code. Because a comment isn't code, your wording can be anything you want. However, to be identified as a comment, you must do one of the following:

>> Start the text with a pound sign (#)

>> Enclose the text in triple quotation marks

If the comment is short (one line), the leading pound sign is sufficient. Often you'll see the pound sign followed by a space, as in the next example, but the space is optional:

```
# This is a Python comment
```

To type a Python comment into your own code

1. **In VS Code, click next to the 1 under the hello.py tab and type the following:**

```
# This is a Python comment in my first Python app.
```

2. **Press Enter.**

The comment you typed appears on line 1, as shown in Figure 4-2. The comment text will be green if you're using the default color theme. Note that the blinking cursor is now on line 2.

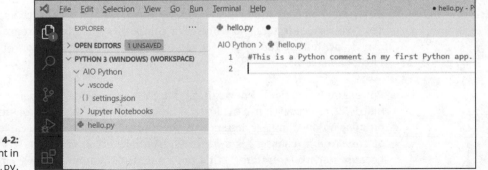

FIGURE 4-2:
A comment in
hello.py.

Building Your First
Python Application

Although you won't use multiline comments just yet, be aware that you can type longer comments in Python by enclosing them in triple quotation marks. These larger comments are sometimes called *docstrings* and often appear at the top of a Python module, function, class, or method definition, which are app building blocks you will learn about a little later in this book. It isn't necessary to type one right now, but here's an example of what one may look like in Python code:

```
"""This is a multiline comment in Python
This type of comment is sometimes called a docstring.
A docstring starts with three double-quotation marks, and also ends with three
    double quotation marks. """
```

At the beginning and end of the comment, you can use three single quotation marks, rather than three double quotation marks, if you prefer.

In VS Code, comments are usually colored differently than code. Short comments that start with # are green, and docstrings are brown, to help them stand out from the Python code that you run.

You can have an unlimited number of comments in your code. If you're waiting for something to happen after you type a comment . . . don't. When you're working in an editor like this, code doesn't do anything until you run it. And right now, all we have is a comment, so even if we did run this code, nothing would happen because comments are for human readers, not computers. Before you start typing code, you need to start with the absolute basics, which would be . . .

Understanding Python Data Types

You deal with written information all the time and probably don't think about the difference between numbers and text. Numbers are amounts, such as 10 or 123.45. Text consists of letters and words. For computers, the big difference is that they can do arithmetic (add, subtract, multiple, divide) with numbers, but not with letters and words.

For example, everyone knows that 1+1 = 2. The same doesn't apply to letters and words. The expression A+A doesn't necessary equal B or AA or anything else because unlike numbers, letters and words aren't quantities. You can buy *12 apples* at the store, because 12 is a quantity, a number. You can't buy a *snorkel apples* because a *snorkel* is a thing — it's not a quantity, a number, or a scalar value.

Numbers

Numbers in Python must start with a number digit, (0-9); a dot (period), which is a decimal point; or a hyphen (-) used as a negative sign for negative numbers. A number can contain only one decimal point. It should not contain letters, spaces, dollar signs, or anything else that isn't part of a normal number. Table 4-1 shows example of good and bad Python numbers.

TABLE 4-1   **Examples of Good and Bad Python Numbers**

Number	Good or Bad?	Reason
1	Good	A whole number (integer)
1.1	Good	A number with a decimal point
1234567.89	Good	A large number with a decimal point and no commas
-2	Good	A negative number, as indicated by the starting hyphen
.99	Good	A number that starts with a decimal point because it's less than 1
$1.99	Bad	Contains a $
12,345.67	Bad	Contains a comma
1101 3232	Bad	Contains a space
91740-3384	Bad	Contains a hyphen
123-45-6789	Bad	Contains two hyphens
123 Oak Tree Lane	Bad	Contains spaces and words
(267)555-1234	Bad	Contain parentheses and hyphens
127.0.0.1	Bad	Only one decimal point is allowed

TIP

If you're worried that the number rules won't let you work with dollar amounts, zip codes, addresses, or anything else, stop worrying. You can store and work with *all* kinds of information, as you'll see shortly.

The vast majority of numbers you use will probably match one of the first four examples of good numbers. However, if you happen to be looking at code used for more advanced scientific or mathematical applications, you may occasionally see numbers that contain the letter *e* or the letter *j*. That's because Python supports three different types of numbers, as discussed in the sections that follow.

Integers

An *integer* is any whole number, positive or negative. There is no limit to its size. Numbers such as 0, -1, and 999999999999999 are all perfectly valid integers. From your perspective, an integer is just any valid number that doesn't contain a decimal point.

Floats

A *floating-point number,* often called a *float,* is any valid number that contains a decimal point. Again, there is no size limit: 1.1 and -1.1 and 123456.789012345 are all perfectly valid floats.

If you work with very large scientific numbers, you can put an *e* in a number to indicate the power of 10. For example, 234e1000 is a valid number, and will be treated as a float even if there's no decimal point. If you're familiar with scientific notation, you know 234e3 is 234,000 (replace the *e3* with three zeroes). If you're not familiar with scientific notation, don't worry about it. If you're not using it in your day-to-day work now, chances are you'll never need it in Python either.

Complex numbers

Just about any kind of number can be expressed as an integer or a float, so being familiar with those is sufficient for just about everyone. Note, though, that Python also supports *complex numbers*. These bizarre little charmers always end with the letter *j*, which is the *imaginary* part of the number. If you have no idea what we're talking about, you're normal — only people deep in math land care about complex numbers. If you've never heard of them before now, chances are you won't be using them in your computer work or Python programming.

Words (strings)

Strings are sort of the opposite of numbers. With numbers, you can add, subtract, multiply, and divide because the numbers represent quantities. Strings are for just about everything else. Names, addresses, and all other kinds of text you see every day would be a string in Python (and in computers in general). It's called a *string* because it's a string of characters (letters, spaces, punctuation marks, and maybe some numbers). To us, a string usually has some meaning, such as a person's name or address. But computers don't have eyes to see with or brains to think with or any awareness that humans even exist, so to a computer, if a piece of information is not something on which it can do arithmetic, it's just a string of characters.

Unlike numbers, a string must always be enclosed in quotation marks. You can use either double (") or single (') quotation marks. All the following are valid strings:

```
"Hi there, I am a string"
'Hello world'
"123 Oak Tree Lane"
"(267)555-1234"
"18901-3384"
```

Note that it's fine to use numeric characters (0-9) as well as hyphens and dots (periods) in strings. Each is still a string because it's enclosed in quotation marks.

WARNING

A word of caution. If a string contains an apostrophe (single quote), the entire string should be enclosed in double quotation marks like this:

```
"Mary's dog said Woof"
```

The double quotation marks are necessary because there's no confusion about where the string starts and ends. If you instead used single quotes, like this:

```
'Mary's dog said Woof'
```

the computer would be too dumb to get that right. It would see the first single quote as the start of the string, the next one (after Mary) as the end of the string, and then it wouldn't know what to do with the rest of the stuff and your app wouldn't run correctly.

Similarly, if the string contains double quotation makes, enclose the entire thing in single quotation marks to avoid confusion. For example:

```
'The dog of Mary said "Woof".'
```

The first single quotation mark starts the string, the second one ends it, and the double quotation marks cause no confusion because they're inside the string.

So what if you have a string that contains both single and double quotation marks, like this:

```
Mary's dog said "Woof".
```

This deserves a resounding *hmm*. Fortunately, the creators of Python realized this sort of thing could happen, so they came up with an escape. The solution involves something called *escape characters* because, in a sense, they allow you to escape (avoid) the special meaning of a character such as a single or double quotation mark. To escape a character, just precede it with a backslash (\). Make sure you use a backslash (the one that leans back toward the previous character, like this \) or it won't work right.

Continuing with the last example, you could enclose the entire thing in single quotation marks, and then escape the apostrophe (which is the same character) by preceding it with a backslash, like this:

```
'Mary\'s dog said "Woof".'
```

Or you could enclose the entire thing in double quotation marks, and escape the quotation marks embedded with the string, like this:

```
"Mary's dog said \"Woof\"."
```

Another common use of the backslash is to use it and *n* (\n) to add a line break on the screen where a user is viewing it (the *user* being anyone who uses the app you wrote). For example, this string

```
"The old pond\nA frog jumped in,\nKerplunk!"
```

would look like this when displayed to a user:

```
The old pond
A frog jumped in,
Kerplunk!
```

Each \n was converted to a line break.

Booleans

A third data type in Python isn't exactly a number or a string. It's called a *Boolean* (named after a mathematician named George Boole), and it can be one of two values: either True or False. It may seem odd to have a data type for something that can only be True or False, but doing so is efficient because you can store the True or False value using a single bit, which is the smallest unit of storage in a computer.

In Python code, people store True and False values in *variables* (placeholders in code that we discuss later in this chapter) using a format similar to this:

```
x = True
```

Or perhaps this:

```
x = False
```

You know `True` and `False` are Boolean here because they are not enclosed in quotation marks (as a string would be) and are not numbers. Also, the *initial cap* is required. In other words, the Boolean values `True` and `False` must be written as shown.

Working with Python Operators

As we discuss in the preceding section, with Python and computers in general, it helps to think of information as being one of the following data types: number, string, or Boolean. You also use computers to *operate* on that information, meaning do any necessary math or comparisons or searches or whatever to help you find information and organize it in a way that makes sense to you.

Python offers many different *operators* for working with and comparing types of information. Here we summarize them all for future reference, without going into great detail. Whether you use an operator in your own work depends on the types of apps you develop. For now, it's sufficient just to be aware that they're available.

Arithmetic operators

Arithmetic operators, as the name implies, are for doing arithmetic; addition, subtraction, multiplication, division, and more. Table 4-2 lists Python's arithmetic operators.

TABLE 4-2

Python's Arithmetic Operators

Operator	Description	Example
+	Addition	1 + 1 = 2
-	Subtraction	10 - 1 = 9
*	Multiplication	3 * 5 = 15
/	Division	10 / 5 = 2
%	Modulus (remainder after division)	11 % 5 = 1
**	Exponent	3**2 = 9
//	Floor division	11 // 5 = 2

The first four items in the table are the same as you learned in elementary school. The last three are a little more advanced, so we'll explain them here:

>> The *modulus* is the remainder after division. So, for example, 11 % 5 is 1 because if you divide 11 by 2 you get 5 remainder 1. That 1 is the modulus (sometimes called the *modulo*).

>> The *exponent* is ** because you can't type a small raised number in code. But it just means "raised to the power of." For example, 3**2 is 3^2 (or 3 squared), which is 3*3, or 9, and 3**4 is 3*3*3*3, or 81.

>> *Floor division*, indicated by //, is integer division in that anything after the decimal point is *truncated* (cut off), without any rounding. For example, in regular division 9/5 is 1.8. But 9//5 is 1 because the .8 is just chopped off — it isn't rounded to 2.

Comparison operators

Computers can make decisions as part of doing their work. But these decisions are not judgement call decisions or anything human like that. These decisions are based on absolute facts that are based on comparisons. The *comparison operators* Python offers to help you write code that makes decisions are listed in Table 4-3.

TABLE 4-3

Python Comparison Operators

Operator	Meaning
<	Less than
<=	Less than or equal to
>	Greater than
>=	Greater than or equal to
==	Equal to
!=	Not equal to
is	Object identity
is not	Negated object identity

The first few are self-explanatory, so we won't go into detail there. The last two are tricky because they concern Python objects, which we haven't talked about yet. Talking about Python objects right now would be a big digression, so if you're at all confused about any operators right now, don't worry about it.

Boolean operators

The *Boolean operators* work with Boolean values (True or False) and are used to determine if one or more things is True or False. Table 4-4 summarizes the Boolean operators.

TABLE 4-4

Python Boolean Operators

Operator	Code Example	What It Determines
or	x or y	Either x or y is True
and	x and y	Both x and y are True
not	not x	x is not True

Python Style Guide (PEP 8) recommends always putting whitespace around operators. In other words, you want to use the spacebar on the keyboard to put a space before the operator, type the operator, and then add another space before continuing the line of code. Here is a somewhat simple example. We know you're not familiar with coding just yet so don't worry too much about the meaning of the code. Instead, note the spaces around the = and > (greater than) operators:

```
num = 10
if num > 0:
    print("Positive number")
else:
    print("Negative number")
```

The first line stores the number 10 in a variable named num. Then the if checks to see whether num is greater than (>) 0. If it is, the program prints Positive number. Otherwise, it prints Negative number. So, let's say you change the first line of the program to this:

```
num = -1
```

If you make that change and run the program again, it prints Negative number because -1 is a negative number.

We used num as a sample variable name in this example so we could show you some operators with space around them. Of course, we haven't told you what variables are, so that part of the example may have left you scratching your head. We clear up that part of this business next.

Creating and Using Variables

Variables are a big part of Python and all computer programming languages. A *variable* is simply a placeholder for information that may vary (change). For example, when you go to Amazon's home page, you can see your name and the date you became a customer, as shown in Figure 4-3. The screen may look different when you visit, but the basic information should be on the page somewhere. Both those pieces of information are variables, because they change depending on who is signed in to Amazon.

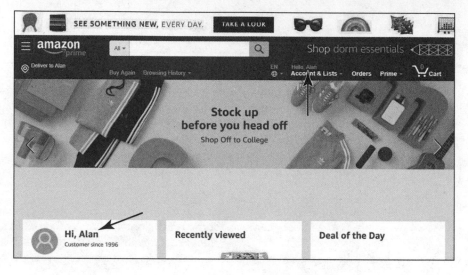

FIGURE 4-3: Your name and the date you became a customer appear on Amazon's home page.

Certainly not everyone who goes to Amazon that day is named Alan and has been a member since 1996. Other people must be seeing other stuff there. But Amazon certainly can't make a custom home page for every one of its millions of users. Most of what's on that page is probably *literal* — meaning everyone who views the page sees the same stuff. Only the information that changes depending on who is viewing the page is stored as a variable.

In your code, a variable is represented by a variable *name* rather than a specific piece of information. Here is another way to think of it. Anytime you buy one or more of some product, the extended price is the unit price times the number of items you bought. In other words

*Quantity * Unit Price = Extended Price*

You can consider Quantity and Unit Price to be variables because no matter what numbers you plug in for Quantity and Unit Price, you get the correct extended price. For example, if you buy three turtle doves for $1.00 apiece, your extended price is $3.00 (3 * $1.00). If you buy two dozen roses for $1.50 apiece, the extended price is $36 because 1.5 * 24 is 36.

Creating valid variable names

In our explanation of variables, we used names like Quantity and Unit Price, and this is fine for a general example. In Python, you can also make up your own variable names, but they must conform to the following rules to be recognized as variable names:

>> The variable name must start with a letter or an underscore (_).

>> After the first character, you can use letters, numbers, or underscores.

>> Variable names are case sensitive, so after you make up a name, any reference to that variable must use the same uppercase and lowercase letters.

>> Variable names cannot be enclosed in, or contain, single or double quotation marks.

>> PEP 8 style conventions recommend that you use only lowercase letters in variable names and use an underscore to separate multiple words.

PEP 8, which we mentioned in previous chapters, is a style guide for writing code, rather than strict must-follow rules. So you often see variable names that don't conform to that last style. *Camel case* formatting — whereby the first letter is lowercase and new words are capitalized — is common, even in Python, for example, `extendedPrice` or `unitPrice`.

Experienced Python purists sometimes get a disgusted look on their face when they see names like these in your code. They would prefer you stick with the PEP 8 style guidelines, which recommend using `extended_price` and `unit_price` as your variable names, on the grounds that the PEP 8 syntax is more readable for human programmers.

Creating variables in code

To create a variable, you use the following syntax (order of things):

```
variablename = value
```

where *variablename* is the name you make up. You can use *x* or *y*, as people often do in math, but in larger programs, it's a good idea to give your variables more meaningful names, such as `quantity` or `unit_price` or `sales_tax` or `user_name`, so that you can remember what you're storing in the variable.

The *value* is whatever you want to store in the variable. It can be a number, a string, or a Boolean `True` or `False` value.

The = sign is the *assignment operator* and is so named because it assigns the value (on the right) to the variable (on the left). For example, in the following:

```
x = 10
```

we are storing the number 10 in a variable named x. In other words, we're assigning the value 10 to the x variable.

And here:

```
user_name = "Alan"
```

we're putting the string Alan in a variable named username.

Manipulating variables

Much of computer programming revolves around storing values in variables and manipulating that information with operators. Time to try some simple examples to get the hang of it. If you still have VS Code open with that one comment displayed, follow these steps in the VS Code editor:

1. Under the line that reads # *This is a Python comment in my first Python app.*, **type this comment and press Enter:**

```
# This variable contains an integer
```

2. **Type the following (don't forget to put a space before and after the = sign) and press Enter:**

```
quantity = 10
```

3. **Type the following and press Enter:**

```
# This variable contains a float
```

4. **Type the following (don't type a dollar sign!) and press Enter:**

```
unit_price = 1.99
```

5. **Type the following and press Enter:**

```
# This variable contains the result of multiplying quantity times unit price
```

6. **Type the following (with spaces around the operators) and press Enter:**

```
extended_price = quantity * unit_price
```

7. **Type the following and press Enter:**

```
# Show the results
```

8. **Finally, type this and press Enter:**

```
print(extended_price)
```

Your Python app creates some variables, stores some values in them, and calculates a new value, extended_price, based on the contents of the quantity and unit_price variables. The last line displays the contents of the extended_price variable on the screen. Remember, the comments don't *do* anything in the program as it's running. The comments are just notes to yourself about what's going on in the program.

Figure 4-4 shows how things should look now. If you made any errors, you may see some wavy lines near errors or stylistic suggestions, such as an extra space or an omitted Enter at the end of a line. When typing code, you must be accurate. You can't type something that looks sort of like what you were supposed to type. When texting to humans, you can make all kinds of typographical errors and your human recipient can usually figure out what you meant based on the context of the message. But computers don't have eyes or brains or a concept of context, so they will generally just not work properly if your code has errors.

```
hello.py  ×
1   # This is a Python comment in my first Python app.
2   # This variable contains an integer
3   quantity = 10
4   # This variable contains a float
5   unit_price = 1.99
6   # This variable contains the result of multiplying quantity times unit price
7   extended_price = quantity * unit_price
8   # Show the results
9   print(extended_price)
10  |
```

FIGURE 4-4:
Your first Python app typed into VS Code.

In other words, if the code is wrong, it won't work when you run it. It's as simple as that — no exceptions.

Saving your work

Typing code is like typing other documents on a computer. If you don't save your work, you may not have it the next time you sit down at your computer and go looking for it. So if you haven't enabled Auto Save on the File menu, as discussed in Chapter 2 of this minibook, choose File⇨Save.

Running your Python app in VS Code

Now you can run the app and see if it works. An easy way to do that is to right-click the `hello.py` filename in the Explorer bar and choose Run Python File in Terminal, as shown in Figure 4-5.

FIGURE 4-5:
Right-click a .py file and choose Run Python File in Terminal.

If your code is typed correctly, you should see the result, `19.9`, in the Terminal window, as shown in Figure 4-6. The result is the output from `print(extended_price)` in the code, and it's `19.9` because the quantity (`10`) times the unit price (`1.99`) is `19.9`.

FIGURE 4-6:
The 19.9 is the
output
from print
(extended_
price)
in the code.

```
PROBLEMS   OUTPUT   DEBUG CONSOLE   TERMINAL

(base) C:\Users\Alan\OneDrive\AIO Python>C:/ProgramData/Anaconda3/python.exe "c:/Users/Alan/OneDrive/AIO Python/hello.py"
19.9

(base) C:\Users\Alan\OneDrive\AIO Python>
```

Suppose your app must calculate the total cost of 14 items that each cost $26.99. Can you think of how to make that happen? You certainly wouldn't need to write a whole new app. Instead, in the code you're working with now, change the value of the quantity variable from 10 to 14. Change the value of the unitprice variable to 26.99 (remember, no dollar signs in your number). Here's how the code looks with those changes:

```python
# This is a Python comment in my first Python app.
# This variable contains an integer
quantity = 14
# This variable contains a float
unit_price = 26.99
# This variable contains the result of multiplying quantity times unit price
extended_price = quantity * unit_price
# Show some results on the screen.
print(extended_price)
```

Save your work (unless you've turned on AutoSave). Then run the app by right-clicking and choosing Run Python File in Terminal once again — just like the first time. The results are again quite a bit of gobbledygook. But you should see the correct answer, 377.85999999999996, in the Terminal window near the bottom of the VS Code window. It doesn't round to pennies and it doesn't even look like a dollar amount. But you need to learn to crawl before you can learn to pole vault, so for now just be happy with getting your apps to run.

Understanding What Syntax Is and Why It Matters

If you look up *syntax* in the dictionary, one definition you might find is "the arrangement of words and phrases to create well-formed sentences in a language." In programming languages like Python, there is no such thing as a well-formed sentence. But Python does have words in the sense that you need a space between each word, just as you do when typing regular text like this, and the order of those words is important.

Syntax is important in human languages because order contributes much to the meaning. For example, compare these three short sentences:

Mary kissed John.

John kissed Mary.

Kissed Mary John.

All three sentences contain the same words, but the meanings are different. The first two make it clear who kissed whom, and the last one is a little hard to interpret.

Proper syntax in programming languages is every bit as important as it is in human languages — even more so, in some ways, because when you make a mistake speaking or writing to someone, that other person can usually figure out what you meant by the context of your words. But computers aren't nearly that smart. Computers don't have brains, can't guess your actual meaning based on context, and in fact the concept of context doesn't even exist for computers. So syntax matters even more in programming languages than in human languages.

Looking back at the earliest code in this chapter, note that all the lines of actual code (not the comments, which start with #) follow this syntax:

```
variablename = value
```

where *variablename* is some name you made up, and *value* is something you are storing in that variable. It works because it's the proper syntax. If you try to do it like this, it won't work:

```
value = variablename
```

For example, the following is the correct way to store the value 10 in a variable named x:

```
x = 10
```

It might seem you could also do it the following way, but it won't work in Python:

```
10 = x
```

If you run the app with that line in it, nothing terrible will happen — you won't break anything. But you will get an error message like the following:

```
File ".../AIO Python/hello.py", line 10
10=x
   ^
SyntaxError: cannot assign to literal
```

The `SyntaxError` part tells you that Python doesn't know what to do with that line of code because you didn't follow the proper syntax. To fix the error, just rewrite the line as

```
x = 10
```

Now let's talk about individual lines of code. In Python, a line of code ends with a line break or a semicolon. For example, this is three lines of Python code:

```
first_name = "Alan"
last_name = "Simpson"
print(first_name, last_name)
```

It would also be acceptable to use a semicolon instead of a line break:

```
first_name = "Alan"; last_name = "Simpson"
print(first_name, last_name)
```

Or, if you prefer:

```
first_name = "Alan"; last_name = "Simpson"; print(first_name, last_name)
```

The code runs the same whether you end each line with a break or a semicolon.

Note how the variable names are all lowercase, and the words are separated by an underscore:

```
first_name
last_name
```

Using all lowercase letters for variable names with words separated by underscores is a *naming convention* in Python. But note that a *convention* is not the same as a *syntax rule*. You could name the variables as follows without breaking any syntax rules:

```
FirstName
LastName
```

The naming convention tries to get programmers to follow basic stylistic guidelines that make the code more readable to other programs, which is especially important when working in programming teams or groups.

So far you've looked at lines of code. There are also *code blocks* where two or more lines of code work together. Here is an example:

```
x = 10
if x == 0:
    print("x is zero")
else:
    print("x is ",x)
print("All done")
```

The == (two equal signs) means "is equal to" in Python and is used to compare values to one another to see if they're equal. That's different from just = (one equal sign), which is the assignment operator for assigning variables.

The first line, x = 10, is just a line of code. Next, the if x == 0 tests to see whether the x variable contains the number 0. If x *does* contain 0, the indented line (print("x is zero") executes and that's what you see on the screen. However, if x does not contain 0, that indented line is skipped and the else: statement executes. The indented line under else: print("x is ",x) executes, but *only* if the x doesn't contain 0. The last line, print("All done!"), executes no matter what, because it's not indented.

So, as you can see, indentations matter a lot in Python. In the preceding code, only one of the indented lines will execute depending on the value in x. You learn about the specifics of using indentations in your code as you progress through the book. For now, just try to remember that syntax and indentations are important in Python, so you must type carefully when writing code.

If you have linting and PEP 8 enabled in your Workspace settings, as described in Chapter 3, you may see wavy underlines in code that appears to be okay. Hovering the mouse pointer over such an underline will usually show a message indicating the problem, as shown in Figure 4-7.

The exact wording and syntax of any error might vary, depending on the version of linting you're using. But as an example, in Figure 4-7, the first part of the message, [pep8], tells you that this error is related to PEP 8 syntax, which says you should put whitespace around operators:

```
[pep8] missing whitespace around operator
```

FIGURE 4-7:
Touching the
mouse pointer
to a red wavy
underline.

```
hello.py
     [pep8] missing whitespace around operator
                                              ion app.
1
2    quantity: int
3    quantity=14
4    # This variable contains a float
5    unit_price = 26.99
```

FIGURE 4-7:
Touching the
mouse pointer
to a red wavy
underline.

The second part just tells you that the variable named quantity contains an integer (int), which is a whole number. That part of the message is information, not an error.

To fix the error, put whitespace around the = sign. In other words, use the spacebar on your keyboard to put a space before and after the = sign.

But now you see a wavy underline under the 14. What's up with that? Well, to find out, simply click or hover the mouse pointer over the green wavy underline and leave the mouse pointer sitting right there until you see an explanation, as in Figure 4-8.

```
hello.py    ×
               [pep8] trailing whitespace
1    # This is a
2    # This vari  14: int
3    quantity = 14
4    # This variable contains a float
5    unit_price = 26.99
6    # This variable contains the result of
7    extended_price = quantity * unit_price
8    # Show the results
9    print(extended_price)
```

FIGURE 4-8:
Touching the
mouse pointer
to a green wavy
underline.

Again, the exact wording of the message may change by the time you read this. But in this example, the message is [pep8] trailing whitespace on top and 14: int on the bottom. The bottom part is just information, telling you that 14 is stored as an integer. The error is the trailing whitespace. In other words, there's a space after the 14 on that line. You can't see it, because it's just a space. To eliminate trailing spaces and fix the error, click the end of that line and press Backspace until the cursor is right up to the 4 in 14.

Other colored errors are stylistic errors. But you won't know the specific error until you hover the mouse pointer over the wavy underline and leave the mouse pointer there until you see the message. And the error won't go away until you take whatever action is required to fix it.

TIP

If PEP 8 errors seem overwhelming while you're trying to learn, turn them off temporarily. Choose File⇨Settings (Windows) or Code⇨Settings (Mac). Then in code view, set python.linting.pyLintEnabled or python.linting.pcodestyleEnabled or both to false.

Putting Code Together

The exercises you've just completed explain how to type, save, run, and change an app, save it again, and run it again. Those tasks define what you'll be doing with any kind of software development in any language, so you should practice them until they become second nature. But don't worry: You don't have to do this one chapter over and over again to get the hang of it. You'll be using these same skills throughout this book as you work your way from beginner to hot-shot twenty-first-century Python developer.

2
Understanding Python Building Blocks

Contents at a Glance

IN THIS CHAPTER

» **Mastering whole numbers**

» **Juggling numbers with decimal points**

» **Simplifying strings**

» **Conquering Boolean True/False**

» **Working with dates and times**

Chapter **1**

Working with Numbers, Text, and Dates

Computer languages in general, and certainly Python, deal with information in ways that are different from what you may be used to in your everyday life. This idea takes some getting used to. In the computer world, *numbers* are numbers you can add, subtract, multiply, and divide. Python also differentiates between whole numbers (integers) and numbers that contain a decimal point (floats). Words (textual information such as names and addresses) are stored as strings, which is short for "a string of characters." In addition to numbers and strings, there are Boolean values, which can be either True or False.

In real life, we also have to deal with dates and times, which are yet another type of information. Python doesn't have a built-in data type for dates and times, but thankfully, a free module you can import any time works with such information. This chapter is all about taking full advantage of the various Python data types.

Calculating Numbers with Functions

A *function* in Python is similar to a function on a calculator, in that you pass something into the function, and the function passes something back. For example, most calculators and programming languages have a square root function: You give them a number, and they give back the square root of that number.

Python functions generally have the syntax:

```
variablename = functionname(param[,param])
```

Because most functions return some value, you typically start by defining a variable to store what the function returns. Follow that with the = sign and the function name, followed by a pair of parentheses. Inside the parentheses you may pass one or more values (called *parameters*) to the function.

For example, the abs() function accepts one number and returns the absolute value of that number. If you're not a math nerd, this just means if you pass it a negative number, it returns that same number as a positive number. If you pass it a positive number, it returns the same number you passed it. In other words, the abs() function simply converts negative numbers to positive numbers.

As an example, in Figure 1-1 (which you can try out for yourself hands-on in a Jupyter notebook, at the Python prompt, or in a .py file in VS Code), we created a variable named x and assigned it the value –4. Then we created a variable named y and assigned it the absolute value of x using the abs() function. Printing x shows its value, –4, which hasn't changed. Printing y shows 4, the absolute value of x as returned by the abs() function.

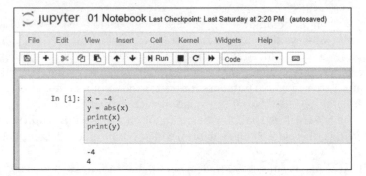

FIGURE 1-1:
Trying out the abs() function.

Even though a function always returns one value, some functions accept two or more values. For example, the round() function takes one number as its first argument. The second argument is the number of decimal places to which you want to round that number, for example, 2 for two decimal places. In the example in Figure 1-2, we created a variable, x, with a whole lot of digits after the decimal point. Then we created a variable named y to return the same number rounded to two decimal places. Then we printed both results.

FIGURE 1-2: Trying out the round() function.

```
In [2]: x = 1.23456789098765432100000000000000000000001
        y = round(x,2)
        print(x)
        print(y)

        1.2345678909876543
        1.23
```

Python has many built-in functions for working with numbers, as shown in Table 1-1. Some may not mean much to you if you're not into math in a big way, but don't let that intimidate you. If you don't understand what a function does, chances are it's not doing something relevant to the kind of work you do. But if you're curious, you can always search the web for *python* followed by the function name for more information. For a more extensive list, search for *python 3 built-in functions*.

TABLE 1-1 Some Built-In Python Functions for Numbers

Built-In Function	Purpose
abs(*x*)	Returns the absolute value of number *x* (converts negative numbers to positive).
bin(x)	Returns a string representing the value of *x* converted to binary.
float(x)	Converts a string or number *x* to the float data type.
format(x, y)	Returns *x* formatted according to the a pattern specified in *y*. This older syntax has been replaced with f-strings in current Python versions.
hex(x)	Returns a string containing *x* converted to hexadecimal, prefixed with 0x.
int(x)	Converts *x* to the integer data type by truncating (not rounding) the decimal portion and any digits after it.
max(x, y, z, ...)	Takes any number of numeric arguments and returns whichever is the largest.
min(x, y, z, ...)	Takes any number of numeric arguments and returns whichever is the smallest.
oct(x)	Converts *x* to an octal number, prefixed with 0o to indicate octal.
round(x, y)	Rounds the number *x* to *y* number of decimal places.
str(x)	Converts the number *x* to the string data type.
type(x)	Returns a string indicating the data type of *x*.

Figure 1-3 shows examples of proper Python syntax for using the built-in math functions.

```
: pi=3.14159265358979
  x=128
  y=-345.67890987
  z=-999.9999
  print(abs(z))
  print(int(z))
  print(int(abs(z)))
  print(round(pi,4))
  print(bin(x))
  print(hex(x))
  print(oct(x))
  print(max(pi,x,y,z))
  print(min(pi,x,y,z))
  print(type(pi))
  print(type(x))
  print(type(str(y)))

  999.9999
  -999
  999
  3.1416
  0b10000000
  0x80
  0o200
  128
  -999.9999
  <class 'float'>
  <class 'int'>
  <class 'str'>
```

FIGURE 1-3: Playing around with built-in math functions at the Python prompt.

You can also *nest* functions — meaning you can put functions inside functions. For example, when z = –999.9999, the expression print(int(abs(z))) prints the integer portion of the absolute value of z, which is 999. The original number is converted to positive, and then the decimal point and everything to its right chopped off.

Still More Math Functions

In addition to the built-in functions you've learned about so far, still others you can import from the math module. If you need them in an app, put import math near the top of the .py file or Jupyter cell to make those functions available to the rest of the code. Or to use them at the command prompt, first enter the **import math** command.

One of the functions in the math module is the sqrt() function, which gets the square root of a number. Because it's part of the math module, you can't use it without importing the module first. For example, if you enter the following, you'll get an error because sqrt() isn't a built-in function:

```
print(sqrt(81))
```

Even if you do two commands like the following, you'll still get an error because you're treating `sqrt()` as a built-in function:

```
import math
print(sqrt(81))
```

To use a function from a module, you have to import the module *and* precede the function name with the module name and a dot. So let's say you have some value, x, and you want the square root. You have to import the `math` module and use `math.sqrt(x)` to get the correct answer, as shown in Figure 1-4. Entering that command shows 9.0 as the result, which is indeed the square root of 81.

FIGURE 1-4:
Using the `sqrt()` function from the math module.

```
In [11]: import math
         z = 81
         print(math.sqrt(81))

         9.0
```

The `math` module offers a lot of trigonometric and hyperbolic functions, powers and logarithms, angular conversions, constants such as `pi` and `e`. We won't delve into all of them because advanced math isn't relevant to most people. You can check them all out anytime by searching the web for *python 3 math module functions*. Table 1-2 offers examples that may prove useful in your own work.

TABLE 1-2   ## Some Functions from the Python Math Module

Built-In Function	Purpose
`math.acos(x)`	Returns the arccosine of x in radians
`math.atan(x)`	Returns the arctangent of x, in radians
`math.atan2(y, x)`	Converts rectangular coordinates (x, y) to polar coordinates (r, theta)
`math.ceil(x)`	Returns the ceiling of x, the smallest integer greater than or equal to x
`math.cos(x)`	Returns the cosine of x radians
`math.degrees(x)`	Converts angle x from radians to degrees
`math.e`	Returns the mathematical constant *e* (2.718281 . . .)
`math.exp(x)`	Returns *e* raised to the power *x*, where *e* is the base of natural logarithms

(continued)

TABLE 1-2 *(continued)*

Built-In Function	Purpose
math.factorial(x)	Returns the factorial of x
math.floor()	Returns the floor of x, the largest integer less than or equal to x
math.isnan(x)	Returns True if x is not a number; otherwise returns False
math.log(x, y)	Returns the logarithm of x to base y
math.log2(x)	Returns the base-2 logarithm of x
math.pi	Returns the mathematical constant pi (3.141592...)
math.pow(x, y)	Returns x raised to the power y
math.radians(x)	Converts angle x from degrees to radians
math.sin(x)	Returns the sine of x, in radians
math.sqrt(x)	Returns the square root of x
math.tan(x)	Returns the tangent of x radians
math.tau()	Returns the mathematical constant tau (6.283185...)

The constants pi, e, and tau are unusual for functions in that you don't use parentheses. As with any function, you can use these functions in expressions (calculations) or assign their values to variables. Figure 1-5 shows some examples of using functions from the math module.

```
In [22]: import math
         pi = math.pi
         e = math.e
         tau = math.tau
         x = 81
         y = 7
         z = -23234.5454
         print(pi)
         print(e)
         print(tau)
         print(math.sqrt(x))
         print(math.factorial(y))
         print(math.floor(z))
         print(math.degrees(y))
         print(math.radians(45))

         3.141592653589793
         2.718281828459045
         6.283185307179586
         9.0
         5040
         -23235
         401.07045659157626
         0.7853981633974483
```

FIGURE 1-5:
More playing around with built-in math functions at the Python prompt.

Formatting Numbers

Over the years, Python has offered different methods for displaying numbers in formats familiar to us humans. For example, most people would rather see dollar amounts expressed in the format $1,234.56 rather than 1234.56006595069540569540595959. The easiest way to format numbers in Python, starting with version 3.6, is to use f-stings.

Formatting with f-strings

Format strings, or f-strings, are the easiest way to format data in Python. All you need is a lowercase *f* or uppercase *F* followed immediately by some text or expressions enclosed in quotation marks. Here is an example:

```
f"Hello {username}"
```

The f before the first quotation mark tells Python that what follows is a format string. Inside the quotation marks, the text, called the *literal part*, is displayed literally (exactly as typed in the f-string). Anything in curly braces is the *expression part* of the f-string, a placeholder for what will appear when the code executes. Inside the curly braces, you can have an *expression* (a formula to perform some calculation, a variable name, or a combination of the two). Here is an example:

```
username = "Alan"
print(f"Hello {username}")
```

When you run this code, the `print` function displays the word `Hello`, followed by a space, followed by the contents of the `username` variable, as shown in Figure 1-6.

FIGURE 1-6:
A super simple f-string for formatting.

```
In [24]: username = "Alan"
         print(f"Hello {username}")
         Hello Alan
```

Here is another example of an expression — the formula `quantity` times `unit_price` — inside the curly braces:

```
unit_price = 49.99
quantity = 30
print(f"Subtotal: ${quantity * unit_price}")
```

The output from that, when executed, follows:

```
Subtotal: $1499.7
```

That $1499.7 isn't an ideal way to show dollar amounts. Typically, we like to use commas in the thousands places, and two digits for the pennies, as in the following:

```
Subtotal: $1,499.70
```

Fortunately, f-strings provide you with the means to do this formatting, as you learn next.

Showing dollar amounts

To get a comma to appear in the dollar amount and the pennies as two digits, you can use a *format string* inside the curly braces of an expression in an f-string. The format string starts with a colon and needs to be placed inside the closing curly brace, right up against the variable name or the value shown.

To show commas in thousands places, use a comma in your format string right after the colon, like this:

```
:,
```

Using the current example, you would do the following:

```
print(f"Subtotal: ${quantity * unit_price:,}")
```

Executing this statement produces this output:

```
Subtotal: $1,499.7
```

To get the pennies to show as two digits, follow the comma with

```
.2f
```

The .2f means "two decimal places, fixed" (never any more or less than two decimal places). The following code will display the number with commas and two decimal places:

```
print(f"Subtotal: ${quantity * unit_price:,.2f}")
```

Here's what the code displays when executed:

```
Subtotal: $1,499.70
```

Perfect! That's exactly the format we want. So anytime you want to show a number with commas in the thousands places and exactly two digits after the decimal point, use an f-string with the format string, .2f.

Formatting percent numbers

Now, suppose your app applies sales tax. The app needs to know the sales tax rate, which should be expressed as a decimal number. So if the sales tax rate is 6.5 percent, it has to be written as 0.065 (or .065, if you prefer) in your code, like this:

```
sales_tax_rate = 0.065
```

It's the same amount with or without the leading zero, so just use whichever format works for you.

This number format is ideal for Python, and you wouldn't want to mess with that. But if you want to display that number to a human, simply using a print() function displays it exactly as Python stores it:

```
sales_tax_rate = 0.065
print(f"Sales Tax Rate {sales_tax_rate}")
Sales Tax Rate 0.065
```

When displaying the sales tax rate for people to read, you'll probably want to use the more familiar 6.5% format rather than .065. You can use the same idea as with fixed numbers (.2f). However, you replace the f for fixed numbers with %, like this:

```
print(f"Sales Tax Rate {sales_tax_rate:.2%}")
```

Running this code multiples the sales tax rate by 100 and follows it with a % sign, as you can see in Figure 1-7.

FIGURE 1-7:
Formatting a percentage number.

```
In [36]: sales_tax_rate = 0.065
         print(f"Sales Tax Rate {sales_tax_rate:.2%}")

         Sales Tax Rate 6.50%
```

In both of the previous examples, we used 2 for the number of digits. But of course you can display any number of digits you want, from zero (none) to whatever level of precision you need. For example, using .1%, as in the following:

```python
print(f"Sales Tax Rate {sales_tax_rate:.1%}")
```

displays this output when the line is executed:

```
Sales Tax Rate 6.5%
```

Replacing 1 with a 9, like this:

```python
print(f"Sales Tax Rate {sales_tax_rate:.9%}")
```

displays the percentage with nine digits after the decimal point:

```
Sales Tax Rate 6.500000000%
```

You don't need to use an f-string only inside a call to the `print` function. You can also execute an f-string and save the result in a variable that you can display later. The format string itself is like any other string in that it must be enclosed in single, double, or triple quotation marks. When using triple quotation marks, you can use either three single quotation marks or three double quotation marks. It doesn't matter which you use as the outermost quotation marks on the format string; the output is the same, as you can see in Figure 1-8.

TIP

For single and double quotation marks, use the corresponding keyboard keys. For triple quotation marks, you can use three of either. Make sure you end the string with exactly the same characters you used to start the string. For example, all the strings in Figure 1-8 are perfectly valid code, and they will all be treated the same.

```python
sales_tax_rate = 0.065
sample1 = f'Sales Tax Rate {sales_tax_rate:.2%}'
sample2 = f"Sales Tax Rate {sales_tax_rate:.2%}"
sample3 = f"""Sales Tax Rate {sales_tax_rate:.2%}"""
sample4 = f'''Sales Tax Rate {sales_tax_rate:.2%}'''

print(sample1)
print(sample2)
print(sample3)
print(sample4)

Sales Tax Rate 6.50%
Sales Tax Rate 6.50%
Sales Tax Rate 6.50%
Sales Tax Rate 6.50%
```

FIGURE 1-8:
An f-string can be encased in single, double, or triple quotation marks.

Making multiline format strings

If you want to have multiline output, you can add line breaks to your format strings in a few ways:

» **Use /n:** You can use a single-line format string with \n any place you want a line break. Just make sure you put the \n in the literal portion of the format string, not inside curly braces. For example:

```
user1 = "Alberto"
user2 = "Babs"
user3 = "Carlos"
output=f"{user1} \n{user2} \n{user3}"
print(output)
```

When executed, this code displays:

```
Alberto
Babs
Carlos
```

» **Use triple quotation marks (single or double):** If you use triple quotation marks around your format string, you don't need to use \n. You can just break the line in the format string wherever you want it to break in the output. For example, look at the code in Figure 1-9. The format string is in triple quotation marks and contains multiple line breaks. The output from running the code has line breaks in the same places.

```
unit_price = 49.95
quantity = 32
sales_tax_rate = 0.065
subtotal = quantity * unit_price
sales_tax = sales_tax_rate * subtotal
total = subtotal + sales_tax
output=f"""
Subtotal:  ${subtotal:,.2f}
Sales Tax: ${sales_tax:,.2f}
Total:     ${total:,.2f}
"""
print(output)


Subtotal:  $1,598.40
Sales Tax: $103.90
Total:     $1,702.30
```

FIGURE 1-9:
A multiline f-string enclosed in triple quotation marks.

As you can see, the output honors the line breaks and even the blank spaces in the format string. Unfortunately, it's not perfect — in real life, we would right align the numbers so that the decimal points line up. All is not lost, though, because with format strings you can also control the width and alignments of your output.

Formatting width and alignment

You can also control the width of your output (and the alignment of content within that width) by following the colon in your f-string with ‹ (for left aligned), ^ (for centered), or › (for right aligned). Put any of these characters right after the colon in your format string. For example, the following will make the output 20 characters wide, with the content right aligned:

```
:>20
```

In Figure 1-9, all the dollar amounts are left aligned, because that's the default. To right align numbers, which is how we usually see dollar amounts, you can use › in an f-string. To make the numbers the same width, specify a number after the › character. For example, in Figure 1-10, each f-string includes ›9, which causes each displayed number to be right aligned and 9 characters wide. The output, which you can see at the bottom of the figure, makes all the numbers align to the right, with their dollar signs neatly aligned to the left. The spaces to the right of each dollar sign make sure each number is exactly 9 characters wide.

FIGURE 1-10: All dollar amounts are right aligned within a width of 9 characters (›9).

```
unit_price = 49.95
quantity = 32
sales_tax_rate = 0.065
subtotal = quantity * unit_price
sales_tax = sales_tax_rate * subtotal
total = subtotal + sales_tax
output=f"""
Subtotal:   ${subtotal:>9,.2f}
Sales Tax: ${sales_tax:>9,.2f}
Total:      ${total:>9,.2f}
"""
print(output)


Subtotal:  $ 1,598.40
Sales Tax: $   103.90
Total:     $ 1,702.30
```

You may look at Figure 1-10 and wonder why the dollar signs are lined up the way they are. Why aren't they aligned right next to their numbers? The dollar signs are part of the literal string, outside the curly braces, so they aren't affected by the ›9 inside the curly braces.

Realigning the dollar signs is a little more complicated than you might imagine, because you can use the `,.2f` formatting only on a number. You can't attach a $ to the front of a number unless you change the number to a string — but then it wouldn't be a number anymore, so `.2f` wouldn't work.

But complicated doesn't mean impossible; it just means inconvenient. You can convert each dollar amount to a string in the current format, stick the dollar sign on that string, and then format the width and alignment on this string. For example, the following code creates a variable named `s-subtotal` containing a dollar sign immediately followed by the dollar amount, with the dollar sign just to the left of the first digit and no spaces after the dollar sign:

```
s_subtotal = "$" + f"{subtotal:,.2f}"
```

In this code, we assume the `subtotal` variable contains some number. Let's say the number is `1598.402`, though it could be any number. The `f"{subtotal:,2f}"` formats the number in a fixed two-decimal-places format with a comma in the thousands place, like this:

```
1,598.40
```

The output is a string rather than a number because an f-string always produces a string.

The following part of the code sticks (concatenates) a dollar sign in the front:

```
"$"+
```

So now the output is $1,598.40. That final formatted string is stored in a new variable named `s_subtotal`. (We added the leading `s_` to remind us that this is the string equivalent of the subtotal number, not the original number.)

To display that dollar amount right aligned with a width of 9 digits, use `>9` in a new format string to display the `s_subtotal` variable, like this:

```
f{s_subtotal:>9}
```

REMEMBER

When you use + with strings, you *concatenate* (join) the two strings. The + only does addition with numbers, not strings.

Figure 1-11 shows a complete example, including the output from running the code. All the numbers are right aligned with the dollar signs in the usual place.

```
# Numerical values
unit_price = 49.95
quantity = 32
sales_tax_rate = 0.065
subtotal = quantity * unit_price
sales_tax = sales_tax_rate * subtotal
total = subtotal + sales_tax

# Format amounts to show as string with leading dollar sign
s_subtotal = "$" + f"{subtotal:,.2f}"
s_sales_tax = "$" + f"{sales_tax:,.2f}"
s_total = "$" + f"{total:,.2f}"

# Output the string with dollar sign already attached
output=f"""
Subtotal:  {s_subtotal:>9}
Sales Tax: {s_sales_tax:>9}
Subtotal:  {s_total:>9}
"""
print(output)


Subtotal:  $1,598.40
Sales Tax:   $103.90
Subtotal:  $1,702.30
```

FIGURE 1-11:
All the dollar amounts neatly aligned.

Grappling with Weirder Numbers

Most of us deal with simple numbers like quantities and dollar amounts all the time. If your work requires you to deal with bases other than 10 or imaginary numbers, Python has the stuff you need to do the job. But keep in mind that you don't need to learn these things to use Python or any other language. You would use these only if your actual work (or perhaps homework) requires it. In the next section, you look at some number types commonly used in computer science: binary, octal, and hexadecimal numbers.

Binary, octal, and hexadecimal numbers

If your work requires dealing with base 2, base 8, or base 16 numbers, you're in luck because Python has symbols for writing these as well as functions for converting among them. Table 1-3 shows the three non-decimal bases and the digits used by each.

TABLE 1-3   **Python for Base 2, 8, and 16 Numbers**

System	Also Called	Digits Used	Symbol	Function
Base 2	Binary	0,1	0b	`bin()`
Base 8	Octal	0,1,2,3,4,5,6,7	0o	`oct()`
Base 16	Hexadecimal or hex	0,1,2,3,4,5,6,7,8,9, A,B,C,D,E,F	0x	`hex()`

Most people never have to work with binary, octal, or hexadecimal numbers. So if all of this is giving you the heebie-jeebies, don't sweat it. If you've never heard of them before, chances are you'll never hear of them again after you've completed this section.

TIP

If you want more information about the various numbering systems, you can use your favorite search engine to search for *binary number* or *octal*, or *decimal*, or *hexadecimal*.

You can use these various functions to convert how the number is displayed at the Python prompt, of course, as well as in an apps you create. At the prompt, just use the print() function with the conversion function inside the parentheses, and the number you want to convert inside the innermost parentheses. For example, the following displays the hexadecimal equivalent of the number 255:

```
print(hex(255))
```

The result is 0xff, where the 0x indicates that the number that follows is expressed in hex, and ff is the hexadecimal equivalent of 255.

To convert from binary, octal, or hex to decimal, you don't need to use a function. Just use print() with the number you want to convert inside the parentheses. For example, print(0xff) displays 255, the decimal equivalent of hex ff. Figure 1-12 shows some more examples you can try at the Python prompt.

```
x=255
# Convert decimal to other number systems
print(bin(x))
print(oct(x))
print(hex(x))

# Show number in decimal number system (no conversion required)
print(0b11111111)
print(0o377)
print(0xff)

0b11111111
0o377
0xff
255
255
255
```

FIGURE 1-12: Messing about with binary, octal, and hex.

Complex numbers

Complex numbers are another one of those weird numbering things you may never have to deal with unless you happen to be into electrical engineering, higher math, or a branch of science that uses them. A *complex number* is one that can be expressed as *a+bi* where *a* and *b* are real numbers, and *i* represents the imaginary number satisfied by the equation $x^2=-1$. There is no real number x whose square equals -1, so that's why it's called an *imaginary number*.

Some branches of math use a lowercase i to indicate an imaginary number. But Python uses j (as do those in electrical engineering because i is used to indicate current).

Anyway, if your application requires working with complex numbers, you can use the `complex()` function to generate an imaginary number, using the following syntax:

```
complex(real,imaginary)
```

Replace *real* with the real part of the complex number, and replace *imaginary* with the imaginary number. For example, in code or the command prompt, try this:

```
z = complex(2,-3)
```

The variable z gets the imaginary number 2–3j. Then use a `print()` function to display the contents of z, like this:

```
print(z)
```

The screen displays the imaginary number 2–3j.

You can tack `.real` or `.imag` onto an imaginary number to get the real or imaginary part. For example, the following produces `2.0`, which is the real part of the number z:

```
print(z.real)
```

And this returns `-3.0`, which is the imaginary part of z:

```
print(z.imag)
```

Once again, if none of this makes sense to you, don't worry. It's not required for learning or doing Python. Python simply offers complex numbers and these functions for people who happen to require them.

TECHNICAL STUFF

If your work requires working with complex numbers, search the web for *python cmath* to learn about Python's `cmath` module, which provides functions for complex numbers.

Manipulating Strings

In Python and other programming languages, we refer to words and chunks of text as *strings,* short for "a string of characters." A string has no numeric meaning or value. (We discuss the basics of strings in Book 1, Chapter 4.) In this section, you learn Python coding skills for working with strings.

Concatenating strings

You can join strings by using a + sign. The process of doing so is called *string concatenation* in nerd-o-rama world. One thing that catches beginners off-guard is the fact that a computer doesn't know a word from a bologna sandwich. So when you join strings, the computer doesn't automatically put spaces where you'd expect them. For example, in the following code, `full_name` is a concatenation of the first three strings.

```
first_name = "Alan"
middle_init = "C"
last_name = "Simpson"
full_name = first_name+middle_init + last_name
print(full_name)
```

When you run this code to print the contents of the `full_name` variable, you can see that Python did join them in one long string:

```
AlanCSimpson
```

Nothing is wrong with this output, per se, except that we usually put spaces between words and the parts of a person's name.

Because Python won't automatically put in spaces where you think they should go, you have to put them in yourself. The easiest way to represent a single space is by using a pair of quotation marks with one space between them, like this:

```
" "
```

If you forget to put the space between the quotation marks, like the following, you won't get a space in your string because there's no space between the quotation marks:

```
""
```

You can put multiple spaces between the quotation marks if you want multiple spaces in your output, but typically one space is enough. In the following example, you put a space between `first_name` and `last_name`. You also stick a period and space after `middle_init`:

```
first_name = "Alan"
middle_init = "C"
last_name = "Simpson"
full_name = first_name + " " + middle_init + ". " + last_name
print(full_name)
```

The output of this code, which is the contents of that `full_name` variable, looks more like the kind of name you're used to seeing:

```
Alan C. Simpson
```

Getting the length of a string

To determine how many characters are in a string, you use the built-in `len()` function (short for *length*). The length includes spaces because spaces are characters, each one having a length of one. An empty string — that is, a string with nothing in it, not even a space — has a length of zero.

Here are some examples. In the first line you define a variable named `s1` and put an empty string in it (a pair of quotation marks with nothing in between). The `s2` variable gets a space (a pair of quotation marks with a space between). The `s3` variable gets a string with some letters and spaces. Then, three `print()` functions display the length of each string:

```
s1 = ""
s2 = " "
s3 = "A B C"
print(len(s1))
print(len(s2))
print(len(s3))
```

Following is the output from that code, when executed. The output makes perfect sense when you understand that `len()` measures the length of strings as the number of characters (including spaces) in the string:

```
0
1
5
```

Working with common string operators

Python offers several operators for working with sequences of data. One weird thing about strings in Python (and in most other programming languages) is that when you're counting characters, the first character counts as 0, not 1. This makes no sense to us humans. But computers count characters that way because it's the most efficient method. So even though the string in Figure 1-13 is five characters long, the last character in that string is the number 4, because the first character is number 0. Go figure.

FIGURE 1-13:
Character positions in a string start at 0, not 1.

Table 1-4 summarizes the Python 3 operators for working with strings.

TABLE 1-4   **Python Sequence Operators That Work with Strings**

Operator	Purpose
x in s	Returns True if x exists somewhere in string s.
x not in s	Returns True if x is not contained in string s.
s * n or n * s	Repeats string s n times.
s[i]	The i th item of string s where the first character is 0.
s[i:j]	A slice from string x beginning with the character at position i through to the character at position j.
s[i:j:k]	A slice of s from i to j with step k.
min(s)	The smallest (lowest) character of string s.
max(s)	The largest (highest) character of string s.
s.index(x[, i[, j]])	The numeric position of the first occurrence of x in string s. The optional i and j limit the search to the characters from i to j.
s.count(x)	The number of times string x appears in larger string s.

Figure 1-14 shows examples of using the string operators in Jupyter Notebook. When the output of a `print()` function doesn't look right, keep in mind two important facts about strings in Python:

» The first character is always number 0.

» Every space counts as one character, so don't skip spaces when counting.

```
: s = "Abracadabra Hocus Pocus you're a turtle dove"
# Is there a lowercase letter t is contained in S?
print("t" in s)
# Is there an uppercase letter t is contained in S?
print("T" in s)
# Is there no uppercase T in s?S
print("T" not in s)
# Print 15 hyphens in a row
print("-" * 15)
# Print first character in string X
print(s[0])
# Print characters 33 - 39 from string x
print(s[33:39])
#Print every third character in s starting at zero
print(s[0:44:3])
#Print lowest character is s (a space is lower than the letter a)
print(min(s))
#Print the highest character is s
print(max(s))
# Where is the first uppercase P?
print(s.index("P"))
# Where is the first lowercase o in the latter half of string s
# Note that the returned value still starts counting from zero
print(s.index("o",22,44))    ·
# How many lowercase letters a are in string s?
print(s.count("a"))
```

```
True
False
True
---------------
A
turtle
AadrHuPuy' tt v

y
18
25
5
```

FIGURE 1-14:
Playing around
with string
operators
in Jupyter
Notebook.

You may have noticed that `min(s)` returns a blank space, meaning that the blank space character is the lowest character in that string. But what exactly makes the space "lower" than the letter *A* or the letter *a*? The simple answer is the letter's *ASCII number*. Every character you can type at your keyboard, and many additional characters, have a number assigned by the American Standard Code for Information Interchange (ASCII).

Figure 1-15 shows a chart with ASCII numbers for many common characters. Spaces and punctuation characters are "lower" than *A* because they have smaller ASCII numbers. Uppercase letters are "lower" than lowercase letters because they have smaller ASCII numbers. Are you wondering what happened to the characters assigned to numbers 0–31? These numbers have characters too, but they are control characters and are essentially non-printing and invisible, such as when you hold down the Ctrl key and press another key.

Number	Character	Number	Character	Number	Character
32	[space]	65	A	97	a
33	!	66	B	98	b
34	"	67	C	99	c
35	#	68	D	100	d
36	$	69	E	101	e
37	%	70	F	102	f
38	&	71	G	103	g
39	'	72	H	104	h
40	(	73	I	105	i
41	)	74	J	106	j
42	*	75	K	107	k
43	+	76	L	108	l
44	,	77	M	109	m
45	-	78	N	110	n
46	.	79	O	111	o
47	/	80	P	112	p
48	0	81	Q	113	q
49	1	82	R	114	r
50	2	83	S	115	s
51	3	84	T	116	t
52	4	85	U	117	u
53	5	86	V	118	v
54	6	87	W	119	w
55	7	88	X	120	x
56	8	89	Y	121	y
57	9	90	Z	122	z
58	:	91	[	123	{
59	;	92	\	124	|
60	<	93	]	125	}
61	=	94	^	126	~
62	>	95	_	127	□
63	?	96	`	128	€
64	@				

FIGURE 1-15: ASCII numbers for common characters.

Python offers two functions for working with ASCII. The `ord()` function takes a character as input and returns the ASCII number of that character. For example, `print(ord("A"))` returns 65, because an uppercase *A* is character 65 in the ASCII chart. The `chr()` function does the opposite. You give it a number, and it returns the ASCII character for that number. For example, `print(chr(65))` displays `A` because *A* is character 65 in the ASCII chart.

Manipulating strings with methods

Every string in Python 3 is considered a *str object* (pronounced "string object"). The shortened word *str* for *string* distinguishes Python 3 from earlier versions of Python, which referred to string as string objects (with the word *string* spelled out, not shortened). This naming convention is a great source of confusion, especially for beginners. Just try to remember that in Python 3, str is all about strings of characters.

Python offers numerous *str methods* (also called *string methods*) to help you work with str objects. The general syntax of str object methods is as follows:

```
string.methodname(params)
```

where *string* is the string you're analyzing, *methodname* is the name of a method from Table 1-5, and *params* refers to any parameters that you need to pass to the method (if required). The leading s in the first column of Table 1-5 means "any string," be it a literal string enclosed in quotation marks or the name of a variable that contains a string.

TABLE 1-5   Built-In Methods for Python 3 Strings

Method	Purpose
s.capitalize()	Returns a string with the first letter capitalized and the rest lowercase.
s.count(x, [y, z])	Returns the number of times string x appears in string s. Optionally, you can add y as a starting point and z as an ending point to search a portion of the string.
s.find(x, [y, z])	Returns a number indicating the first position at which string x can be found in string s. Optional y and z parameters allow you to limit the search to a portion of the string. Returns –1 if none found.
s.index(x, [y, z])	Similar to find but returns a "substring not found" error if string x can't be found in string y.
s.isalpha()	Returns True if s is at least one character long and contains only letters (A-Z or a-z).
s.isdecimal()	Returns True if s is at least one character long and contains only numeric characters (0-9).
s.islower()	Returns True if s contains letters and all those letters are lowercase.
s.isnumeric()	Returns True if s is at least one character long and contains only numeric characters (0-9).
s.isprintable()	Returns True if string s contains only printable characters.
s.istitle()	Returns True if string s contains letters and the first letter of each word is uppercase followed by lowercase letters.
s.isupper()	Returns True if all letters in the string are uppercase.
s.lower()	Returns s with all letters converted to lowercase.
s.lstrip()	Returns s with any leading spaces removed.
s.replace(x, y)	Returns a copy of string s with all characters x replaced by character y.
s.rfind(x, [y, z])	Similar to s.find but searches backward from the start of the string. If y and z are provided, searches backward from position z to position y. Returns –1 if string x not found.

Method	Purpose
s.rindex()	Same as s.rfind but returns an error if the substring isn't found.
s.rstrip()	Returns string x with any trailing spaces removed.
s.strip()	Returns string x with leading and trailing spaces removed.
s.swapcase()	Returns string s with uppercase letters converted to lowercase and lowercase letters converted to uppercase.
s.title()	Returns string s with the first letter of every word capitalized and all other letters lowercase.
s.upper()	Returns string s with all letters converted to uppercase.

You can play around with these methods in a Jupyter notebook, at the Python prompt, or in a .py file. Figure 1-16 shows some examples in a Jupyter notebook using three variables named s1, s2, and s3 as strings to experiment with. The result of running the code appears below the code.

```
s1 = "There is no such word as schmeedledorp"
s2="   a b c   "
s3="ABC"
# Captialize first letter, the rest lowercase
print(s3.capitalize())
# Count the number of spaces in s1
print(s1.count(" "))
# Find the dot in S4
print(s4.find("."))
# Is s2 all lowercase letters?
print(s2.islower())
# Convert s3 to all lowercase
print(s3.lower())
# String leading characters from s2
print(s2.lstrip())
# String leading and trailing characters from s2
print(s2.strip())
# Swap the case of letters in s1
print(s1.swapcase())
# Show s1 in title case (initial caps)
print(s1.title())
# Show s1 uppercase
print(s1.upper())
```

```
Abc
6
3
True
abc
a b c
a b c
tHERE IS NO SUCH WORD AS SCHMEEDLEDORP
There Is No Such Word As Schmeedledorp
THERE IS NO SUCH WORD AS SCHMEEDLEDORP
```

FIGURE 1-16: Playing around with Python 3 string functions.

REMEMBER

Don't bother trying to memorize or even make sense of every string method. Remember instead that if you need to operate on a string in Python, you can do a web search for *python 3 string methods* to find out what's available.

Uncovering Dates and Times

In the world of computers, we often use dates and times for scheduling, or for calculating when something is due or how many days it's past due. We sometimes use *timestamps* to record exactly when a user did something or when an event occurred. There are lots of reasons for using dates and times in Python, but perhaps surprisingly, no built-in data type for them exists like the ones for strings and numbers.

To work with dates and times, you typically need to use the `datetime` module. Like any module, you must import it before you can use it. You do that using `import datetime`. As with **any** import, you can add an alias (nickname) that's easier to type, if you like. For example, `import datetime as dt` would work too. You just have to remember to type `dt` rather than `datetime` in your code when calling upon the capabilities of that module.

The `datetime` module is an abstract base class, which is a fancy way of saying it offers new data types to the language. For dates and times, those data types are as follows:

» **datetime.date:** A date consisting of month, day, and year (but no time information).

» **datetime.time:** A time consisting of hour, minute, second, microsecond, and optionally time zone information if needed (but no date).

» **datetime.datetime:** A single item of data consisting of date, time, and optionally time zone information.

We preceded each type with the full word `datetime` in the preceding list, but if you use an alias, such as `dt`, you can use that in your code instead. We talk about each of these data types separately in the sections that follow.

Working with dates

The `datetime.date` data type is ideal for working with dates when time isn't an issue. You can create a date object in two ways. You can get today's date from the computer's internal clock by using the `today()` method. Or you can specify a year, month, and day (in that order) inside parentheses.

REMEMBER

When specifying the month or day, never use a leading zero for `datetime.date()`. For example, April 1 2020 has to be expressed as `2020,4,1` — if you type `2020,04,01`, it won't work.

For example, after importing the `datetime` module, you can use `date.today()` to get the current date from the computer's internal clock. Or use `date(year, month, day)` syntax to create a date object for some other date. The following code shows both methods:

```
# Import the datetime module, nickname dt
import datetime as dt
# Store today's date in a variable named today.
today = dt.date.today()
# Store some other date in a variable called last_of_teens
last_of_teens = dt.date(2019, 12, 31)
```

Try it by typing the code in a Jupyter notebook, at the Python prompt, or in a `.py` file. Use the `print()` function to see what's in each variable, as shown in Figure 1-17. Your `today` variable won't be the same as in the figure; it will the date you try this.

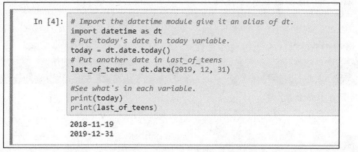

FIGURE 1-17: Experiments with `datetime.date` objects in a Jupyter notebook.

YOUR COMPUTER DATE AND TIME

If your computer is connected to the Internet, its internal date and time should be accurate. That's because it gets that information from NNTP (Network News Transfer Protocol), a standard time that any computer or app can get from the Internet.

The datetime information is tailored to your time zone and takes into account the daylight saving time of your location (if applicable). So in other words, the date and time shown on your computer screen should match what the calendar and the clock on your wall say.

You can isolate any part of a date object by using .month, .day, or .year. For example, in the same Jupyter cell or Python prompt, execute this code:

```
print(last_of_teens.month)
print(last_of_teens.day)
print(last_of_teens.year)
```

Each of the three components of that date appear on a separate line:

```
12
31
2019
```

As you saw on the first printout, the default date display is *yyyy-mm-dd*, but you can format dates and times however you want. Use f-strings, which we discuss earlier in this chapter, along with the directives shown in Table 1-6, which includes the format for dates as well as for times, as we discuss later in this chapter.

TABLE 1-6   **Formatting Strings for Dates and Times**

Directive	Description	Example
%a	Weekday, abbreviated	Sun
%A	Weekday, full	Sunday
%w	Weekday number 0-6, where 0 is Sunday	0
%d	Number day of the month 01-31	31
%b	Month name abbreviated	Jan
%B	Month name full	January
%m	Month number 01-12	01
%y	Year without century	19
%Y	Year with century	2019
%H	Hour 00-23	23
%I	Hour 00-12	11
%p	AM/PM	PM
%M	Minute 00-59	01
%S	Second 00-59	01

Directive	Description	Example
%f	Microsecond 000000-999999	495846
%z	UTC offset	−0500
%Z	Time zone	EST
%j	Day number of year 001-366	300
%U	Week number of year, Sunday as the first day of week, 00-53	50
%W	Week number of year, Monday as the first day of week, 00-53	50
%c	Local version of date and time	Tue Dec 31 23:59:59 2018
%x	Local version of date	12/31/18
%X	Local version of time	23:59:59
%%	A % character	%

TECHNICAL STUFF

Some tutorials tell you to format dates and times by using strftime rather than f-strings, and that's certainly a valid method. We're sticking with the newer f-strings here, however, because we think they'll be preferred over strftime in the future.

When using format strings, make sure you put spaces, slashes, and anything else you want between directives where you want those to appear in the output. For example, this line:

```
print(f"{last_of_teens:%A, %B %d, %Y}")
```

when executed, displays this:

```
Tuesday, December 31, 2019
```

To show the date in the *mm/dd/yyyy* format, use %m/%d/%Y, like this:

```
todays_date = f"{today:%m/%d/%Y}"
```

The output will be the current date for you when you try it, with a format like the following:

```
11/19/2018
```

Table 1-7 shows a few more examples you can try with different dates.

TABLE 1-7 **Sample Date Format Strings**

Format String	Example
%a, %b %d %Y	Sat, Jun 01 2019
%x	06/01/19
%m-%d-%y	06-01-19
This %A %B %d	This Saturday June 01
%A %B %d is day number %j of %Y	Saturday June 01 is day number 152 of 2019

Working with times

If you want to work strictly with time data, use the `datetime.time` class. The basic syntax for defining a time object using the `time` class is

```
variable = datetime.time([hour,[minute,[second,[microsecond]]]])
```

Notice how all the arguments are optional. For example, you can use no arguments:

```
midnight = dt.time()
print(midnight)
```

This code stores the time as 00:00:00, which is midnight. To verify that it's really a time, entering `print(type(midnight))` displays the following:

```
00:00:00
<class 'datetime.time'>
```

The second line tells you that the 00:00:00 value is a `time` object from the `datetime` class.

The fourth optional value you can pass to `time()` is microseconds (millionths of a second). For example, the following code puts a time that's a millionth of a second before midnight in a variable named `almost_midnight` and then displays that time onscreen with a `print()` function:

```
almost_midnight = dt.time(23, 59, 59, 999999)
print(almost_midnight)
23:59:59.999999
```

You can use format strings with the time directives from Table 1-6 to control the format of the time. Table 1-8 shows some examples using 23:59:59:999999 as the sample time.

TABLE 1-8 **Sample Date Format Strings**

Format String	Example
%I:%M %p	11:59 PM
%H:%M:%S and %f microseconds	23:59:59 and 999999 microseconds
%X	23:59:59

Sometimes you want to work only with dates, and sometimes you want to work only with times. Often you want to pinpoint a moment in time using both the date and the time. For that, use the datetime class of the datetime module. This class supports a now() method that can grab the current date and time from the computer clock, as follows:

```
import datetime as dt
right_now = dt.datetime.now()
print(right_now)
```

What you see on the screen from the print() function depends on when you execute this code. But the format of the datetime value will be like this:

```
2019-11-19 14:03:07.525975
```

This means November 19, 2019 at 2:03 PM (with 7.525975 seconds tacked on).

You can also define a datetime using any the following parameters. The month, day, and year are required. The rest are optional and set to 0 in the time if you omit them.

```
datetime(year, month, day, hour, [minute, [second, [microsecond]]])
```

Here is an example using 11:59 PM on December 31 2019:

```
import datetime as dt
new_years_eve = dt.datetime(2019, 12, 31, 23, 59)
print(new_years_eve)
```

Here is the output of that `print()` statement with no formatting:

```
2019-12-31 23:59:00
```

Table 1-9 shows examples of formatting the datetime using directives shown previously in Table 1-6.

TABLE 1-9   **Sample Datetime Format Strings**

Format String	Example
%A, %B %d at %I:%M%p	Tuesday, December 31 at 11:59PM
%m/%d/%y at %H:%M%p	12/31/19 at 23:59
%I:%M %p on %b %d	11:59 PM on Dec 31
%x	12/31/19
%c	Tue Dec 31 23:59:00 2019
%m/%d/%y at %I:%M %p	12/31/19 at 11:59 PM
%I:%M %p on %m/%d/%y	1:59 PM on 12/31/2019

Calculating timespans

Sometimes just knowing the date or time isn't enough. You need to know the duration, or *timespan*, as it's typically called in the computer world. In other words, not the date, not the o'clock, but the "how long" in terms of years, months, weeks, days, hours, minutes, or whatever. For timespans, the Python `datetime` module includes the `datetime.timedelta` class.

A `timedelta` object is created automatically whenever you subtract two dates, times, or datetimes to determine the duration between them. For example, suppose you create a couple of variables to store dates, perhaps one for New Year's Day and another for Memorial Day. Then you create a third variable named `days_between` and put in it the difference you get by subtracting the earlier date from the later date, as follows:

```
import datetime as dt
new_years_day = dt.date(2019, 1, 1)
memorial_day = dt.date(2019, 5, 27)
days_between = memorial_day - new_years_day
```

So what exactly is days_between in terms of a data type? If you print its value, you get 146 days, 0:00:00. In other words, there are 146 days between those dates; the 0:00:00 is time but because we didn't specify a time of day in either date, the time digits are all just set to 0. If you use the Python type() function to determine the data type of days_between, you see it's a timedelta object from the datetime class, as follows:

```
146 days, 0:00:00
<class 'datetime.timedelta'>
```

The timedelta calculation happens automatically when you subtract one date from another to get the time between. You can also define any timedelta (duration) using this syntax:

```
datetime.timedelta(days=, seconds=, microseconds=, milliseconds=, minutes=,
    hours=, weeks=)
```

If you provide an argument, you must include a number after the = sign. If you omit an argument, its value is set to 0.

To get an understanding of how this works, try out the following code. After importing the datetime module, create a date using .date(). Then create a timedelta object using .timedelta. If you add a date and a timedelta, you get a new date — in this case, a date that's 146 days after 1/1/2019:

```
import datetime as dt
new_years_day = dt.date(2019, 1, 1)
duration = dt.timedelta(days=146)
print(new_years_day + duration)
2019-05-27
```

Of course, you can subtract too. For example, if you start with a date of 5/27/2019 and subtract 146 days, you get 1/1/2019, as shown here:

```
import datetime as dt
memorial_day = dt.date(2019, 5, 27)
duration = dt.timedelta(days=146)
print(memorial_day - duration)
2019-01-01
```

It works with datetimes too. If you're looking for a duration that's less than a day, just give both times the same date. For example, consider the following code and the results of the subtraction:

```
import datetime as dt
start_time = dt.datetime(2019, 3, 31, 8, 0, 0)
```

```
finish_time = dt.datetime(2019, 3, 31, 14, 34, 45)
time_between = finish_time - start_time
print(time_between)
print(type(time_between))
```

```
6:34:45
<class 'datetime.timedelta'>
```

We know that 6:34:45 is a time duration of 6 hours 34 minutes and 45 seconds for two reasons. One, it's the result of subtracting one moment of time from another. Two, printing the type() of that data type tells us it's a timedelta object (a duration), not an o'clock time.

Here is another example using datetimes with different dates: One is the current datetime, and the other is a date of birth with the time down to the minute (March 31 1995 at 8:26 AM). To calculate age, subtract the birthdate from the current time, now:

```
import datetime as dt
now = dt.datetime.now()
birthdatetime = dt.datetime(1995, 3, 31, 8, 26)
age = now - birthdatetime
print(age)
print(type(age))
8634 days, 7:55:07.739804
<class 'datetime.timedelta'>
```

The result is expressed as follows:

```
8634 days, 7 hours, 52 minutes, and 1.967031 seconds
```

The tiny seconds value stems from the fact that datetime.now grabs the date and time from the computer's clock down to the microsecond.

You don't always need microseconds or even seconds in your timedelta object. For example, say you're trying to determine someone's age. You could start by creating two dates, one named today for today's date and another named birthdate that contains the birthdate. The following example uses a birthdate of Jan 31, 2000:

```
import datetime as dt
today = dt.date.today()
birthdate = dt.date(2000, 12, 31)
```

```
delta_age = (today - birthdate)
print(delta_age)
```

The last two lines create a variable named delta_age and print what's in the variable. If you run this code, you'll see something like the following output (but it won't be exactly the same because your today date will be whatever today's date is when you run the app):

```
6533 days, 0:00:00
```

Let's say what we really want is the age in years. You can convert timedelta to a number of days by tacking .days onto timedelta. You can put that in another variable called days_old. Printing days_old and its type show you that days_old is an int, a regular old integer you can do math with. For example, in the following code, the days_old variable receives the value delta_age.days, which is delta_age from the preceding line converted to a number of days:

```
delta_age = (today - birthdate)
days_old = delta_age.days
print(days_old, type(days_old))
6533 <class 'int'>
```

To get the number of years, divide the number of days by 365. If you want just the number of years as an integer, use the floor division operator (//) rather than regular division (/). (*Floor division* removes the decimal portion from the quotient, so you get a whole number). You can put the result of that calculation in another variable if you like. For example, in the following code, the years_old variable contains a value calculated by dividing days_old by 365:

```
years_old = days_old // 365
print(years_old)
18
```

So we get the age, in years: 18. If you want the number of months, too, you can ball-park that just by taking the remainder of dividing the days by 365 to get the number of days left. Then floor divide that value by 30 (because on average each month has about 30 days) to get a good approximation of the number of months. Use % rather than / for division to get just the remainder after the division. Figure 1-18 shows the sequence of events in a Jupyter notebook, with comments to explain what's going on.

```
import datetime as dt
# Today's date according to your computer
today = dt.date.today()

# Any birthdate expressed as year, month, day
birthdate = dt.date(2000, 1, 31)

# Duration between the dates as a timedelta
delta_age = (today - birthdate)

# Duration between the dates as a number (of days)
days_old = delta_age.days

# Floor divide days by 365 to get the number of years
years = days_old // 365

# Days left over is remainder of days_old divided by 365.
# Floor divide that remainder by 30 for approximate months.
months = (days_old % 365) // 30

# Print in a format to your liking
print(f"You are {years} years and {months} months old.")

You are 18 years and 9 months old.
```

FIGURE 1-18:
Calculating age in years and months from a timedelta object.

Accounting for Time Zones

As you know, when it's noon in your neighborhood, it doesn't mean its noon every-where. Figure 1-19 shows a map of all the time zones. If you want a closer look, simply search the web for *time zone map*. At any given moment, it's a different day and time of day depending on where you happen to be on the globe. There is a uni-versal time, called the Coordinated Universal Time or Universal Time Coordinated (UTC). You may have heard of Greenwich Mean Time (GMT) or Zulu time used by the military, which is the same idea. All these times refer to the time at the prime meridian on Earth, or 0 degrees longitude, smack dab in the middle of the time zone map in Figure 1-19.

FIGURE 1-19:
Time zones.

These days, most people rely on the Olson Database as the primary source of information about time zones. It lists all current time zones and locations. Do a web search for *Olson database* or *tz database* if you're interested in all the details. There are too many time zone names to list here, but Table 1-10 shows some examples of American time zones. The left column is the official name from the database. The second column shows the more familiar name. The last two columns show the offset from UTC for standard time and daylight saving time.

TABLE 1-10 **Sample Time Zones from the Olson Database**

Time Zone	Common Name	UTC Offset	UTC DST Offset
Etc/UTC	UTC	+00:00	+00:00
Etc/UTC	Universal	+00:00	+00:00
America/Anchorage	US/Alaska	−09:00	−08:00
America/Adak	US/Aleutian	−10:00	−09:00
America/Phoenix	US/Arizona	−07:00	−07:00
America/Chicago	US/Central	−06:00	−05:00
America/New_York	US/Eastern	−05:00	−04:00
America/Indiana/Indianapolis	US/East-Indiana	−05:00	−04:00
America/Honolulu	US/Hawaii	−10:00	−10:00
America/Indiana/Knox	US/Indiana-Starke	−06:00	−05:00
America/Detroit	US/Michigan	−05:00	−04:00
America/Denver	US/Mountain	−07:00	−06:00
America/Los Angeles	US/Pacific	−08:00	−07:00
Pacific/Pago_Pago	US/Samoa	−11:00	−11:00
Etc/UTC	UTC	+00:00	+00:00
Etc/UTC	Zulu	+00:00	+00:00

So why are we telling you all this? Because Python lets you work with two different types of datetimes:

>> **Naïve datetime:** Any datetime that does not include information that relates it to a specific time zone

>> **Aware datetime:** A datetime that includes time zone information

The timedelta objects and dates that you define with .date() are always naïve. Any time or datetime you create as time() or datetime() objects will also by naïve, by default. But with those two you have the option of including time zone information if it's useful in your work, such as when you're showing event dates to an audience in multiple time zones.

Working with Time Zones

When you get the time from your computer's system clock, it's for your time zone, but you don't have an indication of what that time zone *is*. But you can tell the difference between your time and UTC time by comparing .now() for your location to .utc_now() for UTC time, and then subtracting the difference, as shown in Figure 1-20.

```
# Get the datetime module and give it an alias
import datetime as dt

# Get the time from computer clock
here_now = dt.datetime.now()

# Get the UTC datetime right now
utc_now = dt.datetime.utcnow()

# Subtract to see difference
time_difference = (utc_now - here_now)

# Show results
print(f"My time    : {here_now:%I:%M %p}")
print(f"UTC time   : {utc_now:%I:%M %p}")
print(f"Difference: {time_difference}")
```

```
My time    : 01:02 PM
UTC time   : 06:02 PM
Difference: 5:00:00
```

FIGURE 1-20: Determining the difference between your time and UTC time.

When we ran that code, the current time was 1:02PM and the UTC time was 6:02PM. The difference was 5:00:00, which means five hours (no minutes or seconds). Our time is earlier, so our time zone is really UTC – 5 hours.

Note that if you subtract the earlier time from the later time, you get a negative number, which can be misleading, as follows:

```
time_difference = (here_now - utc_now)
Difference: -1 day, 19:00:00
```

That's still five hours, really, because if you subtract 1 day and 19 hours from 24 hours (one day), you still get 5 hours. Tricky business. But keep in mind the left side of the time zone map is east, and the sun rises in the east in each time zone. So when it's rising in your time zone, it's already risen in time zones to the right, and hasn't yet risen in time zones to your left.

If you want to work directly with time zone names, you'll need to import some date utilities from Python's `dateutils` package. In particular, you need `gettz` (short for *get timezone*) from the `tz` class of `dateutil`. So in your code, right after the line where you `import datetime`, use `from dateutil.tz import gettz` like this:

```
# import datetime and dateutil tz
import datetime as dt
from dateutil.tz import gettz
```

Afterwards, you can use `gettz('name')` to get time zone information for any time zone. Replace *name* with the name of the time zone from the Olson database: for example, `America/New_York` for USA Eastern Time, or `Etc_UTC` for UTC Time.

Figure 1-21 shows an example where we get the current date and time using `datetime.now()` with five different time zones — UTC and four US time zones.

```
# import datetime, give it an alias
import datetime as dt
# import timezone helpers from dateutil
from dateutil.tz import gettz

# UTC time right now.
utc=dt.datetime.now(gettz('Etc/UTC'))
print(f"{utc:%A %D %I:%M %p %Z}")

# USA Eastern time.
est = dt.datetime.now(gettz('America/New_York'))
print(f"{est:%A %D %I:%M %p %Z}")

# USA Central time
cst=dt.datetime.now(gettz('America/Chicago'))
print(f"{cst:%A %D %I:%M %p %Z}")

# USA Mountain time
mst=dt.datetime.now(gettz('America/Boise'))
print(f"{mst:%A %D %I:%M %p %Z}")

pst=dt.datetime.now(gettz('America/Los_Angeles'))
print(f"{pst:%A %D %I:%M %p %Z}")
```

```
Friday 11/23/18 06:37 PM UTC
Friday 11/23/18 01:37 PM EST
Friday 11/23/18 12:37 PM CST
Friday 11/23/18 11:37 AM MST
Friday 11/23/18 10:37 AM PST
```

FIGURE 1-21: The current date and time for five different time zones.

All USA times are standard time because no one in the USA is on daylight saving time (DST) in late November. Let's see what happens if we schedule an event for some time in July, when the USA is on back on daylight saving time.

In this code (see Figure 1-22), we import datetime and gettx from dateutil, as we did in the preceding example. But we're not concerned about the current time. We're concerned about an event scheduled for July 4, 2020 at 7:00 PM in our local time zone. So we define that using the following:

```
event = dt.datetime(2020,7,4,19,0,0)
```

```
# import datetime and dateutil tz
import datetime as dt
from dateutil.tz import gettz

# July 4 Event, 7:00 local time (no specific time zone).
event = dt.datetime(2020,7,4,19,0,0)
# Show local date and time
print("Local: " + f"{event:%D %I:%M %p %Z}" + "\n")

event_eastern = event.astimezone(gettz("America/New_York"))
print(f"{event_eastern:%D %I:%M %p %Z}")

event_central = event.astimezone(gettz("America/Chicago"))
print(f"{event_central:%D %I:%M %p %Z}")

event_mountain = event.astimezone(gettz("America/Denver"))
print(f"{event_mountain:%D %I:%M %p %Z}")

event_pacific = event.astimezone(gettz("America/Los_Angeles"))
print(f"{event_pacific:%D %I:%M %p %Z}")

event_utc = event.astimezone(gettz("Etc/UTC"))
print(f"{event_utc:%D %I:%M %p %Z}")
```

```
 Local: 07/04/20 07:00 PM

 07/04/20 07:00 PM EDT
 07/04/20 06:00 PM CDT
 07/04/20 05:00 PM MDT
 07/04/20 04:00 PM PDT
 07/04/20 11:00 PM UTC
```

FIGURE 1-22:
Date and time for a scheduled event in multiple time zones.

We didn't say anything about time zone in the date time, so the time will automatically be for our time zone. That datetime is stored in the event variable.

The following line of code (after the comment, which starts with #) shows the date and time, again local, because we didn't say anything about time zone. We added "Local:" to the start of the text, and added a line break at the end (\n) to visually separate that word from the rest of the output.

```
# Show local date and time
print("Local: " + f"{event:%D %I:%M %p %Z}" + "\n")
```

When the app runs, it displays the following output based on the datetime and our format string:

```
Local: 07/04/20 07:00 PM
```

The remaining code calculates the correct datetime for each of five time zones:

```
name = event.astimezone(gettz("tzname"))
```

The first *name* is just a variable name we made up. In event.astimezone(), the name event refers to the initial event time defined in a previous line. The astimezone() function is a built-in dateutil function that uses the following syntax:

```
.astimezone(gettz("tzname"))
```

In each line of code that calculates the date and time for a time zone, we replace *tzname* with the name of the time zone from the Olson database. As you can see in the output (refer to Figure 1-22), the datetime of the event for five different time zones is displayed. Note that the USA time zones are daylight saving time (such as EDT). Because we happen to be on the east coast and the event is in July, the correct local time zone is Eastern Daylight Time. When you look at the output of the dates, the first one matches our time zone, as it should, and the times for the remaining dates are adjusted for different time zones.

If you're thinking "Eek, what a complicated mess," you won't get any argument from us. None of this strikes us as intuitive, easy, or in the general ballpark of fun. But if you're in a pinch and need some time zone information for your data, the coding techniques you've learned so far should get you want you need.

TECHNICAL STUFF

If you research Python time zones online, you'll probably find that many people recommend using the arrow module rather than the dateutil module. We won't get into all that here, because arrow isn't part of your initial Python installation and this book is hefty enough. (If we tried to cover everything, you'd need a wheelbarrow to carry the book around.)

Chapter **2**

Controlling the Action

So far in this book we've talked a lot about storing information in computers, mostly in variables that Python and your computer can work with. Having the information in a form that the computer can work with is critical to getting a computer to do anything. Think of this as the "having" part — having some information with which to work.

But now we need to turn our attention to the "doing" part — working with that information to create something useful or entertaining. In this chapter, we cover the most important and most commonly used operations for making the computer *do* stuff. We start with something that computers do well, do quickly, and do a lot — make decisions.

Main Operators for Controlling the Action

You control what your program (and the computer) does by making decisions, which often involves making comparisons. You use operators, such as those in Table 2-1 to make comparisons. These operators are often referred to as *relational operators* or *comparison operators* because by comparing items the computer is determining how two items are related.

TABLE 2-1 **Python Comparison Operators for Decision-Making**

Operator	Meaning
==	Is equal to
!=	Is not equal to
<	Is less than
>	Is greater than
<=	Is less than or equal to
>=	Is greater than or equal to

Python also offers three *logical operators*, also called *Boolean operators,* which enable you assess multiple comparisons before making a final decision. These operators use the English word for, well, basically what they mean, as shown in Table 2-2.

TABLE 2-2 **Python Logical Operators**

Operator	Meaning
and	Both are true
or	One or the other is true
not	Is not true

TECHNICAL STUFF

In case you're wondering about that *Boolean* word, it's a reference to a guy named George Boole who, in the mid-1800s, helped establish the algebra of logic, which pretty much laid the foundation for today's computers. Feel free to do a web search for his name to learn more.

All these operators are often used with if...then...else decisions to control what an app or program does. To make such decisions, you use the Python if *statement.*

Making Decisions with if

The word *if* is used a lot in all apps and computer programs to make decisions. The simplest syntax for *if* follows:

```
if condition: do this
do this no matter what
```

So the first do this line is executed only if the condition is true. If the condition is false, that first do this is ignored. Regardless of what the condition turns out to be, the second line is executed next. Note that neither line is indented. Indentation means a lot in Python, as you'll see shortly. But first, let's do a few simple examples with this simple syntax. You can try it for yourself in a Jupyter notebook or .py file.

Figure 2-1 shows a simple example in which the sun variable receives the down string. Then an if statement checks to see whether the sun variable equals the word down and, if it does, prints a Good night! message. Then it just continues on normally to print an I am here message.

FIGURE 2-1:
The result of a simple if when the condition proves true.

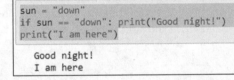

```
sun = "down"
if sun == "down": print("Good night!")
print("I am here")

Good night!
I am here
```

WARNING

Make sure you always use two equal signs with no space between (==) to test equality. This rule is easy to forget. If you type it incorrectly, the code won't work as expected.

If you run the same code with some word other than down in the sun variable, the first print is ignored. But the next line is executed normally because it's not dependent on the condition being true, as shown in Figure 2-2.

FIGURE 2-2:
Result of simple if when the condition proves false.

```
sun = "up"
if sun == "down": print("Good night!")
print("I am here")

    I am here
```

In the second example, it's not true that the sun variable equals down; therefore the rest of that line is ignored and only the next line is executed.

In these two examples, the code to be executed when the condition proves true is on the same line as the if. However, often you want to do more than one thing when the condition proves true. For that, you'll need to indent each line to be executed only if the condition proves true. And code that's not indented below the if is executed whether the condition proves true or not. The recommendation is to indent by four spaces, but that's not a hard-and-fast rule. You just have to remember that each line has to be indented the same amount.

Also, you can use the indented syntax even if only one line of code is to be executed should the condition prove true. In fact, that's the most common way to write an if in Python because most people agree it makes the code more readable from a human perspective. So really, the syntax is

```
if condition:
    do this
    ...
do this no matter what
```

So if the condition proves true, the do this line is executed as are any other lines indented equally to that one. The first un-indented line under the if is executed no matter what. So you could write the simple sun example like this:

```
sun = "down"
if sun == "down":
    print("Good night!")
print("I am here")
```

As you can see in Figure 2-3, this code works the same as putting the code on one line. If sun is down, Good night! prints before the second print is executed. If sun doesn't equal down, the print statement for Good night! is skipped.

FIGURE 2-3: Result of simple if when the condition proves true and then false.

```
sun = "down"
if sun == "down":
    print("Good night!")
print("I am here")

    Good night!
    I am here

sun = "up"
if sun == "down":
    print("Good night!")
print("I am here")

    I am here
```

If you're wondering whether it's better to use a single line or multiple lines in your if statements, it depends on what you mean by *better*. If you mean *better* in terms of which method executes the fastest, the answer is neither. You won't be able to see a speed difference when executing the code. If by *better* you mean easier for a human programmer to read, most people would prefer the second method, with the code indented under the if statement.

Remember, you can indent any number of lines under the if, and those indented lines execute only if the condition proves true. If the condition proves false, none of the indented lines are executed. The unindented code under the indented lines is always executed because it's not dependent on the condition. Here is an example with four lines of code that execute only if the condition proves true:

```
total = 100
sales_tax_rate = 0.065
taxable = True
if taxable:
    print(f"Subtotal : ${total:.2f}")
    sales_tax = total * sales_tax_rate
    print(f"Sales Tax: ${sales_tax:.2f}")
    total = total + sales_tax
print(f"Total    : ${total:.2f}")
```

REMEMBER

You must spell True and False with an initial capital letter and the rest lowercase. If you type it any other way, Python won't recognize it as a Boolean True or False and your code won't run as expected.

Notice that in the if statement we used

```
if taxable:
```

This code is perfectly okay because we made taxable a Boolean that can only be True or False. You may see other people type it as

```
if taxable == True:
```

This line is okay too, and it won't have any negative effect on the code. The == True is just unnecessary because, by itself, taxable is already either True or False.

Anyway, as you can see, we start off with a total variable, a sales_tax_rate variable, and a taxable variable. When taxable is True, all four lines under the if are executed, and you end up with the output shown in Figure 2-4.

When taxable is set to False, all the indented lines are skipped over, and the total shown is the original total without sales tax added, as shown in Figure 2-5.

FIGURE 2-4:
When taxable is
True, sales_tax
is added to
the total.

```
total = 100
sales_tax_rate = 0.065
taxable = True
if taxable:
    print(f"Subtotal : ${total:.2f}")
    sales_tax = total * sales_tax_rate
    print(f"Sales Tax: ${sales_tax:.2f}")
    total = total + sales_tax
print(f"Total    : ${total:.2f}")

    Subtotal : $100.00
    Sales Tax: $6.50
    Total    : $106.50
```

FIGURE 2-5:
When taxable is
False, sales_
tax is not added
into the total.

```
total = 100
sales_tax_rate = 0.065
taxable = False
if taxable:
    print(f"Subtotal : ${total:.2f}")
    sales_tax = total * sales_tax_rate
    print(f"Sales Tax: ${sales_tax:.2f}")
    total = total + sales_tax
print(f"Total    : ${total:.2f}")
    Total    : $100.00
```

**TECHNICAL
STUFF**

The curly braces and .2f stuff in Figures 2-4 and 2-5 are just for formatting, as we discuss in Book 2, Chapter 1, and have nothing to do with the if logic of the code.

Adding else to your if logic

So far you've looked at code examples in which some code is executed if some condition proves true. If the condition proves false, that code is ignored. Sometimes, you may want one chunk of code to execute *if* a condition proves true; *otherwise* (*else*), if it doesn't prove true, you want some other chunk of code to be executed. In that case, you can add an else: to your if. Any lines of code indented under the else: are executed only if the condition did not prove true. Here is the logic and syntax:

```
if condition:
    do indented lines here
    ...
else:
    do indented lines here
    ...
do remaining un-indented lines no matter what
```

Figure 2-6 shows a simple example where we grab the current time from the computer clock using datetime.now(). If the hour of that time is less than 12, the program displays Good morning. Otherwise, it displays Good afternoon. Regardless of the hour, it prints I hope you are doing well! So if you write such a program and run it in the morning, you get the appropriate greeting followed by I hope you are doing well!, as in Figure 2-6.

FIGURE 2-6:
Print an initial
greeting based on
the time of day.

```
import datetime as dt
# Get the current date and time
now = dt.datetime.now()
# Make a decision based on hour
if now.hour < 12:
    print("Good morning")
else:
    print("Good afternoon")
print("I hope you are doing well!")

Good morning
I hope you are doing well!
```

Now you may look at that and say "Wow, that's impressive, Einstein. But what if it's 11:00 at night? Do you really want to say "Good afternoon"? Yet another question deserving of a resounding "Hmm." What we need is an if ... else where multiple else statements are possible. That's where the elif statement, described next, comes into play.

Handling multiple else statements with elif

When if...else isn't enough to handle all the possibilities, there's elif (which, as you may have guessed, is a word made up from else if). An if statement can include any number of elif conditions. You can include or not include a final else statement that executes only if the if and all the previous elifs prove false.

In its simplest form, the syntax for an if with elif and else is

```
if condition:
    do these indented lines of code
    ...
elif condition:
    do these indented lines of code
    ...
do these un-indented lines of code no matter what
```

Given that structure, it's possible that none of the indented code will execute. Take a look at this example:

```python
light_color = "green"
if light_color == "green":
    print("Go")
elif light_color == "red":
    print("Stop")
print("This code executes no matter what")
```

Executing that code results in the following:

```
Go
This code executes no matter what
```

If you change the light color to red, like this:

```python
light_color = "red"
if light_color == "green":
    print("Go")
elif light_color == "red":
    print("Stop")
print("This code executes no matter what")
```

the result is

```
Stop
This code executes no matter what
```

Suppose you change the light color to anything other than red or green, as follows:

```python
light_color = "yellow"
if light_color == "green":
    print("Go")
elif light_color == "red":
    print("Stop")
print("This code executes no matter what")
```

Executing this code produces the following output, because neither color == "green" nor color == "red" proved true, so none of the indented code was executed:

```
This code executes no matter what
```

You can add an `else` option that happens only if the previous conditions all prove false:

```
light_color = "yellow"
if light_color == "green":
    print("Go")
elif light_color == "red":
    print("Stop")
else:
    print("Proceed with caution")
print("This code executes no matter what")
```

The output is

```
Proceed with caution
This code executes no matter what
```

The fact that the `light_color` is yellow prevents the first two `if` conditions from proving true, so only the `else` code is executed. And that's true for anything that you put into the `light_color` variable, except `"red"` or `"green"`, because the `else` isn't looking for a specific condition. It's just playing an "if all else fails, do this" role in the logic.

Ternary operations

Here is another code example, where we set a variable named age to 31. Then we use `if...elif...else` to make a decision about what to display:

```
age = 31
if age < 21:
    beverage = "milk"
elif age >= 21 and age < 80:
    beverage = "beer"
else:
    beverage = "prune juice"

print("Have a " + beverage)
```

Comments are always optional. But adding comments to the code can make it easier to understand, for future reference:

```
age = 31

if age < 21:
    # If under 21, no alcohol
```

```
    beverage = "milk"

elif age >= 21 and age < 80:
    # Ages 21 - 79, suggest beer
    beverage = "beer"

else:
    # If 80 or older, prune juice might be a good choice.
    beverage = "prune juice"

print("Have a " + beverage)
```

REMEMBER

If you're wondering about the rule for indenting comments, there is no rule. Comments are just notes to yourself; they aren't executable code. So they're never executed like code, no matter what their level indentation.

Repeating a Process with for

Decision-making is a big part of writing all kinds of apps — games, artificial intelligence, robotics . . . whatever. But sometimes you need to count or perform a task over and over. For those times, you can use a *for loop*, which enables you to repeat a line of code, or several lines of code, as many times as you like.

Looping through numbers in a range

If you know how many times you want a loop to repeat, using the following syntax may be easiest:

```
for x in range(y):
    do this
    do this
    ...
un-indented code is executed after the loop
```

Replace *x* with any variable name of your choosing. Replace *y* with any number or range of numbers. If you specify one number, the range will be from 0 to 1 less than the final number. For example, run this code in a Jupyter notebook or .py file:

```
for x in range(7):
    print(x)
print("All done")
```

The output is the result of executing print(x) once for each pass through the loop, with x starting at 0. The final line, which isn't indented, executes after the loop has finished looping. So the output is

```
0
1
2
3
4
5
6
All done
```

You might have expected the loop to count from 1 to 7 instead of 0 to 6. However, unless you specify otherwise, the loop always starts counting from 0. If you want to start counting with another number, specify the starting number and the ending number, separated by a comma, inside the parentheses. When you specify two numbers, the first number identifies where the counting starts. The second number is 1 greater than where the loop stops (which is unfortunate for readability but such is life). For example, here is a for loop with two numbers in the range:

```
for x in range(1, 10):
    print(x)
print("All done")
```

When you run this code, the counter starts at 1 and, as mentioned, stops 1 short of the last number:

```
1
2
3
4
5
6
7
8
9
All done
```

If you want the loop to count from 1 to 10, the range is 1,11. This won't make your brain cells any happier, but at least it gets the desired goal of 1 to 10, as shown in Figure 2-7.

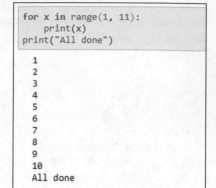

```
for x in range(1, 11):
    print(x)
print("All done")

1
2
3
4
5
6
7
8
9
10
All done
```

FIGURE 2-7:
A loop
that counts
from 1 to 10.

Looping through a string

Using `range()` in a `for` loop is optional. You can replace `range` with a string, and the loop repeats once for each character in the string. The variable x (or whatever you name the variable) contains one character from the string with each pass through the loop, going from left to right. The syntax here is

```
for x in string
    do this
    do this

    ...
do this when the loop is done
```

As usual, replace *x* with any variable name you like. The string should be text enclosed in quotation marks, or it should be the name of a variable that contains a string. For example, type this code into a Jupyter notebook or .py file:

```
for x in "snorkel":
    print(x)
print("Done")
```

When you run this code, you get the following output. The loop prints one letter from the word *snorkel* with each pass through the loop. When the looping was finished, execution fell to the first un-indented line outside the loop.

```
s
n
o
r
k
e
l
Done
```

The string doesn't have to be a literal string. It can be the name of any variable that contains a string. For example, try this code:

```
my_word = "snorkel"
for x in my_word:
    print(x)
print("Done")
```

The result is the same. The only difference is that we used a variable name rather than a string in the for loop. But the code knew that you meant the contents of my_word rather than the literal string my_word, because my_word isn't enclosed in quotation marks.

```
s
n
o
r
k
e
l
Done
```

Looping through a list

In Python, a *list* is basically any group of items, separated by commas, inside square brackets. You can loop through such a list using a for loop. In the following example, the list to loop through is specified in brackets on the first line:

```
for x in ["The", "rain", "in", "Spain"]:
    print(x)
print("Done")
```

This kind of loop repeats once for each item in the list. The x variable gets its value from one item in the list, going from left to right. So, running the preceding code produces the output you see in Figure 2-8.

You can assign the list to a variable, too, and then use the variable name in the for loop rather than the list. Figure 2-9 shows an example where the seven_dwarves variable is assigned a list of seven names. Again, note how the list is contained in square brackets. These make Python treat the variable as a list. The *for* loop then loops through the list, printing the name of one dwarf (one item in the list) with each pass through the loop. We used the variable name dwarf rather than x, but that name can be any valid name you like. We could have used x or little_person or name_of_fictional_entity or goober_wocky or anything else, as long as the name in the first line matches the name used in the for loop.

```
for x in ["The", "rain", "in", "Spain"]:
    print(x)
print("Done")
```

```
The
rain
in
Spain
Done
```

```
seven_dwarves = ["Happy", "Grumpy", "Sleepy", "Bashful", "Sneezy", "Doc", "Dopey"]
for dwarf in seven_dwarves:
    print(dwarf)
print("And Snow White too")
```

```
Happy
Grumpy
Sleepy
Bashful
Sneezy
Doc
Dopey
And Snow White too
```

Bailing out of a loop

Typically, you want a loop to go through an entire list or range of items, but you can also force a loop to stop early if some condition is met. Use the `break` statement inside an `if` statement to force the loop to stop early. The syntax is

```
for x in items:
  if condition:
    [do this ... ]
    break
  do this
```

The square brackets in this example aren't part of the code. They indicate that what is between the brackets is optional. Suppose that someone completed an exam and we want to loop through the answers. But we have a rule that says if an answer is empty, we mark it Incomplete and ignore the rest of the items in the list. In the following, all items are answered (no blanks):

```
answers = ["A", "C", "B", "D"]
for answer in answers:
    if answer == "":
        print("Incomplete")
        break
    print(answer)
print("Loop is done")
```

In the result, all four answers are printed:

```
A
C
B
D
Loop is done
```

Here is the same code, but the third item in the list is blank, as indicated by "", which is an empty string:

```
answers = ["A", "C", "", "D"]
for answer in answers:
    if answer == "":
        print("Incomplete")
        break
    print(answer)
print("Loop is done")
```

Here is the output of running that code:

```
A
C
Incomplete
Loop is done
```

So the logic is, as long as some answer is provided, the if code is not executed and the loop runs to completion. However, if the loop encounters a blank answer, it prints Incomplete and also "breaks" the loop, jumping down to the first statement outside the loop (the final un-indented statement), which prints Loop is done.

Looping with continue

You can also use a continue statement in a loop, which is kind of the opposite of break. Whereas break makes code execution jump past the end of the loop and stop looping, continue makes it jump back to the top of the loop and continue with the next item (that is, after the item that triggered the continue). So here is the same code as the preceding example, but instead of executing a break when execution hits a blank answer, it continues with the next item in the list:

```
answers = ["A", "C", "", "D"]
for answer in answers:
    if answer == "":
        print("Incomplete")
```

```
        continue
    print(answer)
print("Loop is done")
```

The output of that code is as follows. It doesn't print the blank answer, it prints `Incomplete`, but then it goes back and continues looping through the rest of the items:

```
A
C
Incomplete
D
Loop is done
```

Nesting loops

It's perfectly okay to *nest* loops — that is, to put loops inside loops. Just make sure you get your indentations right because the indentations determine which loop, if any, a line of code is located within. For example, in Figure 2-10, an outer loop loops through the words `First`, `Second`, and `Third`. With each pass through the loop, it prints a word and then it prints the numbers 1–3 (by looping through a range and adding 1 to each range value).

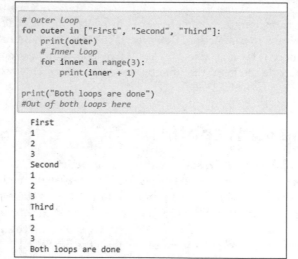

```
# Outer Loop
for outer in ["First", "Second", "Third"]:
    print(outer)
    # Inner Loop
    for inner in range(3):
        print(inner + 1)

print("Both loops are done")
#Out of both Loops here
```
```
First
1
2
3
Second
1
2
3
Third
1
2
3
Both loops are done
```

FIGURE 2-10: Nested loops.

The loops work because each word in the outer list is followed by the numbers 1–3. The end of the loop is the first un-indented line at the bottom, which doesn't print until the outer loop has completed its process.

Looping with while

As an alternative to looping with for, you can loop with while. The difference is subtle. With for, you generally get a fixed number of loops, one for each item in a range or one for each item in a list. With a while loop, the loop keeps going *as long as* (while) some condition is true. Here is the basic syntax:

```
while condition:
    do this ...
    do this ...
do this when the loop is done
```

With while loops, you have to make sure that the *condition* that makes the loop stop happens eventually. Otherwise, you get an infinite loop that just keeps going and going and going until some error causes it to fail, or until you force it to stop by closing the app, shutting down the computer, or doing some other awkward thing.

Here is an example where the while condition runs for a finite number of times due to three things:

>> We create a variable named counter and give it a starting value (65).

>> We say to run the loop *while* counter is less than 91.

>> Inside the loop, we increase counter by 1 (counter += 1). Increasing by 1 repeatedly eventually increases counter to more than 91, which ends the loop.

The chr() function inside the loop displays the ASCII character for the number in counter. Going from 65 to 90 is enough to print all the uppercase letters in the alphabet, as in you see in Figure 2-11.

The easy and common mistake to make with this kind of loop is to forget to increment the counter so that it grows with each pass through the loop and eventually makes the while condition False and stops the loop. In Figure 2-12, we intentionally removed counter += 1 to cause that error. As you can see, the loop keeps printing A. It keeps going until you stop it.

```
counter = 65
while counter < 91:
    print(str(counter) + "=" + chr(counter))
    counter += 1
print("all done")
```

```
65=A
66=B
67=C
68=D
69=E
70=F
71=G
72=H
73=I
74=J
75=K
76=L
77=M
78=N
79=O
80=P
81=Q
82=R
83=S
84=T
85=U
86=V
87=W
88=X
89=Y
90=Z
all done
```

FIGURE 2-11:
Looping while
counter is
less than 91.

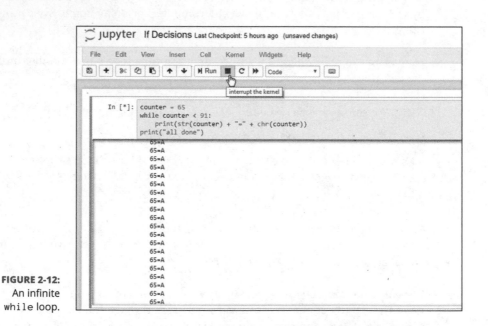

FIGURE 2-12:
An infinite
while loop.

If this happens to you in a Jupyter notebook, don't panic. Just click the square Stop button to the right of Run. (The Stop button displays Interrupt the Kernel, which is nerdspeak for *stop*, when you hover the mouse pointer over it.) All code execution in the notebook will stop. To restart the kernel and get back to square one, click the curved arrow to the right of the Stop button. Then you can fix the error in your code and try again.

Starting while loops over with continue

You can use `if` and `continue` in a `while` loop to skip back to the top of the loop just as you can with `for` loops. Take a look at the code in Figure 2-13 for an example.

```python
import random
print("Odd numbers")
counter = 0
while counter < 10:
    # Get a random number
    number = random.randint(1,999)
    if int(number / 2) == number /2:
        # If it's an even number, don't print it.
        continue
    #Otherwise, if it's odd, print it and increment the couter.
    print(number)
    # Increment the loop counter.
    counter += 1
print("Loop is done")
```

```
Odd numbers
697
449
91
567
949
333
591
699
895
837
Loop is done
```

FIGURE 2-13:
A `while` loop with
`continue`.

A `while` loop keeps going while a variable named `counter` is less than 10. Inside the loop, the variable named `number` is assigned a random number in the range of 1 to 999. Then the following statement checks to see if `number` is even:

```python
if int(number / 2) == number / 2:
```

Remember, the int() function returns only the whole portion of a number. So let's say the random number that's generated is 5. Dividing this number by 2 gets you 2.5. Then int(number) is 2 because the int() of a number drops everything after the decimal point. Because 2 doesn't equal 2.5, the code skips over the continue, prints that odd number, increments the counter, and keeps going.

If the next random number is, say, 12, well, 12 divided by 2 is 6 and int(6) does equal 6 (because neither number has a decimal point). That causes the continue to execute, skipping over the print(number) statement and the counter increment, so it just tries another random number and continues on its merry way. Eventually, it finds 10 odd numbers, at which point the loop stops and the final line of code displays Loop is done.

Breaking while loops with break

You can also break a while loop using break, just as you can with a for loop. When you break a while loop, you force execution to continue with the first line of code under and outside the loop, thereby stopping the loop but continuing the flow with the rest of the action after the loop.

Another way to think of a break is something that allows you to stop a while loop before the while condition proves false. So it allows you to literally break out of the loop before its time. Truthfully, however, we can't remember a situation where breaking out of a loop before its time was a good solution to a problem, so it's hard to come up with a practical example. In lieu of that, we'll just show you the syntax and provide a generic example. The syntax is

```
while condition1:
    do this
    ...
    if condition2:
        break
do this when the loop is done
```

Basically, two things can stop this loop. Either condition1 proves false, or condition2 proves true. Regardless of which of these two things happen, code execution resumes at the first line of code outside the loop, the line that reads do this code when the loop is done in the sample code.

Here is an example where the program prints *up to* ten numbers that are not evenly divisible by 5. It may print fewer than that, though, because when it hits a random number that's evenly divisible by 5, it bails out of the loop. So the only thing you can predict about the example is that it will print between zero and ten numbers that are not evenly divisible by 5. You can't predict how many it will print on any given run, because there's no way to tell if or when it will get a random number evenly divisible by 5 during the ten tries it's allowed:

```python
import random
print("Numbers that aren't evenly divisible by 5")
counter = 0
while counter < 10:
    # Get a random number
    number = random.randint(1,999)
    if int(number / 5) == number / 5:
        # If it's evenly divisible by 5, bail out.
        break
    # Otherwise, print it and keep going for a while.
    print(number)
    # Increment the loop counter.
    counter += 1
print("Loop is done")
```

So the first time you run that app, your output may look something like Figure 2-14. The second time you may get something like Figure 2-15. There's just no way to predict the result because the random number is indeed random and not predictable (which is an important concept in many games).

```python
import random
print("Numbers that aren't evenly divisible by 5")
counter = 0
while counter < 10:
    # Get a random number
    number = random.randint(1,999)
    if int(number / 5) == number / 5:
        # If it's evenly divisble by 5, bail out.
        break
    #Otherwise, print it and keep going for a while.
    print(number)
    # Increment the loop counter.
    counter += 1
print("Loop is done")
```

```
Numbers that aren't evenly divisible by 5
729
754
317
753
327
366
69
813
543
67
Loop is done
```

FIGURE 2-14:
A while loop
with break.

```
import random
print("Numbers that aren't evenly divisible by 5")
counter = 0
while counter < 10:
    # Get a random number
    number = random.randint(1,999)
    if int(number / 5) == number / 5:
        # If it's evenly divisble by 5, bail out.
        break
    #Otherwise, print it and keep going for a while.
    print(number)
    # Increment the loop counter.
    counter += 1
print("Loop is done")
```

```
Numbers that aren't evenly divisible by 5
866
377
197
Loop is done
```

FIGURE 2-15:
The same code as
in Figure 2-14 on
a second run.

Chapter **3**

Speeding Along with Lists and Tuples

S ometimes in code you work with one item of data at a time, such as a person's name or a unit price or a username. Other times, you work with larger sets of data, such as a list of people's names or a list of products and their prices. These sets of data are often referred to as *lists* or *arrays* in most programming languages.

Python has lots of easy, fast, and efficient ways to deal with all kinds of data collections, as you discover in this chapter. As always, we encourage you to follow along in a Jupyter notebook or .py file. The "doing" part helps with the "understanding" part.

Defining and Using Lists

The simplest data collection in Python is a list. We provided examples of these in the preceding chapter. A *list* is any list of data items, separated by commas, inside square brackets. Typically, you assign a name to the list using an = character, just as you would with variables. If the list contains numbers, don't use quotation marks around them. For example, here is a list of test scores:

```
scores = [88, 92, 78, 90, 98, 84]
```

REALLY, REALLY LONG LISTS

All the lists in this chapter are short to make the examples easy and manageable. In real life, however, your lists might contain hundreds or even thousands of items that change frequently. Typing such long lists in the code directly would make the code difficult to work with. Instead, you'd store such lists in external files or external databases, where everything is easier to manage.

All the techniques you learn in this chapter apply to lists stored in external files. The only difference is that you have to write code to pull the data into the list first. But before you start tackling big lists, you need to know all the techniques for working with lists of any size. So stick with this chapter before you move on to managing external data. You'll be glad you did.

If the list contains strings, as always, those strings should be enclosed in single or double quotation marks, as in this example:

```
students = ["Mark", "Amber", "Todd", "Anita", "Sandy"]
```

To display the contents of a list on the screen, you can print it just as you would print any regular variable. For example, executing `print(students)` in your code after defining that list displays the following on the screen:

```
['Mark', 'Amber', 'Todd', 'Anita', 'Sandy']
```

This output may not be exactly what you had in mind. But don't worry, Python offers lots of ways to display lists.

Referencing list items by position

Each item in a list has a position number, starting with 0, even though you don't see any numbers. You can refer to any item in the list by its number using the name for the list followed by a number in square brackets. In other words, use this syntax:

```
listname[x]
```

Replace *listname* with the name of the list you're accessing and replace *x* with the position number of the item you want. Remember, the first item is always 0, not 1. For example, in the following first line, we define a list named `students`, and then print item number 0 from that list. The result, when executing the code, is the name Mark displayed:

```
students = ["Mark", "Amber", "Todd", "Anita", "Sandy"]
print(students[0])
Mark
```

When reading list items aloud, professionals use the word *sub* before the number. For example, *students[0]* would be spoken as "students sub zero."

The next example shows a list named scores. The print() function prints the position number of the last score in the list, which is 4 (because the first one is always 0).

```
scores = [88, 92, 78, 90, 84]
print(scores[4])
84
```

If you try to access a list item that doesn't exist, you get an list index out of range error. The *index* part is a reference to the number inside the square brackets. For example, Figure 3-1 shows a little experiment in a Jupyter notebook where we created a list of scores and then tried to print score[5]. It failed and generated an error because there is no scores[5]. There's only scores[0], scores[1], scores[2], scores[3], and scores[4] because the counting always starts at 0 with the first one in the list.

```
#Define a list of numbers.
scores = [88, 92, 78, 90, 84]

print(scores[5])

---------------------------------------------------------------
IndexError                              Traceback (most recent call last)
<ipython-input-9-240d3b4f5443> in <module>()
      5
      6 #Experiment with the lists
----> 7 print(scores[5])

IndexError: list index out of range
```

FIGURE 3-1: Index out-of-range error because scores[5] doesn't exist.

Looping through a list

To access each item in a list, just use a for loop with this syntax:

```
for x in list:
```

Replace *x* with a variable name of your choosing. Replace *list* with the name of the list.

TIP

An easy way to make the code readable is to always use a plural for the list name (such as `students`, `scores`). Then you can use the singular name (`student`, `score`) for the variable name. You don't need to use subscript numbers (numbers in square brackets) with this approach either. For example, the following code prints each score in the scores list:

```
for score in scores:
    print(score)
```

Remember to always indent the code that's to be executed in the loop. Figure 3-2 shows a more complete example where you can see the result of running the code in a Jupyter notebook.

```
#Define a list of numbers.
scores = [88, 92, 78, 90, 84]
for score in scores:
    print(score)
print("Done")

88
92
78
90
84
Done
```

FIGURE 3-2:
Looping
through a list.

Seeing whether a list contains an item

If you want your code to check the contents of a list to see whether it already contains some item, use `in listname` in an `if` statement or a variable assignment. For example, the code in Figure 3-3 creates a list of names. Then, two variables store the results of searching the list for the names `Anita` and `Bob`. Printing the contents of each variable displays `True` for the one where the name `Anita` is in the list. The test to see whether `Bob` is in the list proves `False`.

```
students = ["Mark", "Amber", "Todd", "Anita", "Sandy"]

# Is Anita in the list?
has_anita = "Anita" in students
print(has_anita)

#Is Bob in the list?
has_bob = "Bob" in students
print(has_bob)

True
False
```

FIGURE 3-3:
Seeing whether
an item is in a list.

Getting the length of a list

To determine how many items are in a list, use the `len()` function (short for *length*). Put the name of the list inside the parentheses. For example, type the following code in a Jupyter notebook or at the Python prompt or whatever:

```
students = ["Mark", "Amber", "Todd", "Anita", "Sandy"]
print(len(students))
```

Running that code produces this output:

```
5
```

The list has five items, though the index of the last item is always 1 less than the number because Python starts counting at 0. So the last item, Sandy, refers to `students[4]` and not `students[5]`.

Adding an item to the end of a list

When you want your code to add an item to the end of a list, use the `.append()` method with the value you want to add inside the parentheses. You can use either a variable name or a literal value inside the quotation marks. For instance, in Figure 3-4, the line `students.append("Goober")` adds the name Goober to the list. The line `students.append(new_student)` adds whatever name is stored in the `new_student` variable to the list. The `.append()` method always adds to the end of the list. So when you print the list, those two new names are at the end.

```
#Create a list of strings (names)
students = ["Mark", "Amber", "Todd", "Anita", "Sandy"]

#Add the name Goober to the list
students.append("Goober")

new_student = "Amanda"
#Add whatever name is in new_student to the list.
students.append(new_student)

#Print the entire list
print(students)

['Mark', 'Amber', 'Todd', 'Anita', 'Sandy', 'Goober', 'Amanda']
```

FIGURE 3-4: Appending two new names to the end of the list.

You can use a test to see whether an item is in a list and then append it only when the item isn't already there. For example, the following code won't add the name Amanda to the list because that name is already in the list:

```python
student_name = "Amanda"

#Add student_name but only if not already in the list.
if student_name in students:
    print(student_name + " already in the list")
else:
    students.append(student_name)
    print(student_name + " added to the list")
```

Inserting an item into a list

Whereas the `append()` method adds an item to the end of a list, the `insert()` method adds an item to the list in any position. The syntax for `insert()` is

```python
listname.insert(position, item)
```

Replace *listname* with the name of the list, *position* with the position at which you want to insert the item (for example, 0 to make it the first item, 1 to make it the second item, and so forth). Replace *item* with the value, or the name of a variable that contains the value, that you want to put in the list.

For example, the following code makes Lupe the first item in the list:

```python
# Create a list of strings (names).
students = ["Mark", "Amber", "Todd", "Anita", "Sandy"]

student_name = "Lupe"
# Add student name to front of the list.
students.insert(0, student_name)

# Show me the new list.
print(students)
```

If you run the code, `print(students)` will display the list after the new name has been inserted, as follows:

```python
['Lupe', 'Mark', 'Amber', 'Todd', 'Anita', 'Sandy']
```

Changing an item in a list

You can change an item in a list using the = assignment operator just like you do with variables. Make sure you include the index number in square brackets to indicate which item you want to change. The syntax is

```
listname[index] = newvalue
```

Replace *listname* with the name of the list; replace *index* with the subscript (index number) of the item you want to change; and replace *newvalue* with whatever you want to put in the list item. For example, take a look at this code:

```
# Create a list of strings (names).
students = ["Mark", "Amber", "Todd", "Anita", "Sandy"]
students[3] = "Hobart"
print(students)
```

When you run this code, the output is as follows, because Anita has been changed to Hobart:

```
['Mark', 'Amber', 'Todd', 'Hobart', 'Sandy']
```

Combining lists

If you have two lists that you want to combine into a single list, use the extend() function with the following syntax:

```
original_list.extend(additional_items_list)
```

In your code, replace *original_list* with the name of the list to which you'll be adding new list items. Replace *additional_items_list* with the name of the list that contains the items you want to add to the first list. Here is a simple example using lists named list1 and list2. After executing list1.extend(list2), the first list contains the items from both lists, as you can see in the output of the print() statement at the end.

```
# Create two lists of Names.
list1 = ["Zara", "Lupe", "Hong", "Alberto", "Jake"]
list2 = ["Huey", "Dewey", "Louie", "Nader", "Bubba"]

# Add list2 names to list1.
list1.extend(list2)

# Print list 1.
```

```
print(list1)

['Zara', 'Lupe', 'Hong', 'Alberto', 'Jake', 'Huey', 'Dewey', 'Louie', 'Nader',
    'Bubba']
```

Easy Parcheesi, no?

Removing list items

Python offers a remove() method so you can remove any value from the list. If the item is in the list multiple times, only the first occurrence is removed. For example, the following code displays a list of letters with the letter *C* repeated a few times. Then the code uses letters.remove("C") to remove the letter *C* from the list:

```
# Create a list of strings.
letters = ["A", "B", "C", "D", "C", "E", "C"]

# Remove "C" from the list.
letters.remove("C")

# Show me the new list.
print(letters)
```

When you execute this code, you'll see that only the first letter *C* has been removed:

```
['A', 'B', 'D', 'C', 'E', 'C']
```

If you need to remove all of an item, you can use a while loop to repeat the .remove as long as the item still remains in the list. For example, this code repeats the .remove as long as "C" is still in the list:

```
while "C" in letters:
    letters.remove("C")
```

If you want to remove an item based on its position in the list, use pop() with an index number rather than remove() with a value. If you want to remove the last item from the list, use pop() without an index number. For example, the following code creates a list, removes the first item (0), and then removes the last item (pop() with nothing in the parentheses). Printing the list proves that those two items have been removed:

```
# Create a list of strings.
letters = ["A", "B", "C", "D", "E", "F", "G"]
```

```
# Remove the first item.
letters.pop(0)
# Remove the last item.
letters.pop()

# Show me the new list.
print(letters)
```

Running the code shows that popping the first and last items did, indeed, work:

```
['B', 'C', 'D', 'E', 'F']
```

When you pop() an item off the list, you can store a copy of that value in some variable. For example, Figure 3-5 shows the same code as the preceding, but it stores copies of what's been removed in variables named first_removed and last_removed. At the end it prints the list, and also shows which letters were removed.

```
# Create a list of strings.
letters = ["A", "B", "C", "D", "E", "F", "G"]

# Make a copy of first list item then remove it from the list.
first_removed = letters.pop(0)
# Make a copy of last list item then remove it from the list.
last_removed = letters.pop()

# Show the new list.
print(letters)
# Show what's been removed.
print(first_removed + " and " + last_removed + " were removed from the list.")

  ['B', 'C', 'D', 'E', 'F']
  A and G were removed from the list.
```

FIGURE 3-5:
Removing list
items with pop().

Python also offers a del (short for *delete*) command that deletes any item from a list based on its index number (position). But again, you have to remember that the first item is 0. So, let's say you run the following code to delete item number 2 from the list:

```
# Create a list of strings.
letters = ["A", "B", "C", "D", "E", "F", "G"]

# Remove item sub 2.
del letters[2]

print(letters)
```

Running that code shows the list again, as follows:

```
['A', 'B', 'D', 'E', 'F', 'G']
```

The letter C has been deleted, which is the correct item to delete because letters are numbered 0, 1, 2, 3, and so forth.

You can also use del to delete an entire list by removing the square brackets and the index number. For example, the code in Figure 3-6 creates a list and then deletes it. Trying to print the list after the deletion causes an error because the list no longer exists when the print() statement is executed. Note that unlike pop, which returns the item you deleted, del just deletes without returning anything.

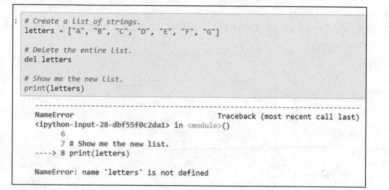

Clearing out a list

If you want to delete the contents of a list but not the list itself, use .clear(). The list still exists, but it contains no items. In other words, it's an empty list. The following code shows how you could test this. Running the code displays [] at the end, which lets you know the list is empty:

```python
# Create a list of strings.
letters = ["A", "B", "C", "D", "E", "F", "G"]

# Clear the list of all entries.
letters.clear()

# Show me the new list.
print(letters)

[]
```

Counting how many times an item appears in a list

You can use the Python count() method to count how many times an item appears in a list. As with other list methods, the syntax is simple:

```
listname.count(x)
```

Replace *listname* with the name of your list, and *x* with the value you're looking for (or the name of a variable that contains that value).

The code in Figure 3-7 counts how many times the letter *B* appears in the list, using a literal B inside the parentheses of .count() like this:

```
grades.count("B")
```

Because B is in quotation marks, you know it's a literal, not the name of some variable.

This code also counts the number of *C* grades, but we stored that value in a variable just to show the difference in syntax. Both counts worked, as you can see in the output of the program at the bottom.

We just counted the *F*'s right in the code that displays the message. There are no *F* grades, so grades.count("F") returns 0, as you can see in the output.

In case you're wondering why we're not counting other grades, it's because the app is just an example to illustrate the Python syntax. We're not trying to create an actual product to count all real grades in a classroom.

```
# Create a list of strings.
grades = ["C", "B", "A", "D", "C", "B", "C"]

# Count the B's
b_grades = grades.count("B")

# Use a variable for value to count.
look_for = "C"
c_grades = grades.count(look_for)

print("There are " + str(b_grades) + " B grades in the list.")
print("There are " + str(c_grades) + " " + look_for + " grades in the list.")

#Count Fs too.
print("There are " + str(grades.count("F")) + " F grades in the list.")

There are 2 B grades in the list.
There are 3 C grades in the list.
There are 0 F grades in the list.
```

FIGURE 3-7: Counting items in a list.

REMEMBER

When trying to combine numbers and strings to form a message, you have to convert the numbers to strings using the str() function. Otherwise, you get an error that reads something like `can only concatenate str (not "int") to str`. In that message, int is short for *integer* and str is short for *string*.

Finding an list item's index

Python offers an .index() method that returns a number indicating the position of an item in a list, based on the index number. The syntax is

```
listname.index(x)
```

As always, replace *listname* with the name of the list you want to search. Replace *x* what whatever you're looking for (either a literal or a variable name, as always). Of course, there's no guarantee that the item is in the list or is in the list only once. If the item isn't in the list, an error occurs. If the item is in the list multiple times, the index of only the first matching item is returned.

Figure 3-8 shows an example where the program crashes at the line `f_index = grades.index(look_for)` because there is no *F* in the list.

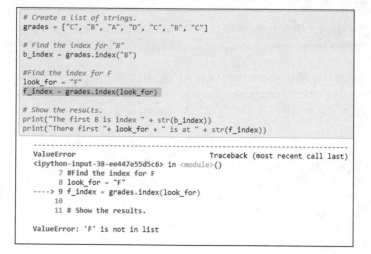

```
# Create a list of strings.
grades = ["C", "B", "A", "D", "C", "B", "C"]

# Find the index for "B"
b_index = grades.index("B")

#Find the index for F
look_for = "F"
f_index = grades.index(look_for)

# Show the results.
print("The first B is index " + str(b_index))
print("There first "+ look_for + " is at " + str(f_index))
```
```
---------------------------------------------------------------------------
ValueError                                Traceback (most recent call last)
<ipython-input-38-ee447e55d5c6> in <module>()
      7 #Find the index for F
      8 look_for = "F"
----> 9 f_index = grades.index(look_for)
     10
     11 # Show the results.

ValueError: 'F' is not in list
```

FIGURE 3-8:
Program fails when trying to find the index of a nonexistent list item.

An easy way to get around this problem is to use an if statement to see whether an item is in the list before you try to get its index number. If the item isn't in the list, display a message saying so. Otherwise, get the index number and show it in a message. That code follows:

```
# Create a list of strings.
grades = ["C", "B", "A", "D", "C", "B", "C"]

# Decide what to look for
look_for = "F"
# See if the item is in the list.
if look_for in grades:
    # If it's in the list, get and show the index.
    print(str(look_for) + " is at index " + str(grades.index(look_for)))
else:
    # If not in the list, don't even try for index number.
    print(str(look_for) + " isn't in the list.")
```

Alphabetizing and sorting lists

Python offers a sort() method for sorting lists. In its simplest form, it alphabet-izes the items in the list (if they're strings). If the list contains numbers, they're sorted smallest to largest. For a simple sort like that, just use sort() with empty parentheses:

```
listname.sort()
```

Replace *listname* with the name of your list. Figure 3-9 shows an example using a list of strings and a list of numbers. We created a new list for each simply by assigning each sorted list to a new list name. Then the code prints the contents of each sorted list.

```
: # Create a list of strings.
  names = ["Zara", "Lupe", "Hong", "Alberto", "Jake", "Tyler"]
  # Create a list of numbers
  numbers = [14, 0, 56, -4, 99, 56, 11.23]

  # Sort the names list.
  names.sort()
  # Sort the numbers list.
  numbers.sort()

  # Show the results
  print(names)
  print(numbers)

  ['Alberto', 'Hong', 'Jake', 'Lupe', 'Tyler', 'Zara']
  [-4, 0, 11.23, 14, 56, 56, 99]
```

FIGURE 3-9:
Sorting strings
and numbers.

TIP

If your list contains strings with a mixture of uppercase and lowercase letters, and if the results of the sort don't look right, try replacing `.sort()` with `.sort(key=lambda s: s.lower())` and then running the code again. See Book 2, Chapter 5 if you're curious about the details.

Dates are a little trickier because you can't just type them in as strings, like `"12/31/2020"`. They have to be the `date` data type to sort correctly. This means using the `datetime` module and the `date()` method to define each date. You can add the dates to the list as you would any other list. For example, in the following line, the code creates a list of four dates:

```
dates = [dt.date(2020,12,31), dt.date(2019,1,31), dt.date(2018,2,28),
    dt.date(2020,1,1)]
```

The computer certainly won't mind if you create the list this way. But if you want to make the code more readable to yourself or other developers, you may want to create and append each date, one at a time. Figure 3-10 shows an example where we created an empty list named `datelist`:

```
datelist = []
```

Then we appended one date at a time to the list using the `dt.date(year,month,day)` syntax.

```
: # Need this modules for the dates.
  import datetime as dt

  # Create a list of dates, empty for starters
  datelist = []
  # Append dates one at time so code is easier to read.
  datelist.append(dt.date(2020,12,31))
  datelist.append(dt.date(2019,1,31))
  datelist.append(dt.date(2018,2,28))
  datelist.append(dt.date(2020,1,1))

  # Sort the dates (earliest to latest) and show formatted.
  datelist.sort()
  for date in datelist:
      print(f"{date:%m/%d/%Y}")

02/28/2018
01/31/2019
01/01/2020
12/31/2020
```

FIGURE 3-10:
Sorting and displaying dates in a nice format.

After the list is created, the code uses `datelist.sort()` to sort the dates into chronological order (earliest to latest). We didn't use `print(datelist)` in that code because that method displays the dates with the data type information included, like this:

```
[datetime.date(2018, 2, 28), datetime.date(2019, 1, 31), datetime.date (2020, 1,
    1), datetime.date(2020, 12, 31)]
```

Not the easiest list to read. So, rather than print the entire list with one `print()` statement, we looped through each date in the list, and printed each one formatted with the f-string %m/%d/%Y. This technique displays each date on its own line in *mm/dd/yyyy* format, as you can see at the bottom of Figure 3-10.

If you want to sort items in reverse order, put `reverse=True` inside the `sort()` parentheses (and don't forget to make the first letter of `True` uppercase). Figure 3-11 shows examples of sorting all three lists in descending (reverse) order using `reverse=True`.

```python
# Need this module for the dates.
import datetime as dt

# Create a list of strings.
names = ["Zara", "Lupe", "Hong", "Alberto", "Jake", "Tyler"]

# Create a list of numbers.
numbers = [14, 0, 56, -4, 99, 56, 11.23]

# Create a list of dates, empty for starters because code is long.
datelist = []
datelist.append(dt.date(2020,12,31))
datelist.append(dt.date(2019,1,31))
datelist.append(dt.date(2018,2,28))
datelist.append(dt.date(2020,1,1))

# Sort strings in reverse order (Z to A) and show.
names.sort(reverse=True)
print(names)
print() # This just adds a blank line to the output.

#Sort numbers in reverse order (largest to smallest) and show.
numbers.sort(reverse=True)
print(numbers)
print() # This just adds a blank line to the output.

# Sort the dates in reverse order (latest to earliest) and show formatted.
datelist.sort(reverse = True)
for date in datelist:
    print(f"{date:%m/%d/%Y}")
```
```
['Zara', 'Tyler', 'Lupe', 'Jake', 'Hong', 'Alberto']

[99, 56, 56, 14, 11.23, 0, -4]

12/31/2020
01/01/2020
01/31/2019
02/28/2018
```

FIGURE 3-11:
Sorting strings, numbers, and dates in reverse order.

Reversing a list

You can also reverse the order of items in a list using the `.reverse` method. This is not the same as sorting in reverse. When you sort in reverse, you still sort: Z–A for strings, largest to smallest for numbers, and latest to earliest for dates. When you reverse a list, you simply reverse the items in the list, no matter their order, without trying to sort them. In the following code, we reverse the order of the names in the list and then print the list.

```
# Create a list of strings.
names = ["Zara", "Lupe", "Hong", "Alberto", "Jake"]
# Reverse the list.
names.reverse()
# Print the list.
print(names)

['Jake', 'Alberto', 'Hong', 'Lupe', 'Zara']
```

Copying a list

If you need to work with a copy of a list so as not to alter the original list, use the `.copy()` method. For example, the following code is similar to the preceding code, except that instead of reversing the order of the original list, we make a copy of the list and reverse that one. Printing the contents of each list shows how the first list is still in the original order whereas the second one is reversed:

```
# Create a list of strings.
names = ["Zara", "Lupe", "Hong", "Alberto", "Jake"]

# Make a copy of the list.
backward_names = names.copy()
# Reverse the copy.
backward_names.reverse()

# Print the list.
print(names)
print(backward_names)

['Zara', 'Lupe', 'Hong', 'Alberto', 'Jake']
['Jake', 'Alberto', 'Hong', 'Lupe', 'Zara']
```

Table 3-1 summarizes the methods you've learned about so far in this chapter. As you will see in upcoming chapters, these methods work with other kinds of *iterables* (a fancy name that means any list or list-like thing that you can go through one at a time).

TABLE 3-1

Methods for Working with Lists

Method	What It Does
append()	Adds an item to the end of the list
clear()	Removes all items from the list, leaving it empty
copy()	Makes a copy of a list
count()	Counts how many times an element appears in a list
extend()	Appends the items from one list to the end of another list
index()	Returns the index number (position) of an element in a list
insert()	Inserts an item into the list at a specific position
pop()	Removes an element from the list, and provides a copy of that item that you can store in a variable
remove()	Removes one item from the list
reverse()	Reverses the order of items in the list
sort()	Sorts the list in ascending order
sort(reverse=True)	Sorts the list in descending order

What's a Tuple and Who Cares?

In addition to lists, Python supports a data structure known as a tuple. Some people pronounce that like "*two*-pull." Some people pronounce it to rhyme with "couple". But it's not spelled *tupple* or *touple,* so our best guess is that it's pronounced "two-pull." (Heck, for all we know, there may not be only one correct way to pronounce it, but that doesn't stop people from arguing about it.)

Anyway, despite the oddball name, a *tuple* is just an immutable list (like that tells you a lot). In other words, a tuple is a list, but you can't change it after it's defined. So why would you want to put immutable, unchangeable data in an app? Consider Amazon. If we could all go into Amazon and change things at will, everything would cost a penny and we'd all have housefuls of Amazon stuff that cost a penny, rather than housefuls of Amazon stuff that cost more than a penny.

The syntax for creating a tuple is the same as the syntax for creating a list, except you don't use square brackets. You have to use parentheses, like this:

```
prices = (29.95, 9.98, 4.95, 79.98, 2.95)
```

Most of the techniques and methods that you learned for using lists back in Table 3-1 *don't* work with tuples because they are used to modify something in a list, and a tuple can't be modified. However, you can get the length of a tuple using len, like this:

```
print(len(prices))
```

You can use .count() to see how many times an item appears in a tuple. For example:

```
print(prices.count(4.95))
```

You can use in to see whether a value exists in a tuple, as in the following sample code:

```
print(4.95 in prices)
```

This returns True if the tuple contains 4.95 or False if it doesn't.

If an item exists in the tuple, you can get its index number. You'll get an error, though, if the item doesn't exist in the list. You can use in first to see whether the item exists before checking for its index number, and then you can return some nonsense value such as –1 if it doesn't exist, as in this code:

```
look_for = 12345
if look_for in prices:
    position = prices.index(look_for)
else:
    position = -1
print(position)
```

You can loop through the items in a tuple and display them in any format you want by using format strings. For example, this code displays each item with a leading dollar sign and two digits for the pennies:

```
# Loop through and display each item in the tuple.
for price in prices:
    print(f"${price:.2f}")
```

The output from running this code with the sample tuple follows:

```
$29.95
$9.98
$4.95
$79.98
$2.95
```

You can't change the value of an item in a tuple using this kind of syntax:

```
prices[1] = 234.56
```

You'll get an error message that reads TypeError: 'tuple' object does not support item assignment. This message is telling you that you can't use the assignment operator, =, to change the value of an item in a tuple because a tuple is immutable, meaning its content cannot be changed.

Any method that alters, or even just copies, data in a list causes an error when you try it with a tuple. So the list methods .append(), .clear(), .copy(), .extend(), .insert(), .pop(), .remove(), .reverse(), and .sort() would fail when working with tuples. In short, a tuple makes sense if you want to *show* data to users without giving them any means to *change* any of the information.

Working with Sets

Python also offers *sets* as a means of organizing data. The difference between a set and a list is that the items in a set have no specific order. Even though you may define the set with the items in a certain order, none of the items get index numbers to identify their position.

To define a set, use curly braces where you use square brackets for a list and parentheses for a tuple. For example, here's a set with some numbers in it:

```
sample_set = {1.98, 98.9, 74.95, 2.5, 1, 16.3}
```

Sets are similar to lists and tuples in a few ways. You can use len() to determine how many items are in a set. Use in to determine whether an item is in a set.

But you can't get an item in a set based on its index number. Nor can you change an item already in the set. You can't change the order of items in a set either. So you can't use .sort() to sort the set or .reverse() to reverse its order.

You can add a single new item to a set using .add(), as in the following example:

```
sample_set.add(11.23)
```

Not that unlike a list, a set never contains more than one instance of a value. So even if you add 11.23 to the set multiple times, the set will still contain only one copy of 11.23.

You can also add multiple items to a set using .update(). But the items you're adding should be defined as a list in square brackets, as in the following example:

```
sample_set.update([88, 123.45, 2.98])
```

You can copy a set. However, because the set has no defined order, when you display the copy, its items may not be in the same order as the original set, as shown in this code and its output:

```
# Define a set named sample_set.
sample_set = {1.98, 98.9, 74.95, 2.5, 1, 16.3}
# Show the whole set
print(sample_set)
# Make a copy and show the copy.
ss2 = sample_set.copy()
print(ss2)

{1.98, 98.9, 2.5, 1, 74.95, 16.3}
{16.3, 1.98, 98.9, 2.5, 1, 74.95}
```

Figure 3-12 shows some sample code and its output. The code creates a set named sample_set and then uses a variety of print() statements to output information. The following line displays the entire set on the screen:

```
print(sample_set)
```

This line displays 6 because the set has six items:

```
print(len(sample_set))
```

And the following line displays True because the number 74.95 is in sample_set:

```
print(74.95 in sample_set)
```

Comments in the code describe what the rest of the lines do. Note this command inside the loop near the end of the code:

```
print(f"{price:>6.2f}")
```

```
# Define a set named sample_set.
sample_set = {1.98, 98.9, 74.95, 2.5, 1, 16.3}
# Show the whole set
print(sample_set)

# Use len to get the length of a set.
print(len(sample_set))

# Use in to determine if the set contains a value
print(74.95 in sample_set)

# Use add() to add one item to a set.
sample_set.add(11.23)

# Use update() to add a [list] to a set.
sample_set.update([88, 123.45, 2.98])

print("\nSample set after .add() and .update()")
print(sample_set)

# Loop through the set and print each item right-aligned and formatted.
print("\nLoop through set and print each item formatted.")
for price in sample_set:
    print(f"{price:>6.2f}")
```

```
{1.98, 98.9, 2.5, 1, 74.95, 16.3}
6
True

Sample set after .add() and .update()
{1.98, 98.9, 2.5, 1, 2.98, 74.95, 11.23, 16.3, 88, 123.45}

Loop through set and print each item formatted.
  1.98
 98.90
  2.50
  1.00
  2.98
 74.95
 11.23
 16.30
 88.00
123.45
```

FIGURE 3-12:
Playing about
with Python sets.

Each number is neatly formatted with two digits, because the code uses the
f-string >6.2f, which right aligns each number with two digits after the decimal
point.

Lists and tuples are two of the most commonly used Python data structures. Sets
don't seem to get as much play as the other two, but it's good to know about them.
A fourth — and widely used — Python data structure is the data dictionary, which
you learn about in the next chapter.

IN THIS CHAPTER

» **Producing a data dictionary**

» **Seeing how to loop through a dictionary**

» **Copying dictionaries**

» **Deleting items in a dictionary**

» **Using multi-key dictionaries**

Chapter **4**

Cruising Massive Data with Dictionaries

ata dictionaries, also called *associative arrays* in some languages, are kind of like lists, which we discuss in Chapter 3 of this minibook. But each item in the list is identified not by its position in the list but by a key. You can define the key, which can be a string or a number. All that matters is that it is unique to each item in the dictionary.

To understand why uniqueness matters, think about phone numbers, email addresses, and Social Security numbers. If two or more people had the same phone number, whenever someone called that number, all those people would get the call. If two or more people had the same email address, all those people would get the same email messages. If two or more people had the same Social Security number, and one of those people was a million dollars behind in their taxes, you better hope you can convince the tax folks that you're not the one who's delinquent, even though your Social Security number is on the past-due bill.

In this chapter, you'll learn all about Python data dictionaries and how to use them in your own applications.

Understanding Data Dictionaries

A *data dictionary* is similar to a list, except that each item in the list has a unique key. The value you associate with a key can be a number, string, list, tuple — just about anything, really. So you can think of a data dictionary as being similar to a table where the first column contains a single item of information unique to that item and the second column, the value, contains information relevant to, and perhaps unique to, that key. In the example in Figure 4-1, the left column contains a key unique to each row. The second column is the value assigned to each key.

Key		Value
"htanaka"	=	"Haru Tanaka"
"ppatel"	=	"Priya Patel"
"bagarcia"	=	"Benjamin Alberto Garcia"
"zmin"	=	"Zhang Min"
"farooqi"	=	"Ayesha Farooqi"
"hajackson"	=	"Hanna Jackson"
"papatel"	=	"Pratyush Aarav Patel"
"hrjackson"	=	"Henry Jackson"

FIGURE 4-1:
A data dictionary with keys in the left column and values in the right.

The left column shows an abbreviation for a person's name. Some businesses use names like these when assigning user accounts and email addresses to their employees.

The value corresponding to each key doesn't have to be a string or an integer. It can be a list, or tuple. For example, in the dictionary in Figure 4-2, the value of each key includes a name, a year (perhaps the year of hire or birth year), a number (for example, the number of dependents the person claims for taxes), and a Boolean `True` or `False` value (which may indicate, for example, whether the person has a company cellphone). For now, it doesn't matter what each item of data represents. What matters is that for each key, you have a list (enclosed in square brackets) that contains four pieces of information about that key.

Key		Value
"htanaka"	=	["Haru Tanaka", 2000, 0, True]
"ppatel"	=	["Priya Patel", 2015, 1, False]
"bagarcia"	=	["Benjamin Alberto Garcia", 1999, 2, True]
"zmin"	=	["Zhang Min", 2017, 0, False]
"farooqi"	=	["Ayesha Farooqi", 2001, 1, True]
"hajackson"	=	["Hanna Jackson", 1998, 0, False]
"papatel"	=	["Pratyush Aarav Patel", 2011, 2, True]
"hrjackson"	=	["Henry Jackson", 2016, 0, False]

FIGURE 4-2:
A data dictionary with lists as values.

A dictionary may also consist of several different keys, each representing a piece of data. For example, rather than have a row for each item with a unique key, you might make each employee their own little dictionary. Then you can assign a key name to each unit of information. The dictionary for htanaka, then, might look like Figure 4-3.

'htanaka'=	'full_name'	=	'Haru Tanaka'
	'year_hired'	=	2000
	'dependents'	=	0
	'has_company_cell'	=	True

The dictionary for another employee might have all the same key names, full_name, year_hired, dependents, and has_company_cell, but a different value for each of those keys, as shown in Figure 4-4.

'ppatel' =	'full_name'	=	'Priya Patel'
	'year_hired'	=	2015
	'dependents'	=	1
	'has_company_cell'	=	False

Each dictionary entry having multiple keys is common in Python, because the language makes it easy to isolate the specific item of data you want using *object.key* syntax, like this:

```
ppatel.full_name = 'Priya Patel'
ppatel.year_hired = 2015
ppatel,dependents = 1
ppatel.has_company_cell = True
```

The key name is more descriptive than using an index based on position, as you can see in the following example.

```
ppatel[0] = 'Priya Patel'
ppatel[1] = 2015
ppatel[2] = 1
ppatel[3]=True
```

Creating a Data Dictionary

The code for creating a data dictionary follows this basic syntax:

```
name = {key:value, key:value, key:value, key:value, ...}
```

The *name* is a name you make up and generally describes to whom or what the key–value pairs refer. The *key:value* pairs are enclosed in curly braces. The *key* is usually a string enclosed in quotation marks, but you can use integers instead. Each colon (:) separates the key name from the value assigned to it. The *value* is whatever you want to store for that key name, and can be a number, string, list — pretty much anything. The ellipsis (...) just means that you can have as many key-value pairs as you want. Just remember to separate *key:value* pairs with commas, as shown in the syntax example.

To make the code more readable, developers often place each *key:value* pair on a separate line. But the syntax is still the same. The only difference is that a line break follows each comma, as in the following:

```
name = {
    key:value,
    key:value,
    key:value,
    key:value,
    ...
}
```

If you want to try it out, open a Jupyter notebook, a .py file, or a Python prompt, and type the following code. Note that we created a dictionary named people that contains multiple *key:value* pairs, each separated by a comma. The keys and values are strings so they're enclosed in quotation marks, and each key is separated from its value with a colon. It's important to keep all that straight; otherwise the code won't work — yes, even one missing or misplaced or mistyped quotation mark, colon, comma, or curly brace can mess up the whole thing:

```
people = {
    'htanaka': 'Haru Tanaka',
    'ppatel': 'Priya Patel',
    'bagarcia': 'Benjamin Alberto Garcia',
    'zmin': 'Zhang Min',
    'afarooqi': 'Ayesha Farooqi',
    'hajackson': 'Hanna Jackson',
    'papatel': 'Pratyush Aarav Patel',
    'hrjackson': 'Henry Jackson'
}
```

Accessing dictionary data

After you've added the data, you can work with it in a number of ways. Using `print(people)` — that is, a `print()` function with the name of the dictionary in the parentheses — you get a copy of the entire dictionary, as follows:

```
print(people)
{'htanaka': 'Haru Tanaka', 'ppatel': 'Priya Patel', 'bagarcia': 'Benjamin
    Alberto Garcia', 'zmin': 'Zhang Min', 'afarooqi': 'Ayesha Farooqi',
    'hajackson': 'Hanna Jackson', 'papatel': 'Pratyush Aarav Patel', 'hrjackson':
    'Henry Jackson'}
```

Typically this is not what you want. More often, you're looking for one specific item in the dictionary. In that case, use this syntax:

```
dictionaryname[key]
```

where *dictionaryname* is the name of the dictionary, and *key* is the key value for which you're searching. For example, if you want to know the value of the `zmin` key, you would enter

```
print(people['zmin'])
```

Think of this line as saying "print people sub zmin," where *sub* just means *the specific key*. When you do that, Python returns the value for that one person — the full name for `zmin`, in this example. Figure 4-5 shows that output after running the code in a Jupyter notebook cell.

```
# Make a data dictionary named people
people = {
    'htanaka': 'Haru Tanaka',
    'ppatel': 'Priya Patel',
    'bagarcia': 'Benjamin Alberto Garcia',
    'zmin': 'Zhang Min',
    'afarooqi': 'Ayesha Farooqi',
    'hajackson': 'Hanna Jackson',
    'papatel': 'Pratyush Aarav Patel',
    'hrjackson': 'Henry Jackson'
    }

print(people['zmin'])

Zhang Min
```

FIGURE 4-5: Printing the value of the `zmin` key in the `people` dictionary.

Note that in the code, zmin is in quotation marks because it's a string. You can use a variable name instead, as long as it contains a string. For example, consider the following two lines of code. The first one creates a variable named person and puts the string 'zmin' into that variable. The next line doesn't require quotation marks because person is a variable name:

```
person = 'zmin'
print(people[person])
```

So what do you think would happen if you executed the following code?

```
person = 'hrjackson'
print(people[person])
```

You would see Henry Jackson, the name (value) that goes with the key 'hrjackson'.

How about if you ran this bit of code?

```
person = 'schmeedledorp'
print(people[person])
```

Figure 4-6 shows what would happen. You get an error because nothing in the people dictionary has the key value 'schmeedledorp'.

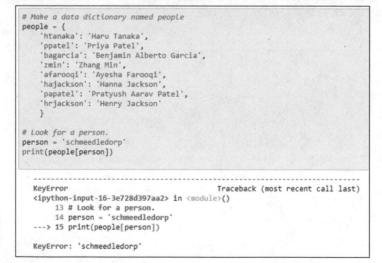

FIGURE 4-6:
Python's way of saying there is no *schmeedledorp*.

Getting the length of a dictionary

The number of items in a dictionary is considered its *length*. As with lists, you can use the len() statement to determine a dictionary's length. The syntax is

```
len(dictionaryname)
```

As always, replace *dictionaryname* with the name of the dictionary you're checking. For example, the following code creates a dictionary, and then stores its length in the howmany variable:

```
people = {
    'htanaka': 'Haru Tanaka',
    'ppatel': 'Priya Patel',
    'bagarcia': 'Benjamin Alberto Garcia',
    'zmin': 'Zhang Min',
    'afarooqi': 'Ayesha Farooqi',
    'hajackson': 'Hanna Jackson',
    'papatel': 'Pratyush Aarav Patel',
    'hrjackson': 'Henry Jackson'
    }
# Count the number of key:value pairs and put in a variable.
howmany = len(people)
# Show how many.
print(howmany)
```

When executed, the print statement shows 8, the value of the hominy variable, as determined by the number of key-value pairs in the dictionary.

TIP

As you may have guessed, an empty dictionary that contains no key-value pairs has a length of 0.

Seeing whether a key exists in a dictionary

You can use the in keyword to see whether a key exists. If the key exists, in returns True. If the key doesn't exist, in returns False. Figure 4-7 shows a simple example with two print() statements. The first one checks to see whether hajackson exists in the dictionary. The second checks to see whether schmeedledorp exists in the dictionary.

As you can see, the first print() statement shows True because hajackson is in the dictionary. The second one returns False because schmeedledorp isn't in the dictionary.

```
# Make a data dictionary named people
people = {
    'htanaka': 'Haru Tanaka',
    'ppatel': 'Priya Patel',
    'bagarcia': 'Benjamin Alberto Garcia',
    'zmin': 'Zhang Min',
    'afarooqi': 'Ayesha Farooqi',
    'hajackson': 'Hanna Jackson',
    'papatel': 'Pratyush Aarav Patel',
    'hrjackson': 'Henry Jackson'
    }

# Is there an hajackson in the people dictionary?
print('hajackson' in people)

# Is there an schmeedledorp in the people dictionary?
print('schmeedledorp' in people)

True
False
```

Getting dictionary data with get()

Having the program crash and burn when you look for something that isn't in the dictionary is a little harsh. A more elegant way to handle that situation is to use the .get() method of a data dictionary. The syntax is

```
dictionaryname.get(key)
```

Replace *dictionaryname* with the name of the dictionary you're searching. Replace *key* with the thing you're looking for. Note that get() uses parentheses, not square brackets. If you look for something that *is* in the dictionary, such as the following, you'd get the same result as you would using square brackets:

```
# Look for a person.
person = 'bagarcia'
print(people.get(person))
```

What makes .get() different is what happens when you search for a non-existent name. You don't get an error, and the program doesn't crash and burn. Instead, get() gracefully returns the word None to let you know that no person named schmeedledorp is in the people dictionary, as you can see in Figure 4-8.

You can pass two values to get(); the second value is what you want get to return if it fails to find what you're looking for. For instance, in the following line of code, we search for schmeedledorp again. But this time, if the code doesn't find that person, it displays not None but the more pompous message Unbeknownst to this dictionary:

```
print(people.get('schmeedledorp', 'Unbeknownst to this dictionary'))
```

```
# Make a data dictionary named people
people = {
    'htanaka': 'Haru Tanaka',
    'ppatel': 'Priya Patel',
    'bagarcia': 'Benjamin Alberto Garcia',
    'zmin': 'Zhang Min',
    'afarooqi': 'Ayesha Farooqi',
    'hajackson': 'Hanna Jackson',
    'papatel': 'Pratyush Aarav Patel',
    'hrjackson': 'Henry Jackson'
    }

# Look for a person.
person = 'schmeedledorp'
print(people.get(person))

None
```

Changing the value of a key

Dictionaries are *mutable,* which means you can change the contents of the dictionary from code (not that you can make the dictionary shut up). The syntax is simply

```
dictionaryname[key] = newvalue
```

Replace `dictionaryname` with the name of the dictionary, `key` with the key that identifies the item, and `newvalue` with whatever you want the new value to be.

For example, supposed Hanna Jackson gets married and changes her name to Hanna Jackson-Smith. You want to keep the same key but change the value. The line that reads `people['hajackson'] = "Hanna Jackson-Smith"` makes the change. The `print()` statement below that line shows the value of `hajackson` after executing that line of code. As you can see in Figure 4-9, the name has indeed been changed to `Hanna Jackson-Smith`.

```
# Print hajackson's current value.
print(people['hajackson'])

# Change the value of the hajackson key.
people['hajackson'] = "Hanna Jackson-Smith"

#Print the hajackson key to verify that the value has changed.
print(people['hajackson'])

Hanna Jackson
Hanna Jackson-Smith
```

FIGURE 4-9:
Changing the
value associated
with a key in a
dictionary.

TECHNICAL STUFF

In real life, the data in a dictionary would probably be stored also in some kind of external file so that it's permanent. Additional code would be required to save the dictionary changes to that external file. But you need to learn these basics before you get into all of that, so let's just forge ahead with dictionaries for now.

Adding or changing dictionary data

You can use the dictionary `update()` method to add a new item to a dictionary or to change the value of a current key. The syntax is

```
dictionaryname.update(key, value)
```

Replace *dictionaryname* with the name of the dictionary. Replace *key* with the key of the item you want to add or change. If the key you specify doesn't exist in the dictionary, it will be added as a new item with the *value* you specify. If the `key` you specify does exist, nothing will be added. The value of the key will be changed to whatever you specify as the *value*.

For example, consider the following Python code that creates a data dictionary named `people` and put two peoples' names into it:

```
# Make a data dictionary named people.
people = {
    'papatel': 'Pratyush Aarav Patel',
    'hrjackson': 'Henry Jackson'
    }

# Change the value of the hrjackson key.
people.update({'hrjackson' : 'Henrietta Jackson'})
print(people)

# Update the dictionary with a new key:value pair.
people.update({'wwiggins' : 'Wanda Wiggins'})
```

The first update line changes the value for `hrjackson` from `Henry Jackson` to `Henrietta Jackson` because the `hrjackson` key already exists in the data dictionary:

```
people.update({'hrjackson' : 'Henrietta Jackson'})
```

The second `update()` reads as follows:

```
people.update({'wwiggins' : 'Wanda Wiggins'})
```

There is no `wwiggins` key in the dictionary, so `update()` can't change the name for `wwiggins`. Instead, the line adds a new key-value pair to the dictionary with `wwigins` as the `key` and `Wanda Wiggins` as the `value`.

The code doesn't specify whether to change or add the value because the decision is made automatically. Each key in a dictionary must be unique; you can't have two or more rows with the same key. So when you do an `update()`, the code first checks to see whether the key exists. If it does, only the value of that key is modified; nothing new is added. If the key doesn't exist in the dictionary, there is nothing to modify so the new key-value is added to the dictionary. That process is automatic, and the decision about which action to perform is simple:

>> If the key already exists in the dictionary, its value is updated because no two items in a dictionary are allowed to have the same key.

>> If the key does *not* already exist, the key-value pair is added because nothing in the dictionary already has that key, so the only choice is to add it.

After running the code, the dictionary contains three items, `paptel`, `hrjackson` (with the new name), and `wwiggins`. Adding the following lines to the end of that code displays everything in the dictionary:

```
# Show what's in the data dictionary now.
for person in people.keys():
    print(person + " = " + people[person])
```

If you add that code and run it again, you get the following output, which shows the complete contents of the data dictionary at the end of that program:

```
papatel = Pratyush Aarav Patel
hrjackson = Henrietta Jackson
wwiggins = Wanda Wiggins
```

As you may have guessed, you can loop through a dictionary in much the same way you loop through lists, tuples, and sets. But you can do some extra things with dictionaries, so let's take a look at those next.

Looping through a Dictionary

You can loop through each item in a dictionary in much the same way you can loop through lists and tuples, but you have some extra options. If you just specify the dictionary name in the `for` loop, you get all the keys, as follows:

```
for person in people:
    print(person)

htanaka
ppatel
bagarcia
zmin
afarooqi
hajackson
papatel
hrjackson
```

If you want to see the value of each item, keep the `for` loop the same, but print *dictionaryname[key]* where *dictionaryname* is the name of the dictionary (`people` in our example) and *key* is whatever name you use right after the `for` in the loop (`person`, in the following example).

```
for person in people:
    print(people[person])
```

Running this code against the sample `people` dictionary lists all the names, as follows:

```
Haru Tanaka
Priya Patel
Benjamin Alberto Garcia
Zhang Min
Ayesha Farooqi
Hanna Jackson
Pratyush Aarav Patel
Henry Jackson
```

You can also get all the names by using a slightly different syntax in the `for` loop: Add `.values()` to the dictionary name, as in the following. Then you can just print the variable name (`person`) inside the loop. The output would be the full name of each person, as in the previous loop example.

```
for person in people.values():
    print(person)
```

Lastly, you can loop through the keys and values at the same time by using `.items()` after the dictionary name in the `for` loop. But you will need two variables after the `for` as well, one to reference the key and the other to reference the value. If you want the code to display both variables as it's looping through the dictionary, you'll need to use those names inside the parentheses of the `print`.

For example, the loop in Figure 4-10 uses two variable names, `key` and `value` (although they could be `x` and `y` or anything else) to loop through `people.items()`. The `print` statement displays both the `key` and the `value` with each pass through the loop. The `print()` also has an equal sign (enclosed in quotation marks) to separate the key from the value. As you can see in the output, you get a list of all the keys followed by an equal sign and the value assigned to that key.

```
# Make a data dictionary named people
people = {
    'htanaka': 'Haru Tanaka',
    'ppatel': 'Priya Patel',
    'bagarcia': 'Benjamin Alberto Garcia',
    'zmin': 'Zhang Min',
    'afarooqi': 'Ayesha Farooqi',
    'hajackson': 'Hanna Jackson',
    'papatel': 'Pratyush Aarav Patel',
    'hrjackson': 'Henry Jackson'
    }

# Loop through .items to get the key and the value.
for key, value in people.items():
    # Show the key and value with = in between.
    print(key, "=", value)
```

```
htanaka = Haru Tanaka
ppatel = Priya Patel
bagarcia = Benjamin Alberto Garcia
zmin = Zhang Min
afarooqi = Ayesha Farooqi
hajackson = Hanna Jackson
papatel = Pratyush Aarav Patel
hrjackson = Henry Jackson
```

FIGURE 4-10: Looping through a dictionary with items() and two variable names.

Data Dictionary Methods

If you've been diligently following along chapter to chapter, you may have noticed that some of the methods for data dictionaries look similar to those for lists, tuples, and sets. So maybe now would be a good time to list, in Table 4-1, all the methods that dictionaries offer. You've already seen some put to use in this chapter. We get to the others a little later.

TABLE 4-1 **Data Dictionary Methods**

Method	What It Does
clear()	Empties the dictionary by remove all keys and values.
copy()	Returns a copy of the dictionary.
fromkeys()	Returns a new copy of the dictionary but with only specified keys and values.
get()	Returns the value of the specified key, or None if it doesn't exist.
items()	Returns a list of items as a tuple for each key-value pair.
keys()	Returns a list of all the keys in a dictionary.
pop()	Removes the item specified by the key from the dictionary, and returns its value.
popitem()	Removes the last key-value pair.
setdefault()	Returns the value of the specified key. If the key doesn't exist, inserts the key with the specified value.
update()	Updates the value of an existing key, or adds a new key-value pair if the specified key isn't already in the dictionary.
values()	Returns a list of all the values in the dictionary.

Copying a Dictionary

If you need to make a copy of a data dictionary to work with, use this syntax:

```
newdictionaryname = dictionaryname.copy()
```

Replace *newdictionaryname* with whatever you want to name the new dictionary. Replace *dictionaryname* with the name of the existing dictionary that you want to copy.

Figure 4-11 shows a simple example in which we created a dictionary named `people`, and then created a dictionary named `peeps2` as a copy of the `people` dictionary. Printing the contents of each dictionary shows that they're identical.

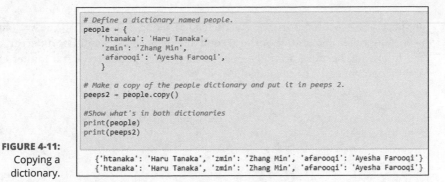

```
# Define a dictionary named people.
people = {
    'htanaka': 'Haru Tanaka',
    'zmin': 'Zhang Min',
    'afarooqi': 'Ayesha Farooqi',
    }

# Make a copy of the people dictionary and put it in peeps 2.
peeps2 = people.copy()

#Show what's in both dictionaries
print(people)
print(peeps2)
```

```
{'htanaka': 'Haru Tanaka', 'zmin': 'Zhang Min', 'afarooqi': 'Ayesha Farooqi'}
{'htanaka': 'Haru Tanaka', 'zmin': 'Zhang Min', 'afarooqi': 'Ayesha Farooqi'}
```

FIGURE 4-11:
Copying a
dictionary.

Deleting Dictionary Items

You can remove data from data dictionaries in several ways. The del keyword
(short for *delete*) can remove any item based on its key. The syntax is as follows:

```
del dictionaryname[key]
```

For example, the following code creates a dictionary named people. Then it uses
del people["zmin"] to remove the item that has zmin as its key:

```
# Define a dictionary named people.
people = {
    'htanaka': 'Haru Tanaka',
    'zmin': 'Zhang Min',
    'afarooqi': 'Ayesha Farooqi',
    }

# Show original people dictionary.
print(people)

# Remove zmin from the dictionary.
del people["zmin"]

# Show what's in people now.
print(people)
```

Printing the contents of the dictionary shows that zmin is no longer in that
dictionary:

```
{'htanaka': 'Haru Tanaka', 'zmin': 'Zhang Min', 'afarooqi': 'Ayesha Farooqi'}
{'htanaka': 'Haru Tanaka', 'afarooqi': 'Ayesha Farooqi'}
```

If you forget to include a specific key with the del keyword and specify only the
dictionary name, the entire dictionary is deleted, even its name. For example,

Cruising Massive Data
with Dictionaries

suppose you executed `del people` instead of using `del people["zmin"]` in the preceding code. The output of the second `print(people)` would be an error, as in the following, because after the `people` dictionary is deleted it no longer exists and its content can't be displayed:

```
{'htanaka': 'Haru Tanaka', 'zmin': 'Zhang Min', 'afarooqi': 'Ayesha Farooqi'}
----------------------------------------------------------
NameError Traceback (most recent call last)
<ipython-input-32-24401f5e8cf0> in <module>()
13
14 # Show what's in people now.
---> 15 print(people)
NameError: name 'people' is not defined
```

To remove all key-value pairs from a dictionary without deleting the entire dictionary, use the `clear` method with this syntax:

```
dictionaryname.clear()
```

The following code creates a dictionary named `people`, puts some key-value pairs in it, and then prints the dictionary so you can see its content. Then, `people.clear()` empties all the data:

```
# Define a dictionary named people.
people = {
    'htanaka': 'Haru Tanaka',
    'zmin': 'Zhang Min',
    'afarooqi': 'Ayesha Farooqi',
    }

# Show original people dictionary.
print(people)

# Remove all data from the dictionary.
people.clear()

#Show what's in people now.
print(people)
```

The output of running this code shows that the `people` data dictionary initially contains three property:value pairs. After using `people.clear()` to wipe the `people` dictionary clear, printing it displays {}, which is Python's way of telling you that the dictionary is empty.

```
{'htanaka': 'Haru Tanaka', 'zmin': 'Zhang Min', 'afarooqi': 'Ayesha Farooqi'}
{}
```

The pop() method offers another way to remove data from a data dictionary. The pop() method actually does two things:

» If you store the results of the pop() method in a variable, that variable gets the value of the popped key.

» Regardless of whether you store the result of the pop() method in a variable, the specified key is removed from the dictionary.

Figure 4-12 shows an example where you first see the entire dictionary in the output. Then adios = people.pop("zmin") is executed, putting the value of the zmin key in a variable named adios. We then print the adios variable so we can see that it contains Zhang Min, the value of the zmin key. Printing the entire people dictionary again proves that zmin has been removed from the dictionary.

```
# Define a dictionary named people.
people = {
    'htanaka': 'Haru Tanaka',
    'zmin': 'Zhang Min',
    'afarooqi': 'Ayesha Farooqi',
    }
# Show original people dictionary.
print(people)

# Pop zmin from the dictionary, store its value in adios variable.
adios = people.pop("zmin")

# Print the contents of adios and people.
print(adios)
print(people)
```

```
{'htanaka': 'Haru Tanaka', 'zmin': 'Zhang Min', 'afarooqi': 'Ayesha Farooqi'}
Zhang Min
{'htanaka': 'Haru Tanaka', 'afarooqi': 'Ayesha Farooqi'}
```

FIGURE 4-12:
Popping an item
from a dictionary.

Data dictionaries offer a variation on pop() that uses this syntax:

```
dictionaryname = popitem()
```

This syntax is tricky because in some earlier versions of Python it would remove an item at random. That's weird unless you're writing a game or something and want to remove things at random. But as of Python version 3.7 (the version used in this book), popitem() always removes the last key-value pair.

If you store the results of popitem in a variable, you *don't* get that item's value, which is different from the way pop() works. Instead, you get both the key and its value. The dictionary no longer contains that key-value pair. So, in other words, if you replace `adios = people.pop("zmin")` in Figure 4-12 with `adios = people.popitem()`, the output will be as follows:

```
{'htanaka': 'Haru Tanaka', 'zmin': 'Zhang Min', 'afarooqi': 'Ayesha Farooqi'}

('afarooqi', 'Ayesha Farooqi')

{'htanaka': 'Haru Tanaka', 'zmin': 'Zhang Min'}
```

Having Fun with Multi-Key Dictionaries

So far you've worked with a dictionary that has one value (a person's name) for each key (an abbreviation of that person's name). But it's not unusual for a dictionary to have multiple key–value pairs for one item of data.

For example, suppose that just knowing the person's full name isn't enough. You want to also know the year the person was hired, his or her date of birth, and whether or not that employee has been issued a company laptop. The dictionary for any one person might look like this:

```
employee = {
    'name': 'Haru Tanaka',
    'year_hired': 2005,
    'dob': '11/23/1987',
    'has_laptop': False
}
```

Or suppose you need a dictionary of products that you sell. For each product, you want to know its name, its unit price, whether or not it's taxable, and how many you currently have in stock. The dictionary might look something like this (for one product):

```
product = {
    'name': 'Ray-Ban Wayfarer Sunglasses',
    'unit_price': 112.99,
    'taxable': True,
    'in_stock'=: 10
}
```

Note that in each example, the key name is in quotation marks. We used single quotes in the sample code, but you can use either single or double quotes. We even enclosed the date in `dob` (date of birth) in quotation marks. If you don't, it may be treated as a set of numbers, as in "11 divided by 23 divided by 1987" which isn't useful information. Booleans are either `True` or `False` (initial caps) with no quotation marks. Integers (2005, 10) and floats (112.99) are not enclosed in quotation marks either.

The value for a property can be a list, tuple, or set; it doesn't have to be a single value. For example, for the sunglasses product, maybe you offer two models, black and tortoise. You could add a colors or model key and list the items as a comma-separated list in square brackets like this:

```
product = {
    'name': 'Ray-Ban Wayfarer Sunglasses',
    'unit_price': 112.99,
    'taxable': True,
    'in_stock': 10,
    'models': ['Black', 'Tortoise']
}
```

Next let's look at how you might display the dictionary data. You can use the simple *dictionaryname*[*key*] syntax to print just the value of each key. For example, using that last product example, the output of this code:

```
print(product['name'])
print(product['unit_price'])
print(product['taxable'])
print(product['in_stock'])
print(product['models'])
```

would be:

```
Ray-Ban Wayfarer Sunglasses
112.99
True
10
['Black', 'Tortoise']
```

You could get fancier by adding descriptive text to each print statement, followed by a comma and the code. You could also loop through the list to print each model on a separate line. And you can use an f-string to format the data. For example, here is a variation on the previous print() statements:

```
product = {
    'name' : 'Ray-Ban Wayfarer Sunglasses',
    'unit_price' : 112.99,
    'taxable' : True,
    'in_stock' : 10,
    'models' : ['Black', 'Tortoise']
}
```

```
print('Name:      ', product['name'])
print('Price:     ', f"${product['unit_price']:.2f}")
print('Taxable: ', product['taxable'])
print('In Stock:', product['in_stock'])
print('Models:')
for model in product['models']:
    print("  " * 10 + model)
```

Here is the output of that code:

```
Name:      Ray-Ban Wayfarer Sunglasses
Price:     $112.99
Taxable:   True
In Stock: 10
Models:
           Black
           Tortoise
```

The " " * 10 on the last line of code means *print a space (" ") ten times.* In other words, indent ten spaces. If you don't put exactly one space between those quotation marks, you won't get 10 spaces. You'll get 10 of whatever is between the quotation marks, which also means you'll get nothing if you don't put anything between the quotation marks.

Using the mysterious fromkeys and setdefault methods

Data dictionaries in Python offer two methods, named fromkeys() and setdefault(), which are the cause of much head-scratching among Python learners — and rightly so because it's not easy to find practical applications for their use. But we'll take a shot at it and at least show you what to expect if you ever use these methods in your code.

The fromkeys() method uses this syntax:

```
newdictionaryname = dict.fromkeys(iterable[,value])
```

Replace *newdictionary* with whatever you want to name the new dictionary. It doesn't have to be a generic name like *product*. It can be something that uniquely identifies the product, such as a UPC (Universal Product Code) or SKU (stock-keeping unit) specific to your business.

Replace the *iterable* part with any iterable — meaning, something the code can loop through; a simple list will do. The *value* part is optional. If omitted, each key in the dictionary gets a value of None, which is simply Python's way of saying *no value has been assigned to this key in this dictionary yet.*

In the following example, we created a dictionary named DWC001 (the SKU for a product in our inventory). We gave it a list of key names, enclosed in square brackets and separated by commas, which makes it a properly defined list for Python. We provided nothing for *value*. The code then prints the new dictionary. As you can see, the last line of code prints the dictionary, which contains the specified key names with each key having a value of None.

```
DWC001 = dict.fromkeys(['name', 'unit_price', 'taxable', 'in_stock', 'models'])
print(DWC001)
{'name': None, 'unit_price': None, 'taxable': None, 'in_stock': None, 'models':
    None}
```

Now, suppose that you don't want to type all those key names. You just want to use the same keys you're using in other dictionaries. In that case, you can use *dictionary*.keys() for your iterable list of key names, as long as *dictionary* refers to another dictionary that exists in the program.

For example, in the following code, we created a dictionary named product that has some key names and nothing specific for the values. Then we used DWC001 = dict.fromkeys(product.keys()) to create a dictionary with the name DWC001 that has the same keys as the generic product dictionary. We didn't specify any values in the dict.fromkeys(product.keys()) line, so each of those keys in the new dictionary will have values set to None.

```
# Create a generic dictionary for products named product.
product = {
    'name': '',
    'unit_price': 0,
    'taxable': True,
    'in_stock': 0,
    'models': []
}
# Create a dictionary named DWC001 that has the same keys as product.
DWC001 = dict.fromkeys(product.keys())

# Show what's in the new dictionary.
print(DWC001)
```

The final print() statement shows what's in the new dictionary. You can see it has all the same keys as the product dictionary, with each value set to None.

```
{'name': None, 'unit_price': None, 'taxable': None, 'in_stock': None, 'models':
    None}
```

The .setdefault() value lets you add a new key to a dictionary, with a predefined value. But .setdefault() only adds a new key and value; it doesn't alter the value for an existing key, even if that key's value is None. So it could come in handy after the fact if you defined other dictionaries and then later wanted to add another property:value pair only to dictionaries that don't already have that property.

Figure 4-13 shows an example in which we created the DWC001 dictionary using the same keys as the product dictionary. After the dictionary is created, setdefault('taxable', True) adds a key named taxable and sets its value to True — but only if that dictionary doesn't already have a key named taxable. It also adds a key named reorder_point and sets its value to 10 but, again, only if that key doesn't already exist.

```
# Create a generic dictionary for products name product.
product = {
    'name': '',
    'unit_price': 0,
    'taxable': True,
    'in_stock': 0,
    'models': []
}
# Create a dictionary for product SKU # DWC001
DWC001 = dict.fromkeys(product.keys())
DWC001.setdefault('taxable',True)
DWC001.setdefault('models',[])
DWC001.setdefault('reorder_point',100)

# Show what's in the new dictionary.
print("Dictionary after fromkeys() and setdefault()")
print(DWC001)

# Change the taxable field from None to True
print("\nDictionary after fromkeys() and setdefault()")
DWC001['taxable']=True

#Print the dictionary after changing taxable to True
print(DWC001)
```

```
Dictionary after fromkeys() and setdefault()
{'name': None, 'unit_price': None, 'taxable': None, 'in_stock': None, 'models': None, 'reorder_point': 100}

Dictionary after fromkeys() and setdefault()
{'name': None, 'unit_price': None, 'taxable': True, 'in_stock': None, 'models': None, 'reorder_point': 100}
```

FIGURE 4-13:
Experimenting with fromkeys and setdefault.

As you can see in the output from the code, after the fromkeys and setdefault operations, the new dictionary has the same keys as the product dictionary plus a new key-value pair, reorder_point: 10, which was added by the second setdefault. The taxable key in that output, though, is still None, because setdefault won't change the value of an existing key. It adds a new key with the default value to a dictionary only if it doesn't already have that key.

So what if you really did want to set the default of taxable to True, rather than None? The simple solution would be to use the standard syntax, *dictionaryname [key] = newvalue* to change the value of the extant taxable key from None to True. The second output in Figure 4-13 proves that changing the value of the key in that manner did work.

Nesting dictionaries

By now it may have occurred to you that any given program you write may require several dictionaries, each with a unique name. But if you just define a bunch of dictionaries with names, how could you loop through the whole kit-and-caboodle without specifically accessing each dictionary by name? The answer is, make each dictionary a key-value pair in some containing dictionary, where the key is the unique identifier for each dictionary (for example, a UPC or SKU for each product). The value for each key would then be a dictionary of all the key-value pairs for that dictionary. So the syntax would be:

```
containingdictionaryname = {
    key: {dictionary},
    key: {dictionary},
    key: {dictionary},
    ...
}
```

That's just the syntax for the dictionary of dictionaries. You have to replace all the italicized placeholder names as follows:

» *containingdictionaryname*: This is the name assigned to the dictionary as a whole. It can be any name you like but should describe what the dictionary contains.

» *key*: Each key value must be unique, such as the UPC or SKU for a product, or the username for a person, or even just some sequential number, as long as it's never repeated.

» *{dictionary}* Enclose all the key-value pairs for that one dictionary item in curly braces, and follow that with a comma if another dictionary follows.

Figure 4-14 shows an example in which we have a dictionary named products (plural, because it contains many products). This dictionary in turn contains four individual products. Each product has a unique key: RB0011, DWC0317, and so forth, which are in-house SKU numbers that the business uses to manage its own inventory. Each of those four products in turn has name, price, and models keys.

The complex syntax with all the curly braces, commas, and colons makes it hard to see what's going on (and hard to type). Outside Python, in a text file, a spreadsheet, a database, or wherever you're putting the data, the same data could be stored as a simple table named Products with the key names as column headings, like the one in Table 4-2.

Multiple product
dictionaries
contained in a
larger products
dictionary.

```
# Create a generic products dictionary to contain multiple product dictionaries.
products = {
    'RB00111': {'name': 'Ray-Ban Sunglasses', 'price': 112.98, 'models': ['black', 'tortoise']},
    'DWC0317': {'name': 'Drone with Camera', 'price': 72.95, 'models': ['white', 'black']},
    'MTS0540': {'name': 'T-Shirt', 'price': 2.95, 'models': ['small', 'medium', 'large']},
    'ECD2989': {'name': 'Echo Dot', 'price': 29.99, 'models': []}
}
```

TABLE 4-2 ## A Table of Products

ID (key)	Name	Price	Models
RB00111	Ray-Ban Sunglasses	112.98	black, tortoise
DWC0317	Drone with Camera	72.95	white, black
MTS0540	T-Shirt	2.95	small, medium, large
ECD2989	Echo Dot	29.99	

Using a combination of f-strings and some loops, you could get Python to display that data from the data dictionaries in a neat, tabular format. Figure 4-15 shows an example of such code in a Jupyter notebook, with the output from that code right below it.

```
# Create a generic products dictionary to contain multiple product dictionaries.
products = {
    'RB00111': {'name': 'Ray-Ban Sunglasses', 'price': 112.98, 'models': ['black', 'tortoise']},
    'DWC0317': {'name': 'Drone with Camera', 'price': 72.95, 'models': ['white', 'black']},
    'MTS0540': {'name': 'T-Shirt', 'price': 2.95, 'models': ['small', 'medium', 'large']},
    'ECD2989': {'name': 'Echo Dot', 'price': 29.99, 'models': []}
}
# This header shows above the output.
print(f"{'ID':<6} {' Name':<17} {'Price':>8}  {' Models'}")
print('-' * 60) # Prints 60 hyphens.
# Loop through each dictionary in the products dictionary
for oneproduct in products.keys():
    # Get the id of one product.
    id = oneproduct
    # Get the name of one product.
    name = products[oneproduct]['name']
    # Get the unit price of one product and format with $
    unit_price = '$' + f"{products[oneproduct]['price']:,.2f}"
    # Create and empty string variable named models
    models = ''
    # Loop through the models list and tack onto models
    # one item from the list followed by a comma and a space.
    for m in products[oneproduct]['models']:
        models += m + ', '
    # If the models variable is more than two characters in length,
    # Peel off the last two characters (last comma and space).
    if len(models) > 2:
        models = models[:-2]
    else:
        # Otherwise, if no models, show <none>.
        models = "<none>"
    # Print all the variables with a neat f-string.
    print(f"{id:<6} {name:<17} {unit_price:>8} {models}")
# Any unidented code down here executed after the loop completes.

ID     Name             Price  Models
------------------------------------------------------------
RB00111 Ray-Ban Sunglasses $112.98 black, tortoise
DWC0317 Drone with Camera   $72.95 white, black
MTS0540 T-Shirt              $2.95 small, medium, large
ECD2989 Echo Dot            $29.99 <none>
```

Printing data
dictionaries
formatted
into rows and
columns.

IN THIS CHAPTER

» **Creating your own function**

» **Including a comment in a function**

» **Seeing how to pass information to a function**

» **Returning values from a function**

» **Understanding anonymous functions**

Chapter **5**

Wrangling Bigger Chunks of Code

I n this chapter, you learn how to better manage larger code projects by creating your own functions. Functions provide a way to compartmentalize your code into small tasks that can be called from multiple places in an app. For example, if something you need to access throughout the app requires a dozen lines of code, chances are you don't want to repeat that code over and over every time you need it. Doing so just makes the code larger than it needs to be. Also, if you want to change something, or if you have to fix an error in that code, you don't want to have to do it repeatedly in a bunch of different places. If all that code were contained in a function, you would have to change or fix it in only one location.

To access the task that the function performs, you *call* the function from your code, just like you call a built-in function such as print. In other words, you just type the name into your code. You can make up your own function names, too. So, think of functions as a way to personalize the Python language so that its commands fit what you need in your application.

Creating a Function

Creating a function is easy. Follow along in a Jupyter notebook cell or .py file if you want to get some hands-on experience.

To create a function, start a new line with def (short for *definition*) followed by a space, and then a name of your own choosing followed by a pair of parentheses with no spaces before or inside. Then put a colon at the end of that line. For example, to create a simple function named hello(), type

```
def hello():
```

This is a function, but it doesn't do anything. To make the function do something, you have to write Python code on subsequent lines. To ensure that the new code is "inside" the function, indent each of those lines.

REMEMBER

Indentations matter big time in Python. There is no command that marks the end of a function. All indented lines below the def line are part of that function. The first un-indented line (indented as far out as the def line) is outside the function.

To make this function do something, put an indented line of code under def. We'll start by just having the function print hello. So, type **print('Hello')** indented under the def line. Now your code looks like this:

```
def hello():
    print('Hello')
```

If you run the code now, nothing will happen. That's okay. Nothing should happen because the code inside a function isn't executed until the functioned is *called*. You call your own functions the same way you call built-in functions: by writing code that calls the function by name, including the parentheses at the end.

For example, if you're following along, press Enter to add a blank line and then type **hello()** (no spaces in there) and make sure it's *not* indented. (You don't want this code to be indented because it's *calling* the function to execute its code; it's not *part of* the function.) So it looks like this:

```
def hello():
    print('Hello')

hello()
```

Still, nothing happens if you're in a Jupyter cell or a .py file because you've only typed the code so far. For anything to happen, you have to run the code in the usual way in Jupyter or VS Code (if you're using a `.py` file in VS Code). When the code executes, you should see the output, which is just the word `Hello`, as shown in Figure 5-1.

FIGURE 5-1:
Writing, and calling, a simple function named `hello()`.

```
def hello():
    print('Hello')

hello()

Hello
```

Commenting a Function

Comments are always optional in code. But it's customary to make the first line under the `def` statement a *docstring* (text enclosed in triple quotation marks) that describes what the function does. It's also common to put a comment, preceded by a # sign, to the right of the parentheses in the first line. Here's an example using the simple `hello()` function:

```
def hello():    # Practice function
    """ A docstring describing the function """
    print('Hello')
```

Because they're just comments, they don't have any effect on what the code does. Comments are just notes to yourself or to programming team members describing what the code is about. Running the code again displays the same results.

As a bonus for VS Code users, when you start typing the function name, VS Code's IntelliSense help shows the `def` statement for your custom function as well as the docstring you typed for it, as shown in Figure 5-2. So you get to create custom help for your own custom functions.

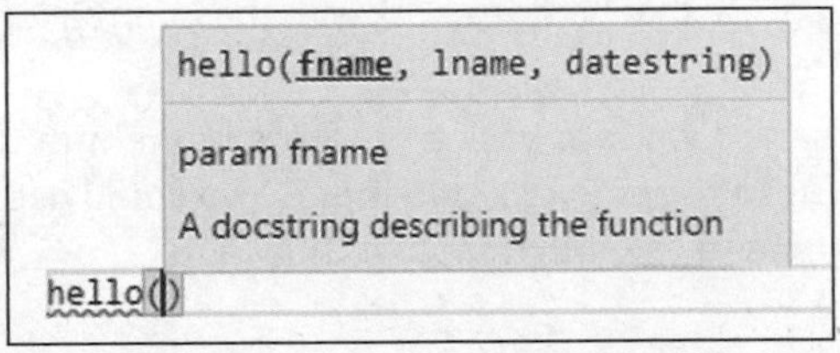

```
hello(fname, lname, datestring)

param fname

A docstring describing the function

hello()
```

Passing Information to a Function

You can pass information to a function for it to work on. To do so, enter a parameter name in the `def` statement for each piece of information you'll be passing to the function. You can use any name for the parameter, as long as it starts with a letter or underscore, followed by a letter, an underscore, or a number. The name should not contain spaces or punctuation. (Parameter names and variable names follow the same rules.) Ideally, the parameter should describe what's being passed in, for code readability, but you can use generic names like x and y, if you prefer.

Any name you provide as a parameter is local only to that function. For example, if you have a variable named x outside the function and another variable named x inside the function, any changes you make to the x variable inside the function won't affect the x variable outside the function.

The technical term for the way variables work inside functions is *local scope*, meaning the scope of the variables' existence and influence stays inside the function and does not extend further. Variables created and modified inside a function literally cease to exist the moment the function stops running, and any variables defined outside the function are unaffected by the goings-on inside the function. This is a good thing because when you're writing a function, you don't have to worry about accidentally changing a variable outside the function that happens to have the same name.

TECHNICAL STUFF

A function can *return* a value, and that returned value *is* visible outside the function. More on how this process works in a moment.

Suppose you want the `hello` function to say `hello` to whoever is using the app (and you have access to that information in some variable). To pass the information into the function and use it there, you would do the following:

>> Put a parameter name inside the function's parentheses to act as a placeholder for the incoming information.

>> Inside the function, use that name to work with the information passed in.

For example, suppose you want to pass a person's name into the `hello` function and then use the name in the `print()` statement. You could use any generic name for both the parameter and the function, like this:

```
def hello(x):   # Practice function
    """ A docstring describing the function """
    print('Hello ' + x)
```

Inside the parentheses of `hello(x)`, the `x` is a parameter, a placeholder for what-ever is being passed in. Inside the function, that `x` refers only to the value passed into the function. Any variables named `x` outside the function are separate from the `x` used in the parameter name and inside the function.

Generic names don't exactly help make your code easy to understand. It would be better to use a more descriptive name, such as `name` or even `user_name`, as in the following:

```
def hello(user_name):   # Practice function
    """ A docstring describing the function """
    print('Hello ' + user_name)
```

In the `print()` function, we added a space after the *o* in *Hello* so there'd be a space between `Hello` and the name in the output.

When a function has a parameter, you have to pass it a value when you call it or it won't work. For example, if you added the parameter to the `def` statement and still tried to call the function without the parameter, as in the following code, run-ning the code would produce an error:

```
def hello(user_name):   # Practice function
    """ A docstring describing the function """
    print('Hello ' + user_name)

hello()
```

The error would read something like the following:

```
hello() missing 1 required positional argument: 'user_name'
```

which is a major nerd-o-rama way of saying the `hello` function expected some-thing to be passed into it.

For this particular function, a string needs to be passed. We know this because we concatenate (add) whatever is passed into the variable to another string (the word `hello` followed by a space). If you tried to concatenate a number to a string, you'd get an error.

The value you pass can be a literal (the exact data you want to pass in) or the name of a variable that contains that information. For example, when you run this code:

```
def hello(user_name):    # Practice function
    """ A docstring describing the function """
    print('Hello ' + user_name)

hello('Alan')
```

the output is Hello Alan because when you called the function with the following line of code, you passed Alan as a string:

```
hello('Alan')
```

You can use a variable to pass data too. For example, in the code in Figure 5-3 we stored the string "Alan" in a variable named this_person. Then we call the function using that variable name. Running that code produces Hello Alan, as shown at the bottom of that figure.

```
def hello(user_name):    # Practice function
    """ A docstring describing the function """
    print('Hello ' + user_name)

# Put a string in a variable named this_person.
this_person = 'Alan'
# Pass that variable name to the function.
hello(this_person)

Hello Alan
```

FIGURE 5-3:
Passing data to a function via a variable.

Defining optional parameters with defaults

In the preceding section we mention that when you call a function that expects parameters without passing those parameters, you get an error. That was a little bit of a lie. You *can* write a function so that passing a parameter is optional, but you have to tell the function what to use if nothing gets passed. The syntax follows:

```
def functioname(parametername=defaultvalue):
```

The only thing that's really different is the = *defaultvalue* part after the parameter name. For example, you could rewrite the sample hello() function with a default value, like this:

```
def hello(user_name = 'nobody'):    # Practice function
    """ A docstring describing the function """
    print('Hello ' + user_name)
```

Figure 5-4 shows the function after making that change, along with the output of testing the function.

First the code calls the function, passing it the value Alan:

```
hello('Alan')
```

So the output is

```
Hello Alan
```

The second line we used to test the function calls the function but doesn't pass in a value. In other words, it calls the function but with no value in the parentheses, like this:

```
hello()
```

Because this line doesn't pass in a value, the function defaults to 'nobody' and the output, as you can see at the bottom of the figure, is

```
Hello nobody
```

FIGURE 5-4:
An optional parameter with a default value added to the hello() function.

```
def hello(user_name = 'nobody'):    # Practice function
    """ A docstring describing the function """
    print('Hello ' + user_name)

hello('Alan')
hello()

Hello Alan
Hello nobody
```

Passing multiple values to a function

So far in all our examples we've passed just one value to the function. But you can pass as many values as you want. Just provide a parameter name for each value, and separate the names with commas.

For example, suppose you want to pass the user's first name, last name, and maybe a date to the function. You could define those three parameters like this:

```
def hello(fname, lname, datestring):    # Practice function
    """ A docstring describing the function """
    print('Hello ' + fname + ' ' + lname)
    print('The date is ' + datestring)
```

Note that none of the parameters is optional. So when calling the function, you need to pass three values, such as this:

```
hello('Alan', 'Simpson', '12/31/2019')
```

Figure 5-5 shows an example of executing code with a hello() function that accepts three parameters.

```
def hello(fname, lname, datestring):    # Practice function
    """ A docstring describing the function """
    msg = "Hello " + fname + " " + lname
    msg += " you mentioned " + datestring
    print(msg)

hello('Alan', 'Simpson', '12/31/2019')

Hello Alan Simpson you mentioned 12/31/2019
```

If you want to use some (but not all) optional parameters with multiple parameters, make sure the optional ones are the last ones entered. For example, consider the following, which would *not* work:

```
def hello(fname, lname='unknown', datestring):
```

If you try to run this code with that arrangement, you get an error that reads something along the lines of

```
SyntaxError: non-default argument follows default argument.
```

This error is trying to tell you that if you want to list both required parameters and optional parameters in a function, you have to put all the required ones first (in any order). Then the optional parameters can be listed after that with their = signs (in any order). So the following would work fine:

```
def hello(fname, lname, datestring=''):
    msg = 'Hello ' + fname + ' ' + lname
    if len(datestring) > 0:
        msg += ' you mentioned ' + datestring
    print(msg)
```

Logically, the code inside the function does the following

» Create a variable named `msg` and put in `Hello` and the first and last name.

» If the `datestring` passed has a length greater than 0, add " you mentioned " and that `datestring` to the `msg` variable.

» Print whatever is in the `msg` variable at this point.

Figure 5-6 shows two examples of calling this version of the function. The first call passes three values, and the second call passes only two. Both work because the third parameter is optional. The output from the first call is the full output including the date, and the output from the second omits the part about the date.

FIGURE 5-6:
Calling the
`hello()` function
with three
parameters, and
again with two
parameters.

```
def hello(fname, lname, datestring=''):
    msg = 'Hello ' + fname + ' ' + lname
    if len(datestring) > 0:
        msg += ' you mentioned ' + datestring
    print(msg)

hello('Alan', 'Simpson', '12/31/2019')
hello('Sammy', 'Schmeedledorp')


Hello Alan Simpson you mentioned 12/31/2019
Hello Sammy Schmeedledorp
```

Using keyword arguments (kwargs)

If you've ever looked at the official Python documentation at Python.org, you may have noticed that they throw around the term *kwargs* a lot. That's short for *keyword arguments* and is yet another way to pass data to a function.

The term *argument* is the technical term for "the value you are passing to a function's parameters." So far, we've used strictly positional arguments. For example, consider these three parameters:

```
def hello(fname, lname, datestring=''):
```

When you call the function like this:

```
hello("Alan", "Simpson")
```

Python assumes "Alan" is the first name, because it's the first argument passed and `fname` is the first parameter in the function. "Simpson", the second argument, is assumed to be `lname` because `lname` is the second parameter in the `def` statement. The `datestring` is assumed to be empty because `datestring` is the third parameter in the `def` statement and nothing is being passed as a third argument.

As an alternative to relying solely on an argument's position in the code to associate it with a parameter name, you can tell the function what's what by using the syntax *parameter = value* in the code calling the function. For example, take a look at this call to `hello`:

```
hello(datestring='12/31/2019', lname='Simpson', fname='Alan')
```

When you run this code, it works fine even though the order of the arguments passed doesn't match the order of the parameter names in the `def` statement. But the order doesn't matter here because the parameter name that each argument goes with is included with the call. Clearly the `'Alan'` argument goes with the `fname` parameter because `fname` is the name of the parameter in the `def` statement.

The same concept applies if you pass variables. Again, the order doesn't matter. In the following example, the values to be passed to the function are first placed in variables named `attpt_date`, `last_name`, and so forth. Then the last line calls the `hello()` function again as in previous examples. But the value assigned to each parameter name is the name of a variable, not a literal value being passed in.

```
appt_date = '12/30/2019'
last_name = 'Janda'
first_name = 'Kylie'
hello(datestring=apt_date, lname=last_name, fname=first_name)
```

Figure 5-7 shows the result of running the code both ways. As you can see, it all works fine. There's no ambiguity about which argument goes with which parameter because the parameter name is specified in the calling code.

```
: def hello(fname, lname, datestring):    # Practice function
      """ A docstring describing the function """
      msg = "Hello " + fname + " " + lname
      msg += " you mentioned " + datestring
      print(msg)

  # Pass in in literal kwargs (identify each by parameter name)
  hello(datestring='12/31/2019', lname='Simpson', fname='Alan')

  # Pass in in kwargs from variables (identify each by parameter name)
  appt_date = '12/30/2019'
  last_name = 'Janda'
  first_name = 'Kylie'
  hello(datestring=appt_date, lname=last_name, fname=first_name)

Hello Alan Simpson you mentioned 12/31/2019
Hello Kylie Janda you mentioned 12/30/2019
```

FIGURE 5-7:
Calling a function with keyword arguments (kwargs).

Passing multiple values in a list

So far we've been passing one piece of data at a time. But you can also pass iterables to a function. Remember an *iterable* is anything that Python can loop through to get values. A list is a simple and perhaps the most commonly used iterable.

The main trick to working with lists is this: If you want to alter the list contents (for example, by sorting the contents), make a copy of the list in the function and then make changes to the copy. You have to work with a copy of the list that was passed because the function doesn't receive the original list in a mutable (changeable) format; it receives only a pointer to the list, which indicates the list's location. Then the function can get the list's contents. The function can do anything it likes with its own copy of the list, but the original list remains unchanged.

After you have a copy of the list inside the function, you can sort that copy using the simple sort() method. Or, if you want to sort in descending order, use sort(reverse=True).

For example, here is a new function named alphabetize() that takes one argument called names. The name of the parameter being passed in is original_list. The entire parameter declaration is original_list=[]. The square brackets indicate an empty list as the default, in case nothing is passed in as a parameter. In other words, we're using =[] to define the default input as an empty list. The function can alphabetize a list of any number of words or names:

```python
def alphabetize(original_list=[]):
    """ Pass any list in square brackets, displays a string with items
    sorted """
    # Inside the function make a working copy of the list passed in.
    sorted_list = original_list.copy()
    # Sort the working copy.
    sorted_list.sort()
    # Make a new empty string for output
    final_list = ''
    # Loop through sorted list and append name and comma and space.
    for name in sorted_list:
        final_list += name + ', '
    # Knock off last comma space if the string is not blank
    final_list = final_list[:-2]
    # Print the alphabetized list.
    print(final_list)
```

The first line defines the function. Note that we used original_list=[] for the parameter. The default value (=[]) is optional, but we put it there so the function doesn't crash if you accidentally call it without passing in a list. Instead, it just creates an empty list. For example, when you start to type the function name in

VS Code, you get both the `def` statement and the docstring as IntelliSense help to remind you how to use the function, as in Figure 5-8.

Because the function can't alter the list directly, it first makes a copy of the original list (the one that was passed) in a new list called `sorted_list`, with this line of code:

```
sorted_list = original_list.copy()
```

At this point, `sorted_list` isn't really sorted; it's still just a copy of the original. The next line of code does the sorting:

```
sorted_list.sort()
```

This function creates a string with the sorted items separated by commas. So the next line creates a new variable name, `final_list` and, after the = sign, starts the variable off as an empty string (two single quotation marks with no space between):

```
final_list = ''
```

This loop loops through the sorted list and adds each item in the list, separated by a comma and a space, to the `final_list` string:

```
for name in sorted_list:
    final_list += name + ', '
```

When that's done, if anything was added to `final_list`, it will have an extra comma and a space at the end. The following statement removes those last two characters, assuming the list is at least two characters in length:

```
final_list = final_list[:-2]
```

The next statement just prints `final_list` so you can see it.

To call the function, you can pass a list inside the parentheses of the function, like this:

```
alphabetize(['Schrepfer', 'Maier', 'Santiago', 'Adams'])
```

As always, you can also pass in the name of a variable that contains the list, as in this example:

```
names = ['Schrepfer', 'Maier', 'Santiago', 'Adams']
alphabetize(names)
```

Either way, the function displays those names in alphabetical order:

```
Adams, Maier, Santiago, Schrepfer
```

Passing in an arbitrary number of arguments

A list provides one way of passing a lot of values into a function. You can also design the function so that it accepts any number of arguments. Note that this method is not particularly faster or better, so use whichever is easiest or makes the most sense. To pass in any number of arguments, use *args as the parameter name, like this:

```
def sorter(*args):
```

Whatever you pass in becomes a tuple named args inside the function. Remember, a tuple is an immutable list (a list you can't change). So again, if you want to change things, you need to copy the tuple to a list and then work on that copy. Here is an example where the code uses the simple statement newlist = list(args). You can read that as *the variable named newlist is a list of all the things that are in the args tuple.* The next line, newlist.sort() sorts the list, and print displays the contents of the list:

```
def sorter(*args):
    """ Pass in any number of arguments separated by commas
    Inside the function, they treated as a tuple named args. """

    # Create a list from the passed-in tuple.
    newlist = list(args)
    # Sort and show the list.
    newlist.sort()
    print(newlist)
```

Figure 5-9 shows an example of running this code with a series of numbers as arguments in a Jupyter cell. As you can see, the resulting list is in sorted order, as expected.

```
def sorter(*args):
    """ Pass in any number of arguments separated by commas
    Inside the function, they treated as a tuple named args """
    # The passed-in
    # Create a list from the passed-in tuple
    newlist = list(args)
    # Sort and show the list.
    newlist.sort()
    print(newlist)

sorter(1, 0.001, 100000,-900,  2)

[-900, 0.001, 1, 2, 100000]
```

FIGURE 5-9:
A function accepting any number of arguments with *args.

Returning Values from Functions

So far, all our functions have displayed output on the screen so you can make sure the function works. In real life, it's more common for a function to *return* some value and put it in a variable specified in the calling code. The line that does the returning is typically the last line of the function followed by a space and the name of the variable (or some expression) that contains the value to be returned.

Here is a variation of the alphabetize function. It contains no print statement. Instead, at the end, it simply returns the alphabetized list (final_list) that the function created:

```
def alphabetize(original_list=[]):
    """ Pass any list in square brackets, displays a string with items
    sorted """
    # Inside the function make a working copy of the list passed in.
    sorted_list = original_list.copy()
    # Sort the working copy.
    sorted_list.sort()
    # Make a new empty string for output
    final_list = ''
    # Loop through sorted list and append name and comma and space.
    for name in sorted_list:
        final_list += name + ', '
    # Knock off last comma space
    final_list = final_list[:-2]
    # Return the alphabetized list.
    return final_list
```

The most common way to use functions is to store whatever they return in some variable. For example, in the following code, the first line defines a variable called random_list, which is just a list containing names in no particular order, enclosed in square brackets (which tells Python it's a list). The second line creates a new variable named alpha_list by passing random_list to the alphabetize() function and storing whatever that function returns. The final print statement displays whatever is in the alpha_list variable:

```
random_list = ['McMullen', 'Keaser', 'Maier', 'Wilson', 'Yudt', 'Gallagher',
    'Jacobs']
alpha_list = alphabetize(random_list)
print(alpha_list)
```

Figure 5-10 shows the result of running the whole kit-and-caboodle in a Jupyter cell.

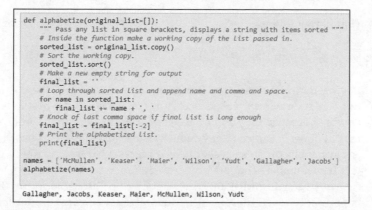

FIGURE 5-10: Printing a string returned by the alphabetize() function.

```
def alphabetize(original_list=[]):
    """ Pass any list in square brackets, displays a string with items sorted """
    # Inside the function make a working copy of the list passed in.
    sorted_list = original_list.copy()
    # Sort the working copy.
    sorted_list.sort()
    # Make a new empty string for output
    final_list = ''
    # Loop through sorted list and append name and comma and space.
    for name in sorted_list:
        final_list += name + ', '
    # Knock of last comma space if final list is long enough
    final_list = final_list[:-2]
    # Print the alphabetized list.
    print(final_list)

names = ['McMullen', 'Keaser', 'Maier', 'Wilson', 'Yudt', 'Gallagher', 'Jacobs']
alphabetize(names)
```

```
Gallagher, Jacobs, Keaser, Maier, McMullen, Wilson, Yudt
```

Unmasking Anonymous Functions

Python supports the concept of *anonymous functions,* also called *lambda functions.* The *anonymous* part of the name is based on the fact that the function doesn't need to have a name (but *can* have one if you want it to). The *lambda* part is based on the use of the keyword *lambda* to define anonymous functions in Python. In other words, when you see the word lambda in Python code, that line of code is defining an anonymous function.

The minimal syntax for defining a lambda expression (with no name) follows:

```
lambda arguments : expression
```

Replace *arguments* with the data being passed into the expression. And replace *expression* with an expression (formula) that defines what you want the anonymous function to return.

A common example of using this syntax is when you're trying to sort strings of text when some of the names start with uppercase letters and some start with lowercase letters, as in these names:

```
Adams, Ma, diMeola, Zandusky
```

Suppose you write the following code to put the names in a list, sort the list, and then print it:

```
names = ['Adams', 'Ma', 'diMeola', 'Zandusky']
names.sort()
print(names)
```

That output follows:

```
['Adams', 'Ma', 'Zandusky', 'diMeola']
```

Having diMeola come after Zandusky seems wrong to us and probably to you. But computers don't always see things the way we do. (Actually, they don't see anything because they don't have eyes or brains, but that's beside the point.) The reason diMeola comes after Zandusky is because the sort is based on ASCII, which is a system in which each character is represented by a number. All lowercase letters have numbers that are higher than uppercase numbers. So, when sorting, all the words starting with lowercase letters come after the words that start with an uppercase letter. If nothing else, this warrants at least a minor *hmm*.

To help with these matters, the Python sort() method lets you include a key= expression inside the parentheses, where you can tell it how to sort. The syntax is as follows:

```
.sort(key = transform)
```

The *transform* part is some variation on the data being sorted. If you're lucky and one of the built-in functions such as len (for *length*) will work, you can use that in place of *transform*, like this:

```
names.sort(key=len)
```

Unfortunately for us, the length of the string doesn't help with alphabetizing. So when you run this line of code, the order is

```
['Ma', 'Adams', 'diMeola', 'Zandusky']
```

The sort is going from the shortest string (the one with the fewest characters) to the longest string. Not helpful at the moment.

You can't write key=lower or key=upper to base the sort on all lowercase or all uppercase letters either, because lower and upper aren't built-in functions (which you can verify quickly by doing a web search for *python 3.7 built-in functions*).

In lieu of a built-in function, you can use a custom function that you define using def. For example, we can create a function named lowercaseof() that accepts a string and returns that string with all its letters converted to lowercase. Here is the function:

```
def lowercaseof(anystring):
    """ Converts string to all lowercase """
    return anystring.lower()
```

We made up the name lowercaseof, and anystring is a placeholder for whatever string you pass to it in the future. The line return anystring.lower() returns that string converted to all lowercase by using the .lower() method of the str (string) object.

**TECHNICAL
STUFF**

Suppose you write this function in a Jupyter cell or .py file. Then you call the function with something like print(lowercaseof('Zandusky')). What you get as output is the string converted to all lowercase, as in Figure 5-11.

FIGURE 5-11:
Putting a
custom function
named lower
caseof() to
the test.

```
: def lowercaseof(anystring):
      """ Converts string to all lowercase """
      return anystring.lower()

  print(lowercaseof('Zandusky'))

  zandusky
```

Okay, so now we have a custom function to convert any string to all lowercase letters. How do we use that as a sort key? Easy. Use key=*transform* the same as before, but replace *transform* with your custom function name. Our function is named `lowercaseof`, so we'd use `.sort(key=lowercaseof)`, as shown in the following:

```python
def lowercaseof(anystring):
    """ Converts string to all lowercase """
    return anystring.lower()

names = ['Adams', 'Ma', 'diMeola', 'Zandusky']
names.sort(key=lowercaseof)
```

Running this code to display the list of names puts them in the correct order, because it based the sort on strings that are all lowercase. The displayed names are the same as before because only the sorting, which took place behind the scenes, used lowercase letters. The original data is still in its original uppercase and lowercase letters.

```
'Adams', 'diMeola', 'Ma', 'Zandusky'
```

If you're still awake and conscious after reading all this, you may be thinking, "Okay, you solved the sorting problem. But I thought we were talking about lambda functions here. Where's the lambda function?" There is no lambda function yet. But this is a perfect example of where you *could* use a lambda function, because the function you're calling, `lowercaseof()`, does all its work with just one line of code: `return anystring.lower()`.

When your function can do its thing with a simple one-line expression like that, you can skip the `def` and the function name and just use this syntax:

```
lambda parameters : expression
```

Replace *parameters* with one or more parameter names that you make up yourself (the names inside the parentheses after `def` and the function name in a regular function). Replace *expression* with what you want the function to return without the word `return`. So in this example, the key, using a lambda expression, would be

```
lambda anystring: anystring.lower()
```

Now you can see why it's an anonymous function. The entire first line with function name `lowercaseof()` has been removed. So the advantage of using the lambda expression is that you don't even need the external custom function. You just need the parameter followed by a colon and an expression that tells it what to return.

Figure 5-12 shows the complete code and the result of running it. You get the proper sort order without the need for a customer external function like `lower-caseof()`. You just use `anystring:  anystring.lower()` (after `lambda`) as the sort key.

FIGURE 5-12:
Using a lambda expression as a sort key.

```
names = ['Adams', 'Ma', 'diMeola', 'Zandusky']
names.sort(key = lambda anystring : anystring.lower())
print(names)
```

```
['Adams', 'diMeola', 'Ma', 'Zandusky']
```

Note that `anystring` is a longer parameter name than most Pythonistas would use. Python folks are fond of short names, even single-letter names. For example, you could replace `anystring` with `s` (or any other letter), as in the following, and the code would work the same:

```
names = ['Adams', 'Ma', 'diMeola', 'Zandusky']
names.sort(key=lambda s: s.lower())
print(names)
```

Way back at the beginning of this section we mentioned that `lambda` functions don't have to be anonymous. You can give them names and call them as you would other functions.

For example, here is a `lambda` function named `currency` that takes any number and returns a string in currency format (that is, with a leading dollar sign, commas between thousands, and two digits for pennies):

```
currency = lambda n: f"${n:,.2f}"
```

Here is one named `percent` that multiplies any number you send to it by 100 and displays it with two digits after the decimal point and a percent sign at the end:

```
percent = lambda n: f"{n:.2%}"
```

Figure 5-13 shows examples of both functions defined at the top of a Jupyter cell. Then a few `print` statements call the functions by name and pass some sample data to them. Each `print()` statement displays the number in the desired format.

```
# Show number in currency format.
currency = lambda n : f"${n:,.2f}"
# Show number in percent format.
percent = lambda n : f"{n:.2%}"

# Test currency function
print(currency(99))
print(currency(123456789.09876543))

# Test percent function
print(percent(0.065))
print(percent(.5))
```

```
$99.00
$123,456,789.10
6.50%
50.00%
```

FIGURE 5-13:
Two anonymous
functions
for formatting
numbers.

The reason you can define those two functions as single-line lambda expressions is because you can do all the work in one line, `f"${n:,.2f}"` for the first one and `f"{n:.2%}"` for the second one. But just because you *can* do it that way, doesn't mean you *must*. You could use regular functions too, as follows:

```
# Show number in currency format.
def currency(n):
    return f"${n:,.2f}"


def percent(n):
# Show number in percent format.
    return f"{n:.2%}"
```

With this longer syntax, you could pass in more information too. For example, you might default to a right-aligned format within a certain width (say 15 characters) so all numbers are right aligned to the same width. Figure 5-14 shows this variation of the two functions.

```
# Show number in currency format, specify width.
def currency(n, w=15):
    """ Show in currency format, width = 15 or width of your choosing """
    s = f"${n:,.2f}"
    # Pad left of output with spaces to width of w.
    return s.rjust(w)

# Show number in percent format, specify width.
def percent(n, w=15):
    """ Show in percent format, width = 15 or width of your choosing """
    # Show number in percent format.
    s = f"{n:.1%}"
    # Pad left of output with spaces to width of w.
    return s.rjust(w)
```

FIGURE 5-14:
Two functions
for formatting
numbers with a
fixed width.

In Figure 5-14, the second parameter is optional and defaults to 15 if omitted. So if you call the currency() function like this:

```
print(currency(9999))
```

you get $9,999.00 padding with enough spaces on the left to make the output 15 characters wide. If you call the currency() function like this instead:

```
print(currency(9999,20))
```

you get $9,999.00 padded with enough spaces on the left to make the output 20 characters wide.

TIP

The .rjust() method used in Figure 5-14 is a Python built-in string method that right justifies content by padding the left side of a string with sufficient spaces to make it the specified width. There's also an .ljust() method that left justifies output by padding the right side. Furthermore, you're not limited to adding blanks spaces. You can add any character you like instead of a space.

We find the whole business of .ljust() and .rjust() confusing at times. When in doubt, just do a web search for *python left justify* or *python right justify* to get the details.

So there you have it, the ability to create your own custom functions in Python. In real life, any time you find that you need access to the same chunk of code — the same bit of logic — over and over again in your app, don't simply copy and paste that chunk of code over and over. Instead, put the code in a function that you can call by name. That way, if you decide to change the code, you don't have to go digging through your app to find all the places that need changing. Just change it in the function where it's all defined in one place.

IN THIS CHAPTER

» **Understanding classes and objects**

» **Learning how to create a class**

» **Initializing an object in a class**

» **Populating an object's attributes**

» **Discovering how to give a class methods**

» **Checking out class inheritance**

Chapter **6**

Doing Python with Class

In the preceding chapter, we talk about functions, which allow you to compartmentalize chunks of code that do specific tasks. In this chapter, you learn about classes, which allow you to compartmentalize code *and* data. You discover all the wonder, majesty, and beauty of classes and objects (okay, maybe we're overselling things a little there). But classes have become a defining characteristic of modern object-oriented programming languages such as Python.

We're aware we threw a whole lot of techno jargon your way in previous chapters. Don't worry. For the rest of this chapter we start off assuming that — like 99.9 percent of people in this world — you don't know a class from an object from a pastrami sandwich.

Mastering Classes and Objects

As you may know, Python is an object-oriented programming language. The concept of object-oriented programming (OOP) has been a major buzzword in the computer world for at least a couple decades. The term *object* stems from the fact that the model resembles objects in the real word in that each object is a thing that has certain attributes and characteristics that make it unique. For example, a chair is an object. Lots of different chairs exist that differ in size, shape, color, and material. But they're all still chairs.

How about cars? We all recognize a car when we see one. (Well, usually.) Even though cars aren't all exactly the same, they all have certain *attributes* (year, make, model, color) that make each unique. They have certain methods in common, where a *method* is an action or a thing the car can do. For example, cars all have go, stop, and turn actions that you control in pretty much the same way.

Figure 6-1 shows the concept where all cars (although not identical) have certain attributes and methods in common. In this case, you can think of the class Car as being a factory that creates all cars. After each car is created, it is an independent object. Changing one car has no effect on the other cars or the Car class.

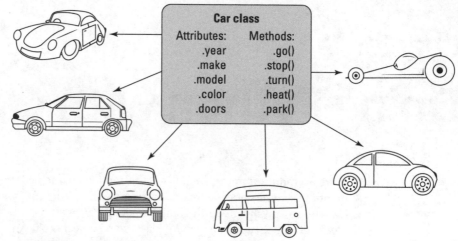

FIGURE 6-1:
Different car objects.

If the factory idea doesn't work for you, think of a class as a type of blueprint. For instance, consider dogs. No, there's no physical blueprint for creating dogs, but there's dog DNA that does pretty much the same thing. The dog DNA can be considered a type of blueprint (like a Python class) from which all dogs are created. Dogs vary in attributes such as breed, color, and size, but they share certain behaviors (methods) such as eat and sleep. Figure 6-2 shows an example of a class of animal called Dog from which all dogs originate.

Even people can be viewed as objects in this manner. For example, perhaps you have a club and want to keep track of its members. Each member is a person, of course. But in code you can create a Member class to store information about each member. Each member would have certain attributes — username, full name, and so forth. You could also have methods such as .archive() to deactivate an account and .restore() to reactivate an account. The .archive() and .restore() methods are behaviors that let you control membership, in much the same way the accelerator, brake, and steering wheel allow you to control a car. Figure 6-3 shows the concept.

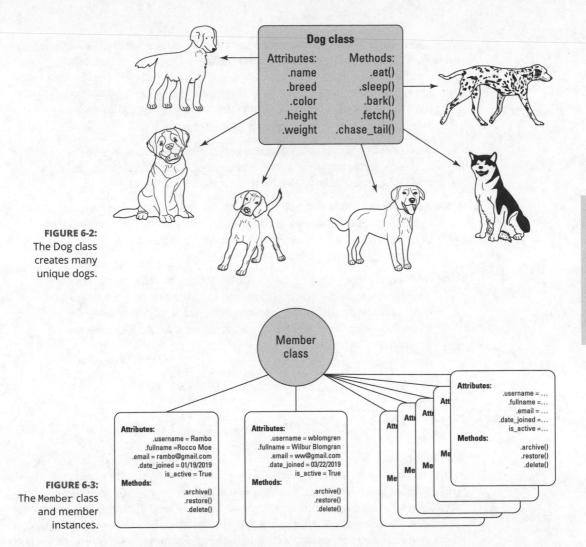

FIGURE 6-2:
The Dog class creates many unique dogs.

FIGURE 6-3:
The Member class and member instances.

The main point is that each instance of a class is an independent object with which you can work. Changing one instance of a class has no effect on the class or on other instances, just as painting one car a different color has no effect on the car factory or on any other cars produced by that factory.

So, going back to initial concepts, all this business of classes and instances stems from a type of programming called *object-oriented programming* (*OOP* for short). Python, like any significant, serious, modern programming language, is object-oriented. The main buzzwords you need to get comfortable with are the ones we've harped on in the last few paragraphs:

>> **Class:** A piece of code from which you can generate a unique object, where each object is a single instance of the class. Think of a class as a blueprint or factory from which you can create individual objects.

>> **Instance:** One unit of data plus code generated from a class as an instance of that class. Each instance of a class is also called an *object* just like all the different cars are objects, all created by some car factory (class).

>> **Attribute:** A characteristic of an object that contains information about the object. Also called a *property* of the object. An attribute name is preceded by a dot, as in member.username which may contain the username for one site member.

>> **Method:** A Python function associated with the class. A method defines an action that an object can perform. You call a method by preceding the method name with a dot and following it with a pair of parentheses. For example member.archive() might be a method that archives (deactivates) the member's account.

Creating a Class

You create your own classes like you create your own functions. You are free to name the class whatever you want, so long as it's a legitimate name that starts with a letter or underscore and contains no spaces or punctuation. It's customary to start a class name with an uppercase letter to help distinguish classes from variables. To get started, all you need is the word class followed by a space, a class name of your choosing, and a colon. For example, to create a new class named Member, use class Member:.

To make your code more descriptive, feel free to put a comment above the class definition. You can also put a docstring below the class line, which will show up whenever you type the class name in VS Code. For example, to add comments for your new Member class, you might type up the code like this:

```
# Define a new class name Member.
class Member:
    """ Create a new member. """
```

That's it for defining a new class. However, it isn't useful until you specify what attributes you want each object that you create from this class to inherit from the class.

EMPTY CLASSES

If you start a class with class *name*: and then run your code before finishing the class, you'll actually get an error. To get around that, you can tell Python that you're just not quite ready to finish writing the class by putting the keyword pass below the definition, as in the following code:

```
# Define a new class name Member.
class Member:
    pass
```

In essence, what you're doing there is telling Python "Hey I know this class doesn't really work yet, but just let it pass and don't throw an error message telling me about it."

Creating an Instance from a Class

To grant to your class the capability to create instances (objects) for you, you give the class an init method. The word *init* is short for *initialize*. As a method, it's really just a function defined inside a class. But it must have the specific name __init__ (that's two underscores followed by init followed by two more underscores).

TIP

That __init__ is sometimes spoken as "*dunder init.*" The *dunder* part is short for *double underline*.

The syntax for creating an init method is

```
def __init__(self[, suppliedprop1, suppliedprop2, ...])
```

The def is short for *define*, and __init__ is the name of the built-in Python method that's capable of creating objects from within a class. The self part is just a variable name and is used to refer to the object being created at the moment. You can use the name of your own choosing instead of self. But self would be considered by most a best practice because it's explanatory and customary.

This business of classes is easier to learn and understand if you start simply. So, for a working example, you'll create a class named Member, into which you'll pass a username (uname) and full name (fname) whenever you want to create a member. As always, you can precede the code with a comment. You can also put a docstring (in triple quotation marks) under the first line both as a comment but also as an IntelliSense reminder when typing code in VS Code:

```
# Define a class named Member for making member objects.
class Member:
    """ Create a member from uname and fname """
    def __init__(self, uname, fname):
```

When the `def __init__` line executes, you have an empty object named `self` inside the class. The `uname` and `fname` parameters hold whatever data you pass in; you see how that works in a moment.

An empty object with no data doesn't do you much good. What makes an object useful is its attributes: the information it contains that's unique to that object. So, in your class, the next step is to assign a value to each of the object's attributes.

Giving an Object Its Attributes

Now that you have a new, empty `Member` object, you can start giving it attributes and *populate* (store values in) those attributes. For example, let's say you want each member to have a `.username` attribute that contains the user's user name (perhaps for logging in). You have a second attribute named `fullname`, which is the member's full name. To define and populate those attributes, use the following:

```
self.username = uname
self.fullname = fname
```

The first line creates an attribute named `username` for the new instance (`self`) and puts into it whatever was passed into the `uname` attribute when the class was called. The second line creates an attribute named `fullname` for the new `self` object, and puts into it whatever was passed in as the `fname` variable. Add some comments and the entire class looks like this:

```
# Define a new class named Member.
class Member:
    """ Create a new member. """
    def __init__(self, uname, fname):
        # Define attributes and give them values.
        self.username = uname
        self.fullname = fname
```

Do you see what's happening? The `__init__` line creates a new empty object named `self`. Next, the `self.username = uname` line adds an attribute named `username` to the empty object, and puts into that attribute whatever was passed in as `uname`. Then the `self.fullname = fname` line does the same thing for the `fullname` attribute and the `fname` value that was passed in.

The convention for naming things in classes suggests using an initial cap for the class name. Attributes, however, should follow the standard for variables, which is all lowercase with an underscore to separate words within the name.

Creating an instance from a class

When you've created the class, you can create instances (objects) from it using this simple syntax:

```
this_instance_name = Member('uname', 'fname')
```

Replace *this_instance_name* with a name of your own choosing (in much the same way you may name a dog, who is an instance of the Dog class). Replace *uname* and *fname* with the username and full name you want to put into the object that will be created. Make sure you don't indent that code; otherwise, Python will think that new code still belongs to the class's code. It doesn't. It's new code to test the class.

So, for the sake of example, let's say you want to create a member named `new_guy` with the username `Rambo` and the full name `Rocco Moe`. Here's the code for that:

```
new_guy = Member('Rambo', 'Rocco Moe')
```

If you run this code and don't get any error messages, you know it at least ran. But to make sure, you can print the object or its attributes. To see what's really in the `new_guy` instance of `Members`, you can print it as a whole. You can also print just its attributes, `new_guy.username` and `new_guy.fullname`. You can also print `type(new_guy)` to ask Python what type `new_guy` is. This code does it all:

```
print(new_guy)
print(new_guy.username)
print(new_guy.fullname)
print(type(new_guy))
```

Figure 6-4 shows the code and the result of running it in a Jupyter cell.

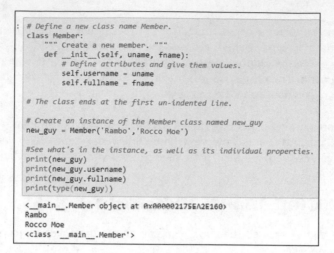

FIGURE 6-4:
Creating a member from the Member class in a Jupyter cell.

```
: # Define a new class name Member.
  class Member:
      """ Create a new member. """
      def __init__(self, uname, fname):
          # Define attributes and give them values.
          self.username = uname
          self.fullname = fname

  # The class ends at the first un-indented line.

  # Create an instance of the Member class named new_guy
  new_guy = Member('Rambo','Rocco Moe')

  #See what's in the instance, as well as its individual properties.
  print(new_guy)
  print(new_guy.username)
  print(new_guy.fullname)
  print(type(new_guy))

  <__main__.Member object at 0x000002175EA2E160>
  Rambo
  Rocco Moe
  <class '__main__.Member'>
```

In the figure, you can see that the first line of output is

```
<__main__.Member object at 0x000002175EA2E160>
```

This output tells you that new_guy is an object created from the Member class. The number at the end is its location in memory. Don't worry about that; you won't need to know about memory locations right now.

The next three lines of output are

```
Rambo
Rocco Moe
<class '__main__.Member'>
```

The first line is the username of new_guy (new_guy.username), and the second line is the full name of new_guy (new_guy.fullname). The last line is the type and tells you that new_guy is an instance of the Member class.

WARNING

Much as we hate to put any more burden on your brain cells right now, the words *object* and *property* are synonymous with *instance* and *attribute*. The new_guy instance of the Member class can also be called an object, and the fullname and username attributes of new_guy can also be called properties of that object.

Admittedly, it can be difficult to wrap your head around all these concepts, but just remember that an object is simply a handy way to encapsulate information about an item that's similar to other items (like all dogs are dogs and all cars are cars). What makes the item unique is its attributes, which won't necessarily be the same as the attributes of other objects of the same type, in much the same way that not all dogs are the same breed and not all cars are the same color.

We intentionally used uname and fname as parameter names to distinguish them from the attribute names username and fullname. However, this isn't a requirement. In fact, if anything, people tend to use the same names for the parameters as they do for the attributes.

Instead of uname for the parameter name, you can use username (even though it's the same as the attribute name). Likewise, you can use fullname in place of fname. Doing so won't alter how the class behaves. You just have to remember that the same name is being used in two different ways, first as a placeholder for data being passed into the class, and then later as an attribute name that gets its value from that passed-in value.

Figure 6-5 shows the same code as Figure 6-4 with uname replaced with username and fname replaced with fullname. Running the code produces the same output as before; using the same name for two different things didn't bother Python one bit.

```
# Define a new class name Member.
class Member:
    """ Create a new member. """
    def __init__(self, username, fullname):
        # Define attributes and give them values.
        self.username = username
        self.fullname = fullname

# The class ends at the first un-indented line.

# Create an instance of the Member class named new_guy
new_guy = Member('Rambo','Rocco Moe')

#See what's in the instance, as well as its individual properties.
print(new_guy)
print(new_guy.username)
print(new_guy.fullname)
print(type(new_guy))

<__main__.Member object at 0x000002175EA2E240>
Rambo
Rocco Moe
<class '__main__.Member'>
```

FIGURE 6-5:
The Member class with username and fullname for both parameters and attributes.

After you type a class name and the opening parenthesis in VS Code, its Intelli-Sense shows you the syntax for parameters and the first docstring in the code, as shown in Figure 6-6. Naming things in a way that's meaningful and including a descriptive docstring in the class makes it easier for you to remember how to use the class in the future.

FIGURE 6-6:
VS Code displays help when you access your own custom classes.

```
 7            self.full  Member(self, username, fullname)
 8
 9       # The class ends   param username
10
11       # Create an insta   Create a new member.
12       new_guy = Member(
```

Changing the value of an attribute

When working with tuples, you can define *key:value* pairs, much like the *attribute:value* pairs you see here with instances of a class. There is one major difference, though: Tuples are immutable, meaning that after they're defined, your code can't change anything about them. This is not true with objects. After you create an object, you can change the value of any attribute at any time using the following simple syntax:

```
objectname.attributename = value
```

Replace `objectname` with the name of the object (which you've already created via the class). Replace `attributename` with the name of the attribute whose value you want to change. Replace `value` with the new value.

Figure 6-7 shows an example in which, after initially creating the `new_guy` object, the following line of code executes:

```
new_guy.username = "Princess"
```

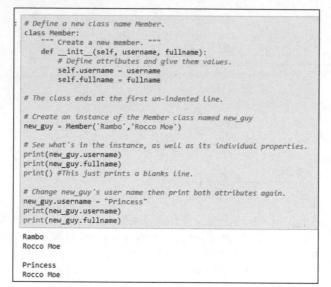

```
# Define a new class name Member.
class Member:
    """ Create a new member. """
    def __init__(self, username, fullname):
        # Define attributes and give them values.
        self.username = username
        self.fullname = fullname

# The class ends at the first un-indented line.

# Create an instance of the Member class named new_guy
new_guy = Member('Rambo','Rocco Moe')

# See what's in the instance, as well as its individual properties.
print(new_guy.username)
print(new_guy.fullname)
print() #This just prints a blanks line.

# Change new_guy's user name then print both attributes again.
new_guy.username = "Princess"
print(new_guy.username)
print(new_guy.fullname)
```

```
Rambo
Rocco Moe

Princess
Rocco Moe
```

FIGURE 6-7: Changing the value of an object's attribute.

The lines of output under that show that `new_guy`'s `username` has indeed been changed to `Princess`. His full name hasn't changed because you didn't do anything to that in your code.

Defining attributes with default values

You don't have to pass in the value of every attribute for a new object. If you're always going to give an attribute some default value at the moment the object is created, you can just use self.*attributename* = *value*, the same as before, in which *attributename* is a name of your own choosing. And *value* can be some value you just set, such as True or False for a Boolean, or today's date, or anything that can be calculated or determined by Python without you providing the value.

For example, let's say that whenever you create a new member, you want to track the date you created that member in an attribute named date_joined. And you want to be able to activate and deactivate accounts to control user logins. So you create an attribute named is_active and decide to start a new member with that attribute set to True.

If you're going to be doing anything with dates and times, you'll want to import the datetime module, so put that at the top of your file, even before the class Member: line. Then you can add the following lines before or after the other lines that assign values to attributes within the class:

```
self.date_joined = dt.date.today()
self.is_active = True
```

Here is how you could add the import and those two new attributes to the class:

```
import datetime as dt

# Define a new class name Member.
class Member:
    """ Create a new member. """
    def __init__(self, username, fullname):
        # Define attributes and give them values.
        self.username = username
        self.fullname = fullname

        # Default date_joined to today's date.
        self.date_joined = dt.date.today()
        # Set is active to True initially.
        self.is_active = True
```

WARNING

If you forget to import datetime at the top of the code, you'll get an error message when you run the code, telling you it doesn't know what dt.date.today() means. Just add the import line to the top of the code and try again.

There is no need to pass any new data into the class for the date_joined and is_active attributes because those attributes get default values from the code.

Note that a default value is just that: It's a value that is assigned automatically when you create the object. But you can change a default value in the same way you would change any other attribute's value, using this syntax:

```
objectname.attributename = value
```

For example, suppose you use the is_active attribute to determine whether a user is active and can log into your site. If a member turns out to be an obnoxious troll and you don't want him logging in anymore, you could just change the is_active attribute to False like this:

```
newmember.is_active = False
```

Giving a Class Methods

Any object you define can have any number of attributes, each given any name you like, to store information *about* the object, such as a dog's breed and color or a car's make and model. You can also define you own methods for any object, which are more like behaviors than facts about the object. For example, a dog can eat, sleep, and bark. A car can go, stop, and turn. A method is really just a function, as you learned in the preceding chapter. What makes it a method is the fact that it's associated with a particular class and with each specific object you create from that class.

Method names are distinguished from attribute names for an object by the pair of parentheses that follow the name. To define what the methods will be in your class, use this syntax for each method:

```
def methodname(self[, param1, param2, ...]):
```

Replace *methodname* with a name of your choosing (all lowercase, no spaces). Keep the word self in there as a reference to the object being defined by the class. Optionally, you can also pass in parameters after self using commas, as with any other function.

REMEMBER

Never type the square brackets ([]). They're shown here in the syntax only to indicate that parameter names after self are allowed but not required.

Let's create a method named .show_date_joined() that returns the user's name and the date the user joined in a formatted string. Here is how you could define this method:

```
# A method to return a formatted string showing date joined.
def show_datejoined(self):
    return f"{self.fullname} joined on {self.date_joined:%m/%d/%y}"
```

The name of the method is show_datejoined. The task of this method, when called, is to simply put together some nicely formatted text containing the member's full name and date joined.

To call the method from your code, use this syntax:

```
objectname.methodname()
```

Replace *objectname* with the name of the object to which you're referring. Replace *methodname* with the name of the method you want to call. Include the parentheses (no spaces). If the class's __init__ method specifies only self, you don't pass anything in. However, if the __init__ specifies additional parameters beyond self, you need to specify values for them. Figure 6-8 shows the complete example.

Note in Figure 6-8 how the show_datejoined() method is defined within the class. Its def is indented to the same level of the first def. The code that the method executes is indented under that. Outside the class, new_guy = Member('Rambo', 'Rocco Moe') creates a new member named new_guy. Then new_guy.show_datejoined() executes the show_datejoined() method, which in turn displays Rocco Moe joined 11/18/20, the day we ran the code.

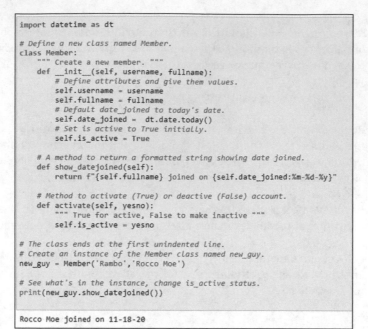

```
import datetime as dt

# Define a new class named Member.
class Member:
    """ Create a new member. """
    def __init__(self, username, fullname):
        # Define attributes and give them values.
        self.username = username
        self.fullname = fullname
        # Default date_joined to today's date.
        self.date_joined = dt.date.today()
        # Set is active to True initially.
        self.is_active = True

    # A method to return a formatted string showing date joined.
    def show_datejoined(self):
        return f"{self.fullname} joined on {self.date_joined:%m-%d-%y}"

    # Method to activate (True) or deactive (False) account.
    def activate(self, yesno):
        """ True for active, False to make inactive """
        self.is_active = yesno

# The class ends at the first unindented line.
# Create an instance of the Member class named new_guy.
new_guy = Member('Rambo','Rocco Moe')

# See what's in the instance, change is_active status.
print(new_guy.show_datejoined())

Rocco Moe joined on 11-18-20
```

FIGURE 6-8:
Changing the value of an object's attributes.

Passing parameters to methods

You can pass data into methods in the same way you do functions: by using parameter names inside the parentheses. However, keep in mind that self is always the first name after the method name, and you never pass data to the self parameter. For example, let's say you want to create a method called .activate() and set it to True if the user is allowed to log in or False when the user isn't. Whatever you pass in is assigned to the .is_active attribute. Here's how to define that method in your code:

```
# Method to activate (True) or deactivate (False) account.
def activate(self, yesno):
    """ True for active, False to make inactive """
    self.is_active = yesno
```

The docstring is optional. However, the docstring would appear on the screen when you're typing relevant code in VS Code, so it would serve as a good reminder about what you can pass in. When executed, this method doesn't display anything on the screen; it just changes the is_active attribute for that member to whatever you passed in as the yesno parameter.

REMEMBER

It helps to understand that a method is really just a function. What makes a method different from a function is the fact that a method is always associated with some class. So a method is not as generic as a function.

Figure 6-9 shows the entire class followed by some code to test it. The line `new_guy = Member('Rambo', 'Rocco Moe')` creates a new member object named `new_guy`. Then `print(new_guy.is_active)` displays the value of the `is_active` attribute, which is `True` because that's the default for all new members.

```
import datetime as dt

# Define a new class named Member.
class Member:
    """ Create a new member. """
    def __init__(self, username, fullname):
        # Define attributes and give them values.
        self.username = username
        self.fullname = fullname
        # Default date_joined to today's date.
        self.date_joined = dt.date.today()
        # Set is active to True initially.
        self.is_active = True

    # A method to return a formatted string showing date joined.
    def show_datejoined(self):
        return f"{self.fullname} joined on {self.date_joined:%m-%d-%y}"

    # Method to activate (True) or deactive (False) account.
    def activate(self, yesno):
        """ True for active, False to make inactive """
        self.is_active = yesno

# The class ends at the first unindented line.

# Create an instance of the Member class named new_guy.
new_guy = Member('Rambo','Rocco Moe')

# Is the new guy active?
print(new_guy.is_active)

# Try out the activate method.
new_guy.activate(False)

# Is the new guy still active?
print(new_guy.is_active)

True
False
```

FIGURE 6-9
Adding and testing an `.activate()` method.

The line `new_guy.activate(False)` calls the `activate()` method for that object and passes to it a Boolean `False`. Then `print(new_guy.is_active)` proves that the call to activate did indeed change the `is_active` attribute for `new_guy` from `True` to `False`.

Calling a class method by class name

As you've seen, you can call a class's method using the following syntax:

```
specificobject.method()
```

An alternative is to use the specific class name, which can help make the code easier for humans to understand:

```
Classname.method(specificobject)
```

Replace *Classname* with the name of the class (which we typically define starting with an uppercase letter), followed by the method name, and then put the specific object (which you've presumably already created) inside the parentheses.

For example, suppose we create a new member named `wilbur` using the `Member` class and this code:

```
wilbur = Member('wblomgren', 'Wilbur Blomgren')
```

Here, `wilbur` is the specific object we created from the `Member` class. We can call the `show_datejoined()` method on that object by using the syntax you've already seen:

```
print(wilbur.show_datejoined())
```

The alternative is to call the `show_datejoined()` method of the `Member` class and pass to it that specific object, `wilbur`, like this:

```
print(Member.show_datejoined(wilbur))
```

The output from both methods is the same (but with the date on which you ran the code):

```
Wilbur Blomgren joined on 11/18/20
```

The latter method isn't faster, slower, better, worse, or anything like that. It's just an alternative syntax you can use, and some people prefer it because starting the line with `Member` makes it clear to which class the `show_datejoined()` method belongs. This in turn can make the code more readable by other programmers or by yourself a year from now when you don't remember any of the things you wrote in the app.

Using class variables

So far you've seen examples of attributes, which are sometimes called *instance variables*, because they're placeholders that contain information that varies from one instance of the class to another. For example, in a Dog class, `dog.breed` may be `Poodle` for one dog but `Schnauzer` for another dog.

Another type of variable you can use with classes is called a *class variable*, which is applied to all new instances of the class that haven't been created yet. Class variables inside a class don't have any tie-in to self because the self keyword always refers to the specific object being created at the moment. To define a class variable, place the mouse pointer above the def __init__ line and define the variable using the standard syntax:

```
variablename = value
```

Replace *variablename* with a name of your own choosing, and replace *value* with the specific value you want to assign to that variable. For example, let's say your code includes a free_days variable that grants people three months (90 days) of free access on sign-up. You're not sure if you want to commit to this forever, so rather than hardcode it into your app (so it's difficult to change), you can just make it a class variable that's automatically applied to all new objects, like this:

```
# Define a class named Member for making member objects.
class Member:
    """ Create a member object """
    free_days = 90

    def __init__(self, username, fullname):
```

Because we define the free_days variable before we define __init__, it's not tied to a specific object in the code.

Now suppose that later in the code, you want to store the date that the free trial expires. You could have an attribute named date_joined that represents the date that the member joined and another attribute named free_expires that represents the date that the user's free membership expires. You could determine the second date by adding the number of free days to the date the member joined. Intuitively, it may seem as though you could add free_days to the date using a simple syntax like this:

```
self.free_expires = dt.date.today() + dt.timedelta(days=free_days)
```

But if you tried to run this code, you'd get an error saying Python doesn't recognize the free_days variable name (even though it's defined right at the top of the class). Instead, you must precede the variable name with the class name or self. For example, this would work:

```
self.free_expires = dt.date.today() + dt.timedelta(days=Member.free_days)
```

Figure 6-10 shows the bigger picture. We removed some of the code from the original class to trim it and make it easier to focus on the new stuff. The `free_days = 365` line near the top sets the value of the `free_days` variable to 365. (We used 90 days in the previous example, but this is a new example, and we want to illustrate how the same code works with any number of days you specify in the `free_days` variable.) Then, later in the code, the `__init__` method uses `Member.free_freedays` to add that number of days to the current date. Running this code by creating a new member named `wilbur` and viewing his `date_joined` and `free_expires` attributes shows the current date (when you run the code) and the date 365 days after that.

```
import datetime as dt
# Define a new class name Member.
class Member:
    # Default number of free days.
    free_days = 365

    """ Create a new member. """
    def __init__(self, username, fullname):
        self.date_joined = dt.date.today()
        # Set an expiration date
        self.free_expires = dt.date.today() + dt.timedelta(days = Member.free_days)

# The class ends at the first un-indented line.

# Create an instance of the Member class named new_guy.
wilbur = Member('wblomgren', 'Wilbur Blomegren')

print(wilbur.date_joined)
print(wilbur.free_expires)

2020-11-18
2021-11-18
```

FIGURE 6-10:
The free_days variable is a class variable in the Member class.

What if you later decide that giving people 90 free days is plenty. You could just change the 365 day value back to 90 in the class directly. Since it's a variable, you can do it on-the-fly, like this, outside the class:

```
#Set a default for free days.
Member.free_days = 90
```

When you run this code, you still create a user named `wilbur` with `date_joined` and `free_days` variables. But this time, `wilbur.free_expires` will be 90 days after the `datejoined`, not 365 days.

Using class methods

Recall that a method is a function that's tied to a particular class. So far, the methods you've used, such as `.show_datejoined()` and `.activate()`, have been *instance methods,* because you always use them with a specific object — a specific instance of the class. With Python, you can also create class methods.

As the name implies, a *class method* is a method associated with the class as a whole, not specific instances of the class. In other words, class methods are similar in scope to class variables in that they apply to the whole class and not just individual instances of the class.

As with class variables, you don't need the `self` keyword with class methods because that keyword always refers to the specific object being created at the moment, not to all objects created by the class. So for starters, if you want a method to do something to the class as a whole, don't use def *name*(`self`) because the `self` immediately ties the method to one object.

It would be nice if all you had to do to create a class method is exclude the word `self`, but unfortunately it doesn't work that way. To define a class method, you first need to type this into your code:

```
@classmethod
```

The @ at the start of this defines `classmethod` as a decorator — yep, yet another term to add to your ever-growing list of nerd-o-rama buzzwords. A *decorator* is generally something that alters or extends the functionality of that to which it is applied.

Below that line, define your class method using this syntax:

```
def methodname(cls,x, ...):
```

Replace *methodname* with the name you want to give your method. Leave the `cls` as-is because it's a reference to the class as a whole (because the `@classmethod` decorator defined it as such behind-the-scenes). After `cls`, you can have commas and the names of parameters that you want to pass to the method, just as you can with regular instance methods.

For example, suppose you want to define a method that sets the number of free days just before you start creating objects, so that all objects get the same `free_days` amount. The following code accomplishes that by first defining a class variable named `free_days` that has a given default value of 0. (The default value can be anything.)

Further down in the class is this class method:

```
# Class methods follow @classmethod decorator and refer to cls rather than
# to self.
@classmethod
def setfreedays(cls,days):
    cls.free_days = days
```

This code tells Python that when someone calls the setfreedays() method on this class, it should set the value of cls.free_days (the free_days class variable for this class) to whatever number of days were passed in. Figure 6-11 shows a complete example in a Jupyter cell (which you can type and try for yourself), and the results of running that code.

```
import datetime as dt

# Define a new class named Member.
class Member:
    # Default number of free days.
    free_days = 365

    """ Create a new member. """
    def __init__(self, username, fullname):
        self.date_joined = dt.date.today()
        # Set an expiration date.
        self.free_expires = dt.date.Today() + dt.timedelta(days - Member.free_days)

    # Class methods follow @classmethod decorator and refer to cls rather than to self.
    @classmethod
    def setfreedays(cls,days):
        cls.free_days = days
```

FIGURE 6-11:
The setfreedays() method is a class method in the Member class.

REMEMBER

It's easy to forget that uppercase and lowercase letters matter a lot in Python, especially since it seems you're using lowercase 99.9 percent of the time. But as a rule, class names start with an initial cap, so any call to the class name must also start with an initial cap.

Using static methods

Just when you thought you may finally be finished learning about classes, it turns out there is another kind of method you can create in a Python class. It's called a static method and it starts with this decorator: @staticmethod.

So that part is easy. What makes a static method different from instance and class methods is that a *static method* doesn't relate specifically to an instance of an object or even to the class as a whole. It is a generic function, and the only reason to define it as part of a class is if you want to use the same name elsewhere in another class in your code.

Wherever you want a static method, you type the `@staticmethod` line. Below that line, you define the static method like any other method, but you don't use `self` and you don't use `cls` because a static method isn't strictly tied to a class or an object. Here's an example of a static method:

```
@staticmethod
def currenttime():
    now = dt.datetime.now()
    return f"{now:%I:%M %p}"
```

So we have a method called `currenttime()` that isn't expecting any data to be passed in and doesn't care about the object or class you're working with. The method just gets the current datetime using `now = dt.datetime.now()` and then returns that information in a nice 12:00 PM format.

Figure 6-12 shows a complete example in which you can see the static method properly indented and typed near the end of the class. When code outside the class calls `Member.currenttime()`, it dutifully returns the time at the moment, without your having to say anything about a specific object from that class.

```
import datetime as dt

# Define a class named Member for making member objects.
class Member:
    # This is a class variable that's the same for all instances.
    free_days = 0

    """ Create a member object from username and fullname """
    def __init__(self, username, fullname):
        # Define properties and assign default values.
        self.datejoined = dt.date.today()
        self.free_expires = dt.date.today() + dt.timedelta(Member.free_days)

    # Class methods follow @classmethods and use cls rather than self.
    @classmethod
    def setfreedays(cls,days):
        cls.free_days = days

    @staticmethod
    def currenttime():
        now = dt.datetime.now()
        return f"{now:%I:%M %p}"

# Class definition ends at last indented line

# Try out the new static method (no object required)
print(Member.currenttime())

03:24 PM
```

FIGURE 6-12:
The Member class now has a static method named currenttime().

Understanding Class Inheritance

People who are into object-oriented programming live to talk about class inheritance and subclasses and so on, stuff that means little or nothing to the average Joe or Josephine on the street. Still, what they're talking about as a Python concept is something you see in real life all the time.

As mentioned, if we consider dog DNA to be a kind of factory or Python class, we can lump all dogs together as members of a class of animals we call dogs. Even though each dog is unique, all dogs are still dogs because they are members of the class we call dogs, and we can illustrate that, as in Figure 6-13.

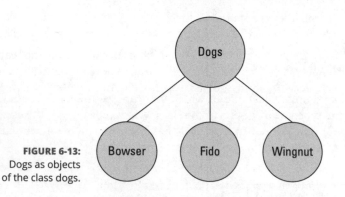

FIGURE 6-13:
Dogs as objects of the class dogs.

So each dog is unique (although no other dog is as good as yours), but what makes dogs similar to one another are the characteristics they *inherit* from the class of dogs.

The notions of class and class inheritance that Python and other object-oriented languages offer didn't materialize out of the clear blue sky just to make it harder and more annoying to learn this stuff. Much of the world's information can best be stored, categorized, and understood by using classes and subclasses and sub-subclasses, on down to individuals.

For example, you may have noticed that other dog-like creatures roam the planet (although they're probably not the kind you'd like to keep around the house as pets). Wolves, coyotes, and jackals come to mind. They are similar to dogs in that they all *inherit* their dogginess from a higher-level class we could call canines, as shown in Figure 6-14.

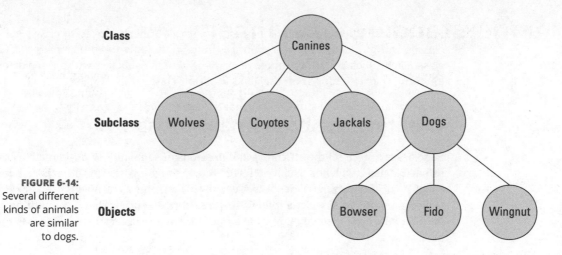

Class

Subclass

FIGURE 6-14:
Several different
kinds of animals
are similar
to dogs.

Objects

Using our dog analogy, we certainly don't need to stop at canines on the way up. We can put mammals above that, because all canines are mammals. We can put animals above that, because all mammals are animals. And we can put living things above that, because all animals are living things. So basically all the things that make a dog a dog stem from the fact that each *inherits* certain characteristics from numerous classes, or critters, that preceded it.

TECHNICAL STUFF

To the biology brainiacs out there, yes we know that Mammalia is a class, Canis is a genus, and below that are species. So you don't need to email or message us on that. We're using *class* and *subclass* terms here just to relate the *concept* to classes, subclasses, and objects in Python.

Obviously the concept doesn't apply just to dogs. The world has lots of different cats too. There's cute little Bootsy, with whom you'd be happy to share your bed, and plenty of other felines, such as lions, tigers, and jaguars, with whom you probably wouldn't.

TIP

If you do a web search for *living things hierarchy* and click Images, you'll see just how many ways there are to classify all living things, and how inheritance works its way down from the general to the specific living thing.

Even our car analogy can follow along with this. At the top, we have transportation vehicles. Under that, perhaps boats, planes, and automobiles. Under automobiles we have cars, trucks, vans, and so forth and so on, down to any one specific car. So classes and subclasses are nothing new. What's new is simply thinking about representing those things to mindless machines that we call computers. So let's see how you would do that.

From a coding perspective, the easiest way to do inheritance is to create subclasses within a class. The class defines things that apply to all instances of that class. Each subclass defines things relevant only to the subclass without replacing anything that's coming from the generic parent class.

Creating the base (main) class

Subclasses inherit all the attributes and methods of some higher-level main class, or parent class, which is usually referred to as the *base class*. This class is just any class, no different from what you've seen in this chapter so far. We'll use a Member class again, but we'll whittle it down to some bare essentials that have nothing to do with subclasses, so you don't have to dig through irrelevant code. Here is the basic class:

```python
# Class is used for all kinds of people.
import datetime as dt


# Base class is used for all kinds of Members.
class Member:
    """ The Member class attributes and methods are for everyone """
    # By default, a new account expires in one year (365 days)
    expiry_days = 365


    # Initialize a member object.
    def __init__(self, firstname, lastname):
        # Attributes (instance variables) for everybody.
        self.firstname = firstname
        self.lastname = lastname
        # Calculate expiry date from today's date.
        self.expiry_date = dt.date.today() + dt.timedelta(days=self.expiry_days)
```

By default, new accounts expire in one year. So this class first sets a class variable name expiry_days to 365 to be used in later code to calculate the expiration date from today's date. As you'll see later, we used a class variable to define expiry_days because we can give it a new value from a subclass.

To keep the code example simple and uncluttered, this version of the Member class accepts only two parameters, firstname and lastname.

Figure 6-15 shows an example of testing the code with a hypothetical member named Joe. Printing Joe's firstname, lastname, and expiry_date shows what you would expect the class to do when passing the firstname Joe and the lastname Anybody. When you run the code, the expiry_date should be one year from the date when you run the code.

```
import datetime as dt
# Class is used for all kinds of people.
import datetime as dt

# Base class is used for all kinds of Members.
class Member:
    """ The Member class attributes and methods are for everyone """
    # By default, a new account expires in one year (365 days)
    expiry_days = 365

    # Initialize a member object.
    def __init__(self, firstname, lastname):
        # Attributes (instance variables) for everybody.
        self.firstname = firstname
        self.lastname = lastname
        # Calculate expiry date from today's date.
        self.expiry_date = dt.date.today() + dt.timedelta(days=self.expiry_days)

# Outside the class now.
Joe = Member('Joe', 'Anybody')
print(Joe.firstname)
print(Joe.lastname)
print(Joe.expiry_date)

    Joe
    Anybody
    2019-12-08
```

FIGURE 6-15: A simplified Member class.

Doing Python with Class

Now suppose our real intent is to make two different kinds of users, Admins and Users. Both types of users will have the attributes that the Member class offers. So by defining those types of users as subclasses of Member, they will automatically get the same attributes (and methods, if any).

Defining a subclass

To define a subclass, make sure you get the cursor below the base class and back to no indentation, because the subclass isn't a part of, or contained within, the base class. To define a subclass, use this syntax:

```
class subclassname(mainclassname):
```

Replace *subclassname* with whatever you want to name this subclass. Replace *mainclassname* with the name of the base class, as defined at the top of the base class. For example, to make a subclass of Member named Admin, use the following:

```
class Admin(Member):
```

To create another subclass named User, add this code:

```
class User(Member):
```

If you leave the classes empty, you won't be able to test them because you'll get an error message telling you the class is empty. But you can put the word pass as the first command in each one. This is your way of telling Python "Yes I know these classes are empty, but let it pass, don't throw an error message." You can

CHAPTER 6 **Doing Python with Class** 241

put a comment above each one to remind you of what each one is for, as in the following:

```
# Subclass for Admins.
class Admin(Member):
    pass

# Subclass for Users.
class User(Member):
    pass
```

When you use the subclasses, you don't have to make any direct reference to the Member class. Admins and Users will both inherit all the Member stuff automatically. So, for example, to create an Admin named Annie, you'd use this syntax:

```
Ann = Admin('Annie', 'Angst')
```

To create a User, do the same thing with the User class and a name for the user. For example:

```
Uli = User('Uli', 'Ungula')
```

To see if this code works, you can do the same thing you did for member Ann. After you create the two accounts, use print() statements to see what's in them. Figure 6-16 shows the results of creating the two users. Ann is an Admin, and Uli is a User, but both automatically get all the attributes assigned to members. (The Member class is directly above the code shown in the image. We left that out because it hasn't changed.)

```
# Subclass for Admins.
class Admin(Member):
    pass

# Subclass for Users.
class User(Member):
    pass

Ann = Admin('Annie', 'Angst')
print(Ann.firstname)
print(Ann.lastname)
print(Ann.expiry_date)
print()
Uli = User('Uli', 'Ungula')
print(Uli.firstname)
print(Uli.lastname)
print(Uli.expiry_date)

Annie
Angst
2019-12-03

Uli
Ungula
2019-12-03
```

FIGURE 6-16:
Creating and testing the Admin and User classes.

So what you've learned here is that the subclass accepts all the different parameters that the base class accepts and assigns them to attributes, same as the Person class. But so far, Admin and User are just members with no unique characteristics. In real life, there will probably be some differences between these two types of users. In the next sections, you learn ways to make these differences happen.

Overriding a default value from a subclass

One of the simplest things you can do with a subclass is to give an attribute that has a default value in the base class some other value. For example, in the Member class we created a variable named expiry_days to be used later in the class to calculate an expiration date. But suppose you want Admin accounts to never expire (or to expire after some ridiculous duration so there's still some date there). Simply set the new expiry_date in the Admin class (and you can remove the pass line because the class won't be empty anymore). Here's how these changes might look in your Admin subclass:

```
# Subclass for Admins.
class Admin(Member):
    # Admin accounts don't expire for 100 years.
    expiry_days = 365.2422 * 100
```

Whatever value you pass will override the default set near the top of the Member class and will be used to calculate the Admin's expiration date.

Adding extra parameters from a subclass

Sometimes members of a subclass have a parameter value that other members don't. In that case, you may want to pass a parameter from the subclass that doesn't exist in the base class. Doing so is a little more complicated than just changing a default value, but it's a common technique so you should be aware of it. Let's work through an example.

For starters, your subclass will need its own def __init__ line that contains everything that's in the base class's __init__, plus any extra stuff you want to pass. For example, let's say admins have some secret code and you want to pass that from the Admin subclass. You still have to pass the first and last name, so your def __init__ line in the Admin subclass will look like this:

```
def __init__(self, firstname, lastname, secret_code):
```

The indentation level will be the same as the lines above it.

Next, any parameters that belong to the base class, `Member`, need to be passed up there using this rather odd-looking syntax:

```
super().__init__(param1, param2, ...)
```

Replace *param1*, *param2*, and so forth with the names of parameters you want to send to the base class. The information you're providing in the parameters should be everything that's already in the `Member` parameters excluding `self`. In this example, `Member` expects only `firstname` and `lastname`, so the code for this example is

```
super().__init__(firstname, lastname)
```

Whatever you didn't provide in the first set of parameters, you can assign to the subclass object using this code:

```
self.secret_code = parametername
```

Replace *parametername* with the name of the parameter that you didn't send up to `Member`. In this case, that would be the `secret_code` parameter. So the code would be:

```
self.secret_code = secret_code
```

Figure 6-17 shows an example in which we created an `Admin` user named `Ann` and passed `PRESTO` as her secret code. Printing all her attributes shows that she does indeed still have the right expiration date plus a secret code. As you can see, we also created a regular `User` named `Uli`. `Uli`'s data isn't affected by the changes to `Admin`.

In our working example, we haven't given regular users a secret code yet. If you try to print a regular user with the Python code as shown, you'll get an error because that Python code isn't yet written to accommodate users that have no secret code.

One solution is to just remember that regular users don't have a secret code. So when using the app, never try to print the secret code for a regular user. But it would be better if the code handled the error gracefully for us. To do so, we would ensure that every user's account is associated with a secret code. For regular users, the secret code will be empty, which prevents them from accessing administrator information. Only admins would have valid secret codes.

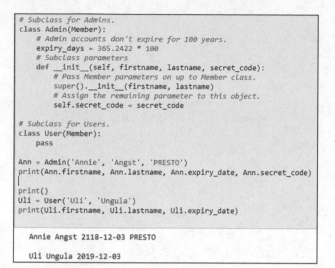

```
# Subclass for Admins.
class Admin(Member):
    # Admin accounts don't expire for 100 years.
    expiry_days = 365.2422 * 100
    # Subclass parameters
    def __init__(self, firstname, lastname, secret_code):
        # Pass Member parameters on up to Member class.
        super().__init__(firstname, lastname)
        # Assign the remaining parameter to this object.
        self.secret_code = secret_code

# Subclass for Users.
class User(Member):
    pass

Ann = Admin('Annie', 'Angst', 'PRESTO')
print(Ann.firstname, Ann.lastname, Ann.expiry_date, Ann.secret_code)

print()
Uli = User('Uli', 'Ungula')
print(Uli.firstname, Uli.lastname, Uli.expiry_date)
```

```
Annie Angst 2118-12-03 PRESTO

Uli Ungula 2019-12-03
```

FIGURE 6-17: The Admin subclass has a new secret_ code parameter.

Should a member join as a regular member and later become an admin, the Python code need only change the empty secret_code to a valid secret_code.

If your class assigns a secret_code to all users (not just admins), you won't get an error when you print the data for a regular user. Instead, the secret code for a regular user will appear as a blank space. To assign a secret code to every member, even when that secret code is blank, add the following to the main Member class:

```
# Default secret code is nothing
self.secret_code = ""
```

So even though you don't do anything with secret_code in the User subclass, you don't have to worry about throwing an error if you try to access the secret code for a User. The User will have a secret code, but it will just be an empty string. Figure 6-18 shows all the code with both subclasses, and also an attempt to print Uli.secret_code, which just displays nothing without throwing an error message.

We left the User subclass with pass as its only statement. In real life, you would probably come up with more default values or parameters for your other subclasses. But the syntax and code is the same for all subclasses. The skills you've learned in this section will work for all your classes and subclasses.

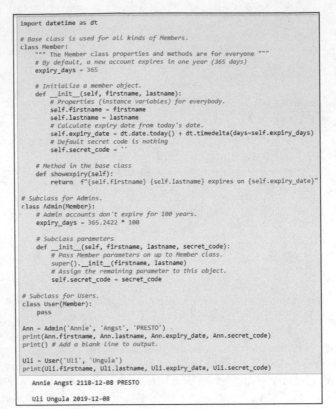

```
import datetime as dt

# Base class is used for all kinds of Members.
class Member:
    """ The Member class properties and methods are for everyone """
    # By default, a new account expires in one year (365 days)
    expiry_days = 365

    # Initialize a member object.
    def __init__(self, firstname, lastname):
        # Properties (instance variables) for everybody.
        self.firstname = firstname
        self.lastname = lastname
        # Calculate expiry date from today's date.
        self.expiry_date = dt.date.today() + dt.timedelta(days=self.expiry_days)
        # Default secret code is nothing
        self.secret_code = ''

    # Method in the base class
    def showexpiry(self):
        return f"{self.firstname} {self.lastname} expires on {self.expiry_date}"

# Subclass for Admins.
class Admin(Member):
    # Admin accounts don't expire for 100 years.
    expiry_days = 365.2422 * 100

    # Subclass parameters
    def __init__(self, firstname, lastname, secret_code):
        # Pass Member parameters on up to Member class.
        super().__init__(firstname, lastname)
        # Assign the remaining parameter to this object.
        self.secret_code = secret_code

# Subclass for Users.
class User(Member):
    pass

Ann = Admin('Annie', 'Angst', 'PRESTO')
print(Ann.firstname, Ann.lastname, Ann.expiry_date, Ann.secret_code)
print() # Add a blank line to output.

Uli = User('Uli', 'Ungula')
print(Uli.firstname, Uli.lastname, Uli.expiry_date, Uli.secret_code)
```

```
Annie Angst 2118-12-08 PRESTO

Uli Ungula 2019-12-08
```

FIGURE 6-18:
The complete
Admin and User
subclasses.

Calling a base class method

Methods in the base class work the same for subclasses as they do for the base class. To try out a method in the base class, add a new method called showexpiry(self) to the bottom of the base class, as follows:

```
class Member:
    """ The Member class attributes and methods are for everyone """
    # By default, a new account expires in one year (365 days)
    expiry_days = 365

    # Initialize a member object.
    def __init__(self, firstname, lastname):
        # Attributes (instance variables) for everybody.
        self.firstname = firstname
        self.lastname = lastname
        # Calculate expiry date from today's date.
        self.expiry_date = dt.date.today() + dt.timedelta(days=self.expiry_days)
```

```
       # Default secret code is nothing
       self.secret_code = ''


   # Method in the base class.
   def showexpiry(self):
       return  f"{self.firstname} {self.lastname} expires on {self.expiry_date}"
```

The showexpiry() method, when called, returns a formatted string containing the user's first and last name and expiration date. Leaving the subclasses untouched and executing the code displays the names and expiry dates of Ann and Uli:

```
Ann = Admin('Annie', 'Angst', 'PRESTO')
print(Ann.showexpiry())


Uli = User('Uli', 'Ungula')
print(Uli.showexpiry())
```

Here is that output, although your dates will differ based on the date you ran the code:

```
Annie Angst expires on 2118-12-04
Uli Ungula expires on 2019-12-04
```

Using the same name twice

You may be wondering about what happens when you use the same name more than once? Python will always opt for the most specific one, the one tied to the subclass. It will use the more generic method from the base class only if nothing in the subclass has that method name.

To illustrate, here's some code that defines a Member class with just a few attributes and methods, to get any irrelevant code out of the way. Comments in the code describe what's going on in the code:

```
class Member:
    """ The Member class attributes and methods """
    # Initialize a member object.
    def __init__(self, firstname, lastname):
        # Attributes (instance variables) for everybody.
        self.firstname = firstname
        self.lastname = lastname


    # Method in the base class
    def get_status(self):
```

```
        return  f"{self.firstname} is a Member."

# Subclass for Administrators
class Admin(Member):
    def get_status(self):
        return  f"{self.firstname} is an Admin."


# Subclass for regular Users
class User(Member):
    def get_status(self):
        return  f"{self.firstname} is a regular User."
```

The Member class, and both the Admin and User classes, have a method named get_status(), which shows the member's first name and status. Figure 6-19 shows the result of running that code with an Admin, a User, and a Member who is neither an Admin nor a User. As you can see, the get_status called in each case is the get_status() associated with the person's subclass (or base class in the case of the person who is a Member but neither an Admin or User).

```
: class Member:
      """ The Member class attributes and methods are for everyone """
      # Initialize a member object.
      def __init__(self, firstname, lastname):
          # Attributes (instance variables) for everybody.
          self.firstname = firstname
          self.lastname = lastname

      # Method in the main class
      def get_status(self):
          return  f"{self.firstname} is a Member."

# Subclass for Administrators
class Admin(Member):
    def get_status(self):
        return  f"{self.firstname} is an Admin."

# Subclass for regular Users
class User(Member):
    def get_status(self):
        return  f"{self.firstname} is a regular User."

# Create an admin
Ann = Admin('Annie', 'Angst')
print(Ann.get_status())

#Create a user
Uli = User('Uli', 'Ungula')
print(Uli.get_status())

# Create a member (neither Admin or User)
Manny = Member("Mindy", "Membo")
print(Manny.get_status())

Annie is an Admin.
Uli is a regular User.
Mindy is a Member.
```

FIGURE 6-19:
Three methods with the same name, get_status().

Python has a built-in `help()` method that you can use with any class to get more information about that class. For example, at the bottom of the code in Figure 6-19, add this line:

```
help(Admin)
```

When you run the code again, you'll see some information about that Admin class, as shown in Figure 6-20.

```
help(Admin)

Help on class Admin in module __main__:

class Admin(Member)
 |  Admin(firstname, lastname)
 |
 |  The Member class attributes and methods are for everyone
 |
 |  Method resolution order:
 |      Admin
 |      Member
 |      builtins.object
 |
 |  Methods defined here:
 |
 |  get_status(self)
 |
 |  ----------------------------------------------------------------------
 |  Methods inherited from Member:
 |
 |  __init__(self, firstname, lastname)
 |      Initialize self.  See help(type(self)) for accurate signature.
 |
 |  ----------------------------------------------------------------------
 |  Data descriptors inherited from Member:
 |
 |  __dict__
 |      dictionary for instance variables (if defined)
 |
 |  __weakref__
 |      list of weak references to the object (if defined)
```

FIGURE 6-20: Output from help(Admin).

You don't need to worry about all the details in Figure 6-20 right now. The most important section is the one titled *Method resolution order*, which looks like this:

```
Method resolution order:
    Admin
    Member
    builtins.object
```

The method resolution order tells you that if a class (and its subclasses) all have methods with the same name (such as get_status), a call to get_status() from an Admin user will cause Python to look in Admin for that method and, if it exists, use it. If no get_status() method was defined in the Admin subclass, Python looks in the Member class and uses that one, if found. If neither of those had a get_status method, it looks in builtins.object, which is a reference to certain built-in methods that all classes and subclasses share.

So the bottom line is, if you do store your data in hierarchies of classes and sub-classes, and you call a method on a subclass, Python will use that subclass method if it exists. If not, Python will use the base class method if it exists. If that also doesn't exist, it will try the built-in methods. And if all else fails, it will throw an error because it can't find the method your code is trying to call. Usually the main reason for this type of error is that you simply misspelled the method name in your code, so Python can't find it.

An example of a built-in method is `__dict__`. The `dict` is short for *dictionary*, and those are double-underscores surrounding the abbreviation. Referring to Figure 6-20, executing the following command:

```
print(Admin.__dict__)
```

doesn't cause an error, even though we've never defined a method named `__dict__`. That's because there is a built-in method with that name, and when called with `print()`, it shows a dictionary of methods (both yours and built-in ones) for that object. The method resolution order isn't something you have to get too involved with this early in the learning curve. Just be aware that if you try to call a method that doesn't exist at any of those three levels, such as this:

```
print(Admin.snookums())
```

you will get an error that looks something like this:

```
---> print(Admin.snookums())
AttributeError: type object 'Admin' has no attribute 'snookums'
```

This error is telling you that Python has no idea what `snookums()` is about. As mentioned, in real life, this kind of error is usually caused by misspelling the method name in your code.

Classes (and to some extent, subclasses) are heavily used in the Python world, and what you've learned here should make it easy to write your own classes, as well as to understand classes written by others. You'll want to learn one more core Python concept before you finish this book: how Python handles errors, and things you can do in your own code to better handle errors.

IN THIS CHAPTER

» **Discovering exceptions**

» **Finding out how to handle errors gracefully**

» **Making sure your app doesn't crash**

» **Checking out**
`try ... except ... else ... finally`

» **Learning to raise your own exceptions**

Chapter **7**

Sidestepping Errors

We all want our programs to run perfectly all the time. But sometimes, situations in the real world stop a program from running. The problem isn't with you or your program. Usually, the person using the program did something wrong. Error handling is all about anticipating these problems, catching the error, and then informing users of the problem so they can fix it.

The techniques we describe here aren't for fixing bugs in your code. You have to fix that type of error yourself. We're talking strictly about errors in the environment in which the program is running, over which you have no control. *Handling* the error is simply a way of replacing the tech-speak error message that Python normally displays, which is meaningless to most people, with a message that tells them in plain English what's wrong and, ideally, how to fix it.

Again, the user will be fixing *the environment in which the program* is running — they won't be fixing your code.

Understanding Exceptions

In Python (and all other programing languages) the term *exception* refers to an error that isn't due to a programming error. Rather, it's an error in the real world that prevents the program from running properly. As a simple example, let's have your Python app open a file. The syntax for that is easy:

```
name = open(filename)
```

Replace *name* with a name of your own choosing, same as a variable name. Replace *filename* with the name of the file. If the file is in the same folder as the code, you don't need to specify a path to the folder because the current folder is assumed.

Figure 7-1 shows an example. We used VS Code for this example so that you can see the contents of the folder in which we worked. The folder contains a file named showfilecontents.py, which is the file that contains the Python code we wrote. The other file is named people.csv.

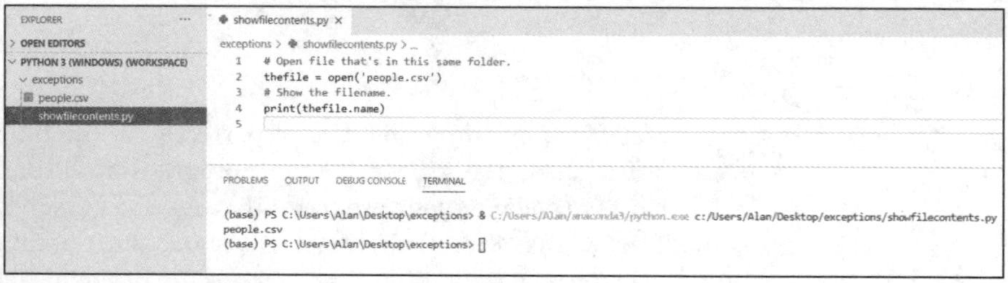

FIGURE 7-1: The show filecontents. py and people. csv files in a folder in VS Code.

The showfilecontents file contains code. The people.csv file contains data (information about people). Figure 7-2 shows the content of the people.csv file in Excel (top) so it's easy for you to read and in a text editor (bottom), which is how it looks to Python and other languages. The file's content doesn't matter much right now; what you're learning here will work in any external file.

The Python code is just two lines (excluding the comments), as follows:

```
# Open file that's in this same folder.
thefile = open('people.csv')
# Show the filename.
print(thefile.name)
```

The first line of code opens the file named people.csv. The second line of code displays the filename (people.csv) on the screen. Running that simple show-filecontents.py file (by right-clicking its name in VS Code and choosing Run

Python File in Terminal) displays people.csv on the screen — assuming a file named people.csv exists in the folder to open. This assumption is where exception handling comes in.

	A	B	C	D	E
1	Username	FirstName	LastName	Role	DateJoined
2	Rambo	Rocco	Moe	0	3/1/2019
3	Ann	Annie	Angst	0	6/4/2019
4	Wil	Wilbur	Blomgren	0	2/28/2019
5	Lupe	Lupe	Gomez	1	4/2/2019
6	Ina	Ina	Kumar	1	1/15/2019
7					

people.csv ☒

```
1  Username,FirstName,LastName,Role,DateJoined
2  Rambo,Rocco,Moe,0,3/1/2019
3  Ann,Annie,Angst,0,6/4/2019
4  Wil,Wilbur,Blomgren,0,2/28/2019
5  Lupe,Lupe,Gomez,1,4/2/2019
6  Ina,Ina,Kumar,1,1/15/2019
7
```

FIGURE 7-2:
The contents of the people.csv file in Excel (top) and a text editor (bottom).

Suppose that for reasons beyond your control, the people.csv file isn't there because some person or automated procedure failed to put it there. Or perhaps someone misspelled the filename. It's easy to accidentally type, say, .cvs rather than .csv for the filename. Running the app *raises an exception* (which in English means "displays an error message"), as you can see in the Terminal window at the bottom of Figure 7-3. The exception reads

```
Traceback (most recent call last):
  File "c:/ Users/ acsimpson/ Desktop/ exceptions/ showfilecontents.py", line 2,
 in <module>
    thefile = open('people.csv')
FileNotFoundError: [Errno 2] No such file or directory: 'people.csv'
```

FIGURE 7-3:
The show filecontents. py file raises an exception.

`Traceback` is a reference to the fact that if there were multiple exceptions, they'd all be listed, with the most recent listed first. In this case, there is just one exception. The `File` part tells you where the exception occurred, in line 2 of the show-filecontents.py file. The following part shows you the line of code that caused the error:

```
thefile = open('people.csv')
```

And finally, the exception itself is described:

```
FileNotFoundError: [Errno 2] No such file or directory: 'people.csv'
```

The generic name for this type of error is `FileNotFoundError`. Many exceptions are also associated with a number (`ERRNO 2` in this example). But the number can vary depending on the operating system environment, so it's typically not used for handling errors. In this case, the main error is `FileNotFoundError`, and the fact that's its `ERRNO 2` where we're sitting right now doesn't matter.

TECHNICAL STUFF

Some people use the phrase *throw an exception* rather than *raise an exception*. The two phrases mean the same thing.

The last part tells you *exactly* what went wrong: `No such file or directory: 'people.csv.'` In other words, Python can't do the `open('people.csv')` business because there is no file named `people.csv` in the current folder.

You could correct this problem by changing the code, but `.csv` is a common file extension for files that contain comma-separated values. It would make more sense to change the name of `people.cvs` to `people.csv` so it matches what the program is looking for and the `.csv` extension is well known.

Handling Errors Gracefully

The best way to handle a file not found error is to replace what Python normally displays with something the person using the app is more likely to understand. To do that, you can code a *try . . . except block* using this basic syntax:

```
try:
    The things you want the code to do
except Exception:
    What to do if it can't do what you want it to do
```

Here's how you can rewrite the `showfilecontents.py` code to handle a missing (or misspelled) file error:

```
try:
    # Open file and show its name.
    thefile = open('people.csv')
    print(thefile.name)
except Exception:
    print("Sorry, I don't see a file named people.csv here")
```

Because the file that the app is supposed to open may be missing, we start with `try:` and then attempt to open the file under that. If the file opens, the `print()` statement runs and displays the filename. But if trying to open the file raises an exception, the program doesn't bomb and display a generic error message. Instead, it displays a message that the average computer user can understand, as shown in Figure 7-4.

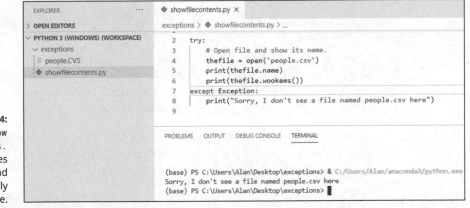

FIGURE 7-4: The show filecontents. py file catches the error and displays a friendly message.

Being Specific about Exceptions

Our previous code example handled the file not found error gracefully. But a larger app might have many places where there's a potential for error, and you want to handle each error differently. To accomplish this, you can define multiple error handlers, as we discuss next.

Suppose that you manually fix the filename so that it's `people.csv` as originally intended. As you saw, when you run the code and there's no error, the output is just the filename. Below the line that prints the filename, we've added another line of code:

```
try:
    # Open file and show its name.
    thefile = open('people.csv')
    print(thefile.name)
    print(thefile.wookems())
except Exception:
    print("Sorry, I don't see a file named people.csv here")
```

When you run this code, the filename isn't a problem, so the output displays `people.csv`, as you'd expect. However, the next line of code, `print(thefile.wookems())`, throws an error because we haven't defined a method named `wookems()`. Unfortunately, the error message is still the same as it was before, even though the cause of the error is that there is no method in Python named `.wookems()`:

```
people.csv
Sorry, I don't see a file named people.csv here
```

So why is the error message saying that the file named `people.csv` wasn't found, when we know it *was* found and that the next line of code is causing the error? The problem is in the `except Exception:` line, which says "if *any* exception is raised in this `try` block, do the code under the `except` line."

To clean this up, you need to replace `Exception:` with the specific exception you want Python to catch. But how do you know what that specific exception is? Easy. The exception raised with no exception handing is

```
FileNotFoundError: [Errno 2] No such file or directory: 'people.csv'
```

The first word is the name of the exception that you can use in place of the generic `Exception` name, like this:

```
try:
    # Open file and show its name.
    thefile = open('people.csv')
    print(thefile.name)
    print(thefile.wookems())
except FileNotFoundError:
    print("Sorry, I don't see a file named people.csv here")
```

Granted, isolating the file not found error doesn't do anything to help with the bad method name. However, the bad method name isn't an exception; it's a programming error that needs to be corrected in the code by replacing `.wookems()`

with the method name you want to use. At least the error message you see isn't the misleading `Sorry, I don't see a file named people.csv here` error. The code works normally and therefore displays the filename when instructed. Then when it reaches the line that contains the bad `.wookem()` method, it throws an error — but not an error related to the filename not being found. It displays the correct error message for this error, `object has no attribute 'wookems'`, as shown in Figure 7-5.

FIGURE 7-5:
The correct error message is displayed.

Again, if you're thinking about handling the `.wookems` error, that's not an exception for which you'd write an exception handler. Exceptions occur when something *outside* the program upon which the program depends isn't available. Programming errors, such as nonexistent method names, are errors inside the program and have to be corrected there by the programmer who wrote the code.

Keeping Your App from Crashing

You can stack up `except:` statements in a `try` block to handle different errors. Just be aware that when the exception occurs, it looks at each one starting at the top. If it finds a handler that matches the exception, it raises that one. If some exception occurred that you didn't handle, you get the standard Python error message. But there's a way around that too.

If you want to avoid all Python error messages, you can start the last exception handler in the code with `except Exception:`. That line means "If the error that occurred wasn't already handled by one of the previous exceptions, use the exception handler instead." In other words, the catch-all exception handler handles any exception that wasn't already handled in the code. For example, here we have two handlers, one for a file not found error and one for everything else:

```
try:
    # Open file and show its name.
    thefile = open('people.csv')
    # Print a couple blank lines then the first line from the file.
    print('\n\n', thefile.readline())
    # Close the file.
    thefile.closed()

except FileNotFoundError:
    print("Sorry, I don't see a file named people.csv here")
except Exception:
    print("Sorry, something else went wrong")
```

We know that you haven't learned about open and readline and close, but don't worry about that. All we care about for now is the exception handling, which is the try: and except: portions of the code.

Running this code produces the following output:

```
Username,FirstName,LastName,Role,DateJoined

Sorry, something else went wrong
```

The first line displays the first line of text from the people.csv file. The second line is the output from the second except: statement, which reads Sorry, something else went wrong. This message is vague and doesn't help you find the problem.

Rather than just print a generic message for an unknown exception, you can capture the error message in a variable and then display the contents of that variable to see the message. As usual, you can name the variable anything you like, though a lot of people use e or err as an abbreviation for *error*.

For example, consider the following rewrite of the preceding code. The generic handler, except Exception, now has an as e at the end, which means "whatever exception gets caught here, put the error message in a variable named e." Then the next line uses print(e) to display the content of the e variable:

```
try:
    # Open file and show its name.
    thefile = open('people.csv')
    # Print a couple blank lines then the first line from the file.
```

```
        print('\n\n', thefile.readline())
        thefile.wigwam()

except FileNotFoundError:
    print("Sorry, I don't see a file named people.csv here")
except Exception as e:
    print(e)
```

Running this code displays the following:

```
Username,FirstName,LastName,Role,DateJoined

'_io.TextIOWrapper' object has no attribute 'wigwam'
```

The first line is just the first line of text from the `people.csv` file. There's no error in the code, and that file is there, so all went well. The second line is

```
'_io.TextIOWrapper' object has no attribute 'wigwam'
```

This isn't plain English, but it's better than "Something else went wrong." At least the part that reads `object has no attribute 'wigwam'` lets you know that the problem has something to do with the word *wigwam*. You handled the error gracefully and the app didn't crash. And you at least got some information about the error that should be helpful to you, even though it may not be helpful to people who are using the app with no knowledge of its inner workings.

Adding an else to the Mix

In our last working example, we used one error handler to handle file not found errors, and a second handler for everything else. But in real life, you may have to handle many more. And if there's no error, you want execution to continue normally. You can use the `else` for the last condition, as follows:

```
try:
    The thing that might cause an exception
catch a common exception:
    Explain the problem
catch Exception as e:
    Show the generic error message
else:
    Continue on here only if no exceptions raised
```

If you convert this code to plain English, the logic of the flow is as follows:

Try to open the file.

If the file isn't there, tell them and stop.

If there's some other error, show the generic error message and stop.

Otherwise

Go on with the rest of the code.

By limiting `try:` to the one thing that's most likely to raise an exception, we can stop the code dead in its tracks before it tries to go any further. But if no exception is raised, the code continues on normally, below the `else`, where the previous exception handlers don't matter anymore. Here is all the code with comments explaining what's going on:

```python
try:
    # Open the file named people.csv
    thefile = open('people.csv')
# Watch for common error and stop program if it happens.
except FileNotFoundError:
    print("Sorry, I don't see a file named people.csv here")
# Catch any unexpected error and stop the program if one happens.
except Exception as err:
    print(err)
# Otherwise, if nothing bad has happened by now, just keep going.
else:
    # File must be open by now if we got here.
    print('\n')  # Print a blank line.
    # Print each line from the file.
    for one_line in thefile:
        print(one_line)
    thefile.close()
    print("Success!")
```

WARNING

As always with Python, indentations matter a lot. Make sure you indent your own code as shown in this chapter. Otherwise, your code will not work right.

Figure 7-6 also shows all the code and the results of running that code in VS Code.

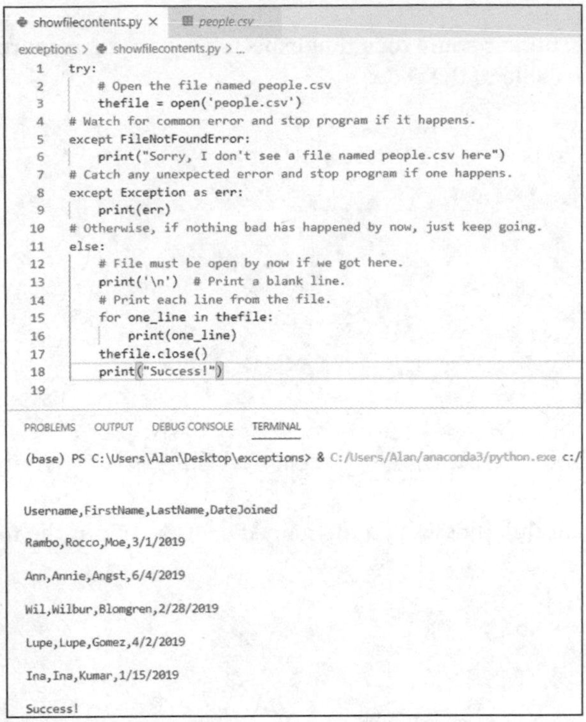

FIGURE 7-6:
Code with
try, exception
handlers, and
an else for when
there are no
exceptions.

Using try . . . except . . . else . . . finally

If you look at the complete syntax for Python exception handling, you'll see one more option at the end, like this:

```
try:
    try to do this
except:
    if x happens, stop here
except Exception as e:
    if something else bad happens, stop here
else:
    if no exceptions, continue on normally here
finally:
    do this code no matter what happened above
```

The `finally` code is executed when the `try` block ends *no matter what*. For example, if you're inside a function and an `except` block uses `return` to exit the function, the `finally` code *still* executes. Without that kind of feature, the `finally` block would be the equivalent of putting its code after and outside the `try` block.

To illustrate, here is some code that expects an external resource named people. csv to be available to the code:

```python
print('Do this first')
try:
    open('people.csv')
except FileNotFoundError:
    print('Cannot find file named people.csv')
except Exception as e:
    print(e)
else:
    print('Show this if there is no exception.')
finally:
    print('This is in the finally block')
print("This is outside the try...except...else...finally")
```

When you run this code with a file named people.csv in the folder, you get this output:

```
Do this first
Show this if no exception.
This is in the finally block
This is outside the try...except...else...finally
```

None of the exception-reporting code executed because the open() statement was able to open the file named people.csv.

If you run this code without a file named people.csv in the same folder, you get the following result:

```
Do this first
Cannot find file named people.csv
This is in the finally block
This is outside the try...except...else...finally
```

This time the code reports that it can't find a file named people.csv. But the app doesn't crash. Rather, it keeps executing the rest of the code.

These examples illustrate that you can control exactly what happens in a small part of a program vulnerable to user errors or other outside exceptions while allowing other code to run normally.

Raising Your Own Exceptions

Python has lots of built-in exceptions for recognizing and identifying errors, as you'll see while writing and testing code, especially when you're first learning. However, you aren't limited to the built-in exceptions. If your app has a vulnerability that isn't covered by the built-in exceptions, you can invent your own.

TECHNICAL STUFF

For a detailed list of all the different exceptions that Python can catch, look at `https://docs.python.org/3/library/exceptions.html` in the Python.org documentation.

The general syntax for raising your own error is

```
raise error
```

Replace *error* with the name of the known error that you want to raise (such as `FileNotFoundError`). Or, if the error isn't covered by one of the built-in errors, you can just use `raise Exception` and that will execute whatever is under `catch Exception:` in your code.

As a working example, let's say you want two conditions to be met for the program to run successfully:

» The `people.csv` file must exist so you can open it.

» The `people.csv` file must contain more than one row of data. The first row contains column names, not data, so if the file has only column headings, we will consider it empty.

Here is an example of how you might handle the exception-handling part of that situation:

```
try:
    # Open the file ]
    thefile = open('people.csv')
    # Count the number of lines in file.
    line_count = len(thefile.readlines())
    # If there are fewer than 2 lines, raise exception.
    if line_count < 2:
        raise Exception
# Handles missing file error.
except FileNotFoundError:
    print('\nThere is no people.csv file here')
```

```
# Handles all other exceptions
except Exception as e:
# Show the error.
    print('\n\nFailed: The error was ' + str(e))
    # Close the file.
    thefile.close()
```

So let's step through the code. The first lines try to open the `people.csv` file:

```
try:
    # Open the file (no error check for this example).
    thefile = open('people.csv')
```

We know that if the `people.csv` file doesn't exist, execution will jump to the following exception handler, which tells the user the file isn't there:

```
except FileNotFoundError:
    print('\nThere is no people.csv file here')
```

Assuming the file was found and no error was thrown, and the file is now open, this next line counts how many lines are in the file:

```
line_count = len(thefile.readlines())
```

If the file is empty, the line count will be 0. If the file contains only column headings, like this:

```
Username,FirstName,LastName,DateJoined
```

the length will be 1. We want the rest of the code to run only if the length of the file is 2 or more. So if the line count is less than 2, the code will raise an exception. You may not know what that exception is, so you tell the app to raise a general exception with `raise Exception` (with an uppercase *E*):

```
if line_count < 2:
    raise Exception
```

The exception handler for general exceptions looks like this:

```
# Handles all other exceptions
except Exception as e:
    # Show the error.
    print('\n\nFailed: The error was ' + str(e))
    # Close the file.
    thefile.close()
```

The e variable grabs the exception, and the next `print` statement displays the exception. So, let's say you run that code and `people.csv` is empty or incomplete. The output would be

```
Failed: The error was
```

Note that there is no explanation of the error because we're using

```
except Exception as e:
```

Remember that `Exception` refers to any error, not an error that has a specific name stored in the variable named e. To throw an error that has an error message associated with it, replace `Exception` with a specific Python exception name. For example, in the following code we've replaced the generic `Exception` with the more specific `FileNotFoundError`:

```
if line_count < 2:
    raise FileNotFoundError
```

But if you do that, the `FileNotFoundError` handler is called and displays There is no people.csv file, which isn't true in this case and it's not the cause of the problem. There is a `people.csv` file; it just doesn't have any data to loop through. What you need is a custom exception handler for that exception.

All exceptions in Python are objects, instances of classes that inherit from the base class `Errors` in Python. To create your own exception, you first have to import the `Exception` class to use as a base class (much like the `Member` class was a base class for different types of users). Then you define your error as a subclass of that base class. This code goes at the top of the file so it's executed before any other code tries to use the custom exception:

```
# Define Python user-defined exceptions
class Error(Exception):
    """Base class for other exceptions"""
    pass

# Your custom error (inherits from Error)
class EmptyFileError(Error):
    pass
```

As before, the word `pass` in each class tells Python "I know this class has no code in it, and that's okay here. You don't need to raise an exception to tell me that."

Now that there exists an exception class called `EmptyFileError`, you can raise *that* exception when the file has insufficient content. Then write a handler to handle that exception:

```
    # If there are fewer than 2 lines, raise exception.
    if line_count < 2:
        raise EmptyFileError
# Handles my custom error for too few rows.
except EmptyFileError:
    print("\nYour people.csv file doesn't have enough stuff.")
```

Figure 7-7 shows all the code.

```
1    # Base class for defining your own user-defined exceptions.
2    class Error(Exception):
3        """Base class for other exceptions"""
4        pass
5
6    # Now define your exception as a subclass of Error.
7    class EmptyFileError(Error):
8        pass
9
10   try:
11       # Open the file (no error check for this example).
12       thefile = open('people.csv')
13       # Count the number of lines in file.
14       line_count = len(thefile.readlines())
15       # If there are are fewer than 2 lines, raise exception.
16       if line_count < 2:
17           raise EmptyFileError
18
19   # Handles missing file error.
20   except FileNotFoundError:
21       print('\nThere is no people.csv file here')
22
23   # Handles my custom error for too few rows.
24   except EmptyFileError:
25       print("\nYour people.csv file doesn't have enough stuff.")
26
27   # Handles all other exceptions
28   except Exception as e:
29       # Show the error.
30       print('\n\nFailed: The error was ' + str(e))
31       # Close the file.
32       thefile.close()
33   else:
34       # This code runs only if no exception above.
35       print('\n') # Print a blank line.
36
37       # File must be open by now if we got here, show content.
38       for one_line in thefile:
39           print(one_line)
40       thefile.close()
41       print("Success!")
```

FIGURE 7-7:
Custom
EmptyFileError
exception added
for exception
handling.

So here is how things will play out when the code runs. If there is no `people.csv` file at all, this error is displayed:

```
There is no people.csv file here.
```

If there is a `people.csv` file but it's empty or contains only column headings, the program displays

```
Your people.csv file doesn't have enough stuff.
```

Assuming neither error happened, the code under the `else:` runs and displays whatever is in the file.

So as you can see, exception handling lets you plan for errors caused by vulnerabilities in your code. We're referring not to bugs in your code or coding errors but to outside resources that the program needs to run correctly.

When outside resources are missing or insufficient, you don't have to let the program just crash and display a nerd-o-rama error message that will baffle your users. Instead, you can catch the exception and show users some text that tells them exactly what's wrong, which will help them fix the problem and run the program again, successfully this time. That's what exception handling is all about.

3

Working with Libraries

Contents at a Glance

Chapter **1**

Working with External Files

P retty much everything stored in your computer, be it a document, program, movie, photograph, and more, is stored in a file. Most files are organized into *folders* (also called *directories*). You can browse through folders and files by using Finder (on a Mac) or File Explorer or Windows Explorer (in Windows).

Python offers many tools for creating, reading from, and writing to many different kinds of files. In this chapter, you learn the most important skills for using Python code to work with files.

Understanding Text and Binary Files

There are basically two types of files:

>> **Text file:** Contains plain text characters. When you open a text file in a text editor, it displays human-readable content. The text may not be in a language

you know or understand, but you will see mostly normal characters that you can type at any keyboard.

>> **Binary file:** Stores information in bytes that aren't quite so human readable. If you open the binary file in a text editor, what you see may resemble Figure 1-1. (We don't recommend that you do this.)

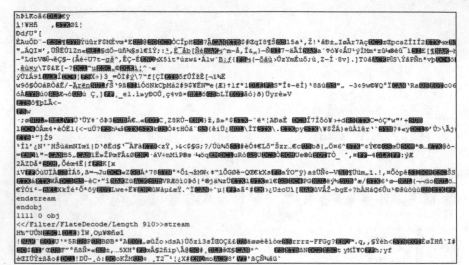

WARNING

If you open a binary file in a text editor and see this gobbledygook, don't panic. Just close the file or program and choose No if asked to save it. The file will be fine, as long as you don't save it.

Figure 1-2 lists examples of different kinds of text and binary files, some of which you may have worked with before. Other files types are available; these are among the most widely used.

Text File

- **Plain text:** .txt, .csv
- **Source code:** .py, .html, .css, .js
- **Data:** .json, .xml

Binary File

- **Executable:** .exe, .dmg, .bin
- **Images:** .jpg, .png, .gif, .tiff, .ico
- **Video:** .mp4, .m4v, .mp4, .mov
- **Audio:** .aif, .mp3, .mpa, .wav
- **Compressed:** .zip, .deb, .tar.gz
- **Font:** .woff, .otf, .ttf
- **Document:** .pdf, .docx, .xlsx

FIGURE 1-2:
Common text and binary files.

As with any Python code, you can use a Jupyter notebook, VS Code, or almost any coding editor to write your Python code. We use VS Code in this chapter simply because its Explorer bar (on the left, when it's open) displays the contents of the folder in which you're currently working.

Opening and Closing Files

To open a file from a Python app, use the syntax:

```
open(filename.ext[,mode])
```

Replace *filename.ext* with the filename of the file you want to open. If the file is not in the same directory as the Python code, you need to specify a path to the file, using forward slashes, even if you're working in Windows. For example, if you want to open the foo.txt on your desktop and your user account name is Alan, you'd use the path C:/Users/Alan/Desktop/foo.txt rather than the more common Windows syntax with backslashes (C:\Users\Alan\Desktop\foo.txt).

The *,mode* is optional (as indicated by the square brackets). Use it to specify what kind of access you want your app to have, using the following single-character abbreviations:

>> **r: (Read):** Opens the file but does not allow Python to make any changes. This is the default mode and is used if you don't specify a mode. If the file doesn't exist, Python raises a FileNotFoundError exception.

>> **r+: (Read/Write):** Opens the file and allows Python to read and write to the file.

>> **a: (Append):** Opens the file and allows Python to add content to the end of the file but not change existing content. If the file doesn't exist, this mode creates the file.

>> **w: (Write):** Opens the file and allows Python to make changes to the file. Creates the file if it doesn't exist.

>> **x: (Create):** Creates the file if it doesn't already exist. If the file does exist, it raises a FileExistsError exception.

REMEMBER

For more information on exceptions, see Book 2, Chapter 7.

You can also specify the type of file you're opening or creating. If you already specified one of the preceding modes, just add this specification as another letter. If you use just one of the following letters on its own, the file opens in Read mode:

>> **t: (Text):** Opens the file as a text file and allows Python to read and write text.

>> **b: (Binary):** Opens the file as a binary file and allows Python to read and write bytes.

You can use the open method in basically two ways. With one syntax you assign a variable name to the file, and use this variable name in code to refer to the file:

```
var = open(filename.ext[,mode])
```

Replace *var* with a name of your choosing (though it's common in Python to use just the letter f as the name).

After the file is open, you can access its content in a few ways, as we discuss a little later in the chapter. For now, we simply copy everything in the file to a variable named *filecontents*, and then we display this content using a simple print() function. So to open quotes.txt, read in all its content, and display that content on the screen, use this code:

```
f = open('quotes.txt')
filecontents = f.read()
print(filecontents)
```

With this method, the file remains open until you specifically close it using the file variable name and the .close() method, like this:

```
f.close()
```

REMEMBER

Make sure that your apps close any files they no longer need open. Failure to do so allows open file handlers to accumulate, which can eventually cause the app to throw an exception and crash, perhaps even corrupting some of the open files along the way.

The second way to open a file, is by using a context manager or contextual coding. *Contextual coding* starts with the word with. You still assign a variable name, but you do so near the end of the line. The last thing on the line is a colon, which marks the beginning of the with block. All indented code below that is assumed to be relevant to the context of the open file (like code indented inside a loop). At the end of contextual coding, you don't need to close the file because Python does it automatically:

```
# ------------------ Contextual syntax
with open('quotes.txt') as f:
    filecontents = f.read()
    print(filecontents)

# The unindented line below is outside the with... block;
print('File is closed: ', f.closed)
```

The following code shows a single app that opens `quotes.txt`, reads and displays its content, and then closes the file. With the first method you have to use `.close()` to close the file. With the second method, the file closes automatically, so no `.close()` is required:

```
# - Basic syntax to open, read, and display file contents.
f = open('quotes.txt')
filecontents = f.read()
print(filecontents)
# Returns True if the file is closed, otherwise False.
print('File is closed: ', f.closed)

# Closes the file.
f.close() #Close the file.
print() # Print a blank line.

# ------------------ Contextual syntax
with open('quotes.txt') as f:
    filecontents = f.read()
    print(filecontents)

# The unindented line below is outside the with... block;
print('File is closed: ', f.closed)
```

The output of this app follows:

```
I've had a perfectly wonderful evening, but this wasn't it.
Groucho Marx
The difference between stupidity and genius is that genius has its limits.
Albert Einstein
We are all here on earth to help others; what on earth the others are here for,
  I have no idea.
W. H. Auden
Ending a sentence with a preposition is something up with which I will not put.
Winston Churchill

File is closed:  False
```

```
I've had a perfectly wonderful evening, but this wasn't it.
Groucho Marx
The difference between stupidity and genius is that genius has its limits.
Albert Einstein
We are all here on earth to help others; what on earth the others are here for,
 I have no idea.
W. H. Auden
Ending a sentence with a preposition is something up with I will not put.
Winston Churchill


File is closed:  True
```

(We can't vouch that these famous quotes were actually said by the people shown.) At the end of the first output, .closed is False because it's tested before the close() closes the file. At the end of the second output, .closed is True without executing a .close() because leaving the code indented under the with: line closes the file automatically.

For the rest of this chapter, we stick with contextual syntax because it's generally the preferred and recommended syntax and a good habit to acquire right from the start.

The previous example works fine because quotes.txt is a simple text file that contains only ASCII characters — the kinds of letters, numbers, and punctuation marks that you can type from a standard keyboard for the English language. Now consider the following code, which attempts to open a .jpg file, which is a graphic image, not a text file:

```
with open('happy_pickle.jpg') as f:
    filecontents = f.read()
    print(filecontents)
```

Attempting to run that code results in the following error:

```
UnicodeDecodeError: 'charmap' codec can't decode byte 0x90 in position 40:
    character maps to <undefined>
```

This message isn't the most helpful one in the world. Suppose we try to open names.txt, which (one would assume) is a text file like quotes.txt, using this code:

```
with open('names.txt') as f:
    filecontents = f.read()
    print(filecontents)
```

We then run this code, and again get a strange error message, like this:

```
UnicodeDecodeError: 'charmap' codec can't decode byte 0x81 in position 45:
    character maps to <undefined>
```

What the heck is going on here?

The first problem is caused because the file type is .jpg, a graphic image, which means the file is a binary file, not a text file. To open a .jpg file, you need b in the mode. Or use rb, which means *read binary*, like this:

```
with open('happy_pickle.jpg', 'rb') as f:
    filecontents = f.read()
    print(filecontents)
```

Running this code doesn't generate an error. But what it does display doesn't look anything like the actual picture:

```
\x07~}\xba\xe7\xd2\x8c\x00\x0e|\xbd\xa8\x121+\xca\xf7\xae\xa5\x9e^\x8d\x89
\x7f\xde\xb4f>\x98\xc7\xfc\xcf46d\xcf\x1c\xd0\xa6\x98m$\xb6(U\x8c\xa6\x83
\x19\x17\xa6>\xe6\x94\x96|g\'4\xab\xdd\xb8\xc8=\xa9[\x8b\xcc`\x0e8\xa3
\xb0;\xc6\xe6\xbb(I.\xa3\xda\x91\xb8\xbd\xf2\x97\xdf\xc1\xf4\xefI\xcdy
\x97d\x1e`;\xf64\x94\xd7\x03
```

If we open happy_pickle.jpg in a graphics app or in VS Code, it looks nothing like that gibberish. Instead, it looks like Figure 1-3.

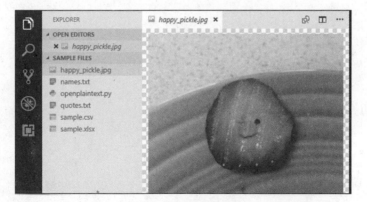

FIGURE 1-3:
How happy_
pickle.jpg is
supposed to look.

So why does the file look so messed up in Python? The print() function displays the raw bytes that make up the file. Displaying raw bytes isn't a problem or an issue; it's just not a good way to work with a .jpg file right now.

The problem with names.txt is different. That file is a text file (.txt), just like quotes.txt. But if you open it and look at its contents, as in Figure 1-4, you'll see that it has a lot of unusual characters that you don't normally see in ASCII (the numbers, letters, and punctuation marks on your keyboard).

FIGURE 1-4: The Names.txt file is text, but with lots of non-English characters.

All those fancy-looking characters tell you that names.txt is not a simple ASCII text file. More likely it's a UTF-8 file, which is basically a text file that uses more than the standard ASCII text characters. To open this file, you have to tell Python to expect UTF-8 characters by using encoding='utf-8' in the open() statement, as shown in Figure 1-5. The output matches the contents of the names.txt file.

```
# readunicode.py ×
1    # Open file with encoding set to utf-8.
2    with open('names.txt','r',encoding='utf-8') as f:
3        # Read entire file into variable named content.
4        content=f.read()
5        # Show that content.
6        print(content)

PROBLEMS    OUTPUT    DEBUG CONSOLE    TERMINAL
Björk Guðmundsdóttir
毛泽东
Борис Николаевич Ельцин
Nguyễn Tấn Dũng
```

FIGURE 1-5: Contents of names.txt displayed.

When opening a file, you need to be aware of three things:

>> For a plain text file (ASCII), you can use r or nothing as the mode.

>> For a binary file, you must specify b in the mode.

>> For a text file with fancy characters, you most likely need to open it as a text file with encoding set to utf-8 in the open() statement.

Reading a File's Contents

Previously in this chapter, you saw how you can use `.read()` to read the contents of an open file. But that's not the only way to read a file. You have three choices:

» `read([size])`: Reads the entire file if you leave the parentheses empty. If you specify a size inside the parentheses, it reads that many characters (for a text file) or that many bytes (for a binary file).

» `readline()`: Reads one line of the contents from a text file — the line ends wherever there's a newline character. (The newline character, \n, ends the line that's displayed and moves the cursor down to the next line.)

» `readlines()`: Reads all the lines of a text file into a list.

People don't type binary files, so any newline characters in a binary file are arbitrary. Therefore, readline() and readlines() are useful only for text files.

Both the read() and readline() methods read in the entire file at once. The only difference is that read reads in the file as one big chunk of data, whereas readlines() reads in the file one line at a time and stores each line as an item in a list. For example, the following code opens quotes.txt, reads in all the contents, and then displays it

```
with open('quotes.txt') as f:
    # Read in entire file
    content = f.read()
    print(content)
```

The content variable stores a copy of everything from the text file. We print the variable to display its contents. The newline character at the end of each line in the file starts a new line on the screen when printing.

Here is the same code using readlines() rather than read:

```
with open('quotes.txt') as f:
    content = f.readlines()
    print(content)
```

The output from this code is

```
["I've had a perfectly wonderful evening, but this wasn't it.\n", 'Groucho
    Marx\n', 'The difference between stupidity and genius is that genius has its
    limits.\n', 'Albert Einstein\n', 'We are all here on earth to help others;
    what on earth the others are here for, I have no idea.\n', 'W. H. Auden\n',
    'Ending a sentence with a preposition is something up with I will not
    put.\n', 'Winston Churchill\n']
```

The square brackets surrounding the output tell you that it's a list. Each item in the list is surrounded by quotation marks and separated by commas. The \n at the end of each item is the newline character that ends the line in the file.

Unlike readlines() (plural), readline() reads just one line from the file. The line extends from the current position in the file to the next newline character. Executing another readline() reads the next line in the file, and so forth. For example, suppose you run this code:

```
with open('quotes.txt') as f:
    content = f.readline()
    print(content)
```

The output is

```
I've had a perfectly wonderful evening, but this wasn't it.
```

Executing another `readline()` after this would read the next line. As you may guess, when it comes to `readline()` and `readlines()`, you're likely to want to use loops to access all the data in a way that gives you more control.

Looping through a File

You can loop through a file using either `readlines()` or `readline()`. The `readlines()` method always reads in the file as a whole. So if the file is very large, your computer may run out of memory (RAM) before the file has been read in. But if you know the size of the file and it's relatively small (maybe a few hundred rows of data or less), `readlines()` is a speedy way to get all the data. That data will be in a list, so you will loop through the list rather than the file. You can also loop through binary files, but they don't have lines of text like text files do. So binary files are read in chunks, as you'll see at the end of this section.

Looping with readlines()

When you read a file with `readlines()`, you read the entire file in one fell swoop as a list. So you don't really loop through the file one row at a time. Rather, you loop through the list of items that `readlines()` stores in memory. The code to do so looks like this:

```python
with open('quotes.txt') as f:
    # Reads in all lines first, then loops through.
    for one_line in f.readlines():
        print(one_line)
```

If you run this code, the output will be double-spaced because each list item ends with a newline, and then `print` always adds its own newline with each pass through the loop. If you want to retain the single spacing, add `end=''` to the `print` statement (make sure you use two single or double quotation marks with no spaces after =). Here's an example:

```python
with open('quotes.txt') as f:
    # Reads in all lines first, then loops through.
    for one_line in f.readlines():
        print(one_line, end='')
```

The output from this code follows:

```
I've had a perfectly wonderful evening, but this wasn't it.
Groucho Marx
The difference between stupidity and genius is that genius has its limits.
Albert Einstein
We are all here on earth to help others; what on earth the others are here for,
    I have no idea.
W. H. Auden
Ending a sentence with a preposition is something up with I will not put.
Winston Churchill
```

Let's suppose you're happy with that output but want to improve it slightly. You want to indent the name below each quote a couple of spaces and add a blank line below the name. How could you do that? Well, Python has a built-in enumerate( ) function that, when used with a list, counts the number of passes through the loop, starting at 0. So instead of the for: loop shown in the preceding example, you write for one_line in enumerate(f.readlines()):. With each pass through the loop, one_line[0] contains the number of that line, one_line[1] contains its contents (the text of the line), and you can see whether the counter is an even number using the modulo operator, %, which returns the remainder after division. So when you calculate % 2 (modulo 2) for an even number, you always get 0. An odd number will always return a non-zero remainder when divided by 2. So you could write the code this way:

```
with open('quotes.txt') as f:
    # Reads in all lines first, then loops through.
    # Count each line starting at zero.
    for one_line in enumerate(f.readlines()):
        # If counter is even number, print with no extra newline
        if one_line[0] % 2 == 0:
            print(one_line[1], end='')
        # Otherwise print a couple spaces and an extra newline.
        else:
            print('  ' + one_line[1])
```

The output is as follows:

```
I've had a perfectly wonderful evening, but this wasn't it.
  Groucho Marx

The difference between stupidity and genius is that genius has its limits.
  Albert Einstein

We are all here on earth to help others; what on earth the others are here for,
    I have no idea.
  W. H. Auden
```

Looping with readline()

If you aren't too sure about the size of the file you're reading or the amount of RAM in the computer running your app, using `readlines()` to read in an entire file can be risky. If there isn't enough memory to hold the entire file, the app will crash when it runs out of memory. To play it safe, you can loop through the file one line at a time so only one line of the contents from the file is in memory at any given time.

To use this method, you open the file, read one line, and put it in a variable. Then loop through the file *as long as* (`while`) the variable isn't empty. Because each line in the file contains some text, the variable won't be empty until after the last line is read. Here is the code for this approach to looping:

```
with open('quotes.txt') as f:
    one_line = f.readline()
    while one_line:
        print(one_line, end='')
        one_line = f.readline()
```

For larger files, this method is the way to go because at no point are you reading in the entire file. The only potential problem is forgetting to include `.readline()` inside the loop to advance to the next row. Otherwise, you end up with in infinite loop that prints the first line over and over. If you ever find yourself in this situation, press Ctrl+C in the Terminal window where the code is running to stop the loop.

You can accomplish the same format, where you indent the name under each quote and add a blank line, by using `.readline()` in Python. In your code, start a counter at 1. Create a loop that reads one row at a time from the text file. Within that loop, increment your counter variable by 1 with each pass through the loop. Then indent and do the extra space on even-numbered lines like this:

```
# Store a number to use as a loop counter.
counter = 1
# Open the file.
with open('quotes.txt') as f:
    # Read one line from the file.
    one_line = f.readline()
    # As long as there are lines to read...
    while one_line:
```

```
# If the counter is an even number, print a couple spaces.
if counter % 2 == 0:
    print('  ' + one_line)
# Otherwise print with no newline at the end.
else:
    print(one_line, end='')
# Increment the counter
counter += 1
# Read the next line.
one_line = f.readline()
```

The output from this loop is the same as for the second readlines() loop, in which each author's name is indented and followed by an extra blank line caused by using print() without the end=''.

Appending versus overwriting files

Any time you work with files, it's important to understand the difference between *write* and *append*. If a file contains information and you open it in write mode and then write more to it, your new content will overwrite (replace) whatever is already in the file. There is no undo for this. So if the content of the file is important, you want to make sure you don't make that mistake. To add content to the end of a file, open the file in append (a) mode, and then use .write to write to the file.

Suppose you want to add the name Peña Calderón to the names.txt file used in the previous section. This name, as well as the names already in this file, use special characters beyond the English alphabet, so you need to set the encoding to UTF-8. Also, if you want to display each name in the file on a separate line, add a \n (newline) to the end of the name you're adding. Your code should look like this:

```
# New name to add with \n to mark end of line.
new_name = 'Peña Calderón\n'
# Open names.txt in append mode with encoding.
with open('names.txt', 'a', encoding='utf-8') as f:
    f.write(new_name)
```

To verify that it worked, start a new block of code, with no indents, so names.txt file closes automatically. Then open the file in read (r) mode and view its contents. Figure 1-6 shows the code for adding the new name and the code to display the names.txt file after adding the name.

```
EXPLORER                    ● AppendToFile.py ✕

⊿ OPEN EDITORS              1   # New name to add with \n to mark end of line.
   ✕ ● AppendToFile.py      2   new_name = 'Peña Calderón\n'
                            3   # Open names.txt in append mode with encoding.
⊿ ENCODING                  4   with open('names.txt', 'a', encoding='utf-8') as f:
   ● AppendToFile.py        5       # Add the new name and \n to the end of the file.
   ▫ names.txt              6       f.write(new_name)
   ● readunicode.py         7
                            8   # File closes automatically after indentations.
                            9   print('\nDone')
                            10  # Re-open the file with encoding and display contents
                            11  with open('names.txt', encoding='utf-8') as f:
                            12      print(f.read())
                            13

                            PROBLEMS   OUTPUT   DEBUG CONSOLE   TERMINAL          2: Python

                            Done
                            Björk Guðmundsdóttir
                            毛泽东
                            Борис Николаевич Ельцин
                            Nguyễn Tấn Dũng
                            Peña Calderón
```

FIGURE 1-6:
A new name appended to the end of the names.txt file.

TIP

Typing special characters such as ñ and ó usually involves holding down the Alt key and typing a three- or four-numeric digit, for example, Alt+164 for ñ or Alt+0243 for ó. Exactly how you do this depends on your operating system and editor. You can do a web search for something like *type tilde n on Windows* or *type accented o on Mac* for details.

Using tell() to determine the pointer location

When you loop through a file, its contents are read top to bottom, and left to right. Python maintains a pointer to keep track of where it is in the file. When you're reading a text file with readline(), the pointer is always the character position of the next line in the file.

If all you've done so far is open the file, the character position will be 0, the start of the file. Each time you execute readline(), the pointer advances to the start of the next row. Here is some code and its output to illustrate:

```
with open('names.txt', encoding='utf-8') as f:
    # Read first line to get started.
    print(f.tell())
    one_line = f.readline()
    # Keep reading one line at a time until there are no more.
    while one_line:
        print(one_line[:-1], f.tell())
        one_line = f.readline()
```

```
0
Björk Guðmundsdóttir 25
毛泽东 36
Борис Николаевич Ельцин 82
Nguyễn Tấn Dũng 104
Peña Calderón 121
```

The first 0 is the position of the pointer right after the file is opened. The 25 at the end of the next line is the position of the pointer after reading the first line. The 36 at the end of the next line is the pointer position at the end of the second line, and so forth, until the 121 at the end, when the pointer is at the end of the file.

If you try to do this with readlines(), you get a different result. Here is the code:

```
with open('names.txt', encoding='utf-8') as f:
    print(f.tell())
    # Reads in all lines first, then loops through.
    for one_line in f.readlines():
        print(one_line[:-1], f.tell())
```

Here is the output:

```
0
Björk Guðmundsdóttir 121
毛泽东 121
Борис Николаевич Ельцин 121
Nguyễn Tấn Dũng 121
Peña Calderón 121
```

The pointer starts out at position 0, as expected. But each line displays 121 at the end because readlines() reads in the entire file when executed, leaving the pointer at the end, position 121. The loop is actually looping through the copy of the file in memory; it's no longer reading through the file.

Moving the pointer with seek()

Whereas the tell() method tells you where the pointer is in an external file, the seek() method enables you to reposition the pointer. The syntax is

```
file.seek(position[,whence])
```

Replace *file* with the variable name of the open file. Replace *position* to indicate where you want to put the pointer. For example, 0 moves the pointer back to the top of the file. The *whence* is optional; you can use it to indicate where in the file to set the pointer position. Your choices are

>> 0: Set the position relative to the start of the file.

>> 1: Set the position relative to the current pointer position.

>> 2: Set the position relative to the end of the file. Use a negative number for *position*.

If you omit the *whence* value, it defaults to 0.

By far, the most common use of seek is to just reset the pointer back to the top of the file for another pass through the file. The syntax for this is simply .seek(0).

Reading and Copying a Binary File

Suppose you have an app that changes a binary file, and you want to always work with a copy of the original file to play it safe. Binary files can be huge, so rather than opening it all at once and risking running out of memory, you can read it in chunks and write it out in chunks. Binary files do not have human-readable content. Nor do they have lines of text. So readline() and readlines() aren't a good choice for looping through binary files, but you can use .read() with a specified size.

Figure 1-7 shows the binarycopy.py file, which makes a copy of any binary file. We'll take you through that code step-by-step so you can understand how it works.

```
binarycopy.py > ...
1   # Specify the file to copy
2   file_to_copy = 'happy_pickle.jpg'
3   #Create new file nane wuth _copy before the extension.
4   name_parts = file_to_copy.split('.')
5   new_file = name_parts[0] + '_copy.' + name_parts[1]
6   # Open the priginal file as read-only binary.
7   with open(file_to_copy,'rb') as original_file:
8       # Create or open file to copy into.
9       with open(new_file,'wb') as copy_to:
10          # Grab a chunk of the original file (4MB).
11          chunk=original_file.read(4096)
12          # Loop though until no more chunks.
13          while len(chunk) > 0:
14              copy_to.write(chunk)
15              # Make sure you read the next chunk in this loop.
16              chunk = original_file.read(4096)
17
18  # Close is automatic after loops, show done message.
19  print('Done!')
```

FIGURE 1-7: The binarycopy. py file copies any binary file.

The first step is to specify the file you want to copy. We chose `happy_pickle.jpg`, which, as you can see in the figure, is in the same folder as the `binarycopy.py` file:

```
# Specify the file to copy.
file_to_copy = 'happy_pickle.jpg'
```

To make an empty file to copy into, you need a filename for the file. The following code takes care of that:

```
# Create new file name with _copy before the extension.
name_parts = file_to_copy.split('.')
new_file = name_parts[0] + '_copy.' + name_parts[1]
```

The first line after the copy splits the existing filename in two at the dot, so `name_parts[0]` contains `happy_pickle` and `name_parts[1]` contains `png`. Then the `new_file` variable gets a value consisting of the first part of the name with `_copy` and a dot attached, and then the last part of the name. So after this line executes, the `new_file` variable contains `happy_pickle_copy.png`.

To make the copy, open the original file in `rb` (read, binary file) mode. Then open the file into which you want to copy the original file in `wb` mode (write, binary). With *write*, Python creates a file of this name if the file doesn't already exist. If the file does exist, Python opens it with the pointer set at 0, so anything that you write into the file will *replace* (not *add to*) the existing file.

In the code you can see that we used `original_file` as the variable name from which to copy, and `copy_to` as the variable name of the file into which you copy data. Indentations, as always, are critical:

```
# Open the original file as read-only binary.
with open(file_to_copy, 'rb') as original_file:
    # Create or open file to copy into.
    with open(new_file, stet'wb') as copy_to:
```

If you use `.read()` to read in the entire binary file, you run the risk of it being so large that it overwhelms the computer's RAM and crashes the program. To avoid this, we've written this program to read in a modest 4MB (4,096 kilobytes) of data at a time. This 4KB chunk is stored in a variable named `chunk`:

```
# Grab a chunk of original file (4MK).
chunk = original_file.read(4096)
```

The next line sets up a loop that keeps reading one chunk at a time. The pointer is automatically positioned to the next chunk with each pass through the loop.

Eventually, it will hit the end of the file where it can't read anymore. When this happens, chunk will be empty, meaning it has a length of 0. So this loop keeps going through the file until it gets to the end:

```
# Loop through until no more chunks.
while len(chunk) > 0:
```

Within the loop, the first line copies the last-read chunk into the copy_to file. The second line reads the next 4KB chunk from the original file. And so it goes until everything from original_file has been copied to the new file:

```
copy_to.write(chunk)
# Make sure you read in the next chunk in this loop.
chunk = original_file.read(4096)
```

All the indentations stop after this line. When the loop is done, the files close automatically, and the last line displays Done! as follows:

```
print('Done!')
```

Figure 1-8 shows the results of running the code. The Terminal pane simply shows Done!. But as you can see, there's now a file named happy_pickle_copy. jpg in the folder. Opening this file will prove that it is a copy of the original file.

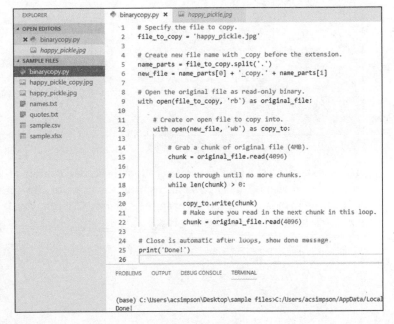

FIGURE 1-8:
Running
binarycopy.py
added happy_
pickle_copy.
jpg to the folder.

Conquering CSV Files

CSV (comma-separated values) is a widely used format for storing and transporting tabular data. *Tabular* means the data can generally be displayed in a table format consisting of rows and columns. In a spreadsheet app such as Microsoft Excel, Apple Numbers, or Google Sheets, the tabular format is obvious, as shown in Figure 1-9.

	A	B	C	D	E
1	Full Name	Birth Year	Date Joined	Is Active	Balance
2	Angst, Annie	1982	1/11/2011	TRUE	$300.00
3	Bónañas, Barry	1973	2/11/2012	FALSE	-$123.45
4	Schadenfreude, Sandy	2004	3/3/2003	TRUE	$0.00
5	Weltschmerz, Wanda	1995	4/24/1994	FALSE	$999,999.99
6	Malaise, Mindy	2006	5/5/2005	TRUE	$454.01
7	O'Possum, Ollie	1987	7/27/1997	FALSE	-$1,000.00
8					
9	Pusillanimity, Pamela	1979	8/8/2008	TRUE	$12,345.67

FIGURE 1-9: A CSV file in Microsoft Excel.

Without the aid of a special program to make the data in the file display in a neat tabular format, each row is just a line in the file. And each unique value is separated by a comma. For instance, opening the file shown in Figure 1-9 in a simple text editor such as Notepad or TextEdit shows what's really stored in the file, as you can see in Figure 1-10.

sample.csv ×

```
Full Name,Birth Year,Date Joined,Is Active,Balance
"Angst, Annie",1982,1/11/2011,TRUE,$300.00
"Bónañas, Barry",1973,2/11/2012,FALSE,-$123.45
"Schadenfreude, Sandy",2004,3/3/2003,TRUE,$0.00
"Weltschmerz, Wanda",1995,4/24/1994,FALSE,"$999,999.99"
"Malaise, Mindy",2006,5/5/2005,TRUE,$454.01
"O'Possum, Ollie",1987,7/27/1997,FALSE,"-$1,000.00"
,,,,
"Pusillanimity, Pamela",1979,8/8/2008,TRUE,"$12,345.67"

```

FIGURE 1-10: A CSV file in a text editor.

In the text editor, the first row, often called the *header*, contains the column headings, or *field names*, that appear across the first row of the spreadsheet. If you look at the names in the second example, the raw CSV file, you'll see that they're enclosed in quotation marks, like this:

```
"Angst, Annie"
```

The quotation marks indicate that the stuff *between* them is all one thing. In other words, the comma between the last and first name is part of the name; it isn't the start of a new column. So the first two columns in this row one are

```
"Angst, Annie", 1982
```

and not

```
Angst, Annie
```

The same is true in all other rows: The name enclosed in quotation marks (including commas) is just one name, not two separate columns of data.

If a string contains an apostrophe, which is the same character as a single quotation mark, you have to use double quotation marks around the string. Otherwise, if you do this:

```
'O'Henry, Harry'
```

the first part of the string is `'O'` and then Python doesn't know what to do with the text after the second single quotation mark. Using double quotation marks alleviates any confusion because there are no other double quotation marks within the name:

```
"O'Henry, Harry"
```

Figure 1-10 also illustrates other considerations when creating CSV files. For example, the Bónañas, Barry name contains some non-ASCII characters. The second-to-last row contains only a bunch of commas. (In a CSV file, if a cell is missing its data, you put the comma that ends the cell with nothing to its left.) The Balance column has dollar signs and commas in the numbers, which don't work with the Python `float` data type. We talk about how to deal with all these issues in the sections to follow.

Although you could work with CSV files using just what you've learned so far, the task will be a lot quicker and easier if you use the `csv` module, which you already have. To use it, just put this near the top of your program:

```
import csv
```

Remember, this line of code doesn't bring in a CSV *file*. It brings in the prewritten code that makes it easier for you to work with CSV files in your own Python code.

Opening a CSV file

Opening a CSV file is no different from opening any other file. Just remember that if the file contains special characters, you need to include `encoding='utf-8'` to avoid an error message. Optionally, when importing data, you probably don't want to read in the newline character at the end of each row, so you can add `new-line=''` to the `open()` statement. Here is how you might comment and code this, except you'd replace `sample.csv` with the path to the CSV file you want to open:

```
# Open CSV file with UTF-8 encoding, don't read in newline characters.
with open('sample.csv', encoding='utf-8', newline='') as f:
```

To loop through a CSV file, you can use the built-in `reader()` function, which reads one row when executed. Again, the syntax is simple:

```
reader = csv.reader(f)
```

Replace `f` with the name you used at the end of your `open` statement (without the colon at the very end).

Optionally, you can also count rows as you go. Just put everything to the right of = in `enumerate()`, as shown in the following (where we've also added a comment above the code):

```
# Create a CVS row counter and row reader.
reader = enumerate(csv.reader(f))
```

Next, you can set up your loop to read one row at a time. Because you put an enumerator on the loop, you can use two variable names in your `for:` loop. The first variable (which we call `i`) keeps track of the counter (which starts at 0 and increases by 1 with each pass through the loop). The second variable, `row`, contains the entire row of data from the CSV file:

```
# Loop through one row at a time, i is counter, row is entire row.
for i, row in reader:
```

Within the loop, you can use a `print()` function to print the value of `i` and `row` with each pass through the loop, like this:

```
import csv
# Open CSV file with UTF-8 encoding, don't read in newline characters.
with open('sample.csv', encoding='utf-8', newline='') as f:
    # Create a CVS row counter and row reader.
    reader = enumerate(csv.reader(f))
```

```
    # Loop through one row at a time, i is counter, row is entire row.
    for i, row in reader:
        print(i, row)
print('Done')
```

The output from this code, using the `sample.csv` file described earlier as input, is as follows:

```
0 ['\ufeffFull Name', 'Birth Year', 'Date Joined', 'Is Active', 'Balance']
1 ['Angst, Annie', '1982', '1/11/2011', 'TRUE', '$300.00']
2 ['Bónañas, Barry', '1973', '2/11/2012', 'FALSE', '-$123.45']
3 ['Schadenfreude, Sandy', '2004', '3/3/2003', 'TRUE', '$0.00']
4 ['Weltschmerz, Wanda', '1995', '4/24/1994', 'FALSE', '$999,999.99']
5 ['Malaise, Mindy', '2006', '5/5/2005', 'TRUE', '$454.01']
6 ["O'Possum, Ollie", '1987', '7/27/1997', 'FALSE', '-$1,000.00']
7 ['', '', '', '', '']
8 ['Pusillanimity, Pamela', '1979', '8/8/2008', 'TRUE', '$12,345.67']
```

Note how the row of column names is row 0. The weird \ufeff before Full Name in that row is the byte order mark (BOM), which is just something Excel sticks in there. Typically you don't care what's in that first row because the real data doesn't start until the second row. So don't give the BOM a second thought; it's of no value to you and it isn't doing any harm.

As you can see, each row is a list of five items separated by commas. In your code, you can refer to each column by its position. For example, row[0] is the first column in the row (the person's name). Then, row[1] is the birth year, row[2] is date joined, row[3] is whether the person is active, and row[4] is the balance.

All the data in the CSV file consists of strings — even if they don't look like strings. But anything and everything coming from a CSV file is a string because a CSV file is a type of text file, and a text file contains only strings (text) — no integers, dates, Booleans, or floats.

In your app, you'll probably want to convert the incoming data to Python data types so you can work with them more effectively or even transfer them to a database. In the next sections, we look at how to do the conversion for each data type.

Converting strings

Technically, you don't have to convert anything from the CSV file to a string. But you may want to chop the file up a bit or deal with empty strings in some way. First, as mentioned, we care only about the data here, not that first row. So inside the loop, you can start with an `if` that doesn't do anything if the current row is row 0. Replace the `print(i, row)` like this:

```
# Row 0 is just column headings, ignore it.
if i > 0:
    full_name = row[0].split(',')
    last_name = full_name[0].strip()
    first_name = full_name[1].strip()
```

This code says "As long as we're not looking at the first row, create a variable named `full_name` and store in it whatever is in the first column split into two separate values at the comma." After that line executes, `full_name[0]` contains the person's last name, which we then put into a variable named `last_name`, and `full_name[1]` contains the person's first name, which we put into a variable named `first_name`. But if you run the code that way, it will bomb, because row 7 doesn't have a name, and Python can't split an empty string at a comma (because the empty string contains no comma).

To get around this, you can tell Python to *try* to split the name at the comma, if it can. But if it bombs when trying, just store an empty string in the `full_name`, `last_name`, and `first_name` variables. Here's that code with some extra comments thrown in to explain what's going on. Instead of printing `i` and the entire row, the code prints the first name and last name (and nothing for the row whose information is missing). The output appears below the code:

```
import csv
# Open CSV file with UTF-8 encoding, don't read in newline characters.
with open('sample.csv', encoding='utf-8', newline='') as f:
    # # Create a CVS row counter and row reader.
    reader = enumerate(csv.reader(f))
    # Loop through one row at a time, i is counter, row is entire row.
    for i, row in reader:
        # Row 0 is just column headings, ignore it.
        if i > 0:
            # Whole name split into two at comma.
            try:
                full_name = row[0].split(',')
                # Last name, strip extra spaces.
                last_name=full_name[0].strip()
                # First name, strip extra spaces.
                first_name=full_name[1].strip()
            except IndexError:
                full_name = last_name = first_name = ""
            print(first_name, last_name)
print('Done!')
```

```
Annie Angst
Barry Bónañas
Sandy Schadenfreude
Wanda Weltschmerz
Mindy Malaise
Ollie O'Possum

Pamela Pusillanimity
Done!
```

Converting to integers

The second column in each row, `row[1]`, is the birth year. As long as the string contains something that can be converted to a number, you can use the simple built-in `int()` function to convert it to an integer. We do have a problem in row 7, which is empty. Python won't automatically convert this to a 0; you have to help it along a bit, as follows:

```
# Birth year integer, zero for empty string.
birth_year = int(row[1] or 0)
```

The code looks surprisingly simple, but that is the beauty of Python: It *is* surprisingly simple. This line of code says "Create a variable named `birth_year` and put in it the second column value, if you can, or if there is nothing to convert to an integer, then just put in a zero."

Converting to date

The third column in our CSV file, `row[2]`, is the date joined, and it appears to have a reasonable date in each row (except the row whose data is missing). To convert the textual date to a Python date, you need to import the `datetime` module by adding `import datetime as dt` near the top of the program. Then the simple conversion is

```
date_joined = dt.datetime.strptime(row[2], "%m/%d/%Y").date()
```

A lot is going on here. First, you create a variable named `date_joined`. The `strptime` code means "string parse for date time." The `[row[2]` code means the third column (because the first column is always column 0). The `"%m/%d/%Y"` tells

Working with External Files

`strptime` that the string date contains the month, a slash, the day of the month, a slash, and then the four-digit year (`%Y`). The `.date()` at the end means "just the date; there is no time here to parse."

One small problem. When the program gets to the row whose date is missing, it will bomb. So once again we'll use a `try` block to convert the date; if it can't come up with a date, it puts in the value `None`, which is Python's word for an empty object.

REMEMBER

In Python, `datetime` is a class, so any date and time you create is an object (of the `datetime` type). You use `' '` for an empty string, but `None` for an empty object.

Here is the code as it stands now with the `import` at top for `datetime`, and `try ... except` to convert the string date to a Python date:

```python
import csv
import datetime as dt
# Open CSV file with UTF-8 encoding, don't read in newline characters.
with open('sample.csv', encoding='utf-8', newline='') as f:
    # Create a CVS row counter and row reader.
    reader = enumerate(csv.reader(f))
    # Loop through one row at a time, i is counter, row is entire row.
    for i, row in reader:
        # Row 0 is just column headings, ignore it.
        if i > 0:
            # Whole name split into two at comma.
            try:
                full_name = row[0].split(',')
                # Last name, strip extra spaces.
                last_name = full_name[0].strip()
                # First name, strip extra spaces.
                first_name = full_name[1].strip()
            except IndexError:
                full_name = last_name = first_name = ""
            # Birth year integer, zero for empty string.
            birth_year = int(row[1] or 0)
            # Date_joined is a date.
            try:
                date_joined = dt.datetime.strptime(row[2], "%m/%d/%Y").date()
            except ValueError:
                date_joined = None
            print(first_name, last_name, birth_year, date_joined)
print('Done!')
```

Here is the output from this code, which now prints `first_name`, `last_name`, `birth_year`, and `date_joined` with each pass through the data rows in the table:

```
Annie Angst 1982 2011-01-11
Barry Bónañas 1973 2012-02-11
Sandy Schadenfreude 2004 2003-03-03
Wanda Weltschmerz 1995 1994-04-24
Mindy Malaise 2006 2005-05-05
Ollie O'Possum 1987 1997-07-27
  0 None
Pamela Pusillanimity 1979 2008-08-08
Done!
```

Converting to Boolean

The fourth column, `row[3]` in each row, contains `TRUE` or `FALSE`. Excel uses all uppercase letters, which are automatically carried over to the CSV file when saving as CSV in Excel. Python uses initial caps, `True` and `False`. Python has a simple `bool()` function for converting data to Boolean. The `bool()` function won't bomb when it hits an empty cell; it just considers that cell `False`. The conversion is as simple as the following:

```
# is_active is a Boolean, automatically False for empty string.
is_active = bool(row[3])
```

Converting to floats

The fifth column in each row contains the balance, which is a dollar amount. In Python, you want the dollar amount to be an actual numeric value, so you can do math. The float data type is good because you can include decimal points for the pennies. But there's one potential snag. Python floats can't contain a dollar sign ($) or a comma (,), so you must remove those from the string. Also, you can't have any leading and trailing spaces. These you can remove easily with the `strip()` method. The following line of code creates a variable named `str_balance` (which is still a string) but with the dollar sign, comma, and any trailing leading spaces removed:

```
# Remove $, commas, leading trailing spaces.
str_balance = (row[4].replace('$', '').replace(',', '')).strip()
```

You can read this second line as "The new string named `str_balance` consists of whatever is in the fifth column after replacing any dollar signs with nothing, replacing any commas with nothing, and stripping all leading and trailing spaces."

Below that line, you can add a comma and then another line to create a float named `balance` that uses the built-in `float()` method to convert the `str_balance` string into a float. Like `int()`, `float()` stores 0 as the value of the float if it can't make sense of the thing it's trying to convert to a float.

The code in Figure 1-11 shows everything in place, including a `print()` line that displays the values of all five columns after the conversion.

Converting from CSV to Objects and Dictionaries

You've seen how to read in data from a CSV file, and how to convert that data from the default string data type to an appropriate Python data type. Chances are, in addition to all this, you may want to organize the data into a group of objects generated from the same class or perhaps into a set of dictionaries inside a larger dictionary.

All the code you've learned so far will be useful, because it's necessary to get the job done. To reduce the code clutter in these examples, we've taken the various bits of code for converting the data and put them into their own functions. This allows you to convert a data item using just the function name with the value to convert in parentheses, such as `balance(row[4])`.

Working with External Files

Importing CSV to Python objects

If you want the data from your CSV file to be organized into a list of objects, write your code as shown here:

```python
import datetime as dt
import csv
# Use these functions to convert any string to appropriate Python data type.
# Get just the first name from full name.
def fname(any):
    try:
        nm = any.split(',')
        return nm[1]
    except IndexError:
        return ''
# Get just the last name from full name.
def lname(any):
    try:
        nm = any.split(',')
        return nm[0]
    except IndexError:
        return ''
# Convert string to integer or zero if no value.
def integer(any):
    return int(any or 0)
# Convert mm/dd/yyyy date to date or None if no valid date.
def date(any):
    try:
        return dt.datetime.strptime(any,"%m/%d/%Y").date()
    except ValueError:
        return None
# Convert any string to Boolean, False if no value.
def boolean(any):
    return bool(any)
# Convert string to float, or to zero if no value.
def floatnum(any):
    s_balance = (any.replace('$','').replace(',',''))
    return float(s_balance or 0)
# Create an empty list of people.
people = []
# Define a class where each person is an object.
class Person:
    def __init__(self, id, first_name, last_name, birth_year, date_joined,
                 is_active, balance):
        self.id = id
        self.first_name = first_name
        self.last_name = last_name
        self.birth_year = birth_year
        self.date_joined = date_joined
```

```
            self.is_active = is_active
            self.balance = balance

    # Open CSV file with UTF-8 encoding, don't read in newline characters.
    with open('sample.csv', encoding='utf-8', newline='') as f:
        # Set up a csv reader with a counter.
        reader = enumerate(csv.reader(f))
        # Skip the first row, which is column names.
        f.readline()
        # Loop through remaining rows one at a time, i is counter, row is
        # entire row.
        for i, row in reader:
            # From each data row in the CSV file, create a Person object with unique
            # id and appropriate data types, add to people list.
            people.append(Person(i, fname(row[0]), lname(row[0]), integer(row[1]),
                      date(row[2]), boolean(row[3]), floatnum(row[4])))

    # When above loop is done, show all objects in the people list.
    for p in people:
        print(p.id, p.first_name, p.last_name, p.birth_year, p.date_joined,
            p.is_active, p.balance)
```

Here's how the code works: The first few lines are the required `imports`, followed by a number of functions to convert the incoming string data to Python data types. This code is similar to previous examples in this chapter. We just separated the conversion code into separate functions to compartmentalize everything a bit:

```
import datetime as dt
import csv
# Use these functions to convert any string to appropriate Python data type.
# Get just the first name from full name.
def fname(any):
    try:
        nm = any.split(',')
        return nm[1]
    except IndexError:
        return ''


# Get just the last name from full name.
def lname(any):
    try:
        nm = any.split(',')
        return nm[0]
    except IndexError:
        return ''
# Convert string to integer or zero if no value.
def integer(any):
    return int(any or 0)
```

```
# Convert mm/dd/yyyy date to date or None if no valid date.
def date(any):
    try:
        return dt.datetime.strptime(any,"%m/%d/%Y").date()
    except ValueError:
        return None

# Convert any string to Boolean, False if no value.
def boolean(any):
    return bool(any)

# Convert string to float, or to zero if no value.
def floatnum(any):
    s_balance = (any.replace('$','').replace(',','')).strip()
    return float(s_balance or 0)
```

The next line creates an empty list named `people` to provide a place to store the objects that the program will create from the CSV file:

```
# Create an empty list of people.
people = []
```

Next, the code defines a class that will be used to generate each `Person` object from the CSV file:

```
# Define a class where each person is an object.
class Person:
    def __init__(self, id, first_name, last_name, birth_year, date_joined,
                 is_active, balance):
        self.id = id
        self.first_name = first_name
        self.last_name = last_name
        self.birth_year = birth_year
        self.date_joined = date_joined
        self.is_active = is_active
        self.balance = balance
```

The reading of the CSV file starts in the next lines. The code opens the `sample.csv` file with encoding. The `newline=''` just prevents the code from sticking the newline character at the end of each row to the last item of data in each row. The `reader` uses an enumerator to keep a count while reading the rows. The `f.readline()` reads the first row, which is just column heads, so that the `for` that follows starts on the second row. The `i` variable in the `for` loop is the incrementing counter, and the `row` is the entire row of data from the CSV file:

```
# Open CSV file with UTF-8 encoding, don't read in newline characters.
with open('sample.csv', encoding='utf-8', newline='') as f:
```

```
# Set up a csv reader with a counter.
reader = enumerate(csv.reader(f))
# Skip the first row, which is column names.
f.readline()
# Loop through remaining rows one at a time, i is counter, row is
# entire row.
for i, row in reader:
```

With each pass through the loop, the code creates a single Person object from the incrementing counter (i) and appends the data in the row. Note how we've called on the functions defined earlier in the code to do the data type conversions. This makes this code more compact and a little easier to read and work with:

```
# From each data row in the CSV file, create a Person object with unique
# id and appropriate data types, add to people list.
people.append(Person(i, fname(row[0]), lname(row[0]), integer(row[1]),
            date(row[2]), boolean(row[3]), floatnum(row[4])))
```

When the loop is complete, the next code simply displays each object on the screen to verify that the code worked correctly:

```
# When above loop is done, show all objects in the people list.
for p in people:
    print(p.id, p.first_name, p.last_name, p.birth_year, p.date_joined,
        p.is_active, p.balance)
```

Figure 1-12 shows the output from running this program. Of course, subsequent code in the program can do anything you need to do with each object; the printing is there to test and verify that the program worked.

Importing CSV to Python dictionaries

If you prefer to store each row of data from the CSV file in its own dictionary, you can use code that's similar to the preceding code for creating objects. You don't need the class definition code, because you won't be creating objects here. Instead of creating a people list, you can create an empty people dictionary to hold all the individual "person" dictionaries, like this:

```
# Create an empty dictionary of people.
people = {}
```

```
34    # Create an empty list of people.
35    people = []
36    # Define a class where each person is an object.
37    class Person:
38        def __init__(self, id, first_name, last_name, birth_year, date_joined, is_active, balance):
39            self.id = id
40            self.first_name = first_name
41            self.last_name = last_name
42            self.birth_year = birth_year
43            self.date_joined = date_joined
44            self.is_active = is_active
45            self.balance = balance
46
47    # Open CSV file with UTF-8 encoding, don't read in newline characters.
48    with open('sample.csv', encoding='utf-8', newline='') as f:
49        # Set up a csv reader with a counter.
50        reader = enumerate(csv.reader(f))
51        # Skip the first row, which is column names.
52        f.readline()
53        # Loop through remaining rows one at a time, i is counter, row is entire row.
54        for i, row in reader:
55            # From each data row in the CSV file, create a Person object with unique id and appropriate data types, add to people list.
56            people.append(Person(i, fname(row[0]), lname(row[0]), integer(row[1]), date(row[2]), boolean(row[3]), floatnum(row[4])))
57
58    # When above loop is done, show all objects in the people list.
59    for p in people:
60        print(p.id, p.first_name, p.last_name, p.birth_year, p.date_joined, p.is_active, p.balance)
61
```

```
PROBLEMS    OUTPUT    DEBUG CONSOLE    TERMINAL

0  Annie Angst 1982 2011-01-11 True 300.0
1  Barry Bónañas 1973 2012-02-11 True -123.45
2  Sandy Schadenfreude 2004 2003-03-03 True 0.0
3  Wanda Weltschmerz 1995 1994-04-24 True 999999.99
4  Mindy Malaise 2006 2005-05-05 True 454.01
5  Ollie O'Possum 1987 1997-07-27 True -1000.0
6  0 None False 0.0
7  Pamela Pusillanimity 1979 2008-08-08 True 12345.67
```

FIGURE 1-12: Reading a CSV file into a list of objects.

As far as the loop goes, again you can use an enumerator (i) to count rows, and you can also use this unique value as the key for each new dictionary you create. The line that starts with newdict= creates a dictionary with the data from one CSV file row, using the built-in Python dict() function. The next line assigns the value of i plus 1 to each newly created dictionary (to start the counting at 1 rather than 0):

```
# Loop through remaining rows one at a time, i is counter, row is entire row.
for i, row in reader:
    # From each data row in the CSV file, create a dictionary item with unique
    # id and appropriate data types, add to people list.
    newdict = dict({'first_name': fname(row[0]), 'last_name': lname(row[0]),
                    'birth_year': integer(row[1]),'date_joined' : date(row[2]),
                    'is_active' : boolean(row[3]), 'balance' : floatnum(row[4])})
    people[i + 1] = newdict
```

To verify that the code ran correctly, you can loop through the dictionaries in the people dictionary and show the *key*:*value* pair for each item of data in each row. Figure 1-13 shows the result of running that code in VS Code:

Here is all the code that reads the data from the CSV files into the dictionaries:

```
import datetime as dt
import csv
# Use these functions to convert any string to appropriate Python data type.
```

```
# Get just the first name from full name.
def fname(any):
    try:
        nm = any.split(',')
        return nm[1]
    except IndexError:
        return ''
# Get just the last name from full name.
def lname(any):
    try:
        nm = any.split(',')
        return nm[0]
    except IndexError:
        return ''
# Convert string to integer or zero if no value.
def integer(any):
    return int(any or 0)
# Convert mm/dd/yyyy date to date or None if no valid date.
def date(any):
    try:
        return dt.datetime.strptime(any, "%m/%d/%Y").date()
    except ValueError:
        return None
# Convert any string to Boolean, False if no value.
def boolean(any):
    return bool(any)
# Convert string to float, or to zero if no value.
def floatnum(any):
    s_balance = (any.replace('$', '').replace(',', '')).strip()
    return float(s_balance or 0)
# Create an empty dictionary of people.
people = {}
# Open CSV file with UTF-8 encoding, don't read in newline characters.
with open('sample.csv', encoding='utf-8', newline='') as f:
    # Set up a csv reader with a counter.
    reader = enumerate(csv.reader(f))
    # Skip the first row, which is column names.
    f.readline()
    # Loop through remaining rows one at a time, i is counter, row is
    # entire row.
    for i, row in reader:
        # From each data row in the CSV file, create a Person object with
        # unique id and appropriate data types, add
        # to people dictionary.
        newdict = dict({'first_name': fname(row[0]), 'last_name': lname(row[0]),
                        'birth_year': integer(row[1]), 'date_joined' date(row[2]),
                        'is_active' : boolean(row[3]), 'balance' :floatnum(row[4])})
        people[i + 1] = newdict
```

```
# When above loop is done, show all objects in the people list.
for person in people.keys():
    id = person
    print(id, people[person]['first_name'], \
                people[person]['last_name'], \
                people[person]['birth_year'], \
                people[person]['date_joined'], \
                people[person]['is_active'], \
                people[person]['balance'])
```

```
30   # Convert string to float, or to zero if no value.
31   def floatnum(any):
32       s_balance = (any.replace('$', '').replace(',', '')).strip()
33       return float(s_balance or 0)
34   # Create an empty dictionary of people.
35   people = {}
36   # Open CSV file with UTF-8 encoding, don't read in newline characters.
37   with open('sample.csv', encoding='utf-8', newline='') as f:
38       # Set up a csv reader with a counter.
39       reader = enumerate(csv.reader(f))
40       # Skip the first row, which is column names.
41       f.readline()
42       # Loop through remaining rows one at a time, i is counter, row is entire row.
43       for i, row in reader:
44           # From each data row in the CSV file, create a Person object with unique id and appropriate data types, add to people list.
45           newdict = dict({'first_name': fname(row[0]), 'last_name': lname(row[0]), 'birth_year': integer(row[1]), \
46                   'date_joined' : date(row[2]), 'is_active' : boolean(row[3]), 'balance' : floatnum(row[4])})
47           people[i + 1] = newdict
48
49   # When above loop is done, show all objects in the people list.
50   for person in people.keys():
51       id = person
52       print(id, people[person]['first_name'], \
53                   people[person]['last_name'], \
54                   people[person]['birth_year'], \
55                   people[person]['date_joined'], \
56                   people[person]['is_active'], \
57                   people[person]['balance'])
58
```

PROBLEMS   OUTPUT   DEBUG CONSOLE   TERMINAL

```
(base) C:\Users\acsimpson\OneDrive\AIO Python\csv_files>C:/Users/acsimpson/AppData/Local/Continuum/anaconda3/python.exe "c:/Users/acsimpson/OneDrive/AIO
1  Annie Angst 1982 2011-01-11 True 300.0
2  Barry Bónañas 1973 2012-02-11 True -123.45
3  Sandy Schadenfreude 2004 2003-03-03 True 0.0
4  Wanda Weltschmerz 1995 1994-04-24 True 999999.99
5  Mindy Malaise 2006 2005-05-05 True 454.01
6  Ollie O'Possum 1987 1997-07-27 True -1000.0
7   0 None False 0.0
8  Pamela Pusillanimity 1979 2008-08-08 True 12345.67
```

FIGURE 1-13:
Reading a CSV file
into a dictionary
of dictionaries.

CSV files are widely used because it's easy to export data from spreadsheets and database tables to this format. Getting data from those files can be tricky at times, but you'll find Python's csv module a big help. The csv module takes care of many of the details, makes it relatively easy to loop through one row at a time, and handles the data however you see fit in your Python app.

Similar to CSV for transporting and storing data in a simple textual format is JSON, or JavaScript Object Notation. You learn all about JSON in the next chapter.

Chapter **2**

Juggling JSON Data

J SON (JavaScript Object Notation) is a common marshalling format for object-oriented data. *Marshalling format* generally means a format used to send data from one computer to another. However, some databases, such as the free Realtime Database at Google's Firebase, store the data in JavaScript Object Notation format as well. The name *JavaScript* at the front sometimes throws people off, especially when you're using Python, not JavaScript, to write your code. But don't worry. The format just got its start in the JavaScript world and is now a widely known general-purpose format used with all kinds of computers and programming languages.

In this chapter, you learn exactly what JSON is, as well as how to export and import data to and from JSON. If you find that all the buzzwords surrounding JSON make you uncomfortable, don't worry. We get through all the jargon first. As you'll see, JSON data is formatted almost the same way as Python data dictionaries, so there won't be a lot of new stuff to learn. Also, you already have the free Python JSON module, which makes it even easier to work with JSON data.

Organizing JSON Data

JSON data is roughly the equivalent of a data dictionary in Python, which makes JSON files fairly easy to work with. JSON data is probably easiest to understand when it's compared to tabular data. For instance, Figure 2-1 shows some tabular data in an Excel worksheet. Figure 2-2 shows the same data converted to JSON format. Each row of data in the Excel sheet has been converted to a dictionary of *key:value* pairs in the JSON file. And there are, of course, lots of curly braces to indicate that the data is dictionary data.

FIGURE 2-1: Some data in an Excel spreadsheet.

	A	B	C	D	E
1	Full Name	Birth Year	Date Joined	Is Active	Balance
2	Angst, Annie	1982	1/11/2011	TRUE	$300.00
3	Bónañas, Barry	1973	2/11/2012	FALSE	-$123.45
4	Schadenfreude, Sandy	2004	3/3/2003	TRUE	$0.00
5	Weltschmerz, Wanda	1995	4/24/1994	FALSE	$999,999.99
6	Malaise, Mindy	2006	5/5/2005	TRUE	$454.01
7	O'Possum, Ollie	1987	7/27/1997	TRUE	-$1,000.00
8					
9	Pusillanimity, Pamela	1979	8/8/2008	TRUE	$12,345.67

FIGURE 2-2: Excel spreadsheet data converted to JSON format.

Exporting data from Excel is just one way to create a JSON file. You can also create a *keyed JSON file*, where each chunk of data has a single key that uniquely identifies it. (No other dictionary in the same file can have the same key.) The key can be a number or text; it doesn't really matter which, as long as it's unique to each item. When you're downloading JSON files created by someone else, it's not unusual for the file to be keyed. For example, on Alan's personal website, he uses the free Google Firebase Realtime Database to count hits per page and other information about each page. The Realtime Database stores the data as shown in

Figure 2-3. Those weird things like -LAOqOxg6kmP4jhnjQXS are all keys that the Firebase generates automatically for each item of data to guarantee uniqueness. The + sign next to each key allows you to expand and collapse the information under each key.

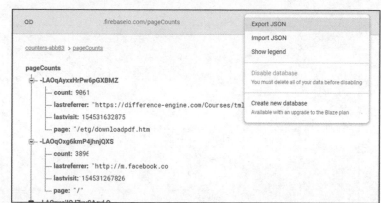

FIGURE 2-3:
Some data
in a Google
Firebase Realtime
Database.

CONVERTING EXCEL TO JSON

In case you're wondering, to convert that sample Excel spreadsheet to JSON, set your browser to www.convertcsv.com/csv-to-json.htm and follow these steps:

1. In Step 1, open the Choose File tab, set the Encoding to UTF-8, click the Choose File button, select your Excel file, and click Open.

2. In Step 2, make sure the First Row Is Column Names option is selected and set Skip # of Lines to 1 to skip the column headings row.

3. In Step 5, click the CSV to JSON button.

4. Next to Save Your Result, type a filename and then click the Download Result button.

The file should end up in your Downloads folder (or to whatever location you normally download) with a .json extension. It's a plain text file, so you can open it with any text editor or a code editor such as VS Code. The converter automatically skips empty rows in Excel files, so your JSON file won't contain any data for empty rows in a spreadsheet. If you often work with Excel, CSV, JSON, and similar types of data, you may want to spend some time exploring the many tools and capabilities that the www.convertcsv.com website provides.

As you can see in the figure, Firebase also has an Export JSON option that downloads the data to a JSON file on your computer. Figure 2-4 shows the data in the downloaded file. You can tell that one is a keyed JSON file because each chunk of data is preceded by a unique key, such as *-LAOqAyxxHrPw6pGXBMZ*, followed by a colon. You can work with both keyed and unkeyed JSON files in Python.

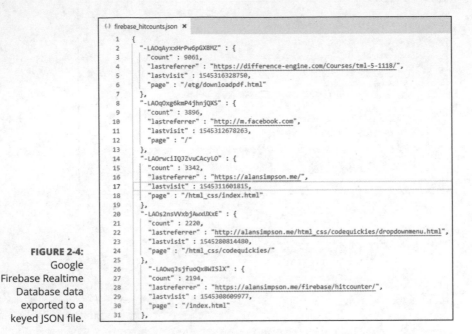

```
{} firebase_hitcounts.json ×
 1    {
 2      "-LAOqAyxxHrPw6pGXBMZ" : {
 3        "count" : 9061,
 4        "lastreferrer" : "https://difference-engine.com/Courses/tml-5-1118/",
 5        "lastvisit" : 1545316328750,
 6        "page" : "/etg/downloadpdf.html"
 7      },
 8      "-LAOqOxg6kmP4jhnjQX5" : {
 9        "count" : 3896,
10        "lastreferrer" : "http://m.facebook.com",
11        "lastvisit" : 1545312678263,
12        "page" : "/"
13      },
14      "-LAOrwciIQJZvuCAcyLO" : {
15        "count" : 3342,
16        "lastreferrer" : "https://alansimpson.me/",
17        "lastvisit" : 1545311601815,
18        "page" : "/html_css/index.html"
19      },
20      "-LAOs2nsVVxbjAwxUXxE" : {
21        "count" : 2220,
22        "lastreferrer" : "http://alansimpson.me/html_css/codequickies/dropdownmenu.html",
23        "lastvisit" : 1545280814480,
24        "page" : "/html_css/codequickies/"
25      },
26      "-LAOwqJsjfuoQx8WISlX" : {
27        "count" : 2194,
28        "lastreferrer" : "https://alansimpson.me/firebase/hitcounter/",
29        "lastvisit" : 1545308609977,
30        "page" : "/index.html"
31      },
```

FIGURE 2-4:
Google Firebase Realtime Database data exported to a keyed JSON file.

Some readers may have noticed that the `Date Joined` field in the JSON file doesn't look like a normal *mm/dd/yyyy* date. The `lastvisit` field from the Firebase database is a `datetime`, even though it doesn't look like a date or time. But don't worry about that. You'll learn how to convert odd-looking serial dates (as they're called) to human-readable format later in this chapter.

Understanding Serialization

When it comes to JSON, the first buzzword you have to learn is serialization. *Serialization* is the process of converting an object (such as a Python dictionary) into a stream of bytes or characters that can be sent across a wire, stored in a file or database, or stored in memory. The main purpose is to save all the information in an object in a way that can be retrieved easily on any other computer. The process of converting the information back to an object is called *deserialization*. To keep things simple you may just consider using these definitions:

>> **Serialize:** Convert an object to a string.

>> **Deserialize:** Convert a string to an object.

The Python standard library includes a `json` module that helps you work with JSON files. Because it's part of the standard library, you just have to put `import json` near the top of your code to access its capabilities. The four main methods for serializing and deserializing `json` are summarized in Table 2-1.

TABLE 2-1

Python JSON Methods for Serializing and Deserializing JSON Data

Method	Purpose
`json.dump()`	Write (serialize) Python data to a JSON file (or stream).
`json.dumps()`	Write (serialize) a Python object to a JSON string.
`json.load()`	Load (deserialize) JSON from a file or similar object.
`json.loads()`	Load (deserialize) JSON data from a string.

Data types in JSON are similar but not identical to data types in Python. Table 2-2 lists how data types are converted between the two languages when serializing and deserializing.

TABLE 2-2

Python and JSON Data Conversions

Python	JSON
dict	object
list, tuple	array
str	string
int and float	number
True	true
False	false
None	null

Loading Data from JSON Files

To load data from JSON files, make sure you import `json` near the top of the code. Then you can use a regular file `open()` method to open the file. As with other kinds of files, you can add `encoding = "utf-8"` if you need to preserve non-ASCII characters in the data. You can also use `newline=""` to avoid bringing in the newline character at the end of each row. The newline character isn't really part of the data; it's a hidden character to end the line when displaying the data on the screen.

To load the JSON data into Python, come up with a variable name to hold the data (we'll use `people`). Then use `json.load()` to load the file contents into the variable, like this:

```python
import json
# This is the Excel data (no keys)
filename = 'people_from_excel.json'
# Open the file (standard file open stuff)
with open(filename, 'r', encoding='utf-8', newline='') as f:
    # Load the whole json file into an object named people
    people = json.load(f)
```

Running this code doesn't display anything on the screen. However, you can explore the `people` object in a number of ways by using un-indented `print()` statements below the last line. For example, the following displays everything in the `people` variable:

```python
print(people)
```

The output starts and ends with square brackets (`[]`), which tell you that `people` is a list. To verify this, you can run this line of code:

```python
print(type(people))
```

Python displays the following:

```python
<class 'list'>
```

This line tells you that the object is an instance of the `list` class. In other words, it's a `list` object, although most people would just call it a list.

Because the object is a list, you can loop through it. Within the loop, you can display the type of each item, like this:

```
for p in people:
    print(type(p))
```

The output follows:

```
<class 'dict'>
<class 'dict'>
<class 'dict'>
<class 'dict'>
<class 'dict'>
<class 'dict'>
<class 'dict'>
```

This is useful information because it tells you that each of the "people" (which we've abbreviated p in that code) in the list is a Python dictionary. So within the loop, you can isolate each value by its key. For example, take a look at this code:

```
for p in people:
    print(p['Full Name'], p['Birth Year'], p['Date Joined'], p['Is Active'],
        p['Balance'])
```

Running this code displays all the data in the JSON file, as in the following. This data came from the Excel spreadsheet shown in Figure 2-1.

```
Angst, Annie 1982 40554 True 300
Bónañas, Barry 1973 40950 False -123.45
Schadenfreude, Sandy 2004 37683 True 0
Weltschmerz, Wanda 1995 34448 False 999999.99
Malaise, Mindy 2006 38477 True 454.01
O'Possum, Ollie 1987 35638 True -1000
Pusillanimity, Pamela 1979 39668 True 12345.67
```

Converting an Excel date to a JSON date

You may be thinking "Hey, waitaminit . . . what's with those 40554, 40950, 37683 numbers in the Date Joined column?" Well, those are serial dates, but you can convert them to Python dates. You'll need to import the xlrd (Excel reader) and datetime modules. Then, to convert that integer in the p['Date Joined'] column to a Python date, use this code:

```
y, m, d, h, i, s = xlrd.xldate_as_tuple(p['Date Joined'],0)
joined = dt.date(y, m, d)
```

To display this date in a familiar format, use an f-string like this:

```
print(f"{joined:%m/%d/%Y}")
```

Here is all the code, including the necessary imports at the top of the file:

```
import json, xlrd
import datetime as dt
# This is the Excel data (no keys)
filename = 'people_from_excel.json'
# Open the file (standard file open stuff)
with open(filename, 'r', encoding='utf-8', newline='') as f:
    # Load the whole json file into an object named people
    people = json.load(f)

# Dictionaries are in a list, loop through and display each dictionary.
for p in people:
    name = p['Full Name']
    byear = p['Birth Year']
    # Excel date pretty tricky, use xlrd module.
    y, m, d, h, i, s = xlrd.xldate_as_tuple(p['Date Joined'], 0)
    joined = dt.date(y, m, d)
    balance = '$' + f"{p['Balance']:,.2f}"
    print(f"{name:<22} {byear}   {joined:%m/%d/%Y} {balance:>12}")
```

Here is the output, which is neatly formatted and looks more like the original Excel data than the JSON data. If you need to display the data in *dd/mm/yyyy* format, change the pattern in the last line of code to %d/%m/%Y.

```
Angst, Annie           1982   01/11/2011       $300.00
Bónañas, Barry         1973   02/11/2012      $-123.45
Schadenfreude, Sandy   2004   03/03/2003         $0.00
Weltschmerz, Wanda     1995   04/24/1994   $999,999.99
Malaise, Mindy         2006   05/05/2005       $454.01
O'Possum, Ollie        1987   07/27/1997    $-1,000.00
Pusillanimity, Pamela  1979   08/08/2008    $12,345.67
```

Looping through a keyed JSON file

Opening and loading a keyed JSON file is the same as opening a non-keyed file. However, after the data is loaded, it's a single dictionary rather than a list of dictionaries. For example, here is the code to open and load the data we exported from Firebase (the original is shown in Figure 2-4). This data contains hit counts for pages in a website, including the page name, the number of hits to date, the last referrer (the last page that sent someone to that page), and the date and time of the last visit. As you can see, the code for opening and loading the JSON data is basically the same. The JSON data loads to an object we named hits:

```
import json
import datetime as dt
# This is the Firebase JSON data (keyed).
filename = 'firebase_hitcounts.json'
# Open the file (standard file open stuff).
with open(filename, 'r', encoding='utf-8', newline='') as f:
    # Load the whole json file into an object named people
    hits = json.load(f)

print(type(hits))
```

When you run this code, the last line displays the data type of the `hits` object, into which the JSON data was loaded, as `<class 'dict'>`. This tells you that the `hits` object is one large dictionary rather than a list of individual dictionaries. You can loop through this dictionary using a simple loop like we did for the non-keyed JSON file:

```
for p in hits:
    print(p)
```

The result, however, is that you don't see much data. All you see is the key for each subdictionary contained in the larger `hits` dictionary:

```
-LAOqAyxxHrPw6pGXBMZ
-LAOqOxg6kmP4jhnjQXS
-LAOrwciIQJZvuCAcyLO
-LAOs2nsVVxbjAwxUXxE
-LAOwqJsjfuoQx8WIS1X
-LAQ7ShbQPqOANbDmm3O
-LAQrS6av1v0PuJGNm6P
-LI0iPwZ7nu3IUgiQORH
-LI2DFNAxVnT-cxYzWR-
```

This output is not an error or a problem. It's just how nested dictionaries work. But don't worry, it's easy to get to the data inside each dictionary. For instance, you can use two looping variables, which we'll call k (for *key*) and v (for *value*), to loop through `hits.items()`:

```
for k, v in hits.items():
    print(k, v)
```

This gives you a different view in which you see each key followed by the dictionary for that key enclosed in curly braces, as shown in Figure 2-5. (The curly braces tell you that the data inside is in a dictionary.)

```
  keyed_json.py  ×
1    import json
2    import datetime as dt
3    # This is the Firebase JSON data (keyed).
4    filename = 'firebase_hitcounts.json'
5    # Open the file (standard file open stuff).
6    with open(filename, 'r', encoding='utf-8', newline='') as f:
7        # Load the whole json file into an object named hits.
8        hits = json.load(f)
9
10   for k, v in hits.items():
11       print(k,v)
12

PROBLEMS    OUTPUT    DEBUG CONSOLE    TERMINAL
-LAOqAyxo4H-Pw6pGXBMZ {'count': 9061, 'lastreferrer': 'https://difference-engine.com/Courses/tml-5-1118/', 'lastvisit': 1545316328750, 'page': '/etg/downloadpdf.html'}
-LAOqOxqg6kmPA1hnjQXS {'count': 3896, 'lastreferrer': 'http://m.facebook.com', 'lastvisit': 1545312678263, 'page': '/'}
-LAOrwc1IQJZvuCAcyLO {'count': 3342, 'lastreferrer': 'https://alansimpson.me/', 'lastvisit': 1545311601815, 'page': '/html_css/index.html'}
-LAOs2nsWxbjAwxUXxE {'count': 2220, 'lastreferrer': 'http://alansimpson.me/html_css/codequickies/dropdownmenu.html', 'lastvisit': 1545280814480, 'page': '/html_css/co
-LAOxq3sjfuoQx8WISlX {'count': 2194, 'lastreferrer': 'https://alansimpson.me/firebase/hitcounter/', 'lastvisit': 1545308609977, 'page': '/index.html'}
-LAQ7ShbQPqOAWbDmm3O {'count': 1154, 'lastreferrer': 'https://alansimpson.me/javascript/code_quickies/clickdropdown/', 'lastvisit': 1544974827730, 'page': '/javascript
-LAQrS6avlv0PuJGNm6P {'count': 1547, 'lastreferrer': '', 'lastvisit': 1545305365597, 'page': '/how/'}
-LI0IPwZ7nu3IUg1QORH {'count': 1439, 'lastreferrer': 'https://www.youtube.com/', 'lastvisit': 1545315903301, 'page': '/datascience/beginner/'}
-LI2DFNAxVnT-cxYzwR- {'count': 1643, 'lastreferrer': '', 'lastvisit': 1545226502089, 'page': '/datascience/cheatsheets/'}
```

FIGURE 2-5:
Output from looping through and displaying keys and values from subdictionaries.

The values for each subdictionary are in the v object of this loop. If you want to access individual items of data, use v followed by a pair of square brackets with the key name (for the field) inside. For example, v['count'] contains whatever is stored as the count: in a given row. Take a look at this code, which displays the data but not the key.

```
for k, v in hits.items():
    # Store items in variables.
    key = k
    hits = v['count']
    last_visit = v['lastvisit']
    page = v['page']
    came_from = v['lastreferrer']
    print(f"{hits} {last_visit} {page:<28} {came_from}")
```

The output is the data from each dictionary, formatted in a way that's a little easier to read, as shown in Figure 2-6.

FIGURE 2-6:
Output showing one value at a time from each dictionary.

```
9061 1545316328750 /etg/downloadpdf.html          https://difference-engine.com/Courses/tml-5-1118/
3896 1545312678263 /                              http://m.facebook.com
3342 1545311601815 /html_css/index.html           https://alansimpson.me/
2220 1545280814480 /html_css/codequickies/         http://alansimpson.me/html_css/codequickies/dropdownmenu.html
2194 1545308609977 /index.html                     https://alansimpson.me/firebase/hitcounter/
1154 1544974827730 /javascript/code_quickies/      https://alansimpson.me/javascript/code_quickies/clickdropdown/
1547 1545305365597 /how/
1439 1545315903301 /datascience/beginner/          https://www.youtube.com/
1643 1545226502089 /datascience/cheatsheets/
```

You may have noticed that we've run into another weird situation with the last-visit column. The date appears in the format *545316328750* rather than the more familiar *mm/dd/yyyy* format. This time we can't blame Excel because these dates were never in Excel. What you're seeing is the Firebase timestamp of when the data item was last written to the database. This date is expressed as a UTC date, including the time down to the nanosecond, which is why the number is so long. Obviously, if people are to understand these dates, you should translate them to Python dates, as we discuss next.

Converting Firebase timestamps to Python dates

As always, the first thing you need to do when working with dates and times in a Python app is to make sure you've imported the datetime module, which we usually do by using the code import datetime as dt, in which the dt is an optional *alias* (a nickname that's easier to type than the full name).

Because the Firebase datetime is UTC-based, we know that we can use the datetime .utcfromtimestamp() method to convert that date to Python time. But there's a catch. If you follow the documentation, you'd expect the following to work:

```
last_visit = dt.datetime.utcfromtimestamp(v['lastvisit'])
```

However, apparently that nanosecond resolution we mentioned in the preceding section is a bit much in Windows and this code raises an OS Error exception. Fortunately, an easy work-around exists. Dividing that lastvisit number by 1,000 trims the last few digits, which gets the number into a lower-resolution datetime that Windows can stomach. All we really care about in this application is the date of the last visit; we don't care about the time. So you can grab just the date and get past the error by writing the code like this:

```
last_visit = dt.datetime.utcfromtimestamp(v['lastvisit']/1000).date()
```

You end up with a simple Python date in the last_visit variable, so you can use a standard f-string to format the date however you like. For example, use the following in your f-string to display the last_visit date:

```
{last_visit: %m/%d/%Y}
```

The dates will be in *mm/dd/yyyy* format in the output, like this:

```
12/20/2018
12/19/2018
12/17/2018
12/20/2018
11/30/2018
12/16/2018
12/20/2018
12/20/2018
12/19/2018
```

Loading unkeyed JSON from a Python string

The load() method we used in the previous examples loaded the JSON data from a file. However, because JSON data is always delivered in a text file, you can copy and paste the entire thing into a Python string. Typically, you give the string a variable name and set it equal to some triple-quoted string (like a Python docstring) that starts and ends with triple quotation marks. Put all the JSON data inside the triple quotation marks as in the following code. To keep the code short, we've included data for only a few people, but at least you can see how the data is structured:

```
import json
# Here the JSON data is in a big string named json_string.
# It starts with the first triple quotation marks and extends
# down to the last triple quotation marks.
json_string = """
{
"people": [
    {
    "Full Name": "Angst, Annie",
    "Birth Year": 1982,
    "Date Joined": "01/11/2011",
    "Is Active": true,
    "Balance": 300
  },
 {
    "Full Name": "Schadenfreude, Sandy",
    "Birth Year": 2004,
    "Date Joined": "03/03/2003",
    "Is Active": true,
    "Balance": 0
  }
]
}
"""
```

Seeing all the data from within your code like this might be nice, but there is one big disadvantage: You can't loop through a string to get to individual items of data. If you want to loop through, you need to load the JSON data from the string into an object. To do this, use json.loads() (where the s in loads is short for *from string*), as in the following code. That peep_data is a name we made up to differentiate the loaded JSON data from the data in the string:

```
# Load JSON data from the big json_string string.
peep_data = json.loads(json_string)
```

Now that you have an object (peep_data), you can loop through and work with the code one bit at a time, like this:

```
# Now you can loop through the peep_data collection.
for p in peep_data['people']:
    print(p["Full Name"], p["Birth Year"], p["Date Joined"],
        p['Is Active'],p['Balance'])
```

Figure 2-7 shows all the code and the result of running that code in VS Code.

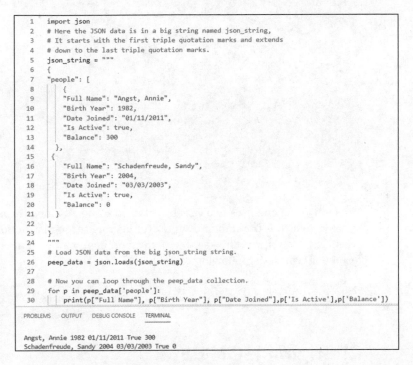

```
1    import json
2    # Here the JSON data is in a big string named json_string,
3    # It starts with the first triple quotation marks and extends
4    # down to the last triple quotation marks.
5    json_string = """
6    {
7    "people": [
8        {
9        "Full Name": "Angst, Annie",
10       "Birth Year": 1982,
11       "Date Joined": "01/11/2011",
12       "Is Active": true,
13       "Balance": 300
14       },
15       {
16       "Full Name": "Schadenfreude, Sandy",
17       "Birth Year": 2004,
18       "Date Joined": "03/03/2003",
19       "Is Active": true,
20       "Balance": 0
21       }
22    ]
23    }
24    """
25    # Load JSON data from the big json_string string.
26    peep_data = json.loads(json_string)
27
28    # Now you can loop through the peep_data collection.
29    for p in peep_data['people']:
30        print(p["Full Name"], p["Birth Year"], p["Date Joined"],p['Is Active'],p['Balance'])

PROBLEMS   OUTPUT   DEBUG CONSOLE   TERMINAL

Angst, Annie 1982 01/11/2011 True 300
Schadenfreude, Sandy 2004 03/03/2003 True 0
```

FIGURE 2-7: Output from showing one value at a time from each dictionary (see bottom of image).

Loading keyed JSON from a Python string

You can store not only unkeyed data but also keyed data in a Python string. In the following example, we used json_string as the variable name again, but the data inside the string is structured differently. The first item has a key of 1 and the second item has a key of 2. But again, the code uses json.loads(json_string) to load this data from the string into a JSON object:

```
import json
# Here the JSON data is in a big string named json_string.
# It starts with the first triple quotation marks and extends
```

```
# down to the last triple quotation marks.
json_string = """
  {
  "1": {
    "count": 9061,
    "lastreferrer": "https://difference-engine.com/Courses/tml-5-1118/",
    "lastvisit": "12/20/2018",
    "page": "/etg/downloadpdf.html"
  },
  "2": {
    "count": 3342,
    "lastreferrer": "https://alansimpson.me/",
    "lastvisit": "12/19/2018",
    "page": "/html_css/index.html"
  }
  }
"""
# Load JSON data from the big json_string string.
hits_data = json.loads(json_string)

# Now you can loop through the hits_data collection.
for k, v in hits_data.items():
    print(f"{k}. {v['count']:>5} - {v['page']}")
```

The loop at the end uses two variables named k and v to loop through hits_data.
items(), which is the standard syntax for looping through a dictionary of dictionaries. The loop prints the key, hit count, and page name from each item, in the
format shown in the following code:

```
1. 9061 - /etg/downloadpdf.html
2. 3342 - /html_css/index.html
```

Changing JSON data

When you have JSON data in a data dictionary, you can use standard dictionary
procedures (originally presented in Book 2, Chapter 4) to manipulate the data in
the dictionary. As you're looping through the data dictionary with key:value variables, you can change the value of any key:value pair using the relatively simple
syntax:

```
value['key'] = newdata
```

Note that *key* and *value* are just the k and v variables from the loop. For example, suppose you're looping through a dictionary created from the Firebase database, which includes a lastvisit field shown as a UTC timestamp number. You want to change this timestamp to a string in a more familiar Python format. Set up a loop as in the following code, in which the first line inside the loop creates a new variable named pydate that contains the date as a Python date. Then the second line replaces the contents of v['lastvisit'] with this date in *mm/dd/yy* format:

```
for k, v in hits_data.items():
    # Convert the Firebase date to a Python date.
    pydate = dt.datetime.utcfromtimestamp(v['lastvisit']/1000).date()
    # In the dictionary, replace the Firebase date with Python date.
    v['lastvisit']= f"{pydate:%m/%d/%Y})"
```

When this loop is complete, all the values in the lastvisit column will be dates in *mm/dd/yyyy* format rather than Firebase timestamp format.

Removing data from a dictionary

To remove data from a dictionary as you're going through the loop, use this syntax:

```
pop('keyname', None)
```

Replace 'keyname' with the name of the column you want to remove. For example, to remove all the lastreferrer key names and data from a dictionary created by the Firebase database JSON example, add the following to the loop:

```
v.pop('lastreferrer', None)
```

Figure 2-8 shows an example where lines 1–8 import Firebase data into a Python object named hits_data. Line 10 starts a loop that goes through each key (k) and value (v) in the dictionary. Line 12 converts the timestamp to a Python date named pydate. Then line 16 replaces the timestring that was in the lastvisit column with that Python date as a string in *mm/dd/yyyy* format. Line 16, v.pop('lastreferrer', None), removes the lastreferrer *key:value* pair from each dictionary. The final loop shows what's in the dictionary after making these changes.

Keep in mind that changes you make to the dictionary in Python have no effect on the file or string from which you loaded the JSON data. If you want to create a new JSON string or file, use the json.dumps() or json.dump() method, discussed next.

```
1    import json
2    import datetime as dt
3    # This is the Firebase JSON data (keyed).
4    filename = 'firebase_hitcounts.json'
5    # Open the file (standard file open stuff).
6    with open(filename, 'r', encoding='utf-8', newline='') as f:
7        # Load the whole json file into an object named hits
8        hits = json.load(f)
9
10   for k, v in hits.items():
11       # Convert the Firebase date to a Python date.
12       pydate = dt.datetime.utcfromtimestamp(v['lastvisit']/1000).date()
13       # In the dictionary, replace the Firebase date with string of Python date.
14       v['lastvisit']= f"{pydate:%m/%d/%Y})"
15       # Remove the entire last referrer column.
16       v.pop('lastreferrer', None)
17
18   # Now look at the lastvisit date in the hits dictionary.
19   for k, v in hits.items():
20       print(k,v)
21
22
```

```
PROBLEMS    OUTPUT    DEBUG CONSOLE    TERMINAL
-LAOqAyxxHrPw6pGXBMZ {'count': 9061, 'lastvisit': '12/20/2018'}, 'page': '/etg/downloadpdf.html'}
-LAOqOxg6kmP4jhnjQXS {'count': 3896, 'lastvisit': '12/20/2018'}, 'page': '/'}
-LAOrwciIQJZvuCAcyLO {'count': 3342, 'lastvisit': '12/20/2018'}, 'page': '/html_css/index.html'}
-LAOs2nsVVxbjAwxUXxE {'count': 2220, 'lastvisit': '12/20/2018'}, 'page': '/html_css/codequickies/'}
-LAOwqJsjfuoQx8wISlX {'count': 2194, 'lastvisit': '12/20/2018'}, 'page': '/index.html'}
-LAQ7ShbQPqOANbDmm3O {'count': 1154, 'lastvisit': '12/16/2018'}, 'page': '/javascript/code_quickies/'}
-LAQrS6av1v0PuJGNm6P {'count': 1547, 'lastvisit': '12/20/2018'}, 'page': '/how/'}
-LI0iPwZ7nu3IUgiQORH {'count': 1439, 'lastvisit': '12/20/2018'}, 'page': '/datascience/beginner/'}
-LI2DFNAxVnT-cXYzWR- {'count': 1643, 'lastvisit': '12/19/2018'}, 'page': '/datascience/cheatsheets/'}
```

FIGURE 2-8: Changing the value of one key in each dictionary, and removing an entire key:value pair from the dictionary.

Dumping Python Data to JSON

So far we've talked about bringing JSON data from the outside world into your app so Python can use its data. Sometimes, you may want to go in the opposite direction, to take some data already in your app in a dictionary format and export it to JSON to pass to another app, the public at large, or whatever. This is where the json.dump() and json.dumps() methods come into play.

The dumps() method creates a JSON string of the data, which is still in memory so you can use print() to see it. For example, the previous code examples imported a Firebase database to a Python dictionary, and then looped through that dictionary changing all the timestamps to *mm/dd/yyyy* dates and removing all the lastreferrer *key:value* pairs. So let's say that you want to create a JSON string of this new dictionary. You could use dumps like the following to create a string named new_dict, and you could also print that string to the console. The last two lines of code outside the loop would be

```
# Looping is done, copy new dictionary to JSON string.
new_dict = json.dumps(hits)
print(new_dict)
```

The new_dict string would show in its native, not-very-readable format, which would look something like this:

```
{"-LAOqAyxxHrPw6pGXBMZ": {"count": 9061, "lastvisit": "12/20/2018)", "page":
          "/etg/downloadpdf.html"}, "-LAOqOxg6kmP4jhnjQXS": {"count": 3896,
          "lastvisit": "12/20/2018)", "page": "/"}, "-LAOrwciIQJZvuCAcyLO":
          {"count": 3342, "lastvisit": "12/20/2018)", "page":
          "/html_css/index.html"}, ... }}
```

We replaced some of the data with ... because you don't need to see all the items to see how unreadable it looks.

Fortunately, the .dumps() method supports an indent= option which you can use to indent the JSON data and make it more readable. Two spaces is usually sufficient. For example, add indent=2 to the preceding code:

```
#Looping is done, copy new dictionary to JSON string.
new_dict = json.dumps(hits, indent=2)
print(new_dict)
```

The output shows the JSON data in a much more readable format:

```
{
  "-LAOqAyxxHrPw6pGXBMZ": {
    "count": 9061,
    "lastvisit": "12/20/2018)",
    "page": "/etg/downloadpdf.html"
  },
  "-LAOqOxg6kmP4jhnjQXS": {
    "count": 3896,
    "lastvisit": "12/20/2018)",
    "page": "/"
  },
  ...
}
```

If you use non-ASCII characters in your data dictionary and you want to preserve them, add ensure_ascii=False to your code, as follows:

```
new_dict = json.dumps(hits, indent=2, ensure_ascii=False)
```

In our example, the key names in each dictionary are already in alphabetical order (count, lastvisit, page). But in your own code, if you want to ensure that the keys in each dictionary are in alphabetical order, add sortkeys=True to your .dumps method as follows:

```
new_dict = json.dumps(hits, indent=2, ensure_ascii=False, sort_keys=True)
```

If you want to output your JSON data to a file, use `json.dump()` rather than `json.dumps()`. You can use `ensure_ascii=False` to maintain non-ASCII characters, and `sort_keys=True` to alphabetize key names. You can also include an `indent=` option, although that would make the file larger, and typically you want to keep files small to conserve space and minimize download time.

As an example, suppose you want to create a file named `hitcounts_new.json` (or, if it already exists, open it to overwrite its contents). You want to retain any non-ASCII characters that you write to the file. Here's the code for that; the `'w'` is required to make sure the file opens for writing data into it:

```
with open('hitcounts_new.json', 'w', encoding='utf-8') as out_file:
```

Then, to copy the dictionary named `hits` as JSON data into this file, use the name you assigned at the end of the code in the preceding line. Again, to retain any no-ASCII characters and optionally to alphabetize the key names in each dictionary, follow that line with this one, indented so that it's contained in the `with` block:

```
json.dump(hits, out_file, ensure_ascii=False, sort_keys=True)
```

Figure 2-9 shows all the code starting with the data that was exported from Firebase, looping through the dictionary that the import created, changing and removing some content, and then writing the new dictionary out to a new JSON file named `hitcounts_new.json`.

```
1   import json
2   import datetime as dt
3   # This is the Firebase JSON data (keyed).
4   filename = 'firebase_hitcounts.json'
5   # Open the file (standard file open stuff).
6   with open(filename, 'r', encoding='utf-8', newline='') as f:
7       # Load the whole json file into an object named hits.
8       hits = json.load(f)
9
10  # Loop through the new hits data dictionary.
11  for k, v in hits.items():
12      # Convert the Firebase date to a Python date.
13      pydate = dt.datetime.utcfromtimestamp(v['lastvisit']/1000).date()
14      # In the dictionary, replace the Firebase date with string of Python date.
15      v['lastvisit'] = f"{pydate:%m/%d/%Y})"
16      # Remove the entire last referrer column.
17      v.pop('lastreferrer', None)
18
19  # Write the modifed data to a JSON file named hitcounts_new.json.
20  with open('hitcounts_new.json', 'w', encoding='utf-8') as out_file:
21      json.dump(hits, out_file, ensure_ascii=False, sort_keys=True)
22
23  print('Done')
```

FIGURE 2-9: Writing modified Firebase data to a new JSON file named `hitcounts_new.json`.

Figure 2-10 shows the contents of the `hitcounts_new.json` file after running the app. We didn't indent the JSON data because files are really for storing or sharing, not for looking at, but you can still see that the `datevisited` values are in *mm/dd/ yyyy* format and the `lastreferrer` *key:value* pair isn't in there because earlier code removed it.

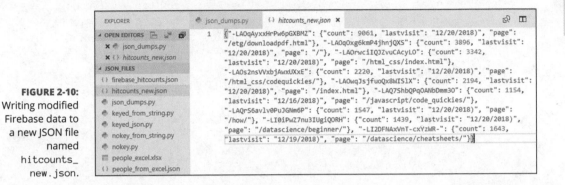

```
{"-LAOqAyxxHrPw6pGXBMZ": {"count": 9061, "lastvisit": "12/20/2018)", "page":
"/etg/downloadpdf.html"}, "-LAOqOxg6kmP4jhnjQXS": {"count": 3896, "lastvisit":
"12/20/2018)", "page": "/"}, "-LAOrwciIQJZvuCAcyLO": {"count": 3342,
"lastvisit": "12/20/2018)", "page": "/html_css/index.html"},
"-LAOs2nsVVxbjAwxUXxE": {"count": 2220, "lastvisit": "12/20/2018)", "page":
"/html_css/codequickies/"}, "-LAOwqJsjfuoQx8WISlX": {"count": 2194, "lastvisit":
"12/20/2018)", "page": "/index.html"}, "-LAQ7ShbQPqOANbDmm3O": {"count": 1154,
"lastvisit": "12/16/2018)", "page": "/javascript/code_quickies/"},
"-LAQrS6avlv0PuJGNm6P": {"count": 1547, "lastvisit": "12/20/2018)", "page":
"/how/"}, "-LI0iPwZ7nu3IUgiQORH": {"count": 1439, "lastvisit": "12/20/2018)",
"page": "/datascience/beginner/"}, "-LI2DFNAxVnT-cxYzWR-": {"count": 1643,
"lastvisit": "12/19/2018)", "page": "/datascience/cheatsheets/"}}
```

FIGURE 2-10: Writing modified Firebase data to a new JSON file named `hitcounts_ new.json`.

JSON is a widely used format for storing and sharing data. Luckily, Python has lots of built-in tools for accessing and creating JSON data. We've covered the most important capabilities here. But don't be shy about doing a web search for *python json* if you want to explore more.

IN THIS CHAPTER

» **Understanding how the web works**

» **Opening web pages from Python**

» **Using Python to post to the web**

» **Web scraping with Python**

Chapter **3**

Interacting with the Internet

As you probably know, the Internet is home to virtually all the world's knowledge. Most of us use the web all the time to find information. We do so using a web browser such as Safari, Google Chrome, Firefox, Opera, Internet Explorer, or Edge. To visit a website, you type a URL (uniform resource locator) into your browser's address bar and press Enter, or you click a link that sends you to the page automatically.

As an alternative to browsing the web with your web browser, you can access its content *programmatically*. In other words, you can use a programming language such as Python to post information to the web, as well as to access web information. In a sense, you make the web your personal database of knowledge from which your apps can pluck information at will. In this chapter, you learn about the two main modules for accessing the web programmatically with Python: `urllib` and `BeautifulSoup`.

Seeing How the Web Works

When you open up your web browser and type in a URL or click a link, that action sends a *request* to the Internet. The Internet directs your request to the appropriate web server, which in turn sends a *response* back to your computer. Typically that response is a web page, but it can be just about any file. Or it can be an error message if what you requested no longer exists at that location. But the important thing is that you, the *user* (a human being), and your *user agent* (the program you're using to access the Internet) are on the *client* side of things. The *server*, which is just a computer, not a person, sends back its response, as illustrated in Figure 3-1.

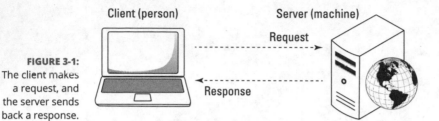

FIGURE 3-1:
The client makes a request, and the server sends back a response.

Understanding the mysterious URL

The URL is a key part of accessing a web page, because that's how the Internet finds the resource you're seeking. On the web, most resources use Hypertext Transfer Protocol (HTTP), and thus their URLs start with `http://` or `https://`. The difference is that `http://` sends stuff across the wire in its raw form, which makes it susceptible to hackers and others who can "sniff out" the traffic. The `https` protocol is *secure* in that the data is *encrypted*, which means it's been converted to a secret code that's not as easy to read. Typically, any site with whom you do business and to whom you transmit sensitive information, such as passwords and credit card numbers, uses `https` to keep that information secret and secure.

The URL for any website can be relatively simple, such as Alan's URL, which is `https://AlanSimpson.me`. Or it can be complex to add more information to the request. Figure 3-2 shows the parts of a URL, some of which you may have noticed in the past.

Note that the order matters. For example, it's possible for a URL to contain a path to a specific folder or page (starting with a slash right after the domain name). The URL can also contain a query string, which is always last and always starts with a question mark (?). After the question mark comes one or more *name=value* pairs, basically the same syntax you've seen in data dictionaries and JSON. If there are multiple *name=value* pairs, they are separated by ampersands.

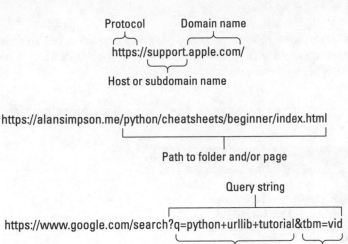

FIGURE 3-2:
Different parts
of URLs.

**TECHNICAL
STUFF**

A # followed by a name after the page name at the end of a URL is called a *frag-ment*, which indicates a particular place on the target page. Behind the scenes in the code of the page is usually a `<a id="`*name*`"></a>` tag that directs the browser to a spot on the page to which it should jump after it opens the page.

Exposing the HTTP headers

When you're using the web, all you care about is the stuff you see on your screen. At a deeper, somewhat hidden level, the two computers involved in the transac-tion are communicating with one another through *HTTP headers*. The headers are not normally visible to the human eye, but they are accessible to Python, your web browser, and other programs. You can choose to see the headers if you want, and doing so can be handy when writing code to access the web.

The product we use most often to view headers is HTTP Headers, which is a Google Chrome extension. If you have Chrome and want to try HTTP Headers for yourself, use Chrome to browse to `https://www.esolutions.se/`, scroll down to Google Chrome Extensions, click HTTP Headers, and install the extension. To see the headers involved whenever you've just visited a site, click the HTTP Headers icon in your Chrome toolbar (it looks like a cloud) and you'll see the HTTP header information (see Figure 3-3).

Two of the most important things in the HTTP headers are at the top, where you see GET followed by a URL. This tells you that a GET request was sent, meaning the URL is just a request for information; nothing is being uploaded to the server. The URL after the word GET is the requested resource. Another type of response is POST, and that means there's some information you're sending to the server, such as when you *post* something on Facebook, Twitter, or any other site that accepts input from you.

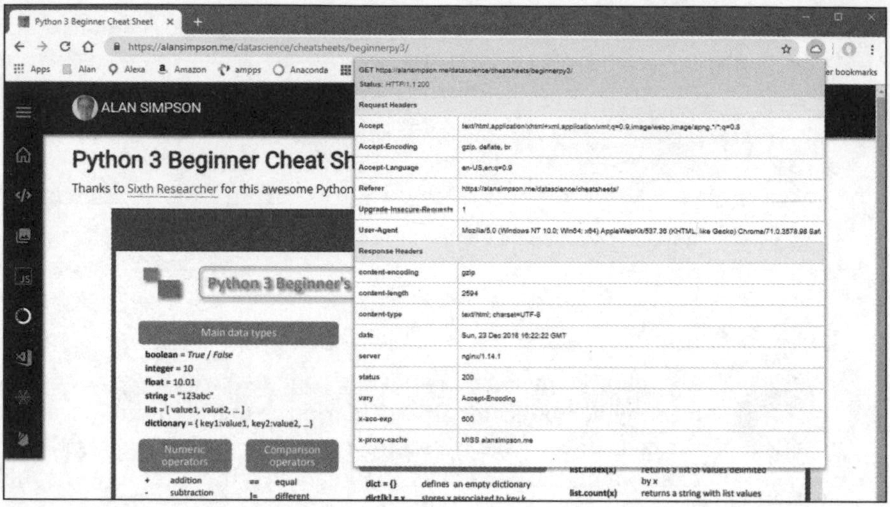

FIGURE 3-3:
Inspecting HTTP headers with Google Chrome.

The line below the GET shows the status of the request. The first part indicates the protocol used. In the example in Figure 3-4, the protocol is HTTP1.1, which just means the web request follows the HTTP version 1.1 rules of communication. The 200 is the status code, which in this case means "okay, everything went well." Common status codes are listed in Table 3-1.

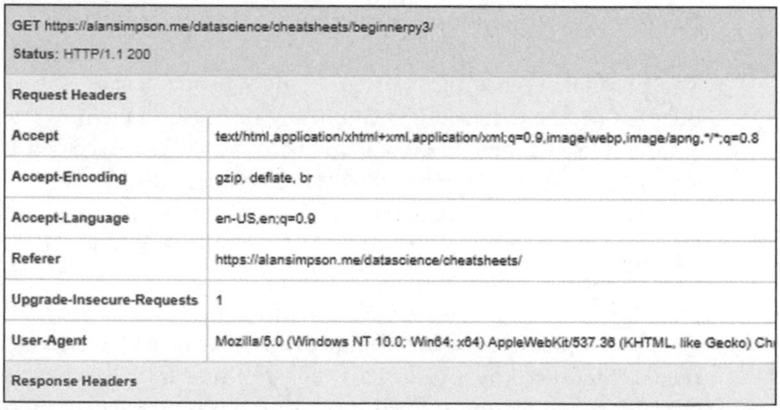

GET https://alansimpson.me/datascience/cheatsheets/beginnerpy3/	
Status: HTTP/1.1 200	
Request Headers	
Accept	text/html,application/xhtml+xml,application/xml;q=0.9,image/webp,image/apng,*/*;q=0.8
Accept-Encoding	gzip, deflate, br
Accept-Language	en-US,en;q=0.9
Referer	https://alansimpson.me/datascience/cheatsheets/
Upgrade-Insecure-Requests	1
User-Agent	Mozilla/5.0 (Windows NT 10.0; Win64; x64) AppleWebKit/537.36 (KHTML, like Gecko) Ch
Response Headers	

FIGURE 3-4:
HTTP headers.

TABLE 3-1 ## Common HTTP Status Codes

Code	Meaning	Reason
200	Okay	No problems exist.
400	Bad Request	The server is available but can't make sense of your request, usually because something is wrong with your URL.
403	Forbidden	The site has detected that you're accessing it programmatically, which it doesn't allow.
404	Not found	Either the URL is wrong or the URL is right but the content that is no longer there.

All of what we've been telling you here matters because it's related to accessing the web programmatically with Python, as you'll see next.

Opening a URL from Python

To access the web from a Python program, you need to use aspects of the `urllib`, or *URL Lib*rary, package. This one library consists of modules, each of which provides capabilities that are useful for different aspects of accessing the Internet programmatically. Table 3-2 summarizes the packages.

TABLE 3-2 ## Packages from the Python `urllib` Library

Package	Purpose
`request`	Opens URLs
`response`	Handles the response that arrived; you don't need to work with it directly
`error`	Handles request exceptions
`parse`	Breaks up the url into smaller chunks
`robotparser`	Analyzes a site's robots.txt file, which grants permissions to bots that are trying to access the site programmatically

Most of the time you'll likely work with the `request` module because it enables you to open resources from the Internet. The syntax for accessing a single package from a library is

```
from library import module
```

where *library* is the name of the larger library, and *module* is the name of the module. To access the capabilities of the `response` module of `urllib`, use the following syntax at the top of your code (the comment line optional):

```
# import the request module from urllib library.
from urllib import request
```

To open a web page, use this syntax:

```
variablename = request.urlopen(url)
```

Replace *variablename* with a variable name of your own choosing. Replace *url* with the URL of the resource you want to access enclosed in single- or double-quotation marks (unless it's stored in a variable). If the URL is already stored in a variable, just the variable name without quotation marks will work.

When running the code, the result will be an HTTPResponse object.

For example, you can run the following code in a Jupyter notebook or any .py file to access a sample HTML page Alan added to his site for this purpose:

```
# Import the request module from urllib library.
from urllib import request
# URL (address) of the desired page.
sample_url = 'https://AlanSimpson.me/python/sample.html'
# Request the page and put it in a variable named thepage.
thepage = request.urlopen(sample_url)
# Put the response code in a variable named status.
status = thepage.code
# What is the data type of the page?
print(type(thepage))
# What is the status code?
print(status)
```

Running this code displays this output:

```
<class 'http.client.HTTPResponse'>
200
```

The variable named `thepage` contains an `http.client.HTTPResponse` object, which is everything the server sent back in response to the request. The `200` is the status code that tells you all went well.

Posting to the web with Python

Not all attempts to access web resources will go as smoothly as the preceding example. For example, type the following URL in your browser's address bar, and press Enter:

```
https://www.google.com/search?q=python web scraping tutorial
```

Google returns a search result of many pages and videos that contain the words *python web scraping tutorial.* If you look at the address bar, you may notice that the URL you typed has changed slightly. The blank spaces have all been replaced with %20, as in the following line of code:

```
https://www.google.com/search?q=python%20web%20scraping%20tutorial
```

The %20 is the ASCII code, in hex, for a space. Those of you familiar with the web may recognize %20 because HTTP doesn't support the use of literal spaces in a URL. The %20 can be converted back to a space, if needed, after the transfer is complete.

Now let's see what happens if you run the same code with the Google URL rather than the original URL. Here is that code:

```
from urllib import request
# URL (address) of the desired page.
sample_url =
    'https://www.google.com/search?q=python%20web%20scraping%20tutorial'
# Request the page and put it in a variable named the page.
thepage = request.urlopen(sample_url)
# Put the response code in a variable named status.
status = thepage.code
# What is the data type of the page?
print(type(thepage))
# What is the status code?
print(status)
```

When you run this code, things don't go so smoothly. You may see several error messages, but the most important message is

```
HTTPError: HTTP Error 403: Forbidden
```

The error isn't with your coding. Rather, it's an HTTP error. Specifically, it's error number 403 for Forbidden. The URL was sent to Google, but it replied "Sorry, you can search our site from your browser, but not from Python code like that." Google, like many other big sites, rejects attempts to access its content programmatically, in part to protect its rights to its content and in part to have some control over incoming traffic.

The good news is, sites that don't allow you to post directly using Python or some other programming language often *do* allow you to post content through their API (application programming interface). You can still use Python as your programming language. You just have to abide by their rules.

An easy way to find out whether a site has such an API is to simply search the web using Google, Bing, or any search engine you like. For example, *post to facebook with python* or *post to twitter with python* or something like that. We won't attempt to provide an example here of doing such a thing, because Facebook tends to change the rules often and anything we say may be outdated by the time you read this. But a web search should get you want you need to know. If you get lots of results, focus on the ones posted most recently.

Scraping the web with Python

Whenever you request a page from the web, it's delivered to you as a web page usually consisting of HTML and content. *HTML* is markup code that, with another language called CSS, tells the browser how to display the content in terms of size, position, font, images, and all other such visual, stylistic matters. In a web browser, you don't see that HTML or CSS code. You see only the content, which is generally contained in blocks of HTML code on the page.

Even though much of the data you see on a web page comes from a database, you don't have permission to access the database directly. However, you can use a technique known as *web scraping* to pull data from the web page for use in some other manner. Python has great web scraping capabilities, and this is a hot topic most people want to learn about. So for the first part of this chapter, we focus on web scraping using the sample page from Figure 3-5 as our working example.

The code that tells the browser how to display that page's content isn't visible in the browser, unless you view the *source code*. In most browsers, you can do that by pressing the F12 key or by right-clicking an empty spot on the page and choosing View Source or Inspect or some other such option. On most web pages, the real content — the stuff you see in the browser — is between the ⟨body⟩ ... ⟨/body⟩ tags. Within the body of the page, there may be sections for a header, a navigation bar footer, perhaps ads, and more. In that particular page, the real meat of the content is between the ⟨article⟩ ... ⟨/article⟩ tags. Each square that you see on the web page in Figure 3-5. is called a *card*, and each card is defined as a link in ⟨a⟩ ... ⟨/a⟩ tags.

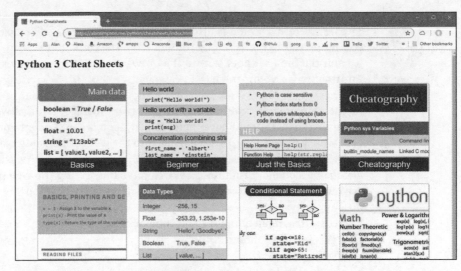

FIGURE 3-5:
Sample page used for web scraping.

Figure 3-6 shows some of the HTML code for the page in Figure 3-3. We're showing code for only the first two links in the page, but all the links follow the same structure. And they are all contained in the section denoted by a pair of `<article> ... </article>` tags.

FIGURE 3-6:
Some of the code from the sample page for web scraping.

```
<body>
    <h1>Python 3 Cheat Sheets</h1>
    <article>
        <a href="http://www.sixthresearcher.com/python-3-reference-cheat-sheet-for-beginners/">
            <img src="../../datascience/python/basics/basics256.jpg" alt="Python Basics Cheat Sheet">
            <span>Basics</span>
        </a>
        <a href="https://alansimpson.me/datascience/python/beginner/">
            <img src="../../datascience/python/beginner/beginner256.jpg" alt="Python Beginner Cheat Sheet">
            <span>Beginner</span>
        </a>
    </article>
</body>
```

Note that each link consists of several tags, as summarized here:

>> `<a> ... </a>`: The a (*anchor*) tags define where the browser should take users when they click the link. The `href=` part of the `<a>` tag is the URL of the page to which users should be taken.

>> `<img>`: The img tag defines the image that appears for each link. The `src=` attribute in the tag defines the *source* of the image — in other words, the location and filename to display for that link.

>> `<span> ... </span>`: At the bottom of the link is text enclosed in `<span> ... </span>` tags. That text appears at the bottom of each link as white text against a black background.

The term *screen scraping* is also used as a synonym for *web scraping*. Although, as you'll see, you're not scraping content from the computer screen. You're scraping it from the file that gets sent to the browser so that the browser can display the information on your screen.

In the Python code, you need to import two modules, both of which come with Anaconda so you should have them. One of them is the `request` module from `url-lib`, which allows you to send a request to the web for a resource and to read what the web serves back. The second is called `BeautifulSoup` (from a song in the book *Alice in Wonderland*). That one provides tools for parsing the web page that you've retrieved for specific items of data in which you're interested.

To get started, open a Jupyter notebook or create a `.py` file in VS Code and type the first two lines as follows:

```
# Get request module from url library.
from urllib import request
# This one has handy tools for scraping a web page.
from bs4 import BeautifulSoup
```

Next, you need to tell Python where the page of interest is located on the Internet. In this case, the URL is

```
https://alansimpson.me/python/scrape_sample.html
```

You can verify this by typing the URL into the address bar of your browser and pressing Enter. But to scrape the page, you'll need to put that URL in your Python code. You can give it a short name, like `page_url`, by assigning it to a variable:

```
# Sample page for practice.
page_url = 'https://alansimpson.me/python/scrape_sample.html'
```

To get the web page at that location into your Python app, create another variable, which we'll call `rawpage`, and use the `urlopen` method of the `request` module to read in the page:

```
# Open that page.
rawpage = request.urlopen(page_url)
```

To make it relatively easy to parse that page in subsequent code, copy it to a `BeautifulSoup` object. We'll name the object `soup` in our code. You'll also have to tell BeautifulSoup how you want the page parsed. You can use html5lib, which also comes with Anaconda:

```
# Make a BeautifulSoup object from the html page.
soup = BeautifulSoup(rawpage, 'html5lib')
```

Parsing part of a page

Most web pages contain lots of code for content in the header, footer, sidebars, ads, and whatever else is going on in the page. The main content is often just in one section. If you can identify just that section, your parsing code will run more quickly. In this example, in which we created the web page ourselves, we put all the main content between a pair of <article> ... </article> tags. In the following code, we assign that block of code to a variable named content. Later code in the page will parse only that part of the page, which can improve speed and accuracy.

```
# Isolate the main content block.
content = soup.article
```

Storing the parsed content

When scraping a web page, your goal is typically to collect specific data of interest. In this case, we want just the URL, image source, and the text for a number of links. We know there will be more than one line. An easy way to store these is to put them in a list, so in the following code we create an empty list named links_list:

```
# Create an empty list for dictionary items.
links_list = []
```

Next the code needs to loop through each link tag in the page content. Each link starts with a <a> tag and ends with a </a> tag. To tell Python to loop through each link individually, use the find_all method of BeautifulSoup in a loop. In the following code, as we loop through the links, we assign the current link to a variable named link:

```
# Loop through all the links in the article.
for link in content.find_all('a'):
```

Each link's code will look something like this, though each will have a unique URL, image source, and text:

```
<a href="https://alansimpson.me/datascience/python/lists/">
    <img src="../datascience/python/lists/lists256.jpg" alt="Python lists">
    <span>Lists</span>
</a>
```

The three items of data we want are as follows:

>> Link url, which is enclosed in quotation marks after the href= in the <a> tag

>> Image source, which is enclosed in quotation marks after src= in the img tag

>> Link text, which is enclosed in <span> ... </span> tags

The following code teases out each component by using the .get() method on BeautifulSoup to isolate something inside the link (that is, between the <a> and </a> tags that mark the beginning and end of each link). The following gets the URL portion of the link and puts it in a variable named url:

```
url = link.get('href')
```

Indent that code under the loop so it's executed for each link. The following code gets the image source and puts it in a variable named img:

```
img = link.img.get('src')
```

The text is between <span> ... </span> text near the bottom of the link. To grab that and put it into a variable named text, add this line of code:

```
text = link.span.text
```

You don't have to use .get() for that because the text isn't in an HTML attribute such as href= or src=. It's just text between <span> ... </span> tags.

Finally, you need to save all that before going to the next link in the page. An easy way to accomplish that is to append all three items of data to the links_list using this code:

```
links_list.append({'url' : url, 'img': img, 'text': text})
```

That's it for storing all the data for one link with each pass through the loop. One caveat: Web browsers are forgiving of errors in HTML code, so there could be mistyped or missing code that could cause the loop to fail. Typically, the error will be in the form of an attribute error, where Python can't find some attribute.

If data is missing, we prefer that Python just skip the bad line and keep going, rather than crash and burn, leaving us with no data. So we should put the whole business of grabbing the parts in a `try:` block, which, if it fails, allows Python to just skip that one link and move to the next:

```python
# Try to get the href, image url, and text.
try:
    url = link.get('href')
    img = link.img.get('src')
    text = link.span.text
    links_list.append({'url' : url, 'img': img, 'text': text})
# If the row is missing anything...
except AttributeError:
    #... skip it, don't blow up.
    pass
```

Figure 3-7 shows all the code as it stands right now. If you run it as shown, the `link_list` will be filled with all the data you scraped, but that doesn't do you much good. Chances are, you want to save that data to use elsewhere. You can do so by saving the data to a JSON file, a CSV file, or both, whatever is most convenient for you. In the sections that follow, we show you both methods.

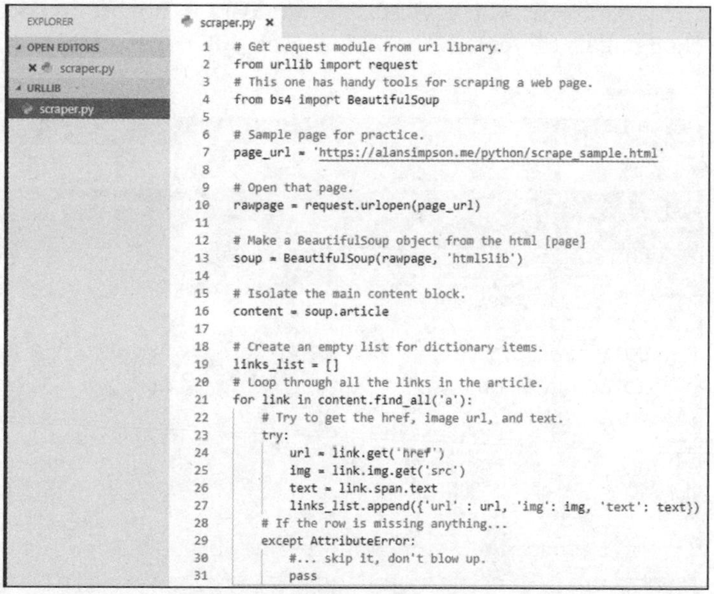

FIGURE 3-7: Web scraping code complete.

Saving scraped data to a JSON file

To save the scraped data to a JSON file, first import the `json` module near the top of your code, like this:

```
# If you want to dump data to the json file.
import json
```

Then, below the loop (not indented, because you don't want to repeat the code for each pass through the loop), first open a file, for writing, using the following code. You can name you file anything you like. We've opted to name ours `links.json`:

```
# Save as a JSON file.
with open('links.json', 'w', encoding='utf-8') as links_file:
```

Then, indented under that line, use `json.dump()` to dump the contents of `links_list` to the JSON file. We typically add `ensure_ascii=false` to preserve any non-ASCII characters, but doing so is optional:

```
json.dump(links_list, links_file, ensure_ascii=False)
```

That's it! After you run the code, you'll have a file named `links.json` that contains all the scraped data in JSON format. If you open the file from VS Code, it will look like one long line, because we didn't add line breaks or spaces to indent. But when you see it as one long line, you can copy and paste it to a site like `json-formatter.org`, which will display the data in a more readable format without changing its content, as shown in Figure 3-8.

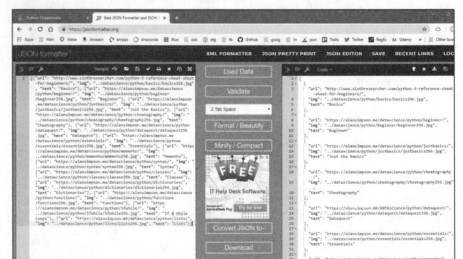

FIGURE 3-8:
Web scraped data in a JSON file.

Saving scraped data to a CSV file

If you prefer to go straight to a CSV file with your scraped data, start by importing the csv module near the top of your code:

```
# If you want to save to CSV.
import csv
```

Then, below and outside the loop that creates links_list, open in write mode a file with the filename of your choosing. In the following code we named ours links.csv. We also used newline='' to avoid putting an extra newline at the end of each row:

```
# Save it to a CSV.
with open('links.csv', 'w', newline='') as csv_out:
```

Indented below that open, create a csv writer that targets the file based on the name you assigned at the end of the with line:

```
csv_writer = csv.writer(csv_out)
```

The first row of a CSV file typically contains field names (also called column headings). So the next step is to add that row to the table, using whatever names you want to apply to headings:

```
# Create the header row
csv_writer.writerow(['url', 'img', 'text'])
```

Then you can write all the data from link_list to the CSV file by looping through link_list and writing the three items of data, separated by commas, to new rows:

```
for row in links_list:
    csv_writer.writerow([str(row['url']),str(row['img']),str(row['text'])])
```

Running the code produces a file named links.csv. If you open that file in Excel or another spreadsheet app, you'll see that the data is neatly organized into a table with columns labeled url, img, and text, as shown in Figure 3-9.

Figure 3-10 shows all the code for scraping both to JSON and CSV. Seeing all the code in the proper order should help you debug your own code, if need be. Note that we removed some comments from the top of the code to get it to all fit in one screenshot.

FIGURE 3-9:
Web scraped
data in Excel.

```
1   from urllib import request
2   from bs4 import BeautifulSoup
3   import json
4   import csv
5
6   # Sample page for practice.
7   page_url = 'https://alansimpson.me/python/scrape_sample.html'
8
9   # Open that page.
10  rawpage = request.urlopen(page_url)
11
12  # Make a BeautifulSoup object from the html [page]
13  soup = BeautifulSoup(rawpage, 'html5lib')
14
15  # Isolate the main content block.
16  content = soup.article
17
18  # Create an empty list for dictionary items.
19  links_list = []
20  # Loop through all the links in the article.
21  for link in content.find_all('a'):
22      # Try to get the href, image url, and text.
23      try:
24          url = link.get('href')
25          img = link.img.get('src')
26          text = link.span.text
27          links_list.append({'url' : url, 'img': img, 'text': text})
28      # If the row is missing anything...
29      except AttributeError:
30          #... skip it, don't blow up.
31          pass
32
33  # Save as a JSON file.
34  with open('links.json', 'w', encoding='utf-8') as links_file:
35      json.dump(links_list, links_file, ensure_ascii=False)
36
37  # Save it to a CSV.
38  with open('links.csv', 'w', newline='') as csv_out:
39      csv_writer = csv.writer(csv_out)
40      # Create the header row
41      csv_writer.writerow(['url','img','text'])
42      for row in links_list:
43          csv_writer.writerow([str(row['url']),str(row['img']),str(row['text'])])
44
45  print('Done')
```

FIGURE 3-10:
The entire
scraper.py
program.

Accessing the web programmatically opens new worlds of possibilities for acquiring and organizing knowledge and is, in fact, part of a field of study called data science. Many specialized tools are available as well, which you'll discover in Book 5.

Before launching into the more advanced and specialized applications of Python in Books 4 and beyond, we need to discuss one more fundamental concept. Throughout these first chapters, you've used many kinds of libraries and modules. But you haven't used all that Python has to offer. In the next chapter, you learn about more Python libraries, packages, and modules, and how to use them to achieve your goals.

Chapter **4**

Libraries, Packages, and Modules

F or the most part, all the chapters leading up to this one have focused on the core Python language, the elements of the language you'll need no matter how you intend to use Python. But as you've seen, many programs start by importing one or more modules. Each module is essentially a collection of prewritten code, which you can use in your own code without having to reinvent that wheel. The granddaddy of all this prewritten specialized code is called the Python standard library.

Understanding the Python Standard Library

The *Python standard library* is basically all the stuff you get when you get the Python language, including all the Python data types such as string, integer, float, and Boolean. Every instance of these data types is an instance of a class defined in the standard library. For this reason, the terms *type, instance,* and *object* are often used interchangeably. An integer is a whole number; it's also a data type in Python. But it exists because the standard library contains a class for integers, and every integer you create is an instance of that class and hence an object (because classes are the templates for things called objects).

The `type()` function in Python usually identifies the type of a piece of data. For example, run these two lines of code at a Python prompt, in a Jupyter notebook, or in a `.py` file:

```
x = 3
print(type(x))
```

The output is

```
<class 'int'>
```

The output tells you that x is an integer and an instance of the `int` class from the standard library. Running this code:

```
x = 'howdy'
print(type(x))
```

produces this output:

```
<class 'str'>
```

That is, x contains data that's the string data type, created by the Python `str` class. The `type()` function works for a float (a numeric value with a decimal point, such as 3.14) and for Booleans (`True` or `False`).

Using the dir() function

The Python standard library offers a `dir()` method that displays a list of all the attributes associated with a type. For example, in the preceding example, the result `<class 'str'>` tells you that the data is the `str` data type. So you know that's a type, and thus an instance of a class called `str` (short for *string*). If you enter this command:

```
dir(str)
```

Something like the following is displayed:

```
['__add__', '__class__', '__contains__', '__delattr__', '__dir__', '__doc__',
    '__eq__', '__format__', '__ge__', '__getattribute__', '__getitem__', '__
    getnewargs__', '__gt__', '__hash__', '__init__','__init_subclass__',
    '__iter__', '__le__', '__len__', '__lt__', '__mod__', '__mul__', '__ne__',
    '__new__', '__reduce__', '__reduce_ex__', '__repr__', '__rmod__', '__rmul__',
    '__setattr__', '__sizeof__', '__str__', '__subclasshook__', 'capitalize',
```

```
'casefold', 'center', 'count', 'encode', 'endswith', 'expandtabs', 'find',
'format', 'format_map', 'index', 'isalnum', 'isalpha', 'isascii',
'isdecimal', 'isdigit', 'isidentifier', 'islower', 'isnumeric',
'isprintable', 'isspace', 'istitle', 'isupper', 'join', 'ljust', 'lower',
'lstrip', 'maketrans', 'partition', 'replace', 'rfind', 'rindex', 'rjust',
'rpartition', 'rsplit', 'rstrip', 'split', 'splitlines', 'startswith',
'strip', 'swapcase', 'title', 'translate', 'upper', 'zfill']
```

Names surrounded by double-underscores, such as __add__ and __class__, are sometimes called *dunder-named* items, where *dunder* is short for *double underscores*. (Dunder-named items are often referred to as *special variables* or *magic methods*.) Each dunder-named item represents something built into Python that plays a role you don't necessarily access directly. For example, the __add__ method is invoked by using the + (addition) operator to add two numbers or join two strings.

The regular functions don't have the double underscores and are typically followed by parentheses. For example, take a look at these lines of code:

```
x = "Howdy"
print(type(x), x.isalpha(), x.upper())
```

The output is

```
<class 'str'> True HOWDY
```

The first part, <class 'str'>, tells you that x contains a string. As such, you can use any of the attributes shown in the output of dir(str) on it. For example, True is the output from x.isalpha() because x does contain alphabetic characters. HOWDY is the output of x.upper(), which converts the string to all uppercase letters.

TIP

Beginners often wonder what good seeing a bunch of names such as 'capitalize', 'casefold', 'center', 'count', 'encode', 'endswith', 'expandtabs', 'find', and 'format' in a dir() output does for them when they don't know what the names mean or how to use them. Well, seeing the names doesn't help much if you don't pursue it any further. You can get more detailed information by using help() rather than dir.

Using the help() function

The Python prompt also offers a help() function with the syntax:

```
help(object)
```

To use it, replace *object* with the object type with which you're seeking help. For example, to get help with `str` objects (strings, which come from the `str` class) enter this command at the Python prompt:

```
help(str)
```

The output will be more substantial information about the topic in the parentheses. For example, where `dir(str)` lists the names of attributes of that type, `help(dir)` provides more detail about each item. For example, `dir(str)` tells you that there's a thing called `capitalize` in the `str` class, but `help(dir)` tells you a bit more about it, as follows:

```
capitalize(self, /)
    Return a capitalized version of the string.
    More specifically, make the first character have upper case and the rest
    lower case.
```

The word `self` just means that whatever word you pass to `capitalize` is what gets capitalized. The `/` at the end marks the end of positional-only parameters, meaning that you can't use keywords with parameters after that as you can when defining your own functions.

What usually works best for most people is a more in-depth explanation and one or more examples. For those, a web search is usually your best bet. Start the search with the word *Python* (so the search engine knows what the search is in reference to) followed by the exact word with which you are seeking assistance. For example, searching for

```
python capitalize
```

provides links to lots of different resources for learning about the `capitalize` function of the `str` object, including examples of its use.

TIP

When you're finished viewing help, you don't have to scroll to the end to get back to the prompt. Simply press Ctrl+C.

A good (albeit technical) resource for the Python standard library is the standard library documentation itself. This information is always available at `https://docs.python.org/` usually under the Library Reference link. But even that wording may change, so if in doubt, just do a web search for *python standard library*. Be forewarned that the library is huge and technical, so don't expect to understand it right off the bat. Instead, use it as an ongoing resource to learn about things that interest you as your knowledge of Python develops.

TECHNICAL STUFF

The documentation that appears at `https://docs.python.org/` will generally be for the current stable version. Links to older versions and to any newer versions that may be in the works when you visit are available from links on the left side of the page.

Exploring built-in functions

Both `dir()` and `help()` are examples of Python built-in functions, which are always available to you in Python, in any app you're creating, as well as at the Python command prompt. These built-in functions are also part of the standard library. In fact, if you do a web search for *Python built-in functions*, some of the search results will point directly to the Python documentation. Clicking one of these results will open a section of the standard library documentation and display a table of all the built-in functions, as shown in Figure 4-1. On that page, you can click the name of any function to learn more about it.

FIGURE 4-1:
Python's built-in functions.

Exploring Python Packages

The Python language supports modular programming, in which a program is broken down into smaller, more manageable components, or modules. And some of those components might already have been created by someone else and can be reused.

Any large project, whether you're working alone or as a team member, can be simplified and streamlined if some components can use code that's already been written, tested, debugged, and deemed reliable by members of the Python programming community. The *packages* you hear about in relation to Python are that kind of code — code that has been developed and nurtured, is trustworthy, and is generic enough to be used as a component of a large project.

Thousands of packages are available for Python. A good resource for finding packages is *PyPi*, a clever name that's easy to remember and short for Python Package Index. You can check it out at https://pypi.org/.

In addition, a program named *pip*, for Pip Installs Packages (another clever name) is a *package manager* that you can use to explore, update, and remove existing packages. To use pip, you have to get to your operating system's command prompt, which is Terminal on a Mac, and cmd.exe or PowerShell in Windows. If you're using VS Code, the simplest way to get to the command prompt is to open VS Code and choose View⇨ Terminal.

If you already have pip, typing this command at a command prompt will tell you which version of pip is currently installed:

```
pip --version
```

The result will likely look something like this (but with your version's numbers and names):

```
pip 18.1 from C:\Users\...\AppData\Local\Continuum\anaconda3\lib\site-packages\
    pip (python 3.7)
```

To see what packages you already have installed, enter this at the operating system command prompt:

```
pip list
```

Most people are surprised at the number of packages that are already installed. One of the advantages of installing Python with Anaconda is that you get lots of great packages in the mix. And you don't have to rely on pip list to find their names. Instead, just open Anaconda Navigator and click Environments in the left column. You'll see a list of all installed packages, along with a brief description and version number for each, as shown in Figure 4-2.

See Book 1 for more information on installing and using Anaconda.

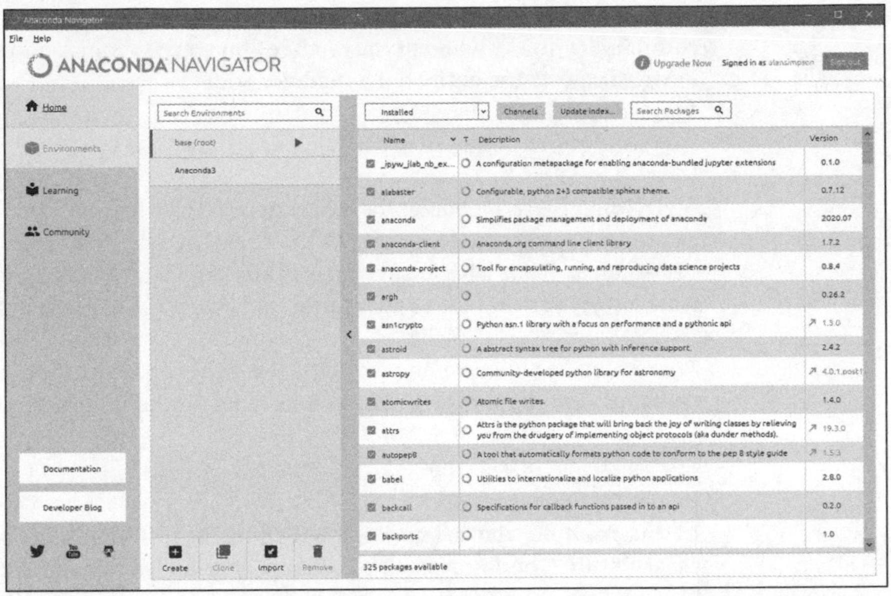

FIGURE 4-2:
Installed packages as viewed in Anaconda.

Although it's okay to use pip to install any packages you don't already have, the one disadvantage is that those packages may not show up in Anaconda Navigator's list of installed packages. To get around that, any time you see an instruction to *pip* something to install it, try replacing *pip* with *conda* (short for Anaconda). This adds the package to your collection, so it will appear both when you do `pip list` and when you look at the list in Anaconda Navigator.

Importing Python Modules

You'll hear the word *module* used with Python all the time. If you think of the standard library as a physical library and a package as a book in that library, a module is one chapter in one book. In other words, a package may contain many modules, and a library may contain many packages. The module is a big part of what makes Python a modular language, because code is grouped together according to function. You don't have to import everything including the kitchen sink to use *some* code. On the other hand, if you need to use several related things, such as functions for working with dates and times, you don't have to import them one at a time. Typically, importing just the entire module will get you what you need.

You can import functionality from modules in a few ways. One of the most common is to simply import the entire module. To do that, just follow the `import` command with the name of the module you want to import. For example, the following imports the entire math module:

```
import math
```

After you import a module, the dir() and help() functions work on that too. For example, if you tried doing dir(math) or help(math) before import math, you'd get an error. That's because that math package isn't part of the standard library. However, if you do import math first and then help(math), it all works.

There may be times when you don't need the whole kit-and-caboodle. In those cases, you can import just what you need using the following syntax:

```
from math import pi
```

In this example, you're importing one thing (pi), so you're not bringing in unnecessary stuff. The latter example, where you added "import pi", is also handy because in your code you can refer to pi as just pi, you don't have to use math.pi.

To see for yourself, at the Python prompt, such as in a VS Code Terminal window, enter the command print(pi) and press Enter. Most likely you'll get an error that reads:

```
NameError: name 'pi' is not defined
```

In other words, pi isn't part of the standard library, which is always available to your Python code. To use pi, you have to import the math module. You can do so in two ways. You can import the entire module by typing the following at the Python prompt:

```
import math
```

But if you do that and then enter

```
print(pi)
```

you'll get the same error again, even though you imported the math package. When you import an entire module and want to use part of it, you have to precede the part you want to use with the name of the module and a dot. For example, if you enter this command:

```
print(math.pi)
```

you get the correct answer:

```
3.141592653589793
```

Be aware that when you import just part of a module, the `help()` and `dir()` functions for the entire module won't work. For example, if you've only executed `from math import pi` in your code and you attempt to execute a `dir(math)` or `help(math)` function, it won't work because Python has only `pi` and not the entire module at its disposal.

You usually use `help()` and `dir()` at the Python prompt for a quick lookup rather than when you're writing an app. So using `from` rather than `import` is more efficient because you're bringing in only what you need.

You can also import multiple items from a package by listing their names, separated by commas, at the end of the `from` command. For example, suppose you need `pi` and square roots in your app. You could import just those into your app using this syntax:

```
from math import pi, sqrt
```

Once again, because you used the `from` syntax for the import, you can refer to `pi` and `sqrt()` in your code by name without the leading module name. For example, after executing that `from` statement, the following code:

```
print(sqrt(pi))
```

displays the following, which, as you may have guessed, is the square root of the number pi:

```
1.7724538509055159
```

You may also notice people importing a module like this:

```
from math import *
```

The asterisk is short for "everything." So in essence, that command is the same as `import math`, which also imports the entire `math` module, but with a subtle difference. When you write `from math import *` you associate the name of everything in the `math` module with that module. So you can use those names without the `math.` prefix. In other words, after you execute the following:

```
from math import *
```

you can do a command like `print(pi)` and it will work, even without using `print(math.pi)`. Although this approach seems smart and convenient, many programmers think it isn't Pythonic. If you're importing lots of modules and using lots of different pieces of each, avoiding module names in code can make it harder for other programmers to read and make sense of that code.

Making Your Own Modules

For all the hoopla about modules, a module is a simple thing. It's just a file with a `.py` extension that contains Python code. That's it. So any time you write Python code and save it in a `.py` file, you've created a module. That's not to say you always have to use that code as a module; you can treat it as a stand-alone app. But if you wanted to create a module with code that you need often in your own work, you could certainly do so. We explain the process in this section.

The module name, without its extension, is the same as the filename.

Suppose that you want three functions to simplify formatting dates and currency values. You can make up any name you like for each function. For our working example, we'll use these three names:

>> `to_date(any_str)`: Pass in any string (*any_str*) date in *mm/dd/yy* or *mm/dd/yyyy* format and the function sends back a Python `datetime.date` that you can use for date calculations.

>> `mdy(any_date)`: Pass in any Python date or datetime, and the function returns a string date formatted in *mm/dd/yyyy* format for display on the screen.

>> `to_curr(any_num, len)`: Pass in any Python float or integer number and the function returns a string with a leading dollar sign, commas in thousands places, and two digits for the pennies. *len* is an optional number for length. If provided, the return value will be padded on the left with spaces to match the length specified.

So here is all the code for all three items:

```
# Contains custom functions for dates and currency values.
import datetime as dt

def to_date(any_str):
    """ Convert mm/dd/yy or mm/dd/yyyy string to datetime.date, or None if
    invalid date. """
```

```
    try:
        if len(any_str) == 10:
            the_date = dt.datetime.strptime(any_str,'%m/%d/%Y').date()
        else:
            the_date = dt.datetime.strptime(any_str,'%m/%d/%y').date()
    except (ValueError, TypeError):
        the_date = None
    return the_date


def mdy(any_date):
    """ Returns a string date in mm/dd/yyyy format. Pass in Python date or
    string date in mm/dd/yyyy format """
    if type(any_date) == str:
        any_date = to_date(anydate)
    # Make sure a datetime is being forwarded
    if isinstance(any_date,dt.date):
        s_date = f"{any_date:'%m/%d/%Y'}"
    else:
        s_date = "Invalid date"
    return s_date


def to_curr(anynum, len=0):
    """ Returns a number as a string with $ and commas. Length is optional """
    s = "Invalid amount"
    try:
        x = float(anynum)
    except ValueError:
        x= None
    if isinstance(x,float):
        s = '$' + f"{x:,.2f}"
        if len > 0:
            s=s.rjust(len)
    return s
```

You can create the same file and name it myfunc.py if you want to follow along.
Note that the file contains only functions. So if you run it, it won't do anything on
the screen because there's no code that calls any of the functions.

To use those functions in a Python app or program you write, first make sure you
copy the myfunc.py file to the same folder as the rest of the Python code you're
writing. Then, when you create a new program, import myfunc as a module just as
you would any other module created by someone else:

```
import myfunc
```

You have to use the module name in front of any of the functions that you call from that module. So if you want to make the code a little more readable, use this instead:

```
import myfunc as my
```

With that as your opening line, you can refer to any function in your custom module with `my.` as the prefix. For example, use `my.to_date()` to call the `to_date` function. Here is a page that imports the module and then tests all three functions using that `my` syntax:

```
# Import all the code from myfunc.py as my.
import myfunc as my

# Need dates in this code
from datetime import datetime as dt

# Some simple test data.

string_date="12/31/2019"
# Convert string date to datetime.date
print(my.to_date(string_date))

today = dt.today()
# Show today's date in mm/dd/yyyy format.
print(my.mdy(today))

dollar_amt=12345.678
# Show this big number in currency format.
print(my.to_curr(dollar_amt))
```

When you run the code, the output should look like this:

```
2019-12-31
'12/27/2018'
$12,345.68
```

We also mentioned that you can skip using the prefix if you import items by name. In this case, that means you could call `to_date()` and `mdy()` and `to_curr()` without using the `my.` prefix. The first line of code would need to be

```
from myfunc import to_date, mdy, to_curr
```

The rest of the code would be the same as in the preceding example, except you can leave off the `my.` prefixes as in the following code:

```
# Import all the code from myfunc.py by name.
from myfunc import to_date, mdy, to_curr

# Need dates in this code
from datetime import datetime as dt

# Some simple test data.

string_date="12/31/2019"
# Convert string date to datetime.date
print(to_date(string_date))

today = dt.today()
# Show today's date in mm/dd/yyyy format.
print(mdy(today))

dollar_amt=12345.678
# Show this big number in currency format.
print(to_curr(dollar_amt))
```

So that's it for Python libraries, packages, and modules. All three represent code written by others that you're allowed to use in any Python code you write. The only real difference is size. A library may contain several packages, a package may contain several modules, and the modules usually contain functions, classes, or other prewritten chunks of code that you're free to use.

In the chapters that follow, you'll see lots of modules and classes because they make Python so modular and applicable to many different types of work and study. But keep in mind that the core principles of the Python language that you've learned in these first three minibooks apply everywhere, whether you're doing data science or AI or robotics. You'll be using that core language to work with code that others have written for that one specialized area.

4

Using Artificial Intelligence

Contents at a Glance

Chapter **1**

Exploring Artificial Intelligence

A rtificial intelligence (AI) has been a much-maligned set of words over the past few years. The popular news media tends to take any small advance in AI out of context and proclaim "smart computers are here!" For example, in 2017, Facebook engineers programmed two programs to value certain objects more than others (balls, blocks, and such) and then had the two programs, through a rules set and a language like English, negotiate with each other to maximize the acquisition of objects that the programs valued.

The programs did not have a language syntax checker and because of the way the programs learned the communication between the programs soon became syntactically incorrect English. (A good example is when a program wanted something, it would say "I want" and the program logic decided that if one "I want" is good, saying many "I want I want I want" should be better.) The news media reported this as a new language (it wasn't). And later, when the programs were shut down because the experiment was finished, some pundit decided instead that the Facebook engineers did so right before the programs had become sentient. Needless to say, this wasn't the case.

This chapter introduces you to the concept of AI and describes its limitations. We explore different AI techniques and then give a bit of history to put the current AI revolution in context.

REMEMBER

Dictionary.com defines *artificial intelligence* as "the theory and development of computer systems able to perform tasks that normally require human intelligence, such as visual perception, speech recognition, decision-making, and translation between languages."

AI Is a Collection of Techniques

The point of this chapter is to demystify AI and describe how useful and cool new AI techniques can be. Note that we said "AI techniques" and not just "AI." General AI, in the sense of robots imitating humans doesn't currently exist (and isn't even close), but we do have a bunch of different algorithms, statistical techniques, and tools that can do some impressive humanlike things, such as learning and adapting to the environment.

In this chapter, we show you three AI techniques:

>> Neural network

>> Machine learning

>> A TensorFlow classifier program with Python

After reading this book, you will become sentient. Oh wait, you've bought this book, so you're already over that threshold. Next, we briefly describe each of the major AI techniques and programs that we delve into in the next three chapters.

Neural networks

Just by the name *neural networks,* you know we're going to talk about brain cells. Human brains have billions of neurons (approximately 80 billion by some counts) and have roughly 10 times the amount of glial cells (which help neurons communicate and play a role in neuron placement). A key to understanding how the brain works is connections. Each neuron has many connections with other neurons (up to 200,000 connections for some neurons in the brain), so it is not just the count of neurons that make people intelligent — it's how they are connected. Neural networks in AI have, in a sense, been reversed-engineered from biological neurons.

ARTIFICIAL INTELLIGENCE IS THE TECHNOLOGY OF THE FUTURE

"What magical trick makes us intelligent? The trick is that there is no trick. The power of intelligence stems from our vast diversity, not from any single, perfect principle."

—MARVIN MINSKY, THE SOCIETY OF MIND (1987)

John Shovic: I had the honor of having lunch and spending an afternoon with Dr. Minsky in 1983 in Pocatello, Idaho. I was working as a VLSI (very large scale integrated circuit) design engineer at American Micro Systems, a company located in Pocatello, and I had just started my Ph.D. work part-time at the University of Idaho. My first AI class was under my belt, and I was beside myself that Dr. Marvin Minsky from the AI Lab at MIT was coming to Pocatello. I made a few phone calls and managed to get him to meet with two of us who had been in the AI class, for lunch and an afternoon meeting. Looking back, I am amazed that he would take this kind of time for us, but that was the kind of guy he was.

It was like we were Rolling Stones fans and Mick Jagger was coming to town to spend time with us. Honestly, much as I would like to spend an afternoon with Mick Jagger, I would rather meet with Dr. Minsky.

I had just finished his book, *Artificial Intelligence,* and I was bursting with questions about his work. He was interested in what we had learned from our AI class at the University of Idaho and was quite complimentary about Dr. John Dickinson, the professor of the AI course, and his choice of subjects. I had a lot of enthusiasm about the topic and was thinking that I might make a career of it. Of all we talked about, I remember one thing clearly. He said (and this is paraphrased), "I started in AI about 20 years ago and I was convinced then that 20 years later we would have true AI. I now think we are still about 20 years from having true AI."

Well, I remember thinking about that day 20 years later, in 2003, and realizing we still weren't there. At that point, I started wondering whether AI will always be the technology of the future. Here I am in 2020, another 17 years later, and we still don't have general AI. But one thing has changed in those years. We now have a bunch of AI techniques for learning and efficient searching that can do some impressive things and may someday lead to the general AI that Dr. Minsky was talking about. Who knows? It may even take less than 20 years!

REMEMBER

Elephants have over 270 billion neurons, but they aren't nearly as densely connected as human neurons. Robert Metcalf, the founder of 3Com and an entrepreneur professor at the University of Texas, famously said (referring to Ethernet) that "the value of a telecommunications network is proportional to the square of the number of connected users of the system." With that squared value of connections coming in, we make up for those missing 190 billion elephant neurons by having ours much more densely connected. (However, is it any surprise that elephants have good memories and a complex social system?)

AI researchers thought (and were right) that if we could reverse-engineer neurons and their connections, we could use this information to construct computer models that could be used to make smarter programs. However, the limitations of the first popular model (Preceptrons) quickly led to general disappointment and the first AI Winter (see the sidebar titled "The AI Winter").

Over the past 30 years, however, much more research has gone into the structure and science behind neural networks, including the study of convolutional neural networks and deep-learning software architectures. This research has led to packages that have immediate application to real-world problems.

THE AI WINTER

The term *AI Winter* was first discussed at the 1984 meeting of the American Association of Artificial Intelligence. Our friend from another sidebar, Dr. Marvin Minsky, warned the business community that enthusiasm for AI had spiraled out of control in the 1980s and that disappointment would certainly follow. Three years after he said that, the multi-billion-dollar AI business collapsed. An *AI Winter* refers to the time when investment and research dollars dried up. In economic terms, this is called a bubble, much like the dot-com bubble in 1999, the real estate bubble that collapsed in 2007, and the Dutch tulip bulb market bubble in Holland in 1637. Overhype leads to over-expectations, which lead to inevitable disappointment.

The AI winter happened again in the 2000s (partially because of the dot-com bubble), and researchers went to great lengths to avoid using the term *AI* in their proposals and papers. It seems to us that we are again approaching such a bubble, but none of us are anywhere near smart enough to know when winter is coming (pardon this, *Game of Thrones* fans). One of the big differences is that a number of AI techniques have moved into the mainstream market, such as Amazon Alexa and Google Home, so AI techniques are much more widely used. Some of the current exuberance and investment in AI is irrational, but this time we have ended up with a lot of good tools that we can continue to use even when the bubble pops.

Neural networks are good models for how brains learn and classify data. Given that, it is no surprise that neural networks show up in machine learning and other AI techniques. Neural networks consist of neurons and, most importantly, the wiring connecting them together. The neurons and connections of those neurons make up a neural network.

When defining a neural network, you define the architecture and layout — creating an arbitrary network of connections. The setting of the network by machine has turned into another field we call *evolutionary computing*, as described in the sidebar. When you set up a network of neurons one of the most important choices you make is the activation function. The neuron activates when a threshold determined by the activation function is crossed. The activation function is one of the key things you define when you build a Python model of neurons in the next chapter.

EVOLUTIONARY COMPUTING

Evolutionary computing is a set of computational algorithms and heuristics (a fancy word for rules of thumb) for global optimization that are inspired by biological evolution. It is derived from machine-learning techniques but differs in that evolutionary computing is generally used to solve problems whose solution is not known by the programmer beforehand. (Machine-learning programs are taught what they are looking for.)

By using evolutionary computing algorithms, you can find guided solutions to problems in a design space (otherwise known as a problem space). Evolutionary computing has been used to create solutions as diverse as better spacecraft antennas and improved bus routing. The process uses computationally intensive algorithms to search a problem space for solutions. Evolutionary computing is computationally intensive because you have a population of solutions that you look at to see which program is getting close to a solution, and then select the new ones to move to the next generation. Survival of the fittest! These population evaluations are difficult for computers to process, which is why so many evolution algorithms require massive parallel computing.

John Shovic: A student in my graduate Advanced Robotics class at the University of Idaho used evolutionary computing to enable a robot named Baxter to pick out red or yellow blocks from one box and move them to another box (as shown in the first photo). He used pictures from the robot arm's cameras and evolutionary computing to try to find an algorithm to identify and locate these blocks so Baxter could find them. Neither Baxter nor the student succeeded in using evolutionary computing algorithms to find a solution. Why? Using evolutionary computing techniques to find a solution to an ill-defined and unconstrained problem requires exponentially greater computing

(continued)

(continued)

resources, and even these still might not come up with a solution. Smaller, constrained problems are a better match for evolutionary techniques.

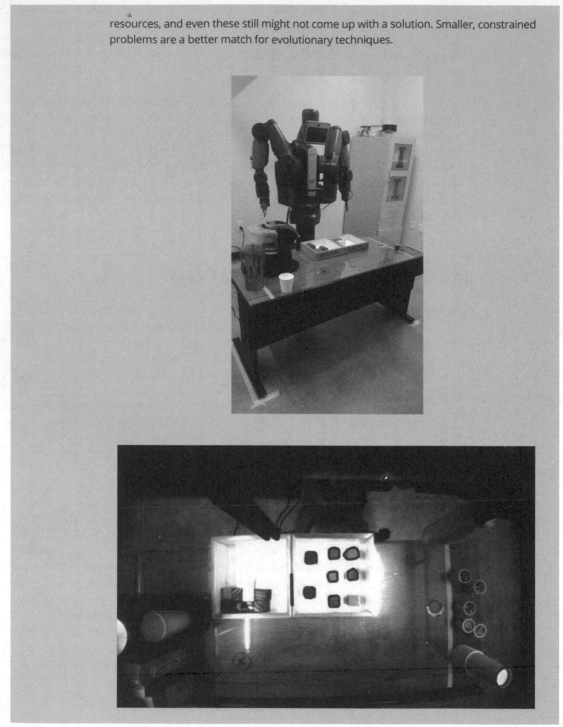

Machine learning

Learning is the classic example of what it means to be human. We learn. We adapt. *Machine learning* is an AI technique that studies the use of computer algorithms and programs that improve automatically through use and experience.

John Shovic: Humans learn quickly and can apply that same learning to different situations. As I write this I am watching my 2-year-old granddaughter, Hazel, eat her first quesadilla. I see that she has learned to find the food on her plate, tell her mom that she likes it, grab the food, bring it to her mouth, and eat it. I wish I could teach my robots to be half as smart as Hazel is at 2. Now I just need to clean the cream cheese off my laptop.

Today, AI researchers have brought quasi-human–level learning to computers in specific tasks, such as image recognition and sound processing ("Alexa, find me a new TV show"), and may get to a level of similar learning in other tasks, such as driving a car.

Machine learning isn't fully automated. You can't say, "Computer, read this book" and expect it to understand what it is reading. Currently, using machine-learning techniques requires large amounts of human-classified and human-selected data, data analysis, and training.

Many different techniques are used in machine learning, such as the following:

>> Statistical analysis

>> Neural networks

>> Decision trees

>> Evolutionary algorithms

Machine learning refers to the different ways of using these learning techniques to emulate and even better the expert systems that ruled AI in the 1980s. In the late 1980s, John wrote his Ph.D. dissertation on how to build a deeply pipelined machine to speed up the evaluation of expert systems. Hardware acceleration of machine learning is still an active area of research today.

In the following chapter, we show you how to use Python to build machines that demonstrate all the important tasks of machine learning.

Exploring Artificial Intelligence

TensorFlow — A framework for deep learning

TensorFlow is an open-source, multi-machine set of APIs (application programming interfaces) used for building, learning, and doing research on deep learning. It hides a lot of the complexity of deep learning, which makes the technology more accessible.

TensorFlow started in 2011 as a proprietary AI environment in the Google Brain group. It has been extensively used at Google and, when it was released to open source, it was embraced immediately by the AI community. Of over 95,000 GitHub source repositories using TensorFlow, only 32 are from Google Research. (GitHub is a popular website where people place their code for applications and projects in a way that other people can use and learn from them.)

TensorFlow gets its name from the way the data is processed. A *tensor* is a multidimensional matrix of data, which is transformed by each TensorFlow layer it moves through. Most college students first learn about matrix mathematics in a linear algebra course. (For a crash course, check out *Linear Algebra For Dummies* by Mary Jane Sterling.)

TIP

So, TensorFlow is built on matrices. And another name for a matrix is a tensor, which is where the name *TensorFlow* comes from.

TensorFlow is Python-friendly and you can use it on many different machines and also in the cloud. It's also easy to understand and easy to use, so you can get your head into AI applications quickly.

Current Limitations of AI

The key word in all of AI is *understanding*. A machine-learning algorithm has been taught to drive a car, for example, but the resulting program does not understand how to drive a car. The emphasis of AI is to perform an analysis of the data, but the human controlling the data still has to interpret it and see whether the data fits the problem. Interpretation also goes far beyond just the data. Humans often can tell whether the data or a conclusion is true or false, even when they can't describe exactly how they know. AI just accepts that the conclusion is true.

Considering that we don't even understand a lot of human behavior and abilities ourselves, it is unlikely that anyone will be developing mathematical models of such behavior soon. And we need those models to start getting AI programs to achieve anything approaching human thought processes.

But with all its limitations, AI is useful for exploring large complex programs to find good solutions.

Now let's go and start using AI in Python!

Exploring Artificial Intelligence

Chapter **2**

Building a Neural Network

Neural networks and various other models of how the brain operates have been around as long as people have been talking about AI. Dr. Marvin Minsky, introduced in Chapter 1 of this minibook, started mainline interest in modeling neurons with his seminal work with perceptrons in 1969. At the time, widespread irrational exuberance about how the perceptron was going to quickly make AI practical attracted a good deal of venture capital to the area. But when many of these ventures failed, investment in neural networks dried up. What's popular, sells.

Fast-forward 37 years from John's conversation with Dr. Minsky in 1983. Today we see renewed interest in neural networks. Better models have been built, but more importantly, we now have useful and economical applications based on neural networks. Will the current market situation lead to another bubble? Most assuredly, but this time the interest in AI should continue because of the application areas that have been developed.

This chapter introduces you to the concept of neural networks and how to implement them in Python. To download the code for this chapter, go to www. dummies.com/go/pythonaiofd2e.

Understanding Neural Networks

These are the six attributes of a neural network:

» Input layer of neurons

» Some number of hidden layers of neurons

» Output layer of neurons connecting to the world

» Set of weights and biases between each neuron level

» Choice of activation function for each hidden layer of neurons

» Choice of loss function to reduce overtraining the network

Figure 2-1 shows the architecture of a two-layer neural network. Note the three layers in this two-layer neural network: The input layer is typically excluded when you count a neural network's layers.

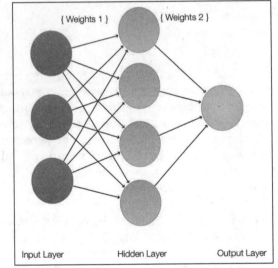

FIGURE 2-1:
A two-layer
neural network.

A *neuron*, as the word is used in AI, is a software model of a nervous system cell that behaves more or less like a brain neuron. The model uses numbers to make one neuron or another more important to the results. These numbers are called *weights*.

By looking at this diagram, you can see that the neurons on each layer are connected to *all* the neurons of the next layer. Weights are given for each inter-neural connecting line.

Layers of neurons

Figure 2-1 shows the input layer, the hidden layer (so-called because it's not directly connected to the outside world), and the output layer. This is a simple network; real networks can be much more complex with many more layers. Deep learning gets its name from the fact that when you have multiple hidden layers, you increase the depth of the neural network.

Note that the layers filter and process information from left to right. This kind of neural network is called a *feed-forward input* because the data feeds in only one direction.

Now that we have a network, how does it learn? The neural network receives an example and guesses at the answer (by using whatever default weights and biases that it starts with). If the answer is wrong, it backtracks and modifies the weights and biases in the neurons, in an effort to fix the error. This process is called *backpropagation* and simulates what people do when performing a task using an iterative trial-and-error approach. See Figure 2-2.

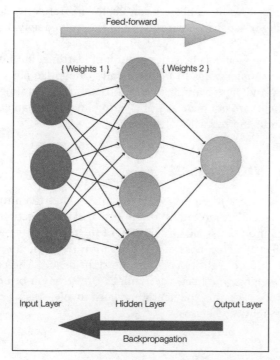

FIGURE 2-2:
Feed-forward and backpropagation.

BACKPROPAGATION

In the human brain, learning happens because of the addition of new connections (synapses) and the modification of those connections based on external stimuli.

In AI research, the methods used to propagate from results to previous layers (also called *feedback*) have changed over the years. Some experts think that the latest surge of AI applications and the exit from the last AI Winter (see Book 4, Chapter 1) is due to the algorithms and techniques now used for backpropagation.

Backpropagation is a mathematically complex topic. For a more detailed description of the math and how it is used, check out *Machine Learning For Dummies*, by John Paul Mueller and Luca Massaron.

After you do this process many times, the neural network begins to get better (learns) and provides better answers with each iteration, or *epoch*. The process can take days or weeks and lots of computer power for complex tasks.

Although it may take days or weeks to train a neural net, after it is trained, it can be duplicated with little effort by copying the topology, weights, and biases of the trained network. When you have a trained neural net, you can use it easily again and again (while not consuming much computer power), until you need something different. As a result, engineers can deploy neural networks in products at low cost. Training is expensive, but the use of the trained network is not.

Neural networks do model some types of human learning, but humans have significantly more complex ways to hierarchically categorize objects (such as categorizing horses and pigs as animals) with little effort. Neural networks (and the deep learning field) are not good at transferring knowledge and results from one type of situation to another without retraining.

Weights and biases

Looking at the network in Figure 2-1, you can see that the output of this neural network is dependent on only the weights of the connections and the *biases* (adjusting the neuron threshold up or down) of the neurons themselves. Although the weights affect the steepness of the activation function curve (more on that later), the bias shifts the entire curve to the right or left. The program's modification of the weights and biases determines the strength of predictions of the individual neurons. Training the neural network involves using the input data to fine-tune the weights and biases.

The activation function

In building our first neural network, an important topic is the activation function. The *activation function* is the software function that determines whether information passes through (thus activating the neuron) or is stopped by the individual neuron (thus deactivating the neuron). However, you use the function not only as a gate (open or shut) but also to transform the input signal to the neuron in some useful way.

Many types of activation functions are available. For our simple neural network, we will use one of the most popular ones — the sigmoid function. A sigmoid function has a characteristic *S* curve, as shown in Figure 2-3.

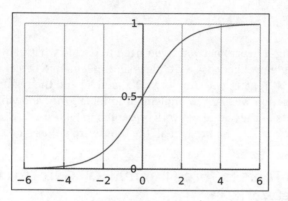

FIGURE 2-3:
An example of a sigmoid function.

Remember we talked about neuron bias earlier in this chapter? If you apply a 1.0 value bias to the curve in Figure 2-3, the curve shifts to the right, making the (0,0.5) point move to (1,0.5).

Loss function

The loss function is the last piece of the puzzle that needs to be explained. The *loss function* compares the result of our neural network to the desired results. Put another way, the loss function tells us how good our current results are. Using a loss function is a good way to avoid *overtraining* the network, in which the network ends up being able to operate only on the training data.

In addition to using the loss function to reduce overtraining, we also transmit the result of the loss function to our backpropagation channel to improve our neural network.

We will use a function that finds the derivative of the loss function showing the quality of our result (the slope of the curve is the first derivative, calculus fans) to figure out what to do with our neuron weights. This changing of bias and weights from the loss function calculation is a major part of the learning activity of the network.

You've been introduced to all the parts of our neural network, so it's time to build an example.

Building a Simple Neural Network in Python

Before building a neural network, you need to decide what you want it to learn. For our example, we'll choose a simple goal: Implement a three-input XNOR gate (an exclusive NOR gate) with inputs X1, X2, and X3 and the result as Y1. Table 2-1 shows the function we want to implement in table form, showing the inputs and desired outputs of the neural network presented in Figure 2-1. Note that an exclusive NOR function returns 1 only if all the inputs are either 0 or 1.

TABLE 2-1   **The Truth Table (a Three-Input XNOR Gate) for the Neural Network**

X1	X2	X3	Y1
0	0	0	1
0	0	1	0
0	1	0	0
0	1	1	0
1	0	0	0
1	0	1	0
1	1	0	0
1	1	1	1

USES OF XNOR FUNCTIONS

XNOR gates are used in a number of applications, both in software and hardware. You can use an XNOR gate as part of a one-bit adder that adds one bit to another bit (and provides a carry bit to string them together to make big adders) or strings bits together to build a pseudo-random number generator.

The coolest XNOR gate application we've heard about involves coding algorithms and the Reed-Solomon error-correction algorithm. Reed-Solomon algorithms mix up your data by using XNOR gates and some additional data (redundant data), resulting in more robust data to transmit long distances (such as from Pluto, our former ninth planet). Long transmission distances can have all sorts of events that cause noise in the data, corrupting bits and bytes.

When you receive the data, you use XNOR gates again to reconstruct the original data, correcting any errors (up to a point) so you have good data. We can transmit data much farther with less power because the Reed-Solomon code makes the transmission more error-tolerant.

Why do we know anything about this? John worked with a team on chips for Reed-Solomon codes in the 1980s at the University of Idaho for NASA. Our chips and derivatives ended up on projects such as the Hubble Space Telescope and John's personal favorite, the New Horizons space probe, which visited Pluto and Ultima Thule in the Oort Cloud. The incredible pictures from those space probes go through all those little XNOR gates.

The neural-net Python code

We will be using the Python library called NumPy, which provides a great set of functions to help us organize our neural network and simplify the calculations.

Although NumPy is designed to simplify writing code for matrix mathematics (a matrix is also known as a *tensor*) in linear algebra, it also includes a number of higher mathematical functions useful in various types of AI. NumPy is now the preferred library to use and is also a part of SciPy and MatPlotLib, two common scientific packages for analysis and visualization of data.

Following is the Python code using NumPy for the two-layer neural network (refer to Figure 2-2). Using nano (or your favorite text editor), create a file called "2LayerNeuralNetwork.py" and enter the following code:

```python
# 2 Layer Neural Network in NumPy


import numpy as np

# X = input of our 3 input XOR gate
# set up the inputs of the neural network (right from the table)
X = np.array(([0,0,0],[0,0,1],[0,1,0], \
    [0,1,1],[1,0,0],[1,0,1],[1,1,0],[1,1,1]), dtype=float)
# y = our output of our neural network
y = np.array(([1], [0], [0], [0], [0], \
    [0], [0], [1]), dtype=float)

# what value we want to predict
xPredicted = np.array(([0,0,1]), dtype=float)

X = X/np.amax(X, axis=0) # maximum of X input array
# maximum of xPredicted (our input data for the prediction)
xPredicted = xPredicted/np.amax(xPredicted, axis=0)

# set up our Loss file for graphing

lossFile = open("SumSquaredLossList.csv", "w")

class Neural_Network (object):
  def __init__(self):
    #parameters
    self.inputLayerSize = 3   # X1,X2,X3
    self.outputLayerSize = 1 # Y1
    self.hiddenLayerSize = 4 # Size of the hidden layer

    # build weights of each layer
    # set to random values
    # look at the interconnection diagram to make sense of this
    # 3x4 matrix for input to hidden
    self.W1 = \
            np.random.randn(self.inputLayerSize, self.hiddenLayerSize)
    # 4x1 matrix for hidden layer to output
    self.W2 = \
            np.random.randn(self.hiddenLayerSize, self.outputLayerSize)
```

```python
def feedForward(self, X):
  # feedForward propagation through our network
  # dot product of X (input) and first set of 3x4  weights
  self.z = np.dot(X, self.W1)

  # the activationSigmoid activation function – neural magic
  self.z2 = self.activationSigmoid(self.z)

  # dot product of hidden layer (z2) and second set of 4x1 weights
  self.z3 = np.dot(self.z2, self.W2)

  # final activation function – more neural magic
  o = self.activationSigmoid(self.z3)
  return o

def backwardPropagate(self, X, y, o):
  # backward propagate through the network
  # calculate the error in output
  self.o_error = y – o

  # apply derivative of activationSigmoid to error
  self.o_delta = self.o_error*self.activationSigmoidPrime(o)

  # z2 error: how much our hidden layer weights contributed to output
  # error
  self.z2_error = self.o_delta.dot(self.W2.T)

  # applying derivative of activationSigmoid to z2 error
  self.z2_delta = self.z2_error*self.activationSigmoidPrime(self.z2)

  # adjusting first set (inputLayer --> hiddenLayer) weights
  self.W1 += X.T.dot(self.z2_delta)
  # adjusting second set (hiddenLayer --> outputLayer) weights
  self.W2 += self.z2.T.dot(self.o_delta)

def trainNetwork(self, X, y):
  # feed forward the loop
  o = self.feedForward(X)
  # and then backpropagate the values (feedback)
  self.backwardPropagate(X, y, o)


def activationSigmoid(self, s):
  # activation function
  # simple activationSigmoid curve as in the AIO Python book
  return 1/(1+np.exp(-s))
```

```
    def activationSigmoidPrime(self, s):
      # First derivative of activationSigmoid
      # calculus time!
      return s * (1 - s)


    def saveSumSquaredLossList(self,i,error):
      lossFile.write(str(i)+","+str(error.tolist())+'\n')

    def saveWeights(self):
      # save this in order to reproduce our cool network
      np.savetxt("weightsLayer1.txt", self.W1, fmt="%s")
      np.savetxt("weightsLayer2.txt", self.W2, fmt="%s")

    def predictOutput(self):
      print ("Predicted XOR output data based on trained weights: ")
      print ("Expected (X1-X3): \n" + str(xPredicted))
      print ("Output (Y1): \n" + str(self.feedForward(xPredicted)))

myNeuralNetwork = Neural_Network()
trainingEpochs = 1000
#trainingEpochs = 100000

for i in range(trainingEpochs): # train myNeuralNetwork 1,000 times
  print ("Epoch # " + str(i) + "\n")
  print ("Network Input : \n" + str(X))
  print ("Expected Output of XOR Gate Neural Network: \n" + str(y))
  print ("Actual  Output from XOR Gate Neural Network: \n" + \
          str(myNeuralNetwork.feedForward(X)))
  # mean sum squared loss
  Loss = np.mean(np.square(y - myNeuralNetwork.feedForward(X)))
  myNeuralNetwork.saveSumSquaredLossList(i,Loss)
  print ("Sum Squared Loss: \n" + str(Loss))
  print ("\n")
  myNeuralNetwork.trainNetwork(X, y)

myNeuralNetwork.saveWeights()
myNeuralNetwork.predictOutput()
```

Breaking down the code

Some of the following code might seem obtuse the first time through, so in this
section we provide some explanations:

```
# 2 Layer Neural Network in NumPy



import numpy as np
```

If you get an import error when running the preceding code, install the NumPy Python library. To do so on a Raspberry Pi (or an Ubuntu system), type the following in a Terminal window:

```
sudo apt-get install python3-numpy
```

Next, we define all eight possibilities of our X1–X3 inputs and the Y1 output from Table 2-1:

```
# X = input of our 3 input XNOR gate
# set up the inputs of the neural network (right from the table)
X = np.array(([0,0,0],[0,0,1],[0,1,0], \
    [0,1,1],[1,0,0],[1,0,1],[1,1,0],[1,1,1]), dtype=float)
# y = our output of our neural network
y = np.array(([1], [0],  [0],  [0],  [0], \
    [0],  [0],  [1]), dtype=float))
```

We now choose a value to predict. We will predict them all, but the value stored in `xPredicted` will be the answer that we want at the end:

```
# what value we want to predict
xPredicted = np.array(([0,0,1]), dtype=float)

X = X/np.amax(X, axis=0) # maximum of X input array
# maximum of xPredicted (our input data for the prediction)
xPredicted = xPredicted/np.amax(xPredicted, axis=0)
```

Save the Sum Squared Loss results to a file (for further use by Excel) per epoch:

```
# set up our Loss file for graphing

lossFile = open("SumSquaredLossList.csv", "w")
```

Next, we build the `Neural_Network` class for our problem. (Refer to Figure 2-2 for the network we're building.) You can see that each layer is represented by a single line in the code:

```
class Neural_Network (object):
  def __init__(self):
    #parameters
    self.inputLayerSize = 3  # X1,X2,X3
    self.outputLayerSize = 1 # Y1
    self.hiddenLayerSize = 4 # Size of the hidden layer
```

Set all the network weights to random values initially:

```python
# build weights of each layer
# set to random values
# look at the interconnection diagram to make sense of this
# 3x4 matrix for input to hidden
self.W1 = \
        np.random.randn(self.inputLayerSize, self.hiddenLayerSize)
# 4x1 matrix for hidden layer to output
self.W2 = \
        np.random.randn(self.hiddenLayerSize, self.outputLayerSize)
```

The rand function generates an array of random numbers between 0 and 1. Our feedforward() function implements the feed-forward path through the neural network. The feedforward() function multiplies the matrices containing the weights from each layer to the next layer and then applies the sigmoid activation function:

```python
def feedForward(self, X):
  # feedForward propagation through our network
  # dot product of X (input) and first set of 3x4  weights
  self.z = np.dot(X, self.W1)

  # the activationSigmoid activation function – neural magic
  self.z2 = self.activationSigmoid(self.z)

  # dot product of hidden layer (z2) and second set of 4x1 weights
  self.z3 = np.dot(self.z2, self.W2)

  # final activation function – more neural magic
  o = self.activationSigmoid(self.z3)
  return o
```

And now we add the backwardPropagate() function, which implements the real trial-and-error learning that our neural network uses:

```python
def backwardPropagate(self, X, y, o):
  # backward propagate through the network
  # calculate the error in output
  self.o_error = y - o

  # apply derivative of activationSigmoid to error
  self.o_delta = self.o_error*self.activationSigmoidPrime(o)

  # z2 error: how much our hidden layer weights contributed to output
  # error
  self.z2_error = self.o_delta.dot(self.W2.T)
```

```
        # applying derivative of activationSigmoid to z2 error
        self.z2_delta = self.z2_error*self.activationSigmoidPrime(self.z2)

        # adjusting first set (inputLayer --> hiddenLayer) weights
        self.W1 += X.T.dot(self.z2_delta)
        # adjusting second set (hiddenLayer --> outputLayer) weights
        self.W2 += self.z2.T.dot(self.o_delta)
```

To train the network for a particular epoch, we call the `backwardPropagate()` function and the `feedforward()` function each time we train the network:

```
def trainNetwork(self, X, y):
    # feed forward the loop
    o = self.feedForward(X)
    # and then backpropagate the values (feedback)
    self.backwardPropagate(X, y, o)
```

The sigmoid activation function and the first derivative of the sigmoid activation function follow:

```
def activationSigmoid(self, s):
    # activation function
    # simple activationSigmoid curve as in the book
    return 1/(1+np.exp(-s))

def activationSigmoidPrime(self, s):
    # First derivative of activationSigmoid
    # calculus time!
    return s * (1 - s)
```

Then we save the epoch values of the loss function to a file (for Excel use) and also to save the neural weights:

```
def saveSumSquaredLossList(self,i,error):
    lossFile.write(str(i)+","+str(error.tolist())+'\n')

def saveWeights(self):
    # save this in order to reproduce our cool network
    np.savetxt("weightsLayer1.txt", self.W1, fmt="%s")
    np.savetxt("weightsLayer2.txt", self.W2, fmt="%s")
```

Next, we run our neural network to predict the outputs based on the current trained weights:

```
def predictOutput(self):
    print ("Predicted XOR output data based on trained weights: ")
```

```
        print ("Expected (X1-X3): \n" + str(xPredicted))
        print ("Output (Y1): \n" + str(self.feedForward(xPredicted)))

myNeuralNetwork = Neural_Network()
trainingEpochs = 1000
#trainingEpochs = 100000
```

Following is the main training loop that goes through all requested epochs. Change the `trainingEpochs` variable in the preceding code snippet to vary the number of epochs you would like to train your network:

```
for i in range(trainingEpochs): # train myNeuralNetwork 1,000 times
    print ("Epoch # " + str(i) + "\n")
    print ("Network Input : \n" + str(X))
    print ("Expected Output of XOR Gate Neural Network: \n" + str(y))
    print ("Actual Output from XOR Gate Neural Network: \n" + \
        str(myNeuralNetwork.feedForward(X)))
    # mean sum squared loss
    Loss = np.mean(np.square(y - myNeuralNetwork.feedForward(X)))
    myNeuralNetwork.saveSumSquaredLossList(i,Loss)
    print ("Sum Squared Loss: \n" + str(Loss))
    print ("\n")
    myNeuralNetwork.trainNetwork(X, y)
```

Finally, save the results of the training for reuse and to predict the output of our requested value:

```
myNeuralNetwork.saveWeights()
myNeuralNetwork.predictOutput()
```

Running the neural-network code

Now that the code is ready, it's time to train our neural network and examine the results. At a command prompt, enter the following command:

```
python3 2LayerNeuralNetworkCode.py
```

The program starts stepping through 1,000 epochs of training, printing the results of each epoch, and then displaying the final input and output. It also creates the following files of interest:

>> `weightsLayer1.txt`: This file contains the final trained weights for input-layer-to-hidden-layer connections (a 4x3 matrix).

>> `weightsLayer2.txt`: This file contains the final trained weights for hidden-layer-to-output-layer connections (a 1x4 matrix).

>> SumSquaredLossList.csv: This comma-delimited file contains the epoch number and each loss factor at the end of each epoch. We use this to graph the results across all epochs.

Here is the final output of the program for the last epoch, which is 999 because we start at 0:

```
Epoch # 999

Network Input :
[[0. 0. 0.]
 [0. 0. 1.]
 [0. 1. 0.]
 [0. 1. 1.]
 [1. 0. 0.]
 [1. 0. 1.]
 [1. 1. 0.]
 [1. 1. 1.]]
Expected Output of XOR Gate Neural Network:
[[1.]
 [0.]
 [0.]
 [0.]
 [0.]
 [0.]
 [0.]
 [1.]]
Actual  Output from XOR Gate Neural Network:
[[0.93419893]
 [0.04425737]
 [0.01636304]
 [0.03906686]
 [0.04377351]
 [0.01744497]
 [0.0391143 ]
 [0.93197489]]
Sum Squared Loss:
0.0020575319565093496


Predicted XOR output data based on trained weights:
Expected (X1-X3):
[0. 0. 1.]
Output (Y1):
[0.04422615]
```

At the bottom, you see that the expected output is 0.04422615, which is quite close but not quite the expected value of 0. Compare each expected output to the actual output from the network, and you'll see that they match pretty closely. Every time you run the program, the results will be slightly different because you initialize the weights with random numbers at the start of the run.

The goal of neural-network training is to get the answer exactly right but right within a stated tolerance of the correct result. For example, if we say that any output above 0.9 is a 1 and any output below 0.1 is a 0, our network would have given perfect results.

The Sum Squared Loss output value is a measure of all the errors of all the possible inputs.

We graphed the Sum Squared Loss values versus the epoch number, and the result is the graph in Figure 2-4. You can see that the program gets better quite quickly and then tails off.

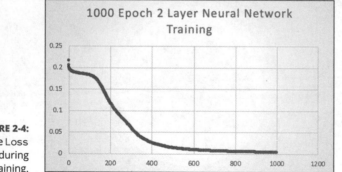

FIGURE 2-4:
The Loss function during training.

Let's try one more experiment and increase the number of epochs to 100,000:

```
Epoch # 99999


Network Input :
[[0. 0. 0.]
 [0. 0. 1.]
 [0. 1. 0.]
 [0. 1. 1.]
 [1. 0. 0.]
 [1. 0. 1.]
 [1. 1. 0.]
 [1. 1. 1.]]
```

```
Expected Output of XOR Gate Neural Network:
[[1.]
 [0.]
 [0.]
 [0.]
 [0.]
 [0.]
 [0.]
 [1.]]
Actual Output from XOR Gate Neural Network:
[[9.85225608e-01]
 [1.41750544e-04]
 [1.51985054e-04]
 [1.14829204e-02]
 [1.17578404e-04]
 [1.14814754e-02]
 [1.14821256e-02]
 [9.78014943e-01]]
Sum Squared Loss:
0.00013715041859631841


Predicted XOR output data based on trained weights:
Expected (X1-X3):
[0. 0. 1.]
Output (Y1):
[0.00014175]
```

The numbers are better but the results in the 1,000 epoch run were good enough according to our accuracy criteria (> 0.9 = 1 and < 0.1 = 0). 1,000 epochs produce data good enough for our stated problem. Increasing our training run to 100,000 epochs improves things only slightly.

Using TensorFlow for the same neural network

TensorFlow is a Python package that supports neural networks based on matrices and flow graphs similar to NumPy. However, unlike NumPy, TensorFlow is designed for use in machine-learning and AI applications and therefore has libraries and functions specifically for those applications.

A *tensor* is a multidimensional matrix of data, which is transformed by each TensorFlow layer it moves through. TensorFlow is Python-friendly and can be used on many different machines and also in the cloud. The capability to run on different machines and architectures makes TensorFlow an excellent choice for general use. As mentioned, neural networks are data-flow graphs and are implemented in terms of performing operations on matrices of data and then moving the resulting data to another matrix. Because matrices are tensors and the data flows from one to another, you can see where the TensorFlow name comes from. Neural network programs are full of matrices.

TensorFlow is one of the best-supported application frameworks, with APIs (application programming interfaces) for Python, C++, Haskell, Java, Go, Rust, and a third-party package for R.

Installing the TensorFlow Python library

To install the TensorFlow software on Windows, Linux, or Raspberry Pi, check out the official TensorFlow link at www.tensorflow.org/install/pip. You can also try Colab and Jupyter Notebook.

TensorFlow is a typical module and API (applications programming interface) for use by Python 3. When you install TensorFlow, many dependencies are also installed.

INTRODUCING TENSORS

As described in Chapter 1 of this minibook, tensors are multidimensional matrices of data. But an additional discussion about the vocabulary of tensors is helpful.

- A *scalar* can be thought of as a single piece of data. Only one piece of data is associated with a scalar. For example, a value of 5 meters or 5 meters/second are examples of a scalar, as is 45 degrees Fahrenheit or 21 degrees Celsius. You can think of a scalar as a point on a plane.

- A *vector* differs from a scalar because it contains at least two pieces of information. An example of a vector is 5 meters east — this describes a distance and a direction. A vector is a one-dimensional matrix (2x1, for example). You can think of a vector as an arrow located on a plane. Plane vectors are the simplest form of tensor. A 3x1 vector gives you the coordinates for 3D space: *x*, *y*, and *z*.

- A *tensor* is a matrix that can be characterized by magnitude and multiple directions. Scalars can be recognized as individual numbers, vectors as ordered sets of numbers, and tensors by a single or multidimensional array of numbers. A vector is a special case of a tensor. For a great non-mathematical introduction to tensors, go to www.youtube.com/watch?v=f5liqUk0ZTw.

Building a Python Neural Network in TensorFlow

For our neural network example in TensorFlow, we will use a network a bit larger than the two-layer neural network we used for NumPy (refer to Figure 2-1), which implemented an XNOR gate. Figure 2-5 shows the new three-layer neural network. Refer to Table 2-1 for the truth table for both networks.

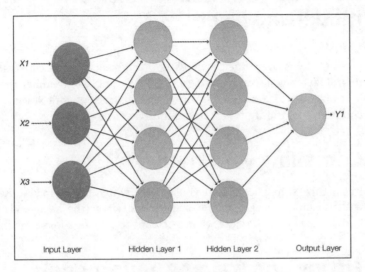

FIGURE 2-5: Our TensorFlow three-layer neural network.

Keras is an open-source neural-network library that enables fast experimentation with neural networks, deep learning, and machine learning. Keras is an indispensable part of TensorFlow. In 2017, Google decided to natively support Keras as the preferred interface for TensorFlow. Keras provides the excellent and intuitive set of abstractions and functions, whereas TensorFlow provides the efficient underlying implementation. NumPy implements the necessary matrix math in the TensorFlow modules.

The five steps to implementing a neural network in Keras with TensorFlow follow:

1. Load and format your data.

2. Define your neural network model and layers.

3. Compile the model.

4. Fit and train your model.

5. Evaluate the model.

Loading your data

The first step, loading your data, is trivial in our model but is often the most complex and difficult part of building an entire program. You have to examine your data (for example, an XOR gate or a database of factors affecting diabetic heart patients) and figure out how to map the data and the results to get to the information and predictions you want.

Defining your neural-network model and layers

In the second step, defining your network, you can see one of the primary advantages of Keras over other frameworks. You basically just construct a stack of the neural layers you want your data to flow through. Remember that TensorFlow is just matrices of data flowing through a neural network stack. In this step, you choose the configuration of your neural layer and activation functions.

Compiling your model

In the third step, you compile your model, which hooks up your Keras layer model with the underlying machine-specific software (the back-end) to run on your hardware. You also choose what you want to use for a loss function.

Fitting and training your model

The real work of training your network takes place in the fourth step. You determine how many epochs you want the program go through. You also accumulate the history of what is happening through all the epochs, and use this information to create your graphs.

Evaluating the model

After training your model, you have to evaluate it. Evaluation refers to running your trained machine-learning model on other data to see how well the model does on data that was not included in your training set.

The Python code using TensorFlow, NumPy, and Keras for the two-layer neural network follows (refer to Figure 2-1). Using nano (or your favorite text editor), open a file called `TensorFlowKeras.py` and enter the following code:

```python
import tensorflow as tf

from tensorflow.keras import layers

from tensorflow.keras.layers import Activation, Dense

import numpy as np

# X = input of our 3 input XOR gate
# set up the inputs of the neural network (right from the table)
X = np.array(([0,0,0],[0,0,1],[0,1,0],
            [0,1,1],[1,0,0],[1,0,1],[1,1,0],[1,1,1]), dtype=float)
# y = our output of our neural network
y = np.array(([1], [0],  [0],  [0],  [0],
            [0],  [0],  [1]), dtype=float)


model = tf.keras.Sequential()

model.add(Dense(4, input_dim=3, activation='relu',
    use_bias=True))
#model.add(Dense(4,  activation='relu', use_bias=True))
model.add(Dense(1, activation='sigmoid', use_bias=True))

model.compile(loss='mean_squared_error',
        optimizer='adam',
        metrics=['binary_accuracy'])

print (model.get_weights())

history = model.fit(X, y, epochs=2000,
        validation_data = (X, y))


model.summary()


# printing out to file
loss_history = history.history["loss"]
numpy_loss_history = np.array(loss_history)
np.savetxt("loss_history.txt", numpy_loss_history,
        delimiter="\n")
```

```
binary_accuracy_history = history.history["binary_accuracy"]
numpy_binary_accuracy = np.array(binary_accuracy_history)
np.savetxt("binary_accuracy.txt", numpy_binary_accuracy, delimiter="\n")



print(np.mean(history.history["binary_accuracy"]))

result = model.predict(X ).round()

print (result)
```

After looking at the code, we will run the neural network and then evaluate the model and results.

Breaking down the code

The first thing to note about our TensorFlow and Keras code is that it's much simpler and easier to understand than the two-layer model we wrote earlier in the chapter in Python using NumPy.

First, we import all the libraries we need to run our example two-layer model. Note that TensorFlow includes Keras by default. And once again we see our friend NumPy as the preferred way of handling matrices:

```
import tensorflow as tf

from tensorflow.keras import layers

from tensorflow.keras.layers import Activation, Dense

import numpy as np
```

Step 1, load and format your data: In this case, we just set up the truth table for the XOR gate with NumPy arrays. Loading and formatting your data can get much more complex when you have large, diverse, cross-correlated sources of data:

```
# X = input of our 3 input XOR gate
# set up the inputs of the neural network (right from the table)
X = np.array(([0,0,0],[0,0,1],[0,1,0],
              [0,1,1],[1,0,0],[1,0,1],[1,1,0],[1,1,1]), dtype=float)
# y = our output of our neural network
y  = np.array(([1], [0],  [0],  [0],  [0],
               [0],  [0],  [1]), dtype=float)
```

Step 2, define your neural network model and layers: This step is where the power of Keras shines. Adding more neural layers and changing their size and activation functions are simple tasks. We also apply a bias (which shifts the activation curve to the right) to our activation function (relu, in this case, with our friend the sigmoid function for the final output layer), which we did not do in our pure Python model because the data we were training on was so simple.

Next, look at the commented model.add statement that follows. When we go to our next three-layer neural network example, we uncomment that single line to add an additional layer to our neural network. We use the relu, which is a simple, general-purpose linear activation function:

```
model = tf.keras.Sequential()

model.add(Dense(4, input_dim=3, activation='relu',
    use_bias=True))
#model.add(Dense(4, activation='relu', use_bias=True))
model.add(Dense(1, activation='sigmoid', use_bias=True))
```

Step 3, compile your model: We are using the same loss function that we used in our pure Python implementation, mean_squared_error. New is the optimizer Adam, which is a method for stochastic optimization. *Stochastic optimization* refers to a set of methods for minimizing or maximizing a value when randomness is present in the program. The default optimizer provides a method for efficiently modifying the weights of the neural layers.

Now we turn to the metrics we want as outputs from the program. binary_accuracy compares the outputs of our network to either a 1 or a 0. You will see values of, say, 0.75, which means six out of eight are correct (because we have eight possible outputs). binary_accuracy means exactly what you would expect from the name:

```
model.compile(loss='mean_squared_error',
        optimizer='adam',
        metrics=['binary_accuracy'])
```

Next we print the starting weights of our model. By default, the network initialization steps use a random method to assign the weights. You can seed that method to use the same starting weights for each run and get the same results, or you can change the method used to generate the weights completely.

```
print (model.get_weights())
```

Step 4, fit and train your model: We chose the number of epochs that would enable us to move towards a binary accuracy of 1.0 most of the time. Here we load the NumPy arrays with the input (X) and our expected output (y). The `validation_data` parameter compares the outputs of the trained network in each epoch and generates `val_acc` and `val_loss` and stores them in the `history` variable:

```
history = model.fit(X, y, epochs=2000,
        validation_data = (X, y))
```

Then we print a summary of the model so we can make sure it was constructed in the way we expected:

```
model.summary()
```

Next, we print the values from the `history` variable, which we will then graph:

```
# printing out to file
loss_history = history.history["loss"]
numpy_loss_history = np.array(loss_history)
np.savetxt("loss_history.txt", numpy_loss_history,
        delimiter="\n")

binary_accuracy_history = history.history["binary_accuracy"]
numpy_binary_accuracy = np.array(binary_accuracy_history)
np.savetxt("binary_accuracy.txt", numpy_binary_accuracy, delimiter="\n")
```

Step 5, evaluate the model: We run the model to predict the outputs from all the inputs of X, using the `round` function to make the outputs either 0 or 1. Note that the `round` function replaces the criteria we used in our pure Python model, which was <0.1 = "0" and >0.9 = "1". We also calculate the average of all the `binary_accuracy` values of all epochs, but the number isn't useful — except to show us that the closer to 1.0, the faster the model succeeded:

```
print(np.mean(history.history["binary_accuracy"]))

result = model.predict(X ).round()

print (result)
```

Now let's move along to some results.

Checking the results

When you run TensorFlow programs, you may see something like this:

WARNING

```
/usr/lib/python3.5/importlib/_bootstrap.py:222: RuntimeWarning: compiletime
    version 3.4 of module 'tensorflow.python.framework.fast_tensor_util' does not
    match runtime version 3.5
return f(*args, **kwds)
/usr/lib/python3.5/importlib/_bootstrap.py:222: RuntimeWarning: builtins.type
    size changed, may indicate binary incompatibility. Expected 432, got 412
return f(*args, **kwds)
```

This output occurs because of a problem with the way TensorFlow was built for your machine. These warnings can be safely ignored. The good folks over at TensorFlow.org say that this issue will be fixed in the next version.

To run the two-layer model, type **python3 TensorFlowKeras.py** in the Terminal window. After watching the epochs march away (you can change the amount of output by setting the Verbose parameter in your model.fit command), we are rewarded with the following:

```
...
Epoch 1999/2000
8/8 [==============================] - 0s 2ms/step - loss: 0.0367 - binary_
    accuracy: 1.0000 - val_loss: 0.0367 - val_binary_accuracy: 1.0000
Epoch 2000/2000
8/8 [==============================] - 0s 2ms/step - loss: 0.0367 - binary_
    accuracy: 1.0000 - val_loss: 0.0367 - val_binary_accuracy: 1.0000

_____
Layer (type)          Output Shape          Param #
=================================================================
dense (Dense)          (None, 4)             16
_____
dense_1 (Dense)        (None, 1)             5
=================================================================
Total params: 21
Trainable params: 21
Non-trainable params: 0
_____
0.8436875
[[1.]
 [0.]
 [0.]
 [0.]
 [0.]
 [0.]
 [0.]
 [1.]]
```

By epoch 2,000, we have achieved the binary accuracy of 1.0, as hoped for, and the results of our `model.predict` function call at the end of the program output matches our truth table. Figure 2-6 shows the loss function and binary accuracy values plotted against the epoch number as the training progressed.

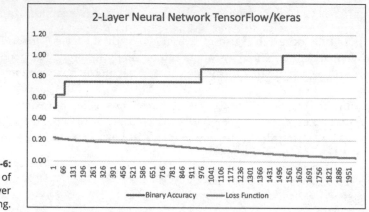

FIGURE 2-6:
Results of the two-layer training.

The new network's loss function (shown in Figure 2-6) is much smoother than the previous network's loss function (refer to Figure 2-4.) This smoother loss function has to do with the activation choice (`relu`) and the optimizer function (ADAM). ADAM (Adaptive Moment Estimation) uses a stochastic algorithm (uses random numbers) to improve the results of the loss function. Also, remember that you will get a somewhat different curve each time because of the random number initial values set in the weights of the individual neurons. You can seed your random number generator to make the random number generator give you the same random numbers each time you run the program. This makes it easier to optimize your performance.

WHY USE A GUI TO RUN TensorFlow?

You'll spend a lot of time coding in text editors to build your models. For simplicity's sake, we exported our data to Excel to produce the graphs in this chapter. Most of the time, we use a Terminal window, but there is a big advantage to using a computer's full GUI (graphical user interface) desktop to open a Terminal window for editing. That big advantage is called TensorBoard. *TensorBoard* is a part of TensorFlow and is available to you in a browser (such as Chrome or Firefox). You point TensorBoard (running in the browser) at your job directory and you can easily do all sorts of visual analysis of your neural network experiments.

With our first neural network in this chapter, we made a big deal about backpropagation and how it was a fundamental part of neural networks. However, Keras handles backpropagation automatically. If you want to modify how Keras is doing backpropagation, you can change the optimization parameter in the `module.compile` command (we used ADAM), but the process requires quite a bit of work. When you run your training for the network, you're using the backpropagation algorithm and optimizing this according to the chosen optimization algorithm and loss function specified when compiling the model.

Note that when the binary accuracy reaches 1.00 (in the example run, at epoch 1556), your network is fully trained in this case.

Changing to a three-layer neural network in TensorFlow and Keras

Now let's add another layer to our neural network. Refer to Figure 2-5 for the new network; Figure 2-7 shows the results. Open the `TensorFlowKeras.py` file in your favorite editor. We will be making a slight change to the following:

```
model.add(Dense(4, input_dim=3, activation='relu',
    use_bias=True))
#model.add(Dense(4, activation='relu', use_bias=True))
model.add(Dense(1, activation='sigmoid', use_bias=True))
```

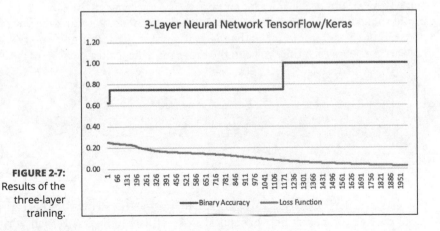

FIGURE 2-7: Results of the three-layer training.

If we remove the comment character in front of the middle layer, we will have a three-layer neural network with four neurons per layer. It's that easy. Here is what the code should look like now:

```
model.add(Dense(4, input_dim=3, activation='relu',
    use_bias=True))
model.add(Dense(4, activation='relu', use_bias=True))
model.add(Dense(1, activation='sigmoid', use_bias=True))
```

When we run the program, we get the results from the three-layer network, which look something like this:

```
8/8 [==============================] - 0s 2ms/step - loss: 0.0153 - binary_
    accuracy: 1.0000 - val_loss: 0.0153 - val_binary_accuracy: 1.0000
Epoch 2000/2000
8/8 [==============================] - 0s 2ms/step - loss: 0.0153 - binary_
    accuracy: 1.0000 - val_loss: 0.0153 - val_binary_accuracy: 1.0000
_____
Layer (type)            Output Shape         Param #
===============================================================
dense (Dense)           (None, 4)             16
_____
dense_1 (Dense)         (None, 4)             20
_____
dense_2 (Dense)         (None, 1)             5
===============================================================
Total params: 41
Trainable params: 41
Non-trainable params: 0
_____
0.930375
[[1.]
 [0.]
 [0.]
 [0.]
 [0.]
 [0.]
 [0.]
 [1.]]
```

You can see that you have three layers in the neural network. The capability to change the neural network quickly and efficiently is one reason why the TensorFlow/Keras software is so powerful. It's easy to tinker with parameters and make changes.

The three-layer run converges to a binary accuracy of 1.00 at about epoch 916, much faster than epoch 1556 in the two-layer run. In addition, the loss function is significantly more sloped than the two-layer example (refer to Figure 2-6).

Just for fun, we ran this program again and changed the number of neurons to 100 per each hidden layer. As expected, the program converged to a binary accuracy of 1.00 much faster than in the previous run (epoch 78 versus epoch 916). Run your own experiments to get a feel for the way the results vary with different parameters, layers, and neuron counts.

Believe it or not, you now understand a great deal about how neural networks and machine learning works. Go forth and train those neurons!

Chapter **3**

Doing Machine Learning

What does it mean to learn something? One definition is "the acquisition and mastery of what is already known about something and the extended clarification of meaning of that knowledge." Another definition is that learning is "a relatively permanent change in a person's knowledge or behavior due to experience."

The second definition best fits with the current state of AI. Our engineering and scientific culture has developed algorithms and programs that can learn things about data and about sensory input and apply that knowledge to new situations. But our machines do not understand anything about what they have learned. They have just accumulated data about their inputs and have transformed that input to some kind of output which we hope means something to the observing humans.

However, even though machines don't understand what they have learned, you can do some impressive problem solving using the machine-learning techniques described in this chapter. And maybe the techniques we are developing now will lead the way to something much more impressive in the future.

What does it mean for a machine to learn something? We use the following rough definition: If a machine can take inputs and transform them to useful outputs, the machine has learned something. For example, if you write a simple program to add two numbers, you have taught that machine something — how to add two numbers.

In this chapter, we focus on machine learning and the use of algorithms and statistical models that progressively improve their performance on a specific task. If this sounds like our neural network experiments in Chapter 2 of this minibook, you are correct. Machine learning involves not only neural networks but also other sophisticated data analysis and statistical techniques. To download the code for this chapter, go to www.dummies.com/go/pythonaiofd2e.

Learning by Looking for Solutions in All the Wrong Places

One of the problems with machine learning and AI in general is figuring out how an algorithm can find the best solution. The operative word is *best*. How do we know a given solution is best? We set specific goals and achieve them (the solution may be just good enough rather than optimal).

Some people compare the problem of finding the best solution to that of trying to find the highest mountain in an area on a foggy day. You get to the top of a mountain and proclaim, "I am on the highest mountain." Well, you're on the highest mountain you can see. But if you define your goal as being on the top of a mountain more than 1,000 feet high, and you're at 1,250 feet, you have met your goal. Meeting a goal such as being above 1,000 feet is called a *local maxima*, and it may or may not be the best maxima available.

Defining a goal for your machine-learning project is a key step in the entire process of building and using a machine-learning program.

In this chapter, we do most of our goal setting (training the machine) with known solutions to a problem. First we train our machine and then we apply the training to new, similar examples of the problem.

The three main types of machine-learning algorithms follow:

>> **Supervised learning:** This type of algorithm builds a model of data that contains both inputs and outputs. The data is known as *training data*. We show this type of machine learning in this chapter.

>> **Unsupervised learning:** For this type of algorithm, the data contains only inputs, and the algorithms look for structures and patterns in the data. The algorithms generally have sophisticated statistical and mathematic goals, not simple goals such as finding a mountain taller than 1,000 meters.

>> **Reinforcement learning:** In this type of algorithm, software takes actions based on a cumulative reward. The algorithm does not assume knowledge of an exact mathematical model and is used when exact models are unavailable. Reinforcement learning is the most complex area of machine learning, and the one that might be most fruitful in the future. Experimenting with reinforcement learning is the area of robotic vision interpretation research using machine learning that is of great interest to co-author John Shovic.

Next, we jump into doing machine learning with Python.

Creating a Machine-Learning Network for Detecting Clothes Types

We use TensorFlow and Keras and the freely available training database called Fashion-MNIST (Modified National Institute of Standards and Technology) to build some machine-learning examples and look at their results. (For more about TensorFlow and Keras, refer to Chapter 2 of this minibook.) The database contains 60,000 fashion products from ten categories. It contains data in 28x28 pixel format, with 6,000 items in each category, as shown in Figure 3-1.

FIGURE 3-1: A small portion of the Fashion-MNIST database.

Fashion-MNIST uses a MNIST-format (a collection of grayscale images with a resolution of 28x28 pixels) fashion database of 60,000 images classified into ten types of apparel:

>> 0: t-shirt/top

>> 1: trouser

>> 2: pullover

>> 3: dress

>> 4: coat

>> 5: sandal

>> 6: shirt

>> 7: sneaker

>> 8: bag

>> 9: ankle boot

We use the same five-step approach we used to build layered networks with Keras in Chapter 2 of this minibook. TensorFlow and Keras.

1. Load and format your data.

2. Define your neural network model and layers.

3. Compile the model.

4. Fit and train your model.

5. Evaluate the model.

Setting up the software environment

Most of the action in this chapter is, as usual, in the command line, because you still have to type code and run software. However, we're going to display some graphics on the screen and use MatPlotLib to evaluate what the machine-learning program is doing, so start a GUI (graphics user interface) if you haven't already.

If you're using a headless Raspberry Pi, either add a keyboard, mouse, and monitor or bring up VNC (virtual network computer) to use your computer monitor as a display for a second computer — the Raspberry Pi, in this case. Many links on the web describe how to do this and how to bring up the GUI on your main computer. For a great source of tutorials on setting up the software and connecting the Raspberry Pi, visit www.raspberrypi.org.

We use VNC on a headless Raspberry Pi in this chapter. Figure 3-2 shows the GUI running on the Raspberry Pi (actually running VNC, but you can't tell from this image).

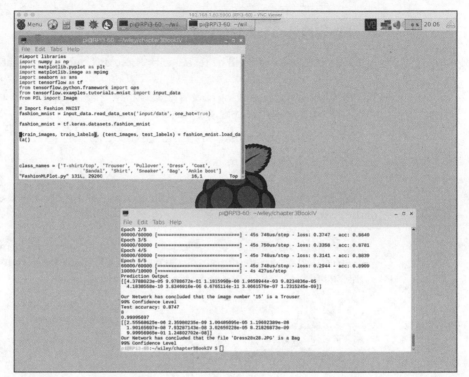

FIGURE 3-2:
A full GUI on the Raspberry Pi.

TIP

If you're missing any of the Python libraries that we use in this example, search the web instructions on installing them on your machine. Every setup is a little different. For example, if you're missing seaborn, search "installing seaborn python library on [*name of your machine*]." If you do a search on "seaborn for the Raspberry Pi," you'll find "sudo pip3 install seaborn."

Getting the data from the Fashion-MNIST dataset

Getting the data is easy, although it will take a while to first load it on your computer. After you run the program for the first time, it will use the Fashion–MNIST data copied to your computer.

Training the network

We will train our machine-learning neural network using all 60,000 images of clothes: 6,000 images in each of the ten categories.

Testing our network

Our trained network will be tested with three different sets of data:

>> A set of 10,000 training photos (unclassified, that is not in the training data) from the Fashion_MNIST data set

>> A selected image from the Fashion_MNIST data set

>> A photo of a woman's dress

This first version of the program will run a test on 10,000 unclassified files from the Fashion_MNIST database.

The Python code using TensorFlow, NumPy, and Keras to perform analysis on the Fashion_MNIST network follows. Using nano (or your favorite text editor), open the FMTensorFlow.py file and enter the following code:

```
#import libraries
import numpy as np
import matplotlib.pyplot as plt
import matplotlib.image as mpimg
import seaborn as sns
import tensorflow as tf
from tensorflow.python.framework import ops
from tensorflow.examples.tutorials.mnist import input_data
from PIL import Image

# Import Fashion MNIST
fashion_mnist = input_data.read_data_sets('input/data',
        one_hot=True)

fashion_mnist = tf.keras.datasets.fashion_mnist

(train_images, train_labels), (test_images, test_labels) \
        = fashion_mnist.load_data()




class_names = ['T-shirt/top', 'Trouser',
        'Pullover', 'Dress', 'Coat',
```

```
            'Sandal', 'Shirt', 'Sneaker', 'Bag', 'Ankle boot']


train_images = train_images / 255.0

test_images = test_images / 255.0


model = tf.keras.Sequential()


model.add(tf.keras.layers.Flatten(input_shape=(28,28)))
model.add(tf.keras.layers.Dense(128, activation='relu' ))
model.add(tf.keras.layers.Dense(10, activation='softmax' ))


model.compile(optimizer=tf.train.AdamOptimizer(),
                    loss='sparse_categorical_crossentropy',
                            metrics=['accuracy'])


model.fit(train_images, train_labels, epochs=5)

# test with 10,000 images
test_loss, test_acc = model.evaluate(test_images, test_labels)

print('10,000 image Test accuracy:', test_acc)
```

Breaking down the code

If you read the description of the TensorFlow and Keras program in Chapter 2, this code should look familiar. In this section, we break the code down into our familiar five-step Keras process.

But first, we import all the libraries needed to run the example two-layer model. Note that TensorFlow includes Keras by default. And once again our friend NumPy is the preferred way of handling matrices:

```
#import libraries
import numpy as np
import matplotlib.pyplot as plt
import matplotlib.image as mpimg
import seaborn as sns
import tensorflow as tf
from tensorflow.python.framework import ops
from tensorflow.examples.tutorials.mnist import input_data
from PIL import Image
```

In step 1, we load and format the data. This time we're using the built-in data set reading capability. The program knows what this data is because of the `import` statement from `tensorflow.examples.tutorials.mnist` in the preceding code:

```
# Import Fashion MNIST
fashion_mnist = input_data.read_data_sets('input/data',
        one_hot=True)

fashion_mnist = tf.keras.datasets.fashion_mnist

(train_images, train_labels), (test_images, test_labels) \
        = fashion_mnist.load_data()
```

Next we give some descriptive names to the ten classes in the `Fashion_MNIST` data:

```
class_names = ['T-shirt/top', 'Trouser',
        'Pullover', 'Dress', 'Coat',
        'Sandal', 'Shirt', 'Sneaker', 'Bag', 'Ankle boot']
```

Then we change the scale of the images from 0–255 to 0.0–1.0:

```
train_images = train_images / 255.0

test_images = test_images / 255.0
```

In step 2, we define the neural network model and layers. Keras makes it very easy to add neural layers and change their sizes and activation functions. We also apply a bias to our activation function (`relu`), in this case with `softmax`, for the final output layer:

```
model = tf.keras.Sequential()


model.add(tf.keras.layers.Flatten(input_shape=(28,28)))
model.add(tf.keras.layers.Dense(128, activation='relu' ))
model.add(tf.keras.layers.Dense(10, activation='softmax' ))
```

In step 3, we compile the model. The loss function `sparse_categorical_cros-sentropy` is used when an individual integer is assigned for each clothes category, as we do in this example. Adam (a method for stochastic optimization) is a good default optimizer because it's well suited for problems that are large in terms of data or parameters or both.

```
model.compile(optimizer=tf.train.AdamOptimizer(),
    loss='sparse_categorical_crossentropy',
        metrics=['accuracy'])
```

The `sparse_categorical_crossentropy` loss function measures the error between categories across the data set. *Categorical* refers to the fact that the data has more than two categories (binary) in the data set. *Sparse* refers to using a single integer to refer to classes (0–9, in our example). *Entropy* (a measure of disorder) refers to the mix of data between the categories.

In step 4, we fit and train the model. We chose five epochs due to the time it takes to run the model for our examples. Feel free to increase the number of epochs. Here we load the NumPy arrays for the input to our network (the data-base `train_images`).

```
model.fit(train_images, train_labels, epochs=5)
```

In step 5, we evaluate the model. The `model.evaluate()` function is used to com-pare the outputs of your trained network in each epoch and generates `test_acc` and `test_loss` for your information in each epoch as stored in the history variable.

```
# test with 10,000 images
test_loss, test_acc = model.evaluate(test_images, test_labels)

print('10,000 image Test accuracy:', test_acc)
```

Results of the training and evaluation

We ran our program on the Raspberry Pi 3B+. (A Raspberry Pi 4B is at least twice as fast.) You can safely ignore the code mismatch warnings and the future depreca-tion announcements at this point.

Here are the results of the program:

```
Epoch 1/5
60000/60000 [==============================] - 44s 726us/step - loss: 0.5009 -
    acc: 0.8244
Epoch 2/5
60000/60000 [==============================]   42s 703us/step - loss: 0.3751 -
    acc: 0.8652
Epoch 3/5
60000/60000 [==============================] - 42s 703us/step - loss: 0.3359 -
    acc: 0.8767
```

```
Epoch 4/5
60000/60000 [==============================] - 42s 701us/step - loss: 0.3124 -
    acc: 0.8839
Epoch 5/5
60000/60000 [==============================] - 42s 703us/step - loss: 0.2960 -
    acc: 0.8915
10000/10000 [==============================] - 4s 404us/step
10,000 image Test accuracy: 0.873
```

Fundamentally, the test results are saying that with our two-layer neural machine-learning network, we're classifying 87 percent of the 10,000-image test database correctly. When we upped the number of epochs to 50, and the accuracy increased to only 88.7 percent — lots of extra computation time with little increase in accuracy.

Testing a single test image

Next we test a single image from the Fashion_MNIST database, which is shown in Figure 3-3. Add the following code to the end of your program and rerun the software:

```
#run test image from Fashion_MNIST data

img = test_images[15]
img = (np.expand_dims(img,0))
singlePrediction = model.predict(img,steps=1)
print ("Prediction Output")
print(singlePrediction)
print()
NumberElement = singlePrediction.argmax()
Element = np.amax(singlePrediction)

print ("Our Network has concluded that the image number '15' is a "
        +class_names[NumberElement])
print (str(int(Element*100)) + "% Confidence Level")
```

Here are the results from a five-epoch run:

```
Prediction Output
[[1.2835168e-05 9.9964070e-01 6.2637120e-08 3.4126092e-04 4.4297972e-06
    7.8450663e-10 6.2759432e-07 9.8717527e-12 1.2729484e-08 1.1002166e-09]]

Our Network has concluded that the image number '15' is a Trouser
99% Confidence Level
```

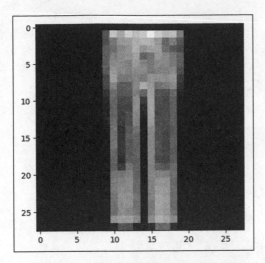

FIGURE 3-3:
Image 15 from
the Fashion-
MNIST test
database.

Woo-hoo! It worked. It correctly identified the picture as a trouser. Remember, however, that we had an overall accuracy level on the test data of only 87 percent.

Testing on external pictures

Next, we test the program using one of our own pictures, taken with an iPhone. See Figure 3-4.

FIGURE 3-4:
Unclassified
dress hanging
on a wall.

Using Preview on a Mac, we converted the picture's resolution from 3024x3024 pixels to 28x28 pixels, as shown in Figure 3-5. Although 28x28 pixels does not result in a clear picture, the photo in Figure 3-5 is clearer than the ones in Figure 3-1 from the Fashion-MNIST database.

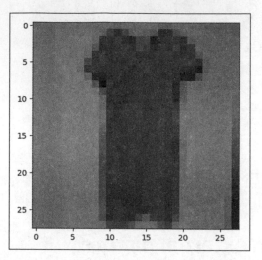

FIGURE 3-5: The dress at 28x28 pixels.

Most of the following code arranges the data from the original JPG picture to fit the picture format required by TensorFlow. You should be able to use this code to easily add your own pictures for more experiments:

```
# read test dress image
imageName = "Dress28x28.JPG"

testImg = Image.open(imageName)
testImg.load()
data = np.asarray( testImg, dtype="float" )


data = tf.image.rgb_to_grayscale(data)
data = data/255.0


data = tf.transpose(data, perm=[2,0,1])



singlePrediction = model.predict(data,steps=1)
print ("Prediction Output")
```

```
print(singlePrediction)
print()
NumberElement = singlePrediction.argmax()
Element = np.amax(singlePrediction)

print ("Our Network has concluded that the file '"
        +imageName+"' is a "+class_names[NumberElement])
print (str(int(Element*100)) + "% Confidence Level")
```

The results, round 1

The results did not make us happy, as you will see shortly. We put the Dress28x28. JPG file in the same directory as our program and ran a five-epoch training run. Here are the results:

```
Prediction Output
[[1.2717753e-06 1.3373902e-08 1.0487850e-06 3.3525557e-11 8.8031484e-09
   7.1847245e-10 1.1177938e-04 8.8322977e-12 9.9988592e-01 3.2957085e-12]]


Our Network has concluded that the file 'Dress28x28.JPG' is a Bag
99% Confidence Level
```

Our neural network machine-learning program, after classifying 60,000 pictures and 6,000 dress pictures, concluded at a 99 percent confidence level . . . *wait for it* . . . that the Dress28x28.JPG photo is a bag. We don't usually laugh at software results but did when we read this one.

So we increased the training epochs to 50 and reran the program. Here are the results from that run:

```
Prediction Output
[[3.4407502e-33 0.0000000e+00 2.5598763e-33 0.0000000e+00 0.0000000e+00
  0.0000000e+00 2.9322060e-17 0.0000000e+00 1.0000000e+00 1.5202169e-39]]
Our Network has concluded that the file 'Dress28x28.JPG' is a Bag
100% Confidence Level
```

The dress is still a bag, but now our program is 100 percent confident that the dress is a bag. Hmm. This illustrates one of the problems with machine learning. Being 100 percent certain that a picture of a dress is a picture of a bag is still 100 percent wrong.

What is the real problem here? The neural network configuration is probably not good enough to distinguish a dress from a bag. Additional training epochs didn't seem to improve the accuracy, so the next thing to try is to increase the number of neurons in our hidden level.

We changed the model layers in our program to use a four-level convolutional-layer model. We love how we can dramatically change the neural network when using Keras and TensorFlow.

A convolutional neural network (CNN) works by scanning images and analyzing the pixels in the image chunk by chunk: for example, with a 5x5 pixel window that moves by a stride length of two pixels each time until it spans the entire message. It's like looking at an image using a microscope; you see only a small part of the picture at any one time, but after moving back and forth you eventually see the entire picture. Using a CNN network on the Raspberry Pi increased the single epoch time from 10 seconds to 1.5 hours, a decrease in performance of 540 times. CNNs use a great deal of computing power.

What other things could you try to improve the accuracy of this machine-learning program? You could use data augmentation (increasing the training samples by rotating, shifting, and zooming the pictures) and a variety of other techniques beyond the scope of this introduction to machine learning.

The CNN model code

The following code has the same overall structure as the last program. The only significant change is the addition of the new layers for the CNN network:

```
#import libraries
import numpy as np
import matplotlib.pyplot as plt
import matplotlib.image as mpimg
import seaborn as sns
import tensorflow as tf
from tensorflow.python.framework import ops
from tensorflow.examples.tutorials.mnist import input_data
from PIL import Image

# Import Fashion MNIST
fashion_mnist = input_data.read_data_sets('input/data',
        one_hot=True)

fashion_mnist = tf.keras.datasets.fashion_mnist
```

```
(train_images, train_labels), (test_images, test_labels) \
        = fashion_mnist.load_data()




class_names = ['T-shirt/top', 'Trouser',
        'Pullover', 'Dress', 'Coat',
        'Sandal', 'Shirt', 'Sneaker', 'Bag', 'Ankle boot']


train_images = train_images / 255.0

test_images = test_images / 255.0


# Prepare the training images
train_images = train_images.reshape(train_images.shape[0], 28, 28, 1)

# Prepare the test images
test_images = test_images.reshape(test_images.shape[0], 28, 28, 1)


model = tf.keras.Sequential()

input_shape = (28, 28, 1)
model.add(tf.keras.layers.Conv2D(32, kernel_size=(3, 3), activation='relu',
    input_shape=input_shape))
model.add(tf.keras.layers.BatchNormalization())

model.add(tf.keras.layers.Conv2D(32, kernel_size=(3, 3), activation='relu'))
model.add(tf.keras.layers.BatchNormalization())
model.add(tf.keras.layers.MaxPooling2D(pool_size=(2, 2)))
model.add(tf.keras.layers.Dropout(0.25))

model.add(tf.keras.layers.Conv2D(64, kernel_size=(3, 3), activation='relu'))
model.add(tf.keras.layers.BatchNormalization())
model.add(tf.keras.layers.Dropout(0.25))

model.add(tf.keras.layers.Conv2D(128, kernel_size=(3, 3), activation='relu'))
model.add(tf.keras.layers.BatchNormalization())
model.add(tf.keras.layers.MaxPooling2D(pool_size=(2, 2)))
model.add(tf.keras.layers.Dropout(0.25))

model.add(tf.keras.layers.Flatten())

model.add(tf.keras.layers.Dense(512, activation='relu'))
model.add(tf.keras.layers.BatchNormalization())
```

```
model.add(tf.keras.layers.Dropout(0.5))

model.add(tf.keras.layers.Dense(128, activation='relu'))
model.add(tf.keras.layers.BatchNormalization())
model.add(tf.keras.layers.Dropout(0.5))

model.add(tf.keras.layers.Dense(10, activation='softmax'))

model.compile(optimizer=tf.train.AdamOptimizer(),
                      loss='sparse_categorical_crossentropy',
                                   metrics=['accuracy'])


model.fit(train_images, train_labels, epochs=5)

# test with 10,000 images
test_loss, test_acc = model.evaluate(test_images, test_labels)

print('10,000 image Test accuracy:', test_acc)

#run test image from Fashion_MNIST data

img = test_images[15]
img = (np.expand_dims(img,0))
singlePrediction = model.predict(img,steps=1)
print ("Prediction Output")
print(singlePrediction)
print()
NumberElement = singlePrediction.argmax()
Element = np.amax(singlePrediction)

print ("Our Network has concluded that the image number '15' is a "
        +class_names[NumberElement])
print (str(int(Element*100)) + "% Confidence Level")
```

The results, round 2

The run on the Raspberry Pi 3B+ took about seven hours to complete. The results
follow:

```
10,000 image Test accuracy: 0.8601
Prediction Output
[[5.9128129e-06 9.9997270e-01 1.5681641e-06 8.1393973e-06 1.5611777e-06
   7.0504888e-07 5.5174642e-06 2.2484977e-07 3.0045830e-06 5.6888598e-07]]

Our Network has concluded that the image number '15' is a Trouser
```

The key number here is the 10,000-image test accuracy, which at 86 percent is lower than the accuracy of our previous, simpler machine-learning neural network (87 percent). Why did this happen? The lower accuracy is probably related to *overfitting* the training data, in which the trained network recognizes the training set better but loses the capability to recognize new test data. This type of issue highlights the fact that using machine-learning programs is an art and a science.

TIP

Choosing which machine-learning neural network to use to work with your data is one of the major decisions you will make in your design. However, understanding activation functions, dropout management, and loss functions will also deeply affect the performance of your machine-learning program. Optimizing all these parameters at once is a difficult task that requires research and experience. Some of this is really rocket science!

Visualizing with MatPlotLib

Now that we've moved to a GUI-based development environment, we're going to run our base code again and analyze the run by using MatPlotLib. We're using a Raspberry Pi for these experiments, but you can use a Mac, a PC, or another Linux system. If you can install TensorFlow, MatPlotLib, and Python on your computer system, you can do these experiments.

To install MatPlotLib on your Raspberry Pi, type `pip3 install matplotlib`.

We add the `history` variable to the output of `model.fit` to collect data. Next, we add MatPlotLib commands to graph the loss and the accuracy from our epochs and then to add figure displays for our two individual image tests.

Using nano (or your favorite text editor), open the `FMTensorFlowPlot.py` file, and enter the following code:

```
#import libraries
import numpy as np
import matplotlib.pyplot as plt
import matplotlib.image as mpimg
import seaborn as sns
import tensorflow as tf
from tensorflow.python.framework import ops
```

```python
from tensorflow.examples.tutorials.mnist import input_data
from PIL import Image

# Import Fashion MNIST
fashion_mnist = input_data.read_data_sets('input/data', one_hot=True)

fashion_mnist = tf.keras.datasets.fashion_mnist

(train_images, train_labels), (test_images, test_labels) = \
    fashion_mnist.load_data()




class_names = ['T-shirt/top', 'Trouser', 'Pullover', 'Dress', 'Coat',
                'Sandal', 'Shirt', 'Sneaker', 'Bag', 'Ankle boot']


train_images = train_images / 255.0

test_images = test_images / 255.0


model = tf.keras.Sequential()


model.add(tf.keras.layers.Flatten(input_shape=(28,28)))
model.add(tf.keras.layers.Dense(128, activation='relu' ))
model.add(tf.keras.layers.Dense(10, activation='softmax' ))


model.compile(optimizer=tf.train.AdamOptimizer(),
                    loss='sparse_categorical_crossentropy',
                            metrics=['accuracy'])


history = model.fit(train_images, train_labels, epochs=2)

# Get training and test loss histories
training_loss = history.history['loss']
accuracy = history.history['acc']
# Create count of the number of epochs
epoch_count = range(1, len(training_loss) + 1)

# Visualize loss history
plt.figure(0)
```

```python
plt.plot(epoch_count, training_loss, 'r--')
plt.plot(epoch_count, accuracy, 'b--')
plt.legend(['Training Loss', 'Accuracy'])
plt.xlabel('Epoch')
plt.ylabel('History')
plt.show(block=False);
plt.pause(0.001)

test_loss, test_acc = model.evaluate(test_images, test_labels)

#run test image from Fashion_MNIST data


img = test_images[15]

plt.figure(1)
plt.imshow(img)
plt.show(block=False)
plt.pause(0.001)

img = (np.expand_dims(img,0))
singlePrediction = model.predict(img,steps=1)

print ("Prediction Output")

print(singlePrediction)

print()

NumberElement = singlePrediction.argmax()

Element = np.amax(singlePrediction)


print ("Our Network has concluded that the image number '15' is a "

            +class_names[NumberElement])

print (str(int(Element*100)) + "% Confidence Level")


print('Test accuracy:', test_acc)
```

```
# read test dress image
imageName = "Dress28x28.JPG"

testImg = Image.open(imageName)

plt.figure(2)
plt.imshow(testImg)
plt.show(block=False)
plt.pause(0.001)
testImg.load()
data = np.asarray( testImg, dtype="float" )


data = tf.image.rgb_to_grayscale(data)
data = data/255.0


data = tf.transpose(data, perm=[2,0,1])



singlePrediction = model.predict(data,steps=1)

NumberElement = singlePrediction.argmax()
Element = np.amax(singlePrediction)
print(NumberElement)
print(Element)
print(singlePrediction)

print ("Our Network has concluded that the file '"+imageName+"' is a "
    +class_names[NumberElement])
print (str(int(Element*100)) + "% Confidence Level")

plt.show()
```

The results of running the program is shown in Figure 3-6. The window labeled Figure 0 shows the accuracy data for each of the five epochs of the machine-learning training. You can see the accuracy slowly increase with each epoch. The window labeled Figure 1 shows the test picture for the first recognition test (the program found a pair of trousers, which is correct). Finally, the window labeled Figure 2 shows the dress picture, which is still incorrectly identified as a bag. Harumph.

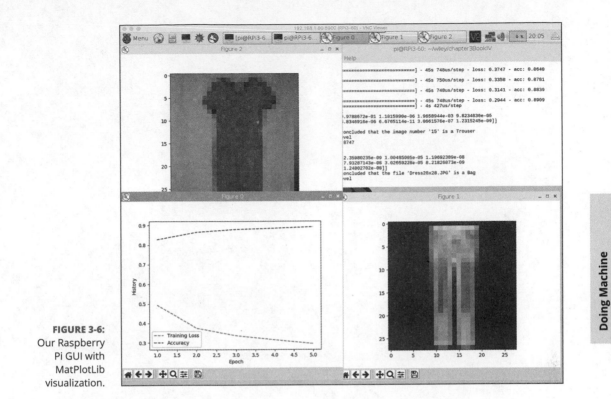

FIGURE 3-6:
Our Raspberry
Pi GUI with
MatPlotLib
visualization.

Learning More Machine Learning

You've built and experimented with machine learning and neural networks, and seen how useful and powerful Python can be. The next step? We recommend you check out *Machine Learning For Dummies* by John Paul Mueller and Luca Massaron and *Deep Learning with Python* by François Chollet (Manning Publications). And for a great beginner's overview of the AI field, read *Artificial Intelligence For Dummies* by John Paul Mueller and Luca Massaron.

Next, you explore using Python with some other AI applications.

Chapter **4**

Exploring AI

After reading the previous three chapters, you've learned quite a bit about using some of the basics of artificial intelligence, specifically neural networks and machine learning. AI has a lot more to it than these two topics, though. We could look at advanced searching (not Google searching but rather looking at big problem spaces and trying to figure out solutions to the problem using AI). We could also look at the problem of autonomous robotics (which we touch upon in Book 7), but that topic is complicated.

Instead, in this chapter, we talk about other ways of doing AI software beyond the Raspberry Pi. Remember how it took us seven hours to run five epochs of training on our large neural network? Sounds like we could use something more powerful to accomplish more training in less time. That's what this chapter is about. To download the code for this chapter, go to www.dummies.com/go/pythonaiofd2e.

Limitations of the Raspberry Pi and AI

The Raspberry Pi is an inexpensive, full-blown computing device. The Raspberry Pi 3B+, which we use throughout this book, has the following major specifications:

» CPU: Broadcom quad-core 64-bit processor @ 1.4GHz

» GPU: Broadcom Videocore-IV

» RAM: 1GB SDRAM

» Networking: Gigabit Ethernet, 802.11b/g/n/ac Wi-Fi

» Storage: SD card

These specs stack up very well for a \$35 computer but not so much for a dedicated AI computer. The Raspberry Pi doesn't have enough RAM or a sophisticated GPU (graphics processing unit). Figure 4-1 shows the Raspberry Pi 3B+ processing chip. The new Raspberry Pi 4B with 8GB of RAM costs about \$70, has more than eight times the RAM, and will generally run about two times faster in most applications. The GPU in the Raspberry Pi (the Videocore-IV) has four GPUs and could be used to accelerate machine-learning applications.

FIGURE 4-1:
The Raspberry Pi processing chip containing the Videocore-IV.

Two mitigating circumstances keep the Raspberry Pi in the running when it comes to experimenting with AI. One, you can buy an AI Accelerator, which can plug into the USB ports of the Raspberry Pi. Two, you can use the Raspberry Pi to control processors and AI hardware located in the cloud.

THE BROADCOM VIDEOCORE-IV ON THE RASPBERRY PI 3B+

The Videocore-IV is a low-power mobile graphics processor. It's a two-dimensional DSP (digital signal processor) that is set up basically as a four-GPU core unit. These GPU core units are called *slices* and can be roughly compared to GPU computer units, such as those used by AMD and Nvidia (which can have 256, 512, or more individual GPU units, far outclassing the Videocore 4 units) to power their GPU cards, which are popular with AI researchers and hobbyists.

The Videocore-IV processor is designed to be used in video encoding and decoding applications, not so much for AI use. However, some researchers have made use of the four slices to accelerate neural network processing on the Raspberry Pi to achieve up to about three times the performance of the four-core main processor used alone.

One of the main barriers to using the Videocore on the Raspberry Pi for AI applications is that the specifications, development tools, and product details have been available only under NDAs (non-disclosure agreements), which do not go along with open-source development. However, you can now get full documentation and the complete source code for the Raspberry Pi 3B+ graphics stack under a nonrestrictive BSD license, which should provide a path forward.

TIP

Remember from Chapter 3 of this minibook that the bulk of computer time in building a machine-learning AI system was for training and, when that training was done, it didn't take a lot of processing to characterize an unclassified picture. Therefore, you could train on one big machine and then deploy on a simpler computer such as the Raspberry Pi in the actual product. This approach doesn't work all the time (especially if you want the program to keep learning as it runs, such as in reinforcement learning) but when it does work, it allows you to deploy sophisticated machine-learning programs on much simpler and less expensive hardware.

Performing AI analysis or training on small computers connected to a network is called *edge computing* or computing on the edge of the network.

Adding Hardware AI to the Raspberry Pi

A number of companies have started to build specialized AI compute sticks (USB dongles that have processors in the stick rather than just memory), many of which can be used on the Raspberry Pi. Typically, Python libraries or wrappers, and often

TensorFlow Python libraries, support using these sticks. Two of the most interesting sticks follow:

>> **The Intel Neural Compute Stick (NCS):** The NCS stick plugs into the USB port of the Raspberry Pi or other computer and provides hardware support for deep learning-based analysis (refer to Chapters 1–3 in this minibook).

For example, from your small Raspberry Pi computer system, you can use Amazon Cloud to perform image analysis, processing, and classification, thus moving a computationally expensive task from your Raspberry Pi to the cloud. However, performing the analysis with your trained deep-learning neural network by using a NCS stick can possibly allow you to disconnect your device from the Internet entirely. The NCS stick runs around 60 times faster than doing image analysis on the Raspberry Pi and costs less than $100. Figure 4-2 shows the Intel Neural Compute Stick 2.

FIGURE 4-2:
The Intel Neural
Compute Stick 2.

You can do facial recognition, text analysis, monitoring, and maintenance using this NCS stick. Pretty cool!

WARNING

Note that the NCS stick performs analysis and conducts inferences on data, *but it is not used for training models!* You still need to build and train the models. It has a good interface with Keras and TensorFlow, so training is possible in a reasonable fashion.

Think of the NCS stick as an accelerator for use by your final project when the training is complete.

>> **The Google Edge TPU accelerator:** The Google Edge TPU (tensor processing unit) has a USB type-C socket that you can plug into a Linux-based system to provide accelerated machine-learning analysis and inferences. (That's why they call the TPU an accelerator.) Does the word *tensor* sound familiar?

WARNING

Tensors are matrices, as in our neural network examples in Chapters 2 and 3 of this minibook. Figure 4-3 shows the Google Edge TPU accelerator.

Much like the Intel NCS stick, this device is all about executing trained machine-learning models. You still train the machine-learning networks using other techniques, and then execute the model on the stick.

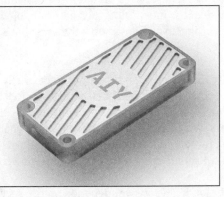

FIGURE 4-3:
The Google Edge TPU accelerator.

In the next few years, this type of specialized hardware for running machine-learning models will explode. You'll see multiple different architectures and solutions from Google, Intel, Nvidia, AMD, Qualcomm, and a number of other smaller companies around the world. Everyone is starting to climb on the AI accelerator bandwagon.

AI in the Cloud

Those in the tech industry love to use buzzwords such as the *cloud*. Often, the use of such language results in arbitrary and nebulous terms that leave consumers (or even sophisticated technical people) unsure what they mean. When your data or programs are running in the cloud, they're just running on computers in a data center.

Some people define the cloud as software or services that run on the Internet rather than on your local machine. This is correct to a degree, but nothing really runs on the Internet; it runs on machines *connected* to the Internet. Understanding that in-the-cloud software runs on servers and is not just "out there" quickly demystifies the cloud and its functions.

If you have two computers networked together and use one of the computers for a data server, you have your own cloud. Companies such as Western Digital and Dell help consumers build their own cloud-based computing systems. Bill Wachsmuth, a manager at Western Digital, states, "Cloud computing is a huge growth market for data storage. We can take existing drives, modify the control software, and repackage the same hardware to aid cloud computing and storage."

By using the cloud, you can use services and storage unavailable to you on your local network and (in one of the most important game changers of cloud computing) you can ramp your usage up and down on a dynamic basis depending on your computing needs.

Using the cloud requires Internet access, but not necessarily 100 percent of the time. (You can fire off a cloud process and then come back to it later.) The requirement to be connected to the Internet continuously limits the cloud in applications such as self-driving cars, which aren't guaranteed to have good Internet access all the time. This "fire and forget" mode is useful for IoT (Internet of Things) devices for which you want to conserve power (such as battery-powered devices).

So, how do you use the cloud? The answer depends on the service and vendor, but in machine-learning applications, the most common method is to set up Python on a computer that calls cloud-based functions and applications. All cloud vendors provide examples.

Great consumer examples of cloud usage are the Amazon Echo and Alexa. They listen to you, compress the speech data, send it to the Amazon AWS cloud, translate and interpret your data, and then send it back with a verbal response or a command (to, for example, turn on your lights). All that processing occurs in the cloud. When your Internet connection goes down, these devices can do little except say "I am having problems connecting to the Internet."

A number of cloud providers for storage and services exist. The top four cloud providers for AI at the time of this writing follow:

>> Google Cloud

>> Amazon Web Services

>> IBM Cloud

>> Microsoft Azure

Google Cloud

Google Cloud is probably the most AI-focused cloud provider. You can gain access to TPUs (tensor processing units) in the cloud, which, like the Google TPU stick described previously, can accelerate your AI applications. Much of Google Cloud's functionality reflects the core skill set of the company — search.

For example, the Cloud Vision API can detect objects, logos, and landmarks in images. Some excellent students at the University of Idaho are building a Smart City application called ParkMyRide, which uses a Raspberry Pi–based solar-powered camera to take pictures of the street and the Google Cloud Vision API to determine street parking availability. The software sends a picture of the street to Google and gets back the number of cars found and where they are in the picture. They then supply this information to a smartphone app that displays the information graphically. Pretty neat.

Other featured services of Google Cloud are video content search applications and speech-to-text/text-to-speech packages (think Google Home —similar to Amazon Alexa). Like Amazon and Microsoft, Google is using its own AI-powered applications to create services for customers to use.

Amazon Web Services

Amazon Web Services (AWS) is focused on supplying businesses with their consumer AI expertise. Many of these cloud services are built on consumer product versions. So, for example, as Alexa improves, the cloud services improve. In a sense, the millions of Alexa consumers are training Alexa to be a better product.

Amazon has not only text and natural language offerings but also machine-learning visualization and creation tools, vision recognition, and analysis.

IBM Cloud

IBM Cloud has received a bad rap for being hard to use. There were so many options on so many different platforms that it was almost impossible to figure out where to start. In the past couple of years, however, IBM Cloud has improved. IBM merged its three big divisions (IBM BlueMix cloud services, SoftLayer data services, and the Watson AI group) under the Watson brand. More than 170 services are available, so initially setting up applications and programs is still hard, but there is much better control and consistency over the process.

Watson Studio, their machine-learning environment, is used to build and train AI models in one integrated environment. IBM also provides huge searchable knowledge catalogs and has one of the better IoT management platforms.

One of the cool services in Watson Studio is Watson Personality Insights, which predicts personality characteristics, needs, and values through written text. What would Watson Personality make of the authors of this book? We should run the text of this book through Watson and see the diagnosis.

Microsoft Azure

Microsoft Azure has an emphasis on developers. Similar to Amazon and Google, Microsoft's AI applications are built on consumer products they have produced. They break down their AI offerings into three categories:

>> AI services

>> AI tools and frameworks

>> AI infrastructures

Azure also has support for specialized FPGA (field-programmable gate arrays — think hardware that can be changed by programming on the fly) and has built out the infrastructure to support a wide variety of accelerators. Microsoft is one of the largest customers of Intel Neural Network chips.

Microsoft Azure has products for machine learning, IoT toolkits, and management services, and a full and rich set of data services, including databases, support for GPUs and custom silicon AI infrastructure, and a container service that can turn your inside applications into cloud apps.

Microsoft Azure is the one to watch for spectacular innovations.

AI on a Graphics Card

Graphics cards, such as the Nvidia graphics chip in Figure 4-4, have been an integral part of the PC experience for decades. People often hunt for the latest and greatest graphics card to make their PCs better gaming machines. Although CPU speed is important, the quality and architecture of the graphics card makes a bigger difference. Why? Computing high-resolution graphics is computationally expensive, and the way to solve the computational speed problem is to build graphics cards out of computers designed to do graphics. These high-quality graphics cards can evaluate machine-learning neural networks very efficiently. Thus was born the GPU (graphics processing unit), a specialized computer core designed to work with graphics.

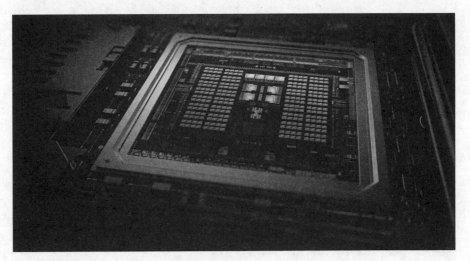

FIGURE 4-4:
Nvidia 256 Core
GPU chip.

Nvidia and others started building graphics cards that contained multiple GPUs, which dramatically improved video resolution and frame rates in games. One thing to remember is that graphics algorithms are constructed using data structures called matrices (or tensors) that are processed in pipelines.

Wait. Tensors? Matrices? This sounds suspiciously like the kind of data structures we use in AI and machine learning. The graphic-processing similarities between machine-learning and deep-learning algorithms have made GPUs useful and effective because they can quickly solve matrix equations, the type of calculation used to train neural networks.

Regardless of the type of neural network used, all programming techniques and modules rely on performing complex statistical operations. During training (learning) operations, a multitude of images or data points are fed to the network and then trained with the correct classification or correct answer. You have to correlate millions of tensors (matrices) and tensor elements to build a trained network that will get the right result.

To speed up the training, these operations can be done in parallel, which turns out to be a good use of the many parallel GPUs on a graphics board.

Exploring AI

An individual GPU core is much simpler than a CPU core because the GPU core is designed for a specific purpose rather than a general one. This simplicity makes it cheaper to build multicore GPU chips than to build multicore CPU chips.

The proliferation of graphics cards with many GPU cores makes these graphics cards perfect for machine-learning applications. The combination of a powerful multicore CPU and many GPUs can dramatically accelerate machine-learning programs. TensorFlow in particular has versions of the software designed to work with GPU boards, removing a lot of the complication of using these boards.

To put this processing power in perspective, the Raspberry Pi 3B+ has 4 processor cores and, in some sense, 4 GPU cores. One of the latest GPU boards from Nvidia has 3,584 cores. By using a large core count GPU board, you can do a lot of fast training and evaluation of machine-learning networks, but you won't speed up operations such as database access or general computational tasks. Executing these tasks requires more complex CPU cores.

The GPU-based boards are not the last step in the evolution of specialized computers and hardware to support AI applications. We are seeing even more specialized chips. At last count, more than 50 companies are working on chips that accelerate AI functions.

When we discussed the Microsoft Azure cloud offering, we mentioned that Microsoft has built out infrastructure to support AI acceleration hardware in the cloud. This development is one of the big reasons to watch what Microsoft is doing.

The future lies in more and more specialized hardware, especially as this hardware gets easier and easier to deal with from the user software side.

Where to Go for More AI Fun in Python

If you're interested in furthering your knowledge and abilities in machine learning and AI, check out the following sources for project inspiration:

» "Is Santa Claus Real?," Varun Vohra, https://towardsdatascience.com/is-santa-claus-real-9b7b9839776c

» "Keras and deep learning on the Raspberry Pi," Adrian Rosebrock, www.pyimagesearch.com/2017/12/18/keras-deep-learning-raspberry-pi/

» "MouseAir – Using AI on the Raspberry Pi to Entertain your Cat," John Shovic, www.switchdoc.com/2019/11/mouseair-raspberry-pi-cat-toy/

» "How to easily Detect Objects with Deep Learning on Raspberry Pi," Sarthak Jain, https://medium.com/nanonets/how-to-easily-detect-objects-with-deep-learning-on-raspberrypi-225f29635c74

» "Building a Cat Detector using Convolutional Neural Network," Venelin Valkov, https://medium.com/@curiousily/tensorflow-for-hackers-part-iii-convolutional-neural-networks-c077618e590b

» "Real time Image Classifier on Raspberry Pi Using Inception Framework," Bapi Reddy, https://medium.com/@bapireddy/real-time-image-classifier-on-raspberry-pi-using-inception-framework-faccfa150909

In the *Dummies* tradition, you'll accelerate your learning in these important technologies by not only reading but also building programs and modifying other people's programs.

5

Doing Data Science

Contents at a Glance

Chapter **1**

Understanding the Five Areas of Data Science

Data science affects our lives in more ways than you may think. When you use Google or Bing or DuckDuckGo, you're using a sophisticated application of data science. The suggestions for other search terms that come up when you're typing? They come from data science. Medical diagnoses and interpretations of images and symptoms are examples of data science. Doctors rely on data science interpretations more and more these days.

As with most of the topics in this book, data science looks intimidating to the uninitiated. Inferences, data graphs, and statistics, oh my! However, just as in previous chapters on artificial intelligence, if you dig in and look at some examples, you can get a handle on what data science is and isn't.

In this chapter, we introduce you to the use of Python in data science and talk about just enough theory to get you started. If nothing else, we want to leave you with an understanding of the process of data science and give you a better idea of what's behind some of the results of big data analysis that are touted in the news. For example, one study says coffee is bad for you but another says the opposite — and sometimes the studies are based on the same data! The hardest part of data science and statistics is determining what the results mean, beyond simple interpretations — and are worthy of their own book. At the end of our data science journey, you'll know more about the processes involved in analyzing results.

There's a mystery to data science and big data, but with a little knowledge and a little Python, we can penetrate the veil and do some real data analysis.

Python and its myriad tools and libraries can make data science much more accessible to non-computer scientists. One thing to remember is that most scientists (including data scientists) are not necessarily experts in computer science. They like to use tools that simplify coding and enable them to focus on getting answers and performing data analysis.

Working with Big, Big Data

The media likes to throw around the notion of "big data" and how people can get insights into consumer (and your) behavior from it. *Big data* refers to complex datasets that are too large for conventional data-processing software (databases, spreadsheets, and traditional statistics packages such as SPSS Statistics) to handle. The industry talks about big data using three concepts, called the "three *v*'s": volume, variety, and velocity.

Volume

Volume refers to the size of the dataset. The volume can be really, really big — almost hard-to-believe big. For example, Facebook has more users than the population of China. There are over 250 billion images on Facebook and 2.5 trillion posts. That's a lot of data.

And what about the upcoming world of IoT (Internet of Things)? Gartner, one of the world's leading analysis companies, estimates 22 billion devices by 2022. That's 22 billion devices producing thousands of pieces of data. Imagine that you're sampling the temperature in your kitchen once a minute for a year — that's over ½ million data points. Add the humidity to the measurements and now you have 1 million data points. Multiply that by five rooms and a garage, all with temperature and humidity measurements, and your house is producing 6 million pieces of data from just one IoT device per room. The amount of data generated gets crazy quickly.

And look at your smartphone. Imagine how many pieces of data it produces in a day. Location, usage, power levels, and cellphone connectivity constantly spews out of your phone into databases and your apps and application dashboards such as Blynk.

Data science is how we make use of all this data.

Variety

Photos and images are different data types from temperature and humidity or location information. In a sense, the information is concentrated in, say, temperature and more smeared out in images. Photos are sophisticated data structures and are hard to interpret and harder still for machines to classify correctly. As you will see in Book 7, a computer has a shot at distinguishing a cat from a dog, but try to throw a baby Yoda into the picture and the computer doesn't have the context to know what the baby Yoda is. The computer has only the context (or, in other words, the training) to tell apart a cat or a dog. Computer vision and interpretation are tough problems.

TECHNICAL STUFF

Let's talk about voice for a minute. Amazon's Alexa is very good at translating voice to text but not as good at assigning meaning to the text. One reason is the lack of context (environmental factors such as social cues, tone, and body language), but another reason is the many ways that people ask for things, make comments, and so on. Alexa (and Amazon) is keeping track of all the queries and then doing data science on them to find the types of things that people are asking for and the variety of ways they ask for them. All that information gathering could be for nefarious reasons, but it could also be to build a system that better services the consumer.

Data science has a much better chance of identifying patterns when the voice has been translated to text because text is easier to search and analyze than audio. However, in this translation we lose a lot of information about tone of voice, emphasis, and so on.

Velocity

Velocity refers to how fast the data is changing and how fast it is being added to the data piles. Facebook users upload about 1 billion pictures a day, so in the next couple of years Facebook will have over 1 trillion images. Facebook is a high-velocity dataset. A low-velocity dataset (not changing at all) might be the set of temperature and humidity readings from your house in the last five years. Needless to say, high-velocity datasets require different techniques than low-velocity datasets.

Managing volume, variety, and velocity

The management of volume, variety, and velocity is a complex topic. Data scientists have developed many methods for processing data. The three V's describe the dataset and give you an idea of the data parameters. The process of gaining insights in data is called *data analytics*. In the next chapters, we focus on gaining knowledge about analytics and learning how to use Python to ask data analytics questions. After doing data science for a few years, you'll be *vvvery* good at managing this process.

Cooking with Gas: The Five-Step Process of Data Science

We generally can break down the process of doing science on data (especially big data) into five steps:

1. Capture the data.

2. Process the data.

3. Analyze the data.

4. Communicate the results.

5. Maintain the data.

We finish this introductory chapter by talking about each of these steps so you can get a handle on the flow of the data science process and a feel for the complexity of the tasks.

Capturing the data

To have something to do analysis on, you must capture data. In any real-world situation, you probably have a number of potential sources of data, such as company records, public databases, or your own gathered data. Inventory them and decide what to include in your project. But before you can know what to include, you have to carefully define your business questions and goals. With well-defined goals, it's easier to know if you have achieved them.

If you can, combine your data sources so it's easy to get to the information you need to find insights and build all those nifty reports you just can't wait to show off to management.

Processing the data

Processing the data is the part of data science that should be easy but almost never is. Some data scientists spend months massaging and manipulating their data so they can process and trust it. You need to identify anomalies and outliers, eliminate duplicates, remove missing entries, and determine what data is inconsistent. You need to clean and process your data carefully so that you don't remove data important to your upcoming analysis work or introduce bias that will destroy your ability down the line to make good inferences or get good answers.

WARNING

One more data-processing issue to worry about: According to Marketing Week in 2015, 60 percent of consumers provide intentionally incorrect information when submitting data online. (We humbly admit to doing this all the time to online marketing forms and even to political pollsters, especially when we sense a political agenda in the questions. Bad boys we are.)

Even good data scientists have been accused of cherry-picking data while cleaning it to support a hypothesis. You have to be careful in processing your data to maintain the integrity and validity of your analysis. Expect to spend a lot of time completing this step.

Understand that it takes only a small amount of disproportionate information to dramatically devalue a database. More food for thought.

Analyzing the data

By the time you've expended all that energy to get to the point of looking at the data to see what you can find, you would think that asking the questions would be relatively simple. It's not. Analyzing big datasets for insights and inferences or asking complex questions requires the most human intuition in all of data science. Some questions, such as "What is the average money spent on cereal in 2020?" can be easily defined and calculated, even on huge amounts of data. But useful questions, such as, "How can I get more people to buy Sugar Frosted Flakes?" is the $64,000 question.

A question such as that has layers and layers of complexity. You want a baseline of how much Sugar Frosted Flakes your customers are currently buying. That answer should be easy to get. Then you have to define what you mean by *more people*. Do you mean *more people* or *more revenue*? Change the price to $0.01 per box, and you will have lots more people buying Sugar Frosted Flakes. What you really want is more revenue or, specifically, more margin (margin = price − cost). But the difficult part of the question is how do you motivate people to buy more Sugar Frosted Flakes? And is the answer in the data you have collected?

REMEMBER

The hard part of analysis is making sure we're asking the right question in the right way of the right kind of data.

Analyzing the data requires skill and experience in statistical techniques such as linear and logistic regressions and finding correlations between different data types by using a variety of probability algorithms and formulas such Naïve Bayes (cool name!). Although a full discussion of these techniques is beyond the scope of this book, we go through some examples later in this minibook.

Communicating the results

After you've crunched and mangled your data into the format you need and then analyzed the data to answer your questions, you need to present the results to management or the customer. Most people visualize and understand information better and faster when they see it in a graphical format rather than just in text.

Data science people use two major Python packages to communicate results: the R language and MatPlotLib. We use MatPlotLib to display our big data graphics and if you've read Book 4, you've experienced MatPlotLib firsthand.

Maintaining the data

Maintaining the data is the step in data science that many people ignore. After they've asked their first round of questions and received their first round of answers, many professionals basically move on to the next project. However, there's a reasonable chance that at some point, perhaps much later, they will have to ask more questions about the same data.

REMEMBER

Be sure to archive and document the following information so you can restart a project quickly or, even more likely, reuse parts of the project for a new one:

» Data and sources

» Models you used to modify the data (including any exception data and "data throw-out criteria")

» Queries and results

In many business, especially in the medical and financial service areas, there are legal reasons for preserving data and the means used to get to the conclusions.

Chapter **2**

Exploring Big Data

In this chapter, you discover some of the tools and processes that data scientists use to format, process, and query data.

A number of Python-based tools and libraries (such as R) are available, but we decided to use NumPy for three reasons. First, it is one of the two most popular tools to use for data science in Python. Second, many AI-oriented projects use NumPy (such as the one in the last chapter). And third, the highly useful Python data science package, Pandas, is built on NumPy.

Pandas is turning out to be an important package in data science. It encapsulates data in a more abstract way, making it easier to manipulate, document, and understand the transformations you make in the base datasets.

MatPlotLib is a good Python-centric package for visualizing the results of big data analysis but requires a steep learning curve. However, this has been ameliorated to some degree by new add-on Python packages, such as seaborn and plotly.

You'll use these three packages as your introduction to data science. To download the code for this chapter, go to www.dummies.com/go/pythonaiofd2e.

Introducing NumPy, Pandas, and MatPlotLib

Anytime you look at the scientific computing and data science communities, three key Python packages keep coming up: NumPy, Pandas, and MatPlotLib. We discuss all three in this section.

NumPy

NumPy adds tools for big-data manipulation to Python, such as large-array manipulation functions and high-level mathematical functions. NumPy is best at handling basic numerical computation such as means and averages. It also excels at the creation and manipulation of multidimensional arrays known as tensors or matrices. In Book 4, you use NumPy extensively in manipulating data and tensors in neural networks and machine learning. It's an exceptional tool for artificial intelligence applications.

TIP

You can find numerous good tutorials for using and installing NumPy on the web. Following are some good step-by-step ones:

» **Python Numpy — Introduction to ndarray [Part 1]** (www.machinelearning plus.com/python/numpy-tutorial-part1-array-python-examples/): A good introduction to matrices (also known as tensors) and how they fit into NumPy

» **NumPy Tutorial** (www.tutorialspoint.com/numpy): A nice overview of NumPy, including where it comes from and how to use it

» **NumPy Tutorial: Learn with Example** (www.guru99.com/numpy-tutorial. html): Less theory, but a bunch of great examples to fill in the practical gaps after looking at the first two tutorials

Here's a simple example of a NumPy program. This program builds a 2x2 matrix, and then performs various matrix-oriented operations on the maxtrix:

```
import numpy as np

x = np.array([[1,2],[3,4]])
print(np.sum(x))  # Compute sum of all elements; prints "10"
print(np.sum(x, axis=0))  # Compute sum of each column; prints "[4 6]"
print(np.sum(x, axis=1))  # Compute sum of each row; prints "[3 7]"
```

TIP

If you're installing NumPy on the Raspberry Pi, use this command first:

```
sudo apt-get install python3-numpy
```

Pandas

Python is great for manipulating and preparing data, but not so great for data analysis and modeling. Pandas fills this gap.

Pandas provides fast, flexible, and expressive data structures to make working with relational or labeled data more intuitive. We think that it's the fundamental building block for doing real-world data analysis in Python. Pandas performs well with tabular types of data (such as SQL tables or Excel spreadsheets) and is really good with time-series data (such as temperature taken hourly). Pandas is yet is another example of the power of using Python libraries to make your problem solving easier.

Remember our discussion on data massaging? Dealing with missing or bad data? Data massaging is one of things that Pandas is designed for and does well. It also allows for complex hierarchical data structures, which can be accessed in an intuitive way using Pandas functions. You can merge and join datasets as well as convert many types of data into the ubiquitous Pandas datatype, the DataFrame.

Pandas is based on NumPy and shares the speed of that Python library, achieving a large speed increase when compared to straight Python code, especially code that loops thorough data.

TECHNICAL STUFF

Pandas DataFrames are a way to store data in rectangular grids that can be easily examined. A DataFrame can contain other DataFrames, a one-dimensional series of data, a NumPy tensor (an array — here we go again with similarities to Book 4 on neural networks and machine learning), and dictionaries for tensors and matrices.

In addition to specifying data for your DataFrame, you can specify indexes and column names, which makes the code more understandable for data analysis and manipulation. You can access, delete, and rename your DataFrame components as you bring in more structures and join more related data into your DataFrame structure.

MatPlotLib

MatPlotLib is a library that adds data visualization functions to Python. MatPlotLib complements the use of NumPy in data analysis and scientific programs. It provides a Python object-oriented API (application programming interface) for embedded plots inserted in applications by using general-purpose GUI programs. MatPlotLib is also available in a procedural version for MatLab called PyLab.

With MatPlotLib, you can make elaborate and professional-looking graphs. You can even build live graphs that update while your application is running. This feature can be handy in machine-learning applications and data-analysis applications, where it's good to see the system making progress toward some goal. With a real-time display, you may also see when the results are good enough or when further training is providing little benefit.

Doing Your First Data Science Project

Time for us to put NumPy and Pandas to work on a simple data science project. We will be working with data from the Kaggle website (www.kaggle.com). Kaggle, whose tag line is "Your Home for Data Science," is a Google-owned online community of data scientists and users. Kaggle allows users to find datasets, download the data, and use the data under very open licenses, in most cases. Kaggle also supports a robust set of competitions for solving machine-learning problems, often posted by companies that actually need the solution. Kaggle has good discussion communities that are helpful for beginners (www.kaggle.com/discussion).

Diamonds are a data scientist's best friend

For this first problem, we chose the diamonds database because it has a fairly simple structure and only about 54,000 elements — easy for our Raspberry Pi computer to use. You can download it at www.kaggle.com/shivam2503/diamonds. Using Kaggle is free, but you do have to register and sign in.

The *metadata* (data describing data) consists of ten variables, which you can also think of as column headers. See Table 2-1.

TABLE 2-1

Columns in the Diamond Database

Column Header	Type of Data	Description
Index counter	Numeric	Specific index of record
carat	Numeric	Carat weight of the diamond
cut	Text	Cut quality of the diamond, in increasing order of fair, good, very good, premium, and ideal
color	Text	Color of the diamond, with D the best and J the worst
clarity	Text	How obvious inclusions are in the diamond, from best to worst, with FL equal to flawless and I3 equal to level 3 inclusions: FL, IF, VVS1, VVS2, VS1, VS2, SI1, SI2, I1, I2, I3
depth	Numeric	Percentage depth: The height of a diamond, measured from the culet (the bottom tip of the cut diamond) to the table (the flat facet on top of the cut diamond), divided by its average girdle diameter
table	Numeric	Percentage table: The width of the diamond's table expressed as a percentage of its average diameter
price	Numeric	Price of the diamond
x	Numeric	Length in mm
y	Numeric	Width in mm
x	Numeric	Depth in mm

If you were to use data as a training set for a machine-learning program, you would create a program using NumPy and TensorFlow similar to the one in Book 4, Chapter 2. In this chapter, we create a set of simple Pandas-based data analysis programs to read the data and ask some questions.

We use a DataFrame (2D-labeled data structure with columns that can be of different types) because it makes it easier to visualize 2D data.

TIP

If you're installing NumPy and Pandas on the Raspberry Pi, type the following commands (commands for other computers will be similar):

```
sudo apt-get install python3-numpy
sudo apt-get install python3-pandas
```

Now, using nano (or your favorite text editor), open a file called FirstDiamonds.py and enter the following code:

```python
# Diamonds are a Data Scientist's Best Friend

#import the pandas and numpy libraries
import numpy as np
import pandas as pd


# read the diamonds CSV file
# build a DataFrame from the data
df = pd.read_csv('diamonds.csv')


print (df.head(10))
print()

# calculate the total value of the diamonds
sum = df.price.sum()
print ("Total $ Value of Diamonds: ${:0,.2f}".format( sum))

# calculate the mean price of the diamonds

mean = df.price.mean()
print ("Mean $ Value of Diamonds: ${:0,.2f}".format(mean))

#   summarize the data
descrip = df.carat.describe()
print()
print (descrip)


descrip = df.describe(include='object')
print()
print (descrip)
```

Making sure you have the diamonds.csv file in your directory, run the following command:

```
python3 FirstDiamonds.py
```

You should see the following results:

```
   Unnamed: 0  carat       cut color clarity  depth  table  price     x
   y     z
0          1   0.23      Ideal     E     SI2   61.5   55.0    326  3.95
   3.98  2.43
```

```
1            2    0.21    Premium    E    SI1    59.8    61.0    326    3.89
     3.84  2.31
2            3    0.23      Good     E    VS1    56.9    65.0    327    4.05
     4.07  2.31
3            4    0.29    Premium    I    VS2    62.4    58.0    334    4.20
     4.23  2.63
4            5    0.31      Good     J    SI2    63.3    58.0    335    4.34
     4.35  2.75
5            6    0.24  Very Good    J    VVS2   62.8    57.0    336    3.94
     3.96  2.48
6            7    0.24  Very Good    I    VVS1   62.3    57.0    336    3.95
     3.98  2.47
7            8    0.26  Very Good    H    SI1    61.9    55.0    337    4.07
     4.11  2.53
8            9    0.22      Fair     E    VS2    65.1    61.0    337    3.87
     3.78  2.49
9           10    0.23  Very Good    H    VS1    59.4    61.0    338    4.00
     4.05  2.39

Total $ Value of Diamonds: $212,135,217.00
Mean $ Value of Diamonds: $3,932.80

count    53940.000000
mean         0.797940
std          0.474011
min          0.200000
25%          0.400000
50%          0.700000
75%          1.040000
max          5.010000
Name: carat, dtype: float64

           cut   color clarity
count    53940   53940   53940
unique       5       7       8
top      Ideal       G     SI1
freq     21551   11292   13065
```

That's a lot of data for a short piece of code!

Breaking down the code

Now we step through our data science code to see how all the code elements play together:

```
# Diamonds are a Data Scientist's Best Friend
```

First, we import all the needed libraries:

```
#import the pandas and numpy libraries
import numpy as np
import pandas as pd
```

Next, we read the diamonds file into a Pandas DataFrame. Note that we didn't have to format and manipulate the data in this file. Working with the data in the original file is not normal in real data science. Getting your data where you want it to be will often require a significant amount of time — sometimes as much time as the entire rest of the project:

```
# read the diamonds CSV file
# build a DataFrame from the data
df = pd.read_csv('diamonds.csv')
```

For a sanity check, we print the first ten rows in the DataFrame:

```
print (df.head(10))
print()
```

Then we calculate a couple of values from the column named price. Note that we get to use the actual column name as part of the DataFrame object. It's great that you can do this with Python!

```
# calculate the total value of the diamonds
sum = df.price.sum()
print ("Total $ Value of Diamonds: ${:0,.2f}".format( sum))

# calculate the mean price of the diamonds

mean = df.price.mean()
print ("Mean $ Value of Diamonds: ${:0,.2f}".format(mean))
```

Next we run the built-in describe function to describe and summarize the data about the carat DataFrame element:

```
# summarize the data
descrip = df.carat.describe()
print()
print (descrip)
```

The next statement prints a description for all nonnumeric columns in our DataFrame, specifically, the cut, color, and clarity columns:

```
descrip = df.describe(include='object')
print()
print (descrip)
```

Visualizing the data with MatPlotLib

Now we move to the data visualization with MatPlotLib. In Book 4, we use MatPlotLib to draw some graphs related to the way the machine-learning program improved its accuracy during training. Here we use MatPlotLib to show some interesting things about the dataset.

TIP

To install MatPlotLib on your Raspberry Pi, type **sudo pip3 install matplotlib**.

WARNING

When your program uses MatPlotLib, you need to run the program from a Terminal window inside the Raspberry Pi GUI. You can use VNC to get a GUI if you're running your Raspberry Pi headless.

One of the useful features of Pandas and MatPlotLib is that the NumPy and DataFrame types are compatible with common graphic formats such as .jpg and .gif images, so you can deal with image data.

Diamond clarity versus carat size

Our first plot is a scatter plot showing diamond clarity versus diamond carat size. Using nano (or your favorite text editor), open a file called Plot_ClarityVSCarat.py and enter the following code:

```
# Looking at the Shiny Diamonds

#import the pandas and numpy libraries
import numpy as np
import pandas as pd
import matplotlib.pyplot as plt

# read the diamonds CSV file
# build a DataFrame from the data
df = pd.read_csv('diamonds.csv')


import matplotlib.pyplot as plt

carat = df.carat
clarity = df.clarity
plt.scatter(clarity, carat)
plt.show()  # or plt.savefig("name.png")
```

Run your program. The result is shown in Figure 2-1. Now, how is that for ease in plotting? Pandas and MatPlotLib go hand-in-hand.

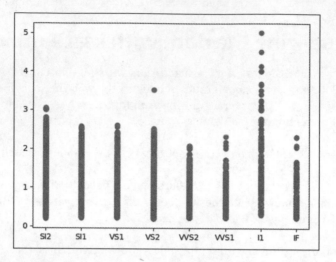

FIGURE 2-1:
Diamond clarity
(horizontal)
versus carat size
(vertical).

Remember that diamond clarity is measured by how obvious the inclusions are in the diamond, from best (FL, flawless) to worst (I3, level-3 inclusions): FL, IF, VVS1, VVS2, VS1, VS2, SI1, SI2, I1, I2, I3. Note that we had no flawless diamonds in our diamond database.

One comment about the value order and the column order. The plot is presenting the values in the order in which they appear in the dataset. The first record has clarity SI2, the next has clarity SI1, then VS1, and so on. You can see this if you execute this code:

```
for i in range(20):
    print(df.iloc[i].clarity)
```

You could sort the data by the clarity column, but then you'd get alphabetical order because that column isn't numeric. Probably the real solution is to process the data to convert the clarity values into numeric values. This is an example of how data preprocessing can be harder than the analysis.

You might be tempted to make a statement that the largest diamonds are rated as I1. However, remember that you have no idea how this data was collected so you can't draw such general conclusions. All you can say is that "In this dataset, the clarity I1 has the largest diamonds."

Number of diamonds in each clarity type

Now we present a plot that will show you the distribution of diamonds in each clarity type. Using nano (or your favorite text editor), open up a file called `Plot_CountClarity.py` and enter the following code:

```
# Looking at the Shiny Diamonds

#import the pandas and numpy libraries
import numpy as np
import pandas as pd
import matplotlib.pyplot as plt


# read the diamonds CSV file
# build a DataFrame from the data
df = pd.read_csv('diamonds.csv')


import matplotlib.pyplot as plt

# count the number of each textual type of clarity

clarityindexes = df['clarity'].value_counts().index.tolist()
claritycount= df['clarity'].value_counts().values.tolist()

print(clarityindexes)
print(claritycount)

plt.bar(clarityindexes, claritycount)
plt.show()  # or plt.savefig("name.png")
```

When you run the `Plot_CountClarity.py` program, you see the results shown in Figure 2-2.

Again, remember that diamond clarity is measured by how obvious inclusions are within the diamond: FL,IF, VVS1, VVS2, VS1, VS2, SI1, SI2, I1, I2, I3 (in order from best to worst: FL = flawless, I3= level 3 inclusions). Note that we had no flawless diamonds in our diamond database.

This graph shows that the medium-quality diamonds SI1, VS2, and SI2 are most represented in our diamond dataset.

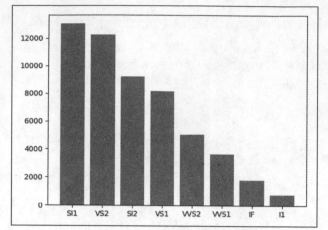

FIGURE 2-2:
Diamond clarity
count in each
type.

Number of diamonds in each color type

We looked at clarity versus size, and now we'll look at color type versus number of diamonds in each clarity type in the pile of diamonds. Using nano (or another text editor), open a file called Plot_CountColor.py and enter the following code:

```
# Looking at the Shiny Diamonds

#import the pandas and numpy libraries
import numpy as np
import pandas as pd
import matplotlib.pyplot as plt

# read the diamonds CSV file
# build a DataFrame from the data
df = pd.read_csv('diamonds.csv')


import matplotlib.pyplot as plt

# count the number of each textual type of color

colorindexes = df['color'].value_counts().index.tolist()
colorcount= df['color'].value_counts().values.tolist()

print(colorindexes)
print(colorcount)

plt.bar(colorindexes, colorcount)
plt.show()  # or plt.savefig("name.png")
```

Run your program. The result is shown in Figure 2-3.

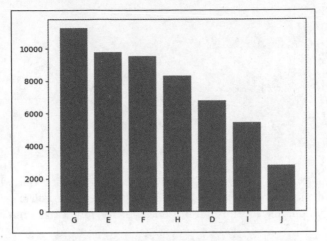

FIGURE 2-3:
Diamond color
count in each
type.

The color G, which is almost colorless, represents about 25 percent of our sample size. The general rule is less color, higher price. The exceptions are pinks and blues, which are outside this color mapping and sample.

Using Pandas heat plots to find correlations

Our last plot is a heat plot, which shows correlations between numeric values inside the database. We take all the numerical values and create a matrix that shows how closely they correlate. To quickly and easily generate this graph, we use another library for Python and MatPlotLib called seaborn, which provides an API built on top of MatPlotLib that integrates with Pandas DataFrames. That integration makes seaborn ideal for data science.

Using nano (or another text editor), create a file called `Plot_Heat.py` and enter the following code:

```
# Looking at the Shiny Diamonds

#import the pandas and numpy libraries
import numpy as np
import pandas as pd

import matplotlib.pyplot as plt
import seaborn as sns

# read the diamonds CSV file
# build a DataFrame from the data
df = pd.read_csv('diamonds.csv')

# drop the index column
df = df.drop('Unnamed: 0', axis=1)
```

```
f, ax = plt.subplots(figsize=(10, 8))
corr = df.corr()
print (corr)
sns.heatmap(corr, mask=np.zeros_like(corr, dtype=np.bool),
        cmap=sns.diverging_palette(220, 10, as_cmap=True),
                    square=True, ax=ax)


plt.show()
```

Run the example Python program `Plot_Heat.py` to find out whether you have seaborn on your Raspberry Pi. If you don't have seaborn, you'll get an import error from Python. If seaborn is not present, type the following command:

```
sudo apt-get install python3-seaborn
```

Run the program and feast on some real data visualization, as shown in Figure 2-4.

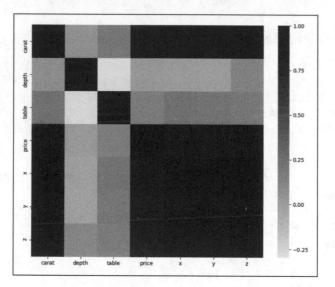

FIGURE 2-4:
Correlation
heat chart.

The first thing to note is that the darker the color, the higher the correlation between the two variables. The diagonal stripe from the top left to the top bottom shows that carat correlates 100 percent with carat. No surprise there. The x, y, and z variables correlate with each other, which says that as the diamonds in the database increase in one dimension, they increase in the other two dimensions as well.

How about price? As carat and size increase, so does price. This makes sense. Interestingly, *depth* — the height of a diamond, measured from the culet (the bottom tip) to the table (the flat facet on the top), divided by its average girdle diameter — does not correlate strongly with price and is somewhat negatively correlated.

It's amazing the amount of inferences you can draw from this kind of a map. Heat maps are fabulous for spotting general cross-correlations in your data.

It would be interesting to see the correlation between color, clarity, and price. But this correlation isn't included on the chart because the color and clarity columns are textual, and you can do correlations only on numerical values. You could fix this by substituting a numerical code (1–8, for example) for each color letter and then regenerating the heat chart. The same technique can be used for diamond clarity. Again, data preprocessing is a time-consuming and sometimes difficult part of doing data science.

IN THIS CHAPTER

» **Accessing really big data**

» **Using Google Cloud BigQuery**

» **Building your first queries**

» **Visualizing results with MatPlotLib**

Chapter **3**

Using Big Data from Google Cloud

U p to this point, you've been dealing with relatively small sets of data. In this chapter, you use big data from the Medicare database and then very big data from NOAA (National Oceanic and Atmospheric Agency) that changes every hour!

Even if you have access to a powerful enough computer to download large datasets like these, not every big dataset can be downloaded. Some datasets can't be downloaded legally. And in the case of the air quality database from NOAA, you would have to download a new version every hour. In cases like these, it's better to leave the data where it is and use the cloud. In addition, when you let the cloud do the database and analysis work, your computer doesn't have to be very big or very fast.

To download the code for this chapter, go to www.dummies.com/go/pythonaiofd2e.

What Is Big Data?

Big data refers to datasets that are too large or complex to be dealt with using traditional data-processing techniques. Data with many cases and many rows offers greater accessibility to sophisticated statistical techniques and generally lead to smaller false discovery rates. A *false discovery rate* is the expected proportion of errors where you incorrectly rejected your hypothesis (in other words, you received false positives).

As mentioned in Chapter 1 of this minibook, big data is becoming more prevalent in our society as the number of computers and sensors proliferate and create more data at an ever-increasing rate. In this chapter, we talk about using the cloud to access these large databases (using Python and Pandas) and then visualizing the results on a Raspberry Pi.

Understanding Google Cloud and BigQuery

In the first program, you access data using Google Cloud and manipulate and analyze the data using Google BigQuery. It is important to understand that you aren't just using data in the cloud, you're also using the data analysis tools in the cloud. Basically, you're using your computer to tell the computers in the cloud what do with the data and how to analyze it. Not much is happening on your local computer.

Google Cloud Platform

Google Cloud Platform is a suite of cloud-computing services that run on the same infrastructure as Google end-user products such as Google Search and YouTube. This cloud strategy has been successfully used at Amazon and Microsoft. Google uses their own internal data services and products to build a cloud offering. With this approach, both the user and the company benefit from advances and improvements to products and clouds.

The Google Cloud Platform has over 100 different APIs (application programming interfaces) and data service products available for data science and artificial intelligence. The primary service we use in this chapter is the Google API called BigQuery.

BigQuery from Google

A REST (representational state transfer) software system defines a set of communication structures to be used for creating web services, typically using http and https requests to communicate. With a REST-based system, different computers and different operating systems can enable the same web service.

A RESTful web service uses URL addresses that ask specific questions in a standard format and get a response just like a browser gets a web page. Additional Python libraries are used to hide the complexity of the queries going back and forth. BigQuery is based on a RESTful web service.

In software engineering, *abstraction* is a technique for arranging complexity in computer systems. It works by establishing a simple layer in the software (such as Python modules) that masks the complex details below the surface. Abstraction in software systems is key to making big systems work and reasonable to program. For example, although a web browser uses HTML to display web pages, layers of software under the HTML are doing such things such as transmitting IP packets or manipulating bits. These lower layers are different if you're using a wired network or a Wi-Fi network. The cool thing about abstraction is that we don't need to know how complex it is. We just use the software.

BigQuery is a serverless model, which means BigQuery has one of the highest levels of abstraction in the cloud community, removing the user's responsibility for bringing new virtual machines online, the amount RAM, the numbers of CPUs, and so on. Scale from one to thousands of CPUs in a matter of seconds, paying only for the resources you use. You can stream data into BigQuery on the order of millions of rows (data samples) per second, which means you can start to analyze the data almost immediately. Google Cloud has a free, 90-day trial with $300 of credit, so you won't have to pay while working on the examples in Book 5.

BigQuery has a large number of public big-data datasets; we access the ones from Medicare and NOAA. We use BigQuery (through the google.cloud library) with the Pandas Python library. The google.cloud Python library maps the BigQuery data into our friendly Pandas DataFrames (described in Chapter 2 of this minibook).

Computer security on the cloud

We would be remiss if we didn't talk just a little bit about maintaining good computer security when using the cloud. Google provides computer security by using the IAM (identity and access management) paradigm throughout its cloud offerings. IAM lets the account owner (who is the administrator) authorize who can take what kind of action on specific resources, giving the owner full control and visibility for simple projects as well as finely grained access extending across an entire enterprise.

We show you how to set up IAM authentication in the sections that follow.

Signing up for BigQuery

Go to `https://cloud.google.com` and sign up for your free trial. Although Google requires a credit card to prove that you're not a robot, it doesn't charge you even when your trial is over unless you manually switch to a paid account. If you exceed $300 during your trial (which you probably won't), Google will notify you but will not charge you. The $300 limit should be more than enough to do a bunch of queries and learn on the BigQuery cloud platform.

Reading the Medicare Big Data

In this section, to start using BigQuery with your own Python programs, you set up a project and download your authentication `.json` file, which contains keys that let you access your account and the data. The Medicare database is the largest easily accessible medical data set in the world. We ask some specific medical queries of this database.

Setting up your project and authentication

To access Google Cloud, you need to set up a project and then receive your authentication credentials from Google.

WARNING

Make sure you follow these directions closely to get the Google authentication correct the first time. When you download your authentication file, don't lose it or delete it. You can't download it a second time. Instead, you have to go through the authentication process again.

If you don't have a Google account, create one. Then go to `www.google.com` and log in,. Next, go to `https://developers.google.com/` and click Google Cloud. Fill out your billing information, and you'll be ready to begin.

The following steps will show you how to set up your project and get your authentication credentials:

1. **Go to** `https://console.developers.google.com/` **and sign in using your account name and password.**

The screen shown in Figure 3-1 appears.

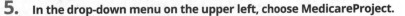

FIGURE 3-1: Google Cloud developer's console page.

2. **Click the My First Project button, in the upper-left corner of the screen.**

3. **On the pop-up screen, click the New Project button in the upper right.**

4. **For the project name, type** MedicareProject **and then click Create.**

You return to the screen shown in Figure 3-1.

5. **In the drop-down menu on the upper left, choose MedicareProject.**

REMEMBER

Make sure you change the selection to MedicareProject and don't leave the default as My First Project. Otherwise, you'll be setting up the APIs and authentication for the wrong project. This mistake is a very common one.

6. **Click the +Enable APIs and Services button (near the top) to enable the BigQuery API.**

The API selection screen appears.

7. **In the search box, search for *BigQuery* and then select BigQuery API. Click Enable.**

Now to get our authentication credentials.

8. **In the right corner of the screen, choose Create Credentials.**

The screen shown in Figure 3-2 appears.

FIGURE 3-2: First credentials screen.

9. **In the drop-down menu, select BigQuery API and then click the No, I'm Not Using Them option below the Are You Planning to Use This API with the App Engine or Compute Engine? section.**

10. **Click the What Credentials Do I Need? button.**

The screen shown in Figure 3-3 appears.

11. **In the Service Account Name box, type** MedicareProject **and then, in the Role drop-down menu, select Project and then select Owner.**

12. **Leave the JSON radio button selected and click Continue.**

A message appears saying that the service account and key have been created. A file named something like MedicareProject-1223xxxxx413.json is downloaded to your computer.

Do not lose this file! It contains your authentication information.

13. **Copy the downloaded file to the directory where you'll be building your Python program file.**

WARNING

Now let's move on to our first example.

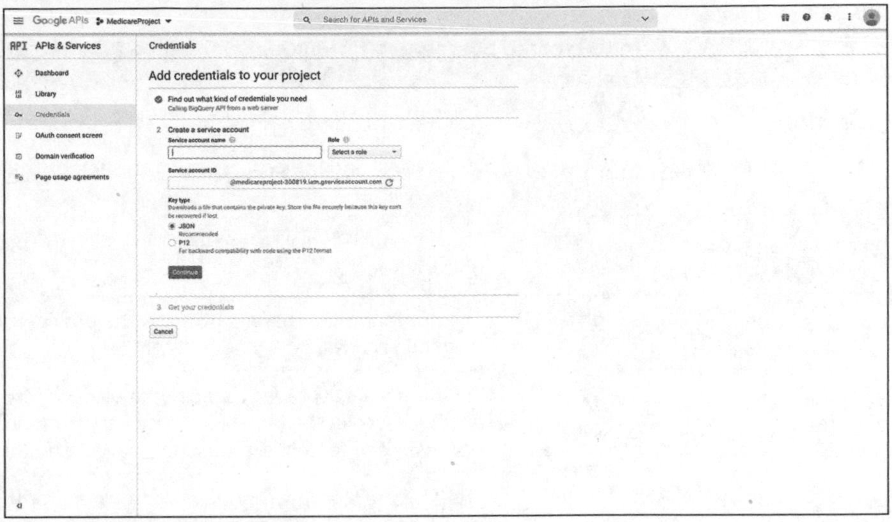

FIGURE 3-3:
Second
credentials
screen.

The first big-data code

The `MedicareQuery1.py` program reads one of the several dozen public-data Medicare datasets and grabs some data for analysis. We will use the `inpatient_charges_2015` dataset and a SQL query to select the information from the dataset that we want to look at and analyze. (Check out the nearby sidebar, "Learning SQL," for more on SQL if you're not already familiar with this ubiquitous query language.)

Table 3-1 shows all the columns in the `inpatient_charges_2015` dataset.

TABLE 3-1 **Columns, Types, and Descriptions of the inpatient_charges_2015 Dataset**

Column	Type	Description
provider_id	STRING	The CMS certification number (CCN) of the provider billing for outpatient hospital services.
provider_name	STRING	The name of the provider.
provider_street_address	STRING	The street address in which the provider is physically located.
provider_city	STRING	The city in which the provider is physically located.
provider_state	STRING	The state in which the provider is physically located.
provider_zipcode	INTEGER	The zip code in which the provider is physically located.

(continued)

TABLE 3-1 *(continued)*

Column	Type	Description
drg_definition	STRING	The code and description identifying the MS-DRG. MS-DRGs are a classification system that groups similar clinical conditions (diagnoses) and the procedures furnished by the hospital during the stay.
hospital_referral_region_description	STRING	The hospital referral region (HRR) in which the provider is physically located.
total_discharges	INTEGER	The number of discharges billed by the provider for inpatient hospital services.
average_covered_charges	FLOAT	The provider's average charge for services covered by Medicare for all discharges in the MS-DRG. These vary from hospital to hospital because of differences in hospital charge structures.
average_total_payments	FLOAT	The average total payments to all providers for the MS-DRG, including the MS-DRG amount, teaching, disproportionate share, capital, and outlier payments for all cases. Also included in average total payments are co-payment and deductible amounts that the patient is responsible for and any additional third-party payments for coordination of benefits.
average_medicare_payments	FLOAT	The average amount that Medicare pays to the provider for its share of the MS-DRG. Average Medicare payment amounts include the MS-DRG amount, teaching, disproportionate share, capital, and outlier payments for all cases. Medicare payments do not include beneficiary co-payments and deductible amounts nor any additional payments from third parties for coordination of benefits.

LEARNING SQL

SQL (Structured Query Language) is a query-oriented language used to interface with databases and to extract information from those databases. Although it was designed for relational database access and management, it has been extended to many other types of databases, including data accessed by BigQuery and Google Cloud.

Here are some excellent tutorials to get your head around how to access data using SQL:

- www.w3schools.com/sql

- www.sql-tutorial.net

- *SQL For Dummies*, 9th Edition, Allen G. Taylor

- *SQL All-in-One For Dummies*, 3rd Edition, Allen G. Taylor

- *SQL in 10 Minutes*, 4th Edition (Sams Publishing), Ben Forta

Using nano (or another text editor), enter the following code and then save it as MedicareQuery1.py:

```
import pandas as pd
from google.cloud import bigquery


# set up the query

QUERY = """
        SELECT provider_city, provider_state, drg_definition,
        average_total_payments, average_medicare_payments
        FROM `bigquery-public-data.cms:medicare.inpatient_charges_2015`
        WHERE provider_city = "GREAT FALLS" AND provider_state = "MT"
        ORDER BY provider_city ASC
        LIMIT 1000
        """

client = bigquery.Client.from_service_account_json(
            'MedicareProject2-122xxxxxf413.json')


query_job = client.query(QUERY)
df = query_job.to_dataframe()

print ("Records Returned: ", df.shape )
print ()
print ("First 3 Records")
print (df.head(3))
```

As soon as you've built this file, replace the MedicareProject2-122xxxxxf413. json file with your own authentication file (which you copied into the program directory earlier).

TIP

When you run the MedicareQuery1.py program, you'll get an import error if the google.cloud library isn't installed. If this happens, type the following in the Terminal window on your computer:

```
sudo pip3 install google-cloud-bigquery
```

When running these programs on a Raspberry Pi, if you see an error that "the pyarrow library is not installed," try the following:

```
sudo pip3 install pyarrow
```

As of November 2020, if installing pyarrow doesn't work, the pyarrow maintainers have not yet fixed the problem with the pip3 pyarrow installation. You will need to move to Windows, another Linux version, or a Mac to run these examples.

Breaking down the code

First, we import our libraries. Note the google.cloud library and the bigquery import:

```
import pandas as pd
from google.cloud import bigquery
```

Next we set up a SQL query to fetch the data into a Pandas DataFrame for analysis:

```
# set up the query

QUERY = """
        SELECT provider_city, provider_state, drg_definition,
        average_total_payments, average_medicare_payments
        FROM `bigquery-public-data.cms:medicare.inpatient_charges_2015`
        WHERE provider_city = "GREAT FALLS" AND provider_state = "MT"
        ORDER BY provider_city ASC
        LIMIT 1000
        """
```

See the structure of the SQL query? We SELECT the columns that we want (as listed in Table 3-1) FROM the bigquery-public-data.cms:medicare.inpatient_charges_2015 database only WHERE the provider_city is GREAT FALLS and the provider_state is MT. Finally, we tell the system to order the results by ascending, alphanumeric order by the provider_city.

Remember to replace the following json filename with your authentication file:

```
client = bigquery.Client.from_service_account_json(
         'MedicareProject2-122xxxxxef413.json')
```

Now we fire off the query to BigQuery:

```
query_job = client.query(QUERY)
```

And translate the results to our good friend the Pandas DataFrame:

```
df = query_job.to_dataframe()
```

Now just a few more code statements to display what we get back from BigQuery:

```
print ("Records Returned: ", df.shape )
print ()
print ("First 3 Records")
print (df.head(3))
```

Run your program `MedicareQuery1.py` and you should see the results of your query as shown next. If you get an authentication error, make sure you put the correct authentication file into your directory. And if necessary, generate another authentication file, paying special attention to the project name selection.

```
Records Returned:  (112, 5)

First 3 Records
  provider_city provider_state
drg_ definition  average_total_payments  average_medicare_payments
0   GREAT FALLS          MT  064 - INTRACRANIAL HEMORRHAGE OR CEREBRAL
   INFA...        11997.11                11080.32
1   GREAT FALLS          MT          039 - EXTRACRANIAL PROCEDURES W/O
CC/MCC         7082.85               5954.81
2   GREAT FALLS          MT  065 - INTRACRANIAL HEMORRHAGE OR CEREBRAL
INFA...        7140.80                6145.38
Visualizing your Data
```

We found 112 records from Great Falls. You can go back and change the query in your program to select your own city and state.

Doing a bit of analysis

You've established a connection to a big-data database. Now let's set up another query. We will search the entire `inpatient_charges_2015` dataset to look for patients with MS_DRG code 554, bone diseases and arthropathies without major complication or comorbidity (in other words, people who have issues with their bones but with no serious issues currently manifesting externally). We find such a diagnosis through one of the most arcane and complicated coding systems in the world: ICD-10, which maps virtually any diagnostic condition to a single code.

ICD CODES

ICD10 is the well-established method for coding medical professional diagnoses for billing and analysis. The latest version of ICD-10 was made mandatory in 2015, resulting in great angst throughout the medical community. It consists of over 155,000 codes, from M79.603 — Pain in Arm, unspecified to S92.4 — Fracture of Greater Toe. These codes are merged into the MS_DRG codes used in the Medicare databases we examine here. When John Shovic had a medical software startup, he developed a love/hate relationship with ICD 10 codes. His favorite codes follow:

- V97.33XD: Sucked into jet engine, subsequent encounter.
- Z63.1: Problems in relationship with in-laws.
- V95.43XS: Spacecraft collision injuring occupant, sequela.
- R46.1: Bizarre personal appearance.
- Y93.D1 Activity, knitting and crocheting.

Create a file called `MedicareQuery2.py` using nano or your favorite text editor, and then copy the following code into the file:

```python
import pandas as pd
from google.cloud import bigquery


# set up the query

QUERY = """
        SELECT provider_city, provider_state, drg_definition,
        average_total_payments, average_medicare_payments
        FROM `bigquery-public-data.cms:medicare.inpatient_charges_2015`
        WHERE drg_definition LIKE  '554 %'
        ORDER BY provider_city ASC
        LIMIT 1000
        """

client = bigquery.Client.from_service_account_json(
            'MedicareProject2-1223283ef413.json')


query_job = client.query(QUERY)
df = query_job.to_dataframe()
```

```
print ("Records Returned: ", df.shape )
print ()
print ("First 3 Records")
print (df.head(3))
```

The only thing different in this program from our previous one is that we added LIKE '554 %', which matches any DRG that starts with 554.

When we ran the program, we got the following results:

```
Records Returned:  (286, 5)

First 3 Records
   provider_city provider_state                               drg_definition
     average_total_payments  average_medicare_payments
0       ABINGTON             PA  554 - BONE DISEASES & ARTHROPATHIES W/O MCC
     5443.67                   3992.93
1         AKRON             OH  554 - BONE DISEASES & ARTHROPATHIES W/O MCC
     5581.00                   4292.47
2        ALBANY             NY  554 - BONE DISEASES & ARTHROPATHIES W/O MCC
     7628.94                   5137.31
```

Now we have some interesting data. Let's do a little analysis. What percent of the total payments for this condition is paid by Medicare? The remainder is usually paid by the patient. We aren't taking third-party billing into account.

Create a file called MedicareQuery3.py using nano or your favorite text editor, and copy the following code into the file:

```
import pandas as pd
from google.cloud import bigquery


# set up the query

QUERY = """
        SELECT provider_city, provider_state, drg_definition,
        average_total_payments, average_medicare_payments
        FROM `bigquery-public-data.cms:medicare.inpatient_charges_2015`
        WHERE drg_definition LIKE  '554 %'
        ORDER BY provider_city ASC
        LIMIT 1000
        """
```

```
client = bigquery.Client.from_service_account_json(
            'MedicareProject2-1223283ef413.json')


query_job = client.query(QUERY)
df = query_job.to_dataframe()

print ("Records Returned: ", df.shape )
print ()

total_payment = df.average_total_payments.sum()
medicare_payment = df.average_medicare_payments.sum()

percent_paid = ((medicare_payment/total_payment))*100
print ("Medicare pays {:4.2f}% of Total for 554 DRG".format(percent_paid))
print ("Patient pays {:4.2f}% of Total for 554 DRG".format(100-percent_paid))
```

The results follow:

```
Records Returned: (286, 5)
Medicare pays 77.06% of Total for 554 DRG
Patient pays 22.94% of Total for 554 DRG
```

Payment percent by state

Next, we select each individual state in our database (not all states are represented) and calculate the percent paid by Medicare by state for a DRG that starts with 554. Call this file MedicareQuery4.py:

```
import pandas as pd
from google.cloud import bigquery


# set up the query

QUERY = """
        SELECT provider_city, provider_state, drg_definition,
        average_total_payments, average_medicare_payments
        FROM `bigquery-public-data.cms:medicare.inpatient_charges_2015`
        WHERE drg_definition LIKE  '554 %'
        ORDER BY provider_city ASC
        LIMIT 1000
        """
```

```
client = bigquery.Client.from_service_account_json(
        'MedicareProject2-1223283ef413.json')


query_job = client.query(QUERY)
df = query_job.to_dataframe()

print ("Records Returned: ", df.shape )
print ()

# find the unique state values

states = df.provider_state.unique()
states.sort()


total_payment = df.average_total_payments.sum()
medicare_payment = df.average_medicare_payments.sum()


percent_paid = ((medicare_payment/total_payment))*100
print("Overall:")
print ("Medicare pays {:4.2f}% of Total for 554 DRG".format(percent_paid))
print ("Patient pays {:4.2f}% of Total for 554 DRG".format(100-percent_paid))

print ("Per State:")

# now iterate over states

print(df.head(5))
state_percent = []
for current_state in states:
    state_df = df[df.provider_state == current_state]

    state_total_payment = state_df.average_total_payments.sum()

    state_medicare_payment = state_df.average_medicare_payments.sum()

    state_percent_paid = ((state_medicare_payment/state_total_payment))*100
    state_percent.append(state_percent_paid)

    print ("{:s} Medicare pays {:4.2f}% of Total for 554 DRG".format
 (current_state,state_percent_paid))
```

Now some visualization

For our last experiment, we use MatPlotLib to visualize the state-by-state data in a graph generated by the `MedicareQuery4.py` program.

TIP

Do you already have seaborn on your Raspberry Pi? (If you've installed MatPlotLib, you probably do.) To find out, run the `MedicareQuery4.py` example Python program. If seaborn isn't installed, you'll see import errors and should then run the following command:

```
sudo apt-get install python3-seaborn
```

Moving to our VNC program so we can have a GUI on our Raspberry Pi, add the following code to the end of the preceding `MedicareQuery4.py` code:

```python
# We could graph this using MatPlotLib with the two lists,
# but we want to use DataFrames for this example

data_array = {'State': states, 'Percent': state_percent}

df_states = pd.DataFrame.from_dict(data_array)

# Now back in dataframe land
import matplotlib.pyplot as plt
import seaborn as sb

print (df_states)

df_states.plot(kind='bar', x='State', y= 'Percent')
plt.show()
```

Figure 3-4 shows the resulting graph from running the `MedicareQuery4.py` program.

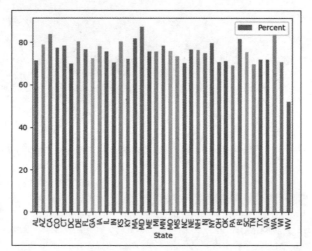

FIGURE 3-4:
Bar chart of Medicare percent paid per state for code 554.

Looking for the Most Polluted City
in the World on an Hourly Basis

Just one more quick example. Another public database on BigQuery called OpenAQ contains air-quality measurements from 47 countries around the world. And this database is updated hourly, believe it or not.

Here is some code that picks up the top three worst polluted cities in the world, as measured by air quality:

```python
import pandas as pd
from google.cloud import bigquery

# sample query from:
QUERY = """
        SELECT location, city, country, value, timestamp
        FROM `bigquery-public-data.openaq.global_air_quality`
        WHERE pollutant = "pm10" AND timestamp > "2017-04-01"
        ORDER BY value DESC
        LIMIT 1000
        """

client = bigquery.Client.from_service_account_json(
                    'MedicareProject2-1223283ef413.json')
query_job = client.query(QUERY)
df = query_job.to_dataframe()

print (df.head(3))
```

Copy this code into a file called PollutedCity.py and run the program. Following is the current result of running the code (as of this writing):

```
     location          city country  value    timestamp
0     Dilovası          Kocaeli    TR  5243.00  2018-01-25 12:00:00+00:00
1  Bukhiin urguu   Ulaanbaatar    MN  1428.00  2019-01-21 17:00:00+00:00
2  Chaiten Norte  Chaiten Norte    CL   999.83  2018-04-24 11:00:00+00:00
```

Dilovasi, Kocaeli, Turkey is not a healthy place to be right now. Doing a quick Google search of Dilovasi finds that cancer rates are three times higher than the worldwide average. This striking difference apparently stems from the environmental heavy metal pollution that has persisted in the area for about 40 years, mainly due to intense industrialization.

John will definitely be checking this on a daily basis.

6

Talking to Hardware

Contents at a Glance

Chapter **1**

Introducing Physical Computing

We think it's more difficult to learn about the software (Python) than the hardware, which is why in the last several hundred pages we've focused on learning how to program in Python. But now it's time for you to learn how to make your computer *do* something with Python. Making your computer do mechanical things — and interact with the world around you — is called *physical computing!*

WARNING

In this chapter, we hook up various sensors and motors to a Raspberry Pi computer. Although the voltages we use — 3.3V and 5V — are not particularly dangerous to people, hooking up things incorrectly can burn out the computer or sensors. For this reason, follow these two rules assiduously:

» **Rule 1:** Turn off *all* power before you hook up or change any wires.

» **Rule 2:** Double-check your connections, especially the power connections, which are power and ground. To find out why these are the most important wires to check, see the next chapter!

Physical Computing Is Fun

One reason why we want to you to learn about physical computing is that little computers doing physical things (typically called *embedded systems*) are everywhere. And we mean everywhere. Look around your kitchen. Your refrigerator has a computer — or maybe two or three if it has a display. Your blender has a computer. Your oven has a computer. Your microwave has a computer. If you use Phillips Hue lights in your house, your light bulbs have a computer. Your car has upwards of 20 computers.

One more example. How about the lowly toaster? If you have a Bagel button or a display on your toaster, it has a computer in there. Why are there so many computers in your house? Because it's significantly less expensive to control gadgets with a computer than with special hardware. (You can buy computers in bulk for about 15¢ each!)

Most of these computers are much simpler and slower and carry much less RAM (random access storage) than your average PC. A PC may have 4GB to 16GB of RAM (1GB equals approximately 1 billion bytes), but the computer running your toaster probably has only about 100 bytes of RAM.

All these little computers are doing physical computing, sensing and interacting with the environment. The refrigerator computer is checking its temperature and then turning on the cooling machinery if necessary, minimizing the amount of electricity it uses. The stove updates its display on the front panel, monitoring the buttons and dials and controlling the temperature so you get a good lasagna for dinner.

What Is a Raspberry Pi?

The functionality of these very small computers was too limited to use in the examples in this book, so we compromised and used the Raspberry Pi, a $35 computer that has an immense amount of hardware and software available for use (especially with Python). It's more complex than a toaster but much simpler than the computer in your TV.

A Raspberry Pi is a popular SBC (single board computer) that has been around since 2012. It was created by the Raspberry Pi Foundation to teach basic science and engineering in schools around the world. It turned out to be wildly popular, with more than 30 million computers sold. A bunch of other Raspberry Pi models are available, from the Raspberry Pi Zero ($5) to the new Raspberry Pi 4B (~$60). We use the Raspberry Pi 3B+ for the projects in the book, but you could also use the 4B.

To demystify some of the technology that we deal with every day, let's talk about the major blocks of hardware on the Raspberry Pi 3B+ computer, as shown in Figure 1-1.

>> **GPIO connector:** General purpose input-output pin connector. We use this connector a lot in the rest of Book 6.

>> **CPU/GPU:** Central processing unit/graphics (for the screen) processing unit. This block is the brains of the gear and tells everything else what to do. Your Python programs are run by this block.

>> **USB ports:** These are standard USB (universal serial bus) ports, the same interfaces you find on big computers. There are many devices you can connect to a USB port, just as on your PC. You will plug your mouse and keyboard into these ports.

>> **Ethernet port:** Just like the Ethernet interface on your computer. Connects to a network via wires.

>> **Wi-Fi:** This block isn't shown on the diagram because it's inside the CPU chip. If you choose to connect with Wi-FI, you don't have to trail Ethernet wires all over just to talk with the Internet.

>> **HDMI out:** You plug your monitor or TV into this port.

>> **Composite video and audio jack:** This jack can supply sound or composite video.

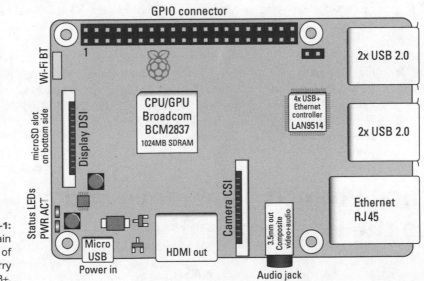

FIGURE 1-1: The main components of the Raspberry Pi 3B+.

>> **microSD card slot:** You plug in your micro SD card with your operating system in this slot.

>> **Status PWR LED:** The red LED shows the status of the power supply. (Note that it doesn't stay on all the time.)

>> **Status ACT LED:** The yellow LED flashes when the Raspberry Pi is accessing the SD card.

>> **Other ports:**

- *Micro USB (universal serial bus):* You plug your 5V power supply in the micro USB connector.

- *Camera CSI (camera serial interface):* You can plug a Raspberry Pi camera into this ribbon cable connector.

- *Display DSI (display serial interface):* This connector is for high-speed connections to a variety of custom displays, a topic well beyond the scope of our book.

To get our computer to do mechanical actions and sense the environment (apart from the computer screen and keyboard), we need a computer and one of two other devices — a sensor or an actuator. A *sensor* is a small piece of electronics that can detect something about the environment (such as temperature or humidity), and an *actuator* is a fancy word for a motor or cable that does things in the real world.

In the remainder of this chapter, you will learn about the necessary ingredients of your first physical computing project, which turns on and off an LED. This first project is the physical computing version of "Hello World" that we all do when we're learning software. Blinking LED, here we come!

TIP

Buy a Raspberry Pi Starter Kit (which comes with a power supply, an operating system, and a case) and get it set up before continuing. We recommend that beginners also get a mouse, keyboard, and monitor to do the setup. More advanced users may want to use the software SSH (Secure SHell) to do a headless setup. Again, the best place to understand how to start is to go to the tutorials on www.raspberrypi.org.

Building Projects That Move and Sense the Environment

At the beginning of the chapter, we talked about computers in the kitchen. All those computers sense the environment (the oven temperature, for example) and most are doing something to affect the environment (your blender chopping up ice for a nice Margarita, for example). You'll be able to build and design your own projects (and believe us, after you get acquainted with the hardware, you'll be able to design wonderful things). You just need to jump in and do your first project.

Then, in further chapters, you build more complex things that will be the launching point to your own projects, all programmed in Python!

WHAT OTHER SMALL COMPUTERS ARE AVAILABLE?

Hundreds of different types of small computers and boards are out there for project building. We chose the Raspberry Pi because of the full support for the Python language, the availability of hundreds of Python libraries, and the number of websites (such as the fabulous `www.raspberrypi.org`) for learning how to set up and use the computer.

Two general categories of small computer systems are accessible to the beginning user: computers based on the Linux operating system (Raspbian, the software on the Raspberry Pi, is a form of Linux) and computers with a much smaller or no operating system. Both versions of computers and operating systems are useful in different applications.

Although Linux is a multitasking, complex operating system that can run with multiple CPU cores, it supports a Windows-like GUI on the Raspberry Pi, making it easy to operate.

Arduinos are small computers that have a small computer and limited amount of RAM. Even though they are much smaller and simpler than the Raspberry Pi, the development boards are about the same price. If you buy the Arduino chips in volume, however, the Arduino type of computer is much less expensive than a Raspberry Pi. An Arduino has many more input/output pins than a Raspberry Pi and has an onboard ADC (analog digital converter), which the Raspberry Pi lacks. In a later chapter, we show you how to create a project with an external ADC and the Raspberry Pi. The project involves a flame. You know that will be fun.

Another class of small computers similar to Arduinos are the SAMD21, ESP8266, and ESP32 boards. These boards can be programmed by the same IDE (integrated development environment) that Arduino devices use. They have much less RAM than the Raspberry Pi, but like the Pi, they come with built-in Wi-Fi (and sometimes Bluetooth) interfaces that make them useful in building projects you want to connect to the Internet, such as IoT (Internet of Things) projects. All these computers are fun to play with, but the Raspberry Pi has a much better environment for Python development and learning.

Sensing the Environment with the Raspberry Pi

By now you have your Raspberry Pi computer set up and running on your monitor, keyboard, and mouse. If not, do that now (remember our friend, www.raspberrypi.org). The next few paragraphs will be a lot more fun if you have a Raspberry Pi computer to work with!

The Raspberry Pi is the perfect platform for physical computing with Python because it has a multiscreen environment, lots of RAM and storage to play with, and the tools we need to build the projects we want.

GPIO pins

A powerful feature of the Raspberry Pi is the row of GPIO (general-purpose input-output) pins along the top. Into this 40-pin header, we can plug a large number of sensors and controllers to do amazing things to expand the Raspberry Pi.

Using Python software, GPIO pins can be designated as input pins or output pins and used for many purposes. Two 5V power pins, two 3.3V power pins, and a number of ground pins have fixed uses. (See the description of voltages in the next chapter.) Figure 1-2 shows the function of each GPIO pin.

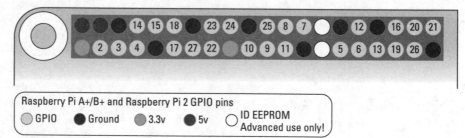

A GPIO pin outputs a 1 or a 0 from the computer to the pin. See the next chapter for more on how this output is accomplished and what it means. Basically, a 1 is 3.3V and a 0 is 0V, but you can think of them just as 1 and 0.

GPIO libraries

A number of GPIO Python libraries can be used for building projects. The one we use throughout the rest of this book is the gpiozero library, which is installed on all Raspberry Pi desktop software releases. The library documentation and installation instructions (if needed) are located on `https://gpiozero.readthedocs.io/en/stable/`.

Now we're going to jump into the "Hello World" physical computing project with our Raspberry Pi.

Buying and assembling the hardware for "Hello World"

To do this project, you need two pieces of Grove hardware:

>> **Pi2Grover board:** This board, shown in Figure 1-3, converts the Raspberry Pi GPIO pin header to Grove connectors. Grove connectors are easy to use, and you can't reverse the power pins! You can buy the Pi2Grover at `https://shop.switchdoc.com` or at Amazon for about $20. (You can get $5.00 off the board at shop.switchdoc.com by using the discount code PI2DUMMIES at checkout.) Lots more on this board in the next chapter.

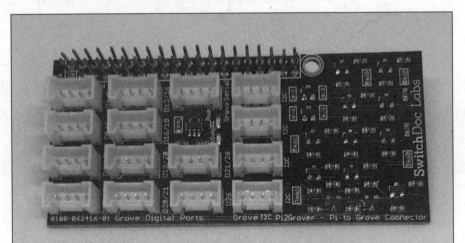

FIGURE 1-3:
The Pi2Grover board.

>> **Grove blue LED module:** This module includes a Grove cable. You can buy this at `https://shop.switchdoc.com` or Amazon for $3. (See Figure 1-4.) The LED module allows you to turn an LED on and off by using the Raspberry Pi.

FIGURE 1-4:
The Grove
blue LED.

For more on Grove connectors, see the next chapter.

For a number of you readers, this will be the first time you've ever assembled a physical computer-based project. The following step-by-step procedure makes the process easy:

1. **Align the Pi2Grover board with the 40-pin GPIO connector on the Raspberry Pi (see Figure 1-5.)**

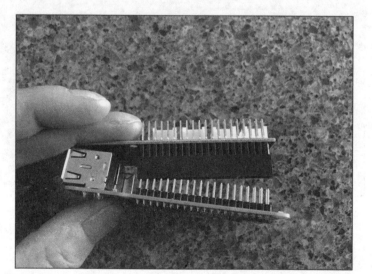

FIGURE 1-5:
Aligning the
Pi2Grover
board with the
Raspberry Pi.

2. **Gently push the Pi2Grover board onto the Raspberry Pi GPIO pins, making sure the pins are aligned (see Figure 1-6).**

No pins should be showing on either end. Make sure the pins on the Raspberry Pi and on top of the Pi2Grover board are not bent.

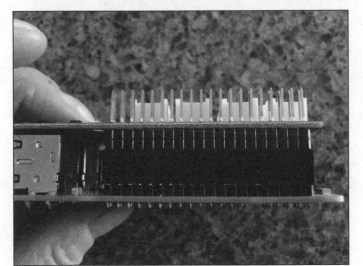

FIGURE 1-6:
The installed
Pi2Grover board.

3. **Plug one end of the Grove cable into the Grove blue LED board (see Figure 1-7).**

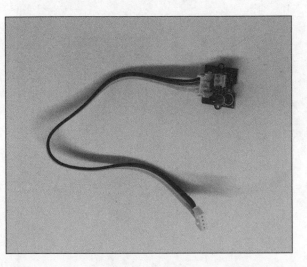

FIGURE 1-7:
A Grove cable
plugged into the
Grove blue LED
board.

4. If necessary, plug the blue LED into the Grove blue LED board, with the flat side of the LED aligned with the flat side of the outline on the board (see Figure 1-8).

Flat side of LED

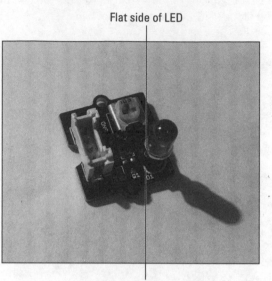

Flat side of outline on board

FIGURE 1-8:
The LED aligned with the outline on the board.

5. Plug the other end of the Grove cable into the slot marked D12/D13 on the Pi2Grover board (see Figure 1-9).

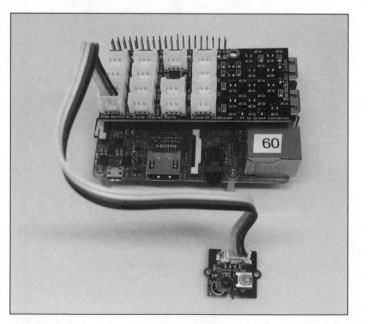

FIGURE 1-9:
The completed "Hello World" project.

We've finished assembling the hardware. Now it's time to create the Python software.

Controlling an LED with Python

Now that we have the hardware connected, we can apply power to the Raspberry Pi. If all is well, the Grove blue LED and a blue power LED on the Pi2Grover board will light, the yellow LED on the Raspberry Pi will flash (during bootup), and the red LED on the Raspberry Pi will light (but may then turn off depending on your power supply).

TECHNICAL STUFF

The Grove blue LED lights when we turn on the Raspberry Pi power because the GPIO pins on the Raspberry Pi power up as inputs. Because the GPIO pin is an input and nothing is driving the GPIO pin (the Grove LED wants an output, not an input to control the LED), the GPIO pin just floats with an undetermined voltage — it's in *tri*-state (neither a 1 nor a 0, but somewhere in-between). Because of the circuitry on the Pi2Grover board, the input will float towards a 1, so the LED turns on. When you turn your GPIO pin to an output in the code, the LED will turn off.

To get started, follow these steps:

TIP

1. **Using your keyboard, open a Terminal window.**

   If you don't know how to open and use a Terminal window and the command line on the Raspberry Pi, go to www.raspberrypi.org/documentation/usage/terminal/ for an excellent tutorial.

2. **Enter the following Python code into a file using the nano text editor (or an editor of your choice). Save it to the file HelloWorld.py.**

```
from gpiozero import LED
from time import sleep

blue = LED(12)

while True:
    blue.on()
    print( "LED On")
    sleep(1)
    blue.off()
    print( "LED Off")
    sleep(1)
```

TIP

For an excellent tutorial on using the nano text editor, visit www.raspberrypi.org/magpi/edit-text/.

3. **Now the big moment. Start your program by running the following on the command line of the Terminal window:**

```
sudo python3 HelloWorld.py
```

The LED blinks on and off once per second and the following appears on the screen in the Terminal window:

```
LED On
LED Off
LED On
LED Off
LED On
LED Off
LED On
LED Off
LED On
LED Off
LED On
```

To stop the program, press Ctrl+C (^C, in geek terms).

TECHNICAL STUFF

The keyword sudo stands for *super user do*. We use sudo in front of the python3 command because some versions of the Raspberry Pi operating system restrict a regular user's access to certain pins and functions. By using sudo, we're running this command as a *super user*, which means it will run regardless. In newer versions of the Raspberry Pi OS, you just type python3 HelloWorld.py. If the program doesn't work, go back to sudo python3 HelloWorld.py.

The following statement imports the LED function from the Python gpiozero library:

```
from gpiozero import LED
```

Then we import the sleep function from the Python time library:

```
from time import sleep
```

Next, we assign an LED on GPIO 12 (remember D12/D13 on the Pi2Grover board?):

```
blue = LED(12)
```

Now we start the loop that will go forever:

```
while True:
```

Turn on the LED:

```
blue.on()
print( "LED On")
```

Wait for one second to go by:

```
sleep(1)
```

Turn off the LED:

```
blue.off()
print( "LED Off")
sleep(1)
```

The program then loops forever — until you stop it.

Wow, you've now entered the world of physical computing. Just wait until the next minibook, where you control robots with Python.

But Wait, There's More

Because we have all this hardware set up, we'll do one more project. This time, we use PWM (pulse width modulation) to vary the brightness of the LED.

TECHNICAL STUFF

Pulse-width modulation is a technique in which you vary the amount of time a signal is at 1 versus at 0. Our LED turns on at 1 and off at 0, so if we vary the time the LED is at 1 versus at 0, we can control the brightness as registered by the human eye. This ratio is called the *duty cycle,* which is shown in Figure 1-10. With a duty cycle of 100 percent, the LED is on 100 percent of the time, and with a duty cycle of 0 percent, it's off all the time. Varying the time the signal is on changes the apparent brightness of the LED. The LED is switched on and off at a default frequency of 100 times per second (Hz), but you can change the frequency.

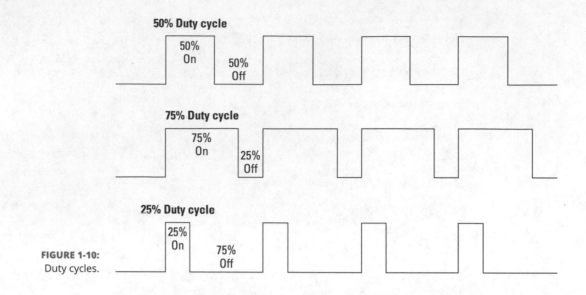

FIGURE 1-10:
Duty cycles.

Enter the following Python code into nano and save it as `HelloWorld2.py`. Note the `PWMLED(12)` function, which connects the LED on GPIO pin 12 to the PWM software:

```python
from gpiozero import PWMLED
from time import sleep

led = PWMLED(12)

while True:
    led.value = 0  # off
    sleep(1)
    led.value = 0.5  # half brightness
    sleep(1)
    led.value = 1  # full brightness
    sleep(1)
```

Run the code, and the brightness will change every second:

```
sudo python3 HelloWorld2.py
```

And use the following code to see a smooth continuous brightening and darkening of the LED:

```python
from gpiozero import PWMLED
from signal import pause
led = PWMLED(12)
led.pulse()
pause()
```

WHY DOES THE LED SEEM TO FLICKER?

When you run your Python program, it's not the only thing running on the Raspberry Pi. Type `ps xaf` at your command-line prompt in the Terminal window, and you'll see that dozens of programs are running.

Because the operating system on the Raspberry Pi is *multitasking* (more than one task is running at a time), sometimes your PWM task (as it is being run in software) doesn't get the CPU quite when it wants. As a result, you see a little jitter in the LED. The Raspberry Pi has two hardware PWM GPIO pins, which also can be used to drive LEDs if you aren't using the audio output on the Raspberry Pi. On a Raspberry Pi 3B+, the flicker is barely noticeable, unless the Raspberry Pi is loaded down with other programs.

Boy, you accomplished a lot in this chapter. You have now started to see the possibilities of physical computing. And you have a blue LED!

Chapter **2**

No Soldering! Using Grove Connectors for Building

G rove is a modular, standardized connecter prototyping system. Grove takes a building-block approach to assembling electronics. Compared to a jumper or solder-based system, Grove is easier to connect, experiment with, and build, and it simplifies the learning process. However, Grove does requires some learning and expertise.

In this chapter, you learn what Grove connections are and what types of Grove connections exist, and you look at example Grove modules for each of the connections.

Working with the Grove System

The *Grove system* consists of a base unit and various modules with standardized connectors. The base unit allows for easy connection to a single-board computer (such as a Raspberry Pi or Arduino). Every Grove module typically addresses a single function, from a button to a sensor for monitoring heart rate.

Selecting a Grove base unit

A *Grove base unit* is a controller or shield to which you attach Grove modules. The base unit provides the processing power, and the modules offer the input sensors and output actuators of your system.

Note that you don't need a base unit to connect Grove modules. Instead, you can use a cable (a Grove-to-pin-header converter) from the pins on the Raspberry Pi or Arduino to the Grove connectors. (We show you how to do this in the "Connecting with Grove Cables" section.) Using header pins, however, is more complicated and prone to error.

Arduino base unit

We mostly talk about the Raspberry Pi in this book, but a number of other computers are out there too, such as the popular Arduino. Several good base unit shields are available for the Arduino that provide a lot of Grove connectors. Figure 2-1 shows the base unit designed to plug into an Arduino Uno. Base units are also available for the Arduino Mega, Due, and others.

FIGURE 2-1:
The Arduino
Uno Grove base
board.

Some Arduino boards, such as the Mini Pro LP (see Figure 2-2), have Grove connectors built right into the board so you don't even need a base unit.

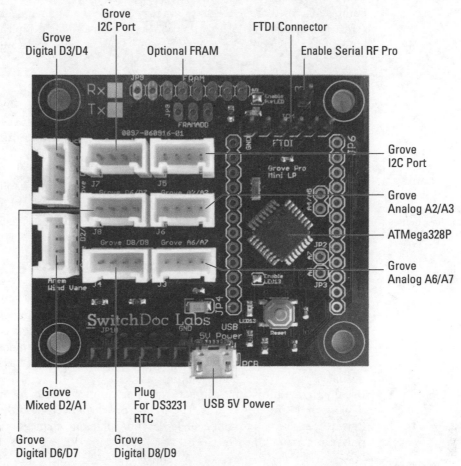

Grove
I2C Port

Grove
Digital D3/D4

Optional FRAM

FTDI Connector

Enable Serial RF Pro

Grove
I2C Port

Grove
Analog A2/A3

ATMega328P

Grove
Analog A6/A7

Grove
Mixed D2/A1

Plug
For DS3231
RTC

USB 5V Power

FIGURE 2-2:
The Arduino
Mini Pro LB board
with Grove.

Grove
Digital D6/D7

Grove
Digital D8/D9

Raspberry Pi base unit

On the Raspberry Pi side, the pickings are much slimmer. Most base unit devices are "too smart," isolating you from the Raspberry Pi hardware and software. The additional hardware layer is a problem when you want to connect to hardware using Python. We prefer a solution that is closer to the Pi hardware for learning and flexibility.

We use the Pi2Grover Raspberry Pi base unit, shown in Figure 2-3. It's basically just a voltage level shifter (from the Raspberry Pi 3.3V to 5V for all the Grove sensors), and it doesn't get in the way of writing drivers in Python.

FIGURE 2-3:
The Pi2Grover
board at work on
the Raspberry Pi.

Error-proofing with a Grove connector

A *Grove connector* is a four-pin standard-size connector that you plug into base units and Grove modules. These standardized connectors are keyed so that you can't plug them in backwards, and the four types of connectors are designed so that if you plug the wrong type of device into the wrong type of base unit, there's no problem. They aren't destroyed; they just won't work. This is a very good thing.

Usually, if you plug things in backwards or connect boards incorrectly, you can damage or destroy the boards. The standardized connectors in the Grove system, however, enable you to connect boards while taking no chances on hooking up the power and ground incorrectly.

WARNING

Note one exception: If you plug in a 3.3V I2C Grove module that is non-5V tolerant into a 5V I2C Grove connector, you could fry the device. In this book, we avoid such situations by making sure everything we do is 5V!

Four types of Grove connectors are available. Figure 2-4 shows the male Grove connector.

All Grove cables are physically identical and can be interchanged. They differ in the signal type they provide. As mentioned, you won't short out power and ground by plugging in the Grove cable in the incorrect Grove connector.

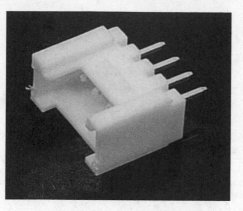

FIGURE 2-4:
A Grove
connector.

All Grove connectors are wired the same. The first pin is signal 1, the second pin is signal 2, the third pin is power, and the forth pin is ground.

The wire colors on Grove cables are always the same, as shown in Figure 2-5:

>> **Yellow:** Connects to Pin 1.

>> **White:** Connects to Pin 2.

>> **Red:** Power on all Grove connectors. Connects to Pin 3.

>> **Black:** Ground on all Grove connectors. Connects to Pin 4.

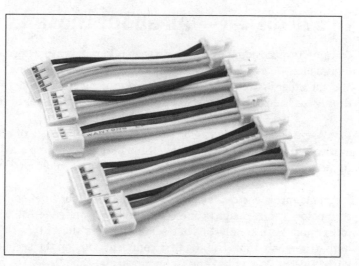

FIGURE 2-5:
5cm-long
Grove cables.

Grove Connectors

Now it's time to wax poetic about the four types of Grove connectors we use when talking about sensors and devices. By using the wrong connector, you may not fry your board, but your project will not work correctly!

Grove digital — All about those 1s and 0s

Computers often communicate with each other and with external devices by using digital bits. We can get information from bits in two ways. One is the value (1 or 0) and the other is timing, such as how long the bit has a value of 1. The thought of timing leads us to the serial Grove ports we talk about later in this chapter.

TECHNICAL STUFF

Many sensors need only one or two bits. A *bit* is the basis of all digital computer hardware and can be either 1 or 0. Although bits are represented by voltage levels, fundamentally we treat bits as having only a 1 or 0 value.

A *digital Grove connector* consists of the standard four lines coming into the Grove connector. The two signal lines (pins 1 and 2) are generically called D0 and D1. Most modules use only D0, but some (such as the LED bar Grove display) use both. Often base units call the first connector D0 and the second D1, and they are wired D0/D1 (D0 on pin 1 and D1 on pin 2) and then D1/D2 (D1 on pin 1 and D2 on pin2), and so on. See Table 2-1 for a description of each pin of the digital Grove connector.

TABLE 2-1   ## The Grove Digital Connector

Pin	Name	Description
1 (yellow)	D0	Primary digital input/output
2 (white)	D1	Secondary digital input/output
3- (red)	VCC	Power for Grove module (5V or 3.3V)
4 (black)	GND	Ground

Some examples of Grove digital modules are switch modules, the fan module, and the LED module. Figure 2-6 shows what the Grove connector looks like on the schematic for the Grove LED module from the previous chapter. These digital modules range from the simple to the very complex.

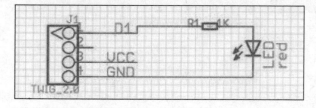

FIGURE 2-6:
A simple digital
Grove module
with LED.

Grove analog: When 1s and 0s aren't enough

A *Grove analog connector* consists of the standard four lines coming into the Grove connector. The two signal lines are generically called A0 and A1. Most modules use only A0. Often base units call the first connector A0 and the second A1, and they are wired A0/A1 and then A1/A2, and so on. This simple voltage divider (which will divide 5V to a lower voltage, such as 2.5V), shown in Figure 2-7, will give you a different analog voltage reading depending on the position of the switch and the voltage present across the green connector on the left side. See Table 2-2 for the descriptions of each pin.

Several examples of Grove analog modules are a potentiometer, a voltage divider, and the Grove air-quality sensor.

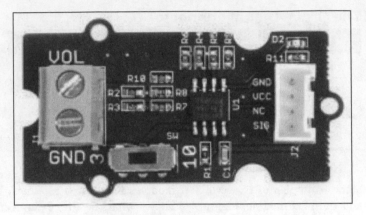

FIGURE 2-7:
A Grove analog simple voltage divider.

TABLE 2-2

The Grove Analog Connector

Pin	Name	Description
1 (yellow)	A0	Primary analog input
2 (white)	A1	Secondary analog input
3 (red)	VCC	Power for Grove module (5V or 3.3V)
4 (black)	GND	Ground

Grove UART (or serial) — bit-by-bit transmission

TECHNICAL STUFF

Remember when we talked about digital signals and how you can convey information not only in the level of the signal (1 or 0) but also in how long it stays at a 1 or 0 (the timing)? This timing information is the basis of sending a serial signal. For example, 8 single bits such as 01000001 sent at a specific speed can represent the letter *A*. The speed at which the bit is sent is called its *baud rate*. (*Baud* comes from Emile Baudot, who was an inventor and a scientist making great progress in the late 1800s with the telegraph.)

The Grove UART (universal asynchronous receiver/transmitter) module is a specialized version of a Grove digital module that uses the digital level (1 or 0) and the timing of the signal to receive and transmit data. It uses Pin 1 and Pin 2 for the serial input and transmit, respectively. The Grove UART (also called a *serial interface*) connector is labeled from the base unit's point of view. In other words, Pin 1 is the RX line (which the base unit uses to receive data, so it is an input) and Pin 2 is the TX line (which the base unit uses to transmit data to the Grove module). Table 2-3 lists a description of each pin on the UART Grove connector.

TABLE 2-3 **The Grove UART Serial Connector**

Pin	Name	Description
1 (yellow)	RX	Serial receive (from the base unit's point of view, not the Grove board's)
2 (white)	TX	Serial transmit (from the base unit's point of view, not the Grove board's)
3 (red)	VCC	Power for Grove module (5V or 3.3V)
4 (black)	GND	Ground

Examples of Grove UART modules are XBee wireless sockets and the 125KHz RFID reader, which is shown in Figure 2-8.

FIGURE 2-8:
A Grove UART
RFID reader.

Grove I2C — Using I2C to make sense of the world

Our favorite devices to plug into little computers are I2C (inter-integrated circuit) sensors. Hundreds of types of inexpensive I2C sensors are on the market. And many types of I2C Grove sensors are available to plug and go!

The sensor shown in Figure 2-9 is a SI1145 sunlight I2C sensor. It measures not only the visible sunlight strength but also the infrared (IR) and ultraviolet (UV) components. This inexpensive sensor can tell you whether you're going to get sunburned as well as if your plants are happy! (The sensor is the little colored chip marked U1; it has a clear top to let light through.)

You just have to love the things you can do these days with computers.

WARNING

Most I2C sensors can be used with both 3.3V and 5V base units, but a few are only 3.3V or only 5.0V. You need to check the specifications. If you connect a 3.3V I2C sensor to your 5V Grove connector, you'll probably destroy the device. See Table 2-4 for the pin descriptions of the Grove connector.

FIGURE 2-9:
The Grove I2C
sunlight sensor.

TABLE 2-4

The Grove I2C Connector

Pin	Name	Description
1 (yellow)	SCL	I2C clock
2 (white)	SDA	I2C data
3 (red)	VCC	Power for Grove module (5V or 3.3V)
4 (black)	GND	Ground

The Grove I2C connector has the standard layout. Pin 1 is the SCL signal and Pin 2 is the SDA signal. Power and ground are the same as the other connectors. Often the I2C bus on a controller (such as the ESP8266, Raspberry Pi, or Arduino) uses just digital I/O pins to implement the I2C bus. The pins on the Raspberry Pi and Arduino, however, have hardware support for the I2C bus. The ESP8266 has a purely software I2C interface, which children of the '90s called "bit banging."

Connecting with Grove Cables

Many lengths of Grove cables are available, from 5cm all the way up to 50cm. (See Figure 2-10.) They have a Grove connector on each end and are interchangeable. You use these to plug your sensors into the Raspberry Pi.

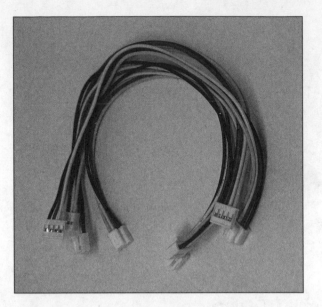

FIGURE 2-10:
20cm Grove
cables.

And if you want to use a device or a sensor that doesn't have a Grove connector, you can use a Grove patch cable. The Grove patch, or adapter, cable converts pin headers to Grove connectors. Two types of Grove adaptor cables are available. The first type is a Grove-connector-to-female-header-pins cable, as shown in Figure 2-11.

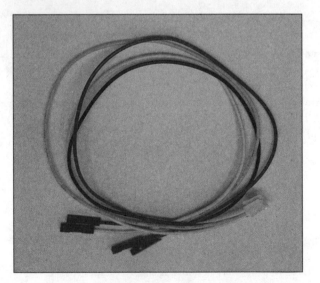

FIGURE 2-11:
Grove female
header cables.

The second type is a Grove-connector-to-male-header-pins cable, as shown in Figure 2-12. For comparison, Figure 2-10 shows normal Grove connectors.

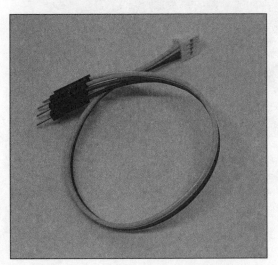

FIGURE 2-12: Grove male header cables.

TIP

WARNING

The power of the patch cable is that you can connect to non-Grove sensors.

To use a patch cable, you have to figure out what pin goes where and that determination is based on the type of sensor and the interface. Grove connectors support four kinds of interfaces, as we talk about earlier in this chapter. Be careful and make sure you check twice before applying power!

An example of the power of the patch!

Now we're going to figure out how to use a Grove patch cable with a real sensor.

SunAirPlus is a solar power controller and data collector. It has an I2C interface on the pin header that we often want to convert to Grove connectors. We connect the cable in the following way (see Figure 2-13):

Pin 1 – Yellow (SCL)

Pin 2 – White (SDA)

Pin 3 – Red (VDD)

Pin 4 – Black (GND)

FIGURE 2-13:
The SunAirPlus
board with the
Grove female
header patch
cable.

Figure 2-14 shows the other end of the adaptor cable plugged into the Pi2Grover adaptor board on the Raspberry Pi.

FIGURE 2-14:
A Grove adaptor
cable attached to
Pi2Grover.

Second example: The Adafruit Ultimate GPS

Now we do a second example with a GPS module that uses a serial interface. The Adafruit Ultimate GPS connects to a Raspberry Pi or an Arduino through a serial interface (UART). To use Grove connectors, we connect the cable in the following way:

Pin 1 – Yellow (TX)

Pin 2 – White (RX)

Pin 3 – Red (VIN)

Pin 4 – Black (GND)

TIP

Note that serial connectors are a bit odd in that you need to connect RX on the Grove connector to TX on the sensor, and TX on the Grove connector to RX on the sensor. (See Figure 2-15.) Flipping these lines is the most common mistake in hooking up a serial interface.

FIGURE 2-15:
A close-up of the Adafruit GPS with a Grove patch cable.

Now that you understand how to hook up Grove modules, cables, and connectors, it's time to start building more complex projects in the next chapter.

Chapter **3**

Sensing the World

S ensors for the Raspberry Pi and other small computers number in the thousands. From detecting people in front of your computer with a passive infrared (PIR) sensor to detecting a myriad of environmental conditions (temperature, humidity, air quality, and so on), your computer can monitor the physical world in many inexpensive ways. In this chapter, you discover how to program your computer to communicate with these sensors.

To download the code for this chapter, go to www.dummies.com/go/pythonaiofd2e.

Understanding I2C

For a computer to talk to sensors, it needs an interface. An *interface* consists of a *hardware interface,* which contains pins, types, and voltage levels, and a *software interface,* which is usually called a driver or an API (application programming interface). In this book, the software interface is a Python module.

You get data to your computer from your outside sensors in four major ways:

» **Digital input:** GPIO pins programmed to be input lines.

» **Analog input:** Analog values that go through an analog-to-digital converter (ADC) to be read by a computer.

>> **Digital I2C:** A general interface used for communicating with sensors. ITC is pronounced "I squared C" for *inter-integrated circuit bus.*

>> **Digital SPI:** An interface using 1s and 0s and timing to produce a *serial peripheral interface.*

In this book, we deal with sensors using digital inputs, analog inputs, and digital I2C interfaces. SPI is a similar interface to I2C that is supported by many sensors. Why not use SPI in this book? Just for simplicity. Most SPI parts also have an I2C interface on the chip.

To understand the I2C interface, let's look at what an I2C bus is. An I2C bus is often used to communicate with chips or sensors that are on the same board or located physically close to the CPU. I2C was developed by Phillips (now NXP Semiconductors). To get around hardware licensing issues (that have largely gone away), the bus is often called TWI (two-wire interface). SMBus, developed by Intel, is a subset of I2C that defines the protocols more strictly. Both the Arduino and the Raspberry Pi support the I2C bus.

Every sensor on the I2C bus has an address. For example, the address of the HDC1080 temperature and humidity sensor we use in this chapter has an address of 0x40. The 0x means that the number that follows is in hexadecimal notation — base 16 instead of base 10 (our normal numbering system).

I2C provides good support for slow, close peripheral devices that need to be addressed only occasionally. For example, a temperature-measuring device generally changes very slowly, so it's a good candidate for an I2C interface, whereas a camera, which generates lots of data quickly and potentially changes often, is not.

I2C uses only two bidirectional open-drain lines: SCL (serial clock line) and SDA (serial data line), similar to two serial data lines next to each other. *Open-drain* means the device can pull a level down to ground (0) but can't pull the line up to Vdd (1). Thus, a requirement of the I2C bus is that both lines are pulled up to Vdd by using a resistor.

Not properly pulling up the lines is the first and most common mistake people make when they first use an I2C bus. The Pi2Grover board we use in this book contains 10K Ohm pullup resistors, so you don't have to worry about connecting pullups to the SDA and SCL signals.

You can connect two types of devices to an I2C bus: master devices and slave devices. Typically, you have one master device (the Raspberry Pi, in our case) and multiple slave sensors, each with an individual 7-bit address, as shown in Figure 3-1.

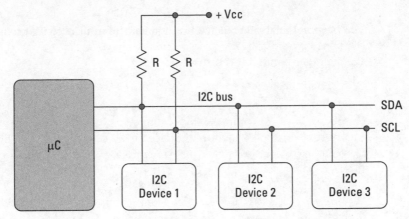

FIGURE 3-1:
The I2C bus.

Multiple devices on common I2C bus

A *protocol* defines how a bus behaves and is used. The I2C protocol uses three types of messages:

>> Digital single message where a master writes data to a slave

>> Digital single message where a master reads data from a slave

>> Digital combined messages, where a master issues at least two reads or writes or both to one or more slaves

Lucky for us, almost all the complexity of dealing with the I2C bus is hidden by Python drivers and libraries.

Enabling I2C on the Raspberry Pi

TIP

To use the I2C bus on the Raspberry Pi, you need to make sure that it's enabled in the operating system. Here is a good tutorial from Adafruit on how to do just that: https://learn.adafruit.com/adafruits-raspberry-pi-lesson-4-gpio-setup/configuring-i2c.

Did you enable I2C correctly? The easy way to check is to type the following command in the Terminal window:

```
sudo i2cdetect -y 1
```

If it returns the following:

```
-bash: i2cdetect: command not found
```

you have not enabled your I2C bus. Repeat the tutorial to fix this.

On the other hand, if it returns this:

```
     0  1  2  3  4  5  6  7  8  9  a  b  c  d  e  f
00:          -- -- -- -- -- -- -- -- -- -- -- -- --
10: -- -- -- -- -- -- -- -- -- -- -- -- -- -- -- --
20: -- -- -- -- -- -- -- -- -- -- -- -- -- -- -- --
30: -- -- -- -- -- -- -- -- -- -- -- -- -- -- -- --
40: -- -- -- -- -- -- -- -- -- -- -- -- -- -- -- --
50: -- -- -- -- -- -- -- -- -- -- -- -- -- -- -- --
60: -- -- -- -- -- -- -- -- -- -- -- -- -- -- -- --
70: -- -- -- -- -- -- -- -- -- -- 
```

you have been successful! The dashes mean there are no sensors on the I2C bus.

The hardware for reading temperature and humidity

To talk to an I2C device, you should have one on the bus. We start with the HDC1080 temperature and humidity sensor, which is shown in Figure 3-2. You can get one of these inexpensive sensors at https://store.switchdoc.com or at www.amazon.com.

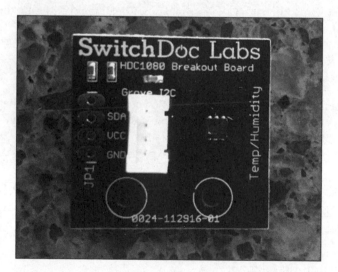

FIGURE 3-2: HDC1080 temperature and humidity sensor.

THE HDC1080 TEMPERATURE AND HUMIDITY SENSOR

The HDC1080 temperature and humidity sensor is an amazing device considering how that it costs about $8. The HDC1080 is located at I2C address 0x40.

The Grove temperature and humidity sensor (HDC1080) utilizes the HDC1080 sensor chip from Texas Instruments and provides excellent measurement accuracy at very low power. The sensor measures humidity based on a novel capacitive sensor. The humidity and temperature sensors are factory calibrated. The innovative WLCSP (wafer-level chip-scale package) simplifies board design with the use of an ultra-compact package. The HDC1080 is functional within the full –40°C to +125°C temperature range, and 0–100 percent relative humidity range. The accuracy of the chip is +/– 3 percent for the relative humidity and +/– 0.2C for the temperature.

Note: If you buy a non-Grove sensor on Amazon, you'll need a female-to-Grove patch cable, as discussed in Chapter 2 of this minibook. The SwitchDoc Labs HDC1080 sensor comes with a Grove connector. In either case, you need the Pi2Grover Raspberry-Pi-to-Grove converter, which was described in Chapters 1 and 2 of this minibook, which is also available at `https://store.switchdoc.com` or at `www.amazon.com`.

Now let's install the HDC1080 I2C sensor on our Raspberry Pi. Follow these steps:

1. **Shut down your Raspberry Pi by typing** `sudo halt` **on the command line (or by choosing Shutdown from the GUI menu). Then, when the yellow LED has stopped blinking, unplug the power from your Raspberry Pi.**

   The `sudo halt` command prepares the SD card on the Raspberry Pi for shutdown. Just unplugging your Raspberry Pi may not always corrupt the card but if it does, repairing the card is a long, technical, irritating process.

   Always shut down the Raspberry Pi before plugging anything into it or pulling anything out of it. Exceptions are USB ports, audio cables, and Ethernet cables, which are designed to support hot-plugging.

   REMEMBER

2. **Plug a Grove cable into the HDC1080, as shown in Figure 3-3.**

   We are using the SwitchDoc Labs HDC1080. If you're using a non-Grove Amazon device, you need to use a Grove patch cable, as described in Chapter 2 of this minibook.

   REMEMBER

FIGURE 3-3:
HDC1080 with
the Grove cable
plugged in.

3. **Plug the other end of the Grove cable into one of the Grove connectors marked I2C on the Pi2Grover plugged on top of your Raspberry Pi. (See Figure 3-4.)**

    Note: The I2C is a bus connected across all I2C connectors, which means you can use any of the four I2C connectors.

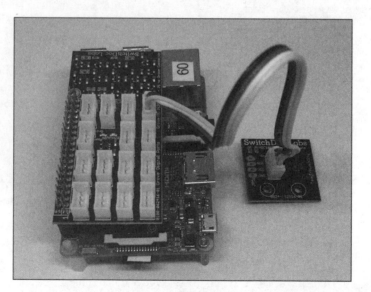

FIGURE 3-4:
The HDC1080
hooked up to the
Raspberry Pi.

4. **Power up the Raspberry Pi and open a Terminal window.**

5. **In the Terminal window, type** `sudo i2cdetect -y 1` **to be rewarded with the following:**

```
     0  1  2  3  4  5  6  7  8  9  a  b  c  d  e  f
00:        -- -- -- -- -- -- -- -- -- -- -- -- --
10: -- -- -- -- -- -- -- -- -- -- -- -- -- -- -- --
20: -- -- -- -- -- -- -- -- -- -- -- -- -- -- -- --
30: -- -- -- -- -- -- -- -- -- -- -- -- -- -- -- --
40: 40 -- -- -- -- -- -- -- -- -- -- -- -- -- -- --
50: -- -- -- -- -- -- -- -- -- -- -- -- -- -- -- --
60: -- -- -- -- -- -- -- -- -- -- -- -- -- -- -- --
70: -- -- -- -- -- -- -- -- --
```

Remember the 0x40 address of the HDC1080? There it is in the output.

Now you're ready to use Python to read the temperature and humidity from this sensor.

Reading temperature and humidity from an I2C device using Python

The use of Python libraries are key to being productive in writing Python applications. We will be using the `SDL_Pi_HDC1080_Python3` library, which is available on github.com at `https://github.com/switchdoclabs/SDL_Pi_HDC1080_Python3`.

To read the temperature and humidity, follow these steps:

1. **First, create a directory in your main directory:**

```
cd
mkdir I2CTemperature
cd I2CTemperature
```

Now you're in the I2CTemperature directory.

2. **Clone the library the `SDL_Pi_HDC1080_Python3` library on the Raspberry Pi.**

Use the following command in the Terminal window:

```
git clone https://github.com/switchdoclabs/SDL_Pi_HDC1080_Python3.git
```

Here git clone clones the git repository and copies it to your Raspberry Pi. If you enter ls in the Terminal window, you'll see the following output:

```
pi@RPi3-60:~/I2CTemperature $ ls
SDL_Pi_HDC1080_Python3
pi@RPi3-60:~/I2CTemperature $
```

3. **Using nano (or your favorite text editor), create a file and name it** temperatureTest.py **and enter the following code:**

```
import sys

sys.path.append('./SDL_Pi_HDC1080_Python3')

import time
import SDL_Pi_HDC1080




# Main Program
print
print ("")
print ("Read Temperature and Humidity from HDC1080 using I2C bus ")
print ("")


hdc1080 = SDL_Pi_HDC1080.SDL_Pi_HDC1080()


while True:

        print ("-----------------")
        print ("Temperature = %3.1f C" % hdc1080.readTemperature())
        print ("Humidity = %3.1f %%" % hdc1080.readHumidity())
        print ("-----------------")

        time.sleep(3.0)
```

4. **Run the code by typing the following:**

```
sudo python3 temperatureTest.py
```

You should see the following output, with new temperature and humidity readings every three seconds:

```
Read Temperature and Humidity from HDC1080 using I2C bus
```

```
------------------
Temperature = 24.2 C
Humidity = 32.9 %
------------------

------------------
Temperature = 24.2 C
Humidity = 32.9 %
------------------

------------------
Temperature = 24.2 C
Humidity = 32.9 %
------------------
```

You're now reading environmental data from an I2C device. Your Raspberry Pi is connected to the real world. Save this project. You'll use it again later in this chapter.

TIP

Try this experiment. Blow on the HDC1080 sensor board and watch the humidity go up! You'll see something like this:

```
------------------
Temperature = 24.2 C
Humidity = 32.9 %
------------------

------------------
Temperature = 24.1 C
Humidity = 33.6 %
------------------

------------------
Temperature = 24.1 C
Humidity = 33.9 %
------------------

------------------
Temperature = 24.1 C
Humidity = 36.3 %
------------------

------------------
Temperature = 24.1 C
Humidity = 36.5 %
------------------
```

Breaking down the program

Now let's look at the temperature and humidity program and see how it works. The first line imports the Python sys library:

```
import sys
```

The next line tells Python to search the SDL_Pi_HDC1080_Python3 directory (created by your clone command in Step 2 in the preceding section) in our current directory so the program can find the library:

```
sys.path.append('./SDL_Pi_HDC1080_Python3')
```

More imports:

```
import time
import SDL_Pi_HDC1080
```

The next few statements print a title for the program's output:

```
# Main Program
print
print ("")
print ("Read Temperature and Humidity from HDC1080 using I2C bus ")
print ("")
```

The next statement defines the hdc1080 object and initializes it:

```
hdc1080 = SDL_Pi_HDC1080.SDL_Pi_HDC1080()
```

These statements read the temperature and humidity and print them to the Terminal window. Note how using the HDC1080 library hides the complexity of using an I2C device:

```
while True:
        print ("-----------------")
        print ("Temperature = %3.1f C" % hdc1080.readTemperature())
        print ("Humidity = %3.1f %%" % hdc1080.readHumidity())
```

Sleep for three seconds and then repeat:

```
print ("-----------------")
time.sleep(3.0)
```

You could add all sorts of different functions to this program, such as turning on a red LED if the temperature gets too hot or turning on a blue LED if the temperature gets too cold.

TIP

You can even tweet the temperature and humidity by using the https://python-twitter.readthedocs.io Python library.

UNDER THE HOOD OF AN I2C DRIVER

I2C devices have not only an address (such as 0x40, the address of our HDC1080) but also registers. You can think of a register as a numbered address in which to write commands and read data. The HDC1080 has eight different registers, as shown in the figure below.

Pointer	Name	Reset value	Description
0x00	Temperature	0x0000	Temperature measurement output
0x01	Humidity	0x0000	Relative Humidity measurement output
0x02	Configuration	0x1000	HDC1080 configuration and status
0xFB	Serial ID	device dependent	First 2 bytes of the serial ID of the part
0xFC	Serial ID	device dependent	Mid 2 bytes of the serial ID of the part
0xFD	Serial ID	device dependent	Last byte bit of the serial ID of the part
0xFE	Manufacturer ID	0x5449	ID of Texas Instruments
0xFF	Device ID	0x1050	ID of the device

(continued)

(continued)

An I2C driver basically reads from these addresses and writes from these addresses to control the HDC1080 and to read the temperature and humidity data. The following figure shows the format of the temperature register located at pointer address 0x00.

Name	Bits		Description
TEMPERATURE	[15:02]	Temperature	Temperature measurement (read only)
	[01:00]	Reserved	Reserved, always 0 (read only)

In the SDL_Pi_HDC1080 Python library, take a look at the Python code to read that I2C register:

```
def readTemperature(self):

    s = [HDC1080_TEMPERATURE_REGISTER] # temp
    s2 = bytearray( s )
    HDC1080_fw.write( s2 )
    time.sleep(0.0625)  # From the data sheet

    #read 2 byte temperature data
    data = HDC1080_fr.read(2)

    buf = array.array('B', data)


    # Convert the data
    temp = (buf[0] * 256) + buf[1]
    cTemp = (temp / 65536.0) * 165.0 - 40
    return cTemp
```

This looks intimidating but it isn't as complicated as it seems. Breaking it down, we first define the function:

```
def readTemperature(self):
```

Then we format the pointer address (0x00 in this case) into a byte array:

```
s = [HDC1080_TEMPERATURE_REGISTER] # temp
s2 = bytearray( s )
```

We first write the register address:

```
HDC1080_fw.write( s2 )
```

We delays 62.5ms, as required by the data sheet. (You can find the data sheet by searching for HDC1080 on www.ti.com.)

```
time.sleep(0.0625)  # From the data sheet
```

We read two bytes:

```
#read 2 byte temperature data
data = HDC1080_fr.read(2)
```

And place the two bytes into a byte array:

```
buf = array.array('B', data)
```

Then we convert the data bytes using the formula in the data sheet:

```
# Convert the data
temp = (buf[0] * 256) + buf[1]
cTemp = (temp / 65536.0) * 165.0- 40
```

And send the temperature back to the calling program:

```
return cTemp
```

You can find many low-level drivers and programs that read from and write to I2C devices on the Raspberry Pi. This driver is one of the most common. Other drivers include Adafruit_i2c, SMBUS, PyComms, and Quick2Wire. You'll typically use the SMBUS library, but once in a while you'll run into a device that requires some non-SMBUS functionality.

Measuring Oxygen and a Flame

The next experiment is more complex. We take a Grove oxygen sensor and place it under a partially sealed glass jar with a lit candle, and then measure the oxygen in the glass jar and watch the level go down as the candle consumes the oxygen. A quick web search tells us that the oxygen should drop about 30 percent before the flame is extinguished, from 21 percent oxygen to about 14.7 percent oxygen. We watch the data on the browser window running on the Raspberry Pi.

We store the information in a CSV file (comma-delimited file), which we will graph later using MatPlotLib. We could also read this data into an Excel spreadsheet and graph it using Excel.

TECHNICAL STUFF

MatPlotLib is a Python library for making publication-quality plots using methods similar to MATLIB. You can output formats such as PDF, Postscript, SVG, and PNG.

You need to the following to do this experiment:

>> **Analog-to-digital converter:** Converts the analog output of the oxygen sensor to digital data for the Raspberry Pi.

>> **Grove oxygen sensor:** Measures the percentage of oxygen in the air and converts it to an analog value (0V–5V).

>> **Candle:** Consumes the oxygen in the bowl. You can use any candle as long as it fits under the bowl.

>> **Large glass bowl:** Covers and seals the candle so we can measure the oxygen.

Analog-to-digital converters (ADC)

An analog-to-digital converter takes an analog signal and converts it to a digital signal (16 bits, in this case) for a computer to read. (See the difference between analog and digital signals in Chapter 2 of this minibook.)

When you have the digital number in the computer, you can convert it back to volts by multiplying the digital number by 5.0/32768.0 to produce a floating-point number representing volts. 32768 is 2 raised to the 15th power, representing 15 bits, with the 16th bit representing the sign. These numbers come from the fact that we're using a 16-bit ADC.

The Grove analog-to-digital converter we use in this experiment, shown in Figure 3-5, is a Grove four-channel, 16-bit analog-to-digital converter available at `https://store.switchdoc.com` and www.amazon.com. Other Grove ADC modules are available, but we wanted to use a 16-bit ADC converter for greater accuracy.

The Grove oxygen sensor

The Grove gas sensor (O_2), shown in Figure 3-6, tests the oxygen concentration in the air. It detects the current oxygen concentration and outputs voltage values proportional to the concentration of oxygen. This would be a fun sensor to use in a greenhouse. What? Another project?

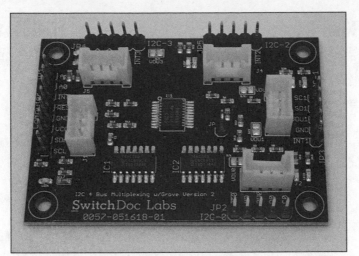

FIGURE 3-5:
The Grove
four-channel,
16-bit ADC.

FIGURE 3-6:
The Grove oxygen
sensor.

You can buy the Grove oxygen sensor for about $55 at www.seeedstudio.com or www.amazon.com.

The sensor value reflects only the approximate trend of oxygen gas concentration in a permissible error range. The Grove gas sensor requires about a 30-minute warm-up. Reading a more exact amount of oxygen would require a more precise and costly instrument.

Hooking up the oxygen experiment

By now, you have quite a bit of experience hooking up Grove devices to the Raspberry Pi. Follow these steps to set up the oxygen sensor:

1. Shut down your Raspberry Pi by typing sudo halt on the command line (or by choosing Shutdown from the GUI menu). Then, when the yellow LED has stopped blinking, unplug the power from your Raspberry Pi.

2. Plug one end of a Grove cable into the Grove oxygen sensor, and plug the other end into the Grove connector marked A1 on the Grove four-channel, 16-bit ADC board.

3. Plug another Grove cable into the Grove connector marked I2C on the Grove four-channel, 16-bit ADC board. Plug the other end of the Grove cable into one of the connectors marked I2C on the Pi2Grover board plugged into the Raspberry Pi, as shown in Figure 3-7.

4. Apply power to the Raspberry Pi.

5. Run the command i2cdetect -y 1 in a Terminal window.

FIGURE 3-7: The complete Raspberry Pi/ ADC/oxygen sensor hookup.

You should see this output:

```
      0  1  2  3  4  5  6  7  8  9  a  b  c  d  e  f
00:            -- -- -- -- -- -- -- -- -- -- -- -- --
10: -- -- -- -- -- -- -- -- -- -- -- -- -- -- -- --
20: -- -- -- -- -- -- -- -- -- -- -- -- -- -- -- --
30: -- -- -- -- -- -- -- -- -- -- -- -- -- -- -- --
40: -- -- -- -- -- -- -- -- 48 -- -- -- -- -- -- --
50: -- -- -- -- -- -- -- -- -- -- -- -- -- -- -- --
60: -- -- -- -- -- -- -- -- -- -- -- -- -- -- -- --
70: -- -- -- -- -- -- -- --
```

Address 0x48 is the Grove four-channel, 16-bit ADC board. If you don't see this output, go back and check your wiring.

Now we'll test the setup by running a simple Python program. First make a new directory for the program:

```
cd
mkdir oxygenProject
cd oxygenProject
git clone https://github.com/switchdoclabs/SDL_Pi_Grove4Ch16BitADC
```

Then use nano to enter the following code into a file called senseOxygen.py in your Terminal window:

```
import time, sys

sys.path.append('./SDL_Pi_Grove4Ch16BitADC/SDL_Adafruit_ADS1x15')

import SDL_Adafruit_ADS1x15

ADS1115 = 0x01    # 16-bit ADC

# Select the gain
gain = 6144  # +/- 6.144V

# Select the sample rate
sps = 250  # 250 samples per second

# Initialize the ADC using the default mode (use default I2C address)
adc = SDL_Adafruit_ADS1x15.ADS1x15(ic=ADS1115)
dataFile = open("oxygenData.csv",'w')

totalSeconds = 0
while (1):
```

```
# Read oxygen channel  in single-ended mode using the settings above
print ("----------------------")
voltsCh1 = adc.readADCSingleEnded(1, gain, sps) / 1000
rawCh1 = adc.readRaw(1, gain, sps)

# O2 Sensor
sensorVoltage = voltsCh1 *(5.0/6.144)
AMP  = 121
K_O2  = 7.43
sensorVoltage = sensorVoltage/AMP*10000.0
Value_O2 = sensorVoltage/K_O2 - 1.05

print ("Channel 1 =%.6fV raw=0x%4X O2 Percent=%.2f" %
      (voltsCh1, rawCh1, Value_O2 ))
print ("----------------------")

dataFile.write("%d,%.2f\n" % (totalSeconds, Value_O2))
totalSeconds = totalSeconds + 1
dataFile.flush()
time.sleep(1.0)
```

WARNING

When you have finished using the oxygen sensor, make sure you put it back in the included capped container and seal the top. Otherwise, humidity will destroy the sensor over time. (We've destroyed these sensors in the past by leaving them unsealed.)

When we ran the program, we got the following the results:

```
----------------------
Channel 1 =2.436375V raw=0x32C2 O2 Percent= 22.05
----------------------

----------------------
Channel 1 =2.436375V raw=0x32C2 O2 Percent= 22.05
----------------------

----------------------
Channel 1 =2.436375V raw=0x32C1 O2 Percent= 22.05
----------------------

----------------------
Channel 1 =2.436375V raw=0x32C2 O2 Percent= 22.05
----------------------

----------------------
Channel 1 =2.436187V raw=0x32C1 O2 Percent= 22.05
----------------------
```

Breaking down the code

Now let's examine the code for this project. In these statements, we set the parameters for the ADC module:

```python
import time, sys

sys.path.append('./SDL_Pi_Grove4Ch16BitADC/SDL_Adafruit_ADS1x15')

import SDL_Adafruit_ADS1x15

# Normal Imports.  Notice the path goes to the subdirectory in your directory.

ADS1115 = 0x01        # 16-bit ADC

# Select the gain
gain = 6144  # +/- 6.144V

# Select the sample rate
sps = 250  # 250 samples per second
```

Then we open the text file to store our data, which we will graph later with Excel or another method:

```python
# Initialize the ADC using the default mode (use default I2C address)
adc = SDL_Adafruit_ADS1x15.ADS1x15(ic=ADS1115)

dataFile = open("oxygenData.csv",'w')
```

Read the data from the ADC. We also show the raw data from which we calculate the voltage:

```python
totalSeconds = 0
while (1):

        # Read oxygen channel  in single-ended mode using the settings above

        print ("---------------------")
        voltsCh1 = adc.readADCSingleEnded(1, gain, sps) / 1000
        rawCh1 = adc.readRaw(1, gain, sps)
```

The `voltsCh1` formula is from the specification of the O2 sensor (www. seeedstudio.com/Grove-Oxygen-Sensor-ME2-O2-f20.html). The formula allows us to calculate O2 percentage given the 16 bits of data from the ADC:

```
# O2 Sensor
sensorVoltage = voltsCh1 *(5.0/6.144)
AMP  = 121
K_O2  = 7.43
sensorVoltage = sensorVoltage/AMP*10000.0
Value_O2 = sensorVoltage/K_O2 - 1.05
```

Here we write the data to the file:

```
print ("Channel 1 =%.6fV raw=0x%4X O2 Percent=%.2f" %
       (voltsCh1, rawCh1, Value_O2 ))
print ("---------------------")

dataFile.write("%d,%.2f\n" % (totalSeconds, Value_O2))
```

We flush the file to make sure the last value is written to the file. We eventually terminate this program with by pressing Ctrl-C:

```
totalSeconds = totalSeconds + 1
dataFile.flush()
```

Interpreting the results

Now that you have built the software, put your candle under the bowl with the oxygen sensor, start your program, and light the candle. See Figure 3-8. After a while, the flame will go out. Stop your program by pressing Ctrl-C.

```
time.sleep(1.0)
```

The data is in the directory that contains your program in a file called oxygen-Data.csv. Use Excel to graph your data. If you need a tutorial on that process, go to www.workzone.com/blog/how-to-make-a-graph-in-excel/.

Looking at the numbers in Figure 3-9, we determined that we started with about 21 percent oxygen and the candle went out at about 15.8 percent oxygen, a reduction of about 25 percent from start to finish. The 15.8 percent ending value is higher than the expected 30 percent reduction of oxygen levels (a 14.7 percent ending value). We suspect that the difference is due to sensor accuracy and candle type. Also note the graph right after the candle went out. The oxygen started to creep up, indicating that the seal wasn't perfect.

To see a video of the experiment, go to https://youtu.be/3amRq1YoVzo.

FIGURE 3-8:
The start of our
O2 experiment.

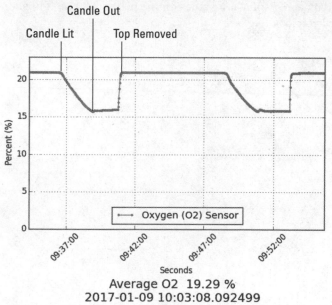

FIGURE 3-9:
The graph of the
data from our O2
experiment.

Building a Dashboard on Your Phone with Blynk

When you drive a car, all the information about your speed, how much fuel remains, and more is on your dashboard. We're going to show you how to construct a simple dashboard so you can view project data on your smartphone. We use the free Blynk app (free for small dashboards; they charge to build more controls). This app is available in the various app stores for Android and iPhone. We use the iPhone for our example, but the process is almost identical for Android phones.

HDC1080 temperature and humidity sensor redux

Earlier in the chapter, you built a temperature and humidity sensing project using a Raspberry Pi. Grab that project now and let's write more software to connect it to Blynk and display our values on the phone. Figure 3-10 shows what the dashboard will look like.

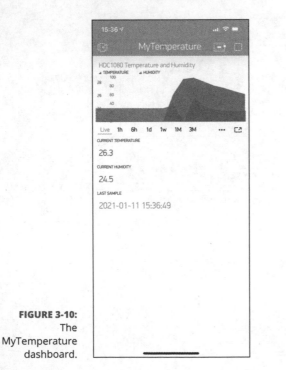

FIGURE 3-10:
The MyTemperature dashboard.

OTHER DASHBOARDS

Blynk is not the only Internet dashboard available. You can also check out the following:

- Freeboard
- XOBXOB
- Adafruit IO
- ThinkSpeak
- IBM Cloud
- Initialstate

All have different strengths and weaknesses, as well as a free option.

Adding the Blynk dashboard

First, we show you how to set up the Blynk app. We do the setup on an iPhone, but the process is similar on an Android phone. And the Python is identical in both cases! Blynk uses the concept of energy, which allows you to use widgets. You start with 2,000 units of energy for experimentation, which is sufficient for this project. You can purchase more if needed.

1. **Install the Blynk app on your mobile phone. Then open the app and create an account.**

See Figure 3-11. You need to set up an account and provide your email address, but you won't be charged for this.

2. **Tap the QR icon to scan a QR (Figure 3-12, left), and then scan the QR code (Figure 3-12, right).**

The MyTemperature app appears on your screen.

3. **After opening the app, tap the nut icon (Figure 3-13, right) to go to project settings.**

4. **RP the E-Mail button to send the authentication token (Auth Token) to your email, as shown in Figure 3-14.**

You can copy and paste the token in an email to yourself (or use the E-Mail button at the bottom of the screen) or into some other secure document. You'll be adding the token to the Python `temperatureTest.py` program file in the next section.

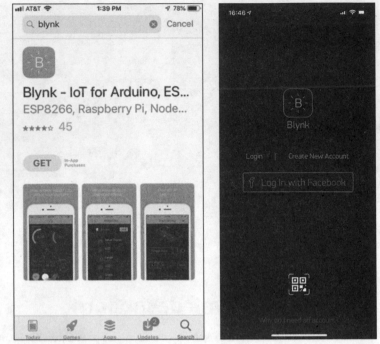

FIGURE 3-11:
Blynk in the App Store (left) and creating a Blynk account (right).

FIGURE 3-12:
Click for QR (left), and then scan the QR to generate your myTemperature app in Blynk.

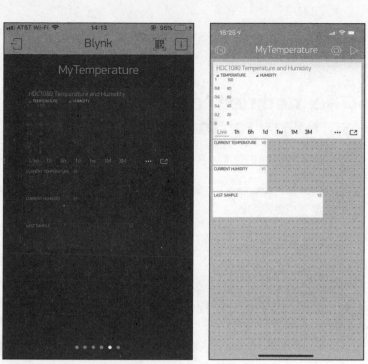

FIGURE 3-13:
The
MyTemperature
app (left) and
the initial screen
of the Blynk app
(right).

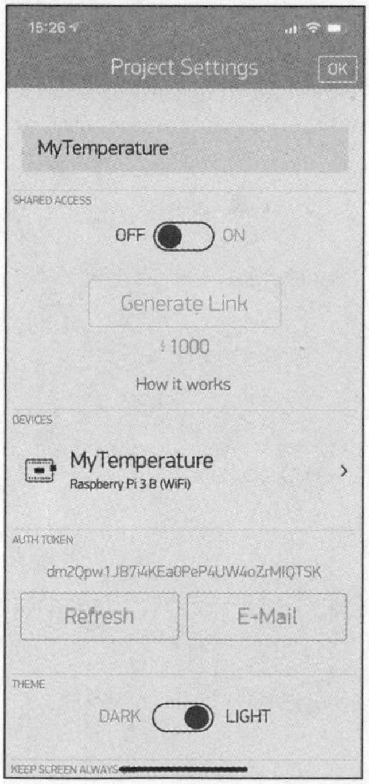

FIGURE 3-14:
The
authentication
token in the
MyTemperature
app project
settings.

You've completed the Blynk myTemperature app installation. Now let's modify the software to support the Blynk app.

The modified temperatureTest.py software for the Blynk app

To modify the software to support the Blynk app, follow these steps:

1. **Create a directory in your main directory by entering the following:**

```
cd
mkdir myTemperature
cd myTemperature
```

Now you're in the myTemperature directory.

2. **Install the Blynk library on the Raspberry Pi by cloning the library located at github.com. Use the following command in the Terminal window:**

```
git clone https://github.com/switchdoclabs/SDL_Pi_HDC1080_Python3.git
```

3. **Use nano (or your favorite editor) to enter the following code into a file named myTemperature.py:**

```
#!/usr/bin/env python3

#imports

import sys

sys.path.append('./SDL_Pi_HDC1080_Python3')

import time
import SDL_Pi_HDC1080

import requests
import json


BLYNK_URL = 'http://blynk-cloud.com/'
BLYNK_AUTH = 'xxxx'

# Main Program
print
print ("")
```

```
print ("Read Temperature and Humidity from HDC1080 using I2C bus and "
       "send to Blynk ")
print ("")

hdc1080 = SDL_Pi_HDC1080.SDL_Pi_HDC1080()

def blynkUpdate(temperature, humidity):
    print ("Updating Blynk")

    try:

        put_header={"Content-Type": "application/json"}
        val = temperature
        put_body = json.dumps(["{0:0.1f}".format(val)])
        r = requests.put(BLYNK_URL+BLYNK_AUTH+'/update/V0',
                         data=put_body, headers=put_header)


        put_header={"Content-Type": "application/json"}
        val = humidity
        put_body = json.dumps(["{0:0.1f}".format(val)])
        r = requests.put(BLYNK_URL+BLYNK_AUTH+'/update/V1',
                         data=put_body, headers=put_header)


        put_header={"Content-Type": "application/json"}
        val = time.strftime("%Y-%m-%d %H:%M:%S")
        put_body = json.dumps([val])
        r = requests.put(BLYNK_URL+BLYNK_AUTH+'/update/V2',
                         data=put_body, headers=put_header)

        return 1

    except Exception as e:
            print ("exception in updateBlynk")
            print (e)
            return 0

while True:

        temperature =  hdc1080.readTemperature()
        humidity = hdc1080.readHumidity()
```

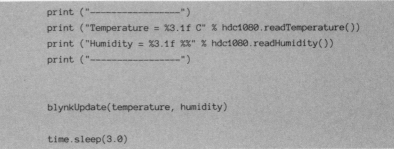

```
        print ("-----------------")
        print ("Temperature = %3.1f C" % hdc1080.readTemperature())
        print ("Humidity = %3.1f %%" % hdc1080.readHumidity())
        print ("-----------------")


        blynkUpdate(temperature, humidity)

        time.sleep(3.0)
```

This code updates your Blynk app every three seconds.

If you update your Blynk app more than once a second, you may be disconnected from the server. Be a good Blynk citizen and keep your updates to less than ten values per second.

4. **Replace the xxxx with the Blynk authorization token you copied in Step 4 in the preceding section.**

   For example, we replaced

   ```
   BLYNK_AUTH = 'xxxx'
   ```

   with

   ```
   BLYNK_AUTH = '445730794c1c4c8ea7852a31555f44444'
   ```

You must use the authorization code you were emailed. The example code shown here will not work.

Breaking down the code

Now let's break down the code section by section. The following code is similar to the HDC1080 code from earlier in this chapter, with the exception of the blynk-Update code:

```
def blynkUpdate(temperature, humidity):
    print ("Updating Blynk")
    try:
```

Why do we have a try: here? Because sometimes the requests library will throw an error if the Internet is being funky. The try: / except: code will trap any error from the requests library and continue to try again.

Next, we set up the required http header for the requests library:

```
put_header={"Content-Type": "application/json"}
```

THE REQUESTS LIBRARY

The Python requests library allows you to use Python to send HTTP/1.1 requests and access the response data of the requests. It's designed to enable humans to interact with http requests without exposing the complexity of the requests. Very Pythonic.

The following code sets the number of digits to the right of the decimal point to only 1 so we won't have long numbers of relatively meaningless digits because of the accuracy of the HDC1080:

```
val = temperature
put_body = json.dumps(["{0:0.1f}".format(val)])
```

The following code transfers the data to the Blynk server in the form of an http request:

```
r = requests.put(BLYNK_URL+BLYNK_AUTH+'/update/V0', data=put_body,
    headers=put_header)
```

Here we print to the Terminal screen any exception. If you get an authentication error, the except: clause will also help you figure out if you've set the Blynk authentication code incorrectly:

```
except Exception as e:
            print ("exception in updateBlynk")
            print (e)
            return 0
```

Next, let's run the program:

```
Sudo python3 myTemperature.py
```

You see this type of output on the terminal screen:

```
------------------
Temperature = 22.6 C
Humidity = 36.8 %
------------------
Updating Blynk
------------------
Temperature = 22.5 C
Humidity = 36.8 %
------------------
Updating Blynk
```

Tap the run icon (left-pointing triangle) at the top-right of your Blynk app on the phone, and then watch the data start to come in. If you don't get data in a few seconds, check your authentication code and make sure you've started the app by tapping the run icon in the upper-right corner of the app.

Your results should look like Figure 3-15.

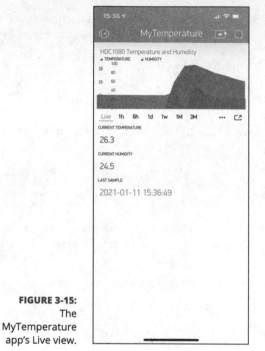

FIGURE 3-15:
The
MyTemperature
app's Live view.

Note that the Live display on the graph can look a little strange. However, your other displays (selected by clicking 1h, 5h, 1d, and so on below the graph) will start filling in and look the way you would expect a graph of your local temperature should look.

Where to Go from Here

In this chapter, you learned a lot about how to connect to the physical world on your Raspberry Pi. To build on your new expertise, we suggest that you make some of the following modifications to your project:

» Add more I2C sensors to your Raspberry Pi. You can choose from hundreds.

» Add a digital sensor to your Pi, such as a PIR detector to detect warm bodies (such as humans) in front of your Raspberry Pi.

» Add an I2C compass and accelerometer to your Pi.

» Build larger and more complex dashboards, and show off your project by sharing your authentication code with your friends.

» Add a motor to make things move. Oh wait! You do that in the next chapter!

Chapter **4**

Making Things Move

Making things move around with Python is undeniably cool. With motors, physical computing goes to a whole new level.

Robots, microwaves, refrigerators, and electric cars use electric motors to move around, blow air, pump coolant, and take you 60 mph wherever you want to go. Electric motors are everywhere — they consume more than half the electric energy produced in the United States.

At its simplest, an electric motor is a machine that converts electrical energy into mechanical energy. In this chapter, we talk about DC (direct current) motors. Direct current is a single, fixed voltage, such as 9V or 5V or 3.3V. Alternating current (AC), on the other hand, is what you get out of your house outlets.

To download the code for this chapter, go to www.dummies.com/go/pythonaiofd2e.

Exploring Electric Motors

All motors use magnets to create motion. All magnets have a north and a south pole. North to north and south to south repel each other whereas north and south attract. Clever people have figured out how to use this fact to create motion. We're all familiar with permanent magnets, like the ones you use to hang things on the front of your refrigerator. However, you can also create magnets (specifically, a magnetic field) by running a current around a coiled wire. By periodically reversing the current through this electromagnet, you can create force, which then becomes motion. There are many ways to build motors, but the electromagnet is the fundamental basis of all of them.

In this chapter, we describe three common types of motors used in small projects and robots:

>> Small DC motors

>> Servo motors

>> Stepper motors

Small DC motors

A *DC motor* has two wires: power and ground. (See Figure 4-1.) When you supply power (putting 5V on the power line, for example), the motor will start spinning. Reverse the power and ground wires, and the motor will spin in the opposite direction.

FIGURE 4-1:
A DC motor on a small robot.

You control the speed of a DC motor by using pulse width modulation (PWM), a technique you saw in Chapter 1 of this minibook for controlling the brightness of an LED. If the power is cycled at 50 percent (half on/half off), the motor will spin at one-half the speed. These DC motors are inexpensive and great for driving wheels. Sometimes we put an encoder on the motor shaft so we can read how far the shaft has turned, giving the computer some feedback that can be useful.

Use a DC motor anytime you want something to be spun at a particular revolutions per minute (RPM), such as a fan or a car wheel.

Servo motors

A *servo motor* is generally a combination of three things: a DC motor, a simple control circuit, and a set of gears. Sometimes a servo motor includes a potentiometer (variable resistor) that will give position feedback like the encoder in the DC motor discussed in the preceding section.

The servo motor is commanded to go to a specific position by using our friend PWM again. However, in this case, a specific pulse wave holds the motor in a specific position and resists a load or a force trying to move the motor. The maximum amount of force that the servo motor can exert against an external force or load is called the *torque rating*. Servos are continuously powered and generally have only about a 180 degree range of motion.

You find servo motors in flaps on model RC (remote control) airplanes, rudder control on RC boats, and some types of robot arms. When you want to move an object and hold it at a specific position, a servo motor is often the answer.

Stepper motors

A *stepper motor* is similar to a servo motor but uses a different method to move the shaft. See Figure 4-2. Whereas a servo motor uses a DC motor, a stepper motor uses multiple-toothed electromagnets surrounding a central-toothed shaft.

Stepper motors use an external controller (you'll use the Raspberry Pi) that sequences the electromagnets surrounding the central shaft to make it turn in steps, hence the name stepper motor. Unlike a servo motor, a stepper motor provides a steady holding torque even when it's not powered up and doesn't require a feedback system to determine its position. As long as the load is within the limits of the servo motor torque, there are no positional errors.

Stepper motors are for slow, precise rotation. 3D printers are a great example of the use of stepper motors.

FIGURE 4-2:
Sun-tracking solar
panels using a
stepper motor.

Next, we get to have some fun showing you how to use Python to control these three types of motors with GPIO (general-purpose input–output) pins and an I2C controller.

Controlling a DC Motor

You can drive DC motors from a Raspberry Pi in lots of different ways. Dozens of robot controllers and motor controller boards will work for this project. The one we use is an I2C controlled board (tying in with our projects from the last chapter), which gives us control over two motors, their individual direction, and their individual speed. Pretty cool.

Here is the parts list:

- » **Pi2Grover Grove interface board:** Buy this at https://shop.switchdoc. com or https://amazon.com.

- » **Grove I2C motor driver:** Available (with a Grove cable) at www.seeedstudio. com or https://amazon.com.

- » **Two small DC motors:** Go to www.adafruit.com/product/711 or https:// amazon.com.

For more on the Pi2Grover board, refer to Chapters 1–3 of this minibook. Let's spend some time on the Grove I2C motor driver because it has a unique way of controlling motors.

Grove I2C motor driver

The Grove I2C motor drive, shown in Figure 4-3, can drive two motors at the same time, all controlled by the I2C bus from the Raspberry Pi. The I2C motor driver handles all the complexity of controlling the DC motors while presenting a simple way of controlling the motors via a Python program.

FIGURE 4-3: The Grove I2C motor driver.

The Grove I2C driver can drive up to 2A for each motor, but we are using motors a lot smaller than that. It can optionally handle 6V to 15V motors, but again, we are using small motors, so we will just use the Raspberry Pi power supply. If you're using bigger motors or want to use an external power supply, you can still use this board.

Figure 4-4 shows the components on the I2C motor driver board. Note that the board has another small computer, an Atmega 8L, which emulates an I2C interface, processes commands coming from your Raspberry Pi, and then controls the motors — all at once. Yet another example of how even boards for little computers have little computers on them. Computers are everywhere!

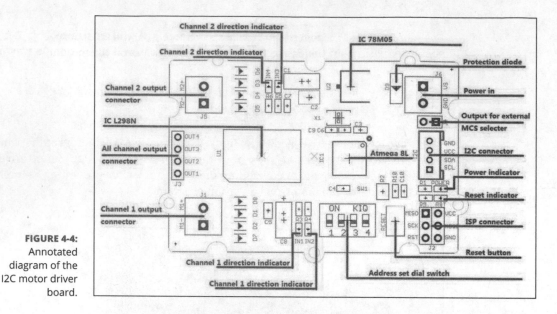

FIGURE 4-4:
Annotated
diagram of the
I2C motor driver
board.

You can see the two motor connections on the left side of the board. LEDs on the board show what the board is currently controlling and powering. Figure 4-5 shows the Adafruit DC motor.

FIGURE 4-5:
The Adafruit DC
motor.

Let's wire the motors and the motor controller and start our engines! Shut down and turn off the power on your Raspberry Pi before you follow these steps:

1. **Loosen the set of two screw terminals on the end of the I2C motor controller board and insert the bare end of the wires on the motors (see Figure 4-6) into the holes.**

Note that with DC motors, it doesn't matter which color wire goes in which screw hole. The motor will just rotate in the opposite direction. Just match the colors into each side as you wire both motors. We added some length to the wires, but that is optional. Figure 4-7 shows the installed motor on your Grove I2C motor drive board.

FIGURE 4-6:
The wires in the I2C motor drive screw terminals.

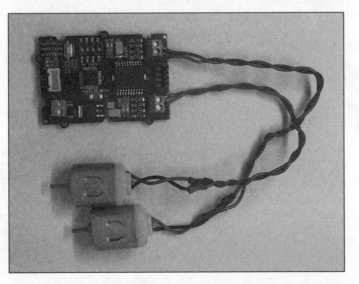

FIGURE 4-7:
Motors installed on the motor drive.

2. **Check that you have the jumper in place on the board (refer to Figure 4-4).**

   The jumper is called *Output for external MCU selector* in the diagram. It comes that way in the package, but make sure anyway. The board won't operate as wired if the jumper is not installed.

3. **Plug one end of a Grove cable into the Grove connector on the Grove I2 motor driver board and plug the other end into an I2C Grove connector on the Pi2Grover board.**

Now, power up the Raspberry Pi so you can start writing some Python! After power up, all five LEDs should be lit on the Grove I2C motor drive board. If not, shut down the Pi again and check your wiring.

Python DC motor software

DC motors are often used for robot wheels, so the words *forward* and *backward* should start to give you some ideas for later in the book when you build a robot car.

The software we use for the Python DC motor experiment will be familiar because it's similar to the I2C project software we dealt with in Chapters 2 and 3.

The use of Python libraries is key to being productive in writing Python applications. We use `SDL_Pi_GroveI2CMotorDrive`, which is available on `https://github.com/switchdoclabs`.

TIP

If your I2C motor driver board and motor don't respond after hookup, try pressing the Reset button on the I2C motor driver board. (The button is in the lower-right corner of Figure 4-4.) Figure 4-8 shows the assembled motor and I2C motor driver board.

To set up the software, follow these steps:

1. **Create a directory in your main directory by entering the following:**

   ```
   cd
   mkdir dcMotor
   cd dcMotor
   ```

   Now you're in the dcMotor directory.

FIGURE 4-8:
The DC motor
setup.

2. **Install the** `SDL_Pi_GroveI2CMotorDrive Python3` **library on the Raspberry Pi by using the following command in your Terminal window to clone the library:**

```
git clone https://github.com/switchdoclabs/SDL_Pi_GroveI2CMotorDrive.git
```

The `git clone` command clones the `git` repository located at the address and copies it to your Raspberry Pi. If you enter `ls` in the terminal window, you'll see the following output:

```
pi@RPi3-60:~/dcMotor $ ls
SDL_Pi_GroveI2CMotorDrive
```

3. **Using nano (or your favorite text editor), create a file called `dcmotorTest.py` and enter the following code:**

```python
import sys
sys.path.append("./SDL_Pi_GroveI2CMotorDrive")


import SDL_Pi_GroveI2CMotorDrive
import time

#"0b1010" defines the output polarity
```

```
#"10" means the M+ is "positive" while the M- is "negative"

MOTOR_FORWARD =  0b1010
MOTOR_BACKWARD =  0b0101


try:

    m= SDL_Pi_GroveI2CMotorDrive.motor_drive()

    #FORWARD
    print("Forward")
    #defines the speed of motor 1 and motor 2;)
    m.MotorSpeedSetAB(100,100)
    m.MotorDirectionSet(MOTOR_FORWARD)
    time.sleep(2)

    #BACK
    print("Back")
    m.MotorSpeedSetAB(100,100)
    #0b0101  Rotating in the opposite direction
    m.MotorDirectionSet(MOTOR_BACKWARD)
    time.sleep(2)

    #STOP
    print("Stop")
    m.MotorSpeedSetAB(0,0)
    time.sleep(1)

    #Increase speed
    for i in range (100):
        print("Speed:",i)
        m.MotorSpeedSetAB(i,i)
        time.sleep(.02)
    print("Stop")
    m.MotorSpeedSetAB(0,0)

except IOError:
    print("Unable to find the I2C motor drive")
    print("Hit Reset Button on I2C Motor Drive and Try Again")
```

This program runs both motors forward at full speed (100), runs them backward at full speed, stops the motors, runs them backward at a slow speed ramping up to full speed, and then stops the motors.

The key aspects of this software are calls to the SDL_Pi_GroveI2CMotorDrive library. The library supports the following functions:

- » MotorSpeedSetAB(*MotorSpeedA*, *MotorSpeedB*): This function sets the motor speed for the A motor (M1) and the B motor (M2). The range for the motor speed is 0–100.

- » MotorDirectionSet(*Direction*): This function controls whether the motors go forward or backward by using the constants set in the program, which are MOTOR_FORWARD = 0b1010 and MOTOR_BACKWARD = 0b0101.

The SDL_Pi_GroveI2CMotorDrive library uses the smbus library, one of many I2C Python libraries available. For example, in the smbus library, you send the command to the I2C board as a block write consisting of the I2C address, a command byte, and then the arguments. Here is the I2C smbus call for setting the motor direction:

```
#Set motor direction
def MotorDirectionSet(self,Direction):
    bus.write_i2c_block_data(self.I2CMotorDriveAdd, self.DirectionSet,
        [Direction,0])
    time.sleep(.02)
```

Time to run the DC motors. Type this in your Terminal window:

```
sudo python3 testMotor.py
```

You are rewarded by seeing the LEDs change and the motors go through the sequence you programmed in Python. You should be able to make your own sequences easily from this example.

WARNING

All these motors take power from the Raspberry Pi when running, so shut down the Pi and then disconnect the DC motors when you're ready to move to the next section.

Running a Servo Motor

A servo motor is a different beast than a DC motor. A servo motor has a DC motor inside, but it also has a controller circuit that allows you to move and hold the DC motor at a specific position. Servo motors are great on a robot arm, where you want the arm to move to a specific position, but not so great for an application that requires a circular motion, such as wheels on a robot.

You control servo motors by using PWM (pulse width modulation). Although you can buy boards that will do PWM (and support bigger servo motors!) under control of your computer, for this small servo we will be using the built-in PWM capability of the GPIO (general purpose input-output) pins of the Raspberry Pi.

Here is the parts list:

>> **Pi2Grover Grove interface board:** Buy this at https://shop.switchdoc. com or https://amazon.com.

>> **SG90 micro servo motor:** Try www.ebay.com or https://amazon.com. These motors are inexpensive, so you may end up having to buy two or more for under $10.

>> **A package of Grove male jumper patch cables:** You want the Grove-4-male-pin-to-Grove-conversion cables, which are available at https://shop. switchdoc.com/products/grove-4-pin-male-jumper-to-grove-4-pin-conversion-cable-5-pcs-per-pack and https://amzn.to/3nyGbic.

We describe the Pi2Grover in Chapters 1, 2, and 3 of this minibook.

The SG90 micro servo motor, shown in Figure 4-9, is a small, inexpensive servo motor available from many sources. It can turn about 90 degrees in each direction, for a total of 180 degrees. It has an operating voltage of 3.0V to 7.0V with a current draw of about 40mA (40 milliamps; a milliamp is 1/1000th of an amp of current) at maximum, so the 5V on the Raspberry Pi can easily operate this servo.

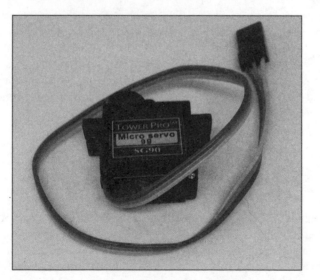

FIGURE 4-9: The SG90 micro servo with wires.

HOW MUCH CURRENT CAN THE RASPBERRY PI SUPPLY TO THE 5V PINS?

Are you wondering how much current the Raspberry Pi 3 can supply to the 5V pins? Unfortunately, there isn't a simple answer to this question because it depends on what is connected to the Raspberry Pi 3 and the type of USB power supply you're using. 250mA is a good number as a general rule, but if you have a beefy 5V USB power supply (say 2.5A), you can go a lot higher, up to 1000mA or more. The Raspberry Pi 3 has a 2.5A fuse on the 5V power supply. The fuse is resettable, so if you pop it, just let it cool down and it will work again.

Most servo motors, including the SG90, have three control wires:

>> Yellow: PWM control signal

>> Red: Power (5V, in our case)

>> Brown: Ground

You use the Grove-male-pin-to-Grove-connector patch cables, shown in Figure 4-10, to make a connection between the three pins on the servo to a Grove connector. Then you can plug the Grove end of the cable into your Raspberry Pi Pi2Grover board.

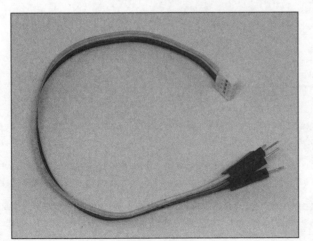

FIGURE 4-10: Grove male-pin-to Grove-connector patch cable.

Now let's connect the wires and make the servo motor rock!

1. **Shut down your Raspberry Pi and remove power.**

2. **Plug one end of the Grove patch cable into your SB90 servo motor (see Figure 4-11), following the wire chart in Table 4-1.**

   Check your wiring carefully. You can damage your Pi and motor if you reverse these wires.

WARNING

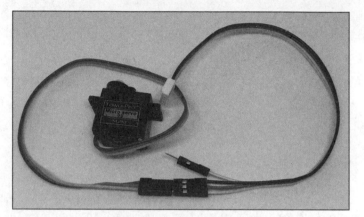

FIGURE 4-11:
Servo motor correctly wired to the patch cable.

TABLE 4-1

Servo Motor to Patch Cable Wiring

SG90 Servo	Grove Patch Cable	Function
Yellow wire	Yellow wire	PWM signal
Red wire	Red wire	Power
Brown wire	Black wire	Ground

3. **Plug the other end of the Grove patch cable into the Pi2Grover Grove connector marked D4/D5.**

4. **Put a piece of electrical tape or blue tape over the unused white exposed pin on the Grove patch cable to keep it from shorting something.**

5. **Put one of the supplied rocker arms on the servo motor gear so you can more easily see its range of motion, as shown in Figure 4-12.**

Now let's look at the Python software.

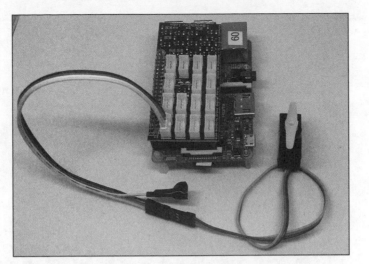

FIGURE 4-12:
Fully connected Pi
and servo motor.

Python servo software

To control the servo motor, we aren't going to use a higher-level servo library
(and there are many available for the Raspberry Pi in Python). Instead, we us GPIO
and the PWM function of the RPi GPIO built-in library. Okay, okay. We *are* using a
library (RPi.GPIO), but we're not adding layers of API (application programming
interface) calls like we normally would do. We're getting down and dirty with the
GPIO pins. To do so, follow these steps:

1. **Create a directory in your main directory by entering the following:**

```
cd
mkdir Servo
cd Servo
```

2. **Using nano (or another text editor), create a file called servoTest.py and
enter the following Python code:**

```
import RPi.GPIO as GPIO
import time


GPIO.setmode(GPIO.BCM)
ServoPin = 4

GPIO.setup(ServoPin, GPIO.OUT)

p = GPIO.PWM(ServoPin, 50)
p.start(7.5)
```

```
    try:
        while True:
            p.ChangeDutyCycle(7.5)   # turn towards 90 degree
            print ("90 degrees")
            time.sleep(1) # sleep 1 second
            print ("0 degrees")
            p.ChangeDutyCycle(2.5)   # turn towards 0 degree
            time.sleep(1) # sleep 1 second
            print ("180 degrees")
            p.ChangeDutyCycle(12.5) # turn towards 180 degree
            time.sleep(1) # sleep 1 second


    except KeyboardInterrupt:
        p.stop()
        GPIO.cleanup()
```

Breaking down the code

Time to go through the code line by line and understand the functionality. The following code sets the pin number to the D4/5 Grove connector on the Pi2Grover board:

```
import RPi.GPIO as GPIO
import time


GPIO.setmode(GPIO.BCM)
ServoPin = 4
```

Next, we use GPIO.OUT to set the GPIO pin to output:

```
GPIO.setup(ServoPin, GPIO.OUT)
```

This command sets an object p to the ServoPin (4) at a frequency of 50Hz.

```
p = GPIO.PWM(ServoPin, 50)
```

Different PWM values move the motor from one end of its range of motion to the other. For our motors, we empirically found that a duty cycle of 2.5 percent moved the motor to its start position at 0 degrees, 7.5 percent positioned the motor at 90 degrees, and 12.5 percent moved the motor to its extreme position of 180 degrees. These values are similar for most small servos. For a good beginner's tutorial on servo motors, go to www.raspberrypi.org/blog/how-to-use-a-servo-motor-with-raspberry-pi/.

```
p.start(7.5)
```

The numbers we use to move the servo in the following code are determined by servo type. For our servo, we use the constant 7.5 and the numbers 2.5 and 12.5:

```
try:
    while True:
        p.ChangeDutyCycle(7.5)  # turn towards 90 degree
        print ("90 degrees")
        time.sleep(1) # sleep 1 second
        print ("0 degrees")
        p.ChangeDutyCycle(2.5)  # turn towards 0 degree
        time.sleep(1) # sleep 1 second
        print ("180 degrees")
        p.ChangeDutyCycle(12.5) # turn towards 180 degree
        time.sleep(1) # sleep 1 second
```

Note how we put the entire body of this program in a try: except: clause. Now, when you press Ctrl-C to exit the program, it will shut down the servo motor and release the GPIO pins back to the operating system. This pin cleanup is a good thing to do when you deal with GPIO pins directly.

```
except KeyboardInterrupt:
    p.stop()
    GPIO.cleanup()
```

Now it's time to run the program. Type the following in a Terminal window:

```
sudo python3 servoTest.py
```

The screen prints the following lines and your servo happily obeys your programmed orders:

```
90 degrees
0 degrees
180 degrees
90 degrees
0 degrees
180 degrees
90 degrees
0 degrees
```

Try different angles and sequences by changing the code and the constants in the p.ChangeDutyCycle function. You won't hurt the servo.

Now we have a servo motor working on our Raspberry Pi. You can see why you use a DC motor for wheels and a servo for non-rotating tasks. In the next mini-book, you see a robot car that uses DC motors to turn the back wheels with the steering of the front wheels. Remember at the beginning when we told you a servo motor can move an robot arm, a flap on an RC airplane, or a rudder on an RC boat? Watching the servo motor go through its programmed sequence should spark ideas about other things to do with a servo motor.

Experiment and build your own magical projects! Now we step right down the line to our last major motor, a stepper motor.

Making a Stepper Motor Step

Stepper motors are a different beast than DC motors or servo motors. A stepper motor can accurately position items by using a digital interface. You can accurately position things with a servo motor too, but the task requires more electronics and positional feedback.

A stepper motor gets around the positional inaccuracy of servo motors by accurately moving from one step to another under command of software. The stepper motor advances the motor one step by sending a specific sequence to two electromagnetic coils. See Figure 4-13. You implement this stepping sequence in the Python software controlling the stepper motor.

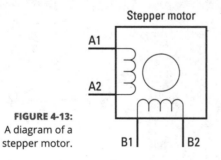

FIGURE 4-13:
A diagram of a
stepper motor.

A stepper motor typically has two coils to move the motor from one step to another.

Tables 4-2 and 4-3 show the sequence for stepping the stepper motor one step forward and backward, respectively. This pattern of steps will be obvious in our Python software.

TABLE 4-2 **Forward Stepping the Stepper**

Coil_A_1 (Pin 12)	Coil_A_2 (Pin 20)	Coil_B_1 (Pin 13)	Coil_B_2 (Pin 21)
1	0	1	0
0	1	1	0
0	1	0	1
1	0	0	1

TABLE 4-3 **Backward Stepping the Stepper**

Coil_A_1 (Pin 12)	Coil_A_2 (Pin 20)	Coil_B_1 (Pin 13)	Coil_B_2 (Pin 21)
1	0	0	1
0	1	0	1
0	1	1	0
1	0	1	0

In Figure 4-14, this digital sequence is graphically portrayed with a logic analyzer connected to the Raspberry Pi GPIO pins used to drive the stepper motor.

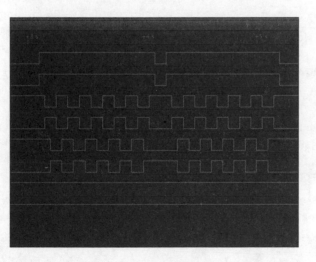

FIGURE 4-14: Logic analyzer showing the motor stepping sequence.

FEEDBACK: WHAT A USEFUL THING!

Feedback occurs when you route a system's output back into its inputs as a loop. Sound complicated? It can be, but the basics are simple. Suppose you publish an article and ask for comments. People supply comments (nice ones, we hope) and you change the article based on some of those comments. That's feedback!

You use feedback in electrical circuits to achieve a better and more accurate positioning of a servo motor, for example. By reading an encoder on the shaft of the servo (an encoder gives you an electrical signal proportional to the position of the shaft), your software can use that feedback to tweak the PWM duty cycle to get a more accurate position.

There are two types of feedback: negative feedback and positive feedback. Good comments and constructive criticism about our article are examples of positive feedback, whereas comments just saying the article is bad are examples of negative feedback.

In electronics, however, you generally tend to like negative feedback and not like positive feedback. We use negative feedback to get closer to the desired position on the shaft. Positive feedback tends to make differences get larger. Ever hear a speaker wail when you put a microphone too close the speaker? That's positive feedback.

Well, now you know all you need to know about stepper motors to build your first project. Here is the parts list:

>> **Pi2Grover Grove interface board:** Buy this at https://shop.switchdoc. com or https://amazon.com. We described the Pi2Grover in Chapters 1, 2, and 3 of this minibook.

>> **28BYJ-48 ULN2003 5V stepper motor:** Try www.ebay.com or https://amzn. to/2BuNDV1. This type of motor is inexpensive, so you may end up having to buy five for $12. Make sure you get the ones with the driver boards (such as the ones at the Amazon.com link).

>> **A package of Grove female patch cables, specifically Grove-connector-to-female-pins:** Available at https://shop.switchdoc.com/products/grove-4-pin-female-jumper-to-grove-4-pin-conversion-cable-5-pcs-per-pack https://amzn.to/3i5u6jf.

The 28BYJ-48, shown in Figure 4-15, is a 5V stepper motor that has 5.625 x 1/64 degrees per step (approximately 0.822 degrees per step). The motor has a driver board with a ULN2003 motor driver chip and, best of all, four LEDs that indicate how your program is changing the GPIO pins connected to the motor.

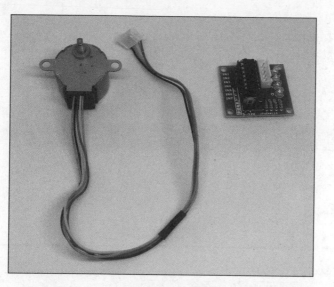

FIGURE 4-15:
The 28BYJ-48 stepper motor and UNL2003 driver board.

The female Grove patch cables, shown in Figure 4-16, connect the stepper motor drive board to the Raspberry Pi.

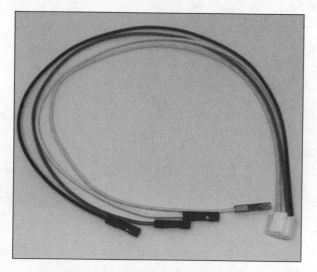

FIGURE 4-16:
A Grove-connector-to-female-pin-header patch cable.

Time to build your stepper motor project! Just follow these steps:

1. **Shut down your Raspberry Pi and remove power.**

2. **Connect a Grove female patch cord to the UNL2003 driver board according to the wire chart in Table 4-4.**

Note that we put a wire tie on the cable to keep things neat and tidy. Look carefully at your red and black wire on the Grove patch cord to make sure it's plugged in correctly, as shown in Figure 4-17.

TABLE 4-4

First Grove Female Patch Cord to UNL2003 Driver Board

Grove Patch Cable	UNL2003 Driver Board	Function
Yellow wire	IN1	Coil A_1
White wire	IN2	Coil B_1
Red wire	+	Power
Black wire	−	Ground

FIGURE 4-17: Closeup of power connections on the UNL2003 driver board.

3. **Connect a second Grove female patch cord to the UNL2003 driver board, as shown in the wire chart in Table 4-5.**

Use a wire tie or a piece of tape to keep the unused red and black wires out of the way, as shown in Figure 4-18.

TABLE 4-5

Second Grove Female Patch Cord to UNL2003 Driver Board

Grove Patch Cable	UNL2003 Driver Board	Function
Yellow wire	IN3	Coil A_2
White wire	IN4	Coil B_3
Red wire	No Connect	
Black wire	No Connect	

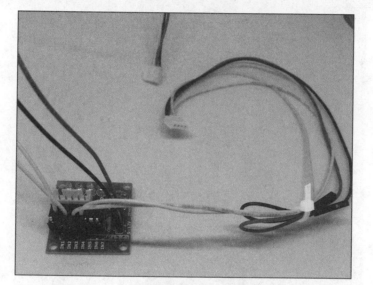

FIGURE 4-18:
Second Grove
patch cable
attached.

4. **Check all your connections again and make sure they look like those in Figure 4-19.**

5. **Plug the 28BYJ-4 stepper motor cable into the UNL2003 driver board connector, as shown in Figure 4-20.**

   The cable is keyed, so it goes in only one way.

6. **Plug the first Grove patch cable (the one with all four wires connected to the UNL2003 driver board) into the Pi2Grover Grove connector marked D12/13.**

FIGURE 4-19:
All patch wires
installed on the
UNL2003 driver
board.

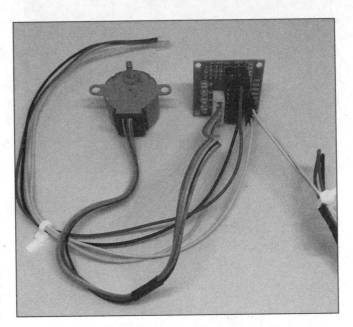

FIGURE 4-20:
Stepper motor
and driver board
connected.

7. **Plug the second Grove patch cable (the one with the yellow and white wires connected) into the Pi2Grove Grove connector marked D20/21.**

The wiring is now complete. The fully wired system is shown in Figure 4-21.

8. **Put a cardboard arrow on your stepper motor shaft so you can more easily see it move, as shown in Figure 4-22.**

FIGURE 4-21:
Fully wired
Raspberry Pi and
stepper motor
project.

FIGURE 4-22:
Stepper motor,
ready to step.

Python stepper software

Similar to what we did with the servo motor, we aren't going to use a higher-level stepper library. Instead, we will control a stepper motor directly by using GPIO pins. Just follow these steps:

1. **Create a directory in your main directory by entering the following:**

```
cd
mkdir Stepper
cd Servo
```

2. **Using nano (or another text editor), create a file called** `stepperTest.py` **and enter the following Python code:**

```
import sys

import RPi.GPIO as GPIO
import time

GPIO.setmode(GPIO.BCM)
GPIO.setwarnings(False)
coil_A_1_pin = 12
coil_B_1_pin = 13
coil_A_2_pin = 20
coil_B_2_pin = 21

GPIO.setup(coil_A_1_pin, GPIO.OUT)
GPIO.setup(coil_A_2_pin, GPIO.OUT)
GPIO.setup(coil_B_1_pin, GPIO.OUT)
GPIO.setup(coil_B_2_pin, GPIO.OUT)


def forward(delay, steps):
  for i in range(0, steps):
    setStep(1, 0, 1, 0)
    time.sleep(delay)
    setStep(0, 1, 1, 0)
    time.sleep(delay)
    setStep(0, 1, 0, 1)
    time.sleep(delay)
    setStep(1, 0, 0, 1)
    time.sleep(delay)
def backwards(delay, steps):
    for i in range(0, steps):
    setStep(1, 0, 0, 1)
```

```
        time.sleep(delay)
        setStep(0, 1, 0, 1)
        time.sleep(delay)
        setStep(0, 1, 1, 0)
        time.sleep(delay)
        setStep(1, 0, 1, 0)
        time.sleep(delay)


def setStep(w1, w2, w3, w4):
  GPIO.output(coil_A_1_pin, w1)
  GPIO.output(coil_A_2_pin, w2)
  GPIO.output(coil_B_1_pin, w3)
  GPIO.output(coil_B_2_pin, w4)

while True:

  try:

    # Delay between steps (milliseconds)
    delay = 10
    # How many Steps forward
    steps = 50
    forward(int(delay) / 1000.0, int(steps))
    # How many Steps backwards
    steps = 50
    backwards(int(delay) / 1000.0, int(steps))

  except KeyboardInterrupt:
    # shut off all coils
    setStep(0,0,0,0)
    sys.exit()
```

The try: except: clause at the end of the program shuts off all GPIO pin outputs and returns them to the operating system for future use when you press Ctrl+C to stop the program.

Breaking down the code

We've written our first stepper motor control software, and now it's time to see how it works. The stepperTest.py code is pretty simple. We set the GPIO outputs to 1 and 0, according to the stepper motor sequences shown in Tables 4-2 and 4-3. You can see the exact sequences in the code in the forward() and backwards() functions.

Now let's run the code and start stepping away. Power up your Pi and open a Terminal window. Note that all four of the LEDs turn on when you power up, as shown in Figure 4-23, but they will be turned off when you run your Python program.

FIGURE 4-23:
The Raspberry
Pi running the
stepper motor.

The stepper motor turns 50 steps to the left and then 50 steps to the right. Try changing those variables in the program to move the stepper motor to other positions. Do you see how these motors can be used in 3D printers and robots to accurately position printing heads, bed height, and robot arms?

With all you've learned in this minibook, you're ready to build a robot that you can control with Python.

7

Building Robots

Contents at a Glance

Chapter **1**

Introducing Robotics

R*obots.* That name has been bandied about for a hundred years. It comes from a Czech word, *robota*, which means "involuntary labor." It was first used in the 1920 play "R.U.R. – Rossum's Universal Robots" by Karel Capek, but it was really Capek's brother Josef who coined the word. Did you know there was a robot in Frank Baum's land of Oz in 1907? He didn't call it a robot, but it's definitely a robot.

Robots are everywhere in today's modern world. Your house is filled with them. How is that possible? To understand what we are talking about, you need to understand the definition of *robot* more in computer-science terms than in Hollywood's.

A Robot Is Not Always Like a Human

Two things to know about robots:

» Robots have only two features, a computer and an actuator.

» Robots are dumb. We call this rule #1. Robots are not people.

Robots have a computer of some kind; think of it as the machine's brain. These brains can vary from IBM's Watson to a small 8-bit processor with a few thousand bytes of RAM. (You will see this with Baxter the Coffee-Making Robot, which has 16 computers inside. But more on that in a moment.)

The computers don't even have to be in the robot itself. You can have a network connection to the computer controlling the robot. Some of these computers run a servo motor or joint, while others control the joints as a group. We can think of the control computer as the robot's brain. This group joint action is similar to the way our joint reflexes work without getting our brain involved.

So, what is an actuator? It is something that physically affects the world outside. Under this definition, a sophisticated IoT (Internet of Things) device connected to a sensor and a database is not really a robot, whereas a computer that controls a toaster actuator to pop up the toasted bread is a robot. As with any definition, you can argue corner cases all day. But this is a good working definition that shows just how varied the body type of a robot can be.

Not Every Robot Has Arms or Wheels

The classic conception of a robot tends to look at least vaguely human. The amazing robots that help assemble cars in factories, for example, have giant arms that pick up car doors, weld metal, place windshields, and do many other assembly line tasks. Smaller arms in manufacturing lines all over the world help to produce small goods as well as large ones.

One of the relatively new categories of robots is called a *cobot* (*collaborative robot*). This type of robot is designed to work closely alongside humans in manufacturing lines. Robots in car lines will hurt you if you get in their way, but cobots will stop if they encounter you. Cobots do tasks to make people more efficient. Baxter the Coffee-Making Robot is an example of a cobot.

Robots don't always have arms (remember the toaster?). Robots can look like microwaves. They can look like cars (yes, self-driving cars, but also like your current car). Modern-day cars are filled with computers doing robotic things. For example, a computer measures how hard you push down on the gas pedal and adjusts the fuel-and-air mixture accordingly. A sensor reads the position of the gas pedal and transmits that signal to a computer, which then controls the engine. No cables physically connect your pedal to a mechanical gas pump or valve. In the 2019 BMW X3s, for example, you can push a button to switch from comfort mode to sport mode, which changes the way the wheel feels (and how much feedback you get from the road), the way the gas pedal responds, and even how the suspension reacts to road conditions. (See Figure 1-1.) In a modern car, more than 20 computers do all sorts of things and talk to each other constantly.

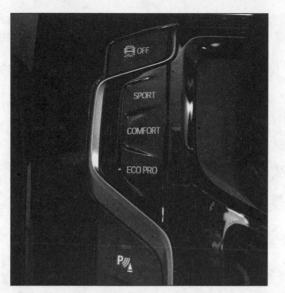

FIGURE 1-1:
Inputs for the
BMW robot
driving system.

When you mention robots, people usually think of the large arms in assembly lines or those fabulous robotic dogs made by Boston Dynamic. However, many other types of robots exist, as you discover in the following sections.

The Wilkinson bread-making robot

Wilkinson Baking (www.wilkinsonbaking.com), in Walla Walla, Washington, has invented a robotic bread-making system (see Figure 1-2) that may bring bread-baking back to local stores and away from giant bread plants. By the way, they claim that their bread requires one-sixth of the fossil fuel needed to get the product to the consumer.

This type of disruption has happened before. Remember when you sent photographic film away to big plants to get it developed? Then suddenly, machines (yes, robots) were built that allowed mom-and-pop stores to get back into the film-development and picture-printing business. Yes, the proliferation of digital cameras took most of that business way, but you can see the point.

Baxter, the coffee-making robot

Baxter is a general-purpose cobot manufactured by Rethink Robotics in 2011 (see Figure 1-3). Although he is a fairly old cobot, he has a fabulous set of sensors and cameras (one in each arm!) and each arm has a different attachment (a gripper on the left and a suction cup on the right). This setup allows students to build some sophisticated projects.

Baxter has more than 16 different computers inside: a main computer (a desktop Dell PC, believe it or not) strapped to his torso and individual computers controlling the joints, cameras, and sensors in both arms. Baxter's brain for the coffee-making program (all in Python) is located across the room and is connected to Baxter by a network connection. The main program in the brain computer uses a distributed ROS (robot operating system) to be controlled and provide information and images to the user and the controlling computer. Take a look at the video at https://youtu.be/zVL8760H768.

Three students in the University of Idaho's Advanced Robotics class were called on to teach Baxter to make coffee in their senior robotics class, and after three months and thousands of lines of code, they succeeded. The team used machine vision techniques to recognize when the coffee was done, connect Baxter to the Amazon AWS Cloud so they could use Alexa ("Alexa, tell Baxter the Robot to make coffee"), and write a variety of pick-and-place code to select a Keurig cup and to deliver a full cup of coffee to the customer's table.

Now that Baxter can do all these tasks, he appears much smarter, but rule #1 still applies ("Robots are dumb"). He can make coffee, but he can't make toaster strudel . . . yet. Next semester.

By the way, we all know what software bugs are. Bugs in robotics projects can be interesting to watch because the robot may do something completely different than what you intended. Software bugs in robotics programs can lead to physical consequences. Spilled coffee in this case.

The Griffin Bluetooth-enabled toaster

You really didn't think we were going to finish these examples of robots without using a toaster, did you? The Griffin Bluetooth-enabled toaster was presented at CES (Consumer Electronic Show) as part of suite of connected kitchen appliances. (See Figure 1-4.) It allows you to program (by app) your desired level of toasty crispness, and it can send your phone a notification when your toast is done. Also, it looks like it never went into production, which is a great disappointment to John because he wants a connected toaster. Really, really wants one. Here is a link to a YouTube video for the toaster: www.youtube.com/watch?v=Z7h8-f-k8C8.

Enough examples. Let's now move into to what makes a robot and how we program them in Python!

FIGURE 1-4:
The Toasteroid
Internet-
connected
toaster.

Understanding the Main Parts of a Robot

All robots have four general types of components:

>> Computers

>> Motors and actuators

>> Communications

>> Sensors

In this section, we describe each component in turn.

Computers

Computers are ubiquitous in robotics. Computers control cameras and motors, interpret the images coming in from the cameras, and read the sensors monitoring the environment around the robot.

These computers are mostly small computers called *embedded systems*. They may have only one dedicated function (such as monitoring the amount of current used for a specific motor), or they may be coordinating an entire set of motors in an arm, telling the other computers what to do.

Higher-level computers in the system are used for planning and receiving orders from other robots (or, say, an assembly line itself) and people. And most of these higher-level computers are programmed in Python.

Motors and actuators

Adding motors and actuators makes a robot more than just a computer (such as your laptop). Motors move things and come in all sorts of types and sizes. (Refer to Book 6 for an introduction to motors.) *Actuator* is a term with a definition that's a bit broader than *motor*'s. A motor is an actuator, and so is a memory wire, which is a type of metal that is heated to make the wire move and expand. Later, when the wire cools down, it goes back to its original size and position. The way the wire expands and contracts is similar to muscle fiber, and it has a lot of uses in the robotic industry. People use memory wire to open ventilation flaps and to change the direction of microphones and sensors. In Book 6, you use Python to make motors move.

Communications

Robots need to communicate. Not just verbally or onscreen, but also in a digital format that other computers and robots understand to coordinate actions and react to the environment. Robots use communication also to offload complex tasks (such as computer vision interpretation) to other computers, sometimes even in the cloud. Many of these communication types (Bluetooth, TCP/IP networks, Wi-Fi) use computers inside the communication device to accomplish the information transfers between the components of the robot and the environment.

Sensors

We'll admit it: We love sensors and are always on the lookout for the latest and greatest ones. Electricity sensors, temperature and humidity sensors, electronic gyroscopes, pressure and touch sensors, people sensors, cameras, and image-processing sensors are becoming more inexpensive and pervasive every day. And many of these sensors and functions are programmed using Python for data-processing and hardware drivers.

In modern robotics and embedded systems, these components all end up mixed together. A motor in a robot will have a computer, communications, and sensors all together in a single board or enclosed box.

Programming Robots

Robots are programmed in many different types of languages. Some robots can be programmed by people moving an arm to a specific set of locations (teaching the robot in a sense). Other robots are programmed to move from one location to another by using procedural statements in a more traditional computer science language.

The most popular programming language in the world for programming robots at a high level (above the motor drivers and low-level program, which are usually done in the C++ language) is Python. Hands down. Baxter is programmed via an API (application programming interface) provided for Python. Programmers use Python to call many robotic functions and image processing as well as to provide movement planning and coordination between robots. Although many robot manufacturers will have their own proprietary software, almost all provide a method for working with Python via libraries and modules.

The best way to jump in and understand the relationship of Python to robots is to build a robot and then write Python to read sensors, understand the environment, and then make decisions on where to move and what tasks to accomplish. By the end of this minibook, you will have a much better understanding of how all these parts — motors, sensors, and software — play together to make your robot move!

Chapter **2**

Building Your First Python Robot

I n this chapter, we build a robot and show you how to use Python to talk to all the parts. Why build the robot first? For two reasons: First, you save money by buying a kit-based robot versus a prebuilt one. Second, by building a robot you get to know how all the parts fit together and work, and how to use Python to control those motors and sensors.

We have chosen a robot based on our friend, the Raspberry Pi single-board computer. You can get robots based on many other types of computers, including the Arduino, but with those smaller computers, you can't do the kind of processing or artificial intelligence applications that you can on the Raspberry Pi.

After all, this is *Python All-in-One For Dummies.* Wouldn't you like to be able to use some of the sophisticated Python tools you learned earlier in this book?

Python programs are available for the Arduino (Circuit Python, for example), but the small processor and memory on the Arduino are limitations. The Raspberry Pi is much better suited for high-level AI applications on robots.

Introducing the Mars Rover PiCar-B

When we were deciding which robot to build in this book, we assembled four different small robot cars. All were similarly priced, and each had drawbacks. After careful consideration, we chose to use the Adeept PiCar-B (shown in Figure 2-1) for several reasons:

>> The assembly manual is clear with lots of pictures and diagrams.

>> The supplied software is compatible with Python 3 (and the Stretch version of the Raspberry Pi operating system).

>> The PiCar-B requires no soldering.

>> The PiCar-B is reasonably priced and has good availability.

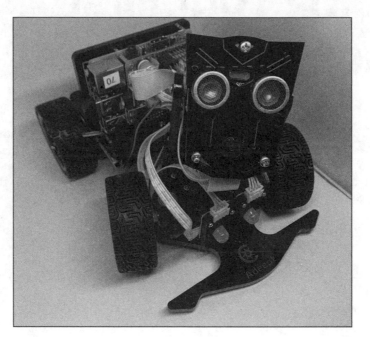

FIGURE 2-1:
The assembled
PiCar-B robot.

What you need for the build

TIP

You need three things to build the robot used in this chapter, in addition to some basic tools (although the kit comes with Allen wrenches and screwdrivers) and some plastic wire ties to bundle the wires after assembly:

» **Raspberry Pi 3B+:** Yes, you could get by with a smaller Raspberry Pi (such as the Raspberry Pi Zero), but we recommend that you get the 3B+ so you can do faster and more sophisticated processing onboard the robot. However, you pay a price for a faster Pi in power consumption and battery life. For our purposes, it's a good tradeoff.

If you want to use a Raspberry Pi 4B in this robot, it will dramatically reduce the battery life, and with some types of batteries the robot may not be able to boot the Pi 4B. (For more information on startup currents, check out this article John wrote about measuring them on the 3B+ and 4B: `www.switchdoc.com/2019/10/raspberry-pi-3b-4b-startup-currents-examined/`.)

Among other places, you can buy the Raspberry Pi 3B+ at Amazon.com, Newark.com, and Adafruit.com.

» **Adeept Raspberry Pi PiCar-B:** The Adeept Raspberry Pi PiCar-B is not quite as available as the Raspberry Pi. When you buy this, make sure you're buying the PiCar-B and *not* the PiCar-A. They added *Mars Rover* to the name of this product in their catalog, so look for the "Adeept Mars Rover PiCar-B."

You can buy the PiCar-B at Amazon.com (`https://amzn.to/36dukPU`), eBay.com, and Adeept.com.

» **18650 LiPo batteries:** The PiCar-B requires two 18650 3.7V LiPo 5000mAh batteries. You can also power the robot by turning off the power switch (or removing the batteries) and supplying power for the Raspberry Pi from the micro USB plug, which then powers both the robot and the Raspberry Pi.

The package we chose has two sets of batteries and a wall charger. You can buy this type of battery at Amazon.com and many, many other places.

Understanding the robot components

Now it's time to look at the components in the PiCar-B. We're not going to focus on the mechanical structure of how the robot is built but rather on each active component, such as sensors and motors. We will also talk about the Python software used to communicate with these components in the Python system test software later in this chapter and in our own robotic software in Chapter 3.

We provide Python code snippets to show you how each of the sensors and motors are controlled. For more complete code and a detailed description, see the "Preparing for running tests on your rover in Python" section, later in this chapter.

Motor controller board

The *motor controller* is designed to interface the Raspberry Pi to the sensors and motors on the PiCar-B. (See Figure 2-2.) The main two chips on the board are the PCA9685, an I2C device that controls up to 16 servo motors (of which 3 are used, so there's lots of room for expansion), and an L289P, which provides power to the main drive motor.) The rest of the board connects the GPIO (general-purpose input-output) pins from the Raspberry Pi to the various sensors and devices. The motor controller board also has a 5.0V power supply that supplies the Raspberry Pi and motors from the LiPo batteries.

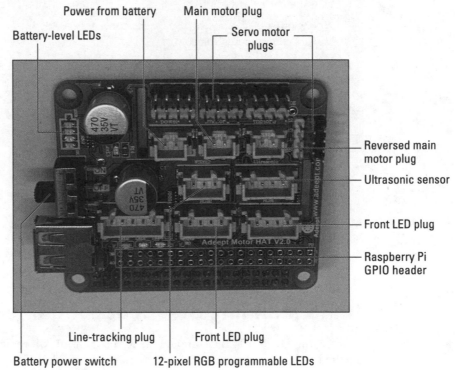

FIGURE 2-2: The PiCar-B motor controller board.

Servo motors

Servo motors are a generally a combination of three things: a DC motor, a simple control circuit, and a gearing set. Sometimes they also include a potentiometer (a variable resistor), which gives positional feedback. See Book 6, Chapter 4 for a description of feedback and its uses.

You control the position by using pulse-width modulation (PWM), a technique that we saw in Book 6, Chapter 1 for controlling the brightness of an LED.

The SG90 micro servo motor supplied with the robot is a small, inexpensive servo motor. (See Figure 2-3.) It has an operating voltage of 3V–7V with a current draw of about 40mA (40 milliamps; a *milliamp* is 1/1000th of an amp of current) at maximum, so the 5V on the Raspberry Pi is sufficient to operate this servo. It can turn about 90 degrees backward and forward for a total of 180 degrees.

FIGURE 2-3:
The SG90 micro servo motor.

Most servo motors have three control wires, and the SG90 is no exception. The three wires are as follows:

» **Yellow:** PWM control signal

» **Red:** Power (5V, in our case)

» **Brown:** Ground

Servos are continuously powered and generally have only about a 180–270 degree range of motion. All three servo motors used by this robot are SC-90 9g micro servos.

These servos are controlled from the PCA9685 I2C chip, so the servos don't use any GPIO lines from the Raspberry Pi. The PCA9685 is on the I2C bus of the Raspberry Pi. (See Chapter 3 in Book 6 for more information about the I2C bus.)

To control a servo motor, we just have to set the PWM value to the position to which we want the servo moved on the appropriate PWM line in the PCA9685:

```
print ("--------------------")
print ("Servo Test - Head Left")
print ("--------------------")
pwm.set_pwm(HEAD_TURN_SERVO, 0, calValues.look_left_max)
time.sleep(1.0)
```

The number passed to the servo motor for position (calValues.look_left_max) is empirically determined later in this chapter and is set by looking at the range of the servo motor as you command it to the left and right. See "Calibrating your servos," later in this chapter.

Drive motor

The main *drive motor* is a DC motor with two wires: power and ground. (See Figure 2-4.) When you supply power (by putting 5V on the power line, for example), the motor will start spinning. Reverse the power and ground wires, and the motor spins in the opposite direction.

FIGURE 2-4:
The main drive
motor.

You control the speed of a DC motor by using pulse-width modulation (PWM), a technique that can be used also to control the brightness of an LED (refer to Book 6, Chapter 1) and servo motors. If the power is cycled at 50 percent (half on/half off), the motor will spin at one-half the speed. Sometimes you will put an encoder on the motor shaft, which allows you to read into a computer how far the shaft has turned, giving the computer some feedback that can be useful.

This motor uses six GPIO lines from the Raspberry Pi to control speed and direction.

The intricacies of controlling this motor are well hidden from the user. Here is the Python code to move the car forward:

```
motor.motor_left(MOTOR_START, forward,left_spd*spd_ad)
motor.motor_right(MOTOR_START,backward,right_spd*spd_ad)
```

TIP

Why are we turning on both a left and right motor when there is only one drive motor in the PiCar-B? The reason is that you can't be sure which way your motor is wired; it may be wired one direction or it may be reversed. (Ours was reversed.) You have two motor plugs on the controller board. If the forward command causes the robot to move backward, you just move the motor to the other motor connection and everything works. Writing the preceding code (using both motor controllers) allows the software to work with either kind of motor.

RGB LED

The front of the robot has two single RGB LEDs, one on each side. (See Figure 2-5.) Each of these big LEDs has three smaller LEDs inside the housing. These smaller LEDs are red, blue, and green and are individually controlled by GPIO lines from the Raspberry Pi (running software PWM code that allows us to mix the R, G, and B LEDs).

FIGURE 2-5:
A single RGB LED.

```
print ()
print ("———————————————")
print ("Left Front LED Test - Red ")
print ("———————————————")
led.side_on(led.left_R)
time.sleep(1.0)
led.side_off(led.left_R)
```

You turn on the LEDs individually and, using other software later in this book, can set the brightness of each LED.

Pixel RGB programmable LEDs

The robot has twelve programmable Pixel RGB LEDs, connected as a string, with two sets of three on the bottom of the robot and two sets of three pointing to the rear. (See Figure 2-6.) These twelve LEDs are connected in serial, like Christmas lights. And like some Christmas lights, if one goes out, all the rest of the string goes too. That is because the Raspberry Pi controls the LEDs by sending a single serial data stream through them. This serial stream is precisely timed, which requires some special code on the Raspberry Pi to make it work.

FIGURE 2-6:
The
12 programmable
RGB LEDs.

The Pixel string of 12 RGB LEDs uses a single GPIO pin coming from the Raspberry Pi:

```
print ()
print ("————————————————")
print ("12 RGB Pixel LED Test - On ")
print ("————————————————")
rainbowCycle(strip, wait_ms=20, iterations=3)
```

PIXEL RGB STRINGS ON THE RASPBERRY PI

The Raspberry Pi has a complex, multifaceted operating system based on Linux. It is a multitasking preemptive operating system, which means virtually any task (and all user tasks) can be interrupted (stopped). Therefore, our serial stream to the Pixel LEDs can be delayed and corrupted. This corruption appears on the Pixel string when some individual LEDs are not set to the correct color.

The library we are using solves this real-time corruption problem by using the PWM and DMA hardware on the Raspberry Pi's processor. The PWM (pulse-width modulation) module can generate a signal with a specific duty cycle to, for example, drive a servo or dim an LED. The DMA (direct memory access) module can transfer bytes of memory between parts of the processor without using the CPU. By using DMA to send a specific sequence of bytes to the PWM module, the Pixel data signal can be generated without being interrupted by the Raspberry Pi's operating system. The use of DMA allows the data to be sent to the LEDs with no participation by the Pi's operating system, so no corruption.

Because the Arduino type of processors don't really have an operating system, it's pretty easy to generate these signals on an Arduino compared to a Raspberry Pi. Processors like the ESP8266 and the ESP32 do have tasks running in the background (such as Wi-Fi) and therefore require special drivers to compensate for that to avoid data corruption and flickering. Note that although the DMA technique works well on the Raspberry Pi 3B+ and 4B, the LEDs do not always work well with older and smaller Raspberry Pi models (A+, 3B, Pi Zero, or Pi Zero W).

This command cycles a rainbow of colors around all 12 LEDs on the back and bottom of the robot. The driver for the RGB Pixel string is complicated, but we'll provide code to easily control the LEDs — and we'll give you some examples of how to use them for other purposes. We really do love these LEDs and use them in many projects.

Pi camera

The camera that comes with in the PiCar-B is the classic Raspberry Pi camera, version 2.1, as shown in Figure 2-7. It has a Sony 8 megapixel sensor and can support pictures up to 3280 x 2464 at 15 frames per second. (The latest camera in the newest Raspberry Pi Foundation model has 12.3 megapixels and a lens bracket but is much too large for our small robotic car.)

FIGURE 2-7:
Raspberry Pi
camera
and cable.

The camera has a good color response and is well supported in Python and with OpenCV, the Open Source Computer Vision package we use later in Chapter 4 of this minibook. The Pi camera talks to the Raspberry Pi via a parallel data ribbon cable connected to the Raspberry Pi board.

The following code opens up a small window on the GUI of the Raspberry Pi, waits 20 seconds, moves the window and resizes it, waits 2 seconds, moves it again and then closes the window:

```
print ()
print ("--------------------")
print ("Open Video Window")
print ("--------------------")
camera.resolution = (1024, 768)
camera.start_preview(fullscreen=False,window=(100,100,256,192))
time.sleep(20)
camera.preview.window=(200,200,256,192)
time.sleep(2)
camera.preview.window=(0,0,512,384)
time.sleep(2)
camera.close()
```

TIP

To view the video from the robot in this chapter, start a GUI (graphics user interface) if you haven't already. If you are running on a headless Raspberry Pi, either add a keyboard, mouse, and monitor or stop now and bring up VNC (virtual network computer). Think of using your computer monitor as a display on a second computer — the Raspberry Pi, in this case. Many links on the web describe how to do this and how to bring up the GUI on your main computer. The official Raspberry Pi Foundation tutorial is at www.raspberrypi.org/documentation/remote-access/vnc/.

We are using VNC on a headless Raspberry Pi in this chapter. Feel free to connect a mouse, a keyboard, and a monitor directly to the Raspberry Pi if you want, but you will be better off using VNC because your robot will be mobile. If you're using VNC to see the GUI of the Raspberry Pi (as we are doing), you need to do the following. Right-click the VNC server icon and then click Options. The VNC Server — Options dialog box appears. Click Troubleshooting in the left sidebar, and then select the Enable Direct Capture Mode check box. See the "Assembling the Robot" section, later in this chapter, for more detail.

Ultrasonic sensor

The ultrasonic detector used in the PiCar-B is a non-contact distance measurement module that works at 40KHz. (See Figure 2-8.)

FIGURE 2-8:
An ultrasonic distance sensor.

When provided a pulse trigger signal longer than 10uS through the signal pin, the unit issues 8 cycles of 40kHz cycle level and detects the echo. The pulse width of the echo signal is proportional to the measured distance. Simple, yet effective.

The formula used is Distance = Echo signal high time * Sound speed (340M/S)/2.

In the following code, the call to ultra.checkdisk() calls the software that sets the transmit GPIO bit and then waits for the returning echo, marking the time received. It then calculates the time of transit and reports the distance in meters, which we convert to centimeters:

```
print ()
print ("--------------------")
print ("Ultrasonic Distance Test")
print ("--------------------")
```

```
average_dist = 0.0
for i in range(0,10):
    distance = ultra.checkdist()
    average_dist = average_distance + distance
    print ("Distance = {:6.3f}cm ".format( distance*100))
    time.sleep(1.0)
average_distance = average_distance / 10
print ("average_dist={:6.3f}cm".format(average_dist*100))
```

Assembling the Robot

The PiCar-B comes with an assembly manual complete with blow out pictures of how things go together. (See Figure 2-9.)

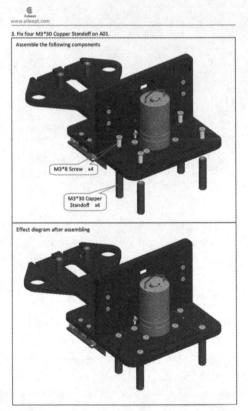

FIGURE 2-9:
An example of the assembly manual diagrams.

It took us about four hours to put together the robot and get to the point to begin testing.

WARNING

Do not go beyond Chapter 2 in the PiCar-B assembly manual. Chapter 3 starts installing all the Adeept software on the Raspberry Pi, and you will want to test the robot using the software in this book to better understand the parts of the robot before continuing.

So, go build your robot and then meet us back here to start testing it. Calibrating your servos is the first step in testing! Then we run a full system test. Figure 2-10 shows the assembled robot.

FIGURE 2-10:
The assembled PiCar-B showing wiring.

TIP

Here are a few helpful tips when building the robot:

» A power switch is on the left side of the motor drive board (viewed from the front of the robot). It shuts off the power from the batteries. (The power switch is not mentioned in the manual.)

» Make sure you use the longer of the two supplied ribbon cables for the Pi camera. The short one will not quite reach.

» Route the wires as shown in Figure 2-10 so the motors won't bind. Use some plastic wire ties to hold things in place, allowing enough room for the servos and housing to turn. A wire wrap enclosure is included that will fit some of the wires in your kit.

PROPERLY TURNING OFF YOUR RASPBERRY PI

Unlike most other computers, the Raspberry Pi does not have an on/off switch. However, like many other computers, just pulling the plug on a Raspberry Pi could have dire consequences, in this case, corrupting the SD card that the Raspberry Pi uses for program and data storage. Before you shut down the Raspberry Pi, type `sudo halt` in a terminal window.

When you run this command, after a bit, the ACT light (the green one) will blink 10 times (at 0.5 second intervals) and then turn off. At this point, you can safely remove the power or pull the plug.

The red power LED will remain on as long as power is applied to the Raspberry Pi.

>> Pay close attention to the orientation of the plastic parts and servos during assembly. Almost all have an asymmetrical top and bottom and need to be oriented correctly to be assembled.

>> Don't drop tiny screws. They're hard to find!

Testing Your Robot

We now have completed the robot assembly. It's time to calibrate the robot and test each one of the sensors, motors, and LEDs.

Calibrating your servos

Now that you've assembled the robot, it's time to start testing things. The first thing to do is to calibrate your servo motors. Why do they need calibration? Although the instructions have you leave the servo motor in the center of their motion range during assembly, they will not necessarily be in the correct place (and might also get moved during the assembly process).

The calibrateServo.py program runs each of the three servos from one end of motion to the other. By watching the motors as they turn, you can write down the max, min, and center numbers of each servo listed on the terminal window display. Then you place these values in the calValues.py program for the rest of the programs to access. The values in calValues.py are right for our robot and will probably be pretty close for yours, but you should run the program to be sure.

The calibrateServo code is as follows:

```python
#!/usr/bin/python3

# calibrate servos
import time

import Adafruit_PCA9685

import calValues

#import the settings for servos


pwm = Adafruit_PCA9685.PCA9685()
pwm.set_pwm_freq(60)


#servo mapping
# pmw 0 head tilt
HEAD_TILT_SERVO = 0
# pwm 1 head turn
HEAD_TURN_SERVO = 1
# pwm 2 wheels turn
WHEELS_TURN_SERVO = 2


if __name__ == '__main__':
    print("---------------------")
    print("calibrate wheel turn")
    print("---------------------")

    for i in range(calValues.turn_right_max,
            calValues.turn_left_max,10):
        pwm.set_pwm(WHEELS_TURN_SERVO,0, i)
        print("servoValue = ", i)
        time.sleep(0.5)

    print("---------------------")
    print("calibrate head turn")
    print("---------------------")
```

```
        for i in range(calValues.look_right_max,
             calValues.look_left_max,10):
          pwm.set_pwm(HEAD_TURN_SERVO,0, i)
          print("servoValue = ", i)
          time.sleep(0.5)


      print("--------------------")
      print("calibrate head up/down")
      print("--------------------")

      for i in range(calValues.look_up_max,
             calValues.look_down_max,10):
          pwm.set_pwm(HEAD_TILT_SERVO,0, i)
          print("servoValue = ", i)
          time.sleep(0.5)
```

The code is pretty straightforward, but the servo program loop needs a little explanation:

```
      for i in range(calValues.turn_right_max,

             calValues.turn_left_max,10):

          pwm.set_pwm(WHEELS_TURN_SERVO,0, i)

          print("servoValue = ", i)

          time.sleep(0.5)
```

This loop steps through the servo range as given in calValues.py from the right to the left, turning the head in steps of 10. This gives you a good idea where the right, left, and center should be (taking into account the robot frame too!), and you can add those values to calValues.py.

The calValues.py file holds the calibration values for the servo motors. You replace the values in this program with your own values from calibrate Servos.py:

```
# Servo calibration values

# head
look_up_max      = 150
look_down_max    = 420
look_tilt_middle = 330

# head turn
```

```
look_right_max    = 200
look_left_max     = 450
look_turn_middle  = 310


# wheels
turn_right_max    = 180
turn_left_max     = 460
turn_middle       = 320


# turn_speed
look_turn_speed   = 5


# motor speed

left_spd   = 100        #Speed of the car
right_spd  = 100        #Speed of the car
```

Preparing for running tests on your rover in Python

Now that you have assembled the PiCar-B and calibrated the servos, it's time to run some tests. We told you to not install the Adeept software, but if you got too excited and did, you need to disable the auto startup of their software.

To do so, open the ~/.config/autostart/car.desktop file and change the following line:

```
Exec=sudo python3 /home/Adeept_PiCar-B/server/server.py
```

to this:

```
#Exec=sudo python3 /home/Adeept_PiCar-B/server/server.py
```

And then reboot your Raspberry Pi by typing sudo reboot.

Installing software for the PiCar-B Python test

Now we download and run the Python test of all the PiCar-B robot functions. Here is a video of what the following Python test software does on the PiCar-B robot: https://youtu.be/UvxRBJ-tFw8.

To download the software for Book 7, Chapter 2, go to www.dummies.com/go/ pythonaiofd2e and click the Code for Book 7 link.

Go into the Book2 Testing directory and then follow these instructions, which are necessary to get the 12 programmable RGB LEDs to work on the Raspberry Pi:

1. **In a Terminal window, type the following:**

```
sudo apt-get install build-essential python3-dev git scons swig
```

This command installs several developer libraries that will allow you to compile the Pixel RGB driver software.

2. **Download the Pixel (also called NeoPixels) code from github using the clone command, which copies all the source code to your local computer:**

```
git clone https://github.com/jgarff/rpi_ws281x.git
```

3. **Change to rpi_ws281x directory and run scons to compile the software:**

```
cd rpi_ws281x
scons
```

4. **Change to the python directory under the rpi-ws2891x directory and install the Python module from there:**

```
cd python
```

5. **Install the Python 3 library file:**

```
sudo python3 setup.py install
```

The PiCar-B Python test code

The Python test file is approximately 370 lines long, so we don't provide a full listing here. The important parts of the file have been discussed along with the individual components and sensors in previous sections in this chapter. A number of other libraries and files are in the Testing directory.

Run the test software (PiCar-B-Test.py) by typing:

```
sudo python3 PiCar-B-Test.py
```

You should immediately see your car start doing the testing sequence, as shown at https://youtu.be/UvxRBJ-tFw8.

Pi camera video testing

Next we need to test the Pi camera on the robot. To prepare for this test, the test must be running in a GUI on your Raspberry Pi. If you're using VNC to display the GUI on another computer, such as your laptop, you must enable a VNC option on the Raspberry Pi. Right-click the VNC server icon and then click Options. The VNC Server — Options dialog box appears. Click Troubleshooting in the left sidebar, and then select the Enable Direct Capture Mode check box. (See Figure 2-11.)

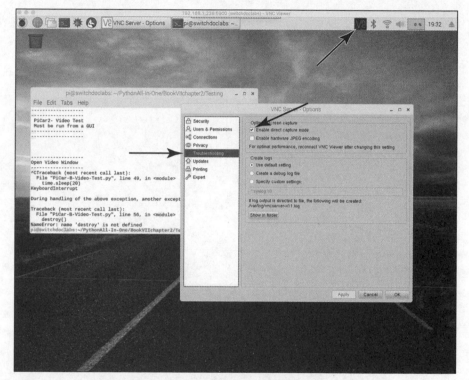

FIGURE 2-11: Setting the VNC viewer option.

You have to set this VNC option because the Raspberry Pi camera takes a small section out of the video display and maps in the picture from the camera rather than rendering it on the screen software. If you're using a monitor, no problem. But for VNC to grab this section and the video, you need to enable the check box to allow VNC to see your video.

The Pi camera test software (`PiCar-B-Video-Test.py`), which is in the Testing directory, follows:

```python
#!/usr/bin/python3

DEBUG = True
VIDEOTEST = True

# runs through a video tests for the PiCar-B

import RPi.GPIO as GPIO
import motor
import ultra
import socket
import time
import threading

import led
import os
import picamera
from picamera.array import PiRGBArray
import cv2


import calValues


if __name__ == '__main__':

    camera = picamera.PiCamera()                #Camera initialization
    camera.resolution = (640, 480)
    camera.framerate = 7
    rawCapture = PiRGBArray(camera, size=(640, 480))


    try:

        print ("--------------------")
        print ("--------------------")
        print (" PiCar2- Video Test")
        print (" Must be run from a GUI")
        print ("--------------------")
        print ("--------------------")
        print ()
        print ()
```

```
        if (VIDEOTEST):

            print ()
            print ("--------------------")
            print ("Open Video Window")
            print ("--------------------")


            camera.resolution = (1024, 768)
            camera.start_preview(fullscreen=False,
                    window=(100,100,256,192))
            time.sleep(20)
            camera.preview.window=(200,200,256,192)
            time.sleep(2)
            camera.preview.window=(0,0,512,384)
            time.sleep(2)
            camera.close()
    except KeyboardInterrupt:
        destroy()
```

This code opens a small window on the GUI of the Raspberry Pi (or on your laptop if you are using VNC), waits 20 seconds, moves the window and resizes it, waits 2 seconds, moves the window again, and then closes the window.

Now you have finished building and testing your robot. In the next chapter, you give the robot a Python brain and start having some fun.

Chapter **3**

Programming Your Robot Rover

O kay, let's review where you are now. You have a basic understanding of robots and (more importantly) the major components of robots. You understand that Python can control these components so that they can work together to accomplish robotic tasks. That's a lot of information.

Next, we show you how to string together these components and software to make a simple robotic brain so that our robot rover can move by itself. The rover won't be a fully functional self-driving car, but after going through this chapter, you will have some sense of how those large self-driving cars are programmed.

Building a Simple, High-Level Python Interface

Let's first make a short Python module that allows us to build more complicated programs while hiding the complexity of dealing with the robot hardware.

Our high-level robotic interface is a python class file called RobotInterface.py. The code length is beyond what we want to list in the book, but it is available at www.dummies.com/go/pythonaiofd2e. We describe a few functions and then show you how to use the rest of the module.

The motorForward() function

The motorForward() function is typical of the motor functions located in the RobotInterface class:

```
def motorForward(self, speed, delay):
    motor.motor_left(self.MOTOR_START, self.forward,speed)
    motor.motor_right(self.MOTOR_START, self.backward,speed)
    time.sleep(delay)
    motor.motor_left(self.MOTOR_STOP, self.forward,speed)
    motor.motor_right(self.MOTOR_STOP, self.backward,speed)
```

This function drives the robot forward for the number of seconds passed into the function in the delay argument. When you call this function, you must use a number in seconds (such as 2) — not milliseconds — in the delay argument.

It basically starts the motors running forward, waits for the time specified in the delay, and then shuts off the motors.

Note that we have two commands to run the motor. (Actually, two commands to start the motor and two to stop it.) As explained in the last chapter, the control board has two motor controllers, and this code will work even if you wire the motors backwards during assembly.

The wheelsLeft function()

This function will turn the front wheels fully left and delay 50ms:

```
def wheelsLeft(self):
    pwm.set_pwm(self.WHEELS_TURN_SERVO, 0, calValues.turn_left_max)
    time.sleep(0.05)
```

The wheelsLeft() function sets WHEELS_TURN_SERVO to the leftmost position of the wheels and then delays 50ms. Why the delay? You will see these delays scattered through the RobotInterface class file. They keep multiple, back-to-back servo commands from exceeding the current capacity of the power supply. By delaying the next servo command by 50ms, the high current transient caused by moving the first servo has a chance to die away before the next servo command is executed.

The wheelsPercent function()

The wheelsPercent() function allows the user to set the servo to a percent of the total range of the servo motor. The functional value goes from full left (0) to full right (100) for the wheels; 50 is approximately in the middle. The values may vary from the middle if your servo has an asymmetric range of motion. If you do, use the wheelsMiddle() function to center your wheels.

This code calculates the total range of motion of the servo motor and then multiplies it by the percentage requested. It then sets the servo motor to the requested range:

```python
def wheelsPercent(self,percent):
    adder = calValues.turn_left_max + (calValues.turn_left_max -
        calValues.turn_right_max)*(percent/100.0)
    pwm.set_pwm(self.WHEELS_TURN_SERVO, 0,int(calValues.turn_right_max + adder))
    time.sleep(0.05)
```

Making a Single Move with Python

Now we're going to string together these functions and make the robot move. First, go to this book's support page at www.dummies.com/go/pythonaiofd2e and download the software for Book 7, Chapter 3.

In the following code, we move the robot a short distance ahead with a motor Forward command and then back to its original position with a motorBackward() command. We hope that you're starting to see the magic of this approach.

Following is the single move code that will move the robot forward and then back:

```python
#!/usr/bin/python3
# Robot Interface Test

import RobotInterface
import time

RI = RobotInterface.RobotInterface()

print ("Short Move Test")

RI.wheelsMiddle()

RI.motorForward(100,1.0)
time.sleep(1.0)
RI.motorBackward(100,1.0)
```

First, we import the `RobotInterface` class library and also the `time` library for `sleep()`. Note how few lines of code are necessary. The complexity of the underlying robot interface libraries are hidden by the using `RobotInterface` module.

```
import RobotInterface
import time
```

Then we initialize the `RobotInterface` module and assign the module to the `RI` object variable:

```
RI = RobotInterface.RobotInterface()
print ("Short Move Test")
```

We center the wheels with the `wheelsMiddle()` function:

```
RI.wheelsMiddle()
```

Now comes the good part. We drive the robot forward for one second, pause a second, and then run it backward for one second, to the robot's original position:

```
RI.motorForward(100,1.0)
time.sleep(1.0)
RI.motorBackward(100,1.0)
```

Pretty simple, right? Name the file `singleMove.py`.

For a video of what you should see when you run this code on your robot in a terminal window, go to `https://youtu.be/UT0PG7z2ccE`.

Our job isn't finished until when? Oh yes, until the documentation is finished. Off to document the `RobotInterface` class functions.

Functions of the RobotInterface Class

In this section, we document the functions of the `RobotInterface` class. We show you the Robot Interface Test program, and then it is off to the races building robot software! The `RobotInterface` class is derived from both original software by the author and from Adeept. We included all the necessary software, so you don't need to install it.

Front LED functions

The following functions control the two LEDs on the front of the robot.

set_Front_LED_On()

The set_Front_LED_On() function sets the front LED to On:

```
set_Front_LED_On(colorLED)
```

Remember that these two front LEDs are tricolor, with red, green, and blue individual LEDs, each of which is individually controllable. The colorLED parameter controls the side of the robot and color to turn on. You set the color and select the side by using the following constants from the RobotInterface class:

```
RobotInterface.left_R
RobotInterface.left_G
RobotInterface.left_B
RobotInterface.right_R
RobotInterface.right_G
RobotInterface.right_B
```

For example, RobotInterface.left_R turns on the red LED on the robot's left side (as viewed when standing behind the robot). You can make multiple calls to this program to turn on all three of the LEDs. Turning on an already on LED does not hurt anything and is ignored.

We could write a more sophisticated driver for the LEDs to drive the LEDs' GPIOs with PWM (pulse-width modulation), allowing even greater color mixing.

WHAT IS RGB?

RGB stands for red green blue, and an RGB LED uses three LEDs (red, green and blue) to produce multiple colors. RGB is an additive color model in which each color is added in various ways to reproduce an array of colors. For example, if you want a red color, you turn the red LED to 100% and the green and blue LEDs to 0%. If you want a white color, you turn all three LEDs to 100%. Most of the time, 100% on is represented by 255 and 0% is 0. A light pink color, for example, is (R=255, G=204, B=229). A good site for choosing RGB colors is www.colorschemer.com/rgb-color-codes/.

Note that unless you're using hardware PWM pins on the Raspberry Pi, the LEDs will flicker when using this technique because of the Raspberry Pi's multitasking operating system. See Book 6, Chapter 1 for a more thorough description of the PWM process and why you would see flickering. You could, however, write Python drivers for the PCA9685 servo driver board problem by using the PWM hardware on the driver board to fix the flickering.

set_Front_LED_Off()

The set_Front_LED_Off() function sets the Front LED to Off:

```
set_Front_LED_Off(colorLED)
```

As mentioned in the preceding section, these two front LEDs are tricolor, with red, green, and blue LEDs, each of which is individually controllable.

The colorLED parameter controls the side of the robot and the color LED to turn off. You set the color and select the side by using the following constants from the RobotInterface class:

```
RobotInterface.left_R
RobotInterface.left_G
RobotInterface.left_B
RobotInterface.right_R
RobotInterface.right_G
RobotInterface.right_B
```

For example, set_Front_LED_Off(RobotInterface.left_R) turns off the red LED on the robot's left side (as viewed from the rear of the robot). You can make multiple calls to this program to turn off all three LEDs. Turning off an already off LED does not hurt anything and is ignored.

Pixel strip functions

The robot has 12 pixel LEDs in four locations. These RGB LEDs, which are called pixels, are controlled by a single serial line that runs through them all. They are programmed by a fairly sophisticated and touchy serial sequence of precisely timed pulses from the Raspberry Pi. Because of the Raspberry Pi operating system, these pulses can't be generated accurately enough using Python and GPIO signals. However, a helpful person named jgarff created a complex driver that uses the DMA (direct memory access) interface on the Raspberry Pi. (The library is named rpi_ws281x and is included in the download from www.dummies.com/go/pythonaiofd2e — very clever coding). We use that driver to generate those pulses. Our RobotInterface software hides all this complexity from the user.

rainbowCycle()

The rainbowCycle() call starts a rainbow cycle that uses all 12 Pixel LEDs and runs through many colors. Although there are only RGB LEDs on each Pixel, the driver creates many different colors by varying the brightness of each LED individually:

```
rainbowCycle(wait_ms = 20, iterations = 3)
```

The wait_ms parameter sets the delay (in milliseconds) between each color change. It defaults to a 20ms delay. The iterations parameter sets the number of full color cycles (each color cycle has 256 different colors) to perform before returning; it defaults to 3 cycles.

colorWipe()

The colorWipe() function sets all 12 Pixel LEDs to the same color or off:

```
colorWipe(color)
```

For example, colorWipe(color(0,0,0)) sets all Pixels to Off. The color parameter specifies the RGB values color to be used using the colorWipe() function. (See the color() function later in this chapter.)

theaterChaseRainbow()

The theaterChaseRainbow() function starts a 40-second pattern of "chasing LEDs" on all 12 LEDs:

```
theaterChaseRainbow(wait_ms = 50)
```

The wait_ms parameter sets the delay, in milliseconds, between each movement. It defaults to 50 milliseconds.

setPixelColor()

The setPixelColor() function sets an individual Pixel (numbered from 0 through 11) to a specific color:

```
setPixelColor(pixel, color, brightness)
```

The color parameter specifies the color to be set by using the color() function, for example, color(255,255,32).

The `brightness` parameter sets the brightness (0–255) for the entire the Pixel string. The color of your selection is scaled by the maximum brightness selected.

color()

The color() function is a helper function that converts the R, G, and B values into a single 24-bit integer used by the internal Pixel driver:

```
color(red, green, blue, white = 0)
```

The `red`, `green`, and `blue` parameters are integers and range from 0 (off) to 255 (fully on). The `white=0` parameter is for RGBW Pixel LEDs. The Pixels on the robot are RGB LEDs.

allLEDSOff()

The `allLEDSOff()` function turns all the LEDs on the robot off, both the front two LEDs and the 12–LED Pixel string:

```
allLEDSOff()
```

Ultrasonic distance sensor function

The ultrasonic distance sensor works by sending a pulse of high-frequency sound and then counting the time before it bounces back to the receiver. Because we know the speed of sound, we can calculate the distance in front of the sensor. The method is not perfect (we would rather be using a laser!), but it's a good starting distance sensor. Ultrasonic sensors are slower than lasers and have a more spread out focus, which leads to inaccurate readings on some complex objects.

fetchUltraDistance()

The `fetchUltraDistance()` function does an measurement from the ultrasonic distance sensor in the head of the robot and returns the distance in centimeters (cm):

```
fetchUltraDistance()
```

Main motor functions

The main motor on our robot drives the back wheels and moves the robot. The motor functions are used to tell how fast and how long to run the main motor.

motorForward()

The `motorForward()` function drives the robot forward at `speed` for the `delay` number of seconds before shutting off the motors:

```
motorForward(speed, delay)
```

The `speed` parameter sets the duty cycle of the PWM GPIO pin driving the interface for the motor. It goes from 0 (off) to 100 (fast).

The `delay` parameter tells the driver how long to run the motor, in seconds.

motorBackward()

The `motorBackward()` function drives the robot backward at `speed` for the `delay` number of seconds before the shutting off the motors:

```
motorBackward(speed, delay)
```

The `speed` parameter sets the duty cycle of the PWM GPIO pin driving the interface for the motor. It goes from 0 (off) to 100 (fast).

The `delay` parameter tells the driver how long to run the motor, in seconds.

stopMotor()

The `stopMotor()` function stops the main motor immediately:

```
stopMotor()
```

This function is useful only if you were driving the motor in another thread. You can think of a *thread* as another entire program running at the same time as your main program. In Chapter 4 of this minibook, we build a threaded program for the robot. This sophisticated programming technique has some significant benefits to writing robot code, which we explore in that chapter.

Servo functions

The servo functions control the three servos on the robot: head-turning, head-tilting, and front wheels servos.

headTurnLeft()

The headTurnLeft() function turns the robot's head all the way to the left:

```
headTurnLeft()
```

"All the way to the left" is defined in the calValues.py file. Refer to Chapter 2 in this minibook for information on the calibration values and how to set them using the calibrateServos.py program.

headTurnRight()

The headTurnRight() function turns the robot's head all the way to the right:

```
headTurnRight()
```

"All the way to the right" is defined in the calValues.py file. Refer to Chapter 2 in this minibook for information on the calibration values and how to set them using the calibrateServos.py program.

headTurnMiddle()

The headTurnMiddle() function turns the robot head to the middle of the front of the robot:

```
headTurnMiddle()
```

"The middle" is defined in the calValues.py file. Refer to Chapter 2 in this minibook for information on the calibration values and how to set them using the calibrateServos.py program.

headTurnPercent()

The headTurnPercent() function turns the head from 0 (all the way to the left) to 100 (all the way to the right):

```
headTurnPercent(percent)
```

The headTurnPercent() function is useful for more precisely aiming the head. Again, "all the way to the left" and "all the way to the right" are defined in the calValues.py file. Refer to Chapter 2 of this minibook for information on the calibration values and how to set them using the calibrateServos.py program.

The percent parameter has values from 0 to 100 and represents the linear percent from left to right. Note that the value 50 may not be quite in the middle because your servos may not be set exactly in the middle of their range.

headTiltDown()

The headTiltDown() function tilts the robot head all the way down:

```
headTiltDown()
```

"All the way down" is defined in the calValues.py file. Refer to Chapter 2 of this minibook for information on the calibration values and how to set them using the calibrateServos.py program.

headTiltUp()

The headTiltUp() function tilts the robot head all the way up:

```
headTiltUp()
```

"All the way up" is defined in the calValues.py file. Refer to Chapter 2 of this minibook for information on the calibration values and how to set them using the calibrateServos.py program.

headTiltMiddle()

The headTiltMiddle() function tilts the robot head so that it points out directly from the front of the robot:

```
headTiltMiddle()
```

"The middle" is defined in the calValues.py file. Refer to Chapter 2 of this minibook for information on the calibration values and how to set them using the calibrateServos.py program.

headTiltPercent()

The headTiltPercent() function turns the head from 0 (all the way down) to 100 (all the way to the up):

```
headTiltPercent(percent)
```

This function is useful for more precisely aiming the head. Again, "all the way down" and "all the way up" are defined in the calValues.py file. Refer to

Chapter 2 of this minibook for information on the calibration values and how to set them using the `calibrateServos.py` program.

The `percent` parameter has values of 0 to 100 and represents the linear percent from down to up. Note that the value 50 may not be quite in the middle because your servos may not be set exactly in the middle of their range (as set by the servo calibration process) and because of the way your robot was built.

wheelsLeft()

The `wheelsLeft()` function turns the robot's front wheels all the way to the left:

```
wheelsLeft()
```

"All the way to the left" is defined in the `calValues.py` file. Refer to Chapter 2 of this minibook for information on the calibration values and how to set them using the `calibrateServos.py` program.

wheelsRight()

The `wheelsRight()` function turns the robot's front wheels all the way to the right:

```
wheelsRight()
```

"All the way to the right" is defined in the `calValues.py` file. Refer to Chapter 2 of this minibook for information on the calibration values and how to set them using the `calibrateServos.py` program.

wheelsMiddle()

The `wheelsMiddle()` function turns the robot's front wheels to the middle:

```
wheelsMiddle()
```

"To the middle" is defined in the `calValues.py` file. Refer to Chapter 2 of this minibook for information on the calibration values and how to set them using the `calibrateServos.py` program.

wheelsPercent()

The `wheelsPercent()` function turns the wheels from 0 (all the way to the left) to 100 (all the way to the right):

```
wheelsPercent(percent)
```

This function is useful for more precisely setting the direction of the robot's front wheels. Again, "all the way to the left and "all the way to the right"" are defined in the `calValues.py` file. Refer to Chapter 2 in this minibook for information on the calibration values and how to set them using the `calibrateServos.py` program.

The `percent` parameter has values from 0 to 100 and represents the linear percent from left to right. Note that the value 50 may not be quite in the middle because your servos may not be set exactly in the middle of their range (as set by the servo calibration process) and because of the way your robot was built.

General servo function

We have included a general function to control all the servos at once. Calling this function moves all servos to the center position.

centerAllServos()

The `centerAllServos()` function puts all the servos to the center of their range, as defined in the `calValues.py` file:

```
centerAllServos()
```

The Python Robot Interface Test

Now that we've defined the robot API (application programming interface), let's run the system test using the `RobotInterface` Python class. This program is useful for two reasons. First, it tests all functions in the `RobotInterface` class. Second, it shows how to use each function in a Python program. This next program, `RITest.py`, is designed to test all the functions of the robot controlled by the `RobotInterface` class.

The code for `RITest.py` follows:

```
#!/usr/bin/python3
# Robot Interface Test

import RobotInterface
import time


RI = RobotInterface.RobotInterface()
```

```
print ("Robot Interface Test")
print ("LED tests")
RI.set_Front_LED_On(RI.left_R)
time.sleep(0.1)
RI.set_Front_LED_On(RI.left_G)
time.sleep(0.1)
RI.set_Front_LED_On(RI.left_B)
time.sleep(1.0)
RI.set_Front_LED_On(RI.right_R)
time.sleep(0.1)
RI.set_Front_LED_On(RI.right_G)
time.sleep(0.1)
RI.set_Front_LED_On(RI.right_B)
time.sleep(1.0)

RI.set_Front_LED_Off(RI.left_R)
time.sleep(0.1)
RI.set_Front_LED_Off(RI.left_G)
time.sleep(0.1)
RI.set_Front_LED_Off(RI.left_B)
time.sleep(1.0)
RI.set_Front_LED_Off(RI.right_R)
time.sleep(0.1)
RI.set_Front_LED_Off(RI.right_G)
time.sleep(0.1)
RI.set_Front_LED_Off(RI.right_B)

time.sleep(1.0)
RI.rainbowCycle(20, 1)
time.sleep(0.5)

# Runs for 40 seconds
RI.theaterChaseRainbow(50)
time.sleep(0.5)

print ("RI.Color(0,0,0)=", RI.Color(0,0,0))
RI.colorWipe(RI.Color(0,0,0))
time.sleep(1.0)
for pixel in range (0,12):
    RI.setPixelColor(pixel,RI.Color(100,200,50),50)
    time.sleep(0.5)

print ("Servo Tests")
RI.headTurnLeft()
time.sleep(1.0)
RI.headTurnRight()
```

```
time.sleep(1.0)
RI.headTurnMiddle()
time.sleep(1.0)

RI.headTiltDown()
time.sleep(1.0)
RI.headTiltUp()
time.sleep(1.0)
RI.headTiltMiddle()
time.sleep(1.0)

RI.wheelsLeft()
time.sleep(1.0)
RI.wheelsRight()
time.sleep(1.0)
RI.wheelsMiddle()
time.sleep(1.0)

print("servo scan tests")
for percent in range (0,100):
    RI.headTurnPercent(percent)
for percent in range (0,100):
    RI.headTiltPercent(percent)
for percent in range (0,100):
    RI.wheelsPercent(percent)

print("motor test")
RI.motorForward(100,1.0)
time.sleep(1.0)
RI.motorBackward(100,1.0)

print("ultrasonic test")
print ("distance in cm=", RI.fetchUltraDistance())

print("general function test")
RI.allLEDSOff()
RI.centerAllServos()
```

Run the program by typing sudo python3 RITest.py in a terminal window. Note that you *have* to use sudo because the Pixel LEDs require root permission (granted by sudo) to correctly run. You see the following output on the Terminal screen while your program is running:

```
Robot Interface Test
LED tests
RI.Color(0,0,0)= 0
Servo Tests
```

```
servo scan tests
motor test
ultrasonic test
distance in cm= 16.87312126159668
general function test
```

Here's a link to the video of the `RobotInterface` class test: `https://youtu.be/1vi-UGao0oI`.

ROS: THE ROBOT OPERATING SYSTEM

We have written a fairly simple interface class for the PiCar-B robot. The RobotInterface module allows us to control the robot from a Python program. If we had more room in this book we would connect our robot to the ROS (robot operating system and pronounced "Ross"). (Actually, an entire book could be written about the use of ROS for a robot like ours.) ROS is designed for controlling robots in a distributed system. Even though it's called the *robot operating system*, it really isn't an operating system.

ROS is *middleware*, which is software designed to manage the complexity of writing software in a complicated and heterogenous (meaning lots of different types of robots and sensors) environment. ROS allows us to treat different robots in a similar manner.

ROS uses a publish-subscribe system, similar to a newspaper. A newspaper publishes stories, but only the people who subscribe to the newspaper see those stories. A subscriber might want a subscription only to the comics or the front page. A robot like ours might publish the current value of the ultrasonic sensor or the current camera image (or even a video stream) and other computers or robots on the network could subscribe to the video stream and see what your robot is seeing. And your robot could subscribe to other sensors (such as a temperature sensor in the middle of the room) or even look at what other robots are seeing.

The power of this technique is that now you can make your robot part of an ecosystem consisting of computers, sensors, and even people making use of your data and contributing information to your robot.

We could build a ROS interface on our robot and then control it remotely and feed sensor data to other computers. To give you an idea of the scalability of this software, you could control the robot car as well as a giant industrial robot and even coordinate the two robots to work together.

In many ways, ROS rocks. Find out more about ROS at `www.ros.org`. John Shovic is standing with his giant industrial ROS-controlled robot in the picture. For a holiday-themed example of the big robot in motion, check out this YouTube video: https://youtu.be/uU5KEzhE7ps.

Coordinating Motor Movements with Sensors

The capability to modify and coordinate motor movements with sensor movements is key to movement in the environment. Sensors give information to be acted upon as well as feedback from our motions. Think of the act of catching a baseball with a glove. Your sensors? Eyes and the sense of touch. Your eyes see the ball and then move your hand and arm to intercept the ball. You're coordinating your movement with a sensor (meaning your eyes). The feedback? Knowing you've caught the ball in your mitt by the feel of it hitting your gloved hand as well as feedback from your vision to know approximately when you will close your hand. You're also updating your internal learning system to become better at catching the ball.

PiCar-B has two sensors that read information from the outside world so that the robot can analyze what it sees. The ultrasonic sensor detects what's in front of the robot and the camera photographs the world. However, programming robot vision is difficult.

Chapter 4 talks about using artificial intelligence for robots to understanding what the camera is seeing, and we will be building an example of how to do this using machine learning. We touch on using camera images for analysis in Chapter 4 of this minibook.

For our next example, we will focus on the simpler sensor, the ultrasonic distance sensor. The following Python code, `simpleFeedback.py`, moves the robot forward or backward depending on the robot's distance from the object in front of it:

```python
#!/usr/bin/python3
# Robot Interface Test

import RobotInterface
import time

DEBUG = True

RI = RobotInterface.RobotInterface()

print ("Simple Feedback Test")

RI.centerAllServos()
RI.allLEDSOff()

# Ignore distances greater than one meter
DISTANCE_TO_IGNORE = 1000.0
# Close to 10cm with short moves
DISTANCE_TO_MOVE_TO = 10.0
# How many times before the robot gives up
REPEAT_MOVE = 10

def bothFrontLEDSOn(color):
    RI.allLEDSOff()
    if (color == "RED"):
        RI.set_Front_LED_On(RI.right_R)
        RI.set_Front_LED_On(RI.left_R)
        return
    if (color == "GREEN"):
        RI.set_Front_LED_On(RI.right_G)
        RI.set_Front_LED_On(RI.left_G)
        return
    if (color == "BLUE"):
        RI.set_Front_LED_On(RI.right_B)
        RI.set_Front_LED_On(RI.left_B)
        return
```

```
try:
    Quit = False
    moveCount = 0
    bothFrontLEDSOn("BLUE")
    while (Quit == False):
        current_distance = RI.fetchUltraDistance()
        if (current_distance >= DISTANCE_TO_IGNORE):
            bothFrontLEDSOn("BLUE")
            if (DEBUG):
                print("distance too far ={:6.2f}cm"
                        .format(current_distance))
        elif (current_distance <= 10.0):
            # reset moveCount
            # the Robot is close enough
            bothFrontLEDSOn("GREEN")
            moveCount = 0
            if (DEBUG):
                print("distance close enough ={:6.2f}cm"
                        .format(current_distance))

            time.sleep(5.0)
            # back up and do it again
            RI.motorBackward(100,1.0)
        else:
            if (DEBUG):
                print("moving forward ={:6.2f}cm"
                        .format(current_distance))
            # Short step forward
            bothFrontLEDSOn("RED")
            RI.motorForward(90,0.50)
            moveCount = moveCount + 1

        # Now check for stopping our program
        time.sleep(1.0)
        if (moveCount > REPEAT_MOVE):
            Quit = True


except KeyboardInterrupt:
    print("program interrupted")

print ("program finished")
```

The `simpleFeedback.py` program is a great example of the use of feedback in robotics. The robot first checks to see if it is less than 1 meter (1000cm) from the wall. If it is, it slowly starts to advance toward the wall in short steps. When it is closer than 10cm to the wall, it stops, waits five seconds, and then backs up about a meter (the distance depends on your flooring and the charge left on the batteries) to repeat the process:

```
if (moveCount > REPEAT MOVE):
    Quit = True
```

It also gives up if it takes more than ten moves to get to the wall, if somehow it has moved farther than 1000cm away from the wall, or if the user has pressed Ctrl+C to interrupt the program.

Note how we use the LEDs to give surrounding people feedback as to what the robot is doing. This visual feedback is an important part of making human–robot interaction more efficient, understandable, and safer.

The main structure of the program is in a Python `while` loop. As long as we haven't interrupted the program (or one of the other quit criteria hasn't been satisfied), our little robot will keep working until the battery goes dead.

Copy the code into `simpleFeedback.py` and give the program a try by executing **sudo python3 simpleFeedback.py**. Here are the printed results:

```
Simple Feedback Test
moving forward = 55.67cm
moving forward = 44.48cm
moving forward = 34.22cm
moving forward = 26.50cm
moving forward = 17.53cm
distance close enough = 9.67cm
moving forward = 66.64cm
moving forward = 54.25cm
moving forward = 43.55cm
moving forward = 36.27cm
moving forward = 28.44cm
moving forward = 21.08cm
moving forward = 13.55cm
distance close enough = 6.30cm
moving forward = 64.51cm
moving forward = 52.89cm
moving forward = 43.75cm
moving forward = 33.95cm
moving forward = 26.79cm
^Cprogram interrupted
program finished
```

You can see the feedback video at https://youtu.be/mzZIMxch5k4.

Play with this code. Try other ideas and different constants and see the different results you get. For example, what happens if you increase the speed of the motors or change the minimum distance to 5cm from 10cm?

Making a Python Brain for Our Robot

Now you're going to create a simple self-driving car. In a sense, you're going to apply the results from the simpleFeedback.py program to create an autonomous vehicle that is not very smart but illustrates the use of feedback in decision making.

The Python brain you are writing is nothing more than a combination of the code for sensing the wall (from earlier in this chapter) and the code for generating a random walk based on the information gained from the ultrasonic sensor. After we tested the code for a while, the robot would get stuck, so we added code to detect when the robot is stuck and to back out in that situation.

Note: Make sure the batteries are fully charged before running this code. When the batteries dip a bit, your motor speed will dramatically decrease. Another way to fix this problem is to use bigger batteries.

Following is the code for the robot brain:

```python
#!/usr/bin/python3
# Robot Brain

import RobotInterface
import time

from random import randint

DEBUG = True

RI = RobotInterface.RobotInterface()

print ("Simple Robot Brain")

RI.centerAllServos()
RI.allLEDSOff()

# Close to 20cm
CLOSE_DISTANCE = 20.0
# How many times before the robot gives up
REPEAT_TURN = 10
```

```python
def bothFrontLEDSOn(color):
    RI.allLEDSOff()
    if (color == "RED"):
        RI.set_Front_LED_On(RI.right_R)
        RI.set_Front_LED_On(RI.left_R)
        return
    if (color == "GREEN"):
        RI.set_Front_LED_On(RI.right_G)
        RI.set_Front_LED_On(RI.left_G)
        return
    if (color == "BLUE"):
        RI.set_Front_LED_On(RI.right_B)
        RI.set_Front_LED_On(RI.left_B)
        return

STUCKBAND = 2.0
# check for stuck car by distance not changing
def checkForStuckCar(cd,p1,p2):

    if (abs(p1-cd) < STUCKBAND):
        if (abs(p2-cd) < STUCKBAND):
            return True
    return False


try:
    Quit = False
    turnCount = 0
    bothFrontLEDSOn("BLUE")

    previous2distance = 0
    previous1distance = 0

    while (Quit == False):
        current_distance = RI.fetchUltraDistance()
        if (current_distance >= CLOSE_DISTANCE ):
            bothFrontLEDSOn("BLUE")
            if (DEBUG):
                print("Continue straight ={:6.2f}cm"
                        .format(current_distance))
            if (current_distance > 300):
                # verify distance
                current_distance = RI.fetchUltraDistance()
                if (current_distance > 300):
                    # move faster
                    RI.motorForward(90,1.0)
            else:
                RI.motorForward(90,0.50)
            turnCount = 0
```

```
    else:
        if (DEBUG):
            print("distance close enough so turn ={:6.2f}cm"
                    .format(current_distance))
        bothFrontLEDSOn("RED")
        # now determine which way to turn
        # turn = 0 turn left
        # turn = 1 turn right
        turn = randint(0,1)

        if (turn == 0): # turn left
            # we turn the wheels right since
            # we are backing up
            RI.wheelsRight()
        else:
            # turn right

            # we turn the wheels left since
            # we are backing up
            RI.wheelsLeft()

    time.sleep(0.5)
    RI.motorBackward(100,1.00)
    time.sleep(0.5)
    RI.wheelsMiddle()
    turnCount = turnCount+1
    print("Turn Count =", turnCount)

# check for stuck car
if (checkForStuckCar(current_distance,
        previous1distance, previous2distance)):
    # we are stuck.  Try back up and try Random turn
    bothFrontLEDSOn("RED")
    if (DEBUG):
        print("Stuck - Recovering ={:6.2f}cm"
                .format(current_distance))
    RI.wheelsMiddle()
    RI.motorBackward(100,1.00)

    # now determine which way to turn
    # turn = 0 turn left
    # turn = 1 turn right
    turn = randint(0,1)


    if (turn == 0): # turn left
        # we turn the wheels right since
```

```
            # we are backing up
            RI.wheelsRight()
        else:
            # turn right

            # we turn the wheels left since
            # we are backing up
            RI.wheelsLeft()
        time.sleep(0.5)
        RI.motorBackward(100,2.00)
        time.sleep(0.5)
        RI.wheelsMiddle()



    # load state for distances
    previous2distance = previous1distance
    previous1distance = current_distance

    # Now check for stopping our program
    time.sleep(0.1)
    if (turnCount > REPEAT_TURN-1):
        bothFrontLEDSOn("RED")
        if (DEBUG):
            print("too many turns in a row")
        Quit = True


except KeyboardInterrupt:
    print("program interrupted")

print ("program finished")
```

This program seems more complex than our ultrasonic sensor program presented earlier in the chapter, but it's not that much harder. We took the same structure of the program (the `while` loop) and added several features.

First, we added a clause to speed up the car when we are far away (over 300cm) from an obstacle. We also reread the distance to make sure we are still 300cm away in case something had changed:

```
if (current_distance >= CLOSE_DISTANCE ):
    bothFrontLEDSOn("BLUE")
    if (DEBUG):
        print("Continue straight ={:6.2f}cm"
            .format(current_distance))
    if (current_distance > 300):
        # verify distance
        current_distance = RI.fetchUltraDistance()
```

```
        if (current_distance > 300):
            # move faster
            RI.motorForward(90,1.0)
    else:
        RI.motorForward(90,0.50)
    turnCount = 0
```

We continue to move in short little hops to move the robot closer to the wall. When the robot gets within about 10cm of the wall, the program decides to turn its front wheels in a random direction and backs up to try a new direction to investigate:

```
if (DEBUG):
    print("distance close enough so turn ={:6.2f}cm"
        .format(current_distance))
bothFrontLEDSOn("RED")
now determine which way to turn
# turn = 0 turn left
# turn = 1 turn right
turn = randint(0,1)
if (turn == 0): # turn left
    # we turn the wheels right since
    # we are backing up
    RI.wheelsRight()
else:
    # turn right
    # we turn the wheels left since
    # we are backing up
    RI.wheelsLeft()
time.sleep(0.5)
RI.motorBackward(100,1.00)
time.sleep(0.5)
RI.wheelsMiddle()
turnCount = turnCount+1
print("Turn Count =", turnCount)
```

We ran the robot for quite a while with just this logic, but the robot would get stuck if part of it was blocked, even though the ultrasonic sensor was still picking up a distance of greater than 10cm.

To fix this problem, we added a running record of the past two ultrasonic distance readings. If we had three readings +/– 2.0cm, the robot would decide it was stuck and back up, turn randomly, and proceed again to wandering. Worked like a champ:

```
if (checkForStuckCar(current_distance,
        previous1distance, previous2distance)):
    # we are stuck. Try back up and try Random turn
    bothFrontLEDSOn("RED")
```

CHAPTER 3 **Programming Your Robot Rover**   625

```
if (DEBUG):
    print("Stuck - Recovering ={:6.2f}cm"
        .format(current_distance))
RI.wheelsMiddle()
RI.motorBackward(100,1.00)

# now determine which way to turn
# turn = 0 turn left
# turn = 1 turn right
turn = randint(0,1)

if (turn == 0): # turn left
    # we turn the wheels right since
    # we are backing up
    RI.wheelsRight()
else:
    # turn right

    # we turn the wheels left since
    # we are backing up
    RI.wheelsLeft()
time.sleep(0.5)
RI.motorBackward(100,2.00)
time.sleep(0.5)
RI.wheelsMiddle()
```

We set the robot down in a room with furniture and a complex set of walls and let it loose by typing **sudo python3 robotBrain.py** in a terminal window. Here are the results from the console:

```
Simple Robot Brain
Continue straight =115.44cm
Continue straight =108.21cm
Continue straight =101.67cm
Continue straight = 95.67cm
Continue straight = 88.13cm
Continue straight = 79.85cm
Continue straight = 70.58cm
Continue straight = 63.89cm
Continue straight = 54.36cm
Continue straight = 44.65cm
Continue straight = 36.88cm
Continue straight = 28.32cm
Continue straight = 21.10cm
distance close enough so turn = 11.33cm
Turn Count = 1
Continue straight = 33.75cm
Continue straight = 25.12cm
```

```
distance close enough so turn = 18.20cm
Turn Count = 1
Continue straight = 40.51cm
Continue straight = 33.45cm
Continue straight = 24.73cm
distance close enough so turn = 14.83cm
Turn Count = 1
Continue straight = 35.72cm
Continue straight = 26.13cm
distance close enough so turn = 18.56cm
Turn Count = 1
Continue straight = 43.63cm
Continue straight = 37.74cm
Continue straight = 27.33cm
Continue straight = 84.01cm
```

You can see the robot drive towards a wall and then turn several times to find a way out and then continue on in the video at https://youtu.be/U7_FJzRbsRw.

A BETTER ROBOT BRAIN ARCHITECTURE

If you look at the robotBrain.py software from a software architectural perspective, one thing jumps out. The main part of the program is a single while loop that polls the ultrasonic and then does one thing at a time (moves, turns, and so on) and then polls it again. This polling and then moving leads to the somewhat jerky behavior of the robot (move a little, sense, move a little, sense, and so on). Although this architecture is the simplest we could use for our example, there are better, albeit more complicated, ways of doing these motions that are beyond the scope of our project today. To improve this program behavior, we again would turn to threads.

You can think of *threads* as separate programs that run at the same time and communicate to each other by using semaphores and data queues. *Semaphores* and *data queues* are simply methods by which a thread can communicate with other threads accurately and consistently. Because multiple threads are running at the same time, you have to be careful how they talk and exchange information. One thread may supply old information to another thread or change data being used by another thread. You also have to make sure that two threads aren't talking to the hardware at the same time. Talking between threads is not complicated, if you follow the rules. For more on threads, see Chapter 4 in this minibook.

(continued)

(continued)

A better architecture for our robot brain would be like this:

- **Motor thread:** This thread controls the motors. It makes them run and stop on command.

- **Sensor thread:** This thread periodically reads the ultrasonic sensor (and any other sensors you may have) so you always have the current distance available.

- **Head thread:** This thread controls the head servos by using commands from the Command thread (described next).

- **Command thread:** This thread is the brains of software. It takes current information from the Sensor thread and sends commands out to the motors in their respective thread.

This architecture leads to a much smoother operation of the robot. You can have the motors running at the same time you're taking sensor values and sending commands. This architecture is used in the Adeept software `server.py` file included with the PiCar-B.

Overview of the Included Adeept Software

The Adeept software supplied with the robot (see Figure 3-1) is primarily a client/server model in which the client is a control panel on another computer and the server runs on the Raspberry Pi on PiCar-B. The control panel allows you to control the robot remotely and has a lot of interesting features, such as object tracking using OpenCV and a radarlike ultrasonic mapping capability. You can also see the video coming from the robot and use that to navigate manually. We've suggested not installing the Adeept software because it will interfere with running your own Python software.

The software installation is complicated, so pay close attention to the instructions.

The software is fun to use, but it doesn't require any actual programming. The software is open source, so you can look inside to see how Adeept is doing things. Be sure to check out `server.py` under the Server directory and look at the way threading is used to get smooth motion and sensing from the robot.

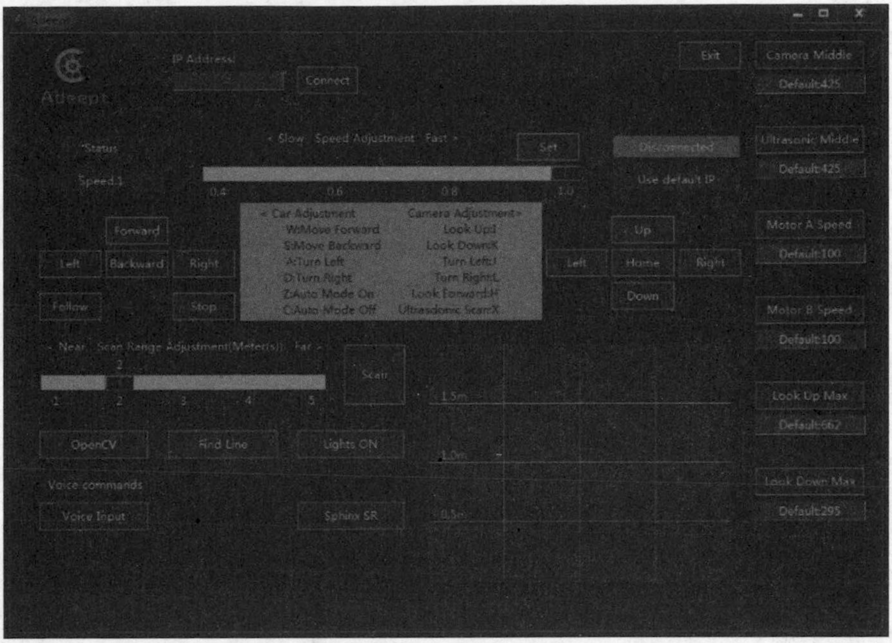

FIGURE 3-1:
Adeept remote
control software.

Where to Go from Here

You now have a small robot that can display complex behavior based on its built-in ultrasonic sensor. You can enhance this robot by adding sensors to the Raspberry Pi. (How about a laser distance finder? Bumper sensors? Light conditions?) Add some of the motors you used in Book 6. You can plug the Pi2Grover on top of the motor controller and use all the Grove devices you have accumulated.

The sky is the limit!

Chapter 4

Using Artificial Intelligence in Robotics

"Artificial Intelligence (AI) is the theory and development of computer systems able to perform tasks that normally require human intelligence, such as visual perception, speech recognition, decision-making, and translation between languages."

—DICTIONARY.COM

So, AI is meant to replace people? Well, not really. Modern AI looks to enhance machine intelligence in certain tasks that are normally performed by people. Even saying "machine intelligence" is somewhat of a misnomer because it's hard to claim that machines have intelligence at all, at least as we think of intelligence in people.

Instead of the philosophical debate, let's focus on this chapter's project, which uses machine-learning AI. We apply the techniques of neural networks to machine vision for our robotic car. In this way, the robot can utilize the Pi camera to understand aspects of its environment.

Making robots see is easy, but making them understand what they are seeing is exceptionally hard. If you want to learn more about computer vision using Python, check out *Computer Vision Projects with OpenCV and Python 3* by Matthew Rever (Packt Publishing).

For a better understanding of the AI techniques in this chapter, read Chapters 1 and 2 in Book 4.

This Chapter's Projects: Going to the Dogs

In this chapter, we show you how to build a machine-learning neural network and train it to recognize cats versus dogs. (This is a skill all robots should have.) To train the network, we use TensorFlow and a 1,000-image subset (500 cats and 500 dogs) of the 25,000 images of cats and dogs in the Kaggle Cats and Dogs database.

TensorFlow is a Python package that supports neural networks and machine learning based on matrices and flow graphs. TensorFlow is similar to NumPy (a Python library that supports large multi-dimensional arrays and a large collection of mathematical functions that operate on these arrays), with one exception: TensorFlow is designed for use in machine-learning and AI applications, so it has libraries and functions designed for those specific applications.

The second project in this chapter uses machine vision to enable your robot to look for a ball and then move toward it like a slow — and dumb — dog. But it is still a good example of what you can do with machine vision using Python.

Refer to Book 4 for examples and information on using TensorFlow in Python and on the Raspberry Pi.

Setting Up the First Project

For the Raspberry Pi, go to www.tensorflow.org/install/pip, download TensorFlow, and install it according to the directions.

Later, if you want to do more experiments with your machine-learning software, download the full Cats and Dogs dataset from www.kaggle.com/c/dogs-vs-cats-redux-kernels-edition/data. Another source of the full data is www.microsoft.com/en-us/download/details.aspx?id=54765.

The truncated list of the Cats and Dogs dataset is located at `https://github.com/switchdoclabs/CatsAndDogsTruncatedData`. The list is about 65MB and is included with our software at `www.dummies.com/go/pythonaiofd2e`.

To make sure that your data is structured for the example programs, run the following command in your program directory to download all the truncated data in the correct directory structures:

```
git clone https://github.com/switchdoclabs/CatsAndDogsTruncatedData.git
```

If you look under the `CatsAndDogsTruncatedData` directory after executing this command, you'll see two directories. The `train` directory contains the cat and dog images that you will use to train your neural network. The `validation` directory contains unclassified images to test your neural network after you've trained it.

Now that the data is ready, let's go train that network.

Machine Learning Using TensorFlow

Our goal in this section is to fully train our machine learning neural network on the difference between cats and dogs, validate the test data, and then save the trained neural network so we can use it on our robot. Then the real fun will begin!

TIP

When you run the following program, if you see `ImportError: No module named 'seaborn'`, type **sudo pip3 install seaborn**.

We started by using a simple two-layer neural network for our cats and dogs machine-learning network. Many more complex networks are available and may give better results, but we were hoping that this would be good enough for our needs. Check out Book 4, Chapter 2 for information on neural networks and TensorFlow.

Using a simple two-layer neural network on the cats and dog dataset did not work well; we achieved about a 51 percent detection rate, and 50 percent is as good as guessing randomly. We needed a more complex neural network that would work better on complex images, so we decided to use a standard six-layer CNN (convolutional neural network) instead. We then changed the model layers in our program to use the six-level convolutional layer model. You just have to love how easy Keras and TensorFlow make it to dramatically change the neural network.

CONVOLUTIONAL NEURAL NETWORKS

Convolutional neural networks (CNNs) work by scanning images and analyzing them chunk by chunk, in a 5x5 pixel window that moves by a length of two pixels each time until it spans the entire image. It's like looking at an image using a microscope; you see only a small part of the picture at any one time, but eventually you scan the entire picture. You then move on to the next image in the dataset. Each loop through all the data is called an *epoch*.

Using a CNN neural network on the Raspberry Pi increased the single epoch time to 1,000 seconds versus 10 seconds on the simple two-layer network, which is 100 times slower. And the analysis program has a CPU utilization of 352 percent, which means it's using 3.5 cores on the Raspberry Pi, a machine that has only 4 cores. (You can think of each core as a smaller computer.) This amounts to a very high CPU utilization of the Raspberry Pi 3B+. The little Raspberry Pi consumes almost 3.8W while running our neural network, up from about 1.5W normally.

You can see the complexity of our new network by looking at the `model.summary()` results:

```
_____
Layer (type) Output Shape Param #
===================================================================
conv2d (Conv2D) (None, 150, 150, 32) 896
_____
max_pooling2d (MaxPooling2D) (None, 75, 75, 32) 0
_____
conv2d_1 (Conv2D) (None, 75, 75, 32) 9248
_____
max_pooling2d_1 (MaxPooling2 (None, 37, 37, 32) 0
_____
conv2d_2 (Conv2D) (None, 37, 37, 64) 18496
_____
max_pooling2d_2 (MaxPooling2 (None, 18, 18, 64) 0
_____
dropout (Dropout) (None, 18, 18, 64) 0
_____
flatten (Flatten) (None, 20736) 0
_____
dense (Dense) (None, 64) 1327168
_____
dropout_1 (Dropout) (None, 64) 0
_____
dense_1 (Dense) (None, 2) 130
===================================================================
```

```
Total params: 1,355,938
Trainable params: 1,355,938
Non-trainable params: 0
```

The last lines are the most interesting. Our CNN has over 1.3 million trainable parameters. Each of those parameters will be modified by our training to produce our trained machine-learning program.

The code

The code to implement this TensorFlow training program is brief. Once again, we see the power of Python libraries in hiding the complexity of the parameter computations for our neural network:

```python
#import libraries
import numpy as np
import matplotlib.pyplot as plt
import matplotlib.image as mpimg
import seaborn as sns
import tensorflow as tf
from tensorflow.python.framework import ops
from tensorflow.examples.tutorials.mnist import input_data
from PIL import Image
from tensorflow.keras.preprocessing.image import ImageDataGenerator

from tensorflow.keras.layers import *

# load data

img_width = 150
img_height = 150
train_data_dir = 'data/train'
valid_data_dir = 'data/validation'

datagen = ImageDataGenerator(rescale = 1./255)

train_generator = datagen.flow_from_directory(
                directory=train_data_dir,
                target_size=(img_width,img_height),
                classes=['dogs','cats'],
                class_mode='binary',
                batch_size=16)

validation_generator = datagen.flow_from_directory(directory=valid_data_dir,
                target_size=(img_width,img_height),
                classes=['dogs','cats'],
```

```
                    class_mode='binary',
                    batch_size=32)

# build model


model = tf.keras.Sequential()


model.add(Conv2D(32, (3, 3), input_shape=(150, 150, 3), padding='same',
    activation='relu'))
model.add(MaxPooling2D(pool_size=(2, 2)))

model.add(Conv2D(32, (3, 3), padding='same', activation='relu'))
model.add(MaxPooling2D(pool_size=(2, 2)))

model.add(Conv2D(64, (3, 3), activation='relu', padding='same'))
model.add(MaxPooling2D(pool_size=(2, 2)))

model.add(Dropout(0.25))
model.add(Flatten())
model.add(Dense(64, activation='relu'))
model.add(Dropout(0.5))
model.add(Dense(2, activation='softmax'))

model.compile(optimizer=tf.train.AdamOptimizer(),
                        loss='sparse_categorical_crossentropy',
                        metrics=['accuracy'])

print (model.summary())

# train model

print('starting training....')
history = model.fit_generator(generator=train_generator,
        steps_per_epoch=2048 // 16,epochs=20,
        validation_data=validation_generator,validation_steps=832//16)

print('training finished!!')

# save coefficients

model.save("CatsVersusDogs.trained")

# Get training and test loss histories
training_loss = history.history['loss']
accuracy = history.history['acc']
```

```
# Create count of the number of epochs
epoch_count = range(1, len(training_loss) + 1)

# Visualize loss history
plt.figure(0)
plt.plot(epoch_count, training_loss, 'r--')
plt.plot(epoch_count, accuracy, 'b--')
plt.legend(['Training Loss', 'Accuracy'])
plt.xlabel('Epoch')
plt.ylabel('History')
plt.grid(True)
plt.show(block=True);
```

Save the code in a file called `CatsVersusDogsTrain.py`.

How the code works

The `CatsVersusDogsTrain.py` code has 93 lines, and it's surprising what we can do with so few lines of code. We will examine each of the major blocks of code in the `CatsVersusDogsTrain.py` program in turn.

First, we import all the libraries:

```
#import libraries
import numpy as np
import matplotlib.pyplot as plt
import matplotlib.image as mpimg
import seaborn as sns
import tensorflow as tf
from tensorflow.python.framework import ops
from tensorflow.examples.tutorials.mnist import input_data
from PIL import Image
from tensorflow.keras.preprocessing.image import ImageDataGenerator

from tensorflow.keras.layers import *
```

Next, we massage the data into tensors (matrices) for training through our neural network. The cat and dog images are stored in separate directories under `data`. We change the images into a 150-by-150-pixel format and then load the image data into the training generator in the format needed by the neural network:

```
# load data

img_width = 150
img_height = 150
```

```
train_data_dir = 'data/train'
valid_data_dir = 'data/validation'

datagen = ImageDataGenerator(rescale = 1./255)

train_generator = datagen.flow_from_directory(
    directory=train_data_dir,
    target_size=(img_width,img_height),
    classes=['dogs','cats'],
    class_mode='binary',
    batch_size=16)

validation_generator = datagen.flow_from_directory(directory=valid_data_dir,
    target_size=(img_width,img_height),
    classes=['dogs','cats'],
    class_mode='binary',
    batch_size=32)
```

Now we build the six-layer neural network that forms the basis of the machine learning model:

```
# build model

model = tf.keras.Sequential()
```

The first layer is a 2D convolutional neural network that starts to extract features from the photograph. We use *RELU* (rectified linear unit) as the neuron activation function. RELU modifies the output from the summed inputs of a neuron to present it to the neuron. For an easy-to-understand introduction to RELU and activation functions in general, check out https://machinelearningmastery. com/rectified-linear-activation-function-for-deep-learning-neural-networks/.

```
model.add(Conv2D(32, (3, 3), input_shape=(150, 150, 3), padding='same',
    activation='relu'))
```

The next layer of our CNN, MaxPooling2D, combines the outputs found in the previous layer:

```
model.add(MaxPooling2D(pool_size=(2, 2)))
```

Next, we add another two layers of convolutional neural networks, each followed by a pooling layer. A *pooling layer* reduces the location sensitivity of a specific feature (such as a cat's nose) by pooling the information in a manner that increases the neural network's capability to see the same feature in other locations in an image:

```
model.add(Conv2D(32, (3, 3), padding='same', activation='relu'))
model.add(MaxPooling2D(pool_size=(2, 2)))
model.add(Conv2D(64, (3, 3), activation='relu', padding='same'))
model.add(MaxPooling2D(pool_size=(2, 2)))
```

One of the problems with neural networks is *overfitting,* when the machine matches the data too closely such that the network won't match any new, slightly different pictures. Dropout layers help here by randomly setting some data to 0. We are removing 25 percent of the data in this layer:

```
model.add(Dropout(0.25))
```

Now we flatten the data into a one-dimensional array to present it to the 64 neurons in the network at the same time, and then use a final densely connected 64-neuron layer:

```
model.add(Flatten())
model.add(Dense(64, activation='relu'))
```

Next, drop out another 50 percent of the input units to help with overfitting. Again, this seems counterintuitive to remove 50 percent of data after training, but it helps the network recognize pictures that aren't in the training set and properly categorize them:

```
model.add(Dropout(0.5))
```

Our output layer, Cat or Dog (`filast model.add` in the code), has two outputs. If the CNN finds a cat, the first output will be a 1 and the second output will be a 0. If the CNN finds a dog, the first output will be a 0 and the second output will be a 1:

```
model.add(Dense(2, activation='softmax'))
model.compile(optimizer=tf.train.AdamOptimizer(),
    loss='sparse_categorical_crossentropy',
    metrics=['accuracy'])
print (model.summary())
# train model
```

The neural network training on 1,000 cat and dog pictures takes about five hours on a Raspberry Pi 3B+:

```
print('starting training....')
history = model.fit_generator(generator=train_generator,
    steps_per_epoch=2048 // 16,epochs=20,
    validation_data=validation_generator,validation_steps=832//16)
print('training finished!!')
```

This next line of code saves the trained neural network model for use later, saving five hours per run! Saving the resulting training is normal for a machine-learning system. Training takes a lot of time, but running the model to categorize new images is fast.

```
# save coefficients
model.save("CatsVersusDogs.trained")
```

We use MatPlotLib to generate a graph that shows how accuracy improves with each epoch:

```
# Get training and test loss histories
training_loss = history.history['loss']
accuracy = history.history['acc']
# Create count of the number of epochs
epoch_count = range(1, len(training_loss) + 1)
# Visualize loss history
plt.figure(0)
plt.plot(epoch_count, training_loss, 'r--')
plt.plot(epoch_count, accuracy, 'b--')
plt.legend(['Training Loss', 'Accuracy'])
plt.xlabel('Epoch')
plt.ylabel('History')
plt.grid(True)
plt.show(block=True);
```

The results

Now after all that neural network training, we can check out the results of running our fully trained network.

WARNING

Install the h5py library before running this program by typing the following. Otherwise, the save statement will not work:

```
sudo apt-get install python-h5py
```

Showtime! Run the following command in the terminal window:

```
python3 CatsVersusDogs.py
```

It takes about five hours on a Raspberry Pi 3B+ to generate 20 epochs of training and save the results into the CatsVersusDogs.training file. A snapshot of the last epoch follows:

```
Epoch 20/20
128/128 [==============================] – 894s 7s/step – loss: 0.0996 – acc:
    0.9609 – val_loss: 1.1069 – val_acc: 0.7356
training finished!!
```

TIP

You can safely ignore warnings from TensorFlow, such as:

```
/usr/lib/python3.5/importlib/_bootstrap.py:222: RuntimeWarning: compiletime
    version 3.4 of module 'tensorflow.python.framework.fast_tensor_util' does not
    match runtime version 3.5
return f(*args, **kwds)
/usr/lib/python3.5/importlib/_bootstrap.py:222: RuntimeWarning: builtins.type
    size changed, may indicate binary incompatibility. Expected 432, got 412
return f(*args, **kwds)
```

These warnings will be fixed in an upcoming version.

After the five-hour-long training, we achieved an accuracy of 96 percent! Pretty good. Figure 4-1 shows how the accuracy improved during training. Remember that test directory of images not used for training? We use those unused but known images for testing how well we're doing.

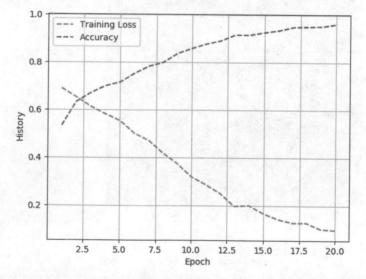

FIGURE 4-1:
Cats and dogs recognition accuracy per epoch.

The shape of the accuracy curve tells us that we might have slightly improved the accuracy rate by running more epochs over several hours, but this is good enough for our example. *Training loss* is an indicator of how many mistakes were made by the neural network during training. Just running more epochs may not improve your accuracy. Eventually, the network may become overfitted and the accuracy numbers will start to go down. Just another example of why machine learning is still an art and not a totally predictive science.

Testing the Trained Network

Time to do a test on a cat/dog image that is not in our training or validation set. We're going to use the trained data from our neural network training session to do a few "cat or dog?" determinations on new pictures that the neural network has not seen.

We chose the cat picture shown in Figure 4-2 because it is a low-contrast, low-quality picture, which should be harder to classify whereas the dog picture, shown in Figure 4-3, is a high-quality picture.

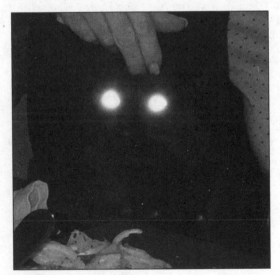

FIGURE 4-2:
Panther the cat on salmon.

The code

The code to use the trained neural network to classify our pictures is even simpler than the code to train the network. Create a file called singleTestImage.py and insert the following code:

```
#import libraries
import numpy as np
```

FIGURE 4-3:
Winston the dog.

```
import tensorflow as tf
from tensorflow.python.framework import ops
from PIL import Image

print("import complete")
# load model

img_width = 150
img_height = 150

class_names = ["Dog", "Cat"]

model = tf.keras.models.load_model("CatsVersusDogs.trained",compile=True)
print (model.summary())

# do cat single image
#imageName = "Cat150x150.jpeg"
imageName = "Dress150x150.JPG"
testImg = Image.open(imageName)
testImg.load()
data = np.asarray( testImg, dtype="float" )

data = np.expand_dims(data, axis=0)
singlePrediction = model.predict(data, steps=1)

NumberElement = singlePrediction.argmax()
Element = np.amax(singlePrediction)
```

CHAPTER 4 **Using Artificial Intelligence in Robotics** 643

```
print(NumberElement)
print(Element)
print(singlePrediction)

print ("Our Network has concluded that the file '"
        +imageName+"' is a "+class_names[NumberElement])
print (str(int(Element*100)) + "% Confidence Level")

# do dog single image
imageName = "Dog150x150.JPG"
testImg = Image.open(imageName)
testImg.load()
data = np.asarray( testImg, dtype="float" )

data = np.expand_dims(data, axis=0)
singlePrediction = model.predict(data, steps=1)

NumberElement = singlePrediction.argmax()
Element = np.amax(singlePrediction)
print(NumberElement)
print(Element)
print(singlePrediction)

print ("Our Network has concluded that the file '"
        +imageName+"' is a "+class_names[NumberElement])
print (str(int(Element*100)) + "% Confidence Level")
```

How the code works

The singleTestImage.py code uses the trained neural network that we generated by the five-hour long training with the cats and dogs dataset earlier in the chapter.

First, we import our libraries, as in the CatsVersusDogsTrain.py program:

```
#import libraries
import numpy as np
import tensorflow as tf
from tensorflow.python.framework import ops
from PIL import Image

print("import complete")
# load model
img_width = 150
img_height = 150
```

Then we set up the class name array so we have classification names for our images:

```
class_names = ["Dog", "Cat"]
```

In the following, we load the training data we generated previously for the neural network machine-learning model, which includes all the neural network layers we used in the training:

```
model = tf.keras.models.load_model(
    "CatsVersusDogs.trained",compile=True)
print (model.summary())
```

Now, we test a single cat image:

```
# do cat single image
imageName = "Cat150x150.jpeg"
testImg = Image.open(imageName)
testImg.load()
```

We then convert our test image to a NumPy array for analysis:

```
data = np.asarray( testImg, dtype="float" )
```

We then expand the dimensions of the array, because the `predict` function looks for an array of images (although we are only giving the program one image to look at):

```
data = np.expand_dims(data, axis=0)
```

Now, we predict whether we have a cat or dog based on our image:

```
singlePrediction = model.predict(data, steps=1)
```

We print out the raw data:

```
NumberElement = singlePrediction.argmax()
Element = np.amax(singlePrediction)
print(NumberElement)
print(Element)

print(singlePrediction)
```

Then we interpret the prediction:

```
print ("Our Network has concluded that the file '"
    +imageName+"' is a "+class_names[NumberElement])
print (str(int(Element*100)) + "% Confidence Level")
```

Next, we do the same with a single dog image:

```
# do dog single image
imageName = "Dog150x150.JPG"
testImg = Image.open(imageName)
testImg.load()
data = np.asarray( testImg, dtype="float" )
data = np.expand_dims(data, axis=0)
singlePrediction = model.predict(data, steps=1)
NumberElement = singlePrediction.argmax()
Element = np.amax(singlePrediction)
print(NumberElement)
print(Element)
print(singlePrediction)
print ("Our Network has concluded that the file '"
    +imageName+"' is a "+class_names[NumberElement])
print (str(int(Element*100)) + "% Confidence Level")
```

The results

Save the code to `singleTestImage.py` and then run it:

```
sudo python3 singleTestImage.py.
```

Here are the results:

```
import complete
WARNING:tensorflow:No training configuration found in save file: the model was
    *not* compiled. Compile it manually.

_____
Layer (type) Output Shape Param #
=====================================================================
conv2d (Conv2D) (None, 150, 150, 32) 896
_____
max_pooling2d (MaxPooling2D) (None, 75, 75, 32) 0
_____
conv2d_1 (Conv2D) (None, 75, 75, 32) 9248
_____
max_pooling2d_1 (MaxPooling2 (None, 37, 37, 32) 0
_____
```

```
conv2d_2 (Conv2D) (None, 37, 37, 64) 18496
_____
max_pooling2d_2 (MaxPooling2 (None, 18, 18, 64) 0
_____
dropout (Dropout) (None, 18, 18, 64) 0
_____
flatten (Flatten) (None, 20736) 0
_____
dense (Dense) (None, 64) 1327168
_____
dropout_1 (Dropout) (None, 64) 0
_____
dense_1 (Dense) (None, 2) 130
=================================================================
Total params: 1,355,938
Trainable params: 1,355,938
Non-trainable params: 0
_____
None
1
1.0
[[ 0. 1.]]
Our Network has concluded that the file 'Cat150x150.jpeg' is a Cat
100% Confidence Level
0
1.0
[[ 1. 0.]]
Our Network has concluded that the file 'Dog150x150.JPG' is a Dog
100% Confidence Level
```

Well, this network worked very well. It identified both the cat and dog as their respective species. See the 100 percent confidence intervals? (A *confidence interval* is an indication from the neural network as to how confident it is in its prediction.) The confidence numbers are actually 99.99 percent or something like that and are rounded to 100 percent by the formatting.

Now that we have the trained model and have tested it with some example images not contained in the training or validation set, it's time to put the network into our robot and use the Pi camera for some dog and cat investigation.

WARNING

A limitation of the way we built this neural network is that it is looking at images of only cats and dogs and determining whether the image is a cat or dog. The network classifies *everything* as either a cat or a dog. If we were to build a more comprehensive network, we would have to train it to differentiate three types of things (between a cat, a dog, and a dress, for example). (See Figure 4-4.) We ran one more test of the network using the much-maligned dress picture from Book 4.

FIGURE 4-4:
A picture of a
dress?

As expected, the network got it wrong because we didn't teach it to understand what a dress is:

```
Our Network has concluded that the file 'Dress150x150.JPG' is a Cat

100% Confidence Level
```

Note that the program reports a confidence level of 100%. It is probably 99.99% or so confident, but the cat-or-dog nature of the training will place the image only in one or the other category so the confidence level means little at this point. There's a lot more to the practice of teaching a machine to learn in a general manner.

If you get an error such as `undefined symbol: cblas_sgemm` when running your program, try running your program using `sudo python3 singleTestImage.py`.

TIP

Taking Cats and Dogs to Our Robot

Time to add a new experience to the last chapter's robot. We are going to install the trained cats and dogs neural network on the PiCar-B robot and use the onboard LEDs to display whether the onboard Pi camera is looking at a cat or a dog.

As mentioned, our neural network classifies everything as a cat or a dog. We will run a neural network classification of the camera image when the ultrasonic sensor changes, which happens when a dog or a cat walks in front of the robot.

John's cat would not cooperate, so we had to use a PowerPoint presentation of various cats and dogs, as shown in Figure 4-5. The robot is staring at the screen, which triggers the ultrasonic sensor.

FIGURE 4-5:
Robot vision neural network test setup.

The code

In the robotVision.py program, we run our trained neural network every time the ultrasonic sensor detects something (a cat or dog, we hope) in front of the robot:

```
#!/usr/bin/python3
#using a neural network with the Robot

#import libraries
import numpy as np
import tensorflow as tf
from tensorflow.python.framework import ops
from PIL import Image


import RobotInterface
import time
import picamera
```

```python
print("import complete")
RI = RobotInterface.RobotInterface()

# load neural network model

img_width = 150
img_height = 150


class_names = ["Dog", "Cat"]
model = tf.keras.models.load_model("CatsVersusDogs.trained",compile=True)



RI.centerAllServos()
RI.allLEDSOff()

# Ignore distances greater than one meter
DISTANCE_TO_IGNORE = 1000.0
# How many times before the robot gives up
DETECT_DISTANCE = 60

def bothFrontLEDSOn(color):
    RI.allLEDSOff()
    if (color == "RED"):
        RI.set_Front_LED_On(RI.right_R)
        RI.set_Front_LED_On(RI.left_R)
        return
    if (color == "GREEN"):
        RI.set_Front_LED_On(RI.right_G)
        RI.set_Front_LED_On(RI.left_G)
        return
    if (color == "BLUE"):
        RI.set_Front_LED_On(RI.right_B)
        RI.set_Front_LED_On(RI.left_B)
        return


def checkImageForCat(testImg):

    # check dog single image
    data = np.asarray( testImg, dtype="float" )

    data = np.expand_dims(data, axis=0)
    singlePrediction = model.predict(data, steps=1)

    print ("single Prediction =", singlePrediction)
    NumberElement = singlePrediction.argmax()
    Element = np.amax(singlePrediction)
```

```python
        print ("Our Network has concluded that the file '"
            +imageName+"' is a "+class_names[NumberElement])

        return class_names[NumberElement]


try:
    print("starting sensing")
    Quit = False
    trigger_count = 0
    bothFrontLEDSOn("RED")

    #RI.headTiltPercent(70)
    camera = picamera.PiCamera()
    camera.resolution = (1024, 1024)
    camera.start_preview(fullscreen=False,
            window=(150,150,100,100))
    # Camera warm-up time
    time.sleep(2)

    while (Quit == False):

        current_distance = RI.fetchUltraDistance()
        print ("current_distance = ", current_distance)
        if (current_distance < DETECT_DISTANCE):
            trigger_count = trigger_count + 1
            print("classifying image")


            camera.capture('FrontView.jpg')
            imageName = "FrontView.jpg"
            testImg = Image.open(imageName)
            new_image = testImg.resize((150, 150))
            new_image.save("FrontView150x150.jpg")

            if (checkImageForCat(new_image) == "Cat"):
                bothFrontLEDSOn("GREEN")
            else:
                bothFrontLEDSOn("BLUE")


            time.sleep(2.0)
            bothFrontLEDSOn("RED")
            time.sleep(7.0)

except KeyboardInterrupt:
        print("program interrupted")

print ("program finished")
```

How it works

Most of the preceding code is straightforward and similar to the robot brain software presented earlier in the chapter. One part that deserves mention, however, is our classifier function:

```python
def checkImageForCat(testImg):

    # check dog single image
    data = np.asarray( testImg, dtype="float" )

    data = np.expand_dims(data, axis=0)
    singlePrediction = model.predict(data, steps=1)

    print ("single Prediction =", singlePrediction)
    NumberElement = singlePrediction.argmax()
    Element = np.amax(singlePrediction)

    print ("Our Network has concluded that the file '"
        +imageName+"' is a "+class_names[NumberElement])

    return class_names[NumberElement]
```

The checkImageForCat function takes the incoming test vision (taken by the Pi camera and then resized into a 150x150-pixel image — the format required by our neural network). See Figure 4-5.

The results

Save the program to a file called robotVision.py. Then, to get your machine to start looking for cats, run the program by typing the following:

```
sudo python3 robotVision.py
```

You should run this program on the Raspberry Pi GUI (either with a monitor or using VNC) so you can see the small camera preview on the screen. It's more interesting to see what the robot is seeing.

Here are some results from our test setup (refer to Figure 4-5):

```
current_distance = 20.05481719970703
classifying image
single Prediction = [[ 0.  1.]]
```

```
Our Network has concluded that the file 'FrontView.jpg' is a Cat
100.00% Confidence Level
current_distance = 20.038604736328125
classifying image
single Prediction = [[ 1. 0.]]
Our Network has concluded that the file 'FrontView.jpg' is a Dog
100.00% Confidence Level
current_distance = 19.977807998657227
```

Overall, the results were pretty good. We found variations in recognition due to lighting, which wasn't a big surprise. Lighting is always a problem. However, the network consistently identified one picture as a dog that was actually a cat, as shown in Figure 4-6.

FIGURE 4-6: The cat who is apparently a dog.

We suspect that the neural network was fooled by the folded ears, but our neural network has 1.3 million parameters, and we can't tell in any particular place where it is going wrong. It's a giant statistical model. After a while, you get a feel for what works and what doesn't in machine learning, but you are out of luck as far as figuring out exactly what this network is doing wrong.

We had a nefarious plan here for a variant of this neural network. We used this neural network to build a kit to use on a new project, the Raspberry Pi–based MouseAir, to launch toy mice when the camera spots a cat but not when it spots a dog. You can see the Pi camera at the top-right corner of the Figure 4-7.

FIGURE 4-7:
MouseAir, an AI
mouse-launching
cat toy.

This project was a lot of fun and included servo motors, the Pi camera, and spinning DC motors, as we discussed earlier in Book 6. Check out these three YouTube videos to see the MouseAir system at work:

```
https://youtu.be/zZQLyIe2vAY

https://youtu.be/7Y6aKJuA1Dc

https://youtu.be/hFZIE97heko
```

There isn't space here to describe the details of the project, but more than 40 customers built the kit and they got pretty good results. Our test cat, Panther, refused to do anything but sit in front of the launcher — unless he was hit, he didn't even respond to the mouse.

Setting Up the Second Project

The chapter's second project uses OpenCV and the RobotInterface Python library to build a new robot brain program that looks for a specifically colored ball and then attempts to move toward the ball until is within about 20cm of the ball. Like a not very smart dog.

To prepare for this project, install OpenCV on your Raspberry Pi by typing the following commands in a terminal window:

```
sudo apt-get install libhdf5-dev libhdf5-serial-dev libhdf5-100
sudo apt-get install libqtgui4 libqtwebkit4 libqt4-test python3-pyqt5
sudo apt-get install libatlas-base-dev
sudo apt-get install libjasper-dev
wget https://bootstrap.pypa.io/get-pip.py
sudo python3 get-pip.py
sudo pip install opencv
sudo pip install opencv-contrib-python==4.1.0.25
```

Now you're ready to go!

The FindAndChaseTheBall.py Python Program

In a lot of ways, the FindAndChaseTheBall program is the most complex program in this book. We are using a sophisticated programming technique called multithreading to get lots of things happening at the same time.

Threads are multiple sections of the program can be run at the same time. In any major operating system (such as the Raspberry Pi OS) dozens of threads (also called *processes*) run at the same time doing operating system functions such as running the display, managing the disk, and handling memory. When we want to run a set of program code (organized in a Python function) at the same time as other functions, we write a thread. Using threads allows a much simpler program structure than trying to interleave all the necessary code in a single sequential block of code.

With our robot, we want to process individual video frames, steer the robot, display on the Raspberry Pi GUI screen, and read distances all at the same time. We suggest that you take a few minutes and read this great introduction to Python threads: www.tutorialspoint.com/python3/python_multithreading.htm.

The communication between threads and the main program is one of the most difficult parts of building threads. There are many potential races between complex threads which can be addressed with programming structures called semaphores and queues, a discussion of which is beyond the scope of this book. But be aware that solutions to these potential problems exist!

The structure of the program

The `FindAndChaseTheBall.py` file is approximately 320 lines long, so we don't provide a full listing here. Instead, go to www.dummies.com/go/pythonaiofd2e and download the software for Book 7, Chapter 4.

In outline form, the `FindAndChaseTheBall.py` program does the following:

1. Start the threads.

2. Display the video results.

3. Read the ultrasonic distance.

4. Look for the blue ball.

5. Figure out how to move toward the ball.

6. Move to the ball until it is 20cm (+/– 2cm) away.

7. Report what is going on to the screen.

8. Stay near the ball.

We have a main program (basically Step 1), which does very little. The work of the program happens in three threads: the ultrasonic thread, the video display thread, and the OpenCV frame analyzer thread. We discuss each one of these threads next.

The ultrasonic thread

The ultrasonic thread, `dis_scan_thread()`, is by far the simplest thread of the program:

```
def dis_scan_thread():        #Get Ultrasonic scan distance
    global dis_data, dis_scan
    while 1:
        while  dis_scan:
            dis_data = RI.fetchUltraDistance()
            #print("dis_data=", dis_data)
            time.sleep(0.2)
        time.sleep(0.2)
```

Note that this thread never ends. That isn't a requirement of a thread (some worker threads finish their job and then quit), but it is typical of a thread to never complete.

The thread uses the RobotInterface library (RI) to read one sample from the ultrasonic sensor on the front of the robot. See the two global variables at the top? The dis_data variable is the current distance, and dis_scan allows other programs to turn scanning on and off.

The time.sleep(0.2) line tells the operating system to pause this thread for 200msec and go ahead with other tasks. Without the sleep statement, the thread would consume the entire single CPU core (the Raspberry 3B+ has four total CPU cores) and waste a bunch of processing power (and real power) getting samples faster than required by our program. Our robot does not move very far in 200msec, so getting distance samples faster than 200msec doesn't make sense in our robot application.

The video display thread

The video display thread, video_thread(), is another fairly simple thread. It has a socket, or pipeline, between this thread and the OpenCV thread. A *socket* is a method for communicating between various threads, even across networks. When you use a browser, you're communicating with the server via sockets (80 for http, 443 for https) that can span many networks. The socket is established in the first four lines of the code:

```
def video_thread():

    context = zmq.Context()
    my_footage_socket = context.socket(zmq.SUB)
    my_footage_socket.bind('tcp://127.0.0.1:5555')
    my_footage_socket.setsockopt_string(zmq.SUBSCRIBE, np.unicode(''))
    while True:
        newframe = my_footage_socket.recv_string()
        img = base64.b64decode(newframe)
        npimg = np.frombuffer(img, dtype=np.uint8)
        source = cv2.imdecode(npimg, 1)
        cv2.imshow("Stream", source)
        cv2.waitKey(1)
```

We use the zmq library to package the data coming from the OpenCV thread into a packet that contains a jpeg image file. The rest of the thread displays on the screen the incoming video frame from the OpenCV thread and then waits until it gets another frame. Note the While True: statement, which means the thread never ends because the While loop will never terminate.

The OpenCV frame analyzer thread

The OpenCV frame analyzer thread, opencv_thread(), does the majority of the work of the program. It looks at each frame coming from the Pi camera (at only

7 frames a second, by the way — you could do more frames per second with a faster computer such as the Raspberry Pi 4). The thread does the following for each video frame coming from the camera:

1. Look for the blue ball.

2. Figure out how to move toward the ball.

3. Move to the ball until it is 20cm (+/– 2cm) away.

4. Report what is going on to the screen.

5. Stay near the ball.

Wow! That's most of the work of the program. This function is long, so let's just look at some of the most interesting parts.

The OpenCV frame analysis

The OpenCV frame thread is looking at each new video frame coming from the camera and performing analysis on the images in the video frame looking for that pesky blue ball:

```
for frame in camera.capture_continuous(rawCapture, format="bgr",
use_video_port=True):
    image = frame.array
    cv2.line(image,(300,240),(340,240),(128,255,128),1)
    cv2.line(image,(320,220),(320,260),(128,255,128),1)


    if True:
        hsv = cv2.cvtColor(image, cv2.COLOR_BGR2HSV)
        mask = cv2.inRange(hsv, colorLower, colorUpper)
        mask = cv2.erode(mask, None, iterations=2)
        mask = cv2.dilate(mask, None, iterations=2)
        cv2.imshow("OpenCV Mask", mask)

        cnts = cv2.findContours(mask.copy(), cv2.RETR_EXTERNAL,
            cv2.CHAIN_APPROX_SIMPLE)[-2]
```

The for loop reads the frame from the Pi camera. Note that as long as the camera is running, the loop never ends. The cv2.line statements first draws a crosshair on the frame. This process is called *overlaying,* and we use it several times in this thread to put text and information on the screen (see Figure 4-8) as well as a bounding box on the target (the ball, we hope).

FIGURE 4-8:
The OpenCV
processed frame.

Next, we create a mask (see Figure 4-9) to find the ball. The OpenCV statements — `cv2.cvtColor()`, `cv2.inRange()`, `cv2.erode()`, and `cv2.dilate()` — look for colors in the range of the ball color (blue in our example), remove some obvious noise to improve the mask, and then display the mask on the screen for the user to see. The mask represents what OpenCV has detected in the appropriate color range and is then used by the `findContours()` function to find some ball-like objects to look at. We check out the biggest blue ball found, determine the position in the video frame, and move the robot towards it.

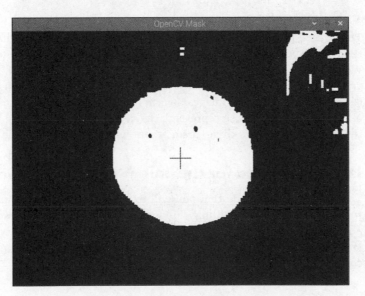

FIGURE 4-9:
The OpenCV
mask frame.

Using Artificial
Intelligence in Robotics

Moving the robot

Now that we've found a ball on the screen (assuming we have — otherwise we keep scanning for one), we figure out the X, Y coordinates on the screen (the upper-left corner of the picture is 0,0 and the lower-right corner is 640x480), and then direct the head to point toward the ball. If the ultrasonic distance numbers are above 20cm, we drive a little towards the calculated direction of the ball and then move to the next video frame to analyze.

Sound simple? It is, but it's still an ugly piece of code because we are moving the head from side to side and up and down, turning the wheels, and driving around. All at once.

```
if radius > 10:
    cv2.rectangle(image,(int(x-radius),int(y+radius)),(int(x+radius),
      int(y-radius)),(255,255,255),1)

    if X < 310:
        mu1 = int((320-X)/3)
        # scale mu1 to 50 (50 is the middle)
        mu1 = int((mu1/320.0)*50.0)
        hoz_mid_orig-=mu1
        if hoz_mid_orig < look_left_max:
            pass
        else:
            hoz_mid_orig = look_left_max
        #print("mu1 = ", mu1)
        #print("hoz_mid_orig=", hoz_mid_orig)
        RI.headTurnPercent(hoz_mid_orig)
```

The preceding section of code checks to see if the radius of the ball is greater than 10 pixels on the screen. If so, it moves the head partially towards the ball. We know the X coordinate of the ball from the OpenCV function cv2.minEnclosingCircle() and the cv2.moments() function. The center of the mask image is called the *moment* of the image. *Moment* is borrowed from those pesky mechanical engineers and in a sense represents the center of gravity of the mask image. (If the image were a pure circle, the moment would be in the middle of the circle.)

Looking around for the ball

The last section of code that you will examine pertains to what happens if the robot has not spotted anything that looks like our blue ball target. We want to do a little searching to find if that blue ball is lurking somewhere we can't see. The simple algorithm we are using works well enough for our example (although we could do a much better job of searching):

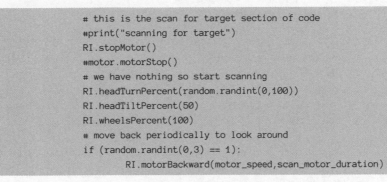

```
                    # this is the scan for target section of code
                    #print("scanning for target")
                    RI.stopMotor()
                    #motor.motorStop()
                    # we have nothing so start scanning
                    RI.headTurnPercent(random.randint(0,100))
                    RI.headTiltPercent(50)
                    RI.wheelsPercent(100)
                    # move back periodically to look around
                    if (random.randint(0,3) == 1):
                            RI.motorBackward(motor_speed,scan_motor_duration)
```

If we don't have a blue ball target, the head randomly scans by moving the robot head and, every three scans, backs up and chooses a different field of view. It's interesting to watch the robot in action and try to figure out better search strategies to implement in the code. Make your robot smarter!

The Main Program

The main part of the `FindAndChaseTheBall.py` program initializes the camera, starts the threads, and sets up the configuration variables. It also brings the robot to a known state by zeroing all the servos and wheels.

The program's configuration

The following section of the main program sets the constants defining the behavior of the robot:

```
####################################
# configuration variables
####################################


distance_stay  = 20 #stay away from target (cm)
distance_range = 2 # accept this error in distance_stay (cm)
dis_data = 0 # current ultrasonic range (cm)

# head turn (hoz) and tilt middles (vtr) - In percent
vtr_mid    = 50
hoz_mid    = 50

# where they start (head turn and tilt)
```

```
hoz_mid_orig= 50
vtr_mid_orig = 50


# sets the max and minimum numbers (in percent) for head tilt and head turn
look_up_max    = 100
look_down_max  = 0
look_right_max = 0
look_left_max  = 100


#motor speed variables - these may have to be tweaked
# depending on the kind of floor
# on which you are operating your robot.


motor_speed = 100
motor_duration = 0.40 # normal approach target duration
turn_motor_duration = 0.50 # during turn duration (needs to be a little longer)
scan_motor_duration = 0.50 # how long to back up during scan for
                           # target operations
```

First we set the distance parameters. The `distance_stay` variable is set to 20cm with a +/– 2cm error in the `distance_range` variable. The error bound of 2cm is important because our robot drive isn't very accurate and will overshoot or under-shoot the 20cm stay distance.

`hoz_mid_orig` and `vt_mid_orig` set the middle value (50%) for the servo motors, all given in percent as we are using the percent driver servo functions from the `RobotInterface` library.

The `motor_speed` and `motor_duration` numbers will change depending on the surface and the battery strength. These numbers are for normal, not flush, car-pets. If you're using the robot on a non-carpeted area, use lower values for the motor durations.

Setting the ball's color

To tell OpenCV the color of the ball, we use the HSV (hue, saturation, value) col-orspace. (Another way of looking at colors is using RGB.) We set two values: `col-orLower` and `colorUpper`. These reflect a color band around the ball color (think blue or a little less blue):

```
colorLower = (65, 66, 97)        #The HSVcolor that openCV will look for
colorUpper = (131, 255, 255)     #bounds for the openCV search
```

Setting these HSV values require some experimentation to get right and depend on the color of your ball and the lighting conditions. Lighting conditions are the bane of every robot machine-vision project; making your lighting consistent and sufficiently bright is difficult. People adapt to differing lighting conditions easily, but robots don't.

To set your ball color correctly, place your ball in front of the robot and start the following program, which is included in the Robot directory in the software download:

```
sudo python3 testColor.py
```

The screen shown in Figure 4-10 appears. Note the mask screen to the left, the video frame from the Pi camera in the middle, and then the mask applied to the Pi camera video frame on the right.

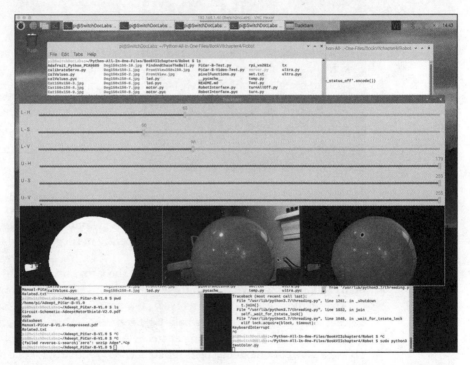

FIGURE 4-10: Screen for the blue ball color configuration.

Adjust the upper two slide bars (representing the lower bound of the color) until your object appears and then adjust the upper bound to 131,255,255. Experiment until you get a nice round mask. Don't be surprised if you have to do this process again after you see your robot in your lighting environment.

Time to do some ball chasing.

Chasing the ball

Put the ball about 1 meter in front of the robot, as shown in Figure 4-11. Then start the ball chase program by typing the following in a terminal window:

```
sudo python3 FindAndChaseTheBall.py
```

FIGURE 4-11:
Raspberry Pi
trying to chase
the ball.

The robot starts looking around and tries to find the ball. After a few seconds, you'll see two windows on your Pi screen. One window shows you the Pi camera video frame, and the other shows you the OpenCV mask generated to find your ball.

You will be amazed at how sophisticated the program seems — until it starts doing stupid things. We will continue to tweak this program and will post updates on the Python All-in-One Archives at https://github.com/switchdoclabs/ Python-All-In-One-Files-Second-Edition.

To see a video of one of our tests, go to https://youtu.be/Copeil-qT6U.

Program notes

Here are few program notes that we wanted to pass along:

» A blue ball may not be the best choice for a ball in every environment. Our robot was picking up the blue ball, but it also headed to a window with a blue tint of light through the curtains, the door to the SwitchDoc Labs laboratory (which has a grow light for the Raspberry Pi SmartGardenSystem, with just enough blue light reflected off the door), and even the overhead light. Not the smartest robot dog in the world. Depending on your environment, a bright green or yellow ball might be best. We suspect yellow would have done well in our test environment.

» The scanning algorithm for finding the ball is rudimentary. A much better ball search algorithm would detect when the robot runs into something and can no longer move forward.

» A method for determining when the robot has fixated on something that is not a ball (such as the window) would be helpful. Figure 4-12 illustrates the problem. You could generate a better image by doing more geometry analysis and size/shape filtering to reject non-ball-like things.

FIGURE 4-12: Missing balls for other targets.

Getting the robot to detect a ball and move towards it was fun. The fact that the robot is not good at the task shows you the complexity of dealing with a real environment and a machine vision system. The robot and program could be improved with a lot of work and more sensors, cameras, and even LIDAR (light detection and ranging), which would make the program a lot more complicated.

Our robot has now been programmed to chase a ball, and that's a good way to end our robot dog saga. Woof!

AI and the Future of Robotics

We think that artificial intelligence is the future of robotics. As the hardware becomes less expensive and the software techniques become easier to use, there will be more and more uses for robots, not only in manufacturing but in the home and on the road.

We expect to see new AI in many new consumer products in the coming years. The only question we have is "How long before we have AI in my toaster?" We'll buy one when they come out.

Index

Symbols and Numerics

D

strip() method, 297

Structured Query Language tables. *See* SQL tables

str(x) function, 89

Style Guide for Python Code, 54. *See also* PEP 8 Guidelines; PEP 20 Guidelines

subclasses
    adding extra parameters from, 243-246
    defining, 241-243
    overriding default value in, 243

subtraction operator, 71

sudo command, 488

sudo halt command, 513, 524, 592

Sum Squared Loss, 382-385

SunAirPlus unit, 505-506

sun-tracking solar panels, 544

super user do command, 488

supervised learning, 400

s.upper() method, 107-109

SVG (Scalable Vector Graphics), 522

SwitchDoc Labs HDC1080 sensor, 3, 513

syntax
    code block, 82
    in datetime module, 110-114
    discussion, 79-80
    errors in
        example, 82-83
        mouse hovering, 82-83
        overview, 79-81
        wording, 82-83
    for functions, 88-90
    with if statements, 129-130
    for importing modules, 61-62
    line breaks and, 81
    naming conventions, 81-82
    object.key, 171-173
    proper, 80-81
    semicolon and, 81
    of str object methods, 107-109

syntax chart, 61-62

T

tabular data, 290, 306, 443

Taylor, Allen G., 464

TCP (Transmission Control Protocol)/IP (Internet Protocol) networks, 577

technology bubble. *See* dot-com bubble

telecommunications network, 362

tell() method, 285-286

temperature and humidity sensor project
    discussion, 511-512
    installation, 512-515
    Python libraries for reading
        code breakdown, 518-519
        mini humidity experiment, 517
        overview, 515-517

temperature-measuring devices, 510

tensor processing unit (TPU), 424-425

TensorBoard extension, 394

TensorFlow
    discussion, 2, 366
    GUI, 394
    ML testing in Cats and Dogs project
        code, 642-644
        code breakdown, 644-646
        overview, 642
        results, 646-648
    ML training in Cats and Dogs project
        CNN model, 633-635
        code, 635-640
        overview, 632-633
        results, 640-642
    neural network project on Keras
        changing to three-layer neural network, 395-397
        checking results, 392-395
        code breakdown, 390-392
        installation, 386
        overview, 386-387
        step 1: loading data, 388, 390
        step 2: defining model and layers, 388, 391
        step 3: compiling, 388, 391
        step 4: fitting and training, 388, 392
        step 5: evaluation, 388-390, 392
    third-party APIs, 386

tensors. *See also* linear algebra; matrix mathematics
    DataFrames and, 443
    discussion, 366, 375, 385, 425
    GPU, 429
    NumPy and, 442
    online tutorials on, 442
    terminology surrounding, 386

W

X

Y

Z

About the Authors

John Shovic has been working with software and electronics since he talked his high school into letting him use their IBM 1130 computer for the entire summer of 1973. That launched him into his lifelong love affair with software. Dr. Shovic has founded multiple companies: Advance Hardware Architectures; TriGeo Network Security; Blue Water Technologies; InstiComm, LLC; and bankCDA. He has also served as a professor of computer science at Eastern Washington University, Washington State University, and the University of Idaho. Dr. Shovic has given more than 70 invited talks and has published over 50 papers on a variety of topics on Arduinos, Raspberry Pis, iBeacons, HIPAA, GLB, computer security, computer forensics, embedded systems, and others. Currently John is proud to be serving as a computer science faculty member, specializing in robotics and artificial intelligence, at the University of Idaho, Coeur d'Alene, Idaho, and is surrounded by a bunch of students who are as excited about technology and computers as he is.

Alan Simpson is the author of more than 100 computer books on databases, programming, and web development. His books have been published throughout the world in over a dozen languages, and have sold millions of copies. Alan left the writing world a few years ago to get out of the ivory tower and into the real working world, first as a developer, and now as a manager, of the apps and DBA team in his county government's IT department. Alan has been called a "master communicator" throughout his extensive career, and his online courses and YouTube videos continue to get rave reviews from his many students and followers.

Authors' Acknowledgments

John Shovic: I would like thank the wonderful staff at Wiley and give full credit to my co-author, Alan. Our technical reviewer, Rod Stephens, did an excellent and thorough job. Our editor, Susan Pink, was the best editor with whom I have every been associated. Thanks to my literary agent Carol Jelen for encouraging me to pursue writing this book. I would like to specifically thank the University of Idaho for their support and suggestions, especially to Dr. Bob Rinker and Dean Larry Stauffer. Great people, great university. Also, no book like this would be complete without my thanking my fabulous students, especially Amanda, Mary, Nikolai, and Doug, who inspire me every day and who had to listen to the chapters of this book as I wrote them.

Alan Simpson: Many thanks to Steve Hayes and everyone else at Wiley for offering me this great opportunity. Thanks to Susan Pink, my intrepid editor. Thanks to my literary agents Carol Jelen and Margot Maley Hutchinson of Waterside Productions. And thanks to my wife Susan for her patience while I was working at all kinds of crazy hours.

Dedication

John Shovic: To my wife, Laurie. She has supported me in so many ways including making sure my socks match in the morning. Thank you!

Alan Simpson: To Susan, Ashley, and Alec.

Publisher's Acknowledgments

Executive Editor: Steve Hayes

Project Editor: Susan Pink

Copy Editor: Susan Pink

Proofreader: Debbye Butler

Technical Editor: Rod Stephens

Production Editor: Tamilmani Varadharaj

Cover Image: © spainter_vfx/ iStock /Getty Images